NEOLITHIC STEPPING STONES

Published in the United Kingdom in 2017 by
OXBOW BOOKS
The Old Music Hall, 106–108 Cowley Road, Oxford OX4 1JE

and in the United States by
OXBOW BOOKS
1950 Lawrence Road, Havertown, PA 19083

Paperback Edition: ISBN 978-1-78570-347-8
Digital Edition: ISBN 978-1-78570-348-5 (epub)

Library of Congress Cataloging-in-Publication Data

Names: Garrow, Duncan, editor. | Sturt, Fraser, editor.
Title: Neolithic stepping stones : excavation and survey within the western seaways of Britain, 2008-2014 / edited by Duncan Garrow and Fraser Sturt.
Description: Oxford ; Philadelphia : Oxbow Books, 2017. | Includes bibliographical references.
Identifiers: LCCN 2017013347 (print) | LCCN 2017027167 (ebook) | ISBN 9781785703485 (epub) | ISBN 9781785703492 (mobi) | ISBN 9781785703508 (pdf) | ISBN 9781785703478 (paperback)
Subjects: LCSH: Stepping Stones Project. | Neolithic period--Great Britain. | Excavations (Archaeology)--Great Britain. | Archaeological surveying--Great Britain. | Great Britain--Antiquities. | Guernsey--Antiquities. | Isles of Scilly (England)--Antiquities. | South Uist (Scotland)--Antiquities.
Classification: LCC GN776.22.G7 (ebook) | LCC GN776.22.G7 N457 2017 (print) | DDC 936.1--dc23
LC record available at https://lccn.loc.gov/2017013347

Printed in Malta by Gutenberg Press Ltd

For a complete list of Oxbow titles, please contact:

UNITED KINGDOM
Oxbow Books
Telephone (01865) 241249, Fax (01865) 794449
Email: oxbow@oxbowbooks.com
www.oxbowbooks.com

UNITED STATES OF AMERICA
Oxbow Books
Telephone (800) 791-9354, Fax (610) 853-9146
Email: queries@casemateacademic.com
www.casemateacademic.com/oxbow

Oxbow Books is part of the Casemate Group

Front and back cover: Excavation underway at An Doirlinn, South Uist (photos: D. Garrow)

NEOLITHIC STEPPING STONES

Excavation and Survey within the Western Seaways of Britain, 2008–2014

DUNCAN GARROW AND FRASER STURT

With contributions by
Hugo Anderson-Whymark, Anwen Cooper, Mike Copper, Elise Fraser, Charles French, Seren Griffiths, Donovan Hawley, Julie Jones, Ceren Kabukcu, Anne Pirie, Henrietta Quinnell, John Renouf, Katharine Sawyer, Rob Scaife, Roger Taylor, Martin Tingle and Jaco Weinstock

Oxford & Philadelphia

Contents

List of figures

List of tables

Acknowledgements

The Stepping Stones project was financed primarily by an Arts and Humanities Research Council award (AH/I021841/1), with key funding also received from the Society of Antiquaries of London, the NERC radiocarbon facility (in kind) and the Universities of Liverpool, Reading and Southampton. We are extremely grateful to all of these bodies for their vital support.

It goes without saying that, on a project such as this which lasted many years and was conducted in several different places, we have a great many people to thank.

First of all, in relation to the project as a whole, we would like to thank: Richard Bradley, Chris Gosden, Tom Higham, Chris Scarre, Alison Sheridan and Alasdair Whittle for their broad academic support for the project right from the start and/or along the way; Doug Baird, Larry Barham, Matthew Fitzjohn, Jess Pearson and Chris Mee for their guidance and support in the project's early stages; Catherine Hardman and Louisa Matthews for technical support and assistance with deposition of the project archive at ADS; Andy Heath for his always good-humoured assistance and creativity in making the Stepping Stones website (and much more besides); Jim Dolwick and Elise Fraser for their post-ex finds assistance; Rose Ferraby for her skill and time in producing our ancient 'landfall' images; Hugo Anderson-Whymark, Sarah Lambert-Gates, Simon Pressey, Jane Read, Jeff Wallis and Alison Wilkins for their skilful illustrative work with the finds; Hugo Anderson-Whymark for applying his enormously wide-ranging expertise to the project in many different ways; Anwen Cooper for her advice on excavation strategy at all three sites and general ability to keep us on the archaeological straight and narrow; and finally Anwen Cooper, Donovan Hawley, Charlie Johns and Niall Sharples for reading and providing insightful comments on various chapters of the final book. We would also like to thank Mette Bundgaard, Julie Gardiner and Claire Litt at Oxbow Books for their help and support in producing the monograph.

In relation to our work in Guernsey specifically, we would like to thank: Barry Cunliffe and Heather Sebire for discussions concerning previous work at L'Erée; Chantal Conneller, Nicolas Fromont, Manu Ghesquière, Donovan Hawley, Ian Kinnes, Cyril Marcigny, Hélène Pioffet and John Renouf for their substantial advice in relation to the Channel Islands and wider French archaeological record; Digimap Guernsey for assistance with mapping data and GPS correction signals; Phil de Jersey, Tanya Walls and Jason Monaghan for the huge amount of support (in many and various ways) that Guernsey Museums gave us over the course of our work at L'Erée; and finally Jan Dockerill for permission to excavate on States of Guernsey land, and Terry Queripel for his kindness in allowing us to dig in his field at all and his considerable assistance whilst we were there.

In relation to our work in South Uist, we we would like to thank: Deborah Anderson, Mark Elliot, Ashley Ferrier, Jane Hamill and Kevin Murphy for their support in enabling the project to happen in the first place right through to deposition of the project archive; John Raven for helpful advice at the start; Catriona MacCuish for her considerable support in organising our Stepping Stones project exhibition and talk at Sgoil Lionacleit, Benbecula; Kate MacDonald and Becky Rennel for being a pair of friendly faces down the pub, helping to put us in touch with volunteers, sharing their site- and region-specific knowledge, and for raising the issue of the site being Neolithic in the first place; Andy Heath and Ashley Shairp for directing, filming, producing and editing our on-site videos at An Doirlinn; Jane Henderson and Phil Parkes for their assistance with the conservation of pottery; Ian Armit, Rosie Bishop, Mike Copper, Cole Henley, Mike Parker Pearson and Niall Sharples for academic advice, support and access to unpublished archives, etc. along the way; Niall Sharples (again) for suggesting that we dug the site in the first place, for coming along to dig, for sharing his extensive knowledge of the islands and taking us on some memorable field trips, and much, much more; and finally Huw Francis (Stòras Uibhist) and Roddy Macleod (North Boisdale grazing committee) for generously allowing us permission to excavate.

In relation to our work in the Isles of Scilly, we we would like to thank: David Mawer, Phil McMahon,

Rebecca Steggles and Val Thomas for their assistance with information about access in the project's early stages; Amanda Martin for her support in organising our Stepping Stones project exhibition at the Isles of Scilly Museum, enabling access to existing archives, arranging and advertising our talks, and much more; Lone Morritson and Jules Webber for their kindness and flexibility in allowing us permission to work on Natural England 'Higher Level Stewardship' land; Trevor Kirk for being a friendly face down the pub, for sharing his local knowledge and accompanying us on our first trip to St Martin's; Terry Perkins, Toby Tobin-Dougan and Steve Walder for sharing their local expertise concerning the location of artefact densities at Old Quay; Keith Low, James Morton, Jackie and Terry Perkins, Val and Graham Thomas, Steve and Julia Walder, Jan and the rest of the St Martin's Stores team, and many other people on St Martin's for their considerable kindness and assistance in many and various ways; Stephen Pendray for his assistance with silcrete thin-sectioning; Chantal Conneller, Manu Ghesquière, Gregor Marchand, Cyril Marcigny and Erick Robinson for their much-needed advice concerning continental European microlith typologies; Ian Dennis, Charlie Johns, Jacqui Mulville and Henrietta Quinnell for academic advice, support and information about various sites along the way; Charlie Johns (again) for suggesting that we dug the site in the first place, for coming out to dig with us, for sharing his extensive knowledge of the islands as well as his limpet hotcake recipes, and much more; and finally Chris Gregory (Duchy of Cornwall) and Steve Walder for very generously allowing us permission to excavate at all.

Excavation teams

It is clear that we could not have excavated the three sites without the assistance of many, many excavators, surveyors and finds handlers along the way. The list is enormous and many names appear more than once; several amazing people even made it to all three sites. We would like to express our huge gratitude to the excavation teams listed below.

L'Erée (2008–2011)

Jon Adams, Tom Adams, Claire Allen, Lucy Barker, Sophie Bourge, Rob Brown, Jonathan Carton, Jenny Cataroche, Charlotte Choizy-Guilloux, Anwen Cooper, Barry Cooper, Terry Coule, Nicky David, Philip de Jersey, Eleanor de Spretter, Cate Frieman, Cara Garrow, Jenny Giddins, Tony Hack, Donovan Hawley, Jack Herdman, Hazel Hill, Reece Horne, Karly Hughes, Kit Hughes, Hannah Johnson, Jody Joy, Sheila Kohring, Dave Lane, Jonathan Last, Hannah Lewendon-Evans, John Lihou, Andrew Mason, Sophie McGregor, Miriam Nathoo, Annie Nettleship, Dan O'Boy, Rodrigo Pacheco-Ruiz, Anna Peacock, Hélène Pioffet, Alex Poudret-Barré, Julie Rigden, Lauren Roth-Brown, Millie Rowe, Emilie Sibbesson, Members of the Junior Société Guernesiaise archaeology section, Tim Sly, Robert Smith, Dan Stansbie, Danni Thornton, Tanya Walls, Margaret White, Rhian Williams, Sue Wood, Tracey Woosley.

An Doirlinn (2012)

Kate Boulden, Will Budd, Jenny Cataroche, Anwen Cooper, Nicky David, Phil de Jersey, Rose Ferraby, Cara Garrow, Joe Garrow, Caroline Godwin, Dave Godwin, Jonathan Last, Robert Lenfert, Kate Macdonald, Mairi Maclean, Catherine Macleod, Lisa Orme, Rodrigo Pacheco-Ruiz, Niall Sharples, Emilie Sibbesson, Dan Stansbie, Mairi Stewart, Tanya Walls, Aaron Wheatley.

Old Quay (2013–2014)

Hugo Anderson-Whymark, Kate Boulden, Will Budd, Anwen Cooper, Hal Dalwood, Nicky David, Ian Dennis, Rose Ferraby, Cara Garrow, Joe Garrow, Caroline Godwin, Dave Godwin, Charlie Johns, Jonathan Last, John Lihou, Lorna Marshall, Anna Peacock, Rodrigo Pacheco-Ruiz, Lizzie Raison, Penny Rogers, Robert Smith, Dan Stansbie, Toby Tobin-Dougan, Linda Wornes.

Chapter 1

Introduction

1.1. Introduction to the Stepping Stones project

This book outlines the results of three excavations conducted between 2008 and 2014 under the auspices of the Neolithic Stepping Stones project: at L'Erée, Guernsey in the Channel Islands, Old Quay, St Martin's in the Isles of Scilly, and An Doirlinn, South Uist in the Outer Hebrides (Figure 1.01). In order to contextualise the significance of these findings, we also explore a series of wider, related themes: the character and archaeological signatures of prehistoric maritime connectivity; the nature and effects of 'island-ness' in later prehistory; the extent and implications of Neolithic/Early Bronze Age (EBA) settlement variability across Britain; and the consequences of geographical biases in archaeological research in terms of our understanding of the prehistoric past.

The project's full title was 'Stepping stones to the Neolithic? Islands, maritime connectivity and the "western seaways" of Britain, 5000–3500 BC'. Its primary focus was the Mesolithic–Neolithic transition on the main offshore island groups within the 'western seaways' – an area of sea extending from the Channel Islands in the south, through the Isles of Scilly and the Isle of Man, around to the Outer Hebrides and Orkney in the north (Figure 1.01). The project represented a research collaboration between the Universities of Liverpool/Reading (Garrow) and the University of Southampton (Sturt). We also worked closely with Cardiff University, Historic Environment, Cornwall Council and three project partner museums: Guernsey Museums and Galleries, the Isles of Scilly Museum and Museum nan Eilean.

In summary, the project as a whole involved the excavation of the three sites (this volume), computer modelling of the sea around that time (Sturt et al. 2013), and the construction of a database of late Mesolithic and early Neolithic sites within the western seaways zone which led to a major radiocarbon dating programme (Garrow et al. 2017). This work was funded predominantly by a grant from the Arts and Humanities Research Council (AH/I021841/1), but money from the Society of Antiquaries of London for excavations at L'Erée (2009–11) and Old Quay (2014) was also crucial to the establishment and subsequent successful completion of the project, as was 'pump-priming' funding from the University of Liverpool (2008), and in-kind funding for dating from the NERC Radiocarbon Facility.

1.2. The Mesolithic–Neolithic transition in Britain, Ireland and north-west France

The processes by which Neolithic practices spread throughout Europe, and – more specifically in relation to this project – ultimately across the Channel to Britain and Ireland, have been much debated over the years (see Thomas 2013 and Anderson-Whymark & Garrow 2015 for recent reviews). In relation to the Mesolithic–Neolithic transition in Britain and Ireland, the two main issues under recent discussion have been the extent and character of migration from the continent (many incoming migrants, none, or just a few?) and the origins and directionality of change (from which parts of the near continent did Neolithic things come, and were 'native' British/Irish people or 'invasive' continental Europeans primarily responsible for their arrival?) (see for example Sheridan 2010, Whittle et al. 2011). A third, more subtle and less discussed, underlying problematic has been the character of the earliest Neolithic material culture in Britain/Ireland – whilst clearly *similar* to material from the continent, it is by no means typologically the same, with certain elements either 'translated' or missing altogether, and precise source areas difficult to pin down (Thomas 2013, 355–384). As Anderson-Whymark & Garrow (2015) stress, many of these recent discussions have been similar to culture-historical ones conducted during the middle decades of the 20th century. Our primary aim in setting up the Stepping Stones project was to understand better the timing and character of change over the 5th and 4th millennia within the crucial western seaways zone, with the intention of shedding new light on age-old problems.

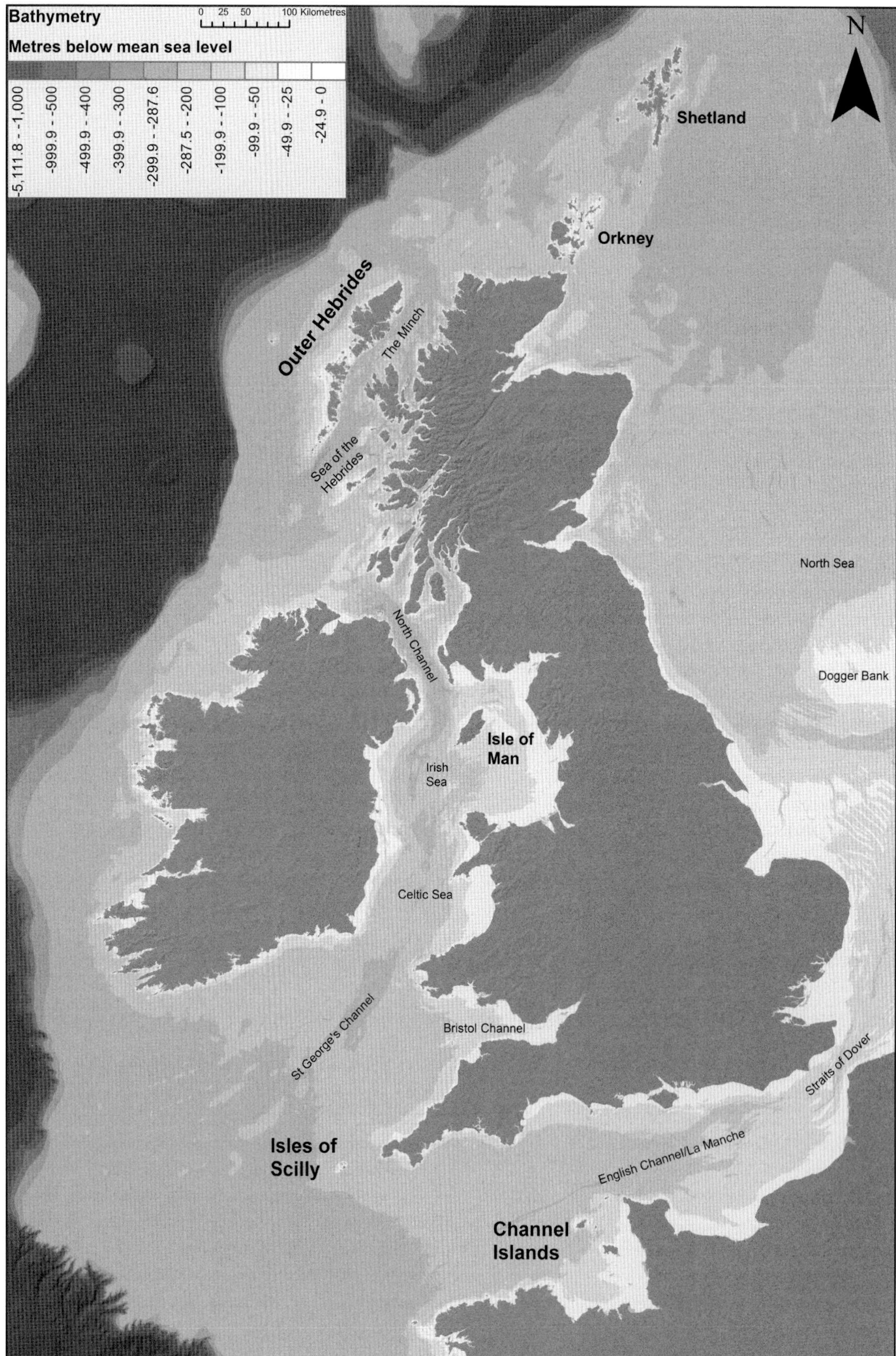

Figure 1.01. Map of the western seaways showing island groups. Topographic and bathymetric data from GEBCO14 (www.gebco.net) and EMODnet (www.emodnet-bathymetry.eu).

Given that they became islands c. 14,000 BC[1] (Ireland) and c. 7000 BC (Britain) (see Sturt 2015 for details), discussions of culture-historical change associated with the start of the Neolithic *must* necessarily involve questions of maritime connectivity and seafaring. As we discuss in more detail in Section 1.3, the western seaways have long been seen as a crucial corridor of interaction. In recent years, Sheridan in particular has stressed connectivity along that route, identifying three main phases and routes of activity leading to the arrival and subsequent development of the Neolithic (e.g. Sheridan 2010, 91). Whittle et al., however, have argued that the dynamics of change were orientated in a quite different direction. Their radiocarbon dating-driven model suggested that 'Neolithic things and practices' arrived in south-east England during the 41st century cal BC, and subsequently spread north and west across Britain, and over to Ireland, in the centuries up to c. 3800–3700 cal BC (Whittle et al. 2011, 836; see also Garrow et al. 2017).

While this newly suggested directionality appears on one level to hand primacy over to the Dover–Calais route, as long as we stay interested in the long-term processes of transition, the western seaways nonetheless remain highly relevant. The best known and most convincing indication of cross-Channel contact between communities in Britain/Ireland and France during the 5th millennium is the small group of cow bones found on an artefactually Mesolithic site at Ferriter's Cove, south-west Ireland, dated to 4495–4195 cal BC at 95% probability (Woodman & McCarthy 2003, 33). Given that there were no native wild cattle in Ireland, it has generally been assumed that these represent the (possibly partial) remains of a cow imported from France (see Thomas 2013, 266–268). Who brought them across the sea, and for what reason, it is impossible to establish. More contentious material indicators of cross-Channel contact *possibly* prior to the start of the Neolithic in Britain and Ireland include the Achnacreebeag pot (which bears distinct similarities to vessels from north-west France) found in an Early Neolithic tomb in western Scotland (Sheridan 2010), a small number of jadeitite axes found across Britain (which derive originally from the Alps and could potentially have been imported during the 5th millennium BC) (Sheridan 2011, 31), possible cereal pollen dating to the 5th millennium cal BC on the Isle of Man (Innes et al. 2003), and the possibly very early causewayed enclosure found at Magheraboy, Co. Sligo, dated to 4115–3850 cal BC (Whittle et al. 2011, 584) (see Anderson-Whymark & Garrow 2015 for a more detailed summary and discussion of all of this evidence). Recent findings including the much-disputed traces of wheat DNA identified in layers dating to the 6th millennium cal BC at Bouldner Cliff, Isle of Wight (Smith et al. 2015), and indeed the Belgian/French-style microliths found at Old Quay, Isles of Scilly (Chapter 3, this volume), can probably also now be added to this list. Once all of this evidence is combined, it becomes clear that, whether or not the location of the first 'full Neolithic' was in south-east England, the western seaways are still crucial to any understanding of maritime connections and the earliest processes of change leading up to the transition.

In light of these wider discussions of the Mesolithic–Neolithic transition in Britain and Ireland, the Channel Islands are able to play an interesting role. This island group is, of course, geographically much closer to France – in between the Normandy and Brittany peninsulas – and part of Britain only as a result of the contingencies of relatively modern politics. The transition occurs there c. 5000 BC (around a thousand years earlier than in Britain/Ireland) and Early Neolithic material culture on the islands is directly comparable to that from mainland France. Our decision to include the Channel Islands in the project was an explicit and intentional one from the outset. The subtly different issues involved in the process of transition there can play a key role in terms of providing perspective on what has at times been, ironically, a somewhat insular debate across the Channel. The particular trajectory of the Channel Islands transition is described fully in Section 1.6. The key issues pertaining to the process across the water in north-west France are, in fact, often surprisingly comparable to those under discussion in Britain and Ireland: the respective roles of incoming farmers and native hunter-gatherers, the effects and meaning of material culture potentially exchanged between these two groups, the visibility (or not) of Early Neolithic settlements (see also Marcigny et al. 2010, Scarre 2011 and Garrow & Sturt 2017).

Our main motivation for focusing attention on the island groups within the western seaways was the fact that – despite the potentially critical importance of this maritime zone – they simply had not featured enough, or even at all, in many previous accounts. While the islands within the seaways could theoretically have been crucial Earliest Neolithic 'stepping stones' on the way across the Channel, broader narratives had been focused almost exclusively on the mainlands either side and so it was impossible to know (see also Garrow et al. 2017). Additionally, a key legacy of the differential histories of research in different regions of Britain and Ireland (see Section 1.7) has been that on some island groups (the Channel Islands, the Isles of Scilly and the Isle of Man in particular) very little at all is known about Early Neolithic settlement (Garrow & Sturt 2011, 66–67). This situation ensured that our work within those island groups especially had the potential to enhance the archaeological record radically, simply by excavating suspected Early Neolithic sites.

One intriguing aspect of working archaeologically on islands is the enhanced visibility (and meaning) of material transformations. While marine-borne culture-historical change should not necessarily occasion more surprise than terrestrial change – in many circumstances in the past, maritime communication may well have been more common and much easier (Garrow & Sturt 2015) – the arrival of people by boat across stretches of water 40–60 km wide often does seem somehow more significant: steps across water to the stepping stones appear more significant than those taken on land up to the bank of the river. Additionally, for many of the stretches of water we are talking about here, the journey *would* often have been a significant event (see Section 1.3). As we discuss in more detail towards the end of this volume, islands provide a particular window onto change, focusing attention very directly on the *process* as well as the outcomes.

1.3. The 'western seaways'

Given Britain and Ireland's physical location on the western edge of the European continental shelf, surrounded by the waters of the Atlantic Ocean, English Channel, Irish, Celtic and North Seas (Figure 1.01), it is unsurprising that the role these seaways played in shaping the archaeological and historical record has been commented on for over a hundred years. As Callaghan and Scarre (2009, 358) note, the importance of the seaways first came to prominence in Fergusson's (1872) wide ranging *Rude Stone Monuments in All Countries; their Ages and Uses*. Fergusson (1872, 37) used classical accounts of Caesar's encounter with the indigenous sailing craft of the Morbihan coast to demonstrate how active these seaways were in the past, and the role they may have played in the transmission of ideas.

While Fergusson gave the sea an important role in his wide ranging antiquarian volume, it was not until the publication of Mackinder's *Britain and British Seas* (1902) that we see a more considered, and potentially more influential, academic engagement. In that volume, Mackinder presented a geopolitical history within which explanations of regional differences and historical trajectories can in part be seen to reflect variable geographic and oceanographic conditions. The text is refreshing for the amount of similarity that can be found between his reading and rendering of space and more recent reconsiderations. In Mackinder's accounts of ocean and sea variability we see glimmers of, for example, Evans's (2003) concept of 'texture', that the specifics of regional environments shape the social histories that play out.

In Mackinder's mind, Britain's variable history could in part be seen to reflect four key divisions:

> there are thus four natural parts of the sea round Britain. To the east and south are the narrow seas between the islands and the continent. To the southwest is the marine antechamber dividing into channels at the Land's End. Spreading four square in the midst of the British Kingdoms is the inland Irish Sea; while for six hundred miles off the north-western shores is the border of the ocean (1902, 23).

Each of these seaways is seen to have a specific character, promoting different forms of interaction. From the perspective of the development of the Neolithic, Mackinder noted:

> the most significant feature of British geography was not the limitless ocean, but the approach of the south-eastern corner of the islands to within sight of the continent. Kent was the window by which England looked into the great world (1902, 10).

He went on to observe that while the channel had some characteristics of being a barrier, it would also have been freely traversed throughout history. Thus in some senses, Mackinder would not have been surprised to hear the results of research by Whittle et al. (2011) into the date of the earliest Neolithic in Britain, where initial developments appear to occur along this stretch of coastline.

While, for Mackinder, Kent was the window onto the wider world, the remaining three seaways offered different qualities of connectivity and communication. The 'marine antechamber' of the western approaches allowed entry into the Irish Sea, a body of water that Mackinder viewed as the 'British Mediterranean' (1902, 10). The connecting Celtic sea and St George's channel to the south (Figure 1.01), and the North Channel and Minch to the north, aided travel along a north–south axis. For Mackinder these waters were about movement and communication, of maritime trade and interaction of a different sort to the short hops across the channel, or the slightly more complex currents of the narrow seas. It is this sense of difference, of a sea that is used in multiple ways, of long distance movement and short distance forays, that stands out from Mackinder's work. Here we see seeds for similar later ideas, such as those of Fox (1932), Crawford (1936) and Childe (1940). In each of these cases the sea was to take on an important role as both conduit and barrier, depending on the history of the group engaging with it. For Crawford (1936) the Western Seaways were a crucial route for the transmission of ideas, while Childe (1946) envisaged them as being as heavily populated with seafarers as the ethnography of Malinoswski (1922) indicated the contemporary waters of the South Pacific were. Fox suggested that 'without doubt' (1932, 20) the western route was the one via which the 'megalithic culture' of the Neolithic reached Britain, based on the distribution of monuments along this coastal fringe, seeing the western seaways as a critical vector through which prehistoric social change was enabled. It is perhaps unsurprising that the cover of *The Personality of Britain* is a map of the coastline of Europe with the seaways prominently represented through strong black arrows.

While we might imagine Mackinder's ideas to be echoed by his close contemporaries, it is more interesting to note the similarity his ideas have with much later publications. Within Mackinder's work we see an attention and focus on maritime space in a similar manner to key recent texts which have attempted to re-engage scholars with the sea. Thus, it is possible to draw parallels with Westerdahl's (1992) 'maritime cultural landscape' and Needham's (2009) 'maritories', both defined on oceanographic and social conditions, with an argument made that these physical differences translate into and explain variability in historical processes. The variability of bodies of water, and peoples' desire to engage with them has thus long been recognised to shape social process. The difficulty lies in understanding how much impact this had, and how to place emphasis within our interpretations.

It can be seen then that, as Callaghan and Scarre (2009, 359) observe, the argument for maritime connections to have existed across the seas around Britain and Ireland has been made for a considerable length of time. While interests may have subtly changed, the issue has now become one of understanding the variable intensity and significance of these connections (as Mackinder argued in 1902). In an effort to provide quantitative boundaries for consideration of these connections, Callaghan and Scarre (2009) conducted a series of seafaring simulations to chart how long journeys from France to Orkney would have taken. For completeness they included rates for both paddling and sailing, with acknowledgement of the fact that there is no direct evidence for sails at this point within north-west Europe. The results indicated that a determined crew could paddle from Brittany to Orkney via south-west Ireland in c. 20 days. This work served to demonstrate how short a timescale might be involved in movement between places if a specific destination was in mind, and a clear purpose to travel established. Within our own previous discussion of maritime connectivity within the western seaways (published prior to the start of the Stepping Stones project: Garrow and Sturt 2011), we suggested that, altogether, the archaeological evidence strongly suggested that people were moving regularly around and across the sea during the 5th and 4th millennia BC. We also highlighted the fact that shorter distance movements might quickly link together to provide a high level of communication.

In their paper Callaghan and Scarre (2009, 259) went on to pose the question 'did the Western Seaways provide an alternative or independent point of entry for Neolithic domesticates, material culture or indeed colonists from the Continent?'. If we are to take anything away from the 144 years of study this topic has received it is hard to conclude anything other than 'yes'. However, this is not to say that it was the most important vector, but as Mackinder (1902) argued, it was one route whose influence may have varied through time. Thus, for the islands considered in our study it is likely that interaction over these bodies of water did have a part to play, perhaps as much, or maybe more so at times, than the short hop over the channel through the Kentish window. The challenge lies in accepting the possibility for communication over the sea, and considering it alongside the other routes through which ideas, material culture and people may have circulated. This helps us to move away from a deterministic binary model of social change, where there is a single point of origin and way of being Neolithic. Instead we can draw upon the more complex world that Mackinder drew attention to and consider how multiple strands might have had a role to play.

1.4. The changing palaeogeography of Britain and Ireland

Given the Stepping Stones project's focus on maritime connectivity and the western seaways, understanding how the land and seascape may have changed over time was a priority. Whilst a considerable amount of research had been carried out into this topic from both a quaternary science (Brooks et al. 2011; Bradley et al. 2011; Shennan and Horton 2002; Shennan et al. 2006; Cohen et al. 2014) and archaeological (Reid 1913; Coles 1998; 1999; Gaffney et al. 2007; 2009) perspective, none of these past studies was at the specific temporal or spatial resolution required to address our research questions. As such a series of palaeogeographic models were created, making use of the latest glacio-isostatic adjustment (GIA) model (Bradley et al. 2011) as well as up-to-date topographic and bathymetric data sources. The detailed method for the production of these models was published in Sturt et al. (2013) and the resulting outputs made freely available both through the article and via the Archaeological Data Service.

Fundamental to an understanding of the changing geography of Europe is knowledge of the fact that the sea is not really level, and has no fixed altitude. All references to sea-level are time and space specific, be that in relation to a particular point on the tidal cycle for a given beach, or more broadly the mean altitude for a body of water over a given period of time. Temperature, weather and tidal state all can cause variances to occur. With regard to the more marked changes which have occurred through time, we can see two key forces at work; glacio-isostasy and glacio-eustacy. Isostasy relates to changes in the altitude of the earth's crust. The principle driver of isostatic changes in north-west Europe is the loading and unloading of the earth's surface by glaciers (glacio-isostatic change). In effect the weight of growing ice-sheets depresses the ground underneath them, and as they begin to melt and retreat the land rebounds. Eustacy refers to the amount of water in the world's oceans and seas. Again the key factor which impacts on eustacy is the amount of water locked on land in ice sheets. As temperatures drop and ice sheets grow the amount of water available in liquid form is reduced. Conversely, as they melt the ice sheets release water back into the seas and eustatic values rise. Figure 1.02 provides a eustatic curve for the study area drawn from Bradley et al. (2011). The interplay between these two drivers help to determine

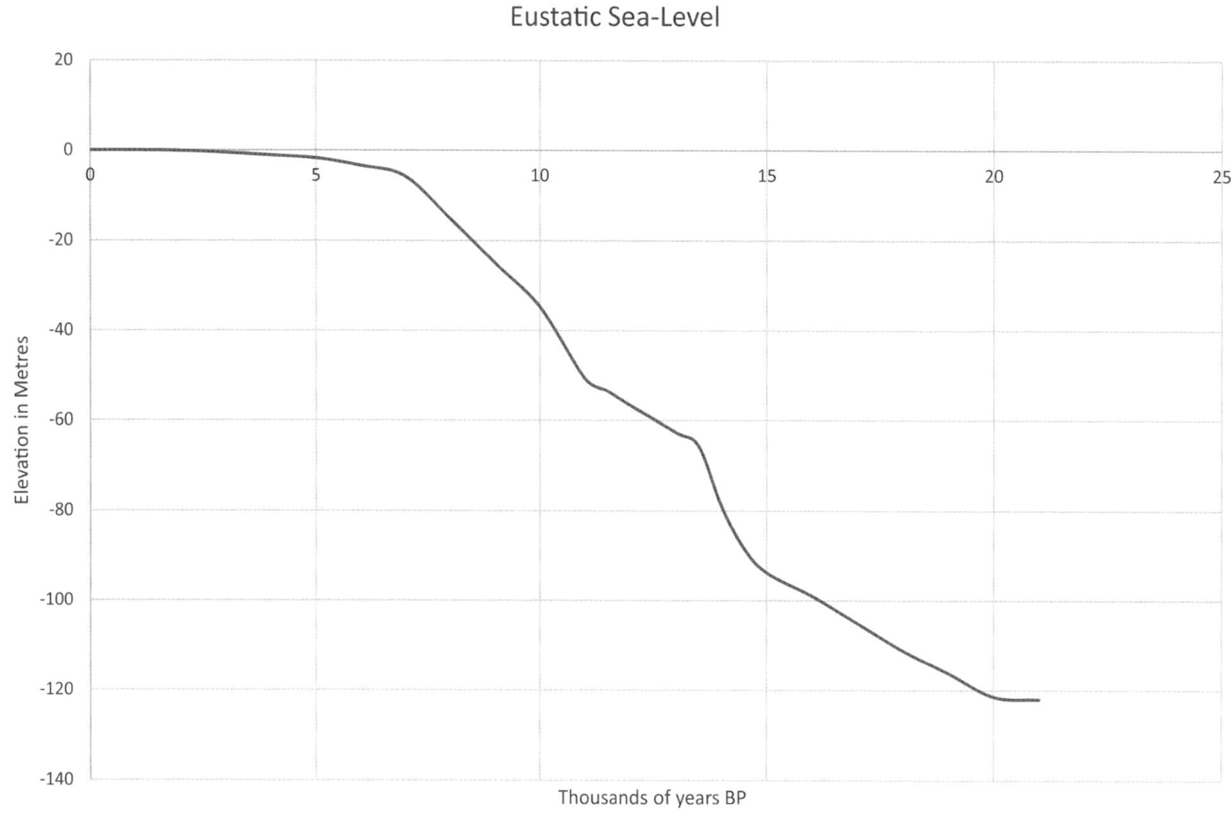

Figure 1.02. Eustatic curve for the study area, drawn from Bradley et al. (2011).

relative sea-level for a given point in space and time. The specifics of how this plays out at the site and regional level can be impacted further by other factors (such as the weight of sediment deposited by large rivers loading a relatively small area of the earth's crust, or tectonics).

Fortunately this process of sea-level variation leaves physical traces in the geological record, through the presence of submerged landscapes, peat deposits and raised beaches. These features can be recorded and dated to create sea-level index points, and the results used to generate a relative sea-level curve for a given area. This record will directly reflect the sea-level history of that specific locale. In turn these records can be collated and broader trends identified. Such work is painstaking and exacting, but has been carried out around the world to great success, and within Britain at frequent points along the coast (Shennan and Horton 2002). Figure 1.03 reproduces relative sea-level curves from different parts of the study area, demonstrating the distinct variability in patterns of sea-level change. However, not all regions retain a sea-level record, and not all areas have been investigated at the level of detailed required to create a robust relative curve. At present within our study region, this remains true of the Channel Islands in particular (although see Goslin et al. 2015 for a record from western Brittany which provides a close proxy).

Data on changes in eustatic values (taken from ice cores and coral reefs) can be combined with isostatic models of the rise and fall of the earth's crust in response to loading to create models of change through time at a range of scales. These models can be tested and refined through comparison to relative sea-level curves. Through this method it is possible to generate testable models for wide areas, and also to move from well constrained regions to less well known areas. As such, it was an appropriate method to adopt within this project, allowing for analysis at large and small spatial scales, and at temporal resolution of 500 year steps (from 20,000 BP to present day). When isostatic rebound values are matched with eustatic data to model the net changes that have occurred since 9000 BC, it becomes clear that parts of Scotland have been rising over the last 11,000 years (as it rebounds from weight that the glacier had placed on it during the last glacial maximum) while southern England has been slowly submerging.

Figure 1.04 provides an overview of the changes that occurred across the whole study region from 9000 BC to AD 1, drawing on Sturt et al. (2013). The seminal work of Coles (1998) and Gaffney et al. (2007) will mean that many readers are familiar with the most significantly visible changes: specifically the submergence of the North Sea and the loss of a permanent land connection between the

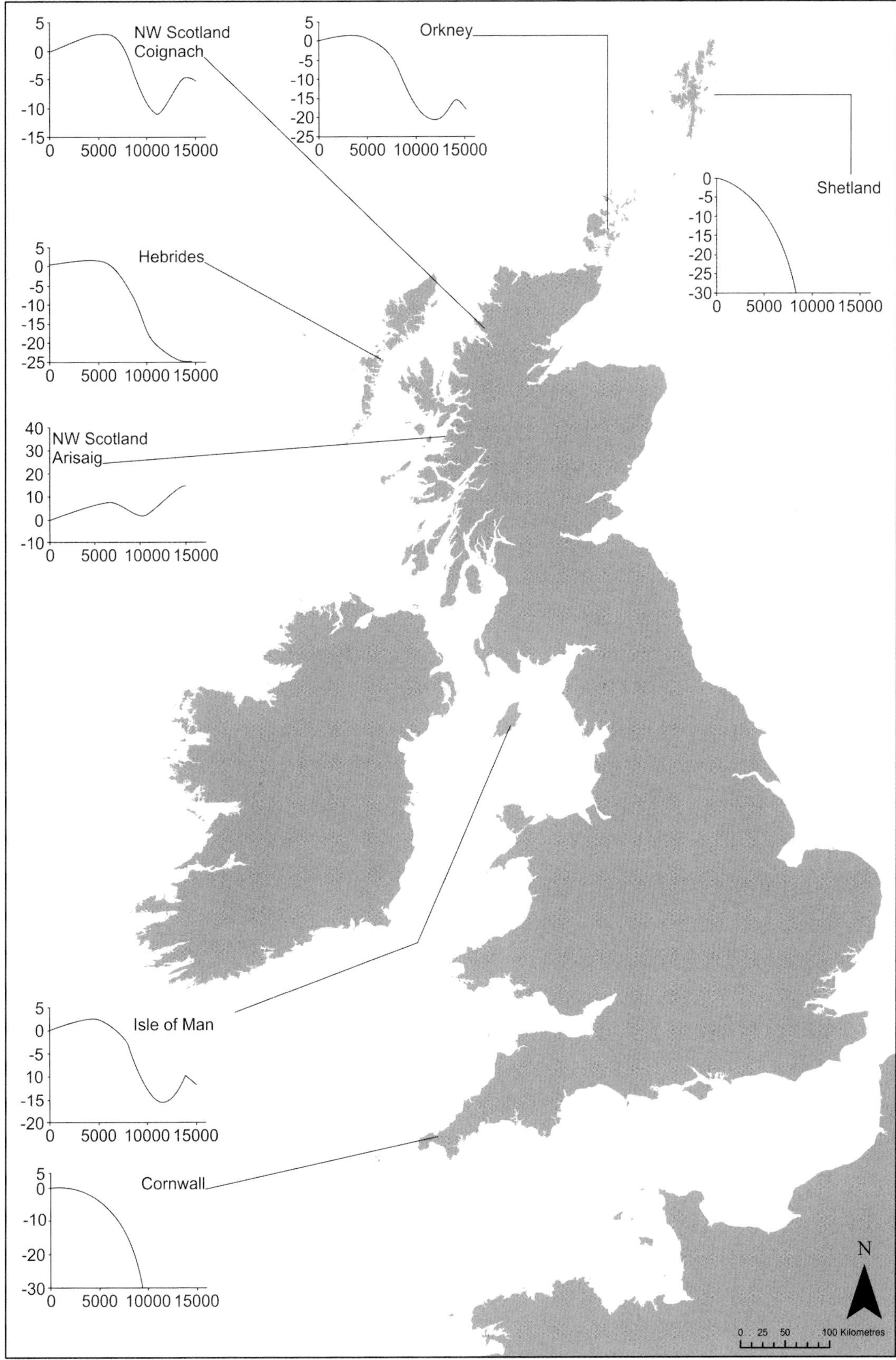

Figure 1.03. Relative sea-level curves from different parts of the study area. Topographic data from GEBCO14 (www.gebco.net). Sea-level curves from Shennan & Horton 2002.

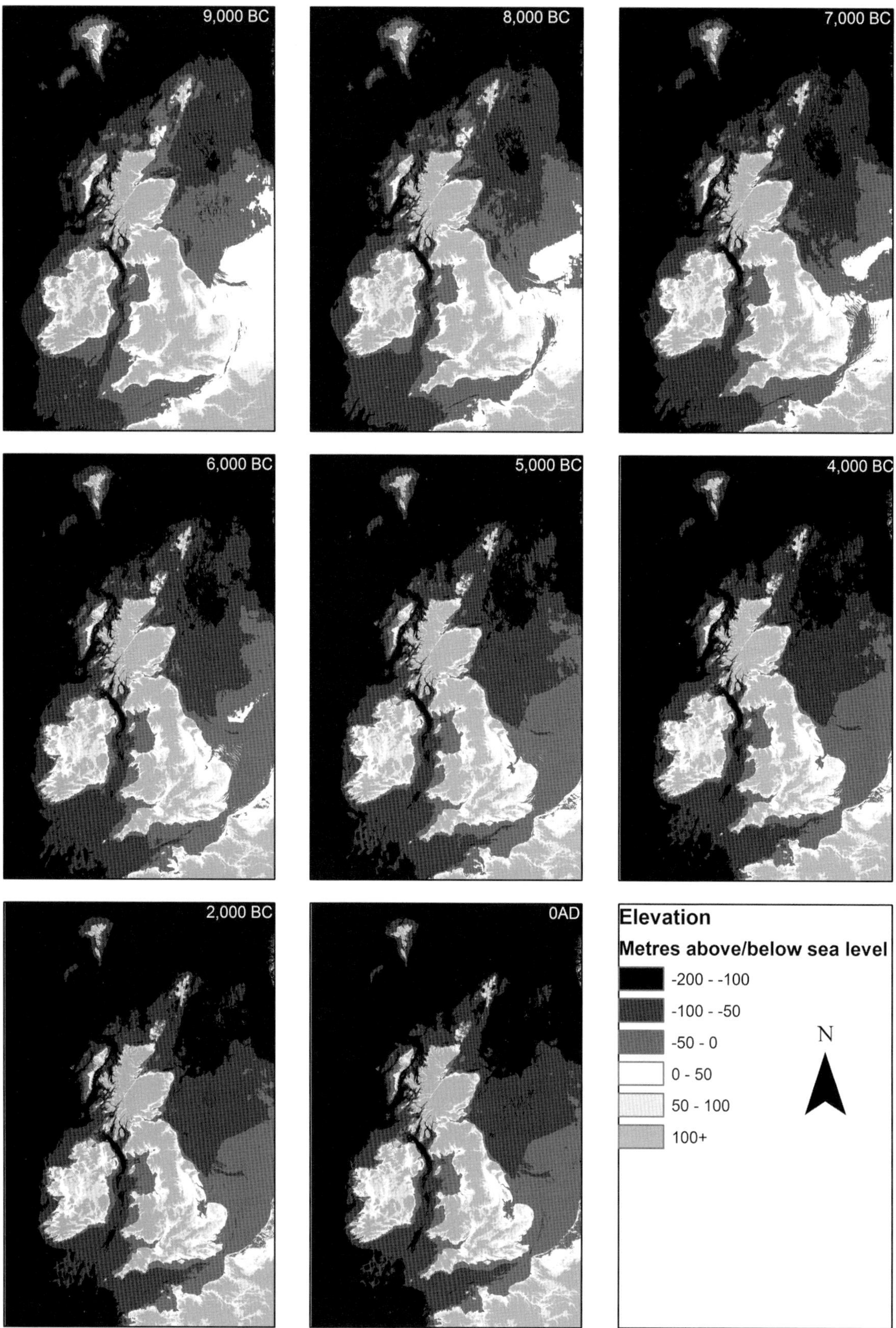

Figure 1.04. Overview of the changes that occurred across the whole study region from 9000 BC to AD 1. Topographic and bathymetric data from GEBCO14 (www.gebco.net), EMODnet (www.emodnet-bathymetry.eu) and the Ordnance Survey © Crown Copyright and Databse Right 2016. Ordnance Survey (Digimap Licence).

continental mainland and Britain c. 9000 years ago has received considerable attention (Coles 1998; Gaffney et al. 2007; Leary 2015). The modelled date for this separation (sometime between 9000 and 8000 years ago) matches well with peat records from the south coast of England (Waller and Kirby 2002) and the Seine Estuary (Frouin et al. 2007) giving a high level of confidence. However, the images given in Figure 1.04 smooth out the process of change. This belies a series of rapid vertical jumps in relative sea-level which are known to have occurred, with the most famous happening 8200 years ago (Hijma and Cohen 2010) where rapid rises of 1–3m are recorded along the Dutch coast.

We have argued elsewhere (Sturt et al. 2013; Sturt 2015) that while the overall picture presented in Figure 1.04 is undoubtedly useful, it can also serve to focus attention on what are seen to be 'big changes' – on the total area of land lost, or changes in physical connections. However, there is even more to be gained by considering the broader implications, not just the timing and tempo of change, but also its characteristics. For example, the loss of a marshy lowland connection between an island and contemporary mainland may have had less impact than associated behaviours in seaways. Did the process of submergence actually increase communication by easing maritime passage rather than preventing it by creating a barrier?

Furthermore, the reconstructions in Figure 1.04 and the eusatic curve given in Figure 1.02 can lead to an assumption that rapid sea-level change is all that we should be concerned with. It is clear that pan-regional significant changes occurred between 21,000 and 6,000 years ago, but then the absolute rate of vertical rise comparatively slowed. However, this does not mean that in all regions the pace of palaeogeographic change slowed at the same time. For low lying coastal areas, even small amounts of vertical change can lead to large differences. As such, the models we produced were deliberately multiscalar in nature, allowing us to reconsider the specifics of each island group at a higher resolution. The results of this work were highly informative and allowed for an improved understanding of the context within which peoples' lives played out. As Mackinder (1902) and Fox (1932) recognised, these differences can prove critical to our understanding of how and why archaeological patterns were formed.

Channel Islands

The absence of a robust relative sea-level curve for the Channel Islands, and its impact on our understanding of the archaeological record, was clearly articulated by Sebire and Renouf (2010). In order to address this issue they pulled together as robust a dataset as possible to allow for discussion of the most significant changes that would have occurred. Advances in computational modelling and the increasing access to higher resolution bathymetric and topographic datasets now allows for this problem to be tackled from a different direction (Sturt et al. 2013; Conneller et al. 2016). Before moving on to to describe the results from our models it is important to highlight a few caveats. First, these models are based on current topography and bathymetry (with data drawn from the states of Guernsey and Jersey, General Bathymetric Chart of the Oceans (www.gebco.net) and the European Marine Observation and Data Network (www.emodnet.eu/bathymetry)). This means that they do not account for erosion and sedimentation that has occurred over the period modelled. This can lead to significant variations, with large Holocene sandbanks (generated by marine processes) leading to 'false islands' being seen in the larger dataset visualised in Figure 1.04. Second, the time steps within the models smooth out change, meaning that although a timeslice might be given for 9000 BP, the changes may have occurred rapidly at the beginning of that time step, or slowly over its course. Thus the dates of change are broadly indicative. In essence, these models are good to think with and show the extent of change, but would always benefit from being ground-truthed and refined.

The paleogeographic story of the Channel Islands is interesting for the differences it reveals (Figure 1.05). As Sebire and Renouf (2010, 376) hypothesised, and has been argued elsewhere (Sturt et al. 2013; Conneller et al. 2016; Garrow and Sturt 2017) it appears likely that Guernsey separated from the mainland of France at sometime between 9000 and 8000 BC. At this point Guernsey and Herm are joined, forming the island of 'Greater Guernsey'. Similarly Alderney is larger in size, but now an island off the North French coast. At this time the intervening seas would have been shallow with large areas of inter-tidal zone. Greater Guernsey appears to break up c. 5000 BC, but was still probably connected through an inter-tidal link until at least 4000 BC. Work by Cazenave (2012, 243) indicates that tidal ranges at this time in this area may have been smaller, but perhaps not significantly so (a reduction of c. 1m). In contrast, Jersey appears to have remained connected until c. 5500 BC, with an inter-tidal link possibly persisting for longer. Recent work by Conneller et al. (2016, 36) also indicates a date of separation at this time. This variable process may well have impacted on the social trajectories of island activity. To be clear, we are not arguing that the process of becoming an island led to isolation, but it may have helped shape the types of activity and the nature of communication that occurred.

Isles of Scilly

Until very recently (Charman et al. 2016), the relative sea-level record for the Isles of Scilly was less robust than more heavily-studied regions along the coast of mainland Britain. This is despite the fact that it represents one of the most visible submerged landscapes in the British Isles, with

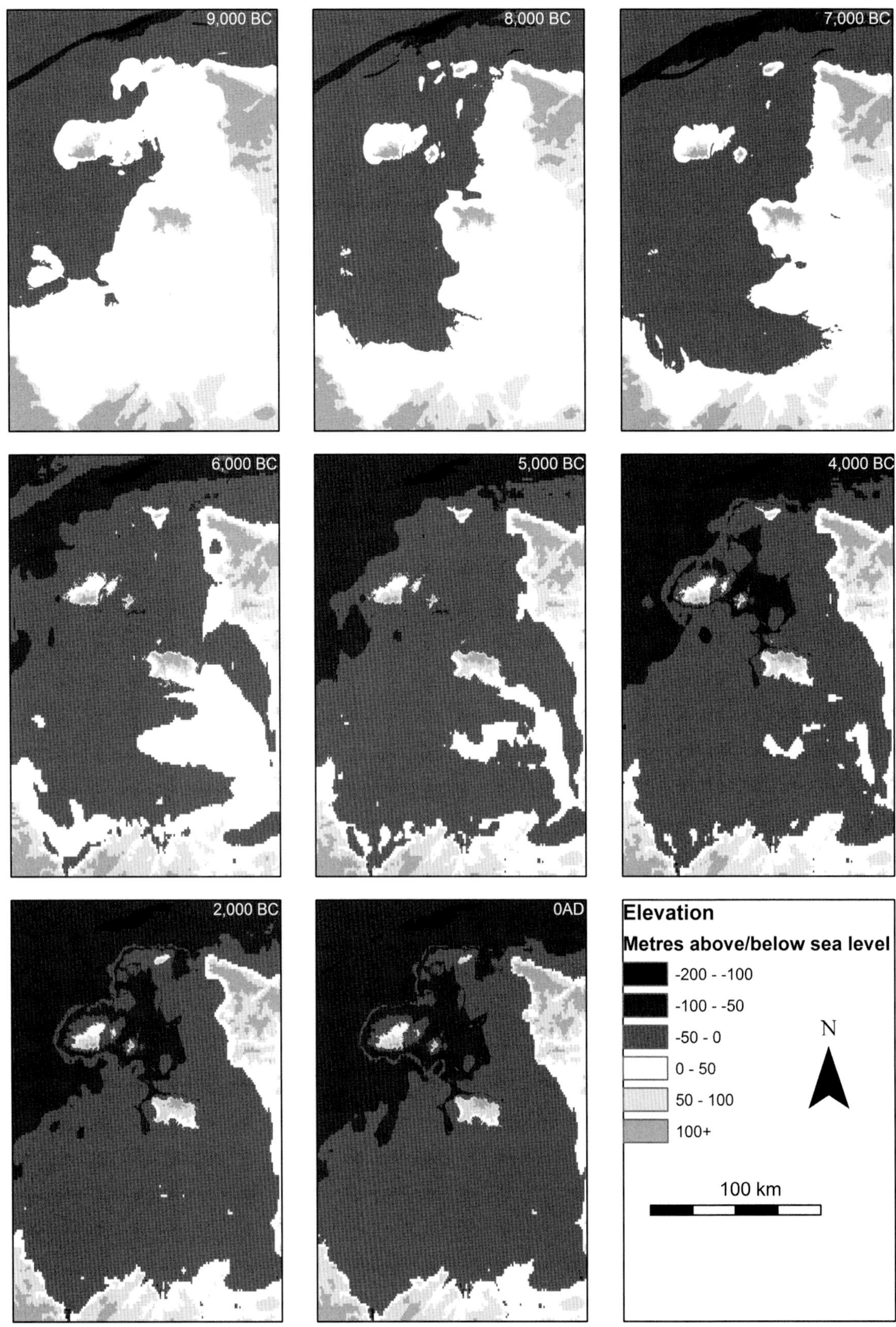

Figure 1.05. Channel Islands palaeogeography. Topographic and bathymetric data from GEBCO14 (www.gebco.net) and EMODnet (www.emodnet-bathymetry.eu) and Digimap Guernsey and Digimap Jersey.

its clear shallow waters allowing visitors to see submerged field systems between the islands of Samson and Tresco. So apparent are these features that they formed the subject of the very first article in the leading archaeological journal *Antiquity* (Crawford 1927). While visiting the islands for a holiday Crawford described 'one of those thrilling moments which occasionally occur in the life of an Archaeologist. Here before us was tangible proof that the land had sunk since prehistoric times' (1927, 6).

These early observations were not acted on in a more concerted manner until Thomas (1985) drew attention back to the islands, their archaeology and its relationship to sea-level. Subsequent work by Ratcliffe and Straker (1996) provided more detailed understanding of the nature of environmental and sea-level change, with much needed radiocarbon dates providing a more secure chronological framework from which models could be created. Most recently, work by Perez (2013; Perez et al. 2015) and Charman et al. (2016) as part of the Lyonesse Project (commissioned by Historic England) has further transformed our understanding, providing 67 new radiocarbon and ten optically stimulated luminescence (OSL) dates (Marshall et al. 2016, 89). These data allowed Charman et al. (2016, 193) to generate a range of palaeogeographic outputs. Significantly the additional sea-level index points gained through this project conform well to the relative sea-level curve generated from the GIA model in our own, adding confidence to the interpretations given below.

In Figure 1.06, the point that absolute rates of vertical sea-level rise do not dictate the extent of palaeogeographic change is amply bourn out. The granite batholith from which Scilly is sculpted rises sharply from the sea, then forms a low lying plateau. Sea-level rise through the early Holocene had comparatively little impact until c. 6000 BC when the single larger island begins to break up. What follows is a slow submergence, and increase in the area of the inter-tidal zone until the modern island of St Mary's breaks off from its more northerly neighbours c. 2500 BC. The most dramatic changes in landscape configuration then occur through the Bronze and Iron Ages over which time the islands begin to take on the form that we recognise today.

This pattern, and that shown in the broader UK wide palaeogeography (Figure 1.04), is significant for the record we uncovered at Old Quay (Chapter 3). As we have discussed previously (Anderson-Whymark et al. 2015, 958), c. 14,000 years ago the Isles of Scilly were a single large island, the end of an archipelago that spread out from Land's End. By 11,000 BC this archipelago had drastically reduced in size, but a chain of islands between Lands End and Scilly remained. The intermediate islands slowly reduce in size until c. 6000 BC when there is clear water between Scilly and mainland Britain. The former islands would have formed highly noticeable reefs (as they do today) and inter-tidal islets.

Outer Hebrides

Figure 1.07 demonstrates how variably the processes of sea-level change have played out. In comparison to the two previous island groups, the Outer Hebrides and north-west Scotland more generally have received considerable attention (Shennan and Horton 2002), due to the direct impact of glaciation and the nature of the environmental record preserved on the islands. For this region, the most significant changes occur over the earlier part of the Holocene, with a large coastal plain stretching south from modern Harris at 9000 BC. This larger landmass begins to reduce in size and break up until 4000 BC when the pace of change slows.

During the Neolithic, the models indicate a large inter-tidal zone and extensive coastal strip down the west coast of South Uist. However, as explained in Section 4.9, these renderings of the past coastline need to be treated with caution. The formation of machair and the rolling coastal dune system will have radically altered its shape. As such, it is possible, indeed probable, that the more extensive coastal plain existed for a longer period of time.

Summary

Within all of the above it is all too easy to focus on the land alone and let the sea recede into the background. Each of the maps discussed here (and presented in more detail, and in colour, in Sturt et al. 2013) also includes information on the changing nature of the connecting seaways. In each instance the sea during the period of interest was configured differently, affording differential access to marine resources, from the large inter-tidal zones and shallow seas surrounding Guernsey, through to the rich Atlantic waters washing the shores of the larger islands in Scilly and the Outer Hebrides.

1.5. Early Neolithic settlement in Britain and Ireland

The main focus of our excavation work on the Stepping Stones project was Early Neolithic *settlement*, although inevitably we captured other types of evidence and periods as well. This decision was made for a number of reasons. Whittle et al.'s work relating to various regions across Britain demonstrated that, in many places, monuments were not straightforwardly the first dated 'Neolithic' element (2011, 841). Consequently, in seeking the earliest Neolithic on island groups around Britain, settlements (and other indications of occupation such as artefact scatters) appeared to have more potential in this regard. Additionally, settlements were also deemed more likely to produce greater amounts and a more varied range of material culture, potentially enabling us to establish important material links with other places – a crucial outcome in a project of this kind. Given the prevalence of acidic soils

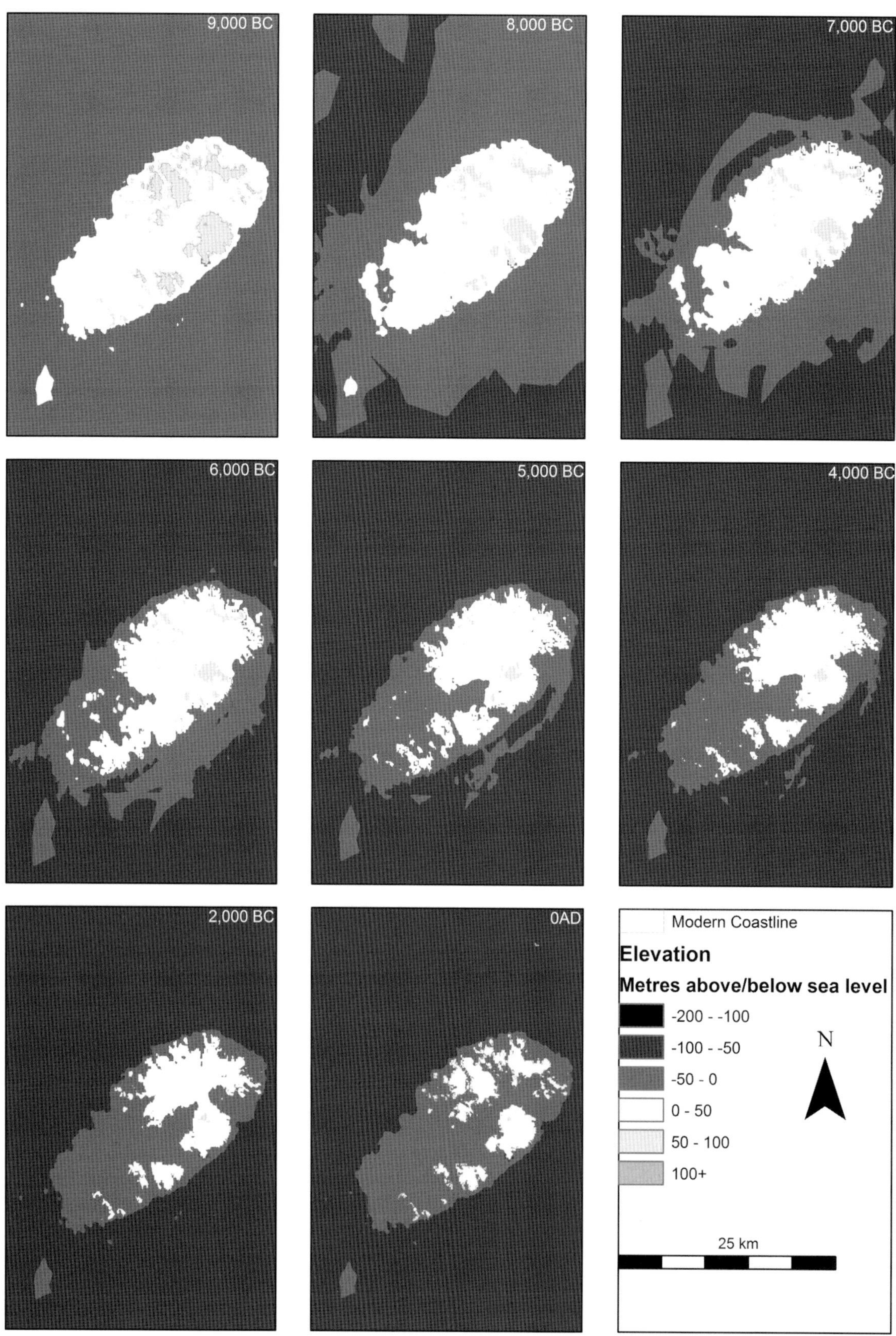

Figure 1.06. Isles of Scilly palaeogeography. Topographic and bathymetric data from GEBCO14 (www.gebco.net), EMODnet (www.emodnet-bathymetry.eu) and the Channel Coastal Observatory (www.channelcoast.org).

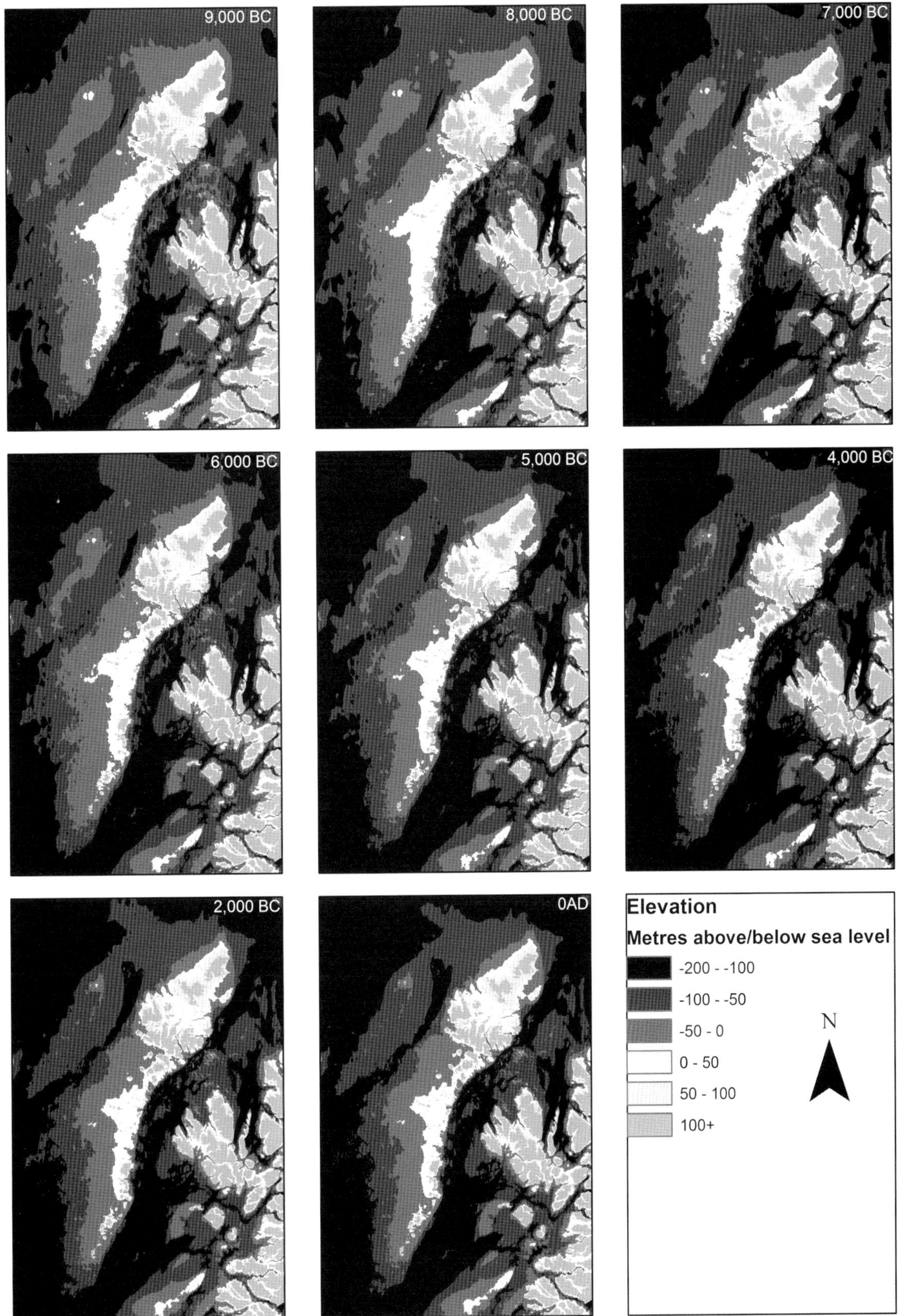

Figure 1.07. Outer Hebrides palaeogeography. Topographic and bathymetric data from GEBCO14 (www.gebco.net), EMODnet (www.emodnet-bathymetry.eu) and the Ordnance Survey © Crown Copyright and Databse Right 2016. Ordnance Survey (Digimap Licence).

around the western seaways zone, and consequent lack of bone survival, settlement sites also seemed more likely than tombs to produce material suitable for radiocarbon dating. Settlements are generally, of course, considerably less visible than monuments, and for that reason, in every one of the island groups, the former had been investigated much less, if at all; put simply, they were in real need of further investigation.

In making a case for focusing on Early Neolithic settlements, it is important also to acknowledge the fact that – in a project looking at the Mesolithic–Neolithic transition – we undoubtedly privileged the latter period in our fieldwork, as so many others have done before us (see Warren 2007). Ideally, we would have been able to investigate promising Late Mesolithic sites within the western seaways as well, but practically this was not possible. Relevant sites simply do not appear in the archaeological record in sufficient numbers (Section 1.6; Garrow & Sturt 2011), and for a research project that needed to produce concrete results speculative excavation was not necessarily the most appropriate approach. Nonetheless, projects that have been designed specifically to enhance the Mesolithic record, both in the Inner Hebrides (Mithen 2001; Hardy & Wickham-Jones 2009) and more recently in Orkney (Lee & Woodward 2009) have demonstrated that very impressive results can be achieved in the right circumstances. Certainly, in future, a project looking specifically at the Late Mesolithic in the western seaways zone could potentially produce a much richer understanding.

The Neolithic settlement landscape in Britain and Ireland has changed significantly over the past twenty years, primarily as a result of the discovery – largely through developer-funded excavation – of numerous new sites. Most impressive, perhaps, has been the remarkable rise in the numbers of known Early Neolithic buildings in Ireland, increasing from 14 in 1996 to 90 in 2014 (Smyth 2014, 1). Early Neolithic buildings, sometimes grouped in localised clusters, have also been recovered in parts of Britain as well, including eastern Scotland (Brophy 2007), north-west Wales (Kenney 2008) and parts of southern England (Booth et al. 2011) (see Thomas 2013, 285–314 for a recent overview). It is interesting to note that all of these have been post-built wooden constructions, even in areas where suitable stone exists.

Within the western seaways, understandings of the Early Neolithic settlement record have also changed, to varying degrees. In Orkney, the picture has been transformed in recent years by the identification of several Early Neolithic buildings, adding to the much better known, and until recently much better represented, Late Neolithic settlement record. These have included both wooden and stone-built architecture (see Richards & Jones 2016 for a summary). Similarly, at the other end of our study zone, several settlements have been excavated recently in the Channel Islands (see Section 1.6). In between, however, the picture has changed very little. In the Isles of Scilly, for example, Old Quay (Chapter 3, this volume) represents the first Neolithic occupation site excavated since the two pits dug at East Porth, Samson in the 1970s (Johns 2012, 59–60). Similarly, An Doirlinn (Chapter 4, this volume) represents the only major Neolithic site excavated in the Outer Hebrides since Henley's review of the evidence in 2003, a fact that is especially surprising given that the settlement record there is fairly well known and archaeologically visible. The settlement record of the Isle of Man also remains sparse and poorly understood (Burrow 1997; Garrow & Sturt 2011).

The *relatively* large increase in the number of Early Neolithic buildings known across Britain and Ireland in recent years has led to a corresponding rise in their prominence within narratives of that period. A number of authors have latched onto the concept of 'house societies' (originally developed in anthropology by Lévi-Strauss), suggesting that these buildings may actually have represented much more than just shelter for their occupants, symbolising the community and working as socially unifying objects in themselves during a time of significant change (e.g. Thomas 2013; Bradley 2013; Richards & Jones 2016). At the same time, there has also been a parallel shift away from the predominant narrative of the 1990s/2000s, which suggested that Neolithic buildings were extremely rare (in most regions at least), and that we must therefore incorporate a much wider spectrum of sites and practices in order to understand fully Neolithic occupation at that time (e.g. Pollard 1999; Whittle 1999; Garrow 2006). While some certainly still acknowledge that these other kinds of site must remain centrally important (e.g. Smyth 2014), 'houses' have definitely been placed back on centre stage. In this light, it is vitally important that we remain mindful of the fact that Neolithic structures have *not* been recovered in many regions, and do not persist *throughout* the Neolithic even in those regions where they have been found. Rather, as many have noted, they tend to have flourished for a fairly short period and then to have disappeared – in the case of the Ireland, for example, their existence was confined to a single century or so within the 1500 year total span of the Neolithic (Smyth 2014, 146). Nonetheless, in comparison to the situation a decade ago, there is now a feeling that Neolithic structures remain out there to be found, and that especially if we employ the right recovery techniques (large-scale open area excavations where possible and targeted work on sites with potential where not) more will be uncovered. This is also the case on the island groups in the western seaways: where relatively extensive programmes of excavation have taken place (e.g. Orkney and the Channel Islands) sites have been indeed found. Our work with the Stepping Stones project has shown that there is also potential elsewhere.

1.6. The Mesolithic, Neolithic and Early Bronze Age archaeology of the Channel Islands, Isles of Scilly and Outer Hebrides

In order to set the scene for the excavation report chapters that follow, in this section we outline briefly the character of the relevant archaeology on the three island groups. As discussed further below, all three excavated sites produced substantial amounts of Neolithic and Early Bronze Age material. The site at Old Quay also revealed a very important assemblage of microliths, whilst L'Erée too produced Mesolithic material. In this section, we therefore cover the Mesolithic, Neolithic and Early Bronze Age periods. As will become clear, the extent and kinds of known archaeology, and histories of excavation, on each of the three island groups are in fact surprisingly different – a first glimpse of the variability of evidence across the western seaways zone.

Channel Islands

The number of known Mesolithic sites in the Channel Islands has increased significantly in recent years, as a result of a sustained programme of investigation, including new collection and archive work in museums (Conneller et al. 2016). Whereas previously, Mesolithic evidence from the islands could be described as 'slender' (Kinnes 1982, 24) or 'extremely sparse' (Patton 1993, 9), a significant number of sites are now known. In his initial review of the evidence, Patton (1993) noted eight Mesolithic sites, but Conneller et al.'s study has increased this number to at least 23. There is a single possible (but uncertain) Early Mesolithic site from the islands, with Late/Final Mesolithic sites (c. 6200–5000 BC) also extremely rare. The vast majority of sites are Middle Mesolithic (c. 8500–6200 BC). Conneller et al. note that the upsurge in site numbers during the Middle Mesolithic closely matches the trend in the adjacent Cotentin peninsula in Normandy (2016, 37). At that time, Jersey would still have been connected to France, but Guernsey/Herm and possibly Sark (which may all still have been joined together) and Alderney would have been islands. Conneller et al. have suggested that 'Greater Guernsey' would have been large enough to allow both terrestrial prey and marine resources to be exploited during the Middle Mesolithic in a similar way to the peninsulas of the mainland, while Alderney may have been a convenient stopping off point for groups used to making sea voyages and may also have been attractive for its flint sources (2016, 41). The significant decrease in site numbers in the Channel Islands for the Late Mesolithic is puzzling, especially given the fact that the opposite appears to be the case on the French-owned islands off Brittany during this period (Marchand 2013; Conneller et al. 2016). We can probably assume that *activity* in the Channel Islands also actually decreased, but it is very difficult to know why this should have been the case.

Neolithic practices arrive on the Channel Islands c. 5000–4800 cal BC (Marcigny et al. 2010; Garrow et al. 2017) in association with Villeneuve-Saint-Germain (VSG) 'cordons' style pottery (see Table 1.01 for details of the French pottery sequence). With the exception of the unusual trapezoidal long mound at Les Fouaillages, Guernsey, all of the Early Neolithic and Middle Neolithic 1 sites[2] on the islands appear to be associated with 'domestic' occupation and 'buildings' rather than with monuments (Table 1.02). Three sites have produced Early Neolithic VSG 'cordons' pottery: Royal Hotel, St Peter Port, Guernsey (a probable settlement with a small post-built structure); L'Ouzière, Jersey (artefacts found in association with a preserved peat horizon); and Les Fouaillages, Guernsey where the pottery has been described as 'transitional VSG/Cerny' (Hélène Pioffet pers. comm.). It is worth noting that the tomb at Les Fouaillages is essentially unique in terms of its architecture (even including sites on the adjacent mainland) and also apparently extremely early in date, being as early as the earliest Carnac mounds in Brittany for example (see Scarre 2011, 92). In addition to these excavated sites, stray finds of 'Cinglais' flint (imported from Normandy) and polished stone rings – both artefact types with strong VSG associations on the French mainland (see Sections 2.5 and 2.6 for further details) – have also been found across the islands (Patton 1995, 31; Marcigny et al. 2010, 123; Fromont 2013). In Britanny, the presence of these artefact types has been used as evidence for the full arrival of the Neolithic (Pailler et al. 2008), but it is

Table 1.01. Neolithic and EBA pottery typologies and their approximate dates in north-west France

Pottery styles in NW France	*Broad period*	*Dates (approximate)*
Rubané récent du Bassin parisien	Early Neolithic	5200–5000 BC
Villeneuve-Saint-Germain ancien	Early Neolithic	5100–5000 BC
Villeneuve-Saint-Germain classique	Early Neolithic	5000–4900 BC
Villeneuve-Saint-Germain 'cordons'	Early Neolithic	4900–4800 BC
Cerny ancien (Néolithique Moyen Ia)	Middle Neolithic	4800–4600 BC
Castellic/Pinacle-Fouaillages/Chambon (Néolithique Moyen Ib)	Middle Neolithic	4600–4300 BC
Néolithique Moyen 2	Middle Neolithic	4300–3500 BC
Néolithique Récent	Late Neolithic	3500–2700 BC
Néolithique Final	Final Neolithic	2700–2300 BC
Chalcolithic/EBA	Chalcolithic/EBA	2500–1600 BC

Table 1.02. Early/Middle Neolithic occupation sites on the Channel Islands

Site	*Island*	*Phase*	*Site type*	*Reference*
Royal Hotel, St Peter Port	Guernsey	VSG 'cordons'	Post-hole structure; artefact-rich layers	Sebire 2012
Les Fouaillages (Phase 1b)	Guernsey	VSG 'cordons'	Artefacts associated with Phase 1b mound of tomb	Kinnes 1982; Pioffet 2013
L'Ouzière	Jersey	VSG 'cordons'	Artefacts associated with a preserved peat layer	Patton & Finlaison 2001
Herm	Herm	Cerny ancien	Beam-slot structures (possible)	C. Scarre & H. Pioffet pers. comm.
Mont Orgeuil	Jersey	Cerny ancien	Artefacts associated with a dark 'occupation layer'	Barton 1984
L'Erée	Guernsey	Pinacle-Fouaillages	Pits, post-holes, hearths	Ch. 2, this volume
Les Fouaillages (Phase 1d)	Guernsey	Pinacle-Fouaillages	Artefacts associated with Phase 1d cists in tomb	Kinnes 1982; Pioffet 2013
La Motte	Jersey	Pinacle-Fouaillages	Artefacts possibly associated with a midden	Warton 1913; Marcigny et al. 2010
Le Pinacle	Jersey	Pinacle-Fouaillages	Occupation layer on axe production site, associated with hearths/middens	Godfray & Burdo 1949; Patton 1991
Guernsey Airport	Guernsey	Middle Neolithic 2	Ditches, post-holes, hearth	Philip de Jersey pers. comm.

equally possible that they were being exchanged between indigenous Mesolithic groups and Neolithic farmers to the east. The presence of these materials and object types in the Channel Islands indicate that the islands' populations were themselves involved in long-distance exchange networks across north-west France. As in so many places elsewhere, it is difficult to say whether Neolithic practices arrived in the Channel Islands through indigenous adoption or migration from France (see also Patton 1995, 21; Bukach 2004, 161) – the seemingly very low levels of Late Mesolithic activity potentially suggest that there, more clearly than in other regions, migration may in fact have been the main driver of change. Given the relatively low numbers of sites early in the Neolithic sequence, it is quite possible that the process of transition was a fairly extended one played out over several centuries.

Two sites in the Channel Islands have produced assemblages of Middle Neolithic 1a 'Cerny ancien' pottery (c. 4800–4600 BC), placing them perhaps a century or two later than those described above: the 'dark occupation layer' found at Mont Orgeuil in Jersey, and two possible beam-slots probably associated with a building on Herm. The subsequent Middle Neolithic 1b phase (c. 4600–4300 BC) is characterised by its own regional 'Pinacle-Fouaillages' pottery style (Constantin 1985; Patton 1992). Sites include the axe production centre and occupation site at Le Pinacle, artefacts possibly associated with a midden at La Motte, a later phase (1d) of the long mound at Les Fouaillages and the settlement site at L'Erée (Chapter 2, this volume).

It is during the Middle Neolithic 2 period that the Channel Islands' best-known Neolithic archaeology appears, in the form of the numerous and often very impressive passage graves scattered across the islands (Patton 1995, 35–63; Sebire 2005, 63–88). Very few of these sites have been radiometrically dated, but on the basis of the small number of radiocarbon dating programmes that have occurred (Schulting, Sebire & Robb 2010; Garrow et al. 2017), and comparisons with tombs in mainland France, it seems likely that most would have been constructed c. 4300–3800 BC. In contrast to previous phases of the Neolithic, occupation sites of any sort are extremely rare – limited to a few ambiguous features found at Guernsey airport (Phil de Jersey pers. comm.) and possibly also the 'midden' at La Motte, Jersey (Patton 1995, 35).

The site excavated at L'Erée (Chapter 2, this volume) represents the only Late/Final Neolithic 'occupation' site on the islands (see for example Patton 1995, 64). Similarly, only a few monuments date to this period – these include a small number of *allées couvertes* gallery grave tombs and the unusual 'cist-in-circle' burial sites which are unique to the Channel Islands (Patton 1995, 78–82). It is likely that the mysterious 'statue menhirs' and perhaps many of the other standing stones known on the islands also date to this phase (Sebire 2005, 78–83). Long-distance connections are again reflected by the presence of flint imported from western France, in this phase from the famous quarries at Grand Pressigny (see also Section 2.5).

The Chalcolithic/Early Bronze Age period is well-represented in the Channel Islands. In addition to Beaker pottery, we are also dealing here with 'Jersey Bowls', an associated Channel Islands-specific style (Hawkes 1937; Patton 1995, 161). Additional plain, coarse-ware, flat-bottomed vessel types characterise the EBA (see Section 2.4). It is possible that a small number of round barrows were constructed on the Channel Islands during this period, but they have not been extensively explored (Sebire 2005, 91–92). Burials of this date were commonly placed in earlier, Neolithic tombs and many Beakers and Jersey Bowls (and other associated items) have been found within them as a result (Patton 1995, 98). 'Cist-in-circles' probably extend into this period as well, and occasional other 'ritual' sites have been identified (e.g. the 'ritual mound/platform' and cists at La Tête de Quennevais: Patton & Finlaison 2001). Occupation evidence is relatively abundant, but is at the same time difficult to interpret. Post-holes, hearths and pits were recovered adjacent to the earlier tomb at Les Fouaillages (Sebire 2005, 91), and substantial Chalcolithic/EBA occupation layers were identified at Le Pinacle, Jersey (Godfray & Burdo 1950) and at Jerbourg, Guernsey, possibly in association with an earthwork rampart (Burns 1988). Chalcolithic/EBA material has also been recovered from deposits variously described as 'occupation debris', 'midden layers', etc. at various other sites across the islands (Table 1.03).

As Table 1.03 demonstrates very clearly, while Late Neolithic/Chalcolithic/EBA 'occupation' sites are fairly numerous, they have not generally produced obvious settlement features such as buildings, but rather midden-type deposits and generalised spreads of material. This pattern broadly echoes that seen in the adjacent regions of mainland France (e.g. Salanova 2000, 27).

In summary, it is possible to determine a number of key themes that emerge from this brief consideration of the Channel Islands evidence:

- The very low visibility of Late Mesolithic occupation on the islands is puzzling in itself, and also makes it difficult to ascertain fully the nature of the Mesolithic–Neolithic transition
- The transition was possibly played out over an extended time-frame, and (like many other regions) may well have involved the (probably very limited) indigenous population and incoming migrants from France
- Early Neolithic/Middle Neolithic 1 settlements appear to be varied in character, and do not closely match the long-house settlements seen on the adjacent mainland (during the VSG phase)
- Middle Neolithic 2 settlements are almost invisible (especially in comparison to the contemporary, highly-visible, passage grave monumental evidence)
- Late Neolithic/Chalcolithic/EBA 'occupation' sites are numerous but their precise character is difficult to define

Isles of Scilly

The known Mesolithic archaeology on the Isles of Scilly, prior to our excavations at Old Quay (Chapter 3, this volume), was very sparse, with the only evidence a few stray flint artefacts and small artefact scatters (Table 1.04). As a result, the general consensus in recent years has been that, during the Mesolithic, the islands were probably visited only on a seasonal basis by groups travelling by boat from the mainland (Ratcliffe 1989, 33; Robinson 2007, 65; Garrow & Sturt 2011; Johns 2012, 46). Following its separation from Cornwall c. 11,500 BC, travel to and from Scilly required an increasing degree of maritime skill. The islands represent a challenging landfall surrounded by rocky reefs, complex tidal patterns and often foggy conditions, which even in small-scale, lightweight Mesolithic boats would sometimes have presented a real threat to life and limb. However, those same rocks and eddies, along with the rapid change from deep to shallow water seen around the islands, may also have been attractive for the variety of marine life they encouraged and supported. As such, it is also possible to see this potentially challenging navigational destination also as an attractive place within the Mesolithic maritime landscape.

The known Neolithic archaeology of Scilly (again prior to our excavations at Old Quay) was similarly thin on the ground. The only excavated features were two pits found in 1971 at East Porth, Samson, one of which contained substantial quantities of Hembury-style Early Neolithic pottery (Johns 2012, 73). In addition, diagnostic Neolithic pottery had also been identified at Old Quay, and at Porth Killier, St Agnes and Bonfire Carn, Bryher (ibid.); undiagnostic pottery in putatively Neolithic fabrics has been found at six more sites (Table 1.05; Section 3.4). A few probably Neolithic flint stray finds were also known (Johns 2012, figure 4.3). There are no known Neolithic monuments on the islands. As a result of these apparently very low levels

Table 1.03. Late Neolithic/Chalcolithic/EBA occupation sites on the Channel Islands

Site	*Island*	*Site type*	*Reference*
Jerbourg	Guernsey	Occupation layer, rampart (?)	Burns 1988
Les Fouaillages	Guernsey	Pits, post-holes, etc.	Sebire 2005, 91
L'Erée	Guernsey	Occupation layer, enclosure (?)	Chapter 2, this volume
Rousse Tower	Guernsey	Occupation layer	Clifton Antiquarian Club 2015
Icho Islet	Jersey	Midden	Hawkes 1937
La Motte	Jersey	Midden	Hawkes 1937
La Moye 1	Jersey	Enclosure/structures	Patton 1984
La Pulente	Jersey	Midden	Hawkes 1937
La Tête de Quennevais	Jersey	Ritual platform, cist	Patton & Finlaison 2001
Le Petit Port	Jersey	Midden	Hawkes 1937
Le Pinacle	Jersey	Occupation layer, rampart (?)	Godfray & Burdo 1950
Les Blanches Banques	Jersey	Occupation layer, hearth	Patton & Finlaison 2001
La Maîtresse Île	Les Minquiers	Midden	Hawkes 1937

Table 1.04. Mesolithic flintwork from the Isles of Scilly prior to the Old Quay excavations

Location	*Artefact type*	*Reference*
Veronica Farm, Bryer	Possible tranchet axe sharpening flake.	Ratcliffe & Thorpe 1991, 24. Isles of Scilly Museum (IOSM). Electrification Project, site 174
The Brow, Bryher	Mesolithic or Neolithic blade and other flints.	Ratcliffe & Thorpe 1991, 24; Johns 2013, 46. IOSM. Electrification Project, RN 1599
The Town, Bryher	Mesolithic or Neolithic 'bladelet' (possible)	Ratcliffe & Thorpe 1991, 24; Johns 2013, 46. IOSM. Electrification Project, site 143
Higher Town, St Martin's	Single platform core	Ratcliffe & Thorpe 1991, 24.
Old Quay, St Martin's	Nine microliths and other flintwork	Ratcliffe & Thorpe 1991, 24; Dennis et al. 2013
Knackyboy Cairn, St Martin's	Borer-needle in association with flints in rock cleft	Johns 2012, 46
Halangy Down, St Mary's	Geometric microlith	Ashbee 1996, 90
Klondyke Fields, St Mary's	Two c. 70mm blades with facetted butts. One exhibits slight edge-retouch and a burin removal. Upper Palaeolithic–Mesolithic? Formerly described erroneously as 'Larnian blades'	IOSM Accession no. 645
Newford Farm, Higher Newford, St Mary's	Probable broken broad blade microlith and a blade (among other flints)	IOSM New accession September 2013
Porthcressa, St Mary's	Unfinished pebble hammer	Johns 2012, 46. IOSM.
New Inn, New Grimsby, Tresco	Mesolithic or early Neolithic bladelet	Ratcliffe & Thorpe 1991, 24. IOSM. Electrification Project, site 169
Scilly: unspecified location	Broken broad blade microlith	IOSM Accession no. 807
Scilly: unspecified location	Obliquely blunted point	Royal Cornwall Museum, Truro
Scilly: unspecified location	Possible late upper Palaeolithic curved-backed 'penknife' point	Johns 2012, 42 & fig. 3.1. Royal Cornwall Museum, Truro

Table 1.05. Sites with Neolithic pottery on the Isles of Scilly

Site	*Island*	*Site type*	*Reference*
East Porth	Samson	Two pits	Johns 2012, 73
Old Quay	St Martin's	Post-holes, pits, hearths, midden, etc.	this volume
Bonfire Carn	Bryher	South Western Bowl sherds	Quinnell 1994
Porth Killier	St Agnes	South Western Bowl sherds	Johns 2012, 60
Veronica Farm	Bryher	Sherds in Neolithic fabric	Quinnell 1994
Periglis Cottage	St Agnes	Sherds in Neolithic fabric	Quinnell 1994
Turk's Head	St Agnes	Sherds in Neolithic fabric	Quinnell 1994
Lower Town	St Martin's	Sherds in Neolithic fabric	Quinnell 1994
Dolphin Town	Tresco	Sherds in Neolithic fabric	Quinnell 1994
Midden	Annet	Sherds in Neolithic fabric (possible)	Robinson 2007, 65

of activity, it has generally been assumed that during the Neolithic, as in the Mesolithic, Scilly was probably occupied only seasonally by sea from mainland Cornwall (Robinson 2007; Johns 2012, 52). However, recently the very valid point has been made that

> with the exception of the tor enclosures and quoits in Penwith and taking into account the small scale of the Islands, the [Neolithic] evidence may not be that different from the mainland – i.e. small pits, pottery and flints – and Cornwall is not considered to have been unpopulated during the Neolithic (Johns 2012, 52).

Given the possible absence of permanent settlement during both Mesolithic and Neolithic, it does not seem particularly meaningful to talk about a 'Mesolithic–Neolithic transition' on the islands. The earliest Neolithic arrives in western Cornwall around c. 3800 cal BC (Whittle et al. 2011, 516).

The Early Bronze Age witnesses a dramatic change in the archaeological record in Scilly, with the widespread appearance of entrance graves, cairns and standing stones. Scillonian entrance graves are small chambered cairns, comprising a roughly circular mound of stone and earth, revetted by a kerb and containing a chamber (Johns 2012, 66). They are found in impressively large numbers on the islands – the Cornwall and Scilly HER records at least 90 entrance graves, including 21 probable and 13 possible examples (Sawyer 2015, 30–31) – and in fact there are far more known from Scilly than on the mainland (ibid.). Whilst entrance graves share some similarities with Neolithic tombs elsewhere, on the basis of an increasing corpus of radiocarbon dates and other associated material culture, they are now generally considered to be Bronze Age in date (Jones & Thomas 2010; Johns 2012, 62; Sawyer 2015, 89). Bone has very occasionally been found within them, but not often. While this may well be predominantly a result of the acidic soils they were constructed on, they have sometimes contained substantial deposits of a dark greasy soil not obviously associated with burial (Johns 2012, 69). Jones & Thomas have suggested that they may have been communal shrines as much as being repositories for the dead (2010, 289).

A total of 384 cairns are recorded in Scilly, the majority of which occur within sometimes very dense cairn-fields (Johns 2012, 70). Few have been excavated and it is therefore difficult to construct a chronological sequence for these monuments. However, it seems probable that most date to the earlier part of the Bronze Age (ibid.; Sawyer 2015, 88). It is likely that many were used for burial – several have contained cists – as well as acting as a mechanism for field clearance (although again, without much excavation having taken place, it is impossible to be certain). Thirteen standing stones are known from the islands (Johns 2012, 71).

Very little is known about the character of EBA settlement on the islands. Occasional finds of probably EBA material have been recovered within small pits (Johns 2012, 73), and it is also thought likely that traces of EBA occupation could underlie some of the many known later settlement sites (ibid., 59). As far as EBA material culture is concerned, five probable findspots of mainland-type vessels are known, including a single Collared Urn and a small number of Trevisker vessels/sherds (Johns 2012, 61–62). The most common prehistoric ceramic in Scilly is a style unique to the islands, best described as 'Scillonian Bronze Age' (see Section 3.4). This is found both in burial-related contexts such as entrance graves and cairns and in domestic contexts such as hut circles and middens (Johns 2012, 61–62). Like the closely related Trevisker style, this pottery appears to have been produced throughout the second millennium BC (ibid.).

The sheer quantities of known EBA archaeology on the islands, combined with the development of an islands-specific type of pottery (and associated lack of mainland styles), have generally been taken as evidence that Scilly was permanently settled (for the first time) during the Early Bronze Age (e.g. Johns 2012, 66; Sawyer 2015, 118).

In summary, the key themes that emerge from this brief consideration of the Isles of Scilly evidence are:

- The known Mesolithic and Neolithic archaeology of the islands is relatively sparse (although excavations at Old Quay have changed this picture to an extent – see Chapter 3)
- Consequently Scilly has generally been thought not to have been permanently settled until the EBA (and thus it does not seem especially appropriate to define a Mesolithic–Neolithic transition specifically on the islands)
- The visibility of the archaeological record changes dramatically during the EBA, with the appearance of entrance graves and cairns in large numbers
- There is, however, still very little clear EBA settlement evidence on the islands

Outer Hebrides

The Mesolithic of the Outer Hebrides had, until very recently, proved elusive archaeologically. Although the presence of micro-charcoal and subtle changes in pollen profiles suggested human occupation of the islands during that period (Edwards 1996; Edwards & Whittington 2000), the first confirmed direct archaeological evidence for the Mesolithic was published only in 2005 – a series of hazelnut shells radiocarbon dated to 7060–6650 and 6510–6090 cal BC recovered at the base of a midden at Northon, Harris (Gregory et al. 2005, 945). The contextual integrity of these nutshells is a little uncertain, as they were found in a layer which also contained barley grains and a sheep bone; consequently, they have been interpreted as being within an originally Mesolithic deposit subsequently cultivated during the Neolithic (ibid.; Gregory et al. 2005, 78–79).

Since this recognition of a Mesolithic element to the multi-period midden at Northton, several more sites have been discovered in the region as a result of a sustained programme of work led by Durham University (Table 1.06). Aird Callanais, Lewis (originally excavated some years before (Flitcroft & Heald 1997)) was recently radiocarbon dated to the Late Mesolithic (Bishop et al. 2014); additionally, new sites at Temple Bay, Tràigh na Beirigh (Sites 2 and 9) and Pabaigh Mòr, Harris, have been identified. All of these sites – shell middens and/or surviving 'old land surfaces' – represent only partially (and, due to the sea, precariously) surviving deposits that have not been extensively excavated. Nonetheless, the identification and subsequent radiocarbon dating of a series of sites extending from possibly as early as the late 8th millenium to the late 5th millennium cal BC represents a hugely significant step change in our

Table 1.06. Mesolithic occupation sites in the Outer Hebrides

Site	*Island*	*Site type*	*Date (approx.) BC*	*Reference*
Aird Calanais	Lewis	Occupation remains, possible hearth	6000–4500	Flitcroft & Heald 1997; Bishop 2014
Northton	Harris	Occupation remains, midden?	7100–6100	Simpson et al. 2006
Pabaigh Mòr	Harris	Shell midden	TBA	Church & Rowley Conwy 2013
Temple Bay	Harris	Midden, land surface, scoop	5700–5400	Church et al. 2012
Tràigh na Beirigh (Site 2)	Harris	Shell midden, old ground surface	6500–6100	Bishop et al. 2014
Tràigh na Beirigh (Site 9)	Harris	Shell midden, old ground surface	TBA	Snape-Kennedy et al. 2014

knowledge of the Mesolithic in the Outer Hebrides. Two substantial projects focused on Inner Hebridean islands, conducted during the late 1990s/early 2000s (Mithen 2000; Hardy & Wickham Jones 2009), demonstrated the wealth of Mesolithic sites that could be found through sustained survey and excavation projects; this work could well provide us with a glimpse of the extent of Mesolithic archaeology that remains to be found in the Outer Hebrides as well.

The Neolithic of the Outer Hebrides is well-known both for its tombs and its settlements, with the latter featuring more prominently in archaeological narratives there than most other regions of Britain. It is widely agreed that the Neolithic tombs found on the islands fall into two main groups – passage graves and Clyde cairns – a division first discussed in detail by Henshall (1972). As their name suggests, the latter can be seen as suggesting close connections with (and even origins in) the west coast of mainland Scotland; the former have been seen by some as a specifically Hebridean instantiation of this widely distributed monument form. The general lack of modern excavations of Neolithic tombs in the Outer Hebrides, and total absence of related radiocarbon dates (Garrow et al. 2017), has ensured that neither the chronological relationship between these two different types of tomb, nor their chronological position within the overall span of the Neolithic, are well understood (Armit 1996, 76; Henley 2003, 168). Armit (ibid.) has observed a general absence in tombs of the highly-decorated Hebridean and Unstan ware pottery styles found on many settlement sites (see below). Several writers have discussed the fact that there is a higher density of tombs in North Uist than elsewhere on the islands, suggesting that this could have been a consequence of social competition and pressure on land in this region at that time (Sharples 1992, 327; Armit 1996, 76; see also Henley 2003, 166).

In contrast to the situation with tombs, with a single exception, all of the known Neolithic settlements in the Outer Hebrides have been excavated recently under modern conditions (Table 1.07). Probably the best known, and certainly the most spectacular site in terms of its surviving archaeology, is Eilean Domhnuill, excavated by Ian Armit and his team in the late 1980s (the site's full monograph publication is close to completion; Armit 2003 presents a concise summary). Eilean Domhnuill is located on a small artificial islet within Loch Olabhat on the north coast of North Uist, connected to the loch shore by a narrow causeway. Eleven separate phases of Neolithic archaeology were identified, with the site's occupation dated to c. 3650–2600 cal BC (Armit 2003, 93; see also Garrow et al.

Table 1.07. Neolithic occupation sites in the Outer Hebrides

Site	*Island*	*Site type*	*Reference*
Allt Chrisal	Barra	Multi-phase buildings, hearths, post-holes, large amounts of material culture, etc.	Branigan & Foster 1995
Northton	Harris	Midden, possible structure	Simpson et al. 2006
Dunasbroc	Lewis	Possible occupation site (single post-hole and pottery/flint/quartz, but not in situ)	McHardy et al. 2009
Eilean nan Luchruban (Pygmies Isle)	Lewis	Possible occupation site (pottery, but not in situ)	Mackenzie 1905; McHardy et al. 2009
Olcote	Lewis	Possible occupation site (Neolithic and Beaker pottery, possibly associated with post-holes under cairn)	Neighbour 2005
Stac Dumhnuill Chaim	Lewis	Possible occupation site (pottery, but not in situ)	McHardy et al. 2009
Loch Arnish	Lewis	Islet site (Neolithic pottery found on loch bed)	Sheridan et al. 2014; Garrow, Sturt & Copper 2017
Loch Bhorgastail	Lewis	Islet site (Neolithic pottery found on loch bed)	Sheridan et al. 2014; Garrow, Sturt & Copper 2017
Loch Langabhat	Lewis	Islet site (Neolithic pottery found on loch bed)	Sheridan et al. 2014; Garrow, Sturt & Copper 2017
Barpa Langais	North Uist	Possible occupation site (post-settings, quartz working debris, base of undated pot, etc.)	Holderness 2007
Bharpa Carinish	North Uist	Three hearths, spreads of ash/charcoal, fragment of stone wall, post-holes	Crone et al. 1993
Eilean an Tighe	North Uist	Islet settlement with multi-phase buildings, hearths, post-holes, large amounts of material culture, etc.	Scott 1951
Eilean Domhnuill	North Uist	Islet settlement with multi-phase buildings, hearths, post-holes, large amounts of material culture, etc.	Armit 2003
Rubh' a' Charnain Moir/Screvan quarry	North Uist	Irregular large pit, lots of pottery, possible stone wall	Downes & Badcock 1998
The Udal	North Uist	Buildings with hearths, post-holes, etc.	Selkirk 1996
An Doirlinn	South Uist	Multi-phase buildings, hearths, post-holes, large amounts of material culture, etc.	Ch 4, this volume
Loch a'Choire	South Uist	Possible occupation site (pottery and flint)	Henley 2012
Bioruaslam	Vatersay	Possible midden (Neolithic sherds associated with otherwise undated midden)	Branigan & Foster 2002

2017). The best-preserved phases contained low stone walls (probably originally built up to roof height with turf), stone-built hearths, post-holes, spreads of occupation debris, etc. The lowest waterlogged levels contained wattlework and other preserved organic remains (Armit 1990, 15). The site produced extremely large quantities of material culture, especially pottery (22,000+ sherds), leading Henley to suggest that the accumulation of material in this way was perhaps a more significant element of the site to its occupants than the architecture (2003, 99). Certainly, many original structural elements had been reconfigured, dismantled and demolished during successive remodelling episodes (Armit 2003, 95). Large quantities of charred cereals and wild plant remains, a sizeable animal bone assemblage, quernstones, polished axes, carved stone balls, worked pumice and many other items were recovered (Armit 1986; 1987; 1988; 1990; see Henley 2003, 44–68 for a concise summary of the evidence). In the context of such material richness, the 'impoverished' (Armit 1992, 313) worked stone assemblage of no more than a few dozen pieces is particularly notable. Armit has suggested that due to seasonally fluctuating water levels the site could not have been occupied all year round (2003, 98), but at the same time emphasised the fact that 'clearly Eilean Domhnuill was a major fixed point in the landscape for a period of around 1000 years, around 40 generations … Whatever else it was, Eilean Domhnuill was *important* and *permanent*' (ibid., emphasis original). Copper has suggested that sites like Eilean Domhnuill with very substantial material repetories may have been locations where feasting and commensality involving relatively large groups of people regularly took place (2015, 450–451).

The impressive architecture and material culture assemblages excavated at Eilean Domhnuill are echoed – albeit in a slightly less well-preserved and somewhat less abundant way – at several other sites (Table 1.07). Eilean an Tighe, another island site that is comparable in many ways, produced multiple phases of occupation, stone-built hearths, spreads of occupation debris, post-holes, a large assemblage of pottery and other material. The site was originally described as a pottery workshop (Scott 1951) but this task-specific interpretation has subsequently been widely dismissed. The archaeology uncovered at Allt Chrisal was also similar, if again less well-preserved – a complex sequence of buildings, stone-built hearths, spreads of occupation debris, substantial amounts of material culture. It is possible that another comparable settlement – consisting of low stone-built walls, substantial hearths, etc. – was recovered at The Udal, but the absence of any formal publication of the site means that it is difficult to be sure (publication of the site's Neolithic phases is currently underway – Beverley Ballin Smith pers. comm.). An Doirlinn (Chapter 4, this volume) can also be placed alongside these substantial settlement sites in terms of the character of the archaeology uncovered. The recent discovery of large amounts of Early Neolithic material underwater, adjacent to islets in several different lochs in Lewis (Sheridan et al. 2014; Garrow, Sturt & Copper 2017), indicates that perhaps many other sites directly comparable to Eilean Domhnuill remain to be found elsewhere – a suggestion made by various writers before (e.g. Armit 1992, 318; Henley 2003, 35; Simpson et al. 2006, 80; Cummings & Richards 2013, 188).

In addition to the substantial settlements described above, several other occupation sites are known through the identification of more ephemeral surviving archaeology (Table 1.07). At Bharpa Carinish, for example, three stone hearths, spreads of ash, post-holes and large amounts of material culture were found; at Rubh' a' Charnain Moir, a large pit containing Neolithic pottery and the possible remains of a wall were identified; and at Barpa Langais post-settings, evidence for quartz working and the base of a pot were recovered. The midden at Northton has already been discussed in relation to its Mesolithic evidence; the Neolithic archaeology there is also difficult to comprehend, but appears to consist of a two-phase midden deposit and a possible stone wall (Simpson et al. 2006, 83). The recovery of Neolithic sherds in association with an otherwise undated midden at Bioruaslam, Vatersay (off Barra), could represent a second Neolithic midden site. Five other sites have produced Neolithic pottery (sometimes along with other finds) and may thus represent the remains of occupation sites of some kind – Loch a'Choire, South Uist and Dunasbroc, Eilean nan Luchrubanall/Pygmies Isle, Olcote and Stac Dumhnuill Chaim, all in Lewis (Table 1.07).

The surviving Neolithic settlement remains of the Outer Hebrides are undeniably impressive, with the best-preserved sites producing complex stratigraphic sequences of stone buildings and very substantial artefactual assemblages. In the past, some writers have chosen to emphasise the differences between sites in order to approach an interpretive understanding of the settlement record across the islands as a whole. Armit's 1996 model has been referred to most often. He stated then that

> it is possible that islet sites like Eilean Domhnuill were permanent bases, occupied all year round, whilst the machair and peatland sites [such as Northton and Allt Chrisal] were more transient or seasonal activity areas. Alternatively, the difference may be based on the relative social status or human resources of the various sites;

he rightly went on to point out that 'the nature of the relationship between these various forms of Neolithic settlement in the Hebrides remains to be established by future research' (Armit 1996, 57). Henley, too, envisaged a fairly heterogenous and mobile settlement pattern, sugesting 'embedded or tethered mobility, characterised by transient and short-lived settlement but rooted in the use of more enduring places at certain times of the year' (2003, 127). Most recently, Simpson et al. have made the very valid point that, given the strong similarities between certain elements of most sites, they may all originally have been much more similar than they now appear – 'apparent differences might ... be a product of site preservation' (2006, 82). Henley's observation that different but apparently roughly contemporary sites have produced very different ceramic assemblages – some producing mainly decorated vessels, others producing much plainer pots (2003, 133) – introduces another interesting element of inter-site variability into the equation. We pick up on both of these points again in detail within Section 4.11.

While most of the better dated Neolithic settlements in the Outer Hebrides appear to witness occupation into the 3rd millennium BC, only four of them (Allt Chrisal, The Udal, Northton and An Doirlinn) continued in use into the Beaker period (Sharples 2009, 154). The Beaker settlement record on the islands nonetheless is extremely rich – as Armit put it, 'the concentration of known settlements with beaker pottery in the Hebrides, specifically the Western Isles, is virtually unparalleled elsewhere in Europe' (1996, 88). In the most recent overview of Beaker settlement evidence, Hamilton & Sharples noted sixteen such sites, of which six have been substantially excavated (2012, 209). A 'typical' Beaker settlement appears to have consisted of one or two 'semi-subterranean, stone-revetted houses, normally oval in shape when well preserved' (ibid., 210). Several sites have also produced substantial Beaker period middens (ibid.). Sharples has argued convincingly that the end of the Late Neolithic period saw a substantial shift in settlement locations (and thus presumably also of settlement practice), with almost everyone moving onto the machair shell sand coastal plains (2009); the precise reasons for this change remain unclear.

In contrast both to the settlement evidence in the Outer Hebrides, and to the mortuary record more widely across Britain, Beaker-associated burials are extremely rare (Armit 1996, 94–99; Sharples 2009, 212). Mortuary practice at that time, when visible at all, is varied – a single possible cist burial is known from Lewis (Hamilton & Sharples 2012, 212), while occasional Beaker burials have been found inserted into middens and were probably also deposited in much earlier Neolithic tombs (Armit 1996, 98–99). Armit notes that around 50 small cists in total have been reported from the islands, mostly from the machair zone, but these are not well dated: pottery, where present, is usually a local variant of the Collared Urn tradition; not one was associated with a Beaker (ibid., 96). Later, non-Beaker Bronze Age settlements are extremely rare and not at present well understood (Hamilton & Sharples 2012, 212).

For the 3rd millennium BC, stone circles represent the main monument form on the islands. Two main clusters or densities are discernible – one around the world famous monument complex at Calanais, Lewis, the other on the eastern side of North Uist (Henley 2003, 259). The former group has been the subject of several excavations, the latter has seen no excavation at all (ibid., 270). The construction of Calanais has been radiocarbon dated to c. 3380–2690 cal BC (Griffiths & Richards 2013, 288). Richards et al. have made the interesting observation that the majority of chambered cairns in the Outer Hebrides contain substantial peristaliths (intermittent circles of large stones around the body of the cairn), suggesting a possible connection between earlier and later Neolithic monument types (2012, 203).

In summary, it is possible to determine a number of key themes that emerge from this brief consideration of the Outer Hebrides evidence:

- The Mesolithic is fairly sparsely represented at present, but initial signs from recent excavations suggest that many more sites could be uncovered if a substantial survey and excavation programme was undertaken
- The Neolithic settlement record is impressive, with several well-preserved and materially rich sites having been excavated (to modern standards)
- The full extent of settlement variability remains to be established, with even the smaller sites producing distinct, recognisable features (suggesting that observed differences could at least to some extent be a consequence of site preservation)
- Neolithic tombs are highly visible in the landscape, but remain poorly understood in terms of chronology and mortuary practice
- The Beaker period is characterised by large numbers of settlements, mostly on the machair, some of which are extremely well-preserved; again, the full extent of settlement variability at this time remains to be established
- The Beaker/EBA burial record is minimal and not well understood; the general absence of Beaker burials is very unusual and appears to relate to an islands-specific role for Beaker pottery

1.7. Volume overview: key themes

There are four key themes that run throughout this volume that we have already touched upon in the preceding sections: 'island-ness' and the sea, material signatures of connectivity, settlement variability across the western seaways and differential traditions of research in different regions. Each of these threads helps to explain how we have come to understand the archaeological record as a discipline. They also form the axis along which are own arguments have developed.

> There is in this aspect of land from the sea ... [t]hat which you thought you knew so well is quite transformed (Hilaire Belloc, *Off Exmouth*).

The concept of 'island archaeology' has been well established since Evans (1973) first encouraged exploration of what he saw as the perfect laboratories for understanding cultural processes. Taking a lead from MacArthur and Wilson's (1967) biogeographical work, Evans thought archaeology could capitalise on the bounded nature of islands, the inherent 'limitation' (1973, 517) that the sea provided, to understand social development better. Even more appealing to Evans (1977) was the fact that different island groups could then be compared to one another. Here the concept of island as petri dish began to emerge. Cherry (1981, 58) was to develop this concept further, hypothesising that island size and remoteness could be used to predict dates for initial colonisation.

These initial forays have now been critiqued (Rainbird 2007, 37; Fleming 2008, 11) for their geographical determinism and correlations. However, as Fleming (2008, 11) notes, 'anyone who has been involved with island archaeologies knows that to make light of their islandness and treat them simply as detached bits of the nearest "mainland", is an equally problematic exercise'.

There are two clear reasons for this. The first may be due to what Fieldhouse (1984, 155) has described as 'sea-blindness' (a state where we are no longer capable of understanding the role of the sea in past, present and future due to our contemporary isolation from it) amongst researchers across a range of disciplines. As the quotation from Belloc (above) indicates, we certainly found something engaging about travelling to and being on an island that shifted our perspective as researchers. This covered everything from the technicalities of excavation logistics through to the experience of arriving in a new place. It included a different relationship to the sea to that which we experience in our day-to-day lives. There is clearly a risk of drifting into a romantic trap at this point, of waxing lyrical about our time in each island group. However, as Sturt (2006) and Lucas (2012) have argued, how we practice archaeology, our experiences on site and the process of encountering archaeological material shapes our understanding of it. In some respects it could be argued that this helped to challenge the state of sea-blindness that we find ourselves within. That which we thought we knew so well was, to a certain extent, transformed. This in turn created a space within which it was possible to more easily consider different ways in which the past may have played out.

The second reason why Fleming's (2008, 11) observation is so apt relates more directly to the archaeological record. Evans' (1977) observation that in some respects islands simplify the task of understanding social development would seem to hold more than a grain of truth. This is not due to the fact that the sea provides a barrier, more that it helps to indicate intentionality. The movement of material culture across space becomes more clearly demarcated, helping us to recognise its potential significance. It is interesting to reflect on the fact that the distance over water between mainland France and Guernsey at the point when we detect the beginnings of Neolithic ways of life is very similar to that from France to Britain. This, and the movement of materials across the region at this time (Anderson-Whymark et al. 2015), clearly indicates that the sea was not a barrier. As such, as Mackinder (1902) might have argued, something else is at play to do with more regional histories of association and connectivity. Consequently, we set out on this project not expecting to find islands as laboratories, but islands and the sea as useful tools through which to think with. How and why did the Mesolithic–Neolithic transition play out in the way it did in these areas? In turn, understanding the dynamic in these locations would better able us to think about the larger bodies of land which surrounded them.

Clearly related to the above is the topic of connectivity. As we have described elsewhere (Garrow and Sturt 2015; Sturt and Garrow 2015) a study of this type challenges us to think about connectivity in a detailed manner. Just as Case's (1969) paper forced researchers to consider what it meant to bring the material culture, flora and fauna of the Neolithic to Britain, so working on islands forces careful consideration of what connectivity means and how it is represented. Islands and discussion of islands often fall between two stools. On the one hand they can be seen as the isolates that Evans (1973) and Cherry (1981) imagined, and at others the centre of hyper-connected maritime routeways (Copat et al. 2010). As Copat et al. (2010) make clear, the reality might be one of fluctuation. Thus rather than presume any particular connectivity state, this project began with a desire to consider how variation might have occurred through time.

Core to any project looking at the Mesolithic/Neolithic transition across such a broad temporal and spatial area will be consideration of settlement variability. Both the Mesolithic and Neolithic are prone to representation through coarse grained stereotypes. These mental models are often 'largely' correct, conveying the broader sense of what we understand as important in the meta-narrative of cultural change. The Neolithic does see a change in the way people lived their lives that involves a shifting relationship to the land, and with that potentially settlement. However, the process of rendering this story at the broad scale runs the risk of smoothing out regional variations that indicate how that process played out. What does the record of Mesolithic and Early Neolithic in neighbouring areas indicate? As discussed in Section 1.5, our understanding of the variability of Neolithic settlement practices across the western seaways has changed radically over the last decade. It now encompases a range of habitation practices which leave very different archaeological signatures, from ephemeral post-built structures through to more substantial stone buildings.

This introductory chapter has been peppered with accounts of how attitudes and approaches to different concepts have changed through time. It is clear that an understanding of how we arrived at particular academic positions is important for appreciating how they might shape our interpretations. This has long been recognised as an issue within studies focused on subjects such as the Mesolithic–Neolithic transition. First, there is a much noted problem (Garrow and Sturt 2011; Thomas 2013) that specialists for each period have placed emphasis on different questions and approaches. Furthermore, the binary nature of terms such as Mesolithic and Neolithic make it hard to recognise (both in the field and conceptually) how a shift from one to the other might occur. Second, given the very extensive spatial scale of this project, we have also had to contend with different traditions of research at a regional and country level. As Bradley (1984, 5) remarked, both spatial and temporal divisions in academic discourse have created the danger that studies 'run the risk of observing a picture dominated by its frame'. Equally, as discussed in Section 1.1, their peripheral geographical location (at least to modern eyes) had, in many respects, led to the island groups we are concerned with here being left out of mainstream accounts and only very rarely being considered alongside one another.

Through working on islands around the western seaways we hoped to challenge (and be challenged by) the issues identified above. The temporal disparity between the development of the Neolithic in the Channel Islands and that seen in mainland Britain, Scilly and the Outer Hebrides forced us to widen our temporal scope and blur the conventional boundaries between Mesolithic and Neolithic. In so doing we had to consider the changing shape of the islands and seaways over this period, and with that the environmental context within which this story plays out. It also forced an engagement with the archaeological record of proximate regions of mainland Europe and Ireland. The sea not only connected these islands in the past, but connected our work to a wider group of researchers and associated literature. This project still has boundaries, a frame within which the following chapters are set. However, it is hoped that through integrating these different threads, the frame compliments rather than dominates the result.

Notes

1 In this book, dates are presented in both 'BC' and 'cal BC' formats. 'BC' is used to indicate fairly approximate dates that are not specifically derived from radiocarbon measurements (e.g. to convey the broad currency of a pottery style). 'Cal BC' is used to indicate dates or date ranges that are directly derived from radiocarbon measurements (e.g. to convey the length of a site phase which has been subject to a detailed dating programme). All radiocarbon dates are given as calibrated dates BC (cal BC) at 95% confidence unless otherwise specified.

2 Please note that we use French chronological divisions for the Neolithic in relation to the Channel Islands throughout this book, as the archaeological record there relates directly to these (and not very closely to British ones). In mainland north-west France, Early Neolithic (Néolithique Ancien) is c. 5200–4800 BC, Middle Neolithic 1 (Néolithique Moyen 1) is c. 4800–4300, and Middle Neolithic 2 (Néolithique Moyen 2) is 4300–3500 BC – see Table 1.01 and Section 2.4 for further details of the French ceramic typologies.

Chapter 2

L'Erée, Guernsey, Channel Islands

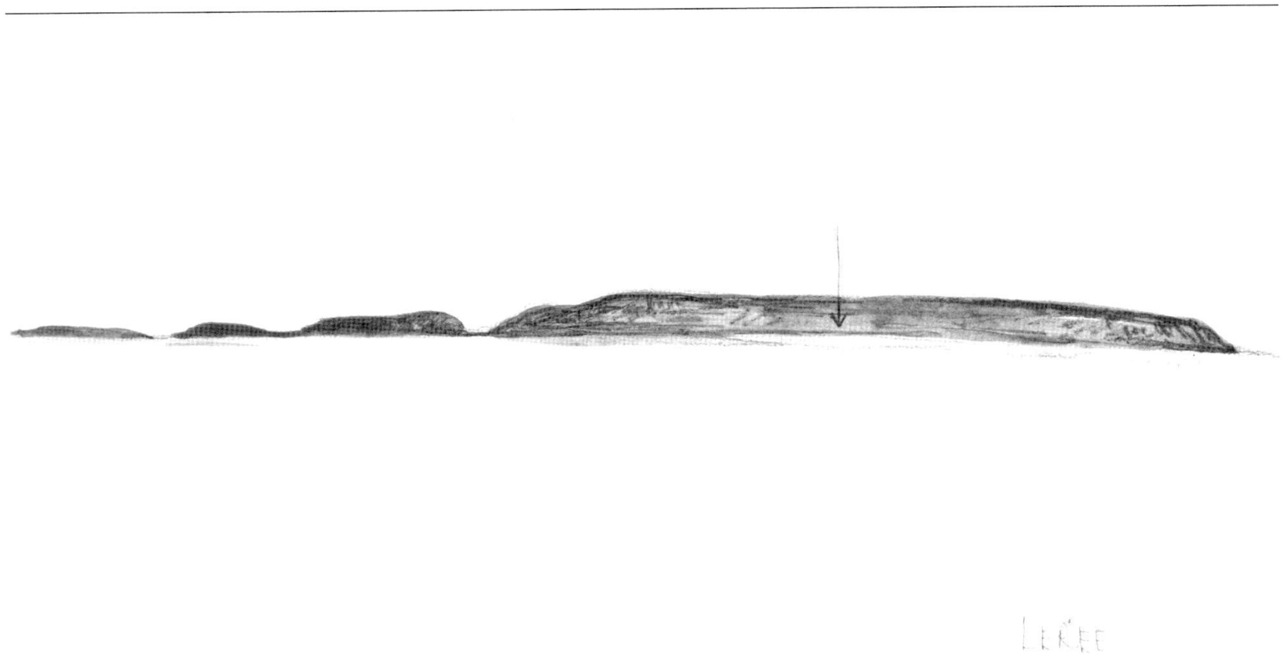

Figure 2.01. L'Erée landfall view. This sketched image shows the 'landfall' view of the site at L'Erée as it would have looked from a boat approaching Guernsey from the north-west c. 4500 BC. It is derived from 3D views of the palaeogeographic models (see Section 1.4) created in ArcScene and re-imagined by Rose Ferraby.

2.1. Introduction

This chapter outlines the results of excavation and survey work undertaken between March 2008 and September 2011 at L'Erée, Guernsey. The site is situated on a promontory on the west coast of Guernsey (Figures 2.01–2.03); the small island of Lihou, which is linked to the mainland by a tidal causeway, lies immediately to the west. Four seasons of excavation and survey at the site revealed evidence of a Middle Neolithic[1] settlement, and large quantities of Late Neolithic, Chalcolithic and Early Bronze Age (henceforth abbreviated to LN/EBA) material culture, associated with a possible ditched enclosure, which must also relate to substantial occupation of some kind.

At a high point on the L'Erée headland, approximately 70m north-east of our main excavation area, lies a passage tomb called Le Creux ès Faïes. The tomb was probably first constructed c. 4300–3800 BC based on evidence from similar tombs elsewhere on the islands and in north-west France (Schulting et al. 2010; Ghesquière & Marcigny 2011). It was also re-used during the Chalcolithic/Early Bronze Age period (c. 2500–1800 BC), when eight Beakers and two barbed and tanged arrowheads were placed within it (Kendrick 1928, 184–185; Salanova 2000, 274–275). It can probably be assumed that human remains were deposited within the tomb during both main phases of its use (and perhaps also in between), but the acidic local geology has ensured that no bones survived and so it is impossible to be certain. The relationship between a tomb used in the Middle Neolithic and then again in the EBA, and a possible settlement site of approximately the same dates immediately adjacent to it, was always a clear point of interest at L'Erée.

Geology and topography

Guernsey lies 40km west of the Contentin peninsula, Normandy and 130km south of Portland Bill, Dorset (Figures 1.01 and 2.02). Guernsey, along with the other Channel Islands, forms part of the French geological region

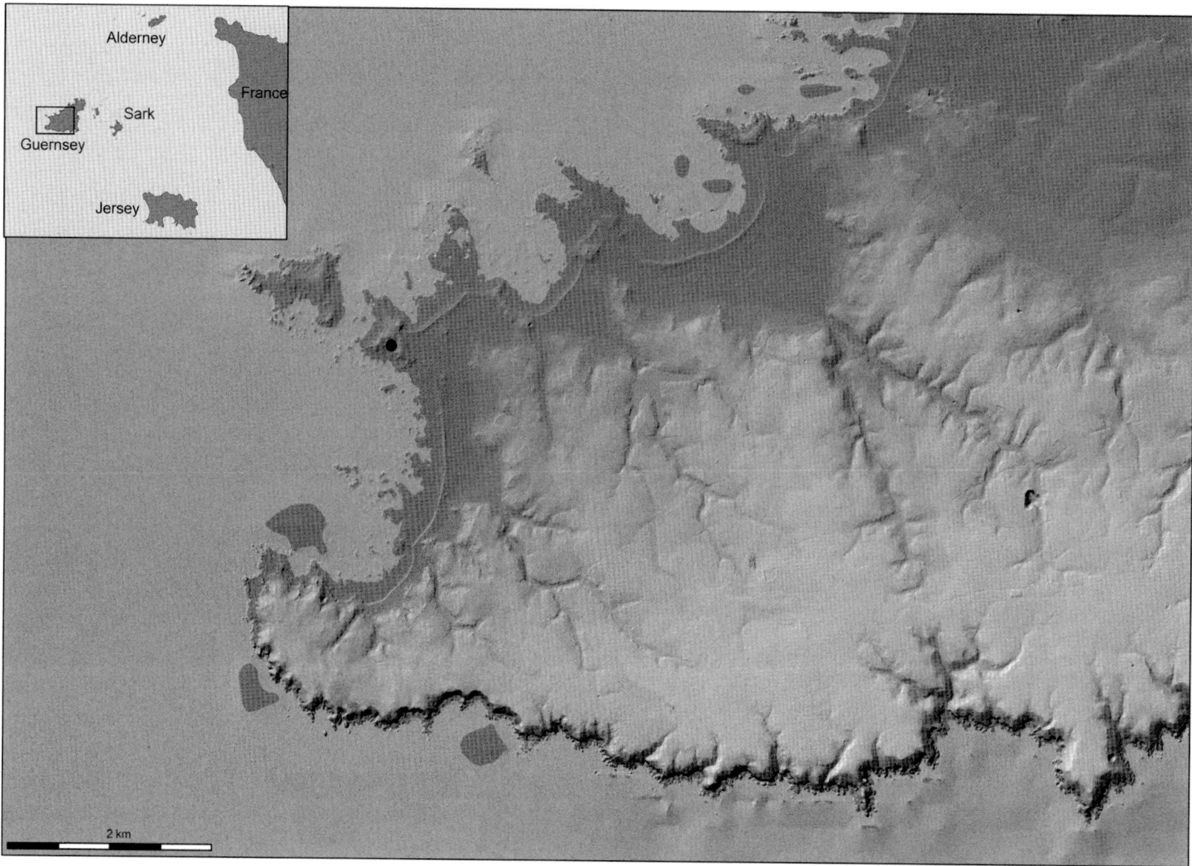

Figure 2.02. L'Erée site location. Digital terrain data courtesey of Digimap Guernsey.

known as the Armorican Massif (Renouf 1985, 90). The solid geology of this massif is composed of Precambrian igneous and metamorphic rocks. Today the island has an area of c. 70 km^2 and its geology can be divided into two: a Southern Metamorphic Complex and a Northern Igneous Complex (Roach 1991, 1). The Southern Metamophic Complex consists largely of metamorphosed igneous and sedimentary rocks of the Pentevrian basement (Roach 1991, 7), cut by numerous minor intrusions. At L'Erée this broad pattern is interrupted with a pluton of Granite (known as the L'Erée Granite (Roach 1991, 11)). The Northern Igneous Complex is comprised predominantly of further plutonic igneous rocks, interspersed by thin screens of sedimentary material, much of which has metamorphosed into schist and quartz.

This pre-quaternary geological pattern has been weathered and masked by soils and sediments bourn of the environmental fluctuations seen over the last 2.6 million years (the Quaternary period). Within the Pleistocene (2.6 million to 11,700 years ago), the various high and low sea-level stands have helped sculpt the landscape with raised beaches apparent from previous elevated sea-levels. Given their southerly location, the Channel Islands never underwent glaciation, instead experiencing peri-glacial conditions within which head material was formed and loess deposits laid down.

Keen (1978) carried out an extensive geological survey of the island, mapping the location and extent of Pleistocene raised beach deposits, along with locations of head and loess material. At L'Eree, Keen (1978, 4) records over 6m of soliflucted head material banked up against the granite headland, reaching elevations up to 25m above Guernsey datum. This rubble head material is frequently overlain by a loess/head interface. Loess deposits are more frequently recorded in situ on the east of the island, but are also found along the western shore, and more broadly as soliflucted sediments moved downslope from their original position. This distribution perhaps tells us more about variability in topography and survival of deposits rather than reflecting the totality of the Pleistocene sedimentary environment. As Antoine et al. (2003, 310) document, the likely of source of loess in this area is from the exposed English Channel during periods of low sea-level, with the predominant winds carrying the loess likely to have come from the west. As such, deposits of loess along the west coast of Guernsey are likely to have originated from that direction.

For the Holocene (11,700 years ago to the present day), Keen (1981) records four major types of deposit across the island: marine deposits, silt and sand, peat and alluvium. These deposits largely relate to changing conditions on the island due to shifts in palaeogeography created by rising sea-levels. Alluvium accumulated in palaeo-valley systems, which along their lower lying reaches were inundated as sea-level rose. As groundwater was driven up by rising sea-level, peat formation occurred in low lying areas: the inter-tidal and submerged coastal peats found extensively along the west coast of Guernsey today represent relics of these environments (Campbell 2000, 12). Marine gravels, silts and sands overlie these alluvial and peat sequences at Vazon and Mare de Carteret (Keen 1981, 10) further documenting the impact of sea-level rise. Finally, wind blown sands have accumulated along the north and west coasts, most notably in extensive sand covers at L'Ancresse. Here the late Pleistocene and early Holocene landsurface now lies buried under metres of sand. Recent work on Herm has provided timings for major phases of dune formation through use of optically stimulated luminescence dating, with 4000, 3000 and 2300 BP identified as major phases of activity (Bailiff et al. 2014, 902). Given its close proximity to Guernsey this offers a useful indicator as to when similar deposits may have been lain down on the north of the island.

This variable geological history has helped shape the current form of Guernsey. Today the island can be characterised as having a rugged exposed coastline, moving from a low-lying northern plain up to a highland plateau in the south (Figure 2.02). The drainage pattern follows this topographic trend, with the majority of streams running from south to north, a characteristic that is likely to have been the same throughout the Holocene. The character of the geology also impacts on the potential resources it offered to past populations. There are no native sources of flint on the island, and as such past inhabitants would have had to have used beach cobbles or imported materials.

As noted in Chapter 1, the Channel Islands have undergone profound palaeogeographic change over the Holocene, moving from being part of the terrestrial extent of a larger Contentin peninsula through to their current island configuration. As Sturt et al. (2013) and Garrow and Sturt (2017) have documented, Guernsey appears to become separated from mainland France at c. 10,000 BC, and from Herm at around 6500 BC. Jersey has a very different relationship with the mainland, perhaps not fully separating until c. 4000 BC. As Sebire and Renouf (2010, 375) have noted, these changes would have seen alteration in tidal patterns. Today the islands exist within a macro-tidal regime of c. 10m. Work by Uehara & Scourse (2006) and Cazenave (2012, 243) suggests a considerable reduction in this range over the early Holocene, with tidal ranges building up to 10m by the present day. The exact nature of this change in tidal range is hard to quantify due to the mismatch between present bathymetry (which is used to calculate palaeotidal range change) and the reality of past landform relief. The amount of sedimentation and erosion that has occurred over this area in the Holocene means that the specifics are hard to determine, but the broader trend of increasing tidal range is still recognisable.

This geological and palaeogeographic history has considerable implications for our understanding of the site at L'Eree. While our excavations took place on the modern coast, during the period of interest the site would have lain considerably further inland. The exact nature of the palaeotopography is hard to determine due to erosion within the modern bay. The impact of this erosion is an 'early' date for inundation of the bay within our models, as relative elevation of the land has been reduced through erosion of infilling material. Renouf and Urry (in Cunliffe & de Jersey 2000, 873) argue that the whole bay within which the site is located was first 'scooped out' during the high sea-levels of the last Warm Stage (the Ipswichian/Emian c. 130,000 years ago). During the following Cold Stage (the Devensian 110,000–11,700 years ago), sea-level fell exposing the bay. A scree of head material formed over this period, derived from the local granitic bedrock. This head material was then overlain by loess. As Renouf and Urry (in Cunliffe & de Jersey 2000, 873) note, the big question is how far out into the modern bay this loess extended, and as such how much the morphology of the headland has changed through time. At present it is not possible to answer this question, but it needs to be borne in mind when considering the potential loss of farmable land in the region and the possible previous extent of the site.

Our understanding of palaeoenvironmental change over the Holocene in Guernsey is relatively poor. Few sequences have been studied in detail, with poor pollen preservation and lack of macrofossil survival posing problems for researchers. Campbell's (2000) thesis stands as the most significant recent investigation of changing Holocene vegetation on the island, with additional consideration of sequences from Alderney. However, the scope of Campbell's thesis was limited by the number of sites he found suitable for sampling. This translated into four locations on Guernsey (two in Vazon Bay, La Grand Mare and Cobo Bay) and two on Alderney (Longis Common and Ile de Raz). The thirty radiocarbon dates acquired for these sites help to unpick local records of vegetation change and tie them into recent comparable studies on neighbouring islands (e.g. work on Jersey by Jones et al. 2004) and the French mainland. The resulting picture is one of slow recolonization by pine, birch and oak of the periglacial landscape of the Younger Dryas during the preboreal (9700–8000 BC). The Boreal 8000–6900 BC) saw increasing quantities of hazel and oak within landscape. This sets the scene for the Atlantic (6900–3500 BC) climatic optimum (also referred to as the Holocene climatic optimum). During this period, Campbell (2000, 306) notes a reduction in tree cover c. 4400–4100 BC which he attributes to Neolithic farming activity, with a later identifiable shift at c. 4000 BC with expansion of Alder Carr. This is interpreted by Campbell (2000, 36) as relating to abandonment/reduced exploitation of the coastal plain by the Neolithic population, matched with a possible move inland.

During the sub-Boreal Campbell (2000, 308) describes a drier oak, hazel and elm woodland, similar to that reported for Jersey at this time (Jones et al. 1990). The beginning of this period witnesses a decline in elm, which again Campbell (2000, 308) finds to be in line with regional records. Interestingly this is interpreted as potentially being the product of increased anthropogenic clearance with a view to generating greater amounts of fodder for cattle. Campbell (2000, 308) indicates a continued increasing level of disturbance through the Middle Neolithic 2 and into the Late Neolithic and Early Bronze Age, with willow carr being cleared away, perhaps for grazing, leading to wider establishment of marsh conditions in lowland areas.

The narrative above, when matched to the images of sea-level change given in Chapter 1, can give a sense that the limited observations gained to date can be resolved into a robust account of the changing nature of Guernsey. This temptation should be resisted, as in reality the discussion above reveals the highly limited nature of supporting data and the considerable need for more targeted environmental work on the island. What has been gained is enough information to tie Guernsey into broader regional sequences and to observe that the wider patterns seem to hold true. However, this does not map onto a detailed understanding of changing patterns of landscape and land use at the resolution required for more archaeologically meaningful accounts. As such, any opportunity to improve this record should be seized upon in future.

Given the site's location on the west coast of Guernsey, it is no surprise that it often bears the full force of Atlantic storms. The damage caused to the archaeology at L'Erée by coastal erosion has long been recognised. As such, there is a sense that important archaeological and environmental archives are being lost, and with them important opportunities to address these lacunae in knowledge.

While today the site sits directly above the beach, overlooking a beautiful seascape out across to a lighthouse marking an outer reef, at the time of the site's Neolithic occupation, we expect it to have been located more than 1km inland (Figure 2.04). The readily apparent erosion of the beach and the depth of deposits on site made it clear that the land extent would have been larger, and the bay most likely infilled, but the sea-level models described in Section 1.4 allow this hypothesis to be supported further. As such, we need to envisage the site at L'Erée not as a beach-side settlement, but one nestled in against a headland, still in fairly close proximity to the sea, but set back a little way from it.

Previous work at the site

The archaeological significance of the site at L'Erée first came to light as a result of the coastal erosion described above. In 1976, in the course of a geological survey of the promontory, John Renouf and James Urry noted the presence of prehistoric pottery and worked flint – material which had eroded out of the sandy cliff onto the beach after a storm (Cunliffe & de Jersey 2000, 870). From that point onwards, staff at Guernsey Museum and other volunteers monitored the site regularly, collecting and conserving the artefacts exposed (Cunliffe & de Jersey 2000, 870; Heather Sebire pers. comm.).

In 1998, as part of a broader targeted programme of work focused on sites under threat of coastal erosion in Guernsey, Barry Cunliffe (in conjunction with Heather Sebire) initiated a small-scale excavation at the site (Cunliffe & de Jersey 2000). Cunliffe's team dug two 4 × 2m trenches close to the eroded cliff edge (Trenches 1 and 2 in Figure 2.03). Two buried soil horizons (assigned to the Early Neolithic and the LN/EBA) and a ditch-like feature were identified. 247 sherds of undiagnostic prehistoric pottery and 296 lithics of Neolithic/EBA date were recovered (ibid., 872–6). Two radiocarbon dates were also obtained, the first (5270–5060 cal BC) on a series of 'charcoal flecks' from the ditch-like feature in Trench 1, the second (4230–3810 cal BC) on unidentified charcoal from a hearth exposed in the cliff section some 55m to the east of Trench 1 (Cunliffe & de Jersey 2000, 892; see also 2.9). Taken together, all of this evidence considerably strengthened previous suggestions that the site was indeed a potentially substantial Neolithic and EBA settlement.

Research objectives

Our work at L'Erée was driven primarily by two initial research objectives, originally defined several years prior to the inception of the broader Neolithic Stepping Stones project. The first was to contextualise the impressive monumental evidence of the Channel Islands by improving our understanding of the contemporary settlement record – only a few Neolithic/EBA settlement sites are known in the Channel Islands, and even fewer have been systematically excavated (Section 1.6). The site at L'Erée appeared to be particularly appropriate in terms of addressing the relationship between settlement and monuments, as it lies immediately beneath one of the best-known passage tombs on the island. Although we could not initially be sure of their exact contemporaneity, the relationship between settlement and monument appeared nevertheless to be very direct. Our second initial aim – which is clearly aligned with those of the subsequent Neolithic Stepping Stones project – was to understand better the broad processes of change by which Neolithic practices spread across the Channel region, from mainland France to the Channel Islands and ultimately to Britain and Ireland, over the course of the fifth and early fourth millennia. The excavation of a promising Neolithic

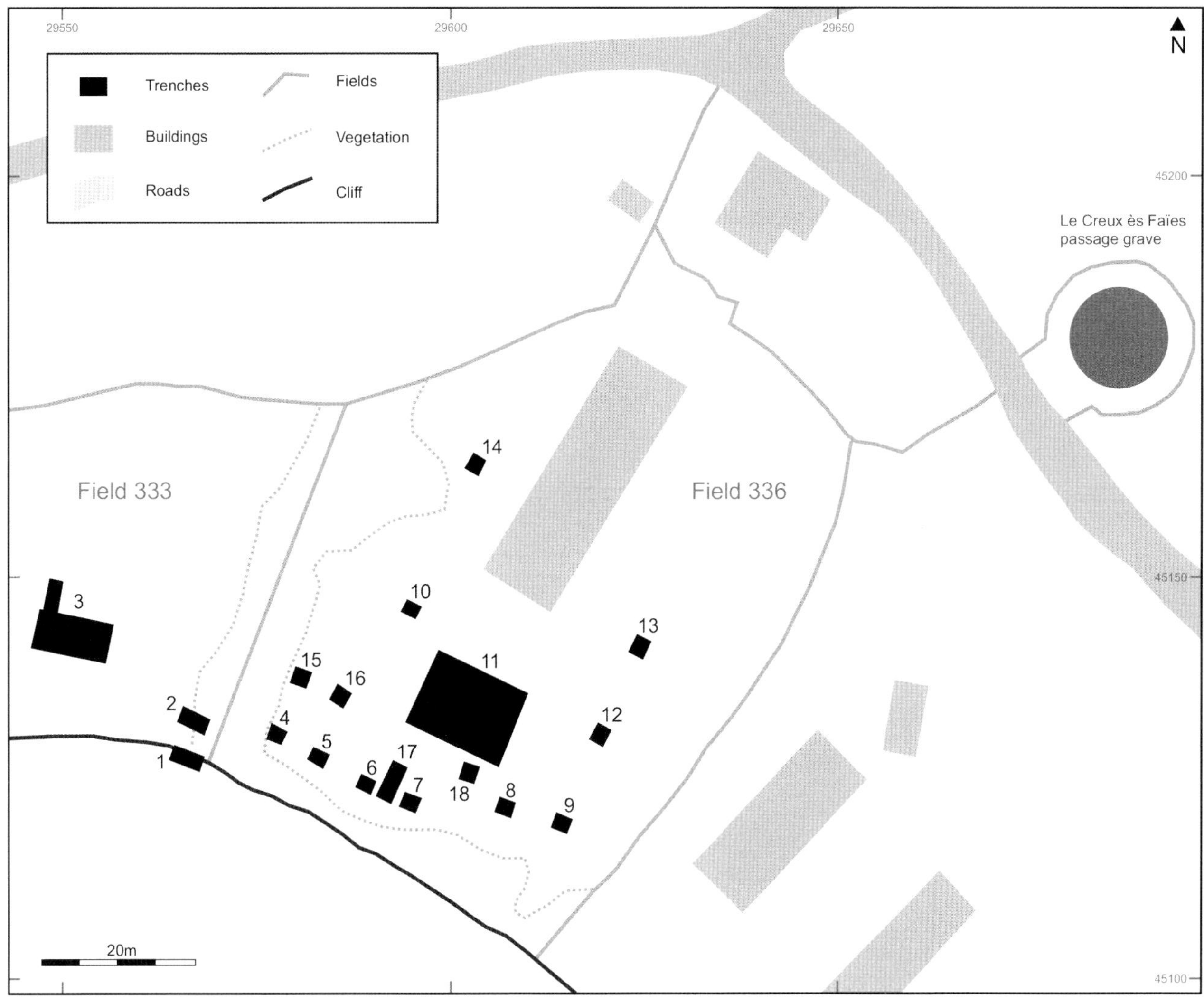

Figure 2.03. L'Erée site location (detailed).

settlement site actually within the Channel itself seemed one way in which to shed light on that process.

2.2. Survey and excavation strategy

Survey strategy

Our first work at the site took place in March 2008, when we carried out an auger survey (to enable rapid assessment of sediment sequences below the surface), a 500mhz ground-penetrating radar survey (to enhance our understanding of the sediments between the auger hole locations, and potentially also to identify features of archaeological interest) and a GPS survey (to capture the topography of the local area). All of this work was focused on Field 333 (Figure 2.03). Together these data supported the observations of Keen (1978) and Renouf (pers. comm.)

Over the course of the next four excavation seasons, we added substantially to this initial survey work. Real Time Kinematic (RTK) GPS was used to provide an accurate record of topography, excavation and borehole locations. Additional auger holes were drilled using an Eijkelkamp hand auger and an Atlas Cobra TT percussion corer. Altogether 28 auger and percussion corer holes were recorded over an area of 7800 m^2. In all years sediments were described according to the conventions of Hodgson (1997), allowing for ease of integration and comparison. The combined geophysical and geotechnical dataset allowed for construction of both a detailed topographic and a 3D deposit model of the study area within the Rockworks 15 and ArcGIS 10.3 software packages. This helped to extend our knowledge of sequences beyond individual trenches and to tie our understanding of the stratigraphic sequence into the broader regional synthesis described above.

Excavation strategy

As is often the case with relatively small-scale research projects of this kind, our excavation strategy necessarily

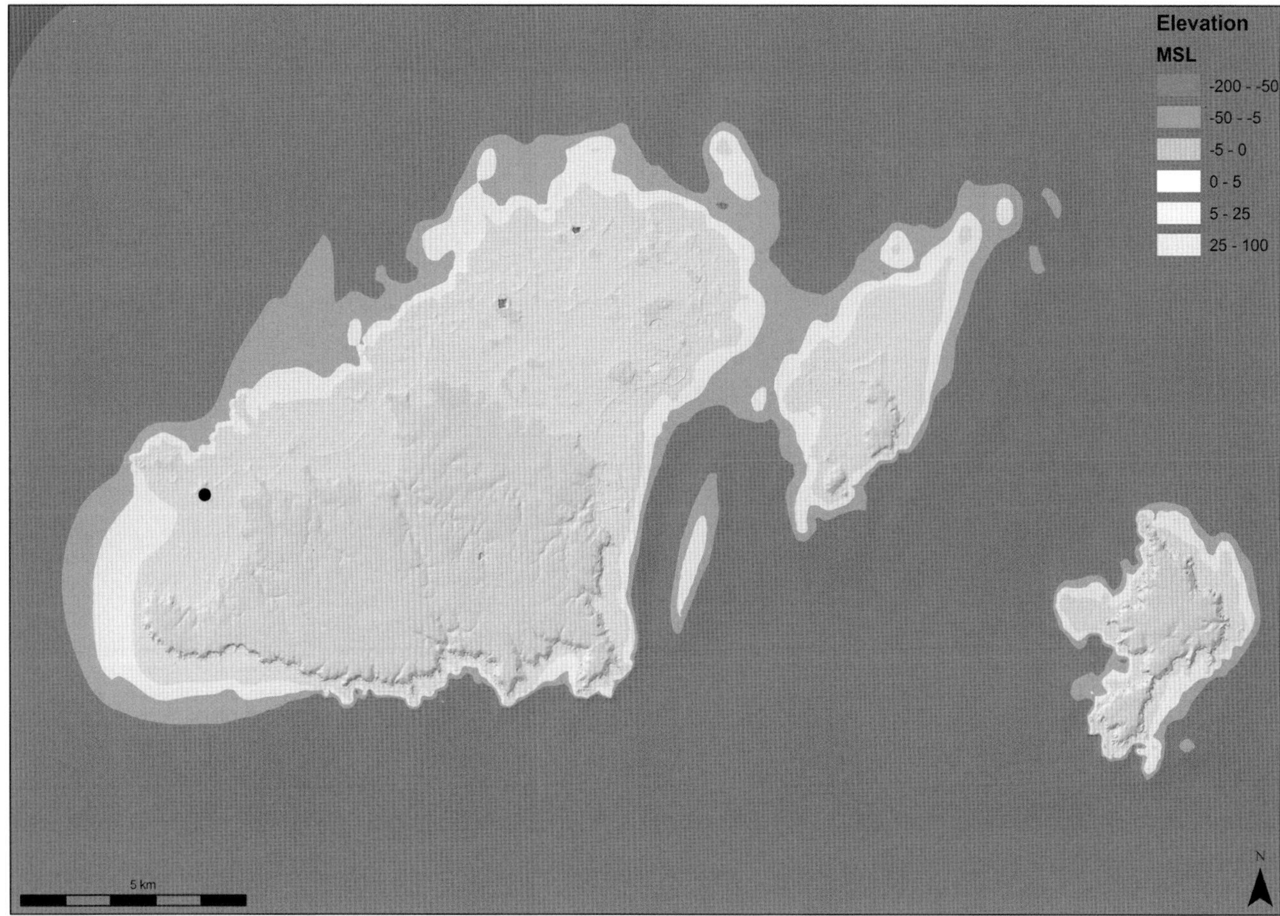

Figure 2.04. L'Eree: geographical location at the time of occupation. Topographic and bathymetric data derived from GEBCO14 (www.gebco.net) and EMODnet (www.emodnet-bathymetry.eu) and Digimap Guernsey and Digimap Jersey and GIA models given in Sturt et al. (2013).

evolved gradually and according to changing circumstances over the course of the 4 years.

In September 2008, our first season of excavation followed on directly from Cunliffe's work in 1998, and from our surveys earlier that year. The location of our work in Field 333 (owned by the States of Guernsey) rather than Field 336 (privately owned) was necessary, since we had not at this stage obtained permission to dig in the latter. Equally, Cunliffe's report suggested that the artefacts his team found had been deposited downslope from their original context by water/wind erosion, and consequently that any settlement relating to that material was likely to be located to the north of his excavations (Cunliffe & de Jersey 2000, 875). In response, we decided to locate our first trench (Trench 3) a short distance upslope of the previous excavation (Figure 2.03). As the deposits in this area had already been evaluated, we decided to open a single large (10 × 5m) trench in order to give ourselves the best possible opportunity of finding (and understanding) any settlement-related features.

In 2009, we were able to obtain permission to excavate in Field 336. Consequently, our main efforts that year were focused there. Since we did not have any direct information about the character of the deposits, or about the distribution of any possible archaeology, we adopted a more evaluative approach, digging eleven 2 × 2m test pits (Trenches 4–14) across the field. This strategy was successful, in that we identified a number of widely-distributed archaeological features. We also dug a small extension to Trench 3 in Field 333, in order to resolve the character of a linear gully feature identified the previous year.

In 2010, we opened a 10 × 5m open area around the main density of features identified in 2009 in Trench 11 (Figure 2.05), a further 4 × 2m trench (Trench 17) in between two 2009 trenches which had contained promising features, and three more test pits (Trenches 15, 16 and 18) in previously unexamined areas of the field.

In 2011, our strategy was straightforward – simply to open up as large an area as we could manage within the given timescale adjacent to the main cluster of features identified in 2009 and 2010 (in Trench 11). This was an L-shaped trench, immediately adjacent to the area we had dug the previous year.

Figure 2.05. Trench 11 under excavation in 2010.

In total, over the 4 years, 238m^2 of the two fields were excavated. This represents approximately 8% of the southern part of the two fields, the area in which the archaeology is concentrated.

Excavation methodology

The western part of L'Erée headland is designated as a 'Ramsar' site due to its ecological importance and sensitivity. Consequently, in Field 333 (within the Ramsar boundary), no mechanical earth-moving machinery was used. The 10 × 5m trench and 5 × 2m extension were both hand-excavated, to a maximum depth of 1.42m. Field 336 lies outside the Ramsar boundary, and so it was possible to employ a mechanical excavator there. In this case, a machine was used only to excavate the upper 0.30–0.40m of the trenches, removing a deposit which, following the 1998 excavations, had been interpreted as a medieval/post-medieval cultivation soil (this interpretation was subsequently confirmed by our own work).

The remaining, lower deposits (which contained substantial amounts of Neolithic/EBA material) were carefully hand excavated – to a maximum depth of 1.70m (in Trench 17), but more usually around 1.40–1.50m (in most other trenches). In order to gain control of finds distributions, excavation of these deposits was carried out in 0.10m spits. In trenches that were larger than 2 × 2m across, the distribution of finds was recorded horizontally as well as vertically, in grid squares; these were labelled with a letter (A–U).

Having outlined our excavation strategy, it is important to keep in mind the fact that the deposits encountered at L'Erée were mostly very deep (up to 1.70m), and contained substantial amounts of prehistoric material culture from a depth of approximately 0.50m. As a result, it was logistically difficult to excavate very large trenches (which would have been better for identifying the relatively ephemeral prehistoric archaeology we encountered), as the majority of the digging needed to be carried out by hand in just three weeks each season.

All trenches were located using a Leica 1200 real time kinematic global position system (RTK GPS) connected to the States of Guernsey correction signal, transmitted via an internet server. The site archive and all relevant interim reports have been deposited in Guernsey Museum under the site codes LER08, LER09, LER10 and LER11. A digital archive for the site can also be accessed via the Archaeology Data Service (doi: 10.5284/1016098).

2.3. Results

The soil sequence

As discussed above, the deposits at L'Erée were deeply stratified and often contained large quantities of prehistoric material culture throughout the majority of the profile. Almost all of the prehistoric features were cut from close to, or at, the base of these, into the loess subsoil. Before describing these features, it is important to convey the character of the stratigraphy which lay above them; these layers contained the majority of the artefacts recovered (mostly LN/EBA material).

The archaeological deposits were deepest close to the present day sea in the southern part of both fields (1.70m maximum in Trench 17), getting shallower upslope away from the sea towards the north (in Trench 14, for example, undisturbed loess deposits were exposed at a depth of only 0.35m). The best-preserved sequence of deposits was visible in Trenches 6, 7 and 17, in the lowest lying part of the site. It is likely that similar deposits had originally extended right across the southern part of the field, but that these had not been quite so well preserved because they were not as deeply buried. In order to illustrate the character of those deposits succinctly, the sequence observed in Trench 6 is described below (see also Figure 2.06). The numbers given in square brackets are the context numbers in Trench 6.

Post-medieval/modern deposits

[1] Modern topsoil 'A1' horizon: a dark brown sandy silt with frequent pebble (4–64mm diameter) and granule (2–4mm diameter) inclusions. In evidence across the entire site ranging in thickness from 8–10cm.

[2] Current 'A/B1' horizon: a very dark greyish brown sandy silt. In evidence across the site ranging in thickness from 1–4cm.

[22] Medieval/post-medieval cultivation soil: mid brown silty sand with frequent pebble inclusions. In evidence across the site, with an average thickness of 0.40m. Interpreted as medieval/post-medieval in date due to the pottery found within it, as well as the numerous pebble inclusions probably resulting from the use of seaweed as a fertilizer.

Prehistoric deposits

[28] LN/EBA 'A2' horizon: pale brownish grey compact sandy silt. Approximately 0.12m thick. Interpreted as the remnant lower part of a LN/EBA topsoil.

[38] LN/EBA Buried soil 'B2' horizon: mottled/laminated pale grey compact sandy silt (loam) with mid-brown silty streaks. Interpreted as a 'B' horizon to the buried soil 'A' horizon [28] described above (i.e. a buried LN/EBA subsoil).

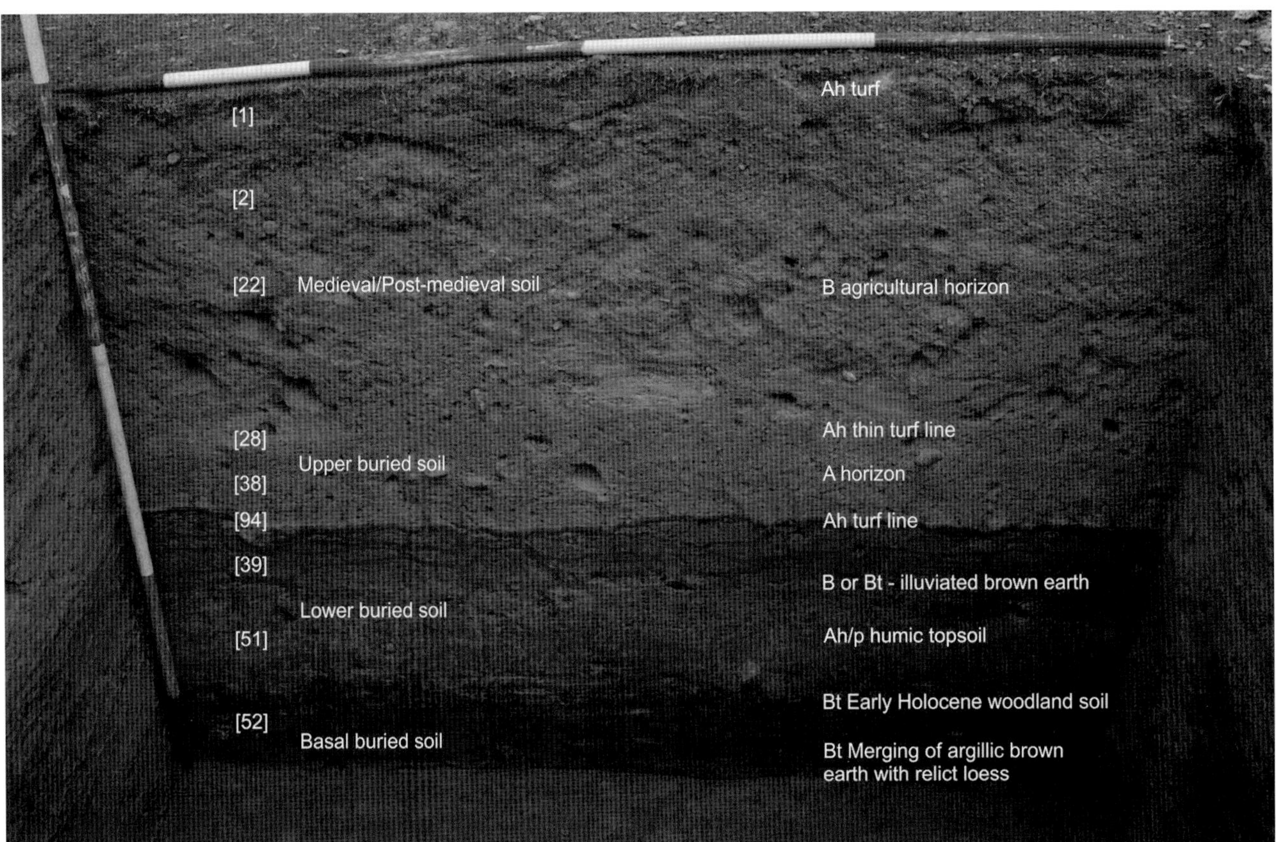

Figure 2.06. The soil sequence at L'Eree, Trench 6 (scale: 2m).

[94] Buried turf: mid reddish brown mineralised very compact sandy silt. Interpreted as a possible turf line to the buried soil 'A' horizon [39] described below.
[39] Late Neolithic buried soil 'A3' horizon: light-mid brownish grey sandy silt loam with numerous bands/ lenses of mid-brown silt caused by solifluction. Interpreted as a third 'A' horizon within the sequence, i.e. a buried topsoil.
[51] Late Neolithic buried soil 'B3' horizon: mottled pale-mid yellow/beige-ish brown sandy silt. Interpreted as the subsoil developed out of in situ loess deposits.
[52] Late Neolithic buried soil 'B/C' horizon: mid-dark brown sandy silt with small lenses/pockets of pale yellow/brown sandy silt. Interpreted as the interface between the subsoil and in situ loess.

During the 2008 excavation this variation was not readily apparent and as such the entire unit (equivalent to [28]–[52]) was viewed and described as a single 'buried soil'. In subsequent years, gradation and variability was more clearly visible, if variably so, leading to the identification of 'upper' [28/38] and 'lower' [39/51] buried soils, with [94] marking the boundary. Below the lower buried soil, in some trenches it became necessary to distinguish an in situ loessic argillic brown earth (referred to as the 'basal' buried soil during excavation). This corresponded to [52] and at times the lower portions of [51] where the interface was hard to distinguish. Groundwater movement up and down the profile and the process of podsolization meant that while the context changes were fairly clear in section, the boundary between units varied across areas of excavation, with lenses of fine silts giving a marbling effect at times making it hard to pinpoint the moment of transition between one numbered context and the next. As described in Section 2.7, this is a cumulative soil profile within which the spatial variability of the processes involved make it difficult to unpick the exact number of buried soil horizons present, with lateral variation in preservation highly likely. In this sense, an understanding of the processes of formation become more significant than attempting to trace a single stabilization layer across the site.

Artefact distributions within the stratified deposits

The vast majority of artefacts recovered at L'Erée came from the buried soils rather than from features (Figures 2.07 and 2.08). Most of the pottery recovered from those soils was LN/EBA, and so it can probably be assumed that most of the associated flint was also of this date. Certain test pits produced extremely high densities of finds, with up to 500 sherds and 800 flints recorded from some 2 × 2m trenches.

In terms of the *vertical* distribution of finds, a certain amount of variability was noted in relation to finds quantities. The lowest 0.20m of the basal soils – generally preserved only in the deepest trenches – contained very few finds. These layers appear to have been associated with the Middle Neolithic phase of occupation, where most of the artefactual material was contained within features (see below and Section 2.4). Higher up the sequence, finds were much more numerous. As discussed in detail within Section 2.4, there was a certain amount of chronological integrity to the vertical distribution of pottery within the buried soils, i.e. Middle Neolithic material at the base, followed by Late Neolithic, Chalcolithic and then EBA material in the upper buried soil levels. However, this patterning was not entirely clear-cut and a degree of mixing of artefact types (intrusive later material in lower/earlier layers, residual early material in upper/later layers) was noted within both pottery and flint assemblages. This mixing, combined with the fact that it was not always possible to distinguish different vertical layers clearly during excavation (see above), makes it very difficult to plot the distribution of material accurately, by phase, across the site. Consequently, all finds – throughout the upper, lower and basal layers – are plotted together in Figures 2.07 and 2.08.

In terms of the *horizontal* distribution of finds across the site, the highest densities can clearly be distinguished within the southern/western parts of Field 336. Intriguingly, the flint and pottery distributions are subtly different. The densest areas of pottery are found in the deepest trenches to the south, closest to the sea, where the best preserved and thickest buried soil layers were located. Flint densities do not follow topography as closely – the highest quantities appear to relate to a single large 'hotspot' in the south-west of Field 336, corresponding with Trenches 5, 6, 7, 16, 17 and the western part of Trench 11. While it is possible that the two materials had different distributions originally, it is thought more likely that their differential patterning has come about at least partly as a consequence of post-depositional factors. The very close relationship between the highest densities of pottery and the best-preserved buried soils appears to be key. It is possible that, in the deepest trenches closest to the cliff section in Field 336 – within which material would have been best protected from later plough truncation and attrition – the pottery simply survived better. In those trenches higher upslope – within which material was not protected from later truncation and attrition – the pottery would not have survived as well. Flint, however, would not have been destroyed by later activity in the same way, and thus despite those subsequent post-depositional processes could have survived across the entirety of the site. If this was indeed the case, the flint distribution should perhaps be considered the 'real' one, reflecting the original densities of both flint and pottery more accurately. Having said all that, it is also important to note that this material was deposited over a long period of time and must be appreciated as a palimpsest – the differential patterns observed could also

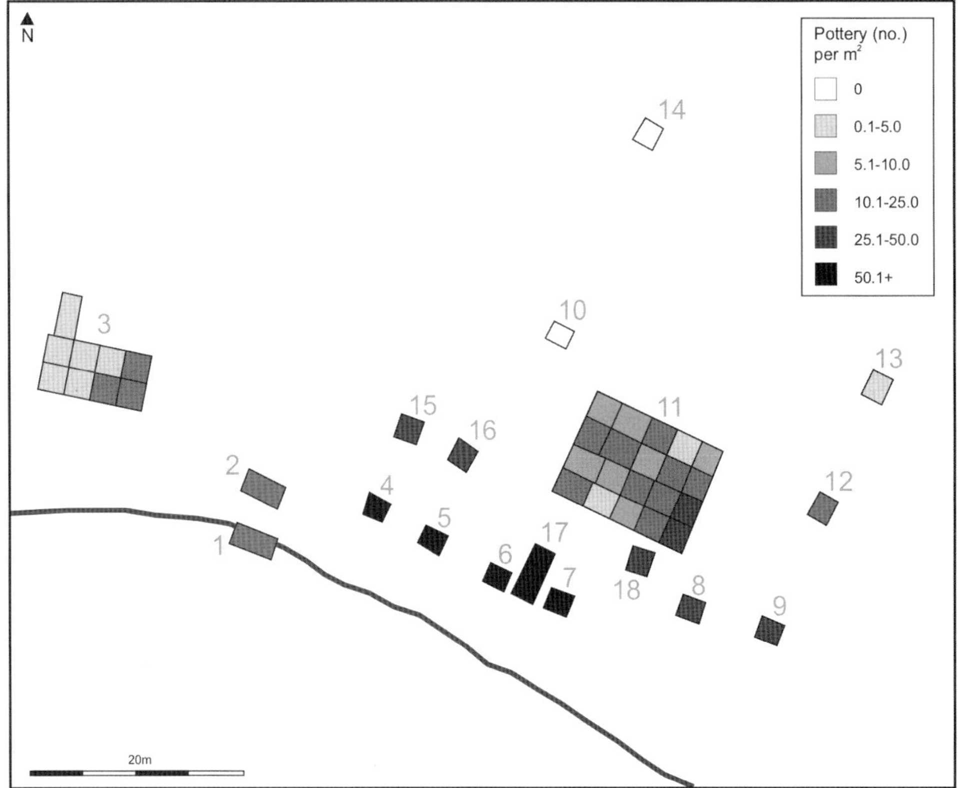

Figure 2.07. Pottery density plot within buried soils.

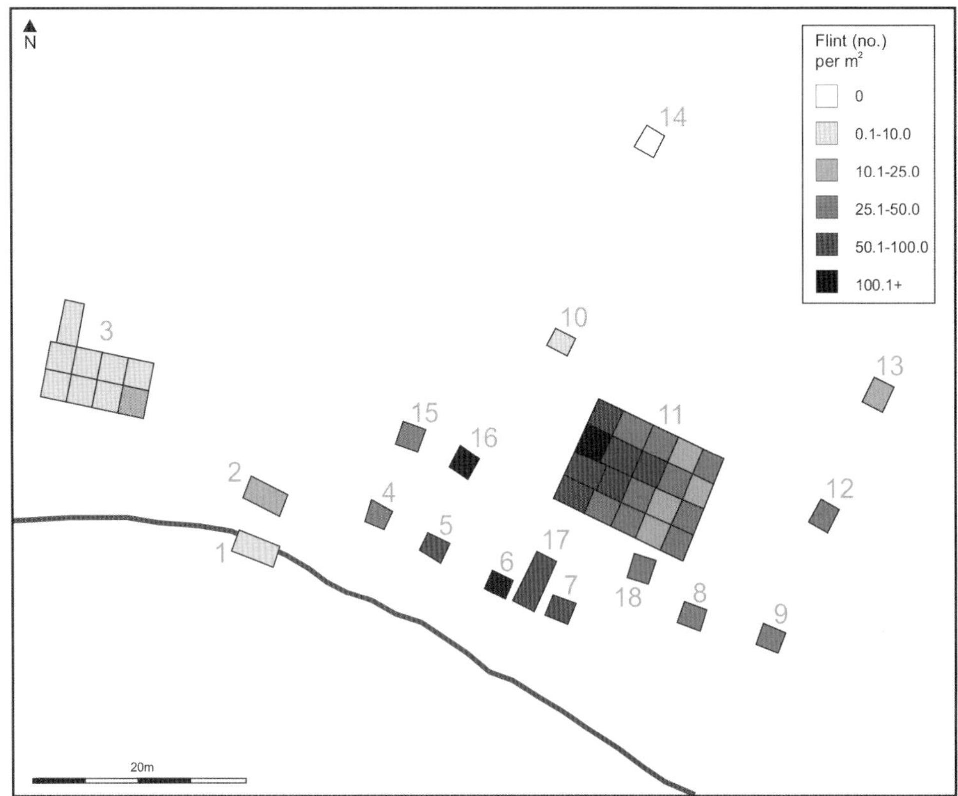

Figure 2.08. Flint density plot within buried soils.

have come about, again at least partly, as a result of different material types having been deposited differentially during different phases.

Whatever the reasons behind the observed material patterning may be, one thing is abundantly clear – very large amounts of both pottery and flint were deposited on the site over a long period of time. If the numbers of finds are scaled up to reflect the fact that only an 8% sample of the site was excavated, we could potentially be talking about tens of thousands of sherds and hundreds of thousands of flints. The processes that led to the accumulation of such large quantities of largely LN/EBA material on the site are difficult to ascertain. The highest densities of material do not closely relate to any of the features uncovered (see below), which in any case were mostly Middle Neolithic in date. The best explanation is perhaps that a massive midden-type deposit was accumulated in the south-western part of Field 336, perhaps over the course of a millennium or so (the dating resolution for Channel Island pottery typologies is at present insufficiently refined to be more precise – see Section 2.4). As we discuss in more detail in Section 2.10, this midden could potentially have related to LN/EBA funerary activity at the Le Creux ès Faïes tomb 70m to the north-east.

Archaeological features

In total, 36 archaeological features were identified and 100% excavated (Table 2.01). Thirty-two of these could be assigned to the Neolithic/EBA, the remaining four were post-medieval or modern. The prehistoric features were:

- ten stake-holes
- seven post-holes
- seven pits
- five hearths
- three ditches

The majority of these were located in Trench 11 (Figures 2.09 and 2.10).

Prehistoric features

The five hearths (F7, F8, F9, F16 and F17) were all clustered towards the northern edge of Trench 11. These were shallow pits (0.09–0.15m deep), ranging in size from 0.55–1.20m across (Figure 2.11). The hearths were characterised by very dark grey/black sandy silt fills that contained abundant charcoal fragments and flecks. They also contained varying numbers of medium-sized stones (0.05–0.15m across). These stones are likely to have been placed originally around each hearth to define an edge to the fire during use; on leaving, people had apparently pushed them on top of the fire presumably to help extinguish it. Three of the hearths contained diagnostic Middle Neolithic 1b pottery of Pinacle-Fouaillages type (see Section 2.4).

All but two of the post- and stake-holes and pits were also found in Trench 11. Despite the fact that, especially towards the north of Trench 11, these were fairly densely clustered, and in some cases formed straight lines, they did not form any obviously coherent patterns suggestive of a formal structure or building (Figure 2.12). The pits closest to the hearths tended also to have dark grey/black, charcoal-rich fills, but those further away were filled with mid-brown/grey sandy silts with only occasional charcoal flecks. Overall, none of these features contained very much at all in the way of artefactual evidence (only 66g of pottery and 119 pieces of flint in total). Again, the diagnostic pottery was Pinacle-Fouaillages type.

One small pit (F34) stood out very clearly from the rest, in that it had been backfilled almost entirely with small unburnt stones within a matrix of light greyish brown sandy silt. This feature was cut from higher up in the sequence than all other prehistoric features in Trench 11. Its stratigraphic position (dug into layer [159]) suggests that it was associated with the LN/EBA occupation of the site. The function of a pit packed full of stones is difficult to determine.

Ditches or ditch-like features were observed in three of our trenches (Trenches 7, 11 and 16) as well as in Cunliffe's Trench 1 (see Figure 2.09). The three ditches, where their full width was revealed, appeared to be similar in both size (1.10–1.60m and 0.30–0.40m deep) and profile (moderately sloping slides, gently curving bases). Given that they were identified in dispersed and mostly small trenches, it is impossible to know what the spatial relationship between these features was. Two of the ditches (F12 and F44) contained large quantities of Late Neolithic pottery (and no later material) suggesting strongly that they date to this phase (see Section 2.4). However, one ditch (F21, Trench 16; Figure 2.13) contained an assemblage of typologically indistinct pottery, residue on which was dated to 4980–4790 cal BC (see Section 2.9); in the buried soil layer immediately above it, only Middle Neolithic type pottery was found. The issues surrounding the dating of this material – and thus also the feature in which it was found – are discussed further in Section 2.4. Given the facts that (a) it appeared on excavation to be cut from fairly high up in the sequence, (b) it was similar in profile and width to other ditches in Trench 1 and 11, and (c) it had an almost directly perpendicular alignment to F44, it is perhaps most likely that ditch F21 was indeed Late Neolithic in date, but had somehow come to contain earlier material (perhaps because it cut through an earlier pit?). However, the possibility that this was in fact a 5th millennium feature cannot be ruled out (see Section 2.10). If indeed the ditches were all contemporary, we could potentially be dealing with a Late Neolithic enclosure (see Section 2.10).

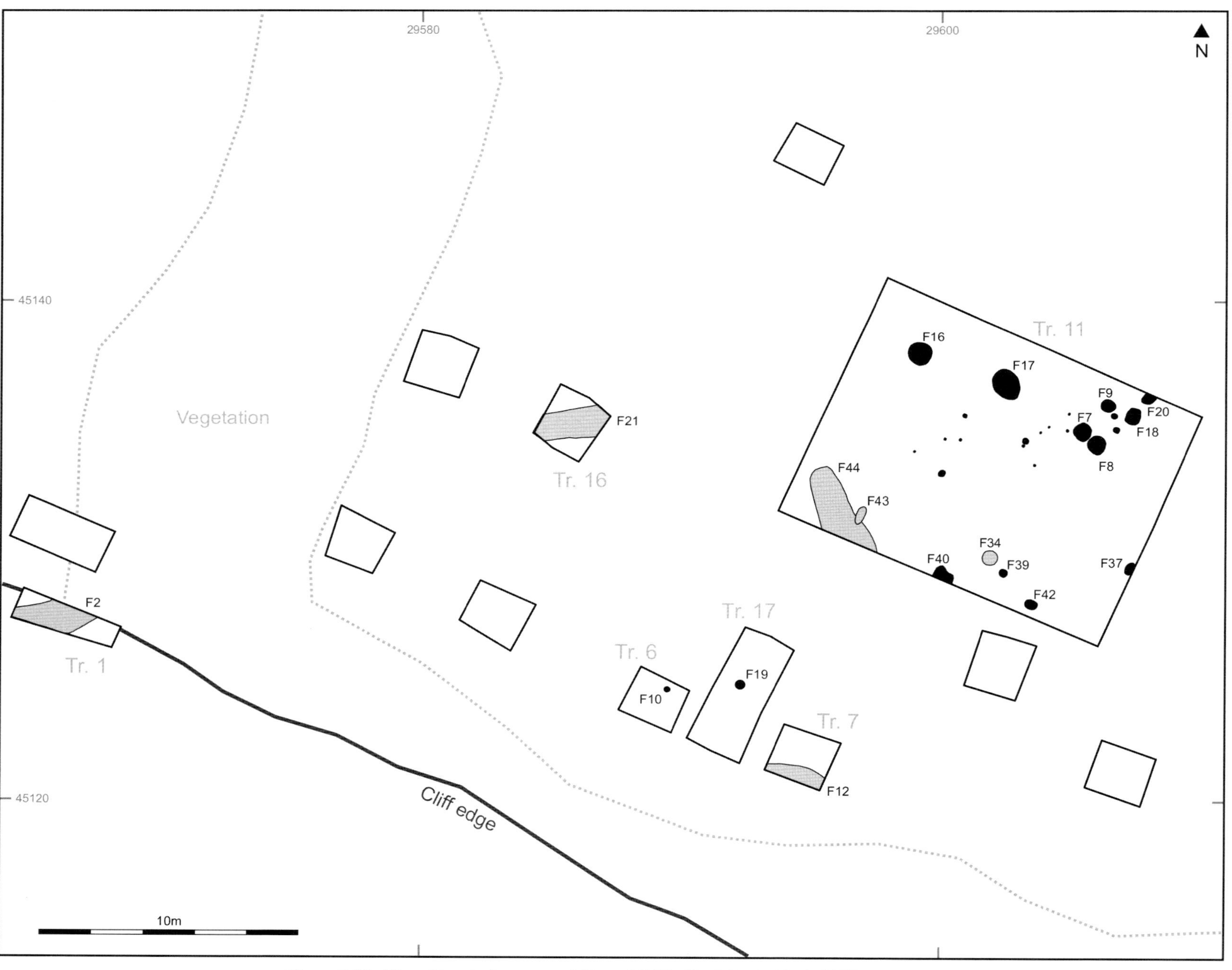

Figure 2.09. All prehistoric features at L'Eree (Middle Neolithic in black, LN/EBA in grey).

Table 2.01. Features excavated at L'Erée – summary

Feature	*Trench*	*Feature type*	*Phase*	*Length (m)*	*Breadth (m)*	*Depth (m)*	*Pottery (no.)*	*Flint (no.)*	*Year*
1	3	Gully	Med/PMed	(9.00)	0.20	0.10	1	0	LER 08
2	3	Post-hole	Med/PMed	0.32	0.32	0.18	0	0	LER 08
7	11	Hearth	MN	0.55	0.55	0.10	0	19	LER 09
8	11	Hearth	MN	0.60	0.60	0.10	5	8	LER 09
9	11	Hearth	MN	0.52	0.50	0.16	5	6	LER 09
10	6	Post-hole	MN	0.22	0.20	0.19	11	9	LER 09
11	11	Post-hole	MN	0.24	0.22	0.14	0	2	LER 09
12	7	Ditch	LN/EBA	(2.00)	(0.50)	0.40	15	0	LER 09
14	10	Pit	Modern	(2.00)	(2.00)	0.70	0	0	LER 09
15	17	Ditch	Modern	(1.50)	1.13	0.85	123	0	LER 10
16	11	Hearth	MN	0.91	0.83	0.09	1	29	LER 10
17	11	Hearth	MN	1.20	1.04	0.15	4	11	LER 10
18	11	Pit	MN	0.70	0.63	0.27	2	6	LER 10
19	17	Post-hole	MN	0.30	0.23	0.29	0	0	LER 10
20	11	Pit	MN	(0.26)	0.54	0.13	0	2	LER 10
21	16	Ditch	LN/EBA	(2.74)	1.10	0.30	18	84	LER 10
22	11	Stake-hole	MN	0.06	0.06	0.07	0	0	LER 10
23	11	Stake-hole	MN	0.06	0.06	0.05	0	1	LER 10
24	11	Stake-hole	MN	0.07	0.07	0.11	0	0	LER 10
25	11	Stake-hole	MN	0.06	0.06	0.06	0	0	LER 10
26	11	Post-hole	MN	0.15	0.15	0.14	0	0	LER 10
27	11	Post-hole	MN	0.24	0.20	0.15	1	0	LER 10
28	11	Stake-hole	MN	0.07	0.07	0.05	0	0	LER 10
29	11	Stake-hole	MN	0.11	0.11	0.07	0	1	LER 10
30	11	Stake-hole	MN	0.05	0.05	0.04	0	0	LER 10
31	11	Stake-hole	MN	0.06	0.06	0.04	0	0	LER 10
33	11	Stake-hole	MN	0.08	0.08	0.08	0	0	LER 10
34	11	Pit	LN/EBA	0.17	0.17	0.27	0	2	LER 11
37	11	Pit	MN	0.33	0.33	0.18	0	0	LER 11
38	11	Post-hole	MN	0.21	0.21	0.08	0	0	LER 11
39	11	Pit	MN	0.37	0.37	0.10	4	1	LER 11
40	11	Pit	MN	(0.24)	0.62	0.90	0	12	LER 11
41	11	Stake-hole	MN	0.08	0.08	0.14	0	0	LER 11
42	11	Post-hole	MN	0.35	0.35	0.48	5	6	LER 11
43	11	Pit	LN/EBA	0.74	0.26	0.10	11	0	LER 11
44	11	Ditch	LN/EBA	(2.24)	1.60	0.40	281	54	LER 11

Medieval/post-medieval/modern features

A shallow gully (F1) and associated post-hole (F2) were identified in Trench 3. These had been cut into the uppermost prehistoric layer, but could not be seen in section within the 'medieval' cultivation layers (which presumably had been heavily ploughed). A sherd of probable LN/EBA pottery and a small flint scraper were found within the post-hole fill. However, due to the facts that (a) the gully ran exactly parallel with the modern field boundary and extended beyond the edge of excavation on either side of a 9m wide trench, and (b) both features had been cut into layers of this date (and could thus easily have contained redeposited prehistoric material), they are interpreted as a part of a medieval or post-medieval field boundary.

A probably 20th century pit (F14) was exposed in Trench 10. It was >2.00m diameter and 0.70m deep, with steeply sloping sides and a flat base. This feature contained large amounts of greenhouse glass and glass bottles, suggesting that it had been dug to dispose of this unwanted broken material, possibly during or immediately after World War 2.

A probable World War 2 military trench (F15), 1.13m wide and 0.85m deep, was observed cut into the upper layers of Trench 17. This feature's southern (beach-facing) side was vertical, its northern (landward) side was steeply sloping, joining a flat-bottomed base. Its fill contained frequent very large pebbles and boulders. Corroded iron and modern glass were found at its base.

2.4. Prehistoric pottery

Anwen Cooper

Introduction

This report analyses an assemblage of 5552 pottery sherds weighing c. 24kg, recovered during four seasons of excavation at L'Erée, Guernsey, between 2008 and 2011 (Figures 2.14–2.17; Table 2.02). Most of the assemblage

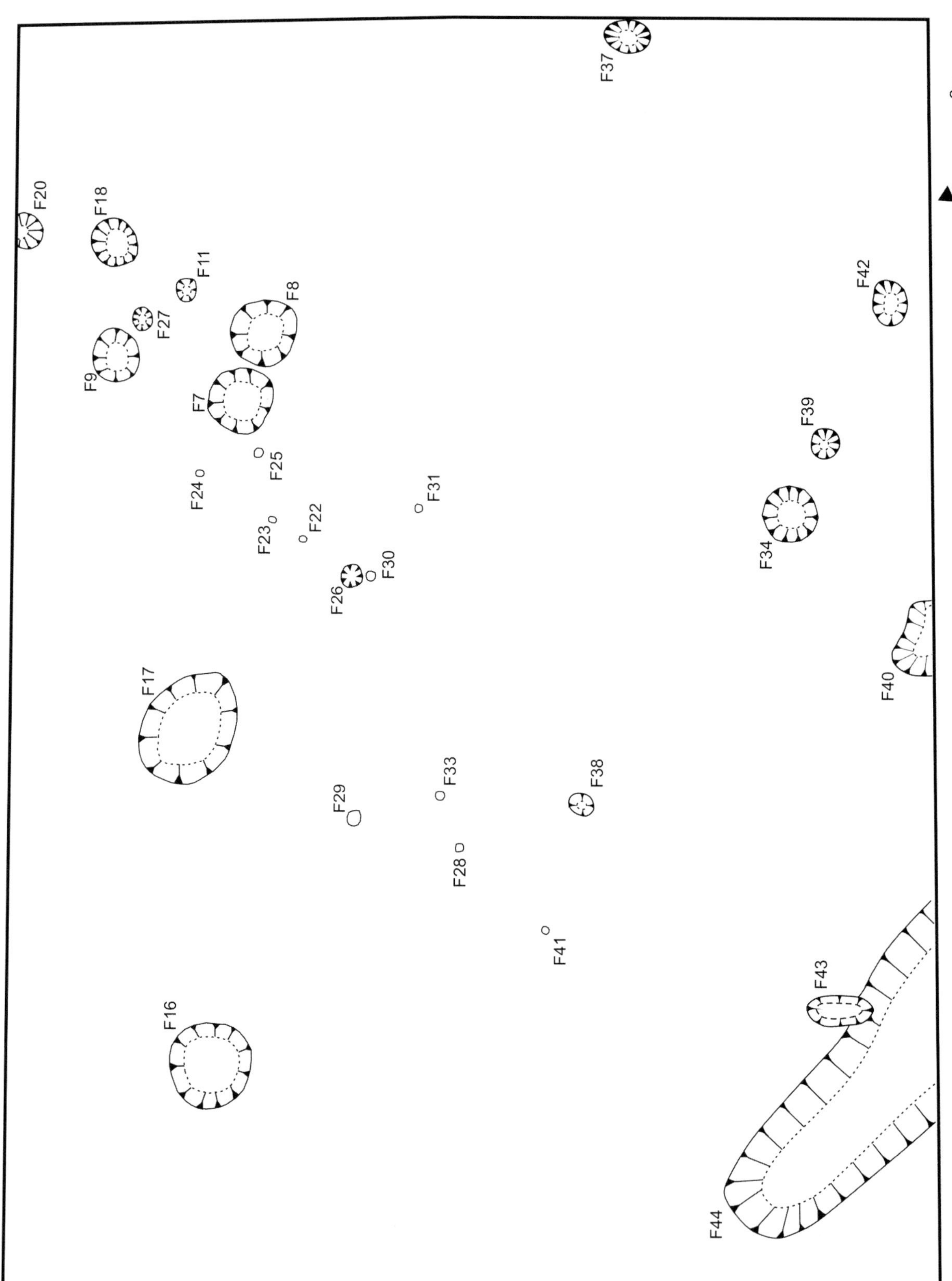

Figure 2.10. Trench 11 features.

Figure 2.11. Hearths F8 and F9, seen in 2009 test pit (top) and hearth F16, seen at edge of 2010 trench (bottom) (scales: 0.5m).

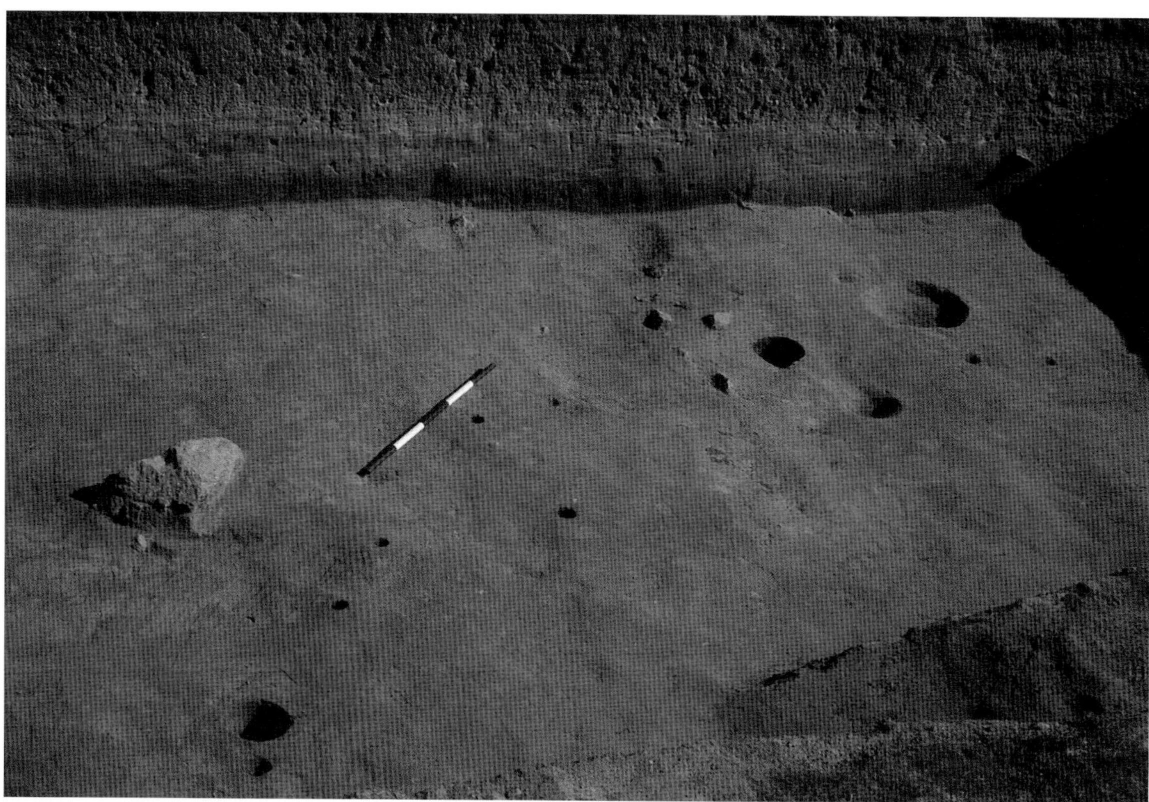

Figure 2.12. Photo of stakeholes and other features at the eastern end of Trench 11. F26 and F30 bottom-left, F18 top-right. Some features, including hearths F7-9, are not visible as they were cut into buried soils higher up that had by this point been removed (scale: 1m).

Figure 2.13. Ditch F21 in Trench 16 (scale: 0.5m).

Table 2.02. Catalogue of illustrated pottery from L'Erée

Illus. no.	*Period*	*Sherd description*	*Trench*	*Context*	*Feature*
1	?MN	Refitting rim sherd with soot	16	130	21
2	MN1b	Reffiting sherds with fine scored line decoration	15	157	–
3	MN1b	Tapered rim sherd	11	162	–
4	MN1b	Flaring folded rim sherd	11	162	–
5	MN1b	Carinated rim sherd	18	107	–
6	MN1b	Bouton au repoussé rim sherd with slashed decoration	11	99	–
7	MN1b	Bouton au repoussé rim sherd (smaller)	11	99	–
8	MN1b	Bouton au repoussé rim sherd (larger)	11	99	–
9	MN1b	Lug bowl sherd	11	115	17
10	MN1b	Refitting perforated lug sherds	11	162	–
11	MN1b	Decorated lug sherd	16	114	–
12	MN1b	Refitting sherds from looped handle	7	54	–
13	MN1b	Fish rib decorated carinated sherd	8	43	–
14	MN1b	Refitting MN carinated bowl sherds with vertical incisions	11	99	–
15	MN1b	Fish rib decorated (dots and slight scoring)	6	80	10
16	MN1b	Sherd with large impressed dots	11	162	–
17	MN1b	Large ?MN bouton au repoussé sherd	11	158	–
18	MN2	?Later MN sherd with flaring rim	11	159	–
19	MN2	Rim sherd from shouldered vessel	11	159	–
20	LN/Chalc	Beaded rim sherd	7	54	–
21	LN/Chalc	Burnished rim sherd	8	42	–
22	LN	Refitting (almost) burnished bowl sherds	11	181	44
23	LN/Chalc	Rim shed with lug	7	54	–
24	LN/Chalc	Rim sherd with lug	7	29	–
25	LN/Chalc	Lug sherd	11	158	–
26	LN/Chalc	Rim sherd with squarish elongated lug	18	106	–
27	LN/Chalc	Squarish rim sherd	11	158	–
28	LN/Chalc	Everted rim sherd	7	54	–
29	Chalc	Large Jersey Bowl rim sherd	11	159	–
30	Chalc	Beaker sherd	6	38	–
31	Chalc	Comb impressed Beaker sherd	11	159	–
32	Chalc	Worn Jersey Bowl sherd	11	159	–
33	Chalc	Carinated Jersey Bowl sherd	11	159	–
34	Chalc	Carinated bowl sherd with vertical incised lines	11	159	–
35	Chalc	Refitting Jersey Bowl sherds with incised decoration	11	99	–
36	Chalc	Small, decorated Jersey Bowl sherd	7	54	–
37	Chalc	Jersey Bowl sherd	11	98	–
38	Chalc	Large, classic Jersey Bowl sherd	7	54	–
39	Chalc	Jersey Bowl sherd with coarse scoring	4	35	–
40	Chalc	Beaded rim sherd	7	84	12
41	Chalc	Shoulder sherd with incised line	9	49	6
42	Chalc	Scored/fingernail impressed sherd	11	159	–
43	BA	Cordoned rim sherd	8	30	–
44	BA	Cordoned rim sherd with finger impressions	8	42	–
45	EBA	Cordoned sherd	6	38	–
46	EBA	Strap handle sherd	7	54	–
47	EBA	Handle fragment	18	106	–
48	Chalc	Sharply carinated ?Jersey Bowl sherd	3	4	–
49	Chalc	Sherd with horizontal/diagonal grain impressions	3	4	–
50	?Chalc	Decorated ?Jersey Bowl sherd	3	4	–

(5034 sherds weighing c. 22kg) derives from 15 test pits (Trenches 4–9 and 12–18) and one larger excavation area (Trench 11) in Field 336. Within these trenches, the vast majority of material was recovered from three buried soil layers. A small but significant component (390 sherds, weighing 2483g – 10.4% of the assemblage by weight) was also recovered from cut features – pits, post-holes, hearths, ditches and gullies – sometimes cut into, but mostly sealed by, these palaeosoils. A further assemblage of 518 prehistoric sherds (2311g in total) was recovered from Trench 3 in the neighbouring field (Field 333). Only one of these sherds was found in a cut feature – a post-hole (F2) within a gully (F1). The remainder were located within a single substantial palaeosoil overlying this feature.

Overall, the material spans the Middle Neolithic 1b (Pinacle-Fouaillages, potentially beginning c. 4600 BC) to the Middle Bronze Age (starting c. 1500 BC). As in the rest of this chapter, French Neolithic phasing terminology (see Table 1.01) is used here for the Middle Neolithic material (see Pioffet 2013 for a recent discussion and definitions of Middle Neolithic pottery periodisation in the Channel Islands). However Channel Islands-specific phasing terminology is used for the Late Neolithic, Chalcolithic and Early Bronze Age material (c. 3500–1500), since Patton (1995) has already set an important precedent for applying these specific definitions to ceramic assemblages of this date on the archipelago. The vast majority of sherds from Field 336 relate either to the Middle Neolithic 1b phase (c. 4600–4000 BC), or to the Late Neolithic/Chalcolithic (c. 3500–2300 BC) through to Early Bronze Age (c. 2300–1500 BC) periods. Occasional sherds relating to the Middle Neolithic 2 phase (beginning in France c. 4300 BC) and possibly also to the Middle Bronze Age period (beginning c. 1500 BC, although very little is known about this period on the Channel Islands (Sebire 2005, 94–5)) were also recovered. The assemblage from Field 333 relates primarily to the Late Neolithic/Chalcolithic period. In common with the vast majority of Neolithic and Bronze Age pottery assemblages on the Channel Islands (Pioffet 2013), most of the material from both fields was small and abraded with an overall mean sherd weight (MSW) of less than 5g.

Methodology

The methodology employed broadly follows guidelines set out by the Prehistoric Ceramics Research Group (2010). All sherds were scanned in order to ascertain their general date and character. Fragments from cut features and from the palaeosoils in Trench 11 were examined in more detail, using a 10× magnification hand lens where pertinent. A record was made of the main formal elements and decorative traits, broad fabric types, surface treatments and any observable residues. Sherds recovered in 2008 were subject to thin-section analysis (Sibbesson 2009). Leading specialists in the prehistoric pottery of Northern France and the Channel Islands (I. Kinnes, C. Marcigny and H. Pioffet) were consulted closely regarding the characterisation of key sherds.

Fabrics

As has been established previously on two separate occasions through thin-section analysis of sherds from excavations at L'Erée (Bukach in Cunliffe & de Jersey 2000; Sibbesson 2009), the overall make-up of fabrics from prehistoric pottery assemblages in the vicinity is fairly conservative. The clay paste was probably sourced locally and was typically sandy and occasionally also micacious. Rock fragments (mainly quartz and feldspar) were the primary added inclusions. One broad distinguishing trait was that sherds from features cut directly into the loess and from the earliest (Middle Neolithic) palaeosoils tended to be predominantly quartz tempered and were more commonly fired in reducing conditions. By contrast those from later (Late Neolithic to Bronze Age) palaeosoils and features tended to be predominantly feldspar tempered and fired in oxidising conditions. Occasional voids indicate the sporadic use of organic tempers. A small number of coarseware sherds included hard reddish clay pellets. Within this broad characterisation, the following subdivisions were made:

Fabrics typically associated with Middle Neolithic 1b contexts

Fabric 1. Hard paste, sometimes with a hackly or laminate structure. Ill-sorted sparse-moderately common inclusions of quartz, feldspar and other rock fragments. Some sherds include small elongated voids indicating the use of organic/vegetable tempers. Many sherds in this fabric have been fired in reducing conditions and are dark grey or brown. Burnishing is a common feature.

Fabric 2. Soft to medium-hard fine paste. Ill-sorted rare to sparse quartz, feldspar and occasionally (most often on coarseware sherds) clay pellet inclusions. Sherds in this fabric are variably but often poorly fired. Finer and coarser versions exist. The finer version is harder and often associated with diagnostically Middle Neolithic 1b (Pinacle-Fouaillages) or Jersey Bowl sherds.

Fabric 3. Hard paste with common fairly well-sorted coarse sand, fine-medium quartz, feldspar and other rock fragments and rare voids (organic component). Most sherds in this fabric have been fired in reducing conditions and are dark (grey, brown or black) in colour. Some sherds are burnished.

Additional fabrics associated with Late Neolithic/ Chalcolithic and EBA contexts

Fabric 4. Hard, sandy paste often with a hackly or laminate structure. Abundant poor to fairly well-sorted moderate to coarse feldspar and rarer quartz inclusions. Sherds in this fabric are typically more uniformly fired in oxidising conditions.

Fabric 5. Moderate to hard sandy paste with variously sorted inclusions of predominantly feldspar, but also other rock fragments and possibly shell.

Fabric 6. Hard, fine, sandy paste with rare fine to moderate inclusions of feldspar and quartz. Common fabric for Beaker sherds.

Fabric 2 was the dominant fabric overall, particularly for material from features cut directly into the loess or from the earliest (basal) palaeosoil. Fabric 4 was the most common fabric for material derived from later cut features or from the subsequent two palaeosoil layers.

Field 336

Since it forms the bulk of the assemblage, the material recovered from palaeosoils is outlined first, followed by that from cut features.

Material from palaeosoils

Finds excavated from within the complex sequence of palaeosoils at L'Erée were recorded as having come essentially from three main layers: (1) an upper buried soil (incorporating lower and upper horizons) situated directly beneath the medieval and post-medieval soil; (2) a lower buried soil (incorporating lower and upper horizons and a turf line), and (3) a basal soil situated directly above and then merging into the loess (see Section 2.3 for further details). These were identifiable in most excavated trenches but most clearly definable in the trenches located downslope, closest to the cliff edge, where the soil layers were thicker. In this analysis, the material from each of these palaeosoils is examined in chronological order. A detailed description is offered of the material from the main trench (Trench 11), the sherds from which were examined in greatest detail. This is followed by a summary of key attributes of the assemblages from the surrounding trenches (Trenches 4–9 and 12–18), the material from which was analysed in less detail.

TRENCH 11

The following analysis of material from Trench 11 focuses primarily on that recovered in 2011. This forms the bulk

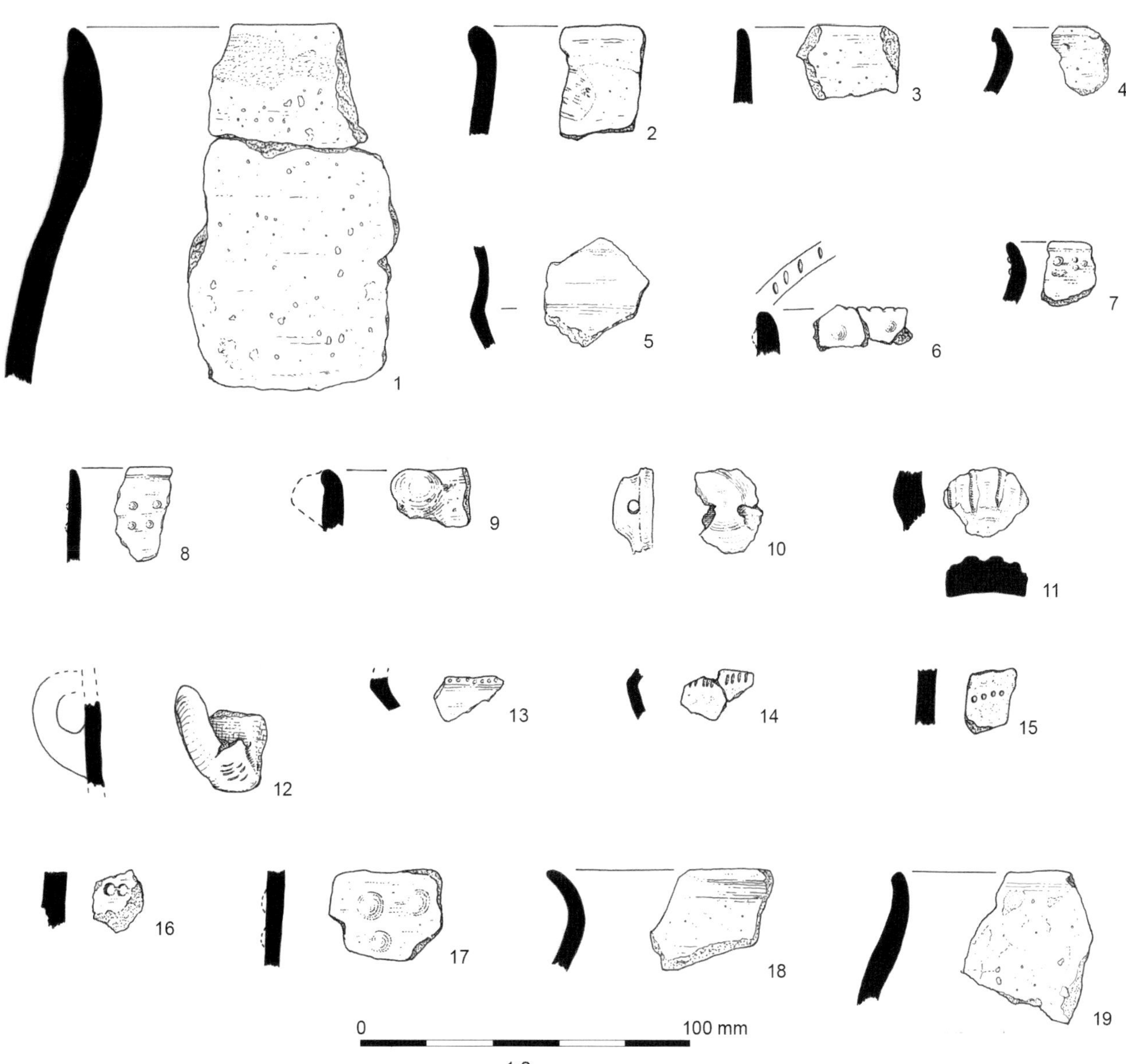

Figure 2.14. Middle Neolithic pottery (drawn by A. Wilkins).

Table 2.03. Trench 11 palaeosol contexts and summaries of pottery recovered

Layer	*LER09 (58 sherds, 196g)*	*LER10 (634 sherds, 2055g)*	*LER11 (1132 sherds, 4674g)*
Upper buried soil (UBS)	[60], [61] (19 sherds, 74g)	[98] (419 sherds, 1552g)	[158] (450 sherds, 2094g)
Lower buried soil (LBS)	[62] (21 sherds, 48g)	[99] (215 sherds, 503g)	[159] (480 sherds, 2125g)
Basal soil (BS)	[73] (28 sherds, 74g)		[162] (202 sherds, c. 470g)

(62% by number, 67% by weight) of the overall assemblage from this trench (Table 2.03). It was also during this season's excavations that the three broad palaeosoil layers were most clearly definable. Distinctive aspects of the assemblages from earlier seasons are highlighted where relevant. It is worth noting that only two soil layers were visible in Trench 11 during the 2010 excavations. Upon examination of the material from these layers, it was clear that the lower context [99] excavated in 2010 corresponded with the basal soil and lower buried soil contexts from 2009 and 2011 ([73]/[62] and [162]/[159]); being higher up-slope, the lower layer(s) were less deep and thus less visible within the 2010 excavation area.

Basal soil material: Most of the sherds from the basal soil contexts in Trench 11 were small, worn and undecorated. Despite their generally weathered appearance, which undoubtedly relates to their occurrence within a soil layer rather than in features, several refitting sherds (broken in antiquity) were present. There was no clear patterning in the overall distribution of sherds within this layer, either across the excavated area or from top to bottom of the deposit, although unsurprisingly the proportion of diagnostically Middle Neolithic 1b sherds increased towards the base. At a broad level, the material from this palaeosoil varied considerably in character. Both coarse and fineware sherds were present, almost certainly relating to bowls of various forms and sizes (no base sherds were recovered from this layer).

A large component of the assemblage was dark (grey, brown or blackish) in colour. Sherds from coarseware vessels were generally poorly-fired and made with a soft to medium-hard fine reddish-brown or brownish-grey (sometimes micacious) paste with rare, ill-sorted, predominantly quartz or feldspar inclusions. Fineware sherds were generally dark grey, brown or black in colour. In some instances it appeared that a brown surface-effect had been achieved carefully through controlled firing (Hélène Pioffet pers. comm.). Several sherds had a dark reddish core, again a feature of differential firing. Some fragments had a distinctive laminate structure and incorporated sparse to moderate, ill-sorted (fine through to coarse) feldspar and quartz inclusions. A few sherds were made from a harder clay matrix including abundant, better-sorted, finer inclusions of quartz sand and other rock fragments. A small but significant proportion of the fineware sherds had burnished surfaces. Only in one case was this on the interior of the vessel. Other sherds had traces of wiping. Soot was the only surface residue noted.

Rim sherds were simple – most were either tapered, rounded or square in profile (Sherd 3). On one sherd, the rim was everted and roughly rolled over (Sherd 4). Several sherds derived from flaring-necked vessels. A number of fineware body sherds clearly related to gently carinated/shouldered vessels.

Within the assemblage from 2011, applied decoration was sparse. There were refitting fragments from a perforated lug (Sherd 10), similar to an example from Le Pinacle (Patton 1995, 142, Vessel A). Another sherd had a large *bouton au repoussé* positioned close to the rim. Beyond this, the main decorative trait was impressed dots of various kinds. One fineware body sherd was adorned with a single row of impressed dots made in wet clay with a blunt point (Sherd 16). One coarseware sherd from a large vessel was marked with two, shallow, crudely impressed dots. It is possible, however, that this sherd derives from the subsequent buried soil layer, since the fabric did not fit well with the remainder of the assemblage.

By contrast, although it was similar in terms of the overall quantity of sherds produced, the 'lower buried soil' assemblage from 2010 [99] produced a greater range of decorated sherds. This included sherds with clusters or rows of small or large *bouton au repoussé*, positioned immediately below the rim (Sherds 6–8), sherds with small vertical incisions along the lip (e.g. Sherd 6), and fragments with rows of comb impressions or small vertical incised lines immediately above the shoulder of the vessel (Sherd 14). One unusual burnished sherd decorated with horizontal incised lines and a row of comb impressions (Sherd 37) resembles closely sherds recovered from Phase I of the Les Fouaillages excavation (Hélène Pioffet pers.comm.). However caution must be applied regarding the dating of sherds from this layer. As mentioned above, layer [99] almost certainly represents an amalgamation of the basal and lower buried soil layers visible elsewhere on the site. The sherds with *bouton au repoussé* and incisions along the lip of the vessel have clear Pinacle-Fouaillages affinities and are almost certainly broadly contemporary with those from the basal soil in 2011. Sherds with vertical incisions along the carination, or horizontal scoring and comb impressions above the shoulder of the vessel, are a feature of Pinacle-Fouaillages assemblages. However similar traits are also present in later assemblages (Middle Neolithic 2 and Chalcolithic) on the Channel Islands, and so are more difficult to place chronologically when encountered in a mixed soil context such as this (see for example Sherd 35 – a less ambiguous Jersey bowl sherd from [99]).

Overall, material associated clearly with the basal soil has broad affinities with Middle Neolithic 1b Pinacle-Fouaillages assemblages recovered from elsewhere on the Channel Islands (Patton 1995, Patton and Finlaison 2001, Pioffet 2013, Sebire 2005). Consequently a date within the mid–late 5th millennium BC seems likely (see also Section 2.9).

Lower buried soil material: Pottery sherds from the lower buried soil [159] (identified only during the 2009 and 2011 excavation seasons in Trench 11) were still more varied in terms of their condition and composition than those from the basal soil. Many fragments were small, worn and undecorated, although a few larger sherds were present. Some patterning was evident in the distribution of sherds within the layer. As might be expected, a greater quantity of abraded Middle Neolithic 1b sherds (similar to those described above) was recovered from the deepest parts of the deposit. Additionally a greater volume of Late Neolithic and Chalcolithic material was found in the south-western and south-eastern corners of Trench 11. The former corresponds with the position of ditch F44 (see below).

The majority of sherds derived from coarseware vessels, although there was also a small fineware component. As with the pottery assemblage from the basal soil layer, the overall range of fabrics was varied. However the material in the lower buried soil layer was more commonly fired in oxidising conditions than the assemblage from the basal soil layer, and was generally more robust in character.

Fragments from jars (straight sided and round shouldered), bowls (including carinated Jersey Bowls: Sherds 32–34) and Beakers (Sherds 30–31) were recorded. In contrast to the assemblage from the basal soil layer, several base sherds were also recovered. Rims were typically simple – rounded, flattened or beaded – and either upright or flaring to varying extents (Sherds 19 and 29). One more pronounced flaring rim (Sherd 18) was similar in form to Middle Neolithic 2 sherds recovered from Guernsey Airport (Hélène Pioffet pers. comm.). Several of the other more gently-carinated plain fineware sherds also resembled Middle Neolithic 2 pot forms from elsewhere on Guernsey (e.g. from Le Déhus, Patton 1995, 150, figure iv.2., vessel B). Soot was present on a small number of sherds.

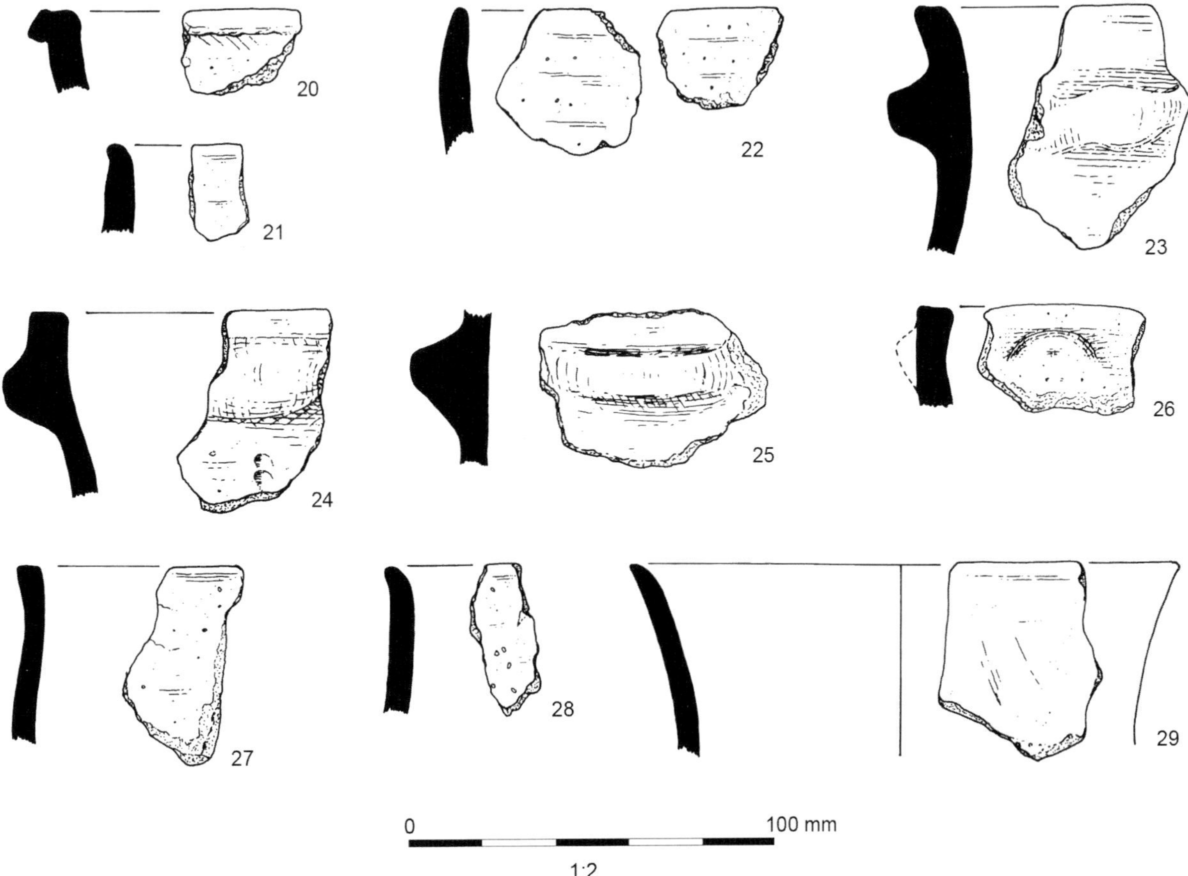

Figure 2.15. Late Neolithic and Chalcolithic (undecorated) pottery (drawn by A. Wilkins).

Very few sherds were decorated. Surface treatments included occasional burnishing on fineware sherds, wiping, and a red surface finish, probably achieved through controlled firing. Heavily abraded *bouton au repoussé* on two fragments and sherds from gently carinated bowls with vertical incisions along the carination (similar to a Middle Neolithic 2 example from Grosnez Hougue, Jersey: Patton 1995, 157, figure iv.16, vessel c), indicate the presence of a small Middle Neolithic component to the lower buried soil assemblage. Beyond this, the main decorative traits were horizontal scored lines, impressed rows or panels of dots and rows of vertical incisions. Several sherds had horizontal scored lines, bordered rows of short vertical incisions or impressed dots, one sherd had an incised horizontal line accentuating a carination, one sherd had rows of short vertical slashes (possibly made with a lithic tool) above the carination, two sherds had simple comb impressed decoration, one sherd had a line scored around the circumference of a square-ish lip, and one coarseware sherd had roughly stabbed marks (Sherds 29 and 31–35). In general, these decorative traits fit well with the characteristics expected for Jersey Bowl and Beaker style vessels. However the decoration present on carinated bowl sherds diverges slightly from that expected for Jersey Bowl vessels in two main respects (see for example the characterisation in Patton 1995, 161). Firstly the rows of impressed dots accompanying the horizontal scored lines were sometimes *below* rather than *above* the scored horizontal lines (as is typical). Secondly, the sherd with rows of incised vertical incisions above the carination but no horizontal scoring (Sherd 34) is not typical of Jersey Bowl decoration. It is possible that this sherd represents a variant of the Jersey Bowl decorative repertoire. Alternatively, this sherd could be residual, belonging instead to the Middle Neolithic 2 assemblage, which does sometimes include vessels with rows of vertical incised lines (though not typically on vessels with such a sharp carination).

Additionally, one sherd from a large jar was decorated with roughly scored lines and fingernail impressions (Sherd 42), and a number of fragments related to simple, usually heavily-abraded, lozenge-shaped (or in one case, round) lugs, positioned horizontally on the body of the vessel. Sherds with lozenge-shaped lugs, roughly scored lines and fingernail impressions are characteristic of Late Neolithic and Chalcolithic 'domestic' assemblages from across the Channel Islands (e.g. Burns 1988, 14; Patton 1995, 163–165; Patton & Finlaison 2001).

Overall, the material from the lower buried soil in Trench 11 spans the Middle Neolithic 1b to Chalcolithic periods. The vast majority of sherds are diagnostically Late Neolithic or Chalcolithic in date, including a small but significant Jersey Bowl and Beaker component. The Middle Neolithic 1b and 2 sherds from this assemblage are almost certainly residual.

Upper buried soil material: Material from the upper buried soil layer in Trench 11 consisted largely of undecorated,

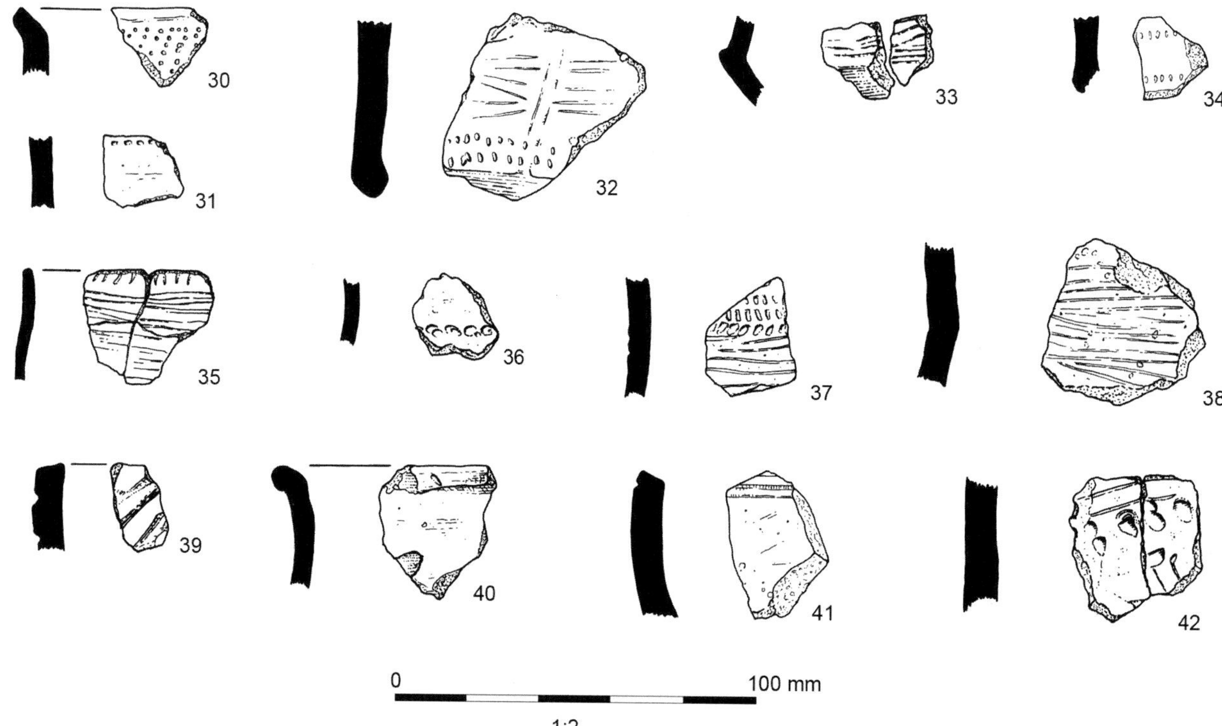

Figure 2.16. Chalcolithic (decorated) pottery (drawn by A. Wilkins).

small and abraded coarseware sherds. Few clearly diagnostic traits (particularly in terms of formal and decorative features) were identified. The few decorated sherds probably relate to the earliest activity associated with this soil layer. Two clear concentrations of sherds were evident. The first was in the south-eastern corner of Trench 11; the second was in the south-western corner of the trench (Square Q) corresponding with the position of ditch F44. Gradation from top to bottom was also evident in the material from this soil horizon. Material recovered from the upper spits of this layer was larger and fairly homogeneous in character, mostly comprising hard, fairly well-fired reddish orange-brown coarseware sherds (mainly c. 1–1.5cm thick) with variably-sorted, common, predominantly feldspar and sometimes quartz inclusions (Fabric 4 was the dominant fabric in this layer). Material recovered from the lower spits of this layer was generally smaller, more worn and more varied in character, and included a larger residual (Middle Neolithic 1b) component.

Fragments from the bodies, necks and rims of a range of jars and bowls together with one sherd from a small vessel with a narrow diameter – a cup? – were recovered. Several possible base sherds were identified but all of these were small and worn and were no longer attached to the body of the vessel. Rims were characteristically simple – square, beaded or rounded – and either upright or everted (e.g. Sherd 27).

In general there was little apparent attention to surface detail. One sherd from this layer had a red finish; a few others were burnished. Lozenge-shaped, horizontally-positioned lugs and plain applied cordons were the main (if rare) decorative traits (Sherd 25). A few sherds were roughly scored. One rim sherd had diagonal incisions along the rim and a cordon running diagonally from just beneath the rim. Otherwise, the majority of decorated sherds from this layer were similar in character to those described for the lower buried soil layer (see above). One sherd was decorated with horizontal scored lines surmounted by chevrons of impressed dots (Sherd 37). The upper buried soil material from 2010 [98] also included sherds with irregular rows of large impressed dots or fingernail impressions and sherds with roughly incised horizontal and diagonal lines similar to examples from the Chalcolithic assemblage at Jerbourg (Burns 1988, 18; Patton 1995, 172). One unusual sherd from [158] was decorated with large applied *boutons* (Sherd 17). Given that residual Middle Neolithic 1b material is present across this layer, it is certainly possible that this sherd is residual and relates to that period of activity (hence its tentative assignation to the Middle Neolithic 1b phase). However the sherd's hard fabric and the lack of clear evidence for the use of the *repoussé* technique characteristic of Middle Neolithic 1b *bouton* sherds could indicate that it could instead belong to a later (Bronze Age?) phase of activity. Unfortunately no decorative parallels could be found from this period.

Overall the material from this layer spans the Middle Neolithic 1b to Early Bronze Age period. However the vast majority of sherds are probably Chalcolithic (2850–2300 BC) or Early Bronze Age in date (2300–1500 BC). Similar assemblages have been identified from the earliest levels of the defences at Jerbourg (Burns 1988, 16–17) and from Early Bronze Age sites elsewhere on the Channel Islands (Patton 1995, 96–97; Patton & Finlaison 2001, 49). However it is also worth noting that the character of Middle Bronze Age pottery from the Channel Islands is less well defined than that for earlier phases; it is certainly possible that the latest material from the upper buried soil layers in Trench 11 extends into this phase.

Material from Trenches 4–9 and 12–18: At a broad level, the prehistoric pottery recovered from the three main soil layers in trenches elsewhere in Field 336 corresponds well with that from the three buried soil layers within Trench 11 (Tables 2.04 and 2.05). Material from the upper buried soil tended to be quite fragmented and probably relates primarily to Chalcolithic and Early Bronze Age activity. That from the lower buried soil mainly spanned the Late Neolithic and Chalcolithic periods. Sherds from the basal soil were mostly small and, at least towards the base of this deposit, were exclusively Middle Neolithic (1b or 2) in date. Exceptions to this scheme were the presence of Early Bronze Age material in the lower buried soil layer in Trenches 6–8, and the presence of potentially Middle Bronze Age sherds in Trenches 8 and 18. As noted for Trench 11, it was sometimes difficult to draw a strict line between the two lower palaeosoil layers (the lower buried soil and basal soil). For this reason excavated contexts commonly spanned these layers. Given the broad overlap with the Trench 11 material, only distinctive aspects of the assemblages from Trenches 4–9 and 12–18 are outlined below.

Overall, there was a broad but thin distribution of Middle Neolithic 1b pottery across these trenches, a particular focus of Late Neolithic and Chalcolithic material in Trench 7, and a slightly looser concentration of Late Neolithic through to Middle Bronze Age material in Trenches 5–7 and 17–18. Elsewhere, material tended to be sparser and more heavily fragmented.

Probably the most distinctive Middle Neolithic 1b sherd from soil layers in the trenches beyond Trench 11 is refitting fragments from a looped decorated handle (Sherd 12). Other noteworthy Middle Neolithic 1b sherds from these trenches include a carinated sherd with tiny impressed (with a fish rib – Ian Kinnes pers. comm.) dots immediately above the carination, refitting sherds from a burnished vessel with fine score marks (not clearly decorative) just below the rim, an oxidised rim sherd from a fine carinated bowl (possibly Middle Neolithic 2 in date), and a small lug, embellished with vertical incisions (Sherds 2, 5, 11 and 13).

Table 2.04. Relationships between palaeosol contexts (not including post-medieval) from Trenches 4–9 and 12–18

	Tr4	*Tr5*	*Tr6*	*Tr7*	*Tr8*	*Tr9*	*Tr12*	*Tr13*	*Tr15*	*Tr16*	*Tr17*	*Tr18*
UBS	[26]	[27], [36]	[28], [38]	[29]	[30]	[31]	[64]	[71]	[111]	[109]	[102]	[106]
LBS	[34], [35] (0–10cm)	[37] (0–10cm)	[39], [51]	[41], [53], [54]	[42], [43]	[48]	[69]	[72]	[113]	[114]	[112]	[107]
BS	[35] (10–30cm)	[37] (10–30cm)	[52]	[54]	[44]				[157]			[120]

Table 2.05. Summary of pottery from Trenches 4–9 and 12–18 (not including material from medieval soil contexts)

	Tr4	*Tr5*	*Tr6*	*Tr7*	*Tr8*	*Tr9*	*Tr12*	*Tr13*	*Tr15*	*Tr16*	*Tr17*	*Tr18*
UBS	24 (308g)	168 (562g)	228 (864g)	77 (486g)	57 (348g)	29 (214g)	30 (94g)	6 (94g)	1 (4g)	99 (261g)	120 (486g)	58 (354g)
LBS	127 (582g)	84 (478g)	97 (430g)	340 (1538g)	104 (672g)	61 (444g)	26 (108g)	4 (20g)	125 (425g)	54 (169g)	413 (1745g)	112 (417g)
BS	4 (8g)	26 (66g)	43 (80g)		4 (12g)				70 (160g)			5 (12g)

NB: where contexts span soil layers and there is no clear point depth-wise at which the assemblage changes, sherd counts are merged.

The Late Neolithic and Chalcolithic sherds recovered from the uppermost 10 cm of the basal soil [54] in Trench 7 represent perhaps the best-preserved and most clearly diagnostic assemblage of this date from the site (Sherds 20, 23, 28, 36 and 38). It is probably no coincidence that this trench lies within the area defined by ditches F12 and F44, which are probably of Late Neolithic date. Other notable sherds of this date from soil layers in Trenches 4–9 and 12–18 include a potentially Late Neolithic upright rim sherd, finely burnished on both the interior and exterior; a Late Neolithic/Chalcolithic rim sherd with an elongated lug (similar to the material from Hougue Mauger – Patton 1995, 164–5); a comb impressed Beaker rim sherd; and a tiny fragment, probably from a larger/more crudely decorated Jersey Bowl (see for example Patton 1995, 171) (Sherds 21, 24, 30 and 39).

Some of the best-preserved diagnostic Early Bronze Age sherds were recovered from the uppermost palaeosoils in Trenches 4–9 and 12–18 (Sherds 43–7). Trench 17 yielded a particularly large assemblage of Early Bronze Age sherds from the uppermost spit of the lower buried soil [112], although this mainly comprised plain coarseware body sherds. Perhaps the most significant sherd of this period is a strap handle fragment from Trench 7 (Sherd 46). While fragments from strap handled vessels are more commonly found on sites of this date in Jersey, a single example has been found previously in Guernsey at L'Erée (Patton 1995, 105). Plain cordoned vessels (Sherds 43 and 45) and vessels with rows of fingernail impressions or impressed lozenges focused along rounded cordons (Sherd 44) have parallels in the Early Bronze Age assemblages from Jerbourg (Burns 1988) and Icho Islet (Patton 1995, 96). Cups and jars with smaller handles such as the fragment from Trench 18 (Sherd 47) have also been recovered from La Roque Qui Sonne (Patton 1995, 103) and La Varde (Patton 1995, 173), both in Guernsey. A fine rim fragment with a small, squarish, elongated horizontal lug was also recovered from the uppermost palaeosoil in Trench 18 (Sherd 26). The fabric of this sherd was similar to that of the Early Bronze Age sherds from the same layer. However, the presence of a lug indicates a Late Neolithic/Chalcolithic date.

It is worth mentioning that the uppermost soil layers in Trenches 8 and 18 produced material of a slightly different character. This was broadly similar in character to the other Early Bronze Age material but included a wider range of fabrics (sherds with a greater proportion of quartz inclusions and hard sandy fragments). It is thus possible that some Middle Bronze Age activity (c. 1500–1000 BC) is represented, although, as mentioned above, the decorative traits of Middle Bronze Age pottery on the Channel Islands overlap with those for Early Bronze Age material and the character of material from the Middle Bronze Age is generally not well defined. It was observed that soot adhered to the surfaces of many of these sherds, perhaps indicating a shift in the use of pottery vessels at this time.

Material from cut features

Pits, post-holes, hearths and gullies associated with the basal soil (Trenches 6 and 11)

Material recovered from these features was sparse, mostly comprising small, abraded and undecorated sherds. Overall this fits well with the assemblage recovered from the basal soil layer in Trench 11 (see above) and is probably all of Middle Neolithic 1b date. Several sherds are notable.

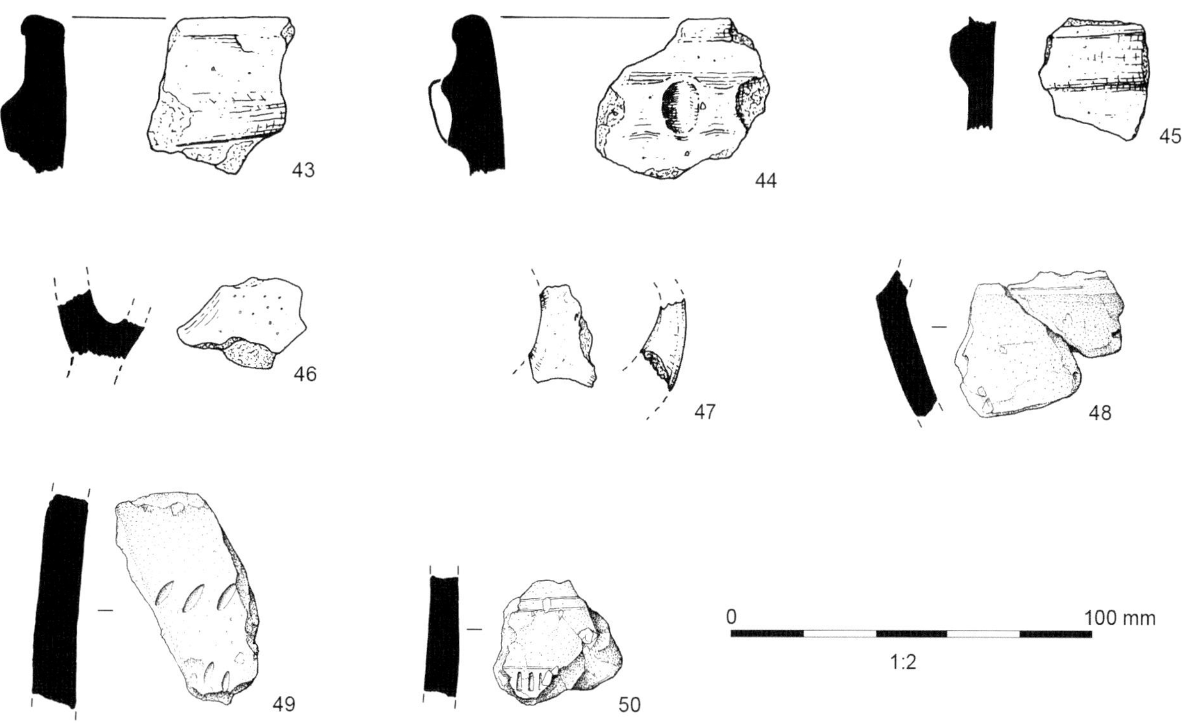

Figure 2.17. Bronze Age pottery (and sherds from Trench 3) (drawn by A. Wilkins).

A burnished fineware sherd impressed with a row of small dots, probably made with the tip of a fish bone (Ian Kinnes pers. comm.) was recovered from a post-hole (F10) in Trench 6 (Sherd 15). Indeed a very similar sherd was recovered from the basal soil [52] in this trench, attesting to the close relationship between the earliest cut features on the site and the development of the earliest soil layer. Two refitting rim sherds decorated with *bouton au repoussé* were recovered from a hearth (F8) in Trench 11. A further *bouton au repoussé* sherd was found in a pit (F39) in the same trench. Additionally a sherd with a small round lug positioned on the rim, probably from a small hemispherical bowl, was recovered from a hearth (F17) in Trench 11 (Sherd 9).

DITCHES (TRENCHES 7, 9, 11 AND 16)

The material recovered from ditches and a 'channel' in Field 336 (Fs 12, 21 and 44 in Trenches 7, 16 and 11 respectively) can be split into two main groups.

The first group is represented by sherds from F12 and F44. In terms of their fabrics and the forms represented, these resemble most closely material from the upper two palaeosoils (the lower and upper buried soil layers). Based on the broad character of this material and on the total absence of either distinctive Jersey Bowl or cordoned sherds (typical of Chalcolithic and Early Bronze Age assemblages respectively), a Late Neolithic origin is likely for this material. Within this group, a further distinction can be made between the material recovered from the shallow and more irregular ditch at the base of the hillslope (F12) and that from the substantial and better defined ditch F44 in Trench 11. The former is highly abraded and includes few diagnostic sherds. The latter includes large, freshly broken and occasionally refitting sherds.

The assemblage recovered from the irregular ditch/gully in Trench 7 was small and abraded and mainly comprised plain body sherds. The presence of base sherds in this assemblage supports a Late Neolithic or later date. Both fine and coarseware vessels in a range of forms (jars and bowls) were represented, although plain coarseware sherds dominated the assemblage. Some attention to surface finish was attested by the presence of several burnished sherds. A sherd from the upper fill [49] of F12 was decorated with a single incised line above the shoulder (Sherd 41). Similar decorative traits are present within the material described as Chalcolithic from Jerbourg (Burns 1988, 19). However more recent studies have raised questions about the dates attributed to the pottery from Jerbourg (e.g. Patton 1995). It is possible that either this simple decorative trait was a feature of both Late Neolithic and Chalcolithic pottery assemblages on Guernsey or otherwise that the material from Jerbourg is earlier than was initially thought.

The material from ditch F44 was similarly homogeneous in terms of the fabrics represented but much less so in terms of the vessel types and forms. Sherds from bowls and large, round-shouldered jars were present. While coarseware sherds dominated, a small but significant quantity of sherds derived from finer or at least more carefully finished vessels. Rims were typically upright or inverted and either rounded or tapered. Several fragments were burnished to varying degrees; others appeared to have a slip coating on inner and/or outer surface (although this may have been achieved through firing). A number of sherds related to round or elongated horizontal lugs. One of the latter was accentuated with a single incised line; another was burnished. Beyond this, very few decorative traits were evident. There were numerous large sherds with fresh breaks in this assemblage. In one instance it was clear that two sherds derived from a single burnished fineware bowl although these did not refit directly (Sherd 22). One other definite refit was identified and with further examination it is possible that other sherds could be refitted. This attests to the likely spatial and temporal proximity of the activity with which these vessels were associated and the ditch in which their broken fragments were deposited. Overall the assemblage from F44 accords well with the Late Neolithic material from Le Déhus (e.g. Patton 1995, 163–164).

The second group of material – that recovered from F21 in Trench 16 – is subtly different in character. The fabric of sherds from this ditch is softer and finer in character than that of material recovered from the other ditch-like features. Although a similar range of inclusions is evident, these are also finer overall and less well sorted. It includes 16 unabraded and in some cases refitting rim and body sherds from a large necked bowl with an everted rim (Sherd 1). Unfortunately these are not sufficiently diagnostic to assign to a specific period. The vessel was irregularly fired and made of a fine, softish paste with ill-sorted predominantly feldspar and quartz inclusions. A collar of soot or charred organic residue clung to the neck sherds. The freshness of the sherds suggests that they were deposited soon after the pot was broken.

The dating of this material is complex for a number of different reasons. Due to the positioning of F21 at right angles to the very similarly shaped and sized ditch in Trench 11 (F44), at first sight it is tempting to suggest that these two features were broadly contemporary, and that the slightly different qualities of the pottery recovered from each represents different components of the Late Neolithic assemblage. This would certainly be the most straightforward interpretation. However, two factors contradict this suggestion: first, the external residue from the neck of this vessel produced a radiocarbon date of 4980–4790 cal BC (see Section 2.9 for details); and second, sherds recovered from the buried soil layers immediately overlying this ditch resemble most closely the Middle Neolithic 1b (Pinacle-Fouaillage) basal soil assemblage, not later material.

In truth, the precise date of the small assemblage from F21 remains ambiguous. It is certainly possible that the charcoal from the vessel neck was derived from 'old wood', and that the actual date of the vessel could therefore be later (although probably not the 1300 years later required to place it in the Late Neolithic). Equally, the absence of clearly Late Neolithic material in the buried soil overlying this ditch is not an unequivocal indication of its early date – residual material was recovered from many layers on the site. One alternative explanation is that the ditch was cut into a much earlier pit, although the facts that the sherds from F21 were large and unabraded, and that refitting sherds were found in close proximity with one another rather than being substantially disturbed, does not support this interpretation very well. For now, therefore, the possible pre-Middle Neolithic 1b ceramic presence must remain a possibility alone (see Section 2.10 for further discussion of a pre-Middle Neolithic 1b presence on the site).

Field 333

The assemblage from Trench 3 in Field 333 corresponds well with the Late Neolithic/Early Bronze Age material from lower buried soil contexts in Field 336. It mainly comprised sherds from coarseware jars (straight sided and round shouldered), bowls (hemispherical and carinated, including Jersey Bowl fragments), and Beakers. The absence of any fragments with cordons or strap handles suggests that the Early Bronze Age component present within assemblages from elsewhere at L'Erée (see above and Cunliffe and de Jersey 2000) is either missing or much less dominant in this assemblage. While it would not be surprising if Middle Neolithic 1b sherds were present within the material from Field 333, this was not verifiable due in part to the overlapping decorative repertoires of Neolithic and Chalcolithic fineware vessels. The vast majority of the assemblage comprised small, worn sherds. However the presence of occasional sherds with minimally-abraded breaks suggests that at least some of the activity represented may have taken place quite close to the excavated area. Key distinguishing traits relative to the Late Neolithic/Chalcolithic material recovered from Field 336, together with clear points of association, are highlighted here.

One distinctive element of the assemblage from Field 333 was the recovery of a greater number of base fragments; these are notably sparse within the assemblage from Field 336. Additionally, a broader range of carinated bowl sherds was observed including one sharply angled example from a large vessel and another with a slight ridge accentuating the carination (Sherd 49). These have parallels within the Chalcolithic assemblage from Jerbourg (Patton 1995, 172).

Distinguishing decorative traits within this material included several sherds with horizontal or zigzag lines of diagonal grain-like impressions (Sherd 50). Similar features are present in the Chalcolithic material from La Varde (Patton 1995, 172–173). The decoration on other fragments showed close affinity with Jersey Bowl sherds from the assemblages recovered in Field 336 and from earlier excavations at L'Erée (Cunliffe and de Jersey 2000, 878) – one sherd was scored with continuous horizontal grooves, another was incised with a single line surmounted by a row of short vertical slashes just above the carination (Sherd 48). It is worth noting, however, that the decoration on this last sherd also accords well with that found on Middle Neolithic 1b material from the Channel Islands. It is certainly possible that the Middle Neolithic 1b occupation represented in Field 336 extended into this area. The single sherd from post-hole F1 was an undiagnostic, plain angled body sherd.

Discussion

The prehistoric pottery from L'Erée represents an important addition to a growing corpus of Neolithic and Bronze Age material recovered from contexts across the Channel Island archipelago (Burns 1988; Patton 1995; Cunliffe and de Jersey 2000; Patton & Finlaison 2001; Sebire 2005, 90; 2012; Pioffet 2013).

Overall, the assemblage provides a clear indication of a long sequence of occupation at L'Erée, spanning the Middle Neolithic to Early Bronze Age periods. The earliest phase of material derives from features – pits, hearths and post-holes – cut directly into the loess. While sparse, this material shows clear affinities with Middle Neolithic 1b (Pinacle-Fouaillages) pottery assemblages across the Channel Islands. Where the form of vessels is apparent, sherds relate exclusively to carinated or hemispherical bowls. The vast majority of sherds were fired in reducing conditions, burnishing is a common feature, and decorative traits include small rounded lugs, rows of impressed dots and *bouton au repoussé.* Material clearly derived from the palaeosoil directly associated with these features (the basal soil layer) is very similar in character, although it includes a greater variety of fabrics, forms and decorative traits. Although the Middle Neolithic 1b assemblage complements rather than adds significantly to assemblages of a similar date from elsewhere in the archipelago (in that the sherds were all small in size and no new decorative traits were identified), it is important in that it derives from stratigraphically secure settlement contexts. As discussed further in Sections 2.9 and 2.10, the radiocarbon dates secured for features containing Pinacle-Fouaillages pottery at L'Erée suggest occupation from 4480–4060 cal BC to 4230–3850 cal BC, putting the currency of this pottery somewhat later than the c. 4600–4300 BC datespan for MN1b pottery suggested previously (Marcigny et al. 2010).

Material spanning the Middle Neolithic 2 to Late Neolithic/Chalcolithic period (c. 4300–2300 BC) derives from the subsequent palaeosoil (the lower buried soil) and from ditches associated directly with this layer. While this includes an element of material probably dating to the Middle Neolithic 2 period, the vast majority of this assemblage is Late Neolithic/Chalcolithic in date.

Potentially Middle Neolithic 2 sherds within this assemblage include occasional fragments from plain, gently carinated vessels with flaring rims and potentially from carinated bowls with small, vertical incisions along the carination. While undecorated globular, hemispherical and carinated vessels are an important component of Middle Neolithic 2 assemblages elsewhere on the Channel Islands (e.g. from Le Déhus chambered tomb), these are unsurprisingly hard to identify within a mixed assemblage (one which spans several continuous periods) of small abraded sherds and it is certainly possible that other fragments relating to this phase of activity are present within the assemblage from the lower buried soil. Fortunately, work at Guernsey Airport (Philip de Jersey and Hélène pers. comm.) has produced a more substantial assemblage of this date. The sherds found there accord well with those of this date from L'Erée; thus our understanding of domestic assemblages of this date will almost certainly improve significantly in the near future. What is clear is that the most distinctive diagnostic traits of Middle Neolithic 2 Channel Island assemblages (as defined by Patton 1995) – miniature vases, vase supports and other heavily decorated vessels – are missing from the L'Erée assemblage. This implies that there was either a hiatus in occupation at L'Erée during the late 5th/earlier 4th millennium BC or otherwise that occupation of the site during this period was significantly more sporadic.

Distinctively Late Neolithic material derives mainly from three ditches or channels cut into the lower buried soil layer, from which Chalcolithic and later material was entirely absent. This includes large, refitting sherds from globular and straight-sided 'flower pot' jars and hemispherical bowls in oxidised fabrics. Round or elongated lugs and burnishing are key decorative traits. Sherds with similar features are present in the associated lower buried soil but since Late Neolithic and Chalcolithic coarseware fabrics are hard to distinguish, and since decorative features are sparse on coarseware vessels, the Late Neolithic component of the buried soil assemblage is more difficult to characterise. The Chalcolithic assemblage from the lower buried soil is relatively substantial, and much more clearly identifiable, due primarily to its inclusion of fineware Beaker and Jersey Bowl sherds. The latter were fairly well represented, if generally by small abraded sherds, and included both typical and potentially new decorative traits. The presence of sherds similar to those from Chalcolithic assemblages at Jerbourg with scored lines and fingernail impressions is an interesting addition to the assemblage and certainly suggests that the two sites were occupied over broadly the same period. What is difficult to establish within mixed soil contexts (like those at L'Erée) is whether the sherds with affinities to the Jerbourg assemblage represent a different (later and less intense?) phase of Chalcolithic activity at the site or whether, alternatively, this material was used alongside Jersey Bowl and Beaker vessels. Overall, the Late Neolithic to Early Bronze Age pottery assemblage from L'Erée adds considerably to our knowledge of assemblages of this date from the Channel Islands. The substantial quantity of this material also suggests that activity at the site during this period was relatively intensive and sustained.

The latest prehistoric material from the site derives from the uppermost spits of the lower buried soil and, primarily, from the upper buried soil. This material has close affinities with Channel Island Early Bronze Age assemblages. Beaded or square rims, plain or decorated cordons and handle fragments (strap handles and smaller, finer examples) are distinctive decorative traits. The vast majority of material of this date is tempered heavily and fairly uniformly with feldspar fragments, although a small (potentially Middle Bronze Age?) element includes a greater proportion of sandy and quartz tempered sherds.

In summary, although the prehistoric assemblage from L'Erée derives largely from mixed palaeosoil contexts – thus many of the sherds are small and abraded – it is significant for three key reasons. Firstly, the material potentially spans a period from the Middle Neolithic to at least the Early Bronze Age (c. 4600–1500 BC), with only a short possible hiatus in the late 5th/earlier 4th millennium BC. Consequently it could be seen as a lynch-pin, linking together assemblages from other more chronologically specific sites both in Guernsey and across the Channel Islands more broadly. Secondly, the material almost certainly derives mainly from settlement activity, providing an important counterpart to the 'ritual' assemblages already known from elsewhere for this period, typically recovered from monumental contexts. Thirdly, although the assemblage does derive largely from palaeosoils and is probably mixed to a certain degree due to the complex formation of these soils, these palaeosoils are consistent across the site and the clear temporal grading of material from top to bottom of the layers suggests that, by and large, disturbance to them has been minimal. Moreover the stratigraphic context of material from cut features is established securely beneath and between these layers.

2.5. Chipped stone

Anne Pirie

Introduction

This report details the results of analysis of 13,860 chipped stone artefacts from L'Erée, recovered over four seasons of excavation (2008–2011) (Figures 2.18 and 2.19; Tables 2.06 and 2.07).

Methodology

The entire assemblage was subject to initial visual inspection, with key artefacts noted and recorded. Following this preliminary scan, a sample of 3334 artefacts from key contexts throughout the sequence was selected for full cataloguing (24% of the total) (see Appendix 1 for full details). This sample included all archaeological features (395 artefacts); material from the full sequence of several of the deeper trenches (Trenches 4, 6, and 11 (Squares C, J, N and Q)); and then a representative additional sample of at least 600 artefacts from each of the different buried soil layers.

Table 2.06. Catalogue of illustrated flint from L'Eree (Figs 2.18–2.19)

Illus. no.	*Description*	*Trench no.*	*Context no.*	*Feature*
1	Used flake, glossy	7	54	–
2	Awl/piercer	6	52	–
3	Asymmetric transverse arrowhead	16	114	–
4	Scraper	11	99	–
5	Scraper (black flint)	11	159	–
6	Knife	11	159	–
7	Scraper	11	162	–
8	Burin	4	35	–
9	Knife/pièce esquillée	11	159	–
10	Scraper (thumbnail)	4	34	–
11	Marginally retouched piece	11	162	–
12	Denticulate	11	162	–
13	Blade tang (Gr. Pressigny flint)	11	158	–
14	Barbed & tanged arrowhead (Gr. Pressigny flint)	7	41	–
15	Anvil	11	158	–
16	Discoidal core	11	158	–
17	Multi platform core	7	54	–
18	Core tablet	11	162	–
19	Bipolar core	4	35	–
20	Single platform core	11	98	–
21	Single platform core core	11	159	–
22	Opposed platform core	11	181	44
23	Sub-pyramidal bladelet core	11	162	–

Table 2.07. Chipped stone assemblages (for trenches catalogued in detail)

Trench no	*4*		*6*		*7*		*9*		*11*		*16*		*Total*	
	No.	*%*	*No.*	*%*	*No.*	*%*	*No.*	*%*	*No.*	*%*	*No.*	*%*	*No.*	*%*
Flakes	196	69.8	567	72.2	233	70.6	27	73.0	1260	72.2	113	73.4	2396	71.9
Flake blades	15	5.3	16	2.0	4	1.2		0.0	30	1.7	8	5.2	73	2.2
Blade (irreg.)	6	2.1	16	2.0	5	1.5		0.0	35	2.0	1	0.6	63	1.9
Blade (reg.)	8	2.8	17	2.2	8	2.4		0.0	34	1.9	1	0.6	68	2.0
Spalls	8	2.8	10	1.3	1	0.3		0.0	21	1.2	1	0.6	41	1.2
Core trimming elements	5	1.8	16	2.0	6	1.8	1	2.7	35	2.0	4	2.6	67	2.0
Indets	18	6.4	85	10.8	49	14.8	5	13.5	171	9.8	9	5.8	337	10.1
<5mm	3	1.1	4	0.5	4	1.2		0.0	5	0.3	3	1.9	19	0.6
Cores	22	7.8	54	6.9	20	6.1	4	10.8	154	8.8	14	9.1	268	8.0
Totals	281		785		330		37		1745		154		3332	
Bl:Fl ratio	28.13		35.82		30.38				35.59		123		37.84	
Total tools	37		70		42		5		217		3		374	
% tools	13.2%		8.9		12.7		13.5		12.4		1.9		11.2	

The sample catalogued in detail was chosen to provide an adequate range across the site, and for each context level. Categories and definitions used follow Inizan et al. (1999). The catalogued sample was 'bulk' catalogued, with a numeric and qualitative summary of the contents of each context entered into an Access database. This includes quantities in each technological category, broad core types and tool classes, as well as descriptive overview of significant cores and tools. Comments are included on raw materials, condition and burning, and regular blade dimensions are recorded.

The remainder of the assemblage was scanned. Scanning was carried out in two ways. Some contexts were scanned in detail (5013 artefacts), with qualitative summaries of technology, cores, tools and raw materials recorded. Other contexts were very quickly scanned (5513), with only diagnostics and total count recorded. The decision as to what level of scanning was carried out was taken randomly. Use of a 10× hand lens to examine artefacts was limited to identified tools, so some categories may be under-identified (e.g. used tools).

The assemblage will be described as a whole, then variability across the site and its levels will be discussed. This discussion is based largely on the catalogued sample, drawing on additional qualitative information from the scanned assemblage where appropriate (see Table 2.06 for cross-reference to Figures 2.18 and 2.19).

Technology

The dominant raw material is a homogeneous flint ranging from light grey to grey-brown or dark grey in colour. There are small numbers of artefacts made from other materials including a very black, opaque flint, a brown grey opaque and very homogenous flint likely to be bathonian flint from Normandy (known widely as 'Cinglais' flint in France), Grand Pressigny flint, quartz, sandstone, jasper, and chert. There is a significant amount of cortex on the artefacts, and many primary pieces. All of the cortex is from rolled pebble exteriors, and it seems likely that most of the raw material was sourced from beach pebbles.

Some of the flints, however, are not derived from beach pebbles. These include the black opaque flint, which occurs in small numbers throughout the assemblage; the 'Cinglais' flint (of which there are only a couple of artefacts, which come from larger nodules than those found as beach pebbles and are likely to have been imported as blanks or tools to the site); and small numbers of artefacts made using Grand Pressigny flint. No cores were found in these materials.

Flakes dominate the lithics, ranging from 69–73% of the catalogued assemblage (Table 2.07). Blades are present in small numbers, and include both regular and irregular specimens in roughly equal quantities. Irregular blades are likely to be a by-product of the general flake industry present at the site. Regular blades, however, are signs of a dedicated blade industry; numbers are very small though, with the blade : flake ratios (using only regular blades) ranging from one blade for every 28–123 flakes (for all trenches catalogued where the assemblage was >25). Blades are variable in width, with most under 16mm wide. Lengths could not be compared because there were too few complete specimens.

Flakes are often irregular hard hammer/bipolar on anvil products, although there are also many finer, more regular flakes. There are a small number of very regular, blade-like flakes with parallel edges and arrises (from 0–5% across the trenches).

There are numerous cores in the assemblage (ranging from 6–9% of the trench assemblages) (Table 2.08). The majority of the cores have some cortex on them, reflecting their beach pebble origin. Nearly all of the cores show only flake removals, although there are two cores with blade removals, and two more that showed partial blade removals from a previous stage of core exploitation. Three of these are opposed platform cores with keeled platforms, and one is a single platform subpyramidal core. Core types present include many bipolar on anvil cores, as well as both single and multiple platform cores, small numbers of irregular discoidal cores and a few tested pebbles. The proportion of these different core types varies across the site and the trenches with, for example, bipolar on anvil cores varying from 21–72% of the core assemblage of the various trenches. The bipolar on anvil technique is used here to split beach pebbles, and many of these cores are essentially half-pebbles; it is also used to further reduce pebbles as seen in many often angular and rather haphazard bipolar cores. Completely exhausted, flat or matchstick shaped bipolar cores are present in only small numbers. Platform cores include small single platform reduced pebbles, often with extensive hinging of removals and sharp platform overhangs, as well as multiple platform cores that are angular, globular and rather disorganised in their reduction – these vary in size but can be amongst the largest cores in the assemblage. Regular single, opposed or change of orientation cores occur very rarely.

Core trimming elements are widely present in small numbers, and include some core tablets from regular platform cores, and some more irregular core trimming elements often removing part of the platform edge/striking face, sometimes including cortex/flaws.

To summarise, there are thus several reduction sequences present in the assemblage. The most common is the production of flakes from small pebble single platform cores using a hard hammer. These are sometimes turned to form additional platforms to extend the life of the core, and platforms are often rejuvenated using core trimming elements, also to extend the removal of the small flakes produced from these cores.

While the relatively small size of the beach pebbles means that fewer blanks will have been produced from each core, it is also true that many, while fairly well used, were not fully exploited. This and the large number of cores in the assemblage probably reflects an abundance of suitable beach pebbles nearby. It may also be that cores were knapped here, with blanks taken elsewhere for use and/or discard.

Bipolar on anvil cores use similar pebbles, and the technique is used at all stages of pebble reduction, from opening through to the final stages. However, these cores are rarely reduced down through controlled bipolar removals to the tiny cores sometimes seen on sites, perhaps because of the abundance of suitable pebbles. A broken anvil was retrieved from the upper buried soil levels in Trench 11, Square Q, in the form of a flat pebble, with evidence of use as an anvil in the form of a central, pitted depression on each side, where cores would have been placed for striking (No. 15).

The multi-platform cores are in some cases further use of the small single platform cores. However, many of them are larger than the single platform cores and show a less organised reduction, with flakes taken off at any and all possible angles. They are globular, angular and very irregular. Removals are likely to be less regular/fine, and in some cases are larger, than those from the single platform cores.

There are a small number of more complex core reduction strategies present at least in part here: discoidal cores, similar to less regular Levallois cores, are used for flake production in some cases; blade cores, usually with opposed removals of fairly narrow blades from keeled platforms, for production of regular blades; rare pressure blades are present, often broader and on dark flint, or very fine grey brown flint (there is no sign of on-site production of these artefacts).

Tools

Tools are mainly on flakes, and are often relatively ad hoc in nature. Many marginally retouched flakes are present (17–37%) (Table 2.09). The other most common retouched tool class is scrapers (14–28%), including endscrapers, sidescrapers and more heavily retouched end-/sidescrapers. Some of these are regular with fine retouch, and some thumbnail scrapers are present. Most common are half-pebbles with regular scraper retouch over 20–70% of the edge. Many of these show signs of heavy use in esquillée type removals, and spall removals, and some scraper bits have been retrieved showing renewal of scraper edges. Other retouched tools include smaller numbers of notches, which are usually scantily retouched and rather ad hoc, with some

Table 2.08. Core types (for trenches catalogued in detail)

Trench no	*4*		*6*		*7*		*9*		*11*		*16*	
	No.	*%*	*No.*	*%*	*No.*	*%*	*No.*	*%*	*No.*	*%*	*No.*	*%*
Bipolar	16	72.7	25	46.3	8	40.0	1	25.0	67	43.8	3	21.4
Bip/plat	1	4.5	2	3.7	1	5.0	1	25.0	10	6.5	1	7.1
Single plat	1	4.5	12	22.2	6	30.0	1	25.0	37	24.2	2	14.3
Multi plat	4	18.2	10	18.5	5	25.0	1	25.0	28	18.3	7	50.0
Tested		0.0	1	1.9		0.0		0.0	4	2.6	1	7.1
Fragment		0.0	3	5.6		0.0		0.0	2	1.3		0.0
Other		0.0	1	1.9		0.0		0.0	8	5.2		0.0
Total	22		54		20		4		153		14	

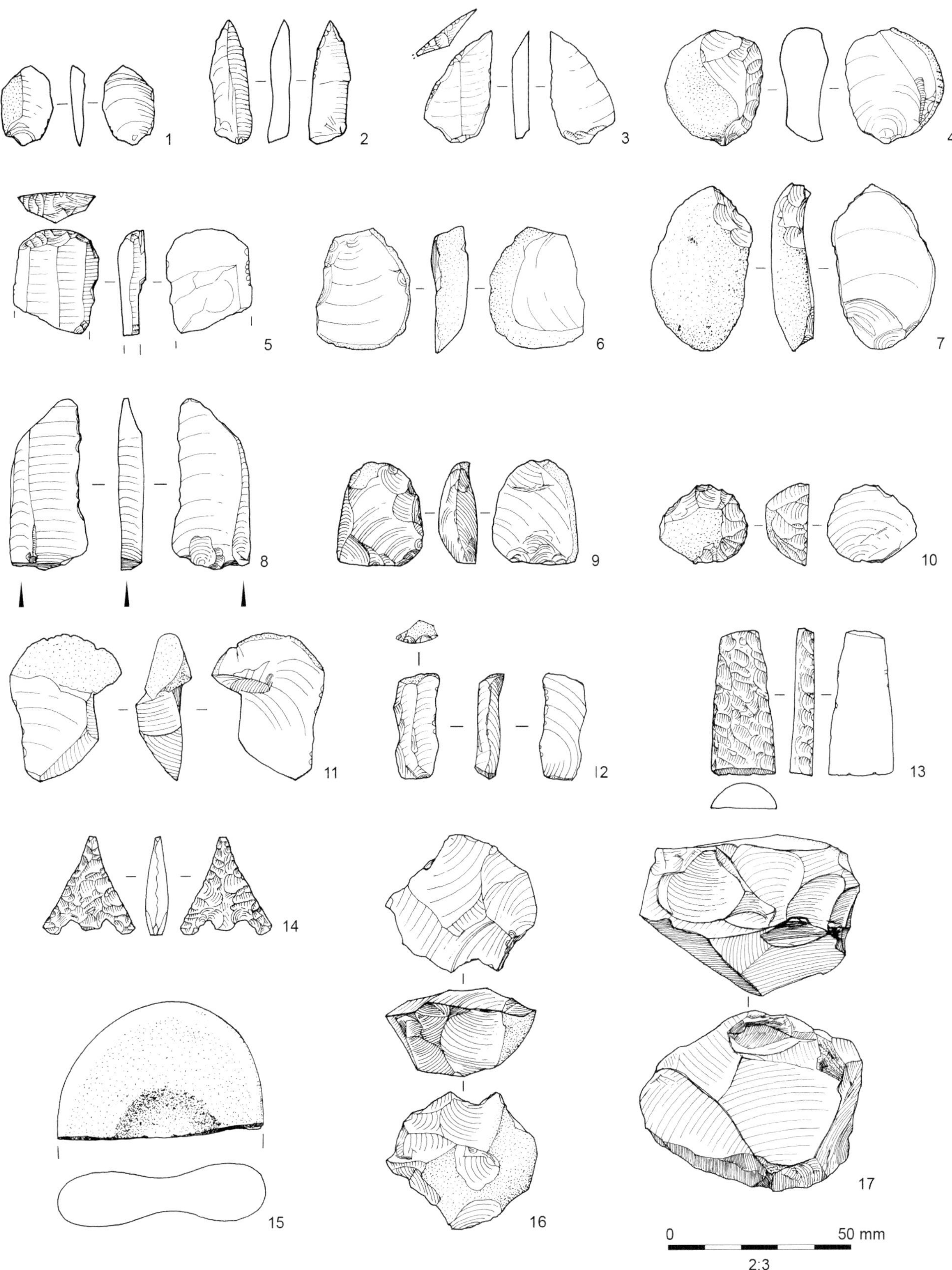

Figure 2.18. Flint (1) (drawn by S. Pressey).

Table 2.09. Tool assemblages (for trenches catalogued in detail)

Trench	*4*		*6*		*7*		*9*		*11*		*16*		*Total*	
	No.	*%*	*No.*	*%*	*No.*	*%*	*No.*	*%*	*No.*	*%*	*No.*	*%*	*No.*	*%*
Marginally ret'd	9	24.3	16	22.9	11	26.2		0.0	52	24.0		0.0	88	23.5
Notch	3	8.1	7	10.0		0.0		0.0	17	7.8	1	33.3	28	7.5
Denticulate		0.0	1	1.4		0.0		0.0	3	1.4		0.0	4	1.1
Scrapers	8	21.6	19	27.1	6	14.3	4	80.0	47	21.7	0	0.0	84	22.5
Microlith		0.0		0.0		0.0		0.0	1	0.5		0.0	1	0.3
Truncation	1	2.7	1	1.4		0.0		0.0	2	0.9	1	33.3	5	1.3
Pièce esq.	6	16.2	8	11.4	5	11.9		0.0	29	13.4		0.0	48	12.8
Burin	2	5.4	3	4.3	2	4.8		0.0	9	4.1		0.0	16	4.3
Used piece	4	10.8	9	12.9	13	31.0	1	20.0	34	15.7		0.0	61	16.3
Point	1	2.7		0.0		0.0		0.0		0.0		0.0	1	0.3
Awl		0.0	3	4.3	2	4.8		0.0	4	1.8	1	33.3	10	2.7
Other	1	2.7		0.0		0.0		0.0	14	6.5		0.0	15	4.0
Fragment	2	5.4	3	4.3	3	7.1		0.0	6	2.8		0.0	14	3.7
Total ret'd	26		52		22		4		147	67.7	3		254	67.9
Total used	11		18		20		1		70	32.3			120	32.1
Total tools	37		70		42		5		217		3	0	374	
% ret.	70.3		74.3		52.4		80.0		67.7	0.3				

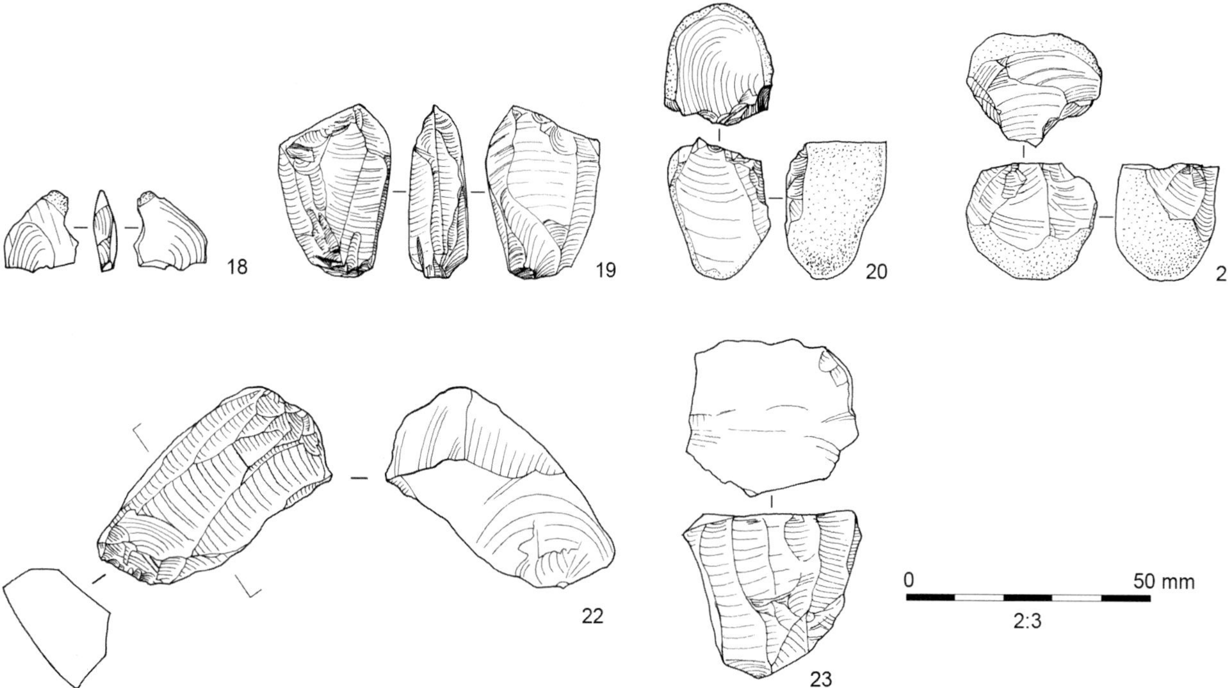

Figure 2.19. Flint (2) (drawn by S. Pressey).

showing signs of opposed notches probably for hafting, and small numbers of truncations and awls, both fairly ad hoc. There are a number of knives on flakes, with usually more extensive scaled retouch along one lateral edge, and four denticulates. One microlith is present, a straight backed fragment on a relatively broad bladelet, and three points. Other tools include a barbed and tanged arrowhead and a fragment of a pressure retouched blade, probably a LN/EBA point, both on Grand Pressigny flint, and one transverse point on a pressure blade in 'Cinglais' flint. Burins are present, in some cases probably created through usewear, but also in some cases formed intentionally; these form up to 7% of each trench's tool assemblage. Several 'chopper cores' were noted, in the form of pebbles with short removals down both faces forming a ridge.

Used tools with no retouch are numerous, making up 16% of the tool assemblage overall. Some of these are glossy tools – and indeed gloss is also present on some retouched tools, including several scrapers, some retouched blades and flakes. Pièces esquillées are numerous, making up 6–17%

of each trench's tools. Most have only limited esquillée removals, and are often on irregular flakes. A few have more extensive removals down one or more faces of the tool.

The tool-kit thus emphasises the use of unretouched blades and, more usually, flakes – with gloss, edge damage, spalling and esquillée removals common. Most retouched tools themselves have small amounts of ad hoc retouch, and often show signs of use wear. The less common more formal tools include scrapers, points and knives.

The non-formal tools and the scrapers are all clearly part of the beach pebble reduction sequence found on site, and in fact scrapers could be said to be a central goal of this reduction sequence. Some endscrapers, as well as the more formal points, may well not be part of this reduction sequence. These may be imports, in some cases part of the pressure blade industry on 'Cinglais' flint and possibly on a black opaque flint brought in very small numbers to the site.

Variability

The assemblage is in many ways fairly constant across the trenches and levels of the site, although some differences were noted, discussed below (Tables 2.10 and 2.11). As discussed above (Sections 2.3 and 2.4), the finds excavated from within the complex sequence of palaeosoils at L'Erée

Table 2.10. Assemblages, by level (for trenches catalogued in detail)

	Upper Buried Soil		*Lower Buried Soil*		*Basal A*		*Basal B*		*Features*	
	No.	*%*	*No.*	*%*	*No.*	*%*	*No.*	*%*	*No.*	*%*
Flakes	436	72.7	587	72.1	509	74.1	455	70.8	269	68.4
Flake blade	10	1.7	18	2.2	13	1.9	11	1.7	11	2.8
Blade (irreg.)	14	2.3	14	1.7	13	1.9	11	1.7	7	1.8
Blade (reg.)	12	2.0	14	1.7	16	2.3	15	2.3	5	1.3
Spalls	9	1.5	15	1.8	7	1.0	5	0.8	2	0.5
core trimming elements	18	3.0	13	1.6	16	2.3	12	1.9	5	1.3
Indeterminates	41	6.8	88	10.8	62	9.0	87	13.5	46	11.7
<5mm	2	0.3	5	0.6		0.0	6	0.9	5	1.3
Cores	58	9.7	60	7.4	51	7.4	41	6.4	43	10.9
Total	600		814		687		643		393	
Fl:Bl	17.50	17.50	22.14	22.14	18.24	18.24	18.12	18.12	23.50	23.50
Total tools	93		91		82		64		21	
Tool %	15.5%		11.2%		11.9%		10.0%		5.3%	
Fl:reg blade	39.08		45.29		33.88		32.13		57.80	

Table 2.11. Tool assemblages, by level (for trenches catalogued in detail)

	Upper Buried Soil		*Lower Buried Soil*		*Basal A*		*Basal B*		*Features*	
	No.	*%*	*No.*	*%*	*No.*	*%*	*No.*	*%*	*No.*	*%*
Marginally retouched	29	31.2	14	15.4	16	19.5	16	25.0	6	28.6
Notch	12	12.9	8	8.8	2	2.4	3	4.7	1	4.8
Denticulate		0.0	1	1.1	3	3.7		0.0		0.0
Sidescraper	3		2		5		1			
Endscraper	4		16		12		4		4	
End/sidescr	5		8		6		5		3	
Total scrapers	12	12.9	26	28.6	23	28.0	10	15.6	7	33.3
Microlith	1	1.1		0.0		0.0		0.0		0.0
Truncation	1	1.1	1	1.1	1	1.2		0.0	1	4.8
Pièce esquillée	13	14.0	14	15.4	12	14.6	6	9.4	1	4.8
Burin	3	3.2	4	4.4	2	2.4	4	6.3	1	4.8
Used	14	15.1	12	13.2	11	13.4	19	29.7	4	19.0
Point	1	1.1		0.0		0.0		0.0		0.0
Awl	1	1.1	4	4.4	1	1.2	3	4.7	1	4.8
Other	4	4.3	2	2.2	8	9.8		0.0		0.0
Fragment	2	2.2	5	5.5	3	3.7	3	4.7		0.0
Total retouched	64		62		57		36		16	
Total used	29		29		25		28		5	
Total tools	93		91		82		64		21	
% retouched	68.8%		68.1%		69.5%		56.3%		76.2%	

were recorded as having come essentially from three main layers: (1) an upper buried soil (incorporating upper and lower horizons) situated directly beneath the medieval and post-medieval soil; (2) a lower buried soil (incorporating upper and lower horizons and a turf line), and (3) a basal soil situated directly above and then merging into the loess (see Section 2.3 for further details). These were identifiable in most excavated trenches but most clearly definable in the deeper trenches located downslope, closest to the cliff edge, where the soil layers were thicker.

Basal soil material

In some trenches, the basal soil layers had been excavated in an 'upper' (A) and a 'lower' (B) portion. Overall, however, the material from basal A and basal B deposits was very similar.

In comparison to the buried soils found higher up in the sequence (see below), there are slightly more signs of a blade industry in the basal levels, where blade:flake ratios are somewhat higher. This was especially marked in the Trench 4 basal levels, where there is one regular blade for every 26 flakes. Platform cores predominate in some basal levels, with basal A levels having the highest single platform core proportions in the site (43%), and a subpyramidal single platform core suggestive of the early Neolithic or the Mesolithic retrieved from the basal B levels. However, in contrast, the basal levels in Trench 4 are dominated by bipolar on anvil technology and all platform cores are rather disorganised multi platform cores, despite the somewhat higher levels of blades present, presumably knapped elsewhere, or on cores that were disposed of elsewhere.

Tool proportions are constant at around 10% or 11% across the basal levels, while tool classes vary, but there is no clear trajectory in terms of proportions of the various largely ad hoc tools present. Basal B levels have more used tools, and quite a few glossy tools (with most of these latter concentrated in Trench 7). Conversely, the basal layers in Trench 4 have higher levels of retouched tools than used tools.

There are few specifically diagnostic tools in the basal levels. The basal A layers contained one truncated denticulate on a blade, and a knife with low, inverse retouch (Trench 11, Sq. Q). Basal levels from Trench 13 contained a used pressure blade on 'Cinglais' flint, glossy and with a burin removal. These all suggest an Early/Middle Neolithic date, which fits well with the pottery recovered from these layers.

Lower buried soil material

Lower buried soil levels have a low regular blade ratio. Cores are mainly bipolar (53%) and there are also a number of cores showing both bipolar and platform use (10%), making a bipolar dominated core assemblage. Platform cores include both single and multiple platform specimens. One core showed previous use as a platform core with bladelet removals before final exploitation using the bipolar on anvil technique.

Retouched tools include numerous scrapers (usually endscrapers) and low proportions of marginally retouched pieces. Tool-kits are fairly constant across the various contexts, except for levels of used and marginally retouched pieces, which vary. A number of more diagnostic artefacts were found in the lower buried soil levels, including a core trimming element from a subpyramidal single platform core, suggestive of the earliest Neolithic or the Mesolithic, as well as the presence of a few pressure blades suggestive of Early Neolithic technology; some of these blades were retouched into endscrapers (Trench 11, Square P) and a transverse point on Cinglais flint (Trench 16), the latter suggestive of the end of the Early Neolithic. A tranchet flake from a flaked axe was retrieved from Trench 17, and two knives with low, scaled inverse retouch along one edge came from Trench 11N, both again likely to date to the earlier or middle Neolithic. The single barbed and tanged arrowhead came from these levels (Trench 7) and was made on Grand Pressigny flint, suggesting a Later Neolithic/EBA date.

Lower buried soil levels are widespread across the site, with some areas of very dense chipped stone (over 100 artefacts/spit) in the west-central area (see Figure 2.08).

Upper buried soil material

Upper buried soil levels again have low proportions of regular blades, although higher than found in the lower buried soil levels. High proportions of cores were retrieved (9%) and also of core trimming elements (3%). Cores here are largely bipolar (46%) with low levels of single platforms (13%). Most of the platform cores are multi platforms, and there are two discoidal cores present as well as one core with opposed platforms.

Upper buried soil levels have a higher tool proportion than other levels within the site (15%). Marginally retouched pieces and notches are more common in these levels than elsewhere in the site, while scrapers are less common.

Tools include glossy pieces (Trenches 6, 11C, 11J, and 11N). Two knives with scaled retouch (Trenches 11C, 11N) and a knife like scraper (Trench 6), as well as a fragment of a point on a probable pressure blade made on Grand Pressigny flint, with pressure retouch covering the dorsal surface (Trench 11K) all suggest the Late Neolithic, while a keeled blade core (later reused as a scraper/ad hoc single platform core) suggests an earlier Neolithic presence (Trench11B). The backed microlith (Trench 11C) indicates an ephemeral Middle Mesolithic presence, as could the thumbnail scrapers (in France these have a primarily Mesolithic, not EBA, association).

Upper buried soil levels are widespread across the site, but usually contain low densities of chipped stone at less than 50 artefacts per spit. The north-west part of Trench 11 contains a concentration of higher densities of artefacts, at 50–99 per spit.

Material from features

Assemblages within the features show interesting differences from the rest of the basal soil lithics. The feature-derived assemblages contain the lowest proportions of blades on the site, with 1 regular blade to 57 flakes. There is a much lower tool level here as well (5%), with retouched tools forming a considerably higher proportion (76%) than used tools with no retouch (with only the basal levels of Trench 4 showing higher levels). Scrapers are particularly important, as are marginally retouched flakes. There are several tools likely to be sickle elements with heavy edgewear and gloss. The features contain the highest core levels in the site (10.9%), and include one blade core with a keeled platform (Trench 11Q) and two discoidal cores (Trench 11Q).

The particularly high levels of cores, together with lower levels of tools and blades, may suggest that the chipped stone assemblages associated with features tend to reflect specific activities, such as knapping, alongside the use of scrapers and retouched flakes, sometimes heavily used.

Discussion

Overall, the technology and tool classes are remarkably constant across the levels at L'Erée. The very low presence of very formal or diagnostic tools is to some extent responsible for this, with only the odd point, blade, core or other tool embodying period-diagnostic qualities – in most cases, even these have long periods of manufacture/use.

The basic technologies of single platform pebble exploitation, multiple platform ad hoc rough flake production and bipolar on anvil technique are used throughout the life of the site, with perhaps a slight shift in proportions from a dominance of platform technology in most of the basal levels, to a dominance of bipolar on anvil technique in lower buried soil and upper buried soil levels. Overall tool-kits also remain constant, with used and ad hoc retouched tools important throughout. Scrapers remain important in all levels, although by the upper buried soil levels they are somewhat less so.

Rare, more diagnostic artefacts are scattered throughout in small numbers and include pressure blades, points, certain scraper forms, and knives as well as certain core forms. There is no clear pattern of distribution throughout the site's levels, with basal, lower buried soil and upper buried soil levels all containing possibly Early/Middle Neolithic artefacts (pressure blades, knives, prismatic opposed blade cores) as well as artefacts more likely to be LN/EBA, and a mix of raw materials.

The distribution of the rare points is no more clear, with the transverse point and the barbed and tanged arrowhead appearing in lower buried soil levels, and the pressure retouched fragment in upper buried soil levels. The lack of points in the basal levels is interesting, possibly suggesting something about the site's function in this early phase. However, points remain rare throughout the assemblage, and while low levels of points are found in certain levels, the particularly low proportions here do suggest that point manufacture and use was not central to the site's activities over the full length of its occupation. It is significant that the rare points found are universally made on probably imported materials, and in some cases, on what may be imported blanks or indeed import of the whole tool – for example, the transverse point on a probable pressure blade.

It may be that some earlier items have been reused in later, upper buried soil levels, such as the double patinated prismatic blade core later reused as a scraper/platform core. However, double patination is rare in the assemblage, and reuse does not explain the entire distribution pattern of artefacts through the levels of the site. It seems likely that the deposits are – at least to some extent – stratigraphically mixed, as seen in the distribution of diagnostic artefacts through the levels.

In addition, some aspects of the assemblage seem to truly reflect a longevity of tradition such as the manufacture and use of scrapers of all sorts, including the relatively rare thumbnail scrapers, or the small numbers of knives with scaled retouch, scattered through all levels. Some of the continuity probably owes much to the qualities of raw material available – for example, the scarcity of longer formal blades.

At L'Erée, the picture is one of a lithic technology responding to very local factors of raw material availability and, probably, site functions, with faint echoes of links to ideas, technologies and resources from further afield throughout the period of occupation. The artefacts that represent these echoes are probably imported to site, with no signs of any home-grown production of these special artefacts.

Regional context

Donovan Hawley

The character of the L'Erée lithic assemblage is typical for Guernsey, being predominantly composed of flint sourced from local beach pebbles. Likewise, on the Armorican Massif littoral zone of the French mainland, raw material of similar quality and provenance makes up the majority of the lithic resource. However, there were also periods during the Neolithic when mined flint of superior quality, Cinglais and Grand Pressigny, was being circulated on the adjacent French mainland; some of this material has also been recovered at L'Erée providing visibility of maritime contacts and helpful additional dating insights for the assemblage. In view of the similar raw material resources and geographical proximity between Guernsey and France, the L'Erée lithic assemblage is compared here with contemporary collections from the Armorican Massif, particularly coastal sites, in order to establish the extent of typological and technological convergence.

As discussed above, and within the pottery report (Section 2.4), the distribution of Neolithic artefacts through all levels suggests that the deposits are, at least to some extent, stratigraphically mixed. Therefore, for the purposes of this section, the assemblage is treated as a time-averaged palimpsest and dating clues and comparisons to mainland assemblages are assessed from the composition and character of the collection, rather than relying on relative stratigraphic location. The review is presented in chronological order from the Early Neolithic period through to the Bronze Age.

A feature of the Early Neolithic (in particular) on the Armorican Massif and its sedimentary margins are the exchange networks of Cinglais flint blades, mined and manufactured in the Plaine de Caen, Normandy. Several pieces of worked Cinglais flint were found during the excavation at L'Erée, including an asymmetric transverse arrowhead (No. 3), a scraper on a blade fragment (No. 5) and a burin (No. 8). The use and circulation of Cinglais flint dates from c. 5200 BC through to the start of Middle Neolithic 1 at c. 4700–4600 BC (Marcigny et al. 2010, 128). After this period, from c. 4600 to 4300 BC, exported Cinglais flint has been found, but with associated debitage, suggesting that rather than the pre-prepared blades of the earlier Villeneuve-Saint-Germain phase, whole nodules or cores were being circulated. Cinglais debitage was absent from L'Erée; while this could be seen as suggesting that the importation of this material dates to the earlier Neolithic, the very low quantities of Cinglais flint overall within the assemblage make it impossible to say with any certainty.

Other elements from L'Erée dating from this period are notably a sub-pyramidal unipolar core (No. 23) and a core trimming element (No. 18) both unlikely to derive from the more expedient lithic working of later (post-MN1) periods. Burins, either on Cinglais flint or local material are typically more common during the Early Neolithic and Middle Neolithic period; their representation at L'Erée (7%) compares favourably with this period in Basse-Normandie (Ghesquière & Marcigny 1998, 60).

On the Armorican Massif, flint working technology changes substantially between the Early Neolithic and the Middle Neolithic 2 period with Cinglais exchange networks diminishing and being replaced by increased exploitation of local resources. The emphasis is typically on flake production, minimal core preparation with scrapers the dominant tool (Ghesquière & Guyodo 2008, 116). The technology at L'Erée appears to follow this pattern with little evidence of blade manufacture and a preponderance of scrapers manufactured on cortical flakes (e.g. Nos 7 and 10). Piercers, pièces esquillées (splintered pieces) and retouched flakes also become more common during this period at the expense of burins. The piercer (No. 2) manufactured on a tertiary blade is similar to one found at the Middle Neolithic 2 coastal site at Lillemer on the northeast Brittany coast (Guyodo et al. 2001).

Notable, not just at L'Erée but also at other domestic sites in Guernsey, is the relative infrequency of arrowheads, especially the transverse type common on mainland sites during the Middle Neolithic. For example, at both the Brittany site of Lillemer and the Cotentin site of Treize Vents these comprise around 10% of the tool count. The reasons for this discrepancy are not immediately evident.

The range of core types in the L'Erée assemblage matches that of mainland coastal sites on the Armorican Massif with a roughly equal mix of single platform (Nos 20 and 21) and multi-platform (No. 17) cores. Through the Middle to Late Neolithic period the bipolar-on-anvil method of core reduction becomes more frequent until it is employed at the same level as direct percussion. The elevated percentage of this technique evident at L'Erée, along with a flake-based industry and scrapers remaining the predominant tool, are compatible with the known Late Neolithic presence at the site.

Towards the end of the 3rd millennium, Grand Pressigny trade networks become established on the mainland. Grand Pressigny is an orange coloured turonian flint, generally containing small inclusions having the appearance of white flecks. The source of this flint, local to the town of Grand Pressigny in the department of Indre et Loire, was a centre of blade production during the 4th and particularly the 3rd millennium BC. On the Armorican Massif these blades are often recycled into other types of tools; this appears also to be the case at L'Erée, where a fragment of broken blade tang (No. 13) and an arrowhead (No. 14) made from this material were recovered. The finely worked barbed and tanged arrowhead must count amongst the finest yet found on the island, adding to the impressive set found in the upper levels at Les Fouaillages. It is invasively pressure flaked on both sides, which would have required a high degree of skill to manufacture; it is impossible to establish whether it was made on the island or on the mainland without finding associated debitage. Arrowheads of this morphology, albeit with square tangs, are considered to originate from the Campaniforme (Beaker) complex dated to between 2600 BC and 2300 BC (Nicolas 2011, 114). The high level of skill involved in the manufacture of this arrowhead reflects the dichotomy in lithic working during the Chalcolithic/Early Bronze Age on the French mainland with expedient use of local beach pebbles and less care taken in the production of tools contrasting with high quality working on imported flint (Ghesquière & Guyodo 2008, 124). This scenario appears to extend to Guernsey during this period with other finely worked arrowheads also being found at Les Fouaillages, Route de Carteret and Jerbourg (Hawley 2017).

To summarise, although direct comparisons with French sites are difficult due to the multi-period nature of the L'Erée assemblage, its composition and character appears to echo mainland trends. The imported Cinglais and Grand Pressigny flint demonstrates that communities living at L'Erée were participating in exchange networks that were in existence during both the early and later parts of the Neolithic period, albeit on a reduced scale compared to the Armorican Massif. In between these periods the assemblage is harder to characterise but there is little to suggest any particular insular island divergence from mainland trends.

2.6. Worked stone

Duncan Garrow & John Renouf

Polished stone ring

A fragment of polished stone ring (Figure 2.20) was recovered from the basal soil layer [99] in Trench 11 during the 2010 season of excavation. The piece recovered represents approximately 12% of the original circular object. It is difficult to be certain of its original dimensions, since both the outer and inner edges are slightly uneven: the ring's outer diameter would probably have been c. 11cm, its inner diameter c. 8cm, and it is 0.5cm thick (in section); the distance between its outer and inner edges is c. 1.5cm. In section, the ring is rectangular with rounded ends.

The object was examined petrologically by David Peacock at the University of Southampton. He identified it as schist or shale, but stated that it is impossible to be certain where on the spectrum of these rocks it lies without further thin section analysis. Digital photos of the object were also examined by Nicolas Fromont (INRAP), who suggested that it could be made, more specifically, from mylonite, a metamorphic rock located in the Saire Valley on the Cotentin peninsula, Normandy that is known to have been used to make stone rings (although again it is impossible to certain without a thin section).

Polished stone rings of this type are strongly associated with the Early Neolithic Villeneuve-Saint-Germain complex (c. 5200–4700 BC) on the French mainland, although their use appears to extend possibly as late as MN2 (c. 4300 BC) in some places (Fromont 2008, 83). In France, the rings are most commonly made from schist, but are also found in many other materials (Fromont 2013). It is thought that they would have been used as bracelets. They are found on settlement sites, in graves, and often as stray finds (ibid.). Both known geological stone sources for, and physical evidence for the manufacture of, stone rings have been identified in eastern Normandy. It has been suggested that during the Early Neolithic period they formed part of a large-scale exchange process across northern France, involving 'Cinglais' flint (see Section 2.5) moving in the opposite direction (Fromont 2008). Stray finds of stone rings in parts of Brittany have been used to identify the presence of the Early Neolithic in the general absence of settlement sites of that date (Pailler et al. 2008; Scarre 2011, 49–53).

The presence of stone rings on the Channel Islands has been discussed by various researchers previously (Kendrick 1928, 55; Patton 1990; 1995, 31; Fromont 2013; Garrow & Sturt 2017). An up-to-date list is presented in Table 2.12, including several previously unlisted finds. Fromont

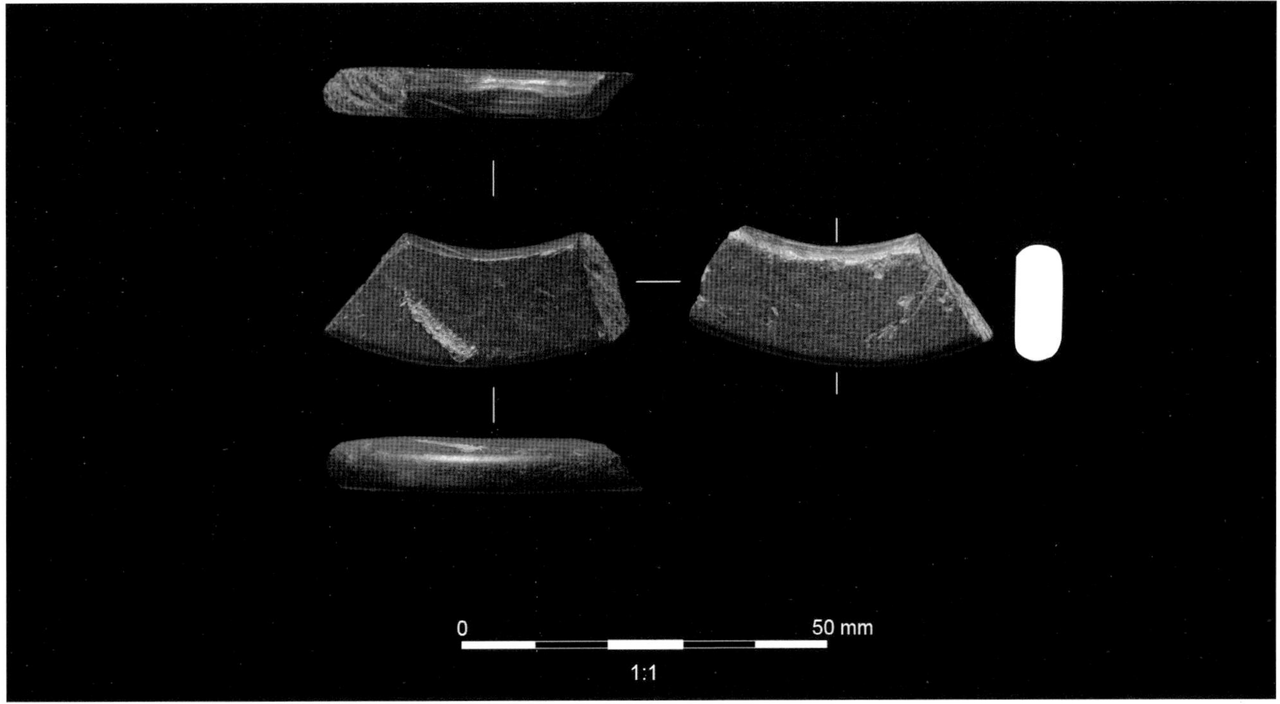

Figure 2.20. Polished stone ring (photo: S. Lambert-Gates).

Table 2.12. Polished stone rings (and ring fragments) from the Channel Islands

Site	*Island*	*Material*	*Context*	*Condition*	*Reference*
Chateau des Marais	Guernsey	schist	Stray find	Fragment (<10%)	Patton 1995, 33
L'Ancresse peat deposits	Guernsey	unknown (now lost)	Stray find	Fragment	Guernsey SMR
Le Déhus passage grave	Guernsey	schist	Tomb	Fragment	Patton 1995, 33
Le Trépied (field), St Andrew's	Guernsey	'dark greenstone'	Stray find	Complete	Kendrick 1928, Patton 1995
L'Erée	Guernsey	schist/mylonite	Settlement	Fragment (10%)	this volume
L'Erée	Guernsey	schist	Stray find	Fragment (10%)	Patton 1995, 33
Les Fouaillages × 7	Guernsey	1 gneiss, 1 serpentine, 1 schist, 4 myolonite	Tomb	Fragments (all <50%)	Patton 1995, 33; Fromont 2013
Mont Cuet, Vale	Guernsey	unknown	Stray find	Fragment (10%)	Guernsey SMR
Port Soif	Guernsey	unknown	Stray find	Fragment (<10%)	Guernsey SMR
Tombeau du Grand Sarrazin	Guernsey	serpentine	Tomb	Fragment (<10%)	Kendrick 1928, Guernsey SMR
Vazon Bay peat	Guernsey	serpentine	Stray find	Fragment (50%)	Kendrick 1928, Patton 1995
Herm	Herm	schist	Settlement	Fragment (15%)	C. Scarre pers. comm.
Jersey (unknown provenance) × 4	Jersey	jadeitite	Stray find	2 complete, 1 frag (30%), 1 frag (<10%)	Patton 1990; 1995, 33
Longueville	Jersey	unknown	Stray find	Fragment (20%)	Patton 1990; 1995, 33
Quennevais	Jersey	unknown	Stray find	Fragment (<10%)	Patton 1990; 1995, 33
Le Coupee × 3	Sark	unknown	Stray find	Fragments (all <10%)	B. Cunliffe, pers. comm.
'North of the island'	Sark	unknown	Stray find	Fragment (<10%)	B. Cunliffe, pers. comm.

Note that materials have not always been confirmed petrologically and so may not be entirely accurate.

(2013, 207) notes that the materials used to make those found on the Channel Islands are varied, reflecting the character of the underlying local geology; it is likely that at least some of them were manufactured and/or quarried locally. Those found on the Channel Islands are mostly towards the larger end of the known size range on the mainland (Fromont 2013, 208), but their shared stylistic attributes strongly suggest that they formed part of the same 'complex'.

In common with many of the other stone rings found on the Channel Islands, at 8cm internal/11cm external diameter, the original ring represented by the fragment found at L'Erée would be classed as 'very large' when compared with the mainland size distributions (compare, for example, with Fromont 2013, figures 28 and 401). Interestingly, however, at 0.5cm thick (*épaisseur*), it is at the same time relatively thin in comparison to the overall distributions (compare with Fromont 2013, figures 29, 402 and 403). In terms of its shape in section, it is directly comparable to Fromont's Villeneuve-Saint-Germain-phase 'Type 5' (Fromont 2013, figure 27).

The stone ring fragment from L'Erée came from the basal buried soil layer [99] in Trench 11. Consequently, it was associated stratigraphically with predominantly Pinacle-Fouaillages (MN1b) style pottery (see Section 2.4). As discussed above, while stone rings are predominantly associated with the Early Neolithic VSG period, they do also seem to have continued in use, if to a more limited extent, into the Middle Neolithic as well (Fromont 2008, 83). Given the low-level presence of other diagnostically VSG material on the site, it is possible that it relates to an Early Neolithic phase of activity on site that was not represented by (visible/surviving) features (see Section 2.10 for further discussion).

Figure 2.21. Quern and rubber-stone (photo: S. Lambert-Gates).

Quernstone and rubber

The quernstone (Figure 2.21) is a large beach stone (granodiorite) with a rounded underside and polished, very slightly dished (4mm deep) upper surface. A rounded triangle in plan, it measures 284mm by 222mm and 59mm thick at its widest points. The rubberstone is a small beach cobble (probably granodiorite) that is highly polished on one side through use; the opposite side was heavily abraded, perhaps through use as a hammerstone. It is rounded sub-square in plan, a squashed oval in section, and measures 92mm by 91mm and 54mm thick.

Interestingly, both objects were found in the same context [47] in Trench 9. This layer was relatively late in the stratigraphic sequence, containing primarily LN/EBA sherds. Very few quernstones/rubbers of this date have previously been recovered from the Channel Islands. A single fragment from a quernstone was found at Royal Hotel, St Peter Port, also in a Chalcolithic layer (Sebire 2012, 234 and 252). In addition, a number of saddle querns and rubber stones/mullers are reported from excavations at Le Pinacle (Godfray & Burdo 1949, 62–79). These were stated to have come from 'Neolithic' layers, but the stratigraphic integrity of the site is not secure (Garrow et al. 2017).

Geological comment

John Renouf

QUERNSTONE

Lithology: Coarse grained plutonic rock with a mix of fe-mg minerals (mostly hornblende with some biotite) feldspars and some quartz. The feldspars are plagioclases and vary in colour from sub-white to very pale salmon pink; they are very variable in colour between these two end colours and are clearly surface weathered. However, I would guess that the fresh rock would appear quite dark grey to grey. The quartz is not abundant and not easy to discern but is vitreous grey. In some areas there is a trace of foliation.

Identification: There is a good correlation of the stone with specimens from the main outcrop of the Perelle Gneiss, which is a granodiorite of extensive outcrop in southern Guernsey (see, for example, the Guernsey geology guide of Roach 1991). The Perelle granodiorite is a gneiss, since it is overall foliated, though the foliation is much more variable in its definition compared to many other members of the Southern Metamorphic Complex of Guernsey; as indicated the foliation of the stone is not very pronounced.

Source: The main outcrop of the Perelle Gneiss in Rocquaine Bay is only some hundreds of metres from the site and is the almost certain source of this stone implement. There is another outcrop of Perelle Gneiss to the west of the Venus Pool on Lihou but there it tends to be rather more variable than within the main outcrop.

RUBBER STONE

Lithology: Coarse grained plutonic rock composed of fe-mg and feldspar. Some scattered larger crystals of feldspar occur up to about 4–5 mm. There is an irregular scattering of a pyrite mineral showing weathering bloom traces. No evident acid feldspar phenocrysts. I cannot make out any definite quartz.

Identification: The petrology of the specimen does not fit any standard rock and I feel it is probably derived from a partially absorbed xenolith within an acid to intermediate plutonic rock such as the Perelle Gneiss, with which its general colour agrees.

Source: There is nothing special about the specimen to preclude its having come from any area of loose rock within a few hundred metres of the site.

2.7. Micromorphology

Charles French

Introduction

The complete soil profile exposed in the deepest trench, Trench 17, afforded the opportunity to sample for combined soil micromorphological and palynological analyses from the full sequence of Neolithic buried soil and thick overlying soil and possible hillwash deposits. Eight sample blocks (samples 27/1–27/6 from monolith 27, and samples 25 & 28) were taken for micromorphological analysis after Murphy (1986), and were described using the terminology of Bullock et al. (1985) and Stoops (2003). Summary descriptions by sample and depth are presented in Tables 2.13 and 2.14 (see also Figure 2.06). I would like to thank Tonko Rajkovaca of the McBurney Geoarchaeology Laboratory, Archaeology Division, University of Cambridge, for making the thin section slides.

Results

Table 2.14 below summarises the thin section descriptions and results.

Interpretation

This is a cumulative soil profile or a sequence of at least five superimposed soils over a depth of *c.* 1.66m, as summarised in Table 2.15.

The basal soil (1) is comprised of a quite thick (c. 12cm) humic horizon over a clay-enriched lower horizon (c. 22+cm thick), with increasingly strong impregnation with amorphous iron down-profile. This lower Bt or argillic horizon blends into

Table 2.13. Soil profile summary

Depth (cm)	*Summary description*
0–10	modern turf, undulating boundary
10–65	dark greyish brown silty sand with frequent rounded pebbles; possibly a former ploughsoil
65–101	yellowish brown to grey sandy silt with three thin turf/stabilisation horizons; possibly later prehistoric ground surfaces
101–141	brownish yellow sandy silt; much rooted; possible Early Neolithic land surface
141–c. 166	yellowish brown sandy silt loess subsoil (or B/C)
c. 166+	gravelly head; geological substrate (C)

Table 2.14. Brief description and interpretations of the micromorphological samples taken from the Trench 17 profile

Sample	*Depth (cm)*	*Main fabric*	*Additional features*	*Interpretation*
28	67–75	bioturbated, pellety humic fine quartz sand	at c. 67–69cm is a thin, undulating and strongly amorphous sesquioxide impregnated horizontal zone; at 69–75, few zones of dusty clay in voids	relict turf line (Ah) over humic A horizon, with minor surface disturbance and/or fine hillwash accretion
25 (1/2 overlap)	c. 84–92	bioturbated, pellety humic fine quartz sand	with a concentration of larger aggregates and greater amorphous sesquioxide impregnation at c. 87–89cm, rare dusty clay in voids and rare very fine charcoal fragments	turf line (Ah) with humic A material above/below, with minor surface disturbance and/or fine hillwash accretion
27/1	75–86	very fine sandy loam	minor pure and dusty clay coatings; a few crescentic void coatings; laminar aspect from greater/lesser amorphous iron, especially between c. 79–83cm	upper part of a B horizon, with effects of fluctuating groundwater table
27/2	86–99	very fine sandy (clay) loam	increasing pure and dusty clay coatings, sometimes micro–laminated; a few pure to dusty crescentic void coatings;	upper 6cm with effect fluctuating groundwater table; possible weaker expression of 87–89cm turf line seen in sample 25;
			86–92cm zone exhibits laminar aspect from greater/lesser amorphous iron	otherwise clay-enriched upper Bt horizon
27/3	99–111	very fine sandy clay loam	common pure to dusty clay in groundmass; few pure to dusty, micro–laminated, crescentic coatings in voids; all clay strongly impregnated with amorphous iron, and 50% of groundmass also	well developed, strongly clay and amorphous iron enriched Bst horizon
27/4	111–122	very fine sandy clay loam	as for sample 3	well developed Bst horizon
27/5	122–134	humic very fine quartz sand	pelllety/bioturbated	humic sand, possibly a relict ploughsoil
27/6	134–146	134–141cm is as for sample 27/5 above; 141–146cm: humic sandy (clay) loam	134–141cm: as for sample 27/5 above; with few fine charcoal fragments and reddish yellow clay; 141–146cm: increasingly strongly impregnated with amorphous sesquioxides	134–141cm: disturbed humic sand, possibly base of a relict ploughsoil (as above); 141–146cm: lower A to weak B to Bts horizon, becoming better developed with depth

Table 2.15. Interpretation of the soil sequence

Depth (cm)	*Horizon*	*Soil sequence no.*	*Soil type*
0–10	Ah	5	Modern turf
10–65	B	5	Medieval/post-medieval agricultural horizon, probably with colluvial additions
65–76	Ah	4	Thin turf line with thin depleted A horizon, with minor surface disturbance and/or colluvial additions
76–87	Ah	3	Thin turf line with thin depleted A horizon
87–122	Poss. Ah over B to Bt to Bst	2	Brown earth soil, subject to illuviation of clay and fine silt, and alternating groundwater table
122–134	Ah/p	1	Humic topsoil, possibly ploughed
134–141	Bt	1	Argillic brown earth or early Holocene woodland soil
141–166	Bt	1	Merging of argillic brown earth Bt with relict loess subsoil or B/C horizon
166+	C	1	Gravelly head drift geological substrate

the loessic-like drift parent material (acting as a B/C horizon), which is dominated by very fine quartz sand, silt and oriented clay, with the whole sequence developed on gravely head drift geology (or C). Significantly the clays are both pure to impure (or dusty), and often exhibit micro-laminae. This organised illuvial fine material was probably once more common, but has suffered removal by the fluctuating groundwater and concomitant leaching effects. Indeed, this latter feature affects the whole trench profile. There is a strong possibility that this weakly acidic soil supported woodland (cf. Fedoroff 1968; Bullock & Murphy 1979), and this is corroborated by the palynological analyses of near-shore peats carried out nearby by Campbell (2000) which indicate an early Holocene wooded environment in the locale.

Interestingly also, the humic sand above this Bt horizon of soil 1 is present as a fine black to reddish brown 'dust' adhering to and inbetween the sand grains. This humic 'dust' feature and the depleted loessic-like Bt horizon beneath was a consistent feature of both the pre- and post-Neolithic soils in recent investigations on the adjacent island of Herm (French 2011). In particular, the humic dust between the sand grains is possibly a consequence of ploughing, aeration and bioturbation (cf. Macphail et al. 1990). For Herm, it has been suggested that the evident additions of organic matter to the A horizon of the early Holocene soil was essential human management to counteract the depletion of these former woodland soils once cleared. This soil was deliberately receiving organic matter and settlement-derived debris to give it much needed nutrients and organic 'body' such that it was usable for arable land.

Above this early Holocene to Neolithic soil there is a superimposed sequence of at least three thin (c. 11–35cm thick), incipient soils which were associated with Late Neolithic to Early Bronze Age cultural material. Each had a period of some stability sufficient to develop a turf horizon. The first of these soils (2; 87–122cm) exhibits a humic Ah over a thin B to Bts horizon with clay illuviation and amorphous sesquioxide impregnation increasing down-profile. The quite strongly developed illuvial clay component suggests that this soil developed over a considerable time period as compared to the two thinner soils (3 & 4) above.

This leaves the question as to how this soil and the succeeding two thinner humic Ah/A horizon soils (3, 76–87cm & 4, 65–76cm) could develop. The rather poorly sorted but consistent very fine to fine sand dominated texture of these soils suggests that there could be a stop/start wind-blown element of soil movement and deposition from bare and exposed soils in the vicinity. The minor dusty clay presence in a few void areas suggests that could have equally have been a hillwash component contributing to these soils, especially given its sloping and embayed topographical position. This hillwash and/or windblown element equally applies to the thicker and more recent soil 5 above.

Particularly evident in the field were rather indistinct but wavy, pale grey horizons in the lower third of the trench profiles. This is probably a reflection of the fluctuating groundwater table conditions of burial on this site, with the greyer colours indicating weak gleying zones, associated with some leaching, weak acidification and iron movement, in effect incipient podzolisation. This was also observed to a lesser extent in some buried soil profiles (ie. in Trench O) on Herm (French 2011).

Thus, there are strong similarities with the prehistoric palaeosoil sequence observed on Herm (French 2011). The development of a weakly acidic but quite developed argillic brown earth soil on a loessic substrate, probably associated with the development of early Holocene woodland cover, is the soilscape presented to Neolithic settlers. Once disturbed, primarily through human activities, it quickly became prone to drying, wind-blow and/or hillwash effects. The only way to counteract this natural tendency and give this soil some stability was through the addition of organic matter, and with it often midden-like, settlement derived rubbish, and/or by allowing a return to turf grassland conditions. Such management was either not always successful nor routinely practiced, such that eroded soil material repeatedly aggraded on this early Holocene soil, thus forming a series of incipient humic fine sandy soils accumulating above to create the thick soil profiles that are observed today.

2.8. Environmental analysis

Julie Jones, Rob Scaife and Fraser Sturt

As noted in Section 2.1, the environmental history of Guernsey is relatively poorly understood. As such, within this project we made a concerted effort to sample what might ordinarily be considered deposits with little chance for recovering environmental data. The rationale was that any additional information that could be gained would make a significant difference. As such, monolith and Kubiena tins were collected for micromorphological and pollen analysis. These were augmented through loss on ignition (LOI) and particle size analysis (PSA) of samples taken down exposed sections in order to understand better the broad environment as captured within the soil and sediment record.

The sampling strategy and methods deployed at L'Erée followed guidelines set out by English Heritage (Campbell et al. 2011). All excavated features were bulk sampled for floatation and wet sieving. For pit and smaller discrete features 100% of the fill was retained, while for larger features (e.g. ditches) a minimum of 30 litres was recovered for analysis.

Methods

During the 2008 excavations it was rapidly noted that whilst the deposits we were encountering closely resembled those described by Cunliffe (Cunliffe & de Jersey 2000), there were some discrepancies. In particular, as discussed in Section 2.2, where Cunliffe identified two stabilised buried soil/turf layers, we only had one clearly identifiable preserved surface. As such, questions emerged as to the nature of site formation process on site and the possibilities of identifying relict, but obscured soil horizons. Following guidelines laid out by English Heritage (2004) for answering such questions, particle size (PSA) and loss on ignition (LOI) analyses were carried out.

PSA

PSA is a laboratory based technique for determining the composition (e.g. silty sand, clay, sandy clay) of a deposit by directly measuring the proportion of different grain sizes within a sample. In this instance samples were analysed using a Coulter laser granulometer, and the ensuing results interpreted with the aid of the grain size and distribution statistics package GRADISTAT, devised by Blott and Pye

(2001). The results of PSA can help to answer questions as to site formation processes; such as whether deposits are Aeolian (wind blown), alluvial or colluvial in nature. This is determined through examining the size of particles present and the degree of sorting. In turn this can be translated into an understanding of process through considering the energy required to move the identified grain sizes (e.g. high energy for large granules, pebbles, cobbles, etc. and low energy for silts and clays) and any differences between the sampled deposit and the local 'parent material' (i.e. is the sample deposit 'local' or has it been transported over a long distance).

LOI

LOI analysis determines the percentage of the sample that is made up of organic material. In this instance this was determined through weighing the sample and then heating it to burn off organic content. The sample was then re-weighed and the percentage change noted. This change in weight can be directly related to the burnt off organic content of the sample. LOI analysis for the samples taken at L'Erée was conducted according to the standards advised by Gale and Hoare (1991, 262–264). The reason for conducting LOI is that organic matter accumulates within topsoils. As such, changes in organic content are one method through which shifting patterns of landform stability verses deposition and erosion (instability) can be determined. Given the research questions relating to site formation processes and potential multiple buried soils of different dates on site, this was considered an appropriate technique to carry out.

Plant macrofossils

To retrieve plant macrofossils, charcoal and molluscs for identification, bulk samples were floated within a siraf system. The flot was collected on a sieve with a mesh size of 250μm, and residues on a mesh of 500μm. Both the flot and heavy residue were air dried and then hand sorted. Surviving organic remains were examined by Julie Jones with plant nomenclature following that given by Stace (2010).

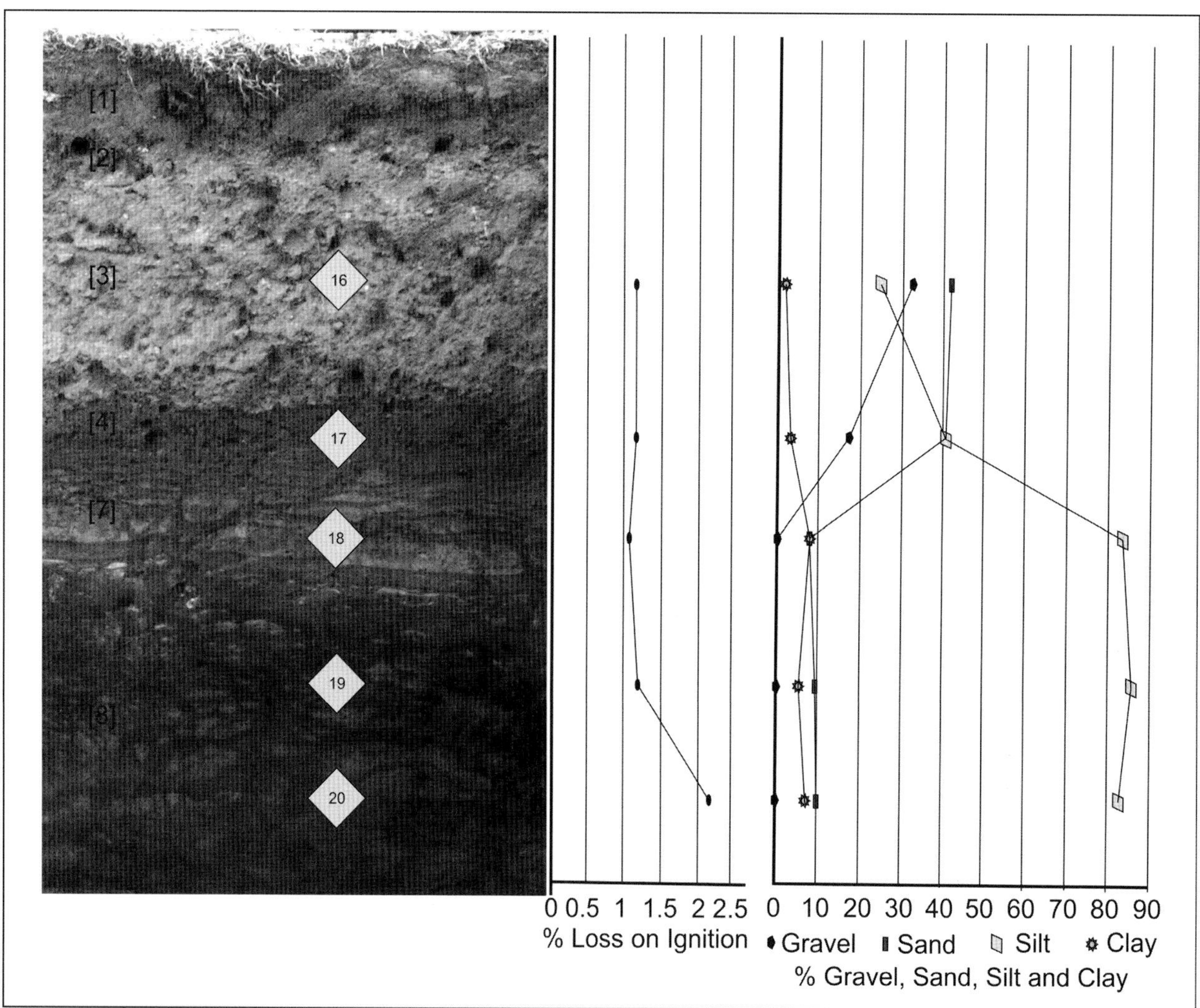

Figure 2.22. Particle size analysis and loss on ignition results. Photo shows contexts (in square brackets) and sample locations (in diamonds) within Trench 3.

Pollen analysis

Monolith samples were taken for each of the main sections exposed in Trenches 3, 11 and 17 and assessed for pollen survival by Rob Scaife. Pollen preparation followed standard methods as described by Moore et al. (1991).

Results

PSA and LOI

Figure 2.22 presents the simplified results from both PSA and LOI analyses. What emerged from these analyses was a quantification of the distinctly different compositions of contexts [3], [4] and [7], with [8] already identified by 'soil texture by feel' in the field. Within these results it was interesting to observe that whilst context [7] and [8] were predominantly silt, rather than having a unimodal distribution, they were in fact trimodal, with notable peaks of sand and clay contained within the deposit. This was interpreted as suggestive of periodic reworking of silt deposits. This reinforced what could be seen visually within the section and the outcome of the micromorphological anlysis described in Section 2.7 (above).

The results of LOI analysis reinforced the picture provided by the PSA analysis. As might be expected the medieval cultivation [3] soil and the upper buried soil [4] had a higher organic content than the lower buried sub soil [7]. However, an increase in organic content in context can be seen for the basal soil [8]. This peak corresponds and supports the interpretation given in Section 2.7 of this as an argillic brown earth.

Plant macrofossils and charcoal

Flotation produced very little organic or charred material for analysis, with only F7 and F8 (both hearths) providing any identifiable plant macrofossils in the form of fragmentary charred hazelnuts (*Corylus avellana*). A number of other samples included charcoal fragments >2mm. These were examined by Dr Eleni Asouti (University of Liverpool) and identified as being gorse (*Ulex europaeus*), hawthorn (*Rosceae maloideae*) and laburnum (*Laburnum anagyroides* type). Details of those samples containing organic and charred remains are given in Table 2.16.

Table 2.16. Organic and charred plant remains from L'Eree-summary

Context	*Feature*	*Sample*	*Feature type*	*Vol (litres)*	*Flot size (ml)*	*Sample composition*	*Charcoal >2mm*	*Plant macro-fossils*	*Charcoal (identifiable)*
LER 09									
74	7	15	Hearth/pit	28	24	60% mineral/40%charcoal	25+	*Corylus avellana* 2 frags	*Rosceae maloideae (hawthorn)*
76	8	16	Hearth/pit	29	200	50% mineral/50%charcoal	400+	*Corylus avellana* 1 frag	*Laburnum anagyroides type*
78	9	17	Hearth/pit	20	9	99% mineral/1%charcoal	<10		*Laburnum anagyroides type*
80	10	18	Post-hole	6	<1	all modern plant debris, leaves, moss			
LER10									
115	17	19	Hearth/pit	38	1	90% mineral, modern plant debris, leaves,seeds/ 10%charcoal			
78	9	20	Hearth/pit		2	95% charcoal/ 5% leaves, plant debris	5		
116	18	21	Pit	29	2	95% charcoal/ 5% leaves, plant debris	<10		*Ulex (gorse)*
117	16	22	Hearth/pit	24	13	2% charcoal/ 98% plant debris, seeds			
82	11	23	Post-hole	2.5	<1	rare plant debris/ rare tiny charcoal			
116	18	43	Pit		4	5% charcoal/ 95% plant debris/seeds	9		
171	39	49	Pit		<1	rare plant debris/ rare tiny charcoal			
LER 11									
160	34	44	Pit	4	2	rare plant debris			
168	37	47	Pit	13	<1	rare plant debris/mineral			
171	39	49	Pit		2	rare plant debris			
173	40	50	Pit	5	<1	rare plant debris/mineral			
177	42	52	Post-hole	27	<1	rare plant debris			
179	43	53	Pit	6	<1	rare plant debris			
181	44	54	Ditch	25	<1	rare plant debris			
183	44	55	Ditch	11	<1	rare plant debris/mineral			

Table 2.17. Radiocarbon measurements from L'Erée

Lab No.	*Material*	*Species*	*Context*	*Radiocarbon age (BP)*	*d¹³C*	*Calibrated date range (cal BC) (95% confidence)*	*Reference*
OxA-7977	Wood charcoal	Unknown; multiple flecks of charcoal used	Ditch/gully F1, Layer [18]	6240 ± 50	-23.9	5320–5060	Cunliffe & de Jersey 2000, 892
OxA-28670	Charred external ?food residue	n/a	Ditch F21, context [130]	5985 ± 36	-22.3	4980–4790	This volume
OxA-28669	Wood charcoal	Rosceae maloideae (hawthorn); young roundwood	Hearth F7, context [74]	5356 ± 36	-25.3	4330–4050	This volume
OxA-28901	Wood charcoal	Ulex (gorse); twig	Pit F18, context [116]	5356 ± 28	-24.4	4320–4060	This volume
Beta-271214	Wood charcoal	Laburnum anagyroides type; young roundwood	Hearth F8, context [76]	5340 ± 40	-22.8	4320–4050	This volume
OxA-28668	Wood charcoal	Rosceae maloideae (hawthorn); young roundwood	Hearth F7, context [74]	5338 ± 34	-24.9	4320–4050	This volume
OxA-28900	Wood charcoal	Laburnum anagyroides type; young roundwood	Hearth F9, context [78]	5260 ± 27	-23.8	4230–3990	This volume
OxA-8328	Wood charcoal	Unknown	Hearth exposed in cliff section 55m to E of Trench 1; no context no. assigned; sample type unspecified	5185 ± 40	-25.2	4220–3820	Cunliffe & de Jersey 2000, 892

Radiocarbon method: Brock et al. 2010.

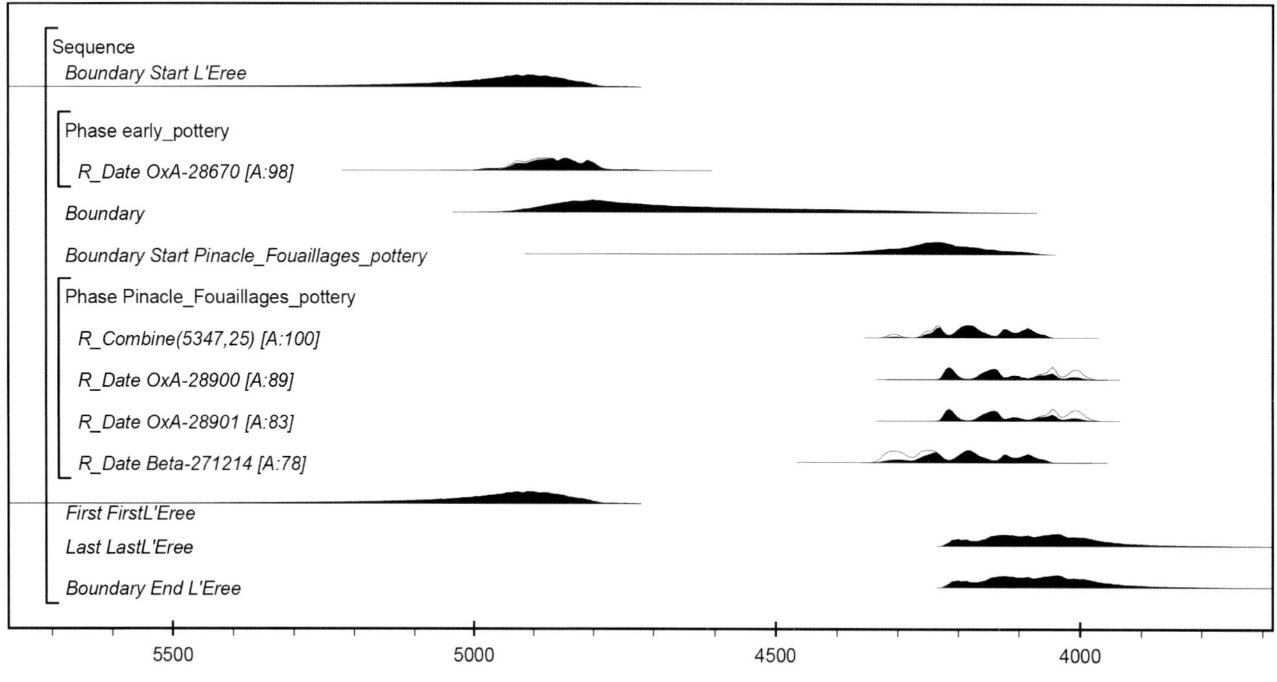

Figure 2.23. Model output for dated samples at L'Erée. The results have been modelled to reflect the pottery typological development, with the result on the potentially VSG sherd modelled as earlier than the results associated with Pinacle-Fouaillages pottery.

Pollen

None of the monolith samples taken from the sections produced enough pollen for a meaningful assessment.

Conclusions

When constructing the sampling strategy and choosing the range of methods to deploy it was understood the chances of success were low. However, the decision was made that given the rarity of excavated Neolithic settlement sites within the region, and the paucity of environmental data, every effort should be made. The result was that our best insights into the changing environment on site derived from consideration of soils and sediments.

2.9. Radiocarbon dating

Duncan Garrow & Seren Griffiths

Eight radiocarbon measurements altogether have been obtained from Neolithic features at L'Erée (Table 2.17 and Figure 2.23). Two of these had been acquired previously as a result of Cunliffe's 1998 excavations at the site (Cunliffe & de Jersey 2000, 892), the remainder were from our own excavations. Since Cunliffe's samples (OxA-7977 and OxA-8328) were not identified to species level and were on charcoal that was not demonstrably shortlife (i.e. they might include an inbuilt age offset, being affected by the 'old wood effect'), these were not included in the models presented here. As a result of the fact that the LN/EBA material from the site was primarily recovered from buried soil contexts rather than in features, it was not possible to secure any suitable samples with which to attempt to date this phase of activity. Radiocarbon dates were obtained for all features on site from which suitable samples were recovered.

Two of the radiocarbon measurements could potentially suggest an early phase of activity on site during the late 6th or early 5th millennium cal BC. However, both are to some extent problematic. The oldest dated sample (OxA-7977) was 'made up of a series of small flecks of charcoal from Cunliffe's layer 18 (Cunliffe & de Jersey 2000, 892) and thus cannot be seen as reliable. The other (OxA-28670) was secured on external food residue on a large, unabraded sherd of pottery within ditch F21, Trench 16. Unfortunately, the sherd itself was not sufficiently diagnostic to place it firmly within either the Early, Middle or Late Neolithic (see Section 2.4). The difficulties in establishing a secure date for the ditch itself have also been discussed (Section 2.3); in summary, it appears most likely to be a Late Neolithic ditch containing potentially earlier material, perhaps as a result of having been cut through an earlier feature. Ultimately though, it must be admitted that the dating of both pottery and ditch have not been satisfactorily resolved. Nonetheless, as discussed in more detail below (Section 2.10), the presence of other items of Early Neolithic VSG-associated material culture from the site support the suggestion of at least some activity there during the earlier 5th millenium cal BC. This sherd could potentially be associated with that phase of activity on site.

The remaining six samples related to hearths/pits, five of which were associated with Pinacle-Fouaillages pottery within Trench 11. The dates from the five features excavated during our own excavations suggest a phase of archaeological activity starting *4480–4060 cal BC (95% probability; or 4330–4140 cal BC, 68% probability)* and ending in *4230–3850 cal BC (95% probability; or 4160–3980 cal BC 68% probability)* (Figure 2.23). It is interesting to note that Cunliffe's hearth (OxA-8328), which was found 'exposed some 55m to the east of Trench 1' (Cunliffe & de Jersey 2000, 892), fell within this date range as well. According to this locational information, this hearth would also have been situated in Field 336; however, given that it was exposed in the eroding cliff face in 1998, it must have been located some distance to the south of the other excavated features. Although Pinacle-Fouaillages pottery cannot yet be tied into a firm radiocarbon chronology (Garrow et al. 2017), it has broadly been assumed to date to the French Middle Neolithic 1b phase, which is generally thought to fall approximately within the c. 4600–4300 BC bracket (Marcigny et al. 2010). The dates produced in association with Pinacle-Fouaillages pottery at L'Erée, however, suggest the possibility of a more extended timeframe within which this type of pottery was in use on the Channel Islands, potentially seeing its use carry on into the last three centuries of the 5th millennium cal BC.

In summary, the radiocarbon dates from L'Erée suggest potentially two main phases of dated Neolithic activity on site, one – tentatively – during the early centuries of the 5th millennium cal BC, the other – securely – during the last few centuries of the 5th millennium cal BC. As discussed, both of these timespans fit fairly well with the VSG and Pinacle-Fouaillages typological attributions of the material culture with which they were associated (see Section 2.10 for further discussion).

2.10. Discussion: Mesolithic to Bronze Age occupation at L'Erée

The prehistoric archaeology at L'Erée falls predominantly into two main phases: Middle Neolithic (c. 4500–4000 BC) and Late Neolithic/Chalcolithic/EBA (c. 3500–1500 BC); the Mesolithic, Early Neolithic and Middle Bronze Age were also represented artefactually (Table 2.18).

Mesolithic

Given that only a single microlith fragment was found, it is difficult to discuss the Mesolithic activity on site in any

Table 2.18. The character of occupation at L'Erée through time

Phase	*Dates BC (approx.)*	*Character of archaeology*	*Occupation type*
Middle Mesolithic	8500–6200	Single microlith	Occasional visit to the site (?)
Early Neolithic	5000–4500	Cinglais flint artefacts, polished stone ring fragment, early 5th millenium ^{14}C date on undiagnostic sherd	Activity not associated with any (identified) features – occasional visits?
Middle Neolithic	4500–4000	Features (hearths, stake-holes, pits) associated with Pinacle-Fouaillages pottery	Repeated, camp-like occupation
Late Neo/Chalcolithic/ EBA	3500–1500	Large amounts of material culture (pottery, flint, etc.) contained within buried soils – midden?	Large-scale (?) gatherings possibly associated with re-use of nearby tomb
Middle Bronze Age	1500–1000	Occasional MBA-type sherds – possibly a continuation of LN/EBA activity?	Occasional visit to the site (?)

detail. Nonetheless, it is interesting to note a Mesolithic presence in the area, adding to the list of 23 sites currently known from the Channel Islands (Conneller et al. 2016; see also Section 1.6). The fact that the piece, a backed bladelet fragment, is very likely to have been Middle Mesolithic in date fits well with broader patterns of activity across the islands at that time. It also potentially links activity at L'Erée directly to the substantial Middle Mesolithic site on Lihou Island, just across the tidal causeway (Conneller et al. 2016).

Early Neolithic

The Early Neolithic phase of activity at L'Erée is also difficult to pin down, and for now must remain a strong possibility only. Three artefacts made from Cinglais flint and a fragment of polished stone ring were found on site. As discussed in Sections 2.5 and 2.6, both of these artefact types are strongly associated on the French mainland with the VSG phase of the Early Neolithic (c. 5100–4800 BC). In addition to these finds, external residue on a sherd of undiagnostic (but conceivably Early Neolithic/Middle Neolithic 1a) pottery – found in a probably Late Neolithic ditch – was radiocarbon dated to 4980–4790 cal BC (see Sections 2.4 and 2.9). Taken together, these things suggest that, although no clearly diagnostic pottery or features were found, some activity probably did occur on site during the Early Neolithic. However, having said that, it is also important to acknowledge (a) that both Cinglais flint and polished stone rings continued in use on the mainland into the Middle Neolithic, albeit on a vastly reduced scale, and (b) that the radiocarbon date was secured on external pottery residue, and thus could potentially have been derived from old wood. As a result, none of these elements can be taken as totally conclusive proof that there was an Early Neolithic phase of activity on site – while it is considered likely, the possibility that all of these things were actually associated with the later, Middle Neolithic phase of activity at L'Erée cannot be ruled out.

Middle Neolithic

During the Middle Neolithic, activity on site becomes somewhat easier to define. A series of occupation-related features were found to contain relatively small amounts of Middle Neolithic 1b 'Pinacle-Fouaillages' type pottery, as did the lowest part of the basal buried soil in some areas. Three of these features were radiocarbon dated to 4480–4060 cal BC to 4230–3850 cal BC (Section 2.9), and thus potentially somewhat later than the usual date range assigned to this and other supposedly contemporary pottery styles (which is c. 4600–4300 BC: see Marcigny et al. 2010). The character of the Middle Neolithic archaeology at L'Erée – a series of hearths, small stake-built 'structures' (but no obvious buildings or houses), ephemeral pits and post-holes, generally low amounts of material culture – suggests non-permanent settlement. We are perhaps talking about a series of short-term, perhaps camp-like, occupations, with the site being returned to intermittently over time.

In putting forward this interpretation, we are mindful of the fact that we have excavated only a relatively small area of a potentially much larger site, and that a sizeable portion of land within L'Erée Bay has subsequently been lost to the sea (Section 2.1). As a consequence of both of these factors, it is possible that more substantial settlement features (including, for example, recognisable structures) may have been present beyond the edge of our excavations. However, having said that, it is important to stress that Middle Neolithic 1b settlement sites in mainland France are directly comparable in terms of their general lack of longhouses or other formal structures (see below) and so it is perfectly possible that our excavations did indeed capture at least a representative sample of the original site. We certainly feel that our interpretation of this phase of archaeology at L'Erée – as the remnants of an impermanently but repeatedly occupied occupation site – is the most appropriate, given the available evidence.

The period over which the occasional visits described above actually occurred is difficult to establish. In this light, it is unfortunate that the three features (two hearths and a pit) containing radiocarbon datable material were all clustered together in one small part of Trench 11 – they were chronologically inseparable in terms of the date ranges obtained. It is however worth noting that another hearth, eroding out of the cliff face south-east of Trench 11, was dated by Cunliffe to 4230–3810 cal BC (see Section 2.9) – features of this date therefore do appear to have been spread across a wide area. The archaeology itself also provides some insight into the site's temporality. It seems unlikely that multiple hearths were used simultaneously, and thus in themselves they imply a number of visits separated in time. Equally, the stratigraphy of the site suggests subtly different sub-phases of occupation. Some of the Middle Neolithic features had clearly been cut into a developed soil that formed a layer 0.15–0.20m thick above the loess subsoil (this layer itself also contained Pinacle-Fouaillages pottery). Others, however, were not visible as features at this level and had potentially therefore been cut from lower down, directly into the loess. The temporal and spatial distinction between these different sub-phases can be seen clearly in Figure 2.24, which shows hearth F17 and pit F9 cut into the slightly later, upper level of Trench 11 (excavated in 2010), but also the earlier, lower level (visible in the bottom of the fully re-excavated 2009 test pit).

What we may be seeing at L'Erée during the Middle Neolithic therefore is several 'bursts' of activity (perhaps consisting of a number of seasonal visits?) which could have been separated from the next 'burst' by years, decades or more. Given the radiocarbon date range for the features at L'Erée (4480–4060 cal BC to 4230–3850 cal BC), it is possible that these visits coincided with the construction and/or use of the Le Creux ès Faïes passage grave 70m away upslope on top of the hill (the tomb has not been independently dated but by comparison with those elsewhere in the region is likely to have been built c. 4300–3800 BC).

Late Neolithic/Chalcolithic/Early Bronze Age

The next main phase of activity at L'Erée relates to the Late Neolithic/Chalcolithic/Early Bronze Age (LN/EBA). Certain stylistic traits are shared between the pottery used during these periods, and our treatment of them (and their associated activity) together in one phase is intentional. The timespan of the Late Neolithic on the Channel Islands is not at present understood in detail, but in mainland France lasts from c. 3500–2500 BC (see Table 1.01). Consequently, between this and the preceding Middle Neolithic phase, we are probably dealing with a hiatus of activity on site lasting between 500 and 1500 years.

The LN/EBA archaeology on site was derived primarily from the sequence of buried soils across the south-western part of Field 336, rather than from features. As

Figure 2.24. Photo showing the different levels in Trench 11: hearth F17 is visible on the left, pit F9 on the right (larger scale: 1m).

discussed in Section 2.3 (and also below), it is possible that this extremely large accumulation of pottery and flint – potentially tens of thousands of sherds and hundreds of thousands of flints – built up over a long period as a result of activity associated with the (re-)use of Le Creux ès Faïes passage tomb nearby.

In addition to this material, four ditch-like features were identified that also appear to date to the Late Neolithic. F2 in Trench 2 was excavated in 1998 and contained quantities of prehistoric flint but no pottery (Cunliffe & de Jersey 2000, 874). F12 (Trench 7) and F44 (Trench 11) were dated to the Late Neolithic specifically on the basis of the fact that they contained no diagnostically Chalcolithic/EBA material (see Section 2.4). F21 (Trench 16) contained a mixed assemblage of pottery, including the sherd dated to 4980–4790 cal BC along with LN/EBA material. Given its shared alignment with F2, and its similar profile to F44, it too has been assigned to the Late Neolithic. F12, only partially exposed in Trench 7, does not clearly relate spatially to the other ditch-like features. However, F2, F21 and F44 could well be related, conceivably forming part of a large enclosure, whose entrance is indicated by the butt-end of F44 in Trench 11 (see Figure 2.09).

As discussed in Section 2.1, the Le Creux ès Faïes passage tomb saw substantial re-use during the Chalcolithic/EBA, with eight Beakers and two barbed and tanged arrowheads placed inside it, probably along with human bone which has not survived. It is possible that the Late Neolithic ditched enclosure – if that is indeed what it is – constructed at the base of the hill beneath the tomb was one of the first elements associated with this later re-use of an originally Middle Neolithic monument. It could potentially have defined an area used for settlement and/or feasting whilst visiting the tomb. Seemingly, the enclosure then came to be filled in: its ditches contain no Chalcolithic/EBA pottery, and the main density of material deposited in the buried soils (Figures 2.07 and 2.08) does not clearly respect its putative location. Nonetheless, activities involving the accumulation of very large amounts of flint and pottery (and no doubt materials such as animal bone which have not survived) continued in the same location for many centuries afterwards.

It is difficult to know exactly what form those activities would have taken – the quantities of material involved imply substantial 'amounts' of occupation and perhaps correspondingly large numbers of people. Given this, it is a little surprising that, beyond the possible Late Neolithic enclosure, only two further features were assigned to this phase: unfortunately, F34 (a somewhat enigmatic stone-filled pit) and F43 (a 'scoop' with no finds) do not enhance our understanding of the site a great deal. It is possible that features did indeed exist outside the area of our excavations, and that the excavated area was simply used for the large-scale dumping of material. The resulting midden-like deposit could conceivably have been an intentionally created 'monumental' feature in its own right.

L'Erée in its regional context

The history of excavation in the Channel Islands has ensured that, from F.C. Lukis's antiquarian explorations in the 19th century to Ian Kinnes's work at Les Fouaillages in the 1980s, monuments have received the vast majority of attention – understandably so, given their impressive character and very obvious presence in the landscape.

The excavation of a Neolithic occupation site at L'Erée adds significantly to our knowledge of the settlement record on the islands. Alongside Le Pinacle (Godfray & Burdo 1949) and Royal Hotel, St Peter Port (Sebire 2012), it represents one of only three substantially excavated settlement sites of that date. Le Pinacle produced significant settlement evidence, including hearths, midden deposits and an occupation layer, as well as large amounts of material culture dating from the Middle Neolithic to the Iron Age, but no clear structures. Patton has made a convincing case that during the Neolithic it was an important axe production site (Patton 1995, 29). Unfortunately, our own recent attempt to radiocarbon date some of the supposedly early features there suggested that the original excavators' phasing was not necessarily secure (Garrow et al. 2017). The stratigraphy of the archaeology at Royal Hotel was also difficult to pin down securely, but in this case because of the far from ideal conditions under which the site was dug (Sebire 2011, 195). Nonetheless, excavations revealed what appears to have been a small, irregular post-built building associated with VSG 'cordons' pottery, along with other post-holes and occupation-related layers (ibid.).

L'Erée appears to have been a settlement of quite different character to both of these other sites. Neolithic settlement evidence from the Channel Islands (summarised in Table 1.02) is in fact of a generally varied character overall. Only a very few of the known sites have produced buildings of any sort. As with our excavations at L'Erée, it is difficult to be certain about the absence of clearly definable structures on most of these since (other than at Le Pinacle) only very small areas had been excavated. However, as far as it is possible to tell from the evidence uncovered so far, it does not seem to have been usual for settlement sites of this date in the Channel Island to have substantial buildings. In neighbouring Brittany and Normandy, the picture is actually very similar – after the VSG phase (which ends c. 4800 BC), substantial houses are rare, and many sites consist solely of pits, post-holes, artefact scatters and often hearth features as well (Hénaff 2002; Marcigny et al. 2010; Scarre 2011, 32–37; Garrow & Sturt 2017, 12).

Interestingly, hearths (like those found at L'Erée) are arguably the most prominent feature of Middle Neolithic sites on the Channel Islands and in mainland France. For example, at Le Pinacle eight 'hearths' 'easily recognisable by their alternate layers of charcoal and ashes mixed with fragments of charred bones' were defined (Godfray & Burdo 1949, 39); whilst four of these were clearly discrete features similar in size to those found at L'Erée, the other four appear from the site plan to have been rather larger 'spreads' of burnt material (ibid., figure 6). Patton and Finlaison provide a second-hand account of two possible hearths observed at La Saline, Jersey: 'these were circular features approximately 1m in diameter, consisting of overlapping granite slabs' (2001, 28); while these are undated, they were found close to and at the same stratigraphic level as a polished axe. Finally, it is worth noting that a single hearth – extremely similar in appearance to those at L'Erée – was found during excavations at Guernsey Airport; it produced a very early radiocarbon date of 5060–4935 cal BC (Phil de Jersey pers. comm.). Close comparisons can also be drawn with several late fifth millennium sites in north-western France, where other hearth features have been found (see for example Marcigny et al. 2010). Perhaps the most directly comparable site is Curnic, Finistère in Brittany, where several hearths were observed eroding out of the cliff face. Giot et al. (1965, 56) described these features as being dark, charcoal-rich subcircular or oval pits, up to 1.00m in diameter and 0.20–0.25m deep, and surrounded by stones – almost exactly like those found at L'Erée.

As far as the Mesolithic–Neolithic transition on the Channel Islands is concerned, the earliest Neolithic presence appears to have been associated with the VSG phase of the Early Neolithic. Features associated with this material have been found at Royal Hotel and Les Fouaillages in Guernsey and L'Ouzière in Jersey. In addition, numerous VSG-associated stray finds (polished stone rings, Cinglais flint) have been recorded across the islands (Garrow & Sturt 2017), including at L'Erée. On the basis of this fairly limited range of evidence, it is difficult to say a great deal about the processes of transition on the islands. Given the apparently very low levels of Late Mesolithic activity on the islands (see Section 1.6) and the very close typological parallels between the earliest Neolithic material culture there and in north-west France, it is tempting to suggest that, in this case, incoming migrants played a greater role in the process than the indigenous population.

The substantial number of stone rings, and less substantial but still significant quantities of Cinglais flint, found across the Channel Islands suggests considerable levels of interaction and clear engagement with long-distance exchange networks across the sea to Normandy, Brittany and beyond, from the very start of the Neolithic. Yet shortly afterwards, people on the islands adopted the island-specific Pinacle-Fouaillages sub-style of pottery and also created the highly unusual, trapezoidal long-mound monument at Les Fouaillages – in both cases distinguishing themselves materially from the mainland. The most straightforward interpretive narrative in this case is that, following initial colonisation of the islands during the Early Neolithic (and associated strong material connections and affiliations with the mainland), during the Middle Neolithic 1 phase, the population of the Channel Islands began to assert their own identity through material culture. Ironically, given the insularity this patterning at first suggests, this trajectory actually fits very well with broader patterns of social fragmentation and increased regionalisation across north-west France at this time (Marcigny et al. 2010, 143–144).

The LN/EBA evidence uncovered at L'Erée appears, at first, somewhat unusual, and is certainly difficult to interpret. However, once a step back is taken to look at the wider regional picture, the site actually appears to fit very well in terms of broader site types and patterning.

It is a relatively common occurrence, both in the Channel Islands (Patton 1995, 98) and in neighbouring regions of France (Salanova 2000, figure 6), to find Middle Neolithic tombs re-used in the Chalcolithic/EBA. Interestingly, other researchers have noted previously that it is also not uncommon to find LN/EBA 'occupation' in close proximity to these re-used tombs, again in both regions (Chancerel & Masson 1991, 183; Patton 1995, 85). The fact that the LN/EBA site at L'Erée consists primarily of a substantial spread of material also situates it firmly within this broader regional picture. In total, thirteen LN/EBA occupation sites have been excavated on the Channel Islands (Table 1.02). Nine of these produced evidence of 'middens' or other similar deposits (variously termed 'occupation layers', 'land surfaces', etc.) that were not clearly associated with any other features. Four sites did produce recognisable features, but these were highly variable in character. Interestingly, given the possible presence of a large ditch-defined enclosure at L'Erée, three of them (Jerbourg, Le Pinacle and La Moye 1) also produced evidence for possible EBA ramparts or other enclosure forms. The picture is very similar in France. Besse (1996, 19), for example, recorded only six possible Beaker 'settlement' sites in the whole of her 'western France' region. Equally, Salanova discussed the dearth of settlement of this date in north-western France, noting that most Beaker sites consist mainly of patches or layers of artefactual material (2000, 26–27). In their more recent account of Basse-Normandy during the Bronze Age, which incorporates many new sites found as a result of development-led excavation, Marcigny and Savary also note that most LN/EBA material is found not in features but as layers or pockets of material (2010, 102). The up-to-date picture they paint of LN/EBA occupation is highly varied, and includes fortified sites, ditched enclosures, quadrangular buildings and, most often, open settlements (ibid.). The EBA ditched enclosure found at Mondeville (Chancerel et al. 2006) provides one possible comparison for our putative enclosure at L'Erée.

The LN/EBA archaeology of the Channel Islands is comparable in some ways to that of the Middle Neolithic. The character of settlements on the islands and in mainland France is similar, while in this case funerary practices are directly comparable as well. The fact that people on the islands were tied into wide-reaching exchange networks during this period too is demonstrated by the minimal, yet significant, presence of Grand Pressigny flint, at L'Erée associated with seemingly special artefacts such as the pressure flaked point and the beautifully-made barbed and tanged arrowhead. At the same time, however, as in the Middle Neolithic, the communities of the Channel Islands also chose to assert their own distinctive identity by producing 'Jersey bowl' pottery that is quite different to anything produced on the mainland. Again, we are dealing with a complimentary mix of long-distance maritime connectivity and the assertion of strong island-specific identities.

Summary

After Le Pinacle, L'Erée represents the most extensively excavated Neolithic/EBA occupation site on the Channel Islands. It has provided further crucial glimpses of potentially both Mesolithic and Early Neolithic activity on the islands, revealing connections across the wider region and all the way over to north-west France from the very start of the Neolithic. In addition, we uncovered evidence of an impermanently occupied Middle Neolithic settlement site, which was probably in use contemporaneously with the immediately adjacent passage grave on top of the hill. The site may well have been visited regularly over perhaps many decades, but apparently no permanent structures were built. From around 4000 BC, the site did not witness any archaeologically visible activity for at least 500 (and perhaps up to 1500) years. During the Late Neolithic, a ditched enclosure was constructed, perhaps relating to activity associated with the first re-use of the Middle Neolithic tomb nearby. The exact nature of this activity is hard to pin down, but whatever it involved, it created substantial amounts of material which then came to be deposited on site. The enclosure was subsequently filled in, but the place it had defined remained a focus for the large-scale accumulation of material, almost certainly relating to activity associated with the known Chalcolithic/EBA use of the tomb. It is possible that, during this period, communities who were usually dispersed across the island congregated to venerate the dead and to carry out activities that involved the breakage of large numbers of pots – large-scale feasting is an immediately obvious possibility.

As discussed in Section 2.2, the substantial depth of the archaeological deposits at L'Erée combined with the associated need to hand-excavate all of our test pits and larger trenches, ensured that even over 4 years we were able only to excavate a relatively small proportion of the site. In future, it would be very interesting to refine our understanding of many things: to establish more fully the (apparently ditch-related) context of the undiagnostic pottery radiocarbon dated to the early 5th millennium; to assess how far the Middle Neolithic hearths and other features extend across the locality, and to establish for certain that – in the area that remains undestroyed by the sea – no substantial buildings were there; and to investigate the putative Late Neolithic enclosure in much more detail, to establish for certain whether or not the ditches identified in small test pits do indeed join up, and what form the enclosure actually takes. It would also be very interesting to secure a series of radiometric dates for construction and early use of the Le Creux ès Faïes passage grave on the hill above the site in order to establish whether or not the Middle Neolithic occupation down below was indeed contemporary. Future work of this kind is not envisaged immediately, but would without doubt be immensely informative.

Note

1 As discussed in Chapter 1, in relation to the Channel Islands we use French chronological divisions for the Neolithic and Bronze Age, as the archaeological record there relates directly to these (not to British ones). See Table 1.01 and Section 2.4 for further details of the French ceramic typologies.

Chapter 3

Old Quay, St Martin's, Isles of Scilly

Figure 3.01. Old Quay landfall view. This sketched image shows the 'landfall' view of the site at Old Quay as it would have looked from a boat approaching the St Martin's area of Scilly from the south c. 3500 BC. It is derived from 3D views of the palaeogeographic models (see Section 1.4) created in ArcScene and re-imagined by Rose Ferraby.

3.1. Introduction

This chapter outlines the results of excavation work undertaken at Old Quay in September 2013 and September 2014. The site is situated on the western side of a prominent headland that forms the southernmost tip of the island of St Martin's (Figures 3.01–3.03); it lies at the base of Cruther's Hill, a prominent local landmark topped by four Bronze Age entrance graves. Two seasons of excavation revealed a substantial artefact scatter (containing Mesolithic and Neolithic material), Neolithic settlement features and a small cluster of Bronze Age features. In addition, charred seeds from a stratigraphically late pit were dated to the 3rd/4th centuries AD. The Mesolithic element of the artefact scatter included an intriguing set of microliths with strong stylistic affinities to types known in northern France and Belgium. The Early Neolithic settlement was represented by a dense cluster of post-holes, pits and a hearth, along with high artefact concentrations in the buried soils nearby, interpreted as a possible midden. The Bronze Age archaeology – a small group of amorphous features – was clearly identified in one test pit only and thus difficult to interpret, but certainly suggestive of occupation during this period as well. The Roman period seeds were a surprising element of the site, given the total absence of any other material culture of that date.

Geology, topography and environment

The Isles of Scilly lie 45km off the south-west coast of Cornwall (Figure 3.02). The islands are formed from the same granite batholith that provides the striking relief of Dartmoor and Bodmin on the mainland. As described in Section 1.4, over the course of the Holocene this topographic high created an archipelago of islands off Lands End, which have progressively submerged due to relative sea-level rise.

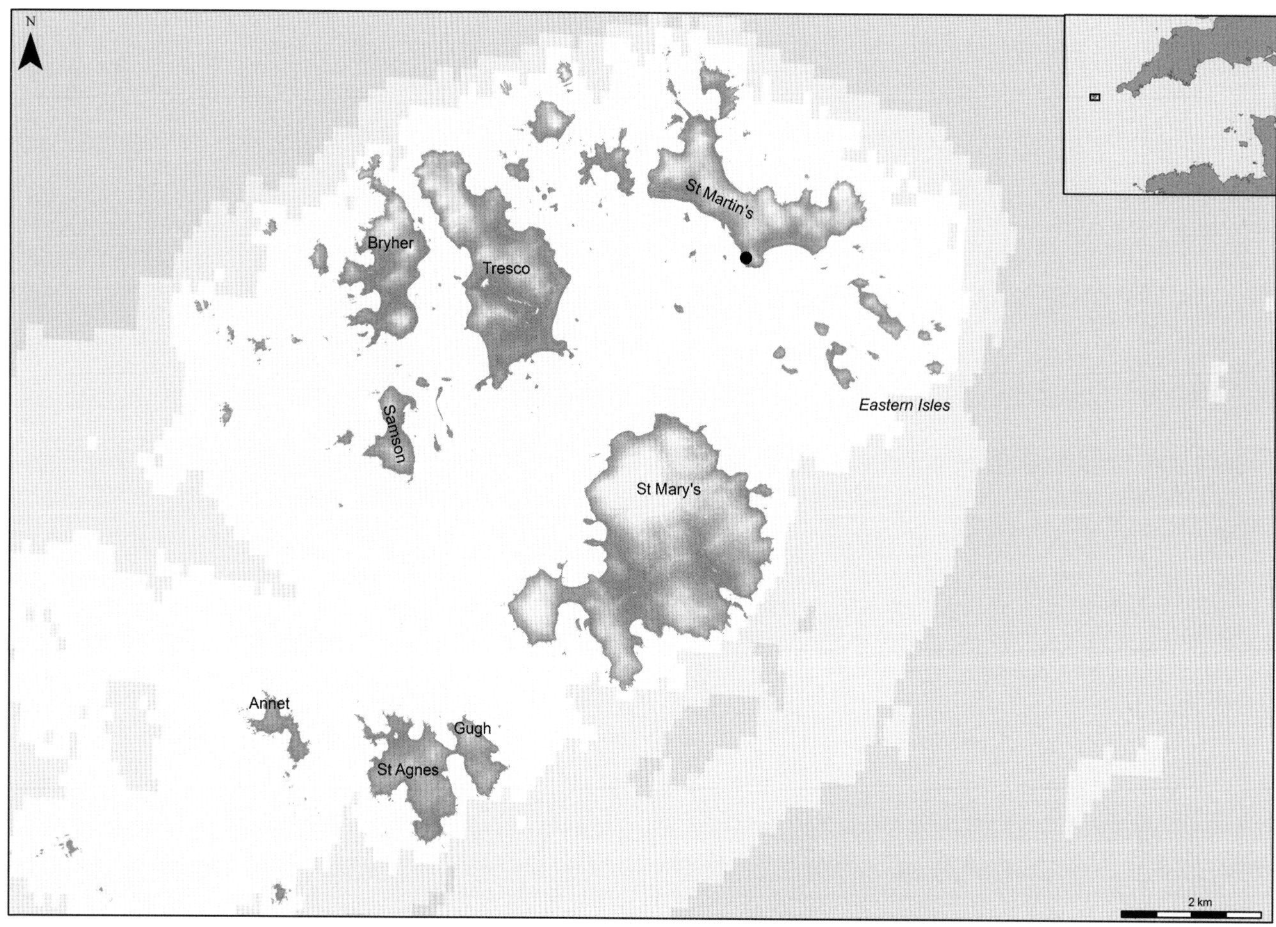

Figure 3.02. Old Quay site location. Topographic and bathymetric data from EMODnet (www.emodnet-bathymetry.eu) and the Channel Coastal Observatory (www.channelcoast.org).

Today this archipelago has been reduced to the c. 200 islands (Charman et al. 2016, 19) that comprise modern Scilly; of these 200, only five are currently inhabited (St Mary's, St Agnes, Bryher, St Martin's and Tresco).

The superficial geology of the islands is dominated by material weathered from the granite bedrock and loess deposits. Within St Mary's two areas of alluvium (Higher Moors and Lower Moors) were identified by the British Geological Survey and subsequently provided a point focus for palaeoenvironmental investigation (Scaife 1980; 1984; Perez 2013; Perez et al. 2015). This has been augmented with data from archaeological excavations and most recently through investigations carried out as part of the Lyonesse Project (Perez 2013; Charman et al. 2016), with additional sampling of submerged and inter-tidal deposits. This dataset has significantly expanded the range of dated deposits on the islands and improved understanding of environmental change.

During the late glacial period (c. 11,400 cal BC) an open landscape prevailed, populated by grasses, sedges and herbs (Charman et al. 2016, 161). By c. 9500 cal BC this had given way to 'significant tree cover' (Charman et al. 2016, 195) with oak and hazel dominating, but with noted presence of willow. It is likely that this tree cover populated the elevated regions, with lowland wetland zones increasing in size as sea-levels rose. Charman et al. (2016, 196) note that there is clear evidence of forest disturbance from as early as 6610–6450 cal BC, with micro-charcoal also evident in their sampled sequences, possibly indicating Mesolithic fires. Charman et al. (ibid.) hypothesise that this could relate to woodland management for red deer. These forest disturbances helped to change the nature of woodland on Scilly, with a decline in oak from this period, and an increase of birch, willow, alder, elm and lime.

A marked decline in tree cover is reported from c. 5000 cal BC onward, again possibly associated with fire events but also potentially connected to the impacts of sea-level rise (Charman et al. 2016, 196). As such, the picture for the Late Mesolithic and Early Neolithic is one of a declining mixed oak, birch and hazel woodland, with increasing amounts of wetland as sea-levels rose. By 3100–2900 cal BC (ibid.), birch had all but disappeared, apparently linked

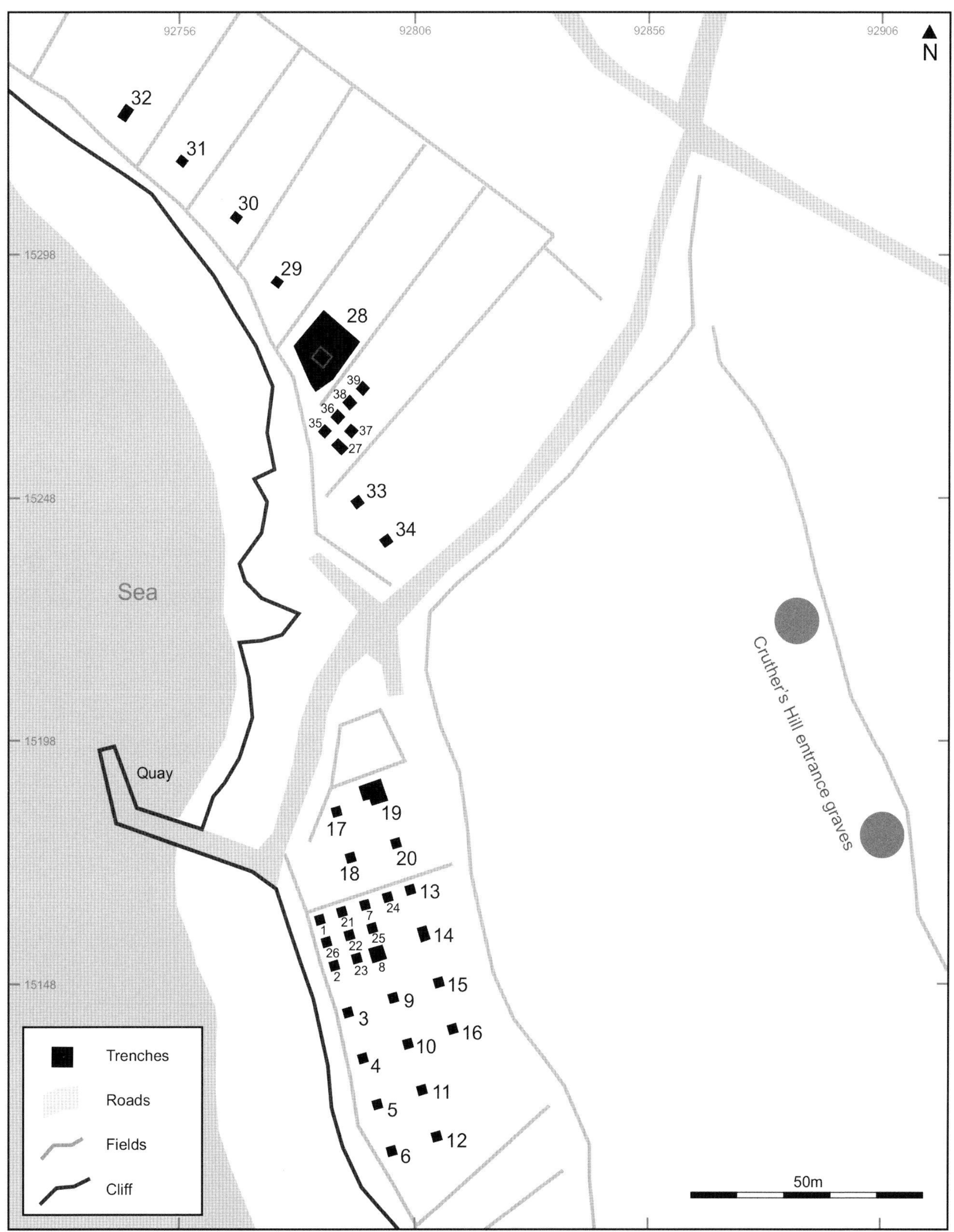

Figure 3.03. Old Quay site location (detailed). Cartographic data from Ordnance Survey © Crown Copyright and Databse Right 2016. Ordnance Survey (Digimap Licence).

to burning/clearance activities which also see a rise in open ground indicators. Charman et al. note that this pattern is not entirely uniform, with the modern island of St Martin's clearly showing evidence for decrease in forest cover from c. 3000 cal BC, but with mixed tree cover remaining for parts of St Mary's. This changes over the next two thousand years, with widespread evidence for open grassland environments across the island group by c. 1000 cal BC (ibid.).

As noted in Section 1.4, the topography and bathymetry of the Isles of Scilly has meant that impact of post-glacial sea-level rise has played out differently here in comparison to our other island groups. Where significant changes occurred through the early Holocene in both the Channel Islands and Outer Hebrides, the most dramatic land/sea reconfigurations occur much later in Scilly. However, just as at L'Erée and An Doirlinn, sea-level change and coastal erosion are very part of the site's current story. This was most recently demonstrated by the dramatic storms over the winter of 2013–14, where severe damage was done to the stone-built Old Quay itself.

According to the sea-level models described in Section 1.4, during the site's occupation, Old Quay would have sat up and above a large low lying plain, more than likely filled with a fine loessic soil (Figure 3.04). This is in stark contrast to its current idyllic setting above the beach and shallow waters of Scilly. With regard to our understanding of the archaeology of Scilly and what the occupants of the site may have been doing, this change in palaeogeographic and oceanographic context is highly significant; these were islands located at the edge of the horizon for any boats hugging the longer shoreline of mainland Britain.

Previous work at the site

As at L'Erée (Chapter 2), the archaeological significance of the site at Old Quay first came to light as a result of coastal erosion. Artefacts have been observed eroding out of the cliff face there since the late 1980s (Ratcliffe 1989; 1994; Johns 2012, 46; Dennis et al. 2013). A short section of the cliff face, incorporating an old land surface and a small pit, was drawn by the Cornwall Archaeology Unit

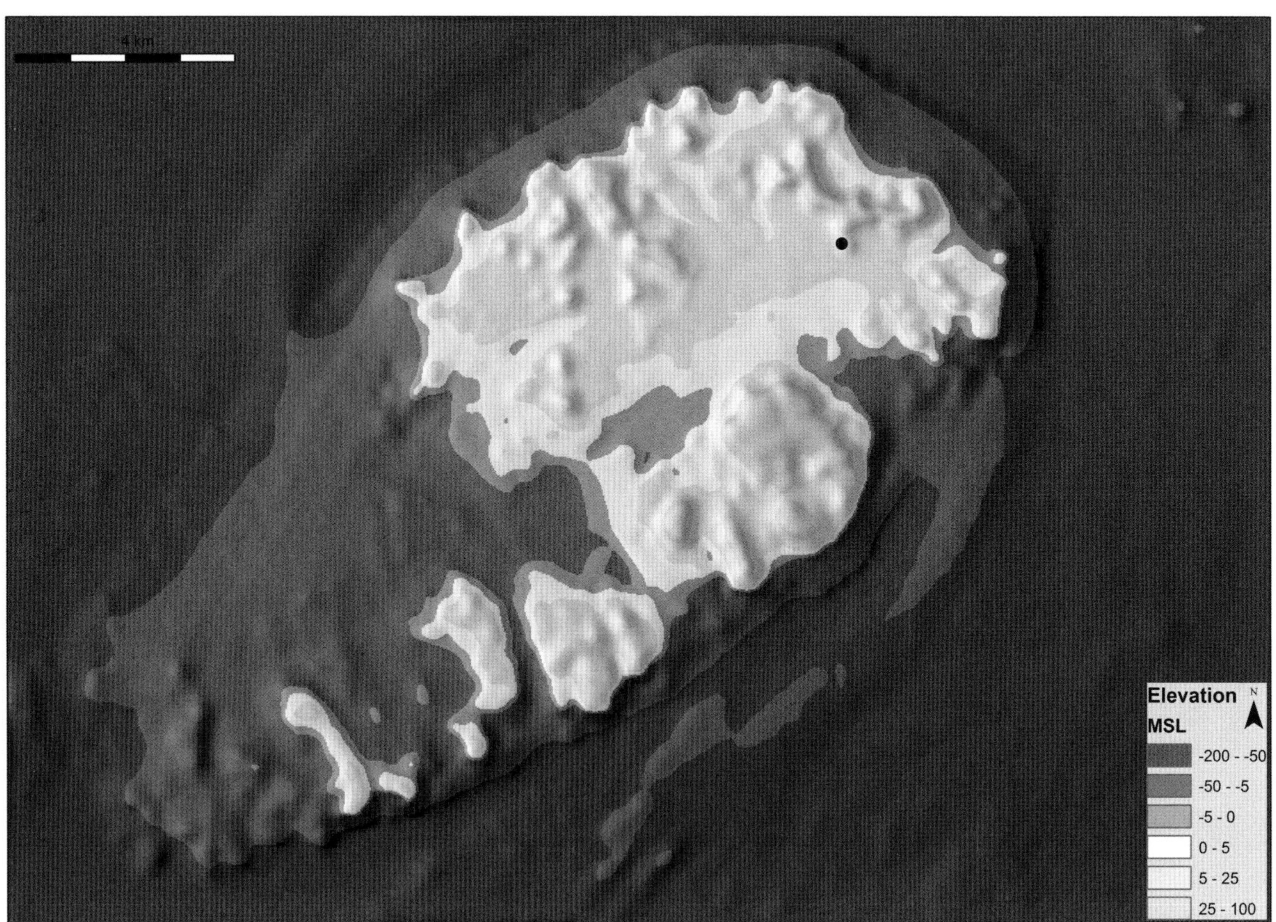

Figure 3.04. Old Quay: geographical location at the time of occupation. Topographic and bathymetric data derrived from GEBCO14 (www.gebco.net), EMODnet (www.emodnet-bathymetry.eu) and the Channel Coastal Observatory (www.channelcoast.org) and GIA models given in Sturt et al. (2013).

in 1993 (Ratcliffe 1994) and the site has been regularly monitored by archaeologists since (Dennis et al. 2013). Old Quay was identified as having potential to be a settlement site, and to shed light on both Mesolithic and Neolithic periods, in the recent *Isles of Scilly Historic Environment Research Framework Resource Assessment* document (Johns 2012).

Research objectives

In consultation with Charlie Johns (Cornwall Council), we decided to focus our Stepping Stones project work in the Isles of Scilly on Old Quay as a result of this promise in relation to both Mesolithic and Neolithic archaeology. It was a relatively easily accessible site that had previously produced material culture from both of the periods we were interested in. Given that no previous excavation work had been undertaken there, our approach was threefold – we aimed to assess the extent of the surviving archaeologial deposits in the area, to recover further quantities of material under controlled archaeological conditions and to establish the presence or absence of any associated archaeological features.

3.2. Excavation strategy and methodology

Our initial work at the site in 2013 was focused on a single large field to the south of Old Quay (Figure 3.03), where previous archaeological monitoring had identified features in the cliff section along with artefactual material. In order (a) to recover further material and establish the extent of the artefact scatter, (b) to assess the character of the buried soils, and (c) to evaluate the field for features, we excavated a series of sixteen 2 × 2m test pits (Trenches 1–16) at 10m intervals across the field (Figure 3.05); this strategy was subsequently extended northwards into the smaller adjacent field as well (Trenches 17–20). On the basis of our findings within these test pits, we excavated a further series of test pits at closer intervals around the main density of finds (Trenches 21–26) and expanded the size of Trench 19 to investigate a cut feature.

Given the scarcity of features identified in these first two fields and the speed at which the excavation progressed during the first three weeks of the 2013 season (meaning that we covered the full extent of this part of the site more quickly than anticipated), we decided to expand our investigations into the large field (sub-divided by hedges

Figure 3.05. Test pits under excavation (Trenches 4 and 10 can be seen in the foreground, the hedged fields containing Trenches 27–39 can be seen top centre) (photo: H. Anderson-Whymark).

into smaller parcels) to the north of Old Quay itself during the final week of the 2013 season. This decision was informed by advice from a number of local people who suggested that the density of finds recovered from the beach after a storm in the vicinity was actually greatest along that section of the promontory. Given the limited time available to us at that stage, we decided simply to excavate one 2 × 2m test pit in the centre of each sub-field (Trenches 27–34) at an average distance of 17m apart. Significant, settlement-related features and deposits (post-holes, pits and a very dense concentration of artefacts within the buried soils) were identified in Trenches 27, 28 and 32 (Figure 3.06). There was time to expand each of these test pits slightly in 2013, but not to investigate the larger area around them in detail.

As a result of the promising character of the archaeology revealed in 2013 (especially in Trenches 27 and 28), we applied for and subsequently received additional funding, enabling us to carry out a further season of work in 2014. In September 2014, we expanded Trench 28 to create an approximately 10 × 14m open area (the maximum size we estimated that we would be able to dig in the time available) and opened up a series of additional test pits (Trenches 35–39) around the dense concentration of material recovered the previous year in Trench 27 (Figure 3.07). Given our limited resources and timeframe we decided not to revisit the isolated Trevisker-associated features in Trench 32; these nonetheless would be a fruitful focus for further investigation in future.

In total, over the two seasons of work at Old Quay (4 and 3 weeks respectively), 310m^2 of the three fields was excavated, representing approximately 11% of the area in which the archaeology is concentrated.

At the time of our investigations, all three fields were under Higher Level Stewardship with Natural England, meaning that the environmental impact of our archaeological work had to be kept to a minimum. During the 2013 season, all of the trenches were entirely hand-dug.

Figure 3.06. Test pit 28 under excavation in 2013.

Figure 3.07. Aerial view of Trenches 28, 36 and 37 under excavation in 2014.

During the 2014 season, the top 0.30–0.40m of topsoil in Trench 28 was removed using a mechanical excavator; lower deposits within that trench, and all of the other trenches, were completely hand-dug. In order to gain control of finds distributions, excavation of all deposits was carried out in 0.10m spits. In the two largest trenches (Trenches 19 and 28), the distribution of finds within the buried soils was recorded horizontally as well, in 2m grid squares. The trenches excavated were between 0.30m and 1.20m deep.

The excavation methodology and recording system was essentially the same as that employed at L'Erée (see Section 2.2). All archaeological deposits were carefully hand-excavated and recorded. Where significant concentrations of flint were identified (in buried soils or in features), 100% of the excavated spoil was passed through 5mm mesh sieves. Separate feature numbers were used to group contexts by feature as well. Features are labelled with an 'F' (e.g. F10) and contexts are depicted in square brackets (e.g. [78]). Plans and sections were drawn at 1:10, 1:20 or 1:50 where appropriate. All of the main contexts and all features were also located digitally in three dimensions with a GPS. All trenches were located using a Leica 1200 and Viva GS15 real time kinematic global position system (RTK GPS) connected to Smartnet reference network. The site archive has now been deposited in the Isles of Scilly Museum under the site codes OLQ13 and OLQ14. Digital copies of the site records, finds tables and other data have also been deposited with the Archaeology Data Service (http://doi.org/10.5284/1016098).

3.3. Results

The soil sequence

The soil sequence at Old Quay was relatively straightforward, and in some ways surprisingly redolent of that seen at L'Erée. It comprised a mottled orange brown coarse and gritty weathered bedrock/glacial head material (known locally as 'ram') overlain by a fine silt loam/loess up to 30cm deep, with evidence of reworking due to solifluxion. In some (but not all) trenches a gradual boundary over 5cm saw the loessic material give way to a darker brown silt loam which varied in thickness from 1–10cm. This horizon reflected a buried topsoil (Ah) horizon, which features had been cut through into the underlying subsoil. This buried soil sequence of loessic material overlain by a preserved topsoil was to produce the majority of prehistoric material from the excavations.

The buried soil sequence was overlain by a grey (eluviated) silty shelly sand with frequent granular inclusions. This varied in depth from 0.15–0.40m across the site and was interpreted as blown sand material enriched and reworked through later agricultural activity (with plough scars and potato trench features clearly evident). Finally this substantially sandy deposit was capped by a very dark grey to black modern topsoil, with frequent rootlets running through it.

Artefact distributions

Artefacts were recovered across the full extent of the investigation area (Figures 3.08 and 3.09). Altogether, 10,739 lithics (94% of the total) and 3,335 sherds of pottery (71% of the total) were recovered within the buried soils rather than in features. Two very dense concentrations of flint were identified: one in the south (in and around Trenches 1, 2, 7, 8 and 21–26) and one in the north (in and around Trenches 27 and 35–39); just a single concentration of pottery was identified, in the same northern area (Table 3.01).

Table 3.01. Summary of main artefact densities at Old Quay

Location	*No.*	*Weight (g)*	*Finds per m²*
Southern concentration – flint	3242	13,494	66
Northern concentration – flint	3337	14,218	128
Northern concentration – pottery	2662	11,532	102

As discussed further in Section 3.5, it is very difficult to pull apart the Mesolithic, Neolithic and Bronze Age elements of the lithic scatter, especially given the relatively small numbers of diagnostic aretfacts recovered. The vast majority of the assemblage was comprised of undiagnostic cores, flakes, scrapers, etc., and thus could potentially have been manufactured in the Mesolithic, Neolithic or Bronze Age. The fact that microliths were found in sizeable numbers within both concentrations, as well as in some of the test pits in between, suggests that we can probably assume that *both* concentrations of lithics had accumulated, at least to some extent, during the Mesolithic occupation of the site. The very high densities of pottery recovered within the northern concentration of material suggest that it must *also* have accumulated during the Neolithic. Consequently, we can assume that, there, a proportion of the flint (found in the same contexts as the pottery) was Neolithic in date. To summarise, the southern artefact concentration probably accumulated mainly during the Mesolithic, while the northern concentration is likely to be a palimpsest of Mesolithic and Neolithic material (the latter including lithics and pottery). The typologically-derived dates for the microliths (5th millennium BC, or earlier) and radiocarbon dates for the Neolithic material (late 4th/early 3rd millennium cal BC) suggest that we are not talking about continuous occupation of the site, but rather two distinct phases (see Section 3.10).

Archaeological features

In total, 67 archaeological features were identified and excavated at Old Quay. Of these, 56 were assigned to the Neolithic and three to the Early Bronze Age. Five more were designated 'probably prehistoric', and a single Late Roman small pit was identified; the remaining two features were post-medieval or modern. No identifiably Mesolithic features were identified. Further details of all features are provided in Table 3.02.

Neolithic

TRENCHES 28, 38 AND 39

Almost all of the Neolithic features were found in Trenches 28, 38 and 39 (Figures 3.10 and 3.11). These were observed across an area of approximately 15 × 8m, but others almost certainly lay beyond our trenches (especially to the north and east). As discussed in further detail below (Sections 3.4 and 3.10), the available dating evidence suggests that this Neolithic activity occurred primarily within the period c. 3350–2900 cal BC, during the British 'Middle Neolithic'.

The most prominent feature was a very large pit (F33) in Trench 28 that extended beyond the south-eastern edge of excavation (visible under the ranging rod on the left-hand side of Figure 3.11). As exposed, it measured 2.75m across × 1.25m wide × 0.50m deep, but it was clearly much larger – a very sizeable feature. The pit contained very dark grey/black fills (with a high charcoal content) towards its base, within which a silvery ash layer [211] could also be seen. The pit's upper fills, mid-brown silty sands, were similar to many of the other features around it. The lower, darker fills contained very large amounts of pottery and flint (F33 contained 738 sherds and 308 flints in total), but interestingly only a very small proportion of the flint debris within it was burnt (see Section 3.5). An irregularly spaced group of stake-holes was clustered on its western side; these may have been associated with the large pit in some way, but their role in relation to it is unclear. All in all, the function of F33 is difficult to ascertain: whilst it contained the remnants of burning, it did not appear to have been used as a fire pit – the natural subsoil at the base of its cut was not scorched. Presumably, therefore, the pit had been used as a secondary dump for burnt material from elsewhere, along with other (unburnt) material culture debris.

Extending across Trench 28 to the west of the large pit was a substantial collection of post-holes and two small pits (F23 and F43). The post-holes varied in size from 0.20m diameter and 0.15m deep to 0.65 diameter and 0.50m deep (Figure 3.12). Almost all of them contained both pottery and flint, but only in small quantities (an average of 8.5 sherds and 3.7 flints per feature). The post-holes did not form a clearly coherent shape in plan, although they could possibly be said to be spread across a roughly rectangular (E–W) area overall. A few of the larger ones contained visible post-pipes, clearly indicating that they had once held posts. A probable explanation for their amorphous form as a group is that they represent a palimpsest, created during multiple episodes of occupation. It seems likely that collectively these post-holes formed part of a small number of temporary structures – perhaps used as shelters during visits to the site.

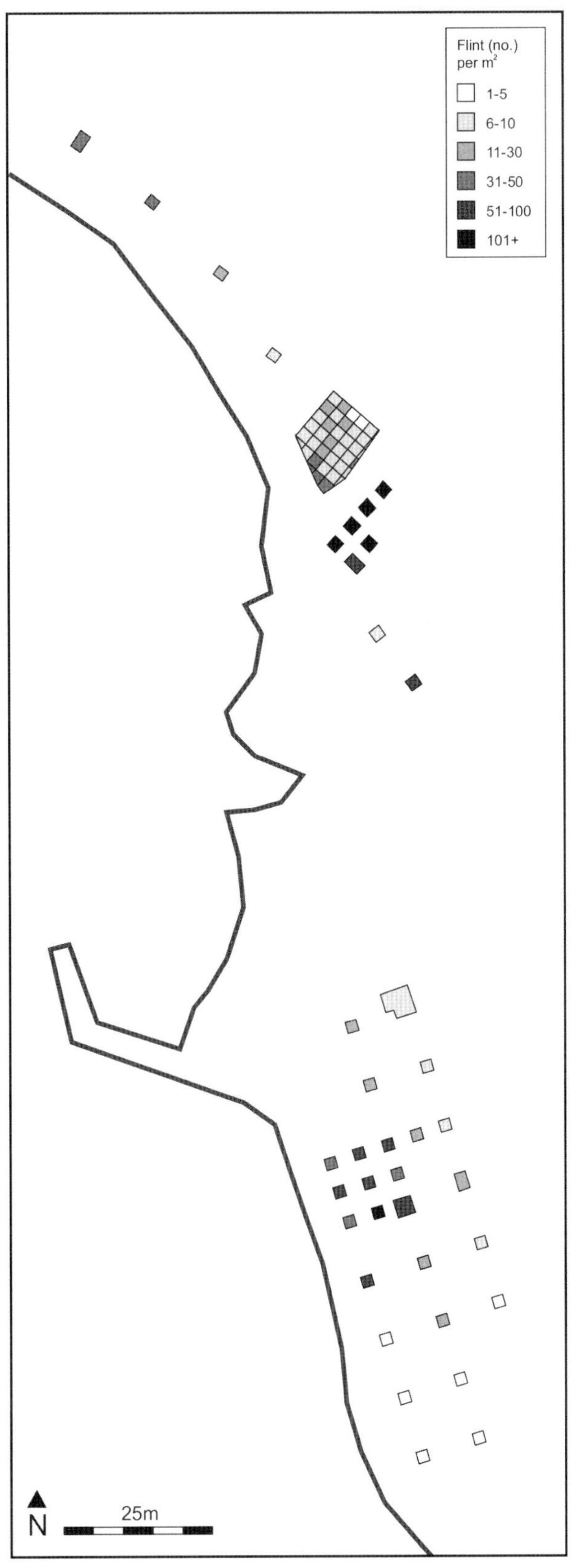

Figure 3.08. Flint density plot within buried soils.

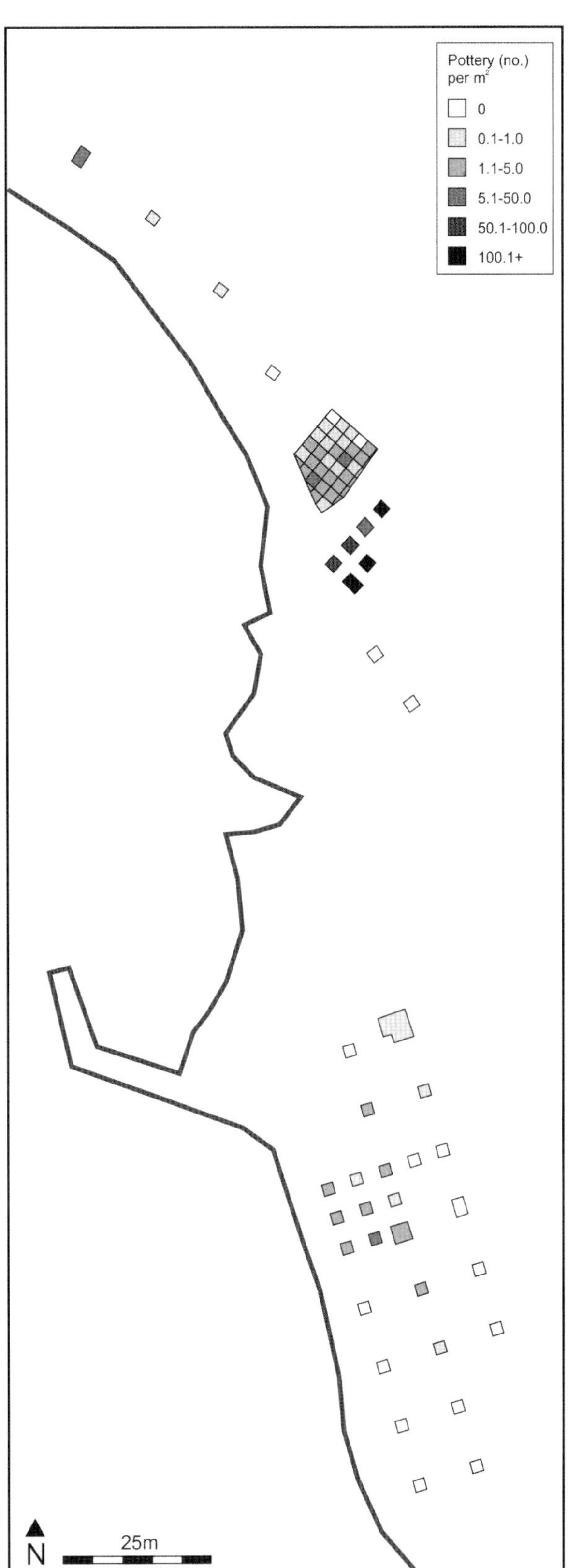

Figure 3.09. Pottery density plot within buried soils.

Table 3.02. Features excavated at Old Quay – summary

Feature	*Trench*	*Feature type*	*Period*	*Length (m)*	*Breadth (m)*	*Depth (m)*	*Pottery (no.)*	*Flint/quartz (no.)*	*Worked stone (no.)*	*Pumice (no.)*
1	12	Pit	Post-Med/Modern	0.59	0.53	0.10	–	–	–	–
2	8	Ditch	?Prehistoric	(1.80)	0.80	0.28	2	62	–	–
3	15	Scoop	Post-Med/Modern	1.10	0.45	0.03	–	5	–	–
4	14	Ditch	?Prehistoric	(2.00)	0.75	0.20	–	3	–	–
5	19	Pit	Neolithic	0.80	0.70	0.25	10	27	–	–
6	beach section	Pit	?Prehistoric	unknown	0.35	0.30	1	–	–	–
7	beach section	Ditch	?Prehistoric	unknown	0.70	0.42	–	–	–	–
8	19	Pit	Neolithic	0.60	0.60	0.10	–	–	–	–
9	19	Pit	Neolithic	1.55	1.49	0.40	–	3	–	–
12	19	Pit	Neolithic	0.25	0.25	0.06	1	–	–	–
14	25	Post-hole	?Prehistoric	0.27	0.27	0.16	–	1	–	–
15	19	Pit	Neolithic	0.62	0.49	0.10	–	–	–	–
16	28	Post-hole	Neolithic	0.20	0.20	0.15	6	3	–	–
17	28	Post-hole	Neolithic	0.34	0.34	0.24	13	3	–	–
18	28	Post-hole	Neolithic	0.25	0.15	0.06	2	0	–	–
19	28	Post-hole	Neolithic	0.38	0.38	0.18	–	–	–	–
20	32	Pit	EBA	2.30	0.79	0.25	11	15	–	–
21	32	Scoop	EBA	(1.35)	(0.30)	0.28	1	4	–	–
22	32	Pit	EBA	0.80	0.30	0.20	1	2	–	–
23	28	Pit	Neolithic	0.60	0.50	0.50	78	16	–	–
24	28	Post-hole	Neolithic	0.30	0.30	0.15	7	1	–	–
25	28	Post-hole	Neolithic	0.28	0.28	0.16	–	1	–	–
26	28	Post-hole	Neolithic	0.30	0.30	0.25	7	4	–	–
27	28	Post-hole	Roman	0.30	0.30	0.07	–	–	–	–
28	28	Post-hole	Neolithic	0.35	0.35	0.19	6	2	–	–
29	28	Post-hole	?EBA	0.40	0.40	0.30	20	7	1	–
30	28	Post-hole	Neolithic	0.30	0.30	0.20	8	14	–	–
31	28	Post-hole	Neolithic	0.40	0.40	0.12	–	–	–	–
32	28	Post-hole	Neolithic	0.33	0.33	0.28	5	–	–	–
33	28	Pit	Neolithic	(2.75)	(1.25)	0.50	738	308	4	3
34	28	Stake-hole	Neolithic	0.12	0.12	0.10	–	–	–	–
36	28	Post-hole	Neolithic	0.30	0.30	0.10	–	–	–	–
37	28	Stake-hole	Neolithic	0.14	0.13	0.22	–	1	–	–
38	28	Stake-hole	Neolithic	0.16	0.15	0.13	–	–	–	–
39	28	Post-hole	Neolithic	0.35	0.30	0.29	2	–	–	–
40	28	Stake-hole	Neolithic	0.13	0.10	0.09	17	12	–	–
41	28	Post-hole	Neolithic	0.25	0.25	0.18	2	–	–	–
42	28	Pit	Neolithic	0.60	0.40	0.18	3	–	–	–
43	28	Post-hole	Neolithic	0.66	0.56	0.39	26	8	1	–
44	28	Post-hole	Neolithic	0.26	0.24	0.09	–	–	–	–
45	28	Post-hole	Neolithic	0.37	0.37	0.36	20	9	–	–
46	28	Post-hole	Neolithic	0.35	0.35	0.15	3	1	–	–
47	28	Post-hole	Neolithic	0.44	0.38	0.35	26	14	–	–
48	28	Post-hole	Neolithic	0.50	0.46	0.45	2	4	–	–
49	28	Post-hole	Neolithic	0.64	0.64	0.51	76	28	–	–
50	28	Post-hole	Neolithic	0.24	0.23	0.15	–	–	1	–
51	28	Stake-hole	Neolithic	0.15	0.15	0.15	–	–	–	–
52	28	Stake-hole	Neolithic	0.15	0.15	0.10	–	1	–	–
54	39	?Hearth	Neolithic	0.50	(0.30)	0.10	130	15	–	–
55	39	Post-hole	Neolithic	0.40	(0.25)	0.04	–	–	–	–
56	38	Pit	Neolithic	(0.60)	0.50	0.20	11	30	–	–
57	38	Post-hole	Neolithic	(0.50)	0.40	0.40	–	27	–	–
58	28	Post-hole	Neolithic	0.23	0.22	0.10	–	–	–	–
59	28	Post-hole	Neolithic	0.30	0.25	0.06	–	–	–	–
60	28	Stake-hole	Neolithic	0.18	0.18	0.12	1	1	–	–
61	28	Stake-hole	Neolithic	0.15	0.15	0.15	–	–	–	–
62	28	Stake-hole	Neolithic	0.20	0.18	0.10	–	3	–	–
63	39	Scoop	Neolithic	(1.30)	(0.70)	0.12	92	42	–	–
64	28	Stake-hole	Neolithic	0.25	0.25	0.08	–	–	–	–

65	38	Scoop	Neolithic	(0.60)	(0.50)	0.08	–	27	–	–
66	38	Post-hole	Neolithic	0.20	0.20	0.12	–	–	–	–
67	38	Post-hole	Neolithic	(0.20)	0.20	0.06	–	–	–	–
68	28	Stake-hole	Neolithic	0.18	0.18	0.12	–	1	–	–
69	39	Post-hole	Neolithic	0.75	(0.45)	0.30	21	18	1	–
70	28	Stake-hole	Neolithic	0.12	0.12	0.10	–	–	–	–
71	28	Stake-hole	Neolithic	0.17	0.13	0.10	–	–	–	–
72	28	Stake-hole	Neolithic	0.17	0.15	0.12	1	2	–	–

At this point, it is worth highlighting the fact that, as Figures 3.10 and 3.11 clearly show, all of these settlement features were built adjacent to a notable spread of sometimes very large rocks. Given their position directly on top of the weathered bedrock material, it seems most likely that the rocks got there through geological not human processes, during the last glacial maximum. However, having said that, it is quite possible that some rocks were subsequently moved around by people (during the Neolithic) to create a better space for living in. The apparently naturally-created, roughly rectangular area (containing no cut features at all) in the northern half of Trench 28 (see Figure 3.10) may well also have been used in this way. Equally, especially towards the southern side of Trench 28, a few smaller rocks were located immediately adjacent to post-holes, suggesting that they may well have been incorporated as structural features in some way.

Across the hedge from Trench 28, a further series of features was located in Trenches 38 and 39. Given that these were seen only within two small 2 × 2m test pits, it was for the most part difficult to be sure of their character: post-holes, small pits/scoops and a single hearth were identified. The hearth (F54) was a very shallow feature (0.10m deep), defined primarily as a localised, apparently circular, highly-scorched patch of natural subsoil. The pits and post-holes were comparable to those in Trench 28. Notably, the upper fills of hearth F54 and scoop F63, both in Trench 39, contained the highest quantities of material (130 and 92 sherds and 15 and 42 flints respectively) in features on the site overall, after F33. It is probable that many more features would be identified in the vicinity if a larger area were opened around Trenches 38 and 39; sadly, time did not allow this in 2014.

As discussed above, very high densities of artefacts were found within the buried soils in the area of Trenches 38 and 39. Notably, unlike the features, these high densities extended southwards into Trenches 27, 35, 36 and 37. The character of the pottery recovered within the buried soils was essentially the same as that within the features, and so we can assume they are broadly contemporary; as discussed, it is likely that a sizeable proportion of the flint was as well. In this case, it seems probable that the very dense build-up of material was a 'midden' or rubbish dump of some kind. Any bone that it may originally have contained would not have survived, whilst previously charcoal-rich soils could have been leached out over time. Although it is difficult to be certain given the small size of the trenches, the fact that Trenches 27, 35, 36 and 37 contained no features at all may suggest that this zone was reserved in the long term for the accumulation of material, rather than for other occupation-related practices involving cut features. In this light, it is notable that mean sherd weights for material from the buried soils in Trenches 27/35–39 were all very low (3–6g), whilst those in the adjacent 2m buried soil squares in Trench 28 were much higher (12–18g). This suggests higher attrition and abrasion rates – possibly as a result of middening – in the former zone.

TRENCH 19

A small cluster of five pits was excavated in Trench 19 (Figures 3.13 and 3.14). The first pit dug in the initial test-pit, F5, produced an assemblage of 27 pieces of worked quartz and 10 fragments of pottery from a curved-sided Neolithic bowl (P9). As a result, a larger trench (5.00 × 4.50m) was opened up around it. Four more features were uncovered (Fs 8, 9, 12 and 15): F9, an amorphous, irregular pit, contained three further pieces of worked quartz; F12 (which was very shallow and thus probably heavily truncated) contained a single, very large fragment (604g) of very coarse pottery from a straight-sided, neutral bowl (P3); the other two pits were empty.

It is difficult to say a great deal about these features. The amorphous character of, and near-absence of finds from, F9, and shallow depth (0.10m) and total absence of finds from F8 and F15, made it difficult to be sure that they were indeed 'real' features. The other two pits could well have been created during a single visit to the site. The pottery within them was not identifiably distinct from the main assemblage, and presumably dates to approximately the same period. The total dominance of quartz (as opposed to flint) from the features within Trench 19 does however make the assemblage stand out from those in and around Trench 28 – this could perhaps be a reflection of timing, the pits having been created during one specific, temporally distinct phase when quartz, not flint, was more widely available or used.

Bronze Age

TRENCHES 31 AND 32

Trench 32, the northernmost test pit, produced three features dating to the Bronze Age (Figures 3.15 and 3.16). The

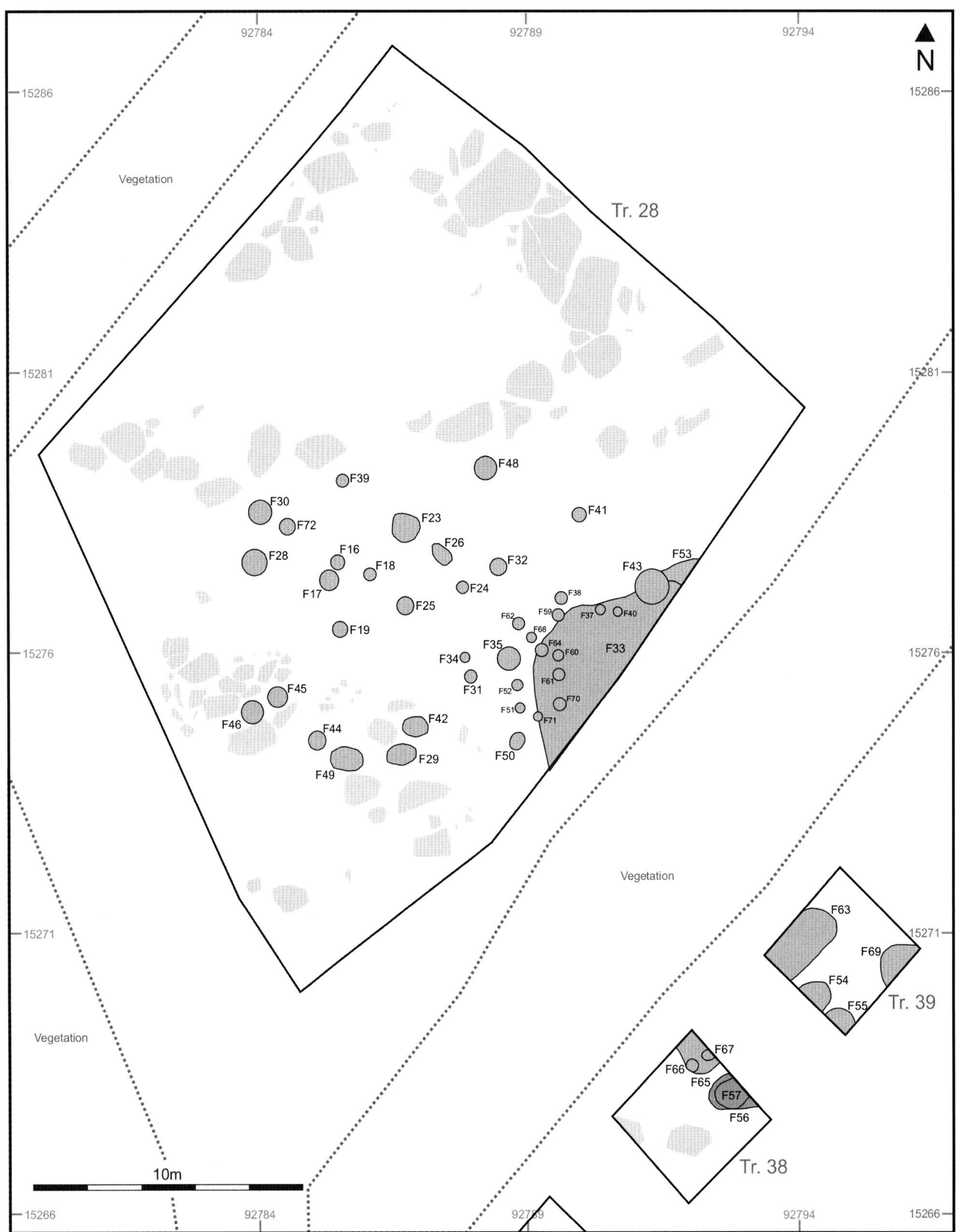

Figure 3.10. Trenches 28, 38, 39: all features. Natural boulders are also shown (light grey).

Figure 3.11. Trench 28, with all features excavated, looking south-west (scales: 2m).

Figure 3.12. Photo of post-hole F49, half-sectioned (scale: 0.5m).

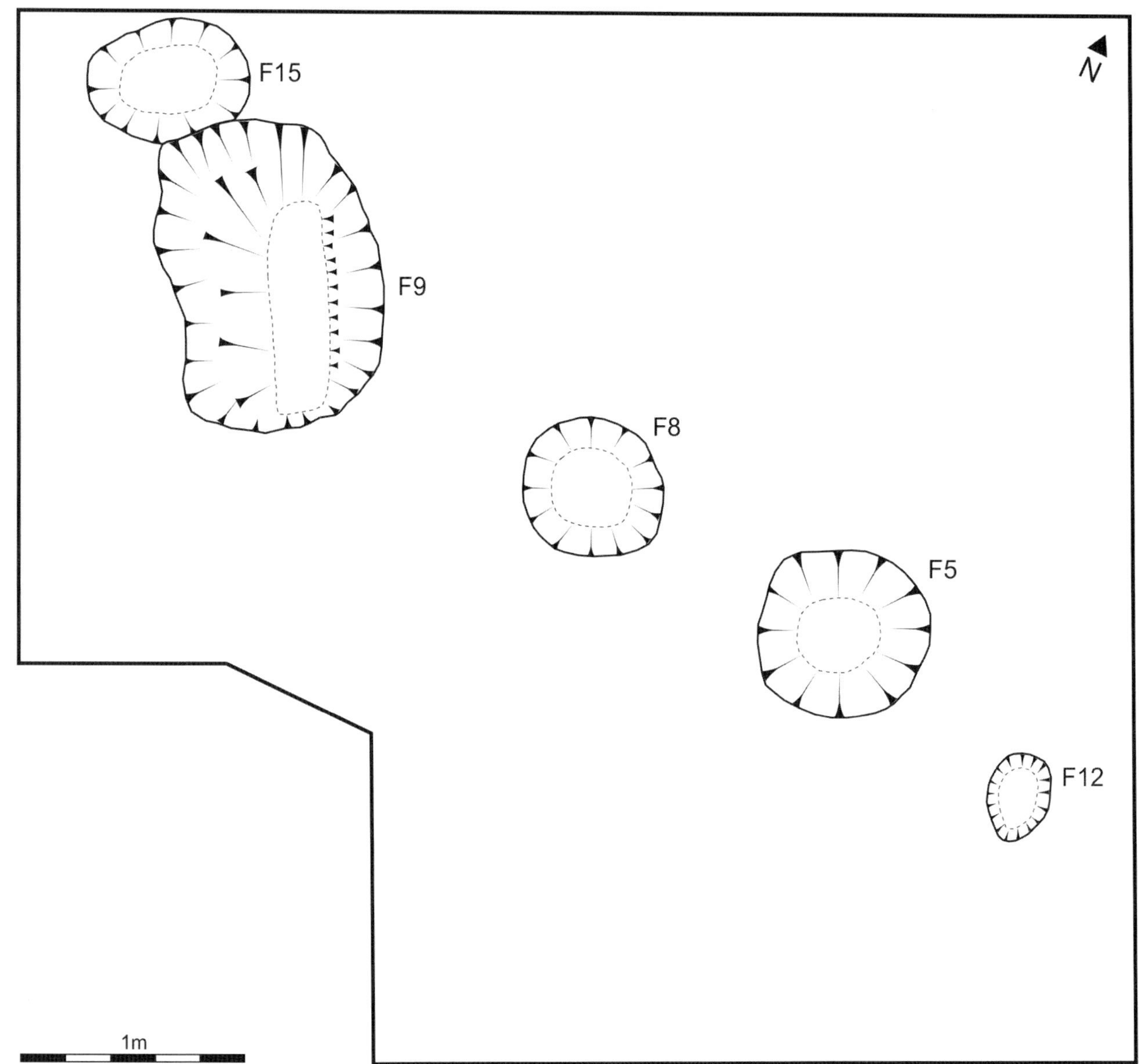

Figure 3.13. Trench 19 features.

largest pit (F20) measured 2.30m × 0.79m (visible) wide × 0.25 deep; it appeared to be circular. The smaller pit (F22), which was 0.80m × 0.30m (visible) wide × 0.20m deep, appeared to have been cut by F20. A somewhat amorphous 1.25m long × 0.30m wide × 0.28m deep stretch of 'gully' (F21) was also discernible within the trench. The two pits (F20 and F22) both contained pottery with Trevisker affinities (see Section 3.4); the 'gully' feature (F21) adjacent to these did not, but (while, like the pits, it did contain a few small sherds of probably residual Neolithic pottery) it is probable that it dates to the same phase. The buried soils above the features in Trench 32 contained further sherds in the same distinctive Bronze Age fabric, as did those in Trench 31. A single sherd (P17) from the buried soils in Trench 32 could potentially be from a Collared Urn (see Section 3.4).

It is difficult to say a great deal about these features without having opened up a larger area around them. They certainly appear to be related to occupation of some sort.

Possibly prehistoric

Trenches 8, 14 and 25

A small cluster of potentially prehistoric features was identified in three adjacent trenches in the southern field (Figure 3.17). F2 in Trench 8 and F4 in Trench 14 possibly represented separate lengths of the same ditch-like feature: they were approximately aligned (oriented SW–NE) and – given the different potential for truncation higher upslope

Figure 3.14. Photo of Trench 19, looking north-west (horizontal scales: 2m).

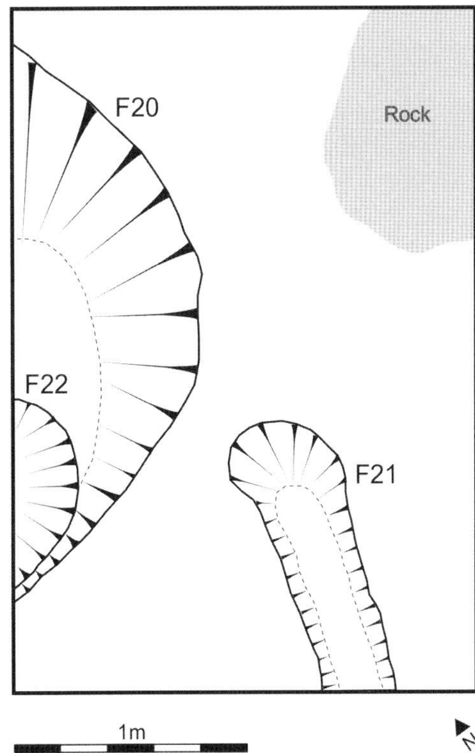

Figure 3.15. Trench 32 features.

in Trench 14 – possibly originally of comparable width and depth. F2 contained two sherds of pottery in a Bronze Age fabric, F4 produced no finds. F14 in Trench 25 was a post-hole, 0.27m diameter and 0.16m deep; it contained a single flint flake. A further ditch-like feature (F7, whose alignment did match that of F2 and F4 fairly well; see Figure 3.17) and a small pit (F6, located immediately west of Trench 1) were identified in the cliff section.

These features certainly would not appear out of place on a prehistoric site. A general spread of sherds made from Bronze Age fabric 2 was noted across the southern field (see Section 3.4) suggesting that there may have been wider activity of that date in the area. It is quite possible that all five of these features should be assigned more specifically to this Bronze Age phase, but given the lack of clear dating evidence within them, they have simply been assigned a possibly prehistoric date.

Roman

A single small, shallow pit (F27) was identified at a higher stratigraphic level in Trench 28 than any of the other features: cut into, rather than sealed by, the lowest buried soil layer [195] (Figure 3.18). The feature contained no finds, other than hundreds of wheat and barley grains recovered during

Figure 3.16. Photo of Trench 32, looking north-east (horizontal scales: 2m).

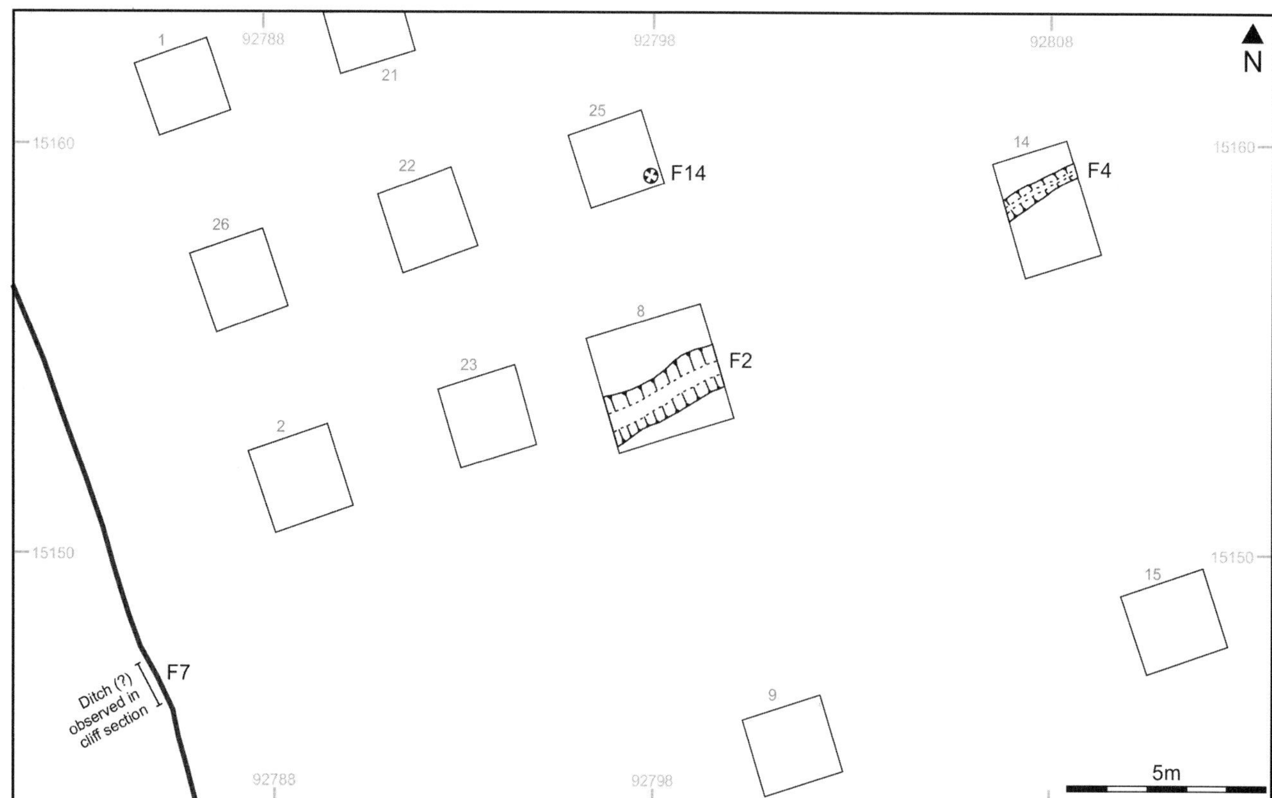

Figure 3.17. Trenches 8, 14 and 25: features.

Figure 3.18. Roman pit F27, half-sectioned (scales: 0.2m). The excavators are standing on buried soil layer [195].

wet-sieving (see Section 3.8). A single barley grain from F27 was radiocarbon dated to the late 3rd/4th centuries AD (see Section 3.9). Another grain, this time wheat, from a second almost certainly Neolithic pit (F29) close by, produced a date with almost exactly the same calibrated range (see Section 3.9). The dating of these grains to the Late Roman period comes as something of a surprise given the total absence of any other material culture of that period from the site.

Post-medieval/modern

Two large, very shallow pits (F1 and F3), assigned to the post-medieval or modern periods, were recorded in the southern field (Trenches 12 and 15). Their function is uncertain but they could both have been stone removal holes – the alteration, movement and destruction of large natural boulders in the field was carried out in living memory (Steve Walder pers. comm.). In total, 414 unstratified sherds of medieval or post-medieval pottery were identified during excavations at Old Quay. These remain with the site archive but are not reported on here.

3.4. Prehistoric pottery

Henrietta Quinnell (with petrographic identification and comment by Roger Taylor)

The total assemblage of prehistoric pottery from Old Quay consisted of 4685 sherds weighing 26,390g, of which most (4638 sherds, 26,151g) was Middle Neolithic (Fabric 1); there were also a few Bronze Age sherds (Fabric 2, 20 sherds, 98g; Fabric 3, 27 sherds, 141g) (Figures 3.19–3.21; Tables 3.03 and 3.04)). After initial examination, selected sherds of the different fabrics were examined under a petrological microscope by Roger Taylor to produce the detailed fabric descriptions given below.

Middle Neolithic

Fabric

The Middle Neolithic fabric (Fabric 1) has inclusions of beach sand up to small pebble size. In general the inclusions project through the body of the fabric, although more attempt has been made to smooth these over on the interiors than exteriors. The quality of this fabric is very variable, with variation even within the same vessel: in larger vessels there are noticeably more inclusions in the thicker, lower part. The matrix is a predominantly smooth clay with a scatter of colourless well rounded polished quartz grains up to 0.2mm and some fine muscovite flakes. Beach sand/gravel has been added to a clay with some marine content, possibly glacially derived; in this sand/gravel, white quartz and feldspar predominate.

Fabric 1 can be broadly divided into three sub-types:

Coarse. Up to 40mm thick, inclusions over 30% and sometimes abundant (over 50%). *Quartz*, white angular to sub-angular grains, 1–8mm, *feldspar* white cleaved grains up to 7mm, composite *quartz-muscovite* and *quartz-feldspar* grains; *matrix* predominantly smooth clay with a scatter of colourless well rounded polished *quartz* grains up to 0.2mm and some fine *muscovite* flakes.

Medium. Up to c. 8mm thick, inclusions between 10% and 30%. *Quartz* – transparent colourless angular to sub-angular 0.1–3.0mm, *feldspar* sparse white sub-angular to sub-rounded 2.5–3.0mm, composite *quartz-muscovite* 3.0mm, *mica* including muscovite and biotite flakes 0.1–0.5mm, *tourmaline* rare black angular 4.0mm, *matrix* predominantly smooth clay with a scatter of well-rounded polished quartz grains 0.2–0.3mm.

Fine. Generally thin, around 4mm, with sparse inclusions usually <3mm but occasional larger ones. The mineralogy is essential the same as in medium and coarse variant, with a high content of finer *quartz* sand 0.2–0.3mm coarser grains up to 0.5mm relatively sparse and well-rounded polished grains quite common.

Table 3.03. Neolithc illustrated vessels (Figures 3.19 and 3.20)

P1 [211] fill F33 Tr 28 Deep bodied straight sided neutral bowl, rim diameter 175–200mm, medium/coarse fabric 1, lug 24 × 18 × 15mm. Drawn from overlapping but not joining sherds, from some of which the interior has split off.
P2 [172] fill F23 Tr 28 Deep bodied straight sided neutral bowl, rim diameter 200–230mm, medium fabric 1, drawn from overlapping sherds, probably originally had lugs.
P3 [103] F12 Tr 19 Body sherd from towards base of deep bodied straight sided bowl, diameter >300mm, coarse fabric 1.
P4 [119] spit 3 Tr 27 Straight/curved sided bowl, rim diameter 250–300mm, fine fabric 1. Lug 11 × 11 × 4mm.
P5 [291] F63 Tr 39 Straight sided bowl, rim diameter 200–240mm, fine fabric 1.
P6 [153] fill F18 Tr 28. Straight sided bowl, rim diameter c 165mm, coarse fabric 1.
P7 [179] fill F26 Tr 28. Curved sided bowl, rim diameter 190mm. Lug 16 × 14 × 10mm.
P8 [119] spit 2 Tr 27 Curved sided bowl, rim diameter c 180mm, medium fabric 1.
P9 [84] F5 Tr 19 Curved sided bowl, rim diameter 180–250mm, medium fabric 1 rim.
P10 [119] spit 1 Tr 27 Shallow open bowl or platter, rim diameter 270–300mm, fine fabric 1.
P11 [238] 10–22cm Tr 38 Curved sided bowl ?, uncertain diameter, fine fabric 1. Lug 9 × 10 × 5mm.
P12 [211] F33 Tr 28 Straight sided (?) bowl, uncertain diameter, fine fabric 1. Lug 12 × 11 × 6mm.
P13 [195] E2 Tr 28 Lug, fine fabric 1, 28 × 12 × 14mm, short incised lines in upper angle between lug and body. Shows clearly the smoothed projection of the end of the lug on the inner body wall.
P14 [119] spit 1 Tr 27 Lug, fine fabric 1, 21 × 12 × 10mm but very irregular.
P15 [119] spit 2 Tr 27 Lug, fine fabric 1, 14 × 12 × 10mm.
P16 [261] fill F49 Tr 28 Projecting oval lug, medium/fine fabric 1, 19 × 14 × 14mm.

Lug dimensions given in the order: width (along vessel), diameter, height, thickness/projection.

Table 3.04. Bronze Age illustrated vessels (Figure 3.21)

P17 [152] subsoil Tr 32 Fabric 3. Undecorated sherd with double angle in wall, possibly from a Collared Urn of which otherwise only a single example is reliably recorded from Scilly, from Normandy Down on St Mary's (Parker Pearson 1990, 14, No 180). The latter vessel is in an imported Cornish fabric, and if the identification of P17, is correct would imply copying of this vessel type.
P18 [169] F22 Tr 32 Fabric 3. Body sherd, two horizontal lines below/bordering two/three diagonal lines, impressed with unusually thick simple twist cord. Some parallels for the type of cord impressions occur occasionally in Cornish Trevisker ware (Quinnell in Nowakowski & Quinnell 2011, 2.80). Cord impressed and incised bordered designs are found regularly on mainland Cornwall Trevisker ware of the 2nd millennium BC: see for example the numerous examples from the settlement at Trethellan, Newquay (Woodward & Cane in Nowakowski 1991; Quinnell 2012).
P19 (not illus) [152] subsoil Tr 32 Fabric 3. Body sherd, single thick cord impressed line as P18.
P20 [159] F20 Tr 32 Fabric 3. Body sherd from large diameter vessel fabric 3, with close set parallel cord impressed lines. Such close set lines occur on Scillonian ceramics of the Earlier Bronze Age, as at Halangy Porth, St Mary's (Ashbee 1983, figure 7).

These fabrics are visually distinctive from the local fabrics found in post-Neolithic contexts in Scilly, in that some inclusions are large and leave the matrix unmixed with added material, with the larger inclusions breaking through roughly smoothed surfaces. The assemblage has not been divided between these fabric sub-types because of the variation within individual vessels and the difficulties of determining category for individual sherds.

Condition, fragmentation and deposition

Most sherds may be described as 'slightly abraded', with some rounding of the sharpness of corners but no alteration in core sherd colour. This condition is probably due to bioturbation factors. Conjoins are virtually absent and there has been no success in matching sherds from contexts such as post-hole fills where all pottery was retrieved, or between different 2 × 2m grid squares in Trench 28. Attempts were made to match larger rim sherds between different contexts but without success.

Some idea of the amount of fragmentation can be obtained from analysis. The mean sherd weight of the whole assemblage is 5.6g. On the whole, features tend to contain a slightly larger sherd size than buried soil layers, but even this is variable. The calculations can distorted when there is a single sherd of large size such as P3 (604g) from pit F12, Trench 19.

There is no indication of any special patterning in deposition such as a concentration of rim or lug sherds. In a few features, all the sherds could come from one single vessel but only represent a small part of it, for example F16 and F43, Trench 28. In F23 all sherds in one fill [172] belong to P3, and all the sherds from the second fill [171] could also belong. Despite 78 sherds weighing 2470g being present, only a small part of this large vessel is present, with all the rim and both the presumed lugs being absent.

The one instance where there may be chronological variation is in pit F29, Trench 28, which produced the shafthole adze which is most likely to be Beaker or Early Bronze Age. The 16 sherds (weighing 254g) in that feature are generally more abraded than those in other cut features.

The assemblage

The assemblage belongs in the South Western or Hembury Bowl tradition of the Early Neolithic in south-west Britain but with some distinctive features. One is its Middle

Neolithic date (see below). The second is the total absence of carinated bowls, found regularly in Early Neolithic assemblages in Devon and Cornwall. The third is the poor quality of the potting and the irregularity of the vessels produced. Decoration is normally rare in South Western Bowl assemblages. Here the only 'decorated' pieces are P13 with incisions on the lug top and an unillustrated sherd from [238] Trench 38 with a single finger nail impression.

The clay is very poorly mixed and poorly fired, with both oxidisation and reduction on many sherds and a very great range of colours. On larger, thicker vessels, it is apparent that, rather than made of coils, vessels were constructed of substantially overlapped pads of clay. Lower parts of vessels generally have more and coarser inclusions than the upper parts. Many sherds have split along badly potted pad joins. Poor quality potting as well as high soil acidity has led to the sherds surviving in a soft and sometimes friable condition. All vessels have similar rims, pointed to rounded: these may vary a little on each sherd and appear more rounded than pointed in thicker coarser vessels. The plan shapes of vessel rims are variable: sizable variation is indicated in individual vessel descriptions. Around 90 rim sherds represent less than 5% of the estimated rim diameter, with around 30 between 5% and 10%; none is larger. The 5–10% rims divide into 8 fine fabric, 17 medium and 4 coarse.

Lugs are the only additional regularly occurring feature, and in general appear small for vessel size. They vary from round to oval and in their degree of projection (Table 3.05). None is perforate. In no case could two lugs be demonstrated to belong to the same vessel: South Western Bowl lugs are most usually paired. It is therefore not possible to assess the similarity of lugs on each vessel. Some lugs, for example that on P4, are so small that they would appear to have had little function, to be only token. Apart from 25 complete lugs detailed in Table 3.05, there are a number of incomplete examples, in medium or coarse fabric, some of which appear to have been of larger size. It is likely that all lugged vessels had paired lugs. A number of broken examples show clearly that lugs were inserted through holes in the vessel wall with the interior portion being smoothed into the wall of the vessel (P13). The lugs illustrated use the convention of the lug (shaded) and the wall profile (black) but close examination shows that most display signs of the method of conversion.

The illustrations (Figures 3.19 and 3.20) depict all sherds with some good indication of vessel shape. P1–3 are examples of straight-sided, deep bodied, neutral bowls (following Cleal 2004). These form a component of the geographically closest large South Western Bowl assemblage, the 550 vessels from Carn Brea near Camborne (Smith in Mercer 1981, figures 72–73). The other forms represented are open bowls, with either curved or straight sides, the staple component of Carn Brea and other South Western Bowl assemblages. P10 is an unusual shallow open bowl, platter or possible lid in fine fabric, with three others, one fine one medium, represented by smaller sherds. A few simple flat dishes are present both at Carn Brea (Smith in Mercer 1981, figure 74, P137) and Helman Tor, near Bodmin (Smith in Mercer 1997, figure 7, P12). Table 3.06 presents the data on shape, size and fabric for the 31 vessels from Old Quay for which this can be estimated. This suggests that curved-sided bowls were the most numerous form but this can only be tentative.

Sherds of Fabric 1, including those of a curve-sided bowl, were found in the cliff face studied during a project on coastal erosion in 1989–1993 (Ratcliffe and Straker 1996; Quinnell 1994, Section 12). In addition to these, two small conjoining sherds in a thin gabbroic fabric came from the cliff face. This gabbroic fabric was similar to the fine gabbroic fabrics found at the tor enclosure of Carn Brea near Camborne (Smith in Mercer 1981), but cannot

Table 3.05. Data for the 25 complete lugs

	8mm	*10mm*	*12mm*	*14mm*	*16mm*	*18mm*	*20mm*	*22mm*	*24mm*	*26mm*	*28mm*	*30mm*
8mm	F 3 F 5 F 5	F 4										
10mm		F 4	F 3 M 6	M 8								
12mm				F 9 F 10	M 12	M 13	F 8					
14mm					M 10 M 9				M 14		M 14	M 14
16mm						M 10 M 10 M 11						
18mm									M 15 M 9			
20mm								C 20	M 13			

Horizontal = width mm; vertical = height mm; F = fine fabric, M = medium fabric C = coarse fabric with the number after each letter the projection in mm from the vessel. 8mm indicates 8–9mm, 10mm 10 = 11mm etc.

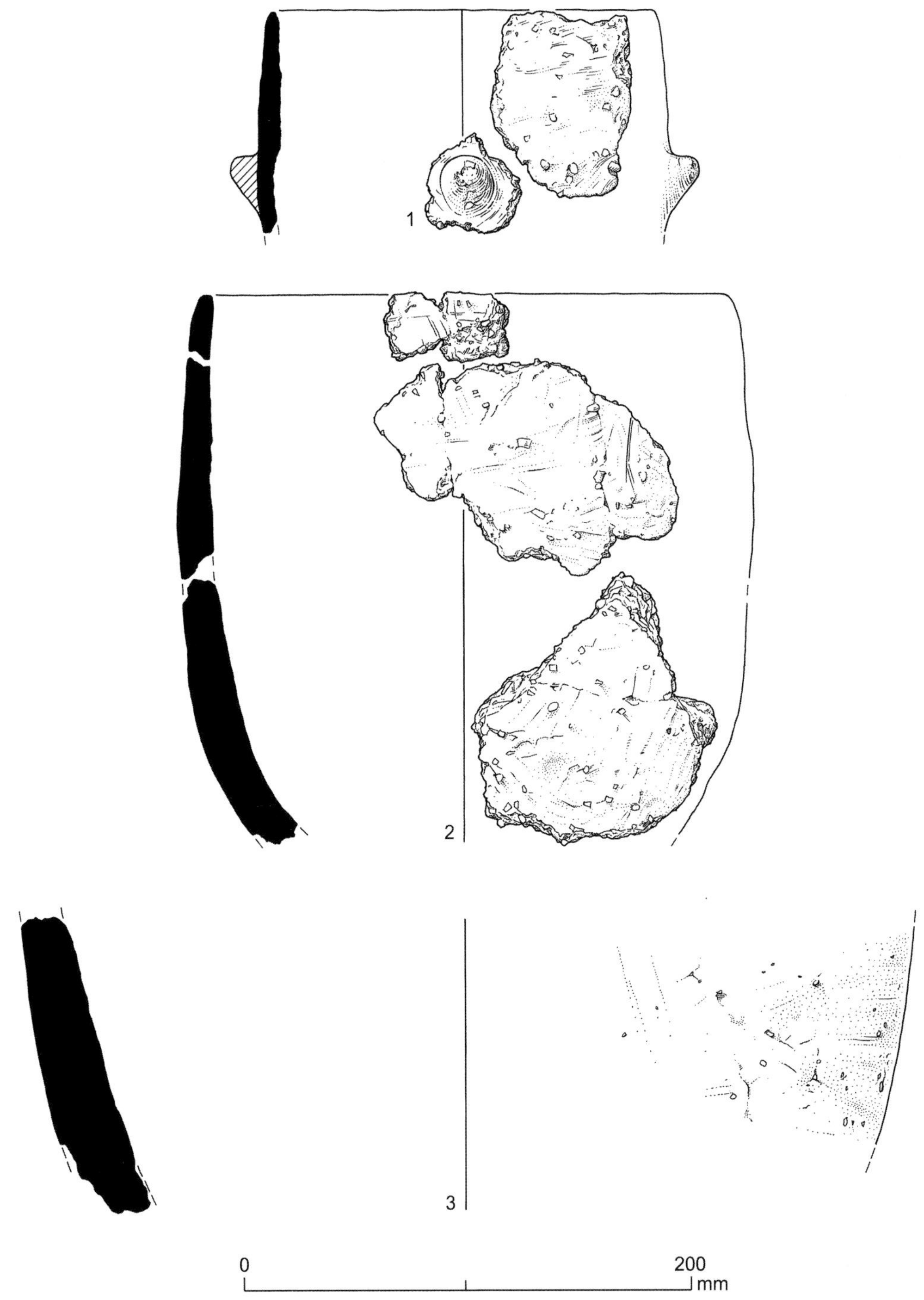

Figure 3.19. Neolithic pottery (1) (drawn by J. Read).

definitely be regarded as Neolithic. Robinson's (2007, 140) suggestion that most of Scillonian Neolithic pottery used mixed gabbroic and granitic material is not supported by the author's observations.

The only other excavated site on Scilly with South Western Bowl ceramics is East Porth, Samson (see Section 1.6). Here a group of pits underlay an Early Medieval site. The pottery from East Porth is generally similar to the fine sub-type of Old Quay. The two illustrated vessels there were deep, curve-sided bowls, one with a small lug set slantwise. The fabric differs a little from Old Quay, with some crushed quartz included with the sparse added beach sand. The previous reconstructions of these East Porth vessels by Thomas (1985, figure 42, nos 2–3) should be regarded only as indicative sketches, while the quasi-carinated bowl from Bant's Carn, St Mary's (ibid, no. 1) is

Table 3.06. Vessel types

	120 mm	*130 mm*	*140 mm*	*160 mm*	*180 mm*	*200 mm*	*220 mm*	*240 mm*	*250 mm*	*300 mm*	*totals*
Curve-sided bowls	F 1		F 1			F 2			F 1		F 5
		M 1	M 3	M 2	M 3	M1				M1	M 11
				C 1		C 1		C 1			C 3
Straight-sided bowls			F 1			F 1					F 2
						M 1					M 1
Open bowl/platter										F1	F1
			M 1				M 1			M 1	M 3
Straight-sided deep-bodied bowls						F 1					F 1
						M 2					M 2
				C 1						C1	C 2
Total	1	1	6	4	3	9	1	1	1	4	31

Diameters centring on 120cm, 130cm etc. Fabric F = fine 8 vessels, M = medium 17 vessels, C = coarse 4 vessels.

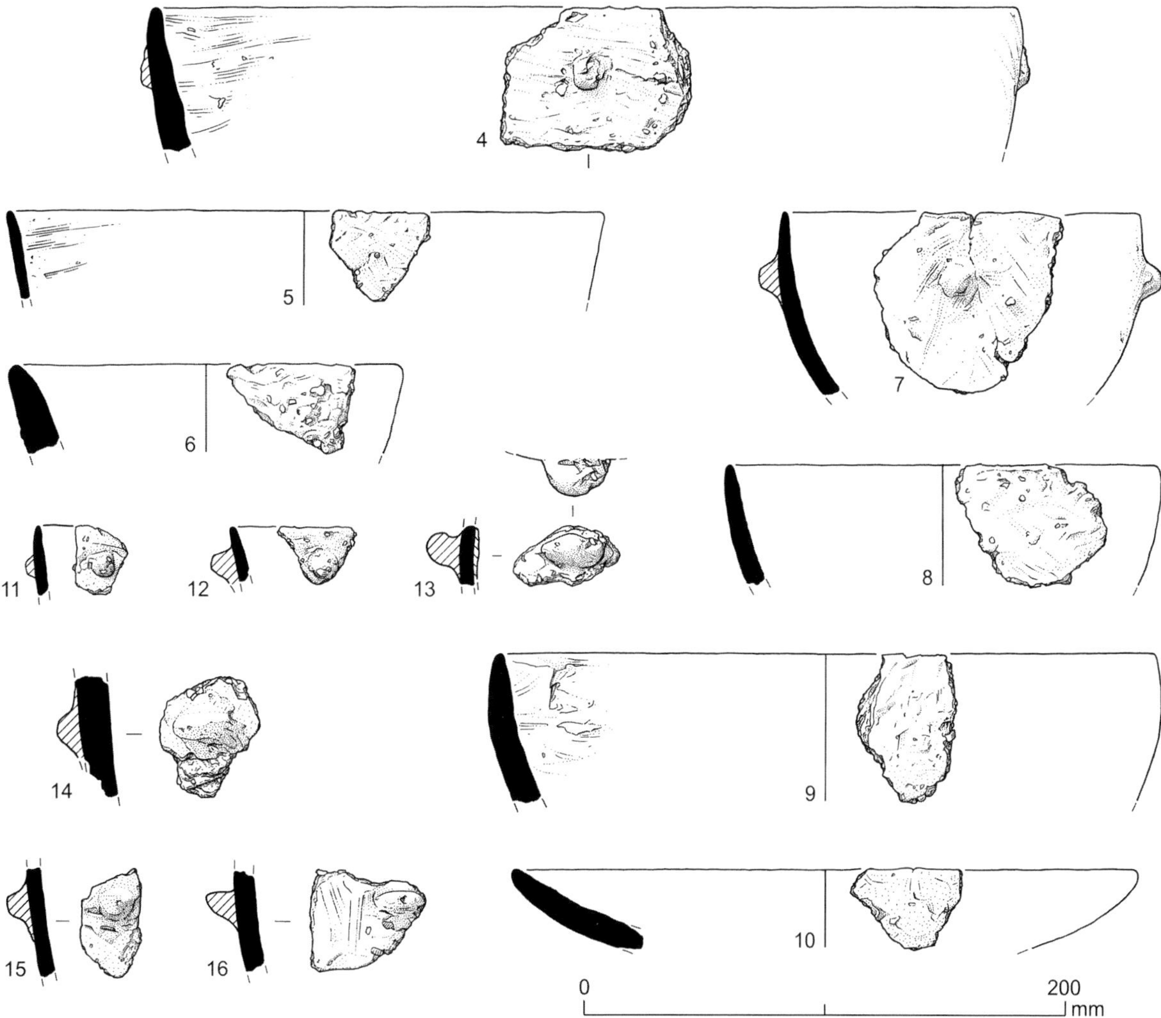

Figure 3.20. Neolithic pottery (2) (drawn by J. Read).

now known to be wrongly identified and is in fact Bronze Age (Johns 2012, 60).

A small collection of South Western Bowl sherds came from coastal observation work at Bonfire Carn, Bryher, probably below a Bronze Age structure (Quinnell 1994, section 3). The sherds can now be seen as in fabrics similar to the finer vessels at Old Quay and included a lug much larger than the Old Quay examples. Otherwise individual or very small groups of sherds in Old Quay type fabrics were recorded at five locations during the 1985 Electrification Project (Quinnell 1994): Lower Town, St Martin's, Dolphin Town, Tresco, Veronica Farm, Bryher, and Periglis Cottage and Turk's Head, St Agnes. Thus South Western Bowl pottery has now been found at eight locations on Scilly; these locations are presented on a map (Griffith and Quinnell 1999, map 52 – the inclusion of Oliver's Battery on this map is erroneous). Robinson (2007, 65) reports South Western Bowl sherds from a midden on Annet, but these have not been seen by the author. Other, older, mistaken attributions, especially those in association with passage graves, have been now been refuted (Johns 2012).

The six radiocarbon dates from pits and post-holes with South Western Bowl pottery at Old Quay calibrate to c. 3350–2900 cal BC (see Section 3.9), a date range generally associated elsewhere with Middle Neolithic Peterborough Ware ceramics. No ceramics of Peterborough style have been identified from Scilly and there are no comparable radiocarbon dates from non-ceramic contexts within the Islands. On the Cornish mainland, sites with South Western/Hembury bowl pottery are not yet recorded with radiocarbon dates which extend later than the 34th century cal BC. A range of Cornish sites with pits have dates for which the later end of their calibration comes between 3400 and 3350 cal BC (Jones and Quinnell 2014, table 30), and this terminal date for the ceramic style is similar for tor and causewayed enclosures in Cornwall and Devon and sites with pits in Devon (Whittle et al. 2011, figure 10.27). Currently therefore in Cornwall and Devon there is no data indicating that South Western/Hembury bowl pottery continued beyond the 34th century cal BC. The site at Old Quay therefore represents a potentially interesting exception.

Middle Neolithic Peterborough pottery occurs in small quantities on sites in Devon, some with appropriate radiocarbon dates as at Hems Valley, Staverton (Quinnell 2014). Three sites with Peterborough Ware pottery, again in small quantities, have been recently identified in Cornwall but await analysis and radiocarbon dates. These are at Helston Travel Lodge (Hood 2009), Tregunnel Hill, Newquay (Quinnell 2016) and the Truro Eastern District Centre (S. Taylor in prep.). Currently it appears that few ceramics were used in the Middle Neolithic of Cornwall and Devon, especially in comparison with the amount of South Western/Hembury bowl pottery in use earlier. The most likely scenario on present data is that use of South Western/Hembury bowl pottery pottery declined for some reason after c. 3300 BC in the south-west peninsula, while potentially still being used in Scilly. This of course would imply a settled population on Scilly from a date within the Early Neolithic, but given the amount of land which would have been available at that date, this does not seem unlikely. It may seem unlikely that South Western/Hembury bowl pottery continued to be made on Scilly for several centuries after this ceased on the mainland, given the evidence from artefacts such as stone axes and the intervisibility between the Islands and the mainland. But it should be remembered that later, in the Bronze Age, a distinct Scillonian ceramic style developed in the Islands, contrasting in shape and decorative detail to the Trevisker ceramics of the mainland. By the Bronze Age it is widely presumed that a permanent population may have been established in Scilly (see Section 1.6). Any definite conclusions about the ceramic styles of Middle Neolithic Scilly and the mainland will however have to await further radiocarbon dates from sites yet to be discovered in both areas.

Bronze Age

Fabric 2. Twenty sherds (98g), all from trenches south of Trench 28. This fabric has high (70%) amounts of coarse beach sand, mostly under 2mm in size. It is well made and generally reduced.
Quartz – angular to sub-angular transparent to translucent grains up to 0.5mm, rarely 3.0mm; *muscovite* and *biotite* as cleavage flakes 0.2–0.3mm; *feldspar* – scatter of white angular to sub-angular grains up to 0.5mm; *tourmaline* – rare black angular grains 0.3mm: *matrix* – finely sandy silty clay with sparse well rounded polished quartz grains up to 0.3mm.

There are no pieces in Fabric 2 with diagnostic forms or decoration, but the fabric is generally similar to that used for Early to Middle Bronze Age assemblages in Scilly (Quinnell 1994, Section 12). Previously no pottery of this date has been identified from the Old Quay area of St Martin's (ibid).

Fabric 3. Twenty-seven sherds (141g), all from Trenches 31 and 32. This fabric has an abundant (up to 50%) amount of granite inclusions, fairly well made

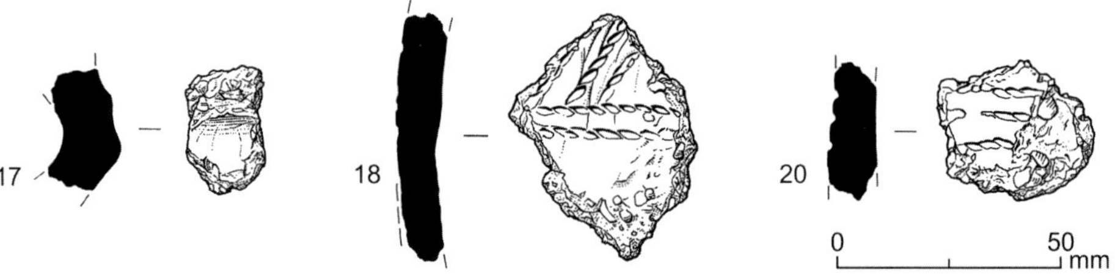

Figure 3.21. Bronze Age pottery (drawn by J. Read).

and generally reduced. A finely sandy micaceous fabric with large composite *quartz/biotite* grains and larger *quartz* grains up to 6mm. Disintegrated granite added to clay with very sparse polished *quartz* grains 0.4mm.

The addition of disintegrated, or sometimes crushed, granite has been found in other Scillonian Bronze Age assemblages, such as that from Dolphin Town, Tresco (Quinnell and Taylor in Taylor & Johns 2009/10). At Old Quay the fabric was used for P17–20 from F20 and F22 and the surrounding subsoil.

General comment

Internal residue on P18, a sherd with Trevisker affinities, produced a radiocarbon date of 1870–1630 cal BC, situating it firmly in the Early Bronze Age. Only a few pieces of Trevisker ware have been found on Scilly, all apparently in Island fabrics: from Porth Hellick Down 'Great Tomb', St Mary's (Hencken 1932, figure 9), from the settlement on Nornour (Butcher 1978, figure 34, no. 134) and possibly from the settlement at Porth Killier, St Agnes (Quinnell in Johns, Ratcliffe & Young in prep.). None of these other pieces has a firm associated radiocarbon date. That from Nornour comes from 'upper levels' (ibid., 69) and can not be closely associated with the only, unsatisfactorily wide, radiocarbon date indicating Early Bronze Age activity (ibid., 66); other dates and finds from the site and ceramic finds from this settlement indicate activity throughout the Bronze Age and beyond. Generally both burial and settlement sites in Scilly have a local ceramic style with decoration of parallel horizontal lines, incised or cord impressed, around the upper parts of vessels belonging to the earlier Bronze Age, replaced during the Middle Bronze Age by mainly plain vessels, some with incised horizontal lines. The excavated settlement at Little Bay on St Martin's (Neal 1983, 49) has these ceramics through a long period of time; the earliest of three radiocarbon dates from this site is c. 2130–1535 cal BC (HAR-4324; 3490 ± 100 BP) and so its date range overlaps with the dated EBA material from Old Quay. The range of dates from Knackyboy Cairn on St Martin's (Sawyer 2015, table 8.1) demonstrates a long sequence of local ceramics, again likely to have been in use contemporary with P18. The presence of P18 in an Island fabric at Old Quay arguably demonstrates some knowledge of contemporary mainland ceramic styles and their occasional copying, but not wholesale adoption, on Scilly.

3.5. Worked flint, chert and quartz

Martin Tingle and Hugo Anderson-Whymark

Introduction

The flint, chert and quartz assemblage from Old Quay – 10,901 pieces in total – was recovered over two seasons of excavation in 2013 and 2014 (Figures 3.22–3.28; Tables 3.07 and 3.13). The 2013 assemblage is composed of 5750 pieces from 34 trenches covering 170m^2 while the 2014 assemblage was composed of 5151 pieces from six trenches covering 130m^2 (Table 3.08). There is considerable variation in the distribution of material: Trench 11 produced only two finds while there were 563 from Trench 8. Most of the material was from the topsoil and buried subsoils, although there were 516 finds from 25 features. The largest trench (Trench 28) covered 119 square metres producing 1617 finds (15% of the entire assemblage) of which 413 pieces were recovered from 19 features.

The excavations produced an assemblage of 433 retouched tools of which 268 (62%) were scrapers; significantly, 80 (18%) were microliths. The microliths were were flake rather than blade based pieces of a type previously unknown in the UK but with clear parallels in northern France (see below). There is a probably substantial Neolithic element within the assemblage but with no clearly diagnostic pieces this is more difficult to characterise.

The worked flint assemblage was visually inspected and then sorted using the classifications outlined by Butler (2005). The finds were aggregated by context, and sorted by artefact type, with burnt or broken examples being recorded separately. Finds were also sorted by stone type. These were then counted and weighed. Tools were separated from flakes, blades and cores for more complete analysis. A detailed

Table 3.07. Catalogue of illustrated flint from Old Quay (Figs 3.22–3.25)

Illus. no.	*Object type*	*Context*	*Trench*	*Feature*
1	Core	98	22	–
2	Core	62	10	–
3	Core	165	34	–
4	Awl	119	27	–
5	Awl	14	4	–
6	Awl	162	26	–
7	Truncation	119	27	–
8	Truncation	24	7	–
9	Truncation	94	23	–
10	Truncation	23	1	–
11	Microburin	102	23	–
12	Serrated flake	199	28	–
13	Serrated blade	242	28	43
14	Serrated flake	119	27	–
15	Serrated blade	195	28	–
16	Serrated blade	242	28	43
17	Serrated flake	119	27	–
18	Serrated flake	211	28	33
19	Serrated flake	242	28	43
20	Scraper	210	28	33
21	Scraper	210	28	33
22	Scraper	210	28	33
23	Scraper	210	28	33
24	Scraper	217	28	33
25	Scraper	217	28	33
26	Scraper (silcrete)	183	17	–

Microliths are detailed separately in Table 3.13.

Table 3.08. Lithics densities by trench

Trench	*Area sq m*	*All lithic finds*	*Finds/m²*
1	4	198	49.5
2	4	165	41.25
3	4	285	71.25
4	4	19	4.75
5	4	6	1.5
6	4	4	1
7	4	245	61.25
8	9	563	62.5
9	4	43	1.75
10	4	110	27.5
11	4	2	0.5
12	4	17	4.25
13	4	35	8.75
14	6	63	15.75
15	4	35	8.75
16	4	17	4.25
17	4	55	13.75
18	4	68	17
19	20	116	5.8
20	4	37	9.25
21	4	355	88.75
22	4	313	78.25
23	4	612	153
24	4	103	25.75
25	4	136	34.1
26	4	273	68.25
27	6	523	87.16
29	4	136	34
30	4	69	17.25
31	4	140	35
32	6	122	20.3
33	4	36	9
34	4	238	59.5
28	119	3259	27.3
35	4	413	103.25
36	4	447	103.25
37	4	553	111.75
38	4	479	119.75
39	4	687	171.75

study was made of the finds from four contexts that made up pit F33 in which flakes were classified by their remaining dorsal cortex following Andrefsky (1998).

Raw materials

The solid geology of St Martin's, and the Isles of Scilly in general, is predominantly granite although there are small exposures of elvan (quartz porphyry) and phyllitic country rock. In addition, it has been noted since the mid-nineteenth century that the northernmost islands have glacial deposits, the dating and extent of which have been the subject of much debate and disagreement (Scourse 1986, 18–22).

It is currently suggested that deposits of glacial material dating from 21,000 BP, originating from the floor of the Irish Sea, are the likely source of extensive deposits of pebble flint found on numerous beaches of the archipelago (Johns 2012, 41). An additional source of flint could be submarine deposits of chalk in the English Channel which occur 50km to the south of the islands.

The Old Quay assemblage is predominantly composed of local material although there is a small element which appears to have been imported from the mainland (Table 3.09). In addition there are even smaller quantities of a dark chert and a dark flint with a coarse brown, unrolled cortex, the origins of which are unknown although it is assumed that they also derive from the glacial deposits.

Locally derived flint cobbles

Almost 98% of the Old Quay assemblage is composed of local beach flint and a flint conglomerate. It varies from pale brown to pale grey, is largely unpatinated and frequently displays the characteristic water rolled outer surface of a beach cobble. These are abundantly available on the beaches of the north and east coast of St Martin's, particularly on and around White Island and Great Bay.

Quartz

Quartz is an essential constituent of granite, and occurs throughout the Isles of Scilly. There are several examples of a milky quartz flakes and possible cores although no recognisable tools were identified.

Greensand chert

Greensand chert is found in archaeological assemblages throughout south-west England, but away from source areas usually in very small quantities. It is more often found within Mesolithic assemblages tending to become much less common on later sites. Like flint, it also occurs in marine deposits within the western approaches, but these are restricted to the sea-bed east of Plymouth (approximately 150km east of the Isles of Scilly). A recent examination of material from Sennan, Cornwall included several pieces of greensand chert with pebble cortex which it was suggested had derived from local beaches (Stewart 2012). If this is accepted then it is possible that similar deposits occur on the beaches of the Isles of Scilly. An alternative source for such material would be East Devon where the outcrops in the Axe valley and around Beer are known to have been subject to extensive prehistoric exploitation. This was the suggested source for two pieces found at Carn Brea (Saville in Mercer 1981, 109). Only 21 pieces were found at Old Quay (17 flakes and 4 retouched tools).

Non-local flint

Within Trench 28 there were 89 pieces of worked flint that appears to derive directly from chalk deposits, with a further 18 pieces from adjacent trenches 35–39. These are dark grey with occasional white speckling and, where present, this material has a rough pale brown cortex. Similar flint has been noted from sites in the east of Devon such as Hembury, Membury and Raddon and it closely resembles the 'non-beach flint' identified in the assemblage at Carn Brea

Table 3.09. Raw materials present at Old Quay

Raw Material	*Source*	*No OLQ13*	*%*	*No OLQ14*	*%*
Flint	Beach pebbles & cobbles, White Island, St Martins	5538	95.70	4964	94.45
Milky Quartz	as above	142	2.50	42	0.80
Flint Conglomerate	as above	33	0.60	9	0.15
Quartzite	as above	20	0.30	84	1.55
Other (granite, Sandstone)	as above	15	0.30	2	0.03
Black chert/flint	as above	6	0.10	8	0.10
Dark flint with rough brown cortex	Unknown glacial deposits	22	0.40	4	0.07
Black ?Portland type Chert	Dorset, Wiltshire or elsewhere	3	0.10	9	0.10
Greensand Chert	?East Devon	9	0.20	14	0.25
Chalk type flint	East Devon			108	2
Silcretes	East Devon			8	0.10
Total		5788		5252	

(Saville 1981, 107). Occasional examples of nodular flint have been noted before in Scillonian assemblages (Robinson 2007, 135). Nodular flint is known to derive from the East Devon coastal chalk at Beer and is also present within inland chalk deposits at Furley/Membury and Widworthy/Wilmington (Newberry 2002).

Portland-type chert

The distribution and use of Portland-type chert in locations away from its various sources is difficult to characterise from written reports since the stone is often mis-identified. At Carn Brea, 57 pieces of 'a dark grey/black probably Portland' chert were identified including a scraper, a piercer and six leaf-shaped arrowheads (Saville 1981, 109). Prior to 2012, the only find of Portland type chert on the Isles of Scilly recorded in the Cornwall HER was a single small core found on 'an exposed land surface' at The Brow, Bryer (SMR No. 7304 - MCO31553).

Portland-type chert in Cornwall is often stated to derive from locally sourced beach pebbles, because some worked pieces from prehistoric sites have been found to exhibit beach pebble cortex (Smith & Harris 1982, Berridge & Roberts 1986). It has been suggested that prior to the existence of the English Channel, chert from the Portland Beds could have been carried westwards by the Channel River and subsequently redeposited in Cornwall and therefore possibly also the Isles of Scilly (Stewart 2012). Given the limited extent of the Portland Beds and the course of the Channel River it is difficult to imagine this process could have transported significant amounts of the material to Cornwall, still less the 280km (in a direct line, 325km following the coast) from Portland to the Isles of Scilly. Once the English Channel came into existence, longshore drift would have been moving beach material in the opposite direction from west to east (Stewart 2012; Stewart in Jones et al. 2012).

Silcretes

Fifteen worked pieces have been identified as silcretes, a surface weathering deposit of lower Tertiary age associated with the flint gravels capping the hills around Sidmouth, East Devon. It forms by the movement of siliceous ground water in a similar way to sarsen. One of the silcrete pieces from F33, Trench 28 was sent for thin sectioning whereupon it was examined with a petrological microscope (×40–400). It was concluded that the source of this specimen was east Devon and that it had formed in a sub-aerial environment (Roger Taylor, pers. comm.).

The use of silcretes as a source for stone tool production is well attested in the southern hemisphere and has recently been reported in Scotland (Ballin & Faithfull 2014) but is previously unknown in south-west England. The small scale working of unusual stone types has been noted before in the south west, in excavations at Beer Head, where knapped glauconite sandstone flakes were found in a large pit associated with Beaker pottery (Tingle 1998, 76). The silcrete assemblage is predominantly composed of waste flakes and core fragments although it also includes a single, large, very finely made scraper (see Figure 3.25, No. 26).

Granites, sandstone and siltstone cobbles

Other stone types were utilised as tools without any form of working (e.g. hammerstones and elongated pebble tools) – these are examined in a separate report (Section 3.6).

Composition and technology

The assemblages from the two seasons of excavation were of a similar size but the excavations in 2013 were largely made up of a dispersed series of 2 × 2m test pits while the 2014 season was centred on a single large trench (Trench 28) and adjacent test pits. It is therefore unsurprising that the results from the two seasons while broadly comparable, included some significant differences. Reflecting these differences, the two assemblages are, where relevant, discussed separately below.

Cores

The 2013 excavations produced 192 cores, along with a further 25 tested nodules and seven split (Tables 3.10

Table 3.10. The lithic assemblage from Trenches 1–20

Category/Trench no.	*1*	*2*	*3*	*4*	*5*	*6*	*7*	*8*	*9*	*10*	*11*	*12*	*13*	*14*	*15*	*16*	*17*	*18*	*19*	*20*	*Total*
Flake	108	93	206	13	3	2	164	353	22	54	1	12	22	49	29	8	33	51	71	23	1316
Blade	1	4	5		1		1	4				1							1	1	19
Bladelet	13	8	11	1			14	30	4	5			2	3	2	1	3	2	5	3	107
Blade-like flake	1		17		1		4	6	1	2			3			1		1	3	1	41
Irregular waste	10	4	11	1	1	1	7	16	2	7		1	1			1	4		29	2	98
Chip	45	41	19				33	106	6	26				1			13	7	2	2	301
Crested blade							1	2	1			1					1				6
Rejuvenation flake tablet								1													1
Split pebble		1	1																		2
Tested nodule/bashed lump		2					1			1				1		1					6
Single platform flake core	5	4	5	1			5	8	2	2				3	1	3	1			1	41
Multiplatform flake core	1	1	4	1		1	3	8	2	2		1		1		1		1	1	1	29
Discoidal/Levallois flake core								1			1	1	1								4
Bipolar flake core								1		1			1						1		4
Core on a flake			1											1							2
Unclassifiable/fragmentary core	2							1		1					1						5
Micro-burin								1					1						1		3
Microlith	5	1	1				2	7		2			1		1			2			23
Truncated flake	1	1					1	2		1											6
End scraper	2	1	2	1			2	5	1	1			1	1	1					1	19
Side scraper		1					1							1							3
End and side scraper							1	2		1						1		2		1	8
Disc scraper	1	2					1		2	1			1	1							9
Thumbnail scraper							1	2		1				1							5
Scraper on a non-flake blank																		1			1
Awl				1						1											2
Piercer			1				1	2													4
Serrated blade/flake	1						1	2													4
Notch								1										1			2
Retouched flake	1		1				1			1			1						1	1	7
Polished axe								1													1
Hammerstone	1	1						1											1		4
Total	198	165	285	19	6	4	245	563	43	110	2	17	35	63	35	17	55	68	116	37	2083

Table 3.11. The lithic assemblage from Trenches 21–34 (2013)

Category/Trench no.	*21*	*22*	*23*	*24*	*25*	*26*	*27*	*28*	*29*	*30*	*31*	*32*	*33*	*34*	*Total*
Flake	178	225	364	80	88	198	356	377	97	45	97	88	28	207	2428
Blade	1	2	2	1	1	3	6	10		1	2	2	1		32
Bladelet	23	26	46	1	5	12	31	34	8	4	4	8	1	10	213
Blade-like flake	1	2	12	2	1	4	9	6	3	1	1	1		5	48
Irregular waste	15	11	16	7	6	12	20	35	17	8	13	2	1	5	168
Chip	107	17	121	5	15	29	31	85			17	12		2	441
Crested blade			5		2		2	1		1	1	1			13
Rejuvenation flake tablet			1					1							2
Split pebble		2	1		1		1								5
Single platform blade core	1		1	1		1	2								6
Tested nodule/bashed lump	2	2	6		1	1	1	4		1			1		19
Single platform flake core	4	1	7	3	1	3	8	9		1	1	2		2	42
Multiplatform flake core	3	1	6	2	1	3	9	8	1	1	2	3	3	1	44
Discoidal/Levallois flake core			1				1	3						1	6
Bipolar flake core		2						1	1						4
Core on a flake						1									1
Unclassifiable/fragmentary core			2				1						1		4
Micro-burin			1												1
Microlith	5	3	4		3	2	6	5	2			1		3	34
Truncated flake	1	3	3				2	2							11
End scraper	7	10	7	1	6	1	14	4	2	2	2	1			57
Side scraper	1	1					1	1							4
End and side scraper			2		2	1	3	6							14
Disc scraper	1				1		1								3
Long end scraper						1	1								2
Thumbnail scraper								6	1	1				1	9
Other scraper								1		1					2
Awl		2				1	5	2	1					1	12
Piercer		1					4	1		1					7
Spurred piece		1						1							2
Serrated blade/flake							4	1							5
Burin					1										1
Notch		1			1			2	2						6
Retouched flake	3		2				4	1	1						11
Fabricator										1					1
Misc. retouch												1			1
Hammerstone	2		2					4							8
Total	355	313	612	103	136	273	523	611	136	69	140	122	36	238	3667

and 3.11). This equates to one core for every 21 struck artefacts, excluding chips, indicating that flint knapping was taking place on site. The cores are predominately aimed at flake production, with only six (all single platform) orientated towards the production of blade and bladelets. The flake cores include broadly equal numbers of single- and multi-platform types (83 and 73 examples, respectively) and in many cases they were regularly worked. Ten cores result from discoidal reduction, including one example of Levallois style working; these cores appeared slightly fresher than the majority of the assemblage and could potentially date from the Later Neolithic. Eight bipolar cores were identified indicating that bipolar reduction formed a small, but significant, part of reduction strategies.

The 2014 excavations produced 50 cores along with six tested nodules and one split pebble with a ratio of 90 flakes to each core (Table 3.12). There were almost twice as many single platform cores as multi-platform examples (32 and 18 respectively). There were no examples of blade cores, bipolar cores or cores resulting from discoidal reduction.

Flakes

The 2013 assemblage was strongly orientated toward the production of small regular flakes. The flakes produced were typically of small proportions, but they vary in shape and thickness. Platform edge abrasion is present on a small proportion of the assemblage and a mixture of hard and soft hammer percussion was employed.

Blades and bladelets formed only 8.8% of the flake assemblage and notably 'blade-like flakes', which exhibit some traits of blades (e.g. parallel sides) but fail to achieve a 2:1 length to breath ratio, are present in very small numbers. This indicates that flake and blade/bladelet components

Table 3.12. Lithics from 2014 excavation - summary

Category	*Tr 28*	*Tr 35*	*Tr 36*	*Tr 37*	*Tr 38*	*Tr 39*	*Total*
Flake	2286	372	455	440	340	582	4475
Blade	14	2	4		1	5	26
Bladelet	6					3	9
Blade-like flake	8	12	5	3	4	12	44
Irregular waste		3	2	3		3	11
Chip	7	4	5		32	28	76
Crested blade							
Rejuvenation flake tablet	1			1			2
Split pebble	1						1
Single platform blade core							
Tested nodule/bashed lump	4		2				6
Single platform flake core	19	2	1	2	6	2	32
Multiplatform flake core	9			4	4	1	18
Discoidal/Levallois flake core							
Bipolar flake core							
Core on a flake							
Unclassifiable/fragmentary core	111	2	9	9	17	14	162
Burin			1			1	2
Microlith	12	2	4	3	1	6	28
Truncated flake							
End scraper	77	6	4	10	10	10	117
Side scraper	6						6
End and side scraper		1					1
Disc scraper					2		2
Long end scraper							
Thumbnail scraper					3		3
Other scraper	1			1			2
Awl	1				1		2
Piercer	4	1	2	1	1	1	10
Spurred piece							
Serrated blade/flake	5						5
Burin					1		1
Notch	1						1
Retouched flake/blade	9		3		2	2	16
Fabricator	1						1
Misc. retouch							
Hammerstone	1						1
Gun flint	1						1
Total	2585	407	497	477	425	670	5061

The total number of lithic finds from 2014 appear elsewhere in the report as 5151 pieces; this includes some unstratified material, natural pebbles and quartz pieces which are not included in this table.

of the assemblage represent distinct products, probably manufactured on separate cores, with distinctly different morphologies.

The blades/bladelets were typically of small proportions with the vast majority measuring 30–40mm in length and very few examples exceeding 50mm. Blade production appears to have been initiated by the removal of a unifacial crested blade, or very occasionally a bifacial crest. Nineteen crested blades were recorded in the assemblage with complete examples measuring between 23 and 46mm in length; these measurements provide an indication of the length of the core face when blade production was initiated and compare well with the size of the blades recovered. All blades appear to have been struck from single platform cores, probably using a soft hammer percussor. Core rejuvenation was infrequently practiced and only three core tablets are present in the assemblage; this probably reflects the limited size of the raw materials and its plentiful availability. Two blades were the product of bipolar percussion and one bipolar core exhibited unifacial crests, indicating that the bipolar technique produced blades and flakes.

The 2014 assemblage is also dominated by the production of small regular flakes although the proportion of blades and bladelets to intact flakes is much lower (1.2%). A small number of 'blade like flakes' are also present but there are no crested blades.

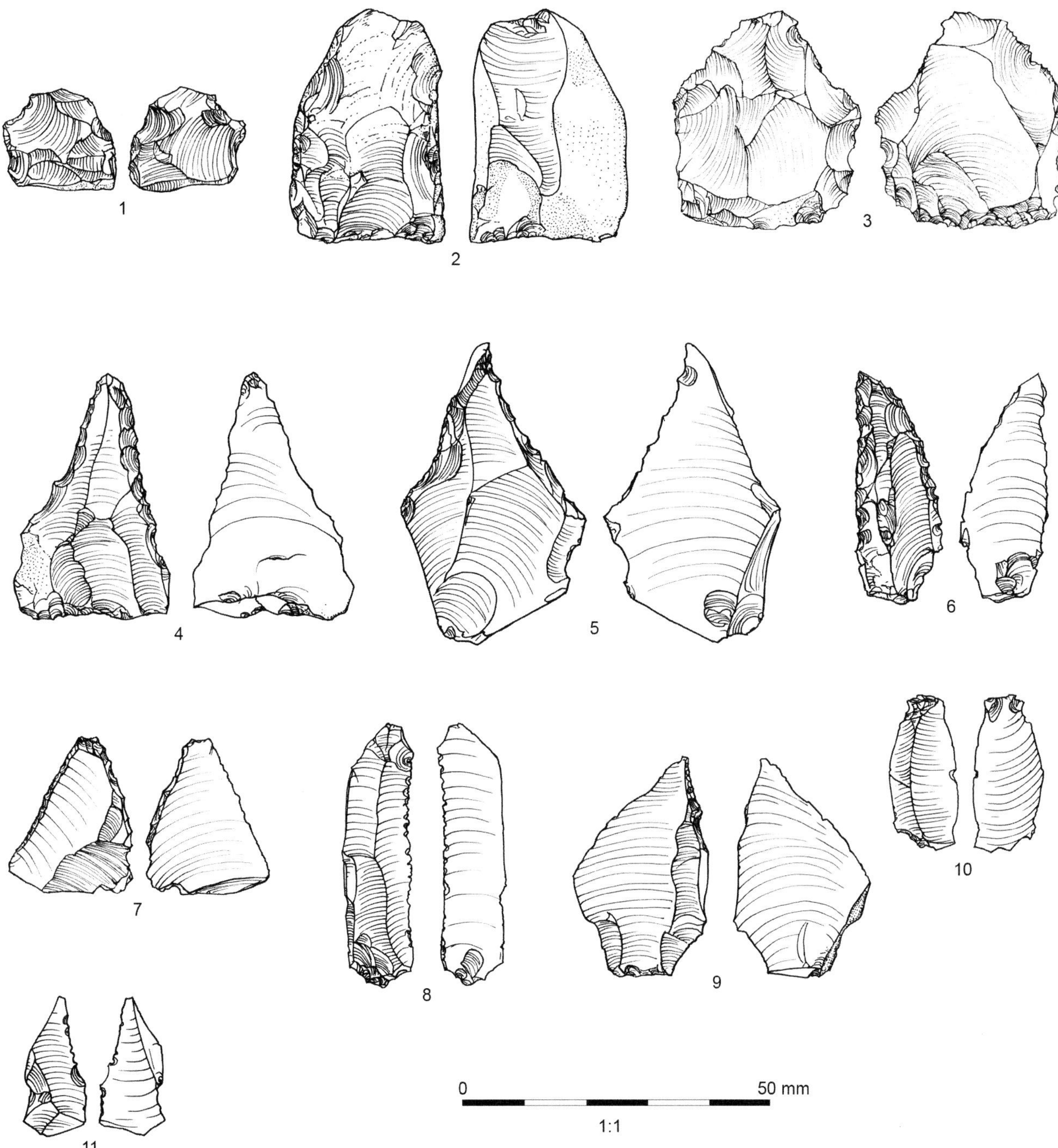

Figure 3.22. Flint cores, awls, truncations (drawn by S. Lambert-Gates).

Retouched tools

In total 477 retouched artefacts were recovered so that, excluding chips, retouched artefacts form 5.5% of the assemblage from 2013 and 2014. The assemblage is dominated by scrapers (268) and microliths (80). There are also piercing tools (34) and a range of other artefacts such as serrated flakes/blades (14), notched flakes (8), edge retouched flakes (34), two burins, two rod-shaped fabricators and a gun flint.

A wide variety of scraper forms are represented, but the majority are simply manufactured on flakes and cannot be dated with any degree of precision. Fourteen thumbnail forms were recovered, all of which exhibit regular pressure flaking; these are likely to date to the Early Bronze Age. Notably six of the thumbnail forms were recovered from Trench 28.

Piercing tools included 21 piercers and 13 awls, which are differentiated essentially by the greater prominence of

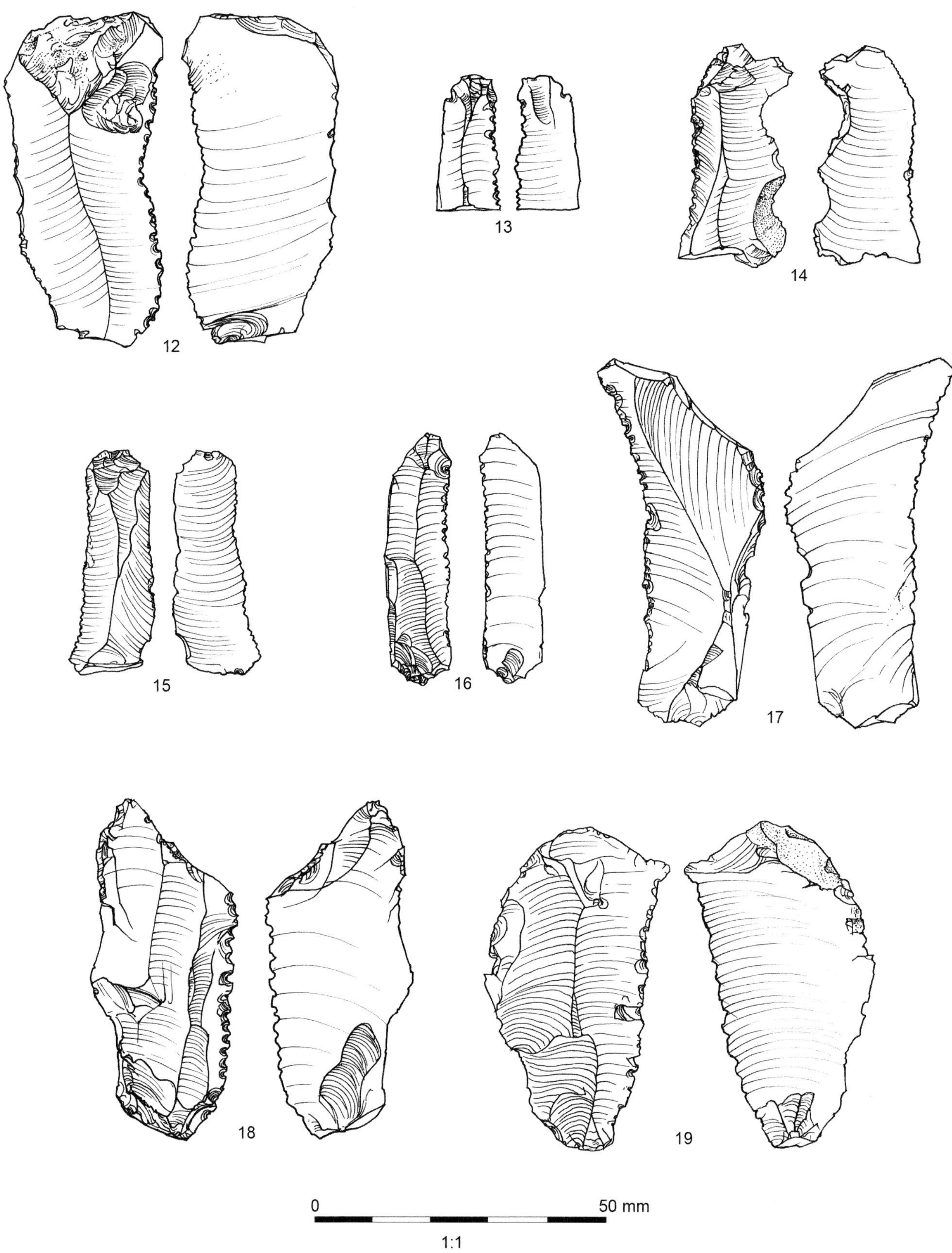

Figure 3.23. Flint serrated flakes (drawn by S. Lambert-Gates).

the working tip of the piercer compared to its abrupt retouch on an awl (Butler 2005, 53). The awls (mean weight 7.2g) are larger than the piercers (mean weight 4g), two of which weigh less than 1g. The awls have truncations between 20° and 45° forming robust points. None of these examples was from a feature fill but there is a distinct concentration in Trench 27 which produced 5 awls and 4 piercers, 26% of all piercing tools.

There are 13 serrated pieces: 5 flakes, 5 blades, 2 bladelets and 1 blade-like flake. One of the flakes is a fragment weighing 0.3g. Two of the blades, a bladelet and a flake exhibit wear gloss and all the serrated blades are more than 40mm in length. Only two of these pieces were found within feature fills, but notably they are serrated blades from the same feature (F43), a Neolithic pit/post-hole in which only four other pieces of worked flint were recovered. As with the piercing tools, the greatest number of serrated pieces was in Trench 27 which produced four (30%).

The 33 edge retouched tools are a miscellaneous collection in which the amount and the location of the retouch varies considerably. The mean weight is 8g but ranges from 24g to 0.5g. Some may be uncompleted tools or the fragmentary remains of damaged retouched tools that cannot be positively identified.

The notched flakes vary from a small fragment weighing 0.8g which may be an unsnapped micro burin notch, to a combined notch and piercing tool weighing 50g. The remainder are small notches on regular flakes and one example of a proximal notch on a blade-like flake.

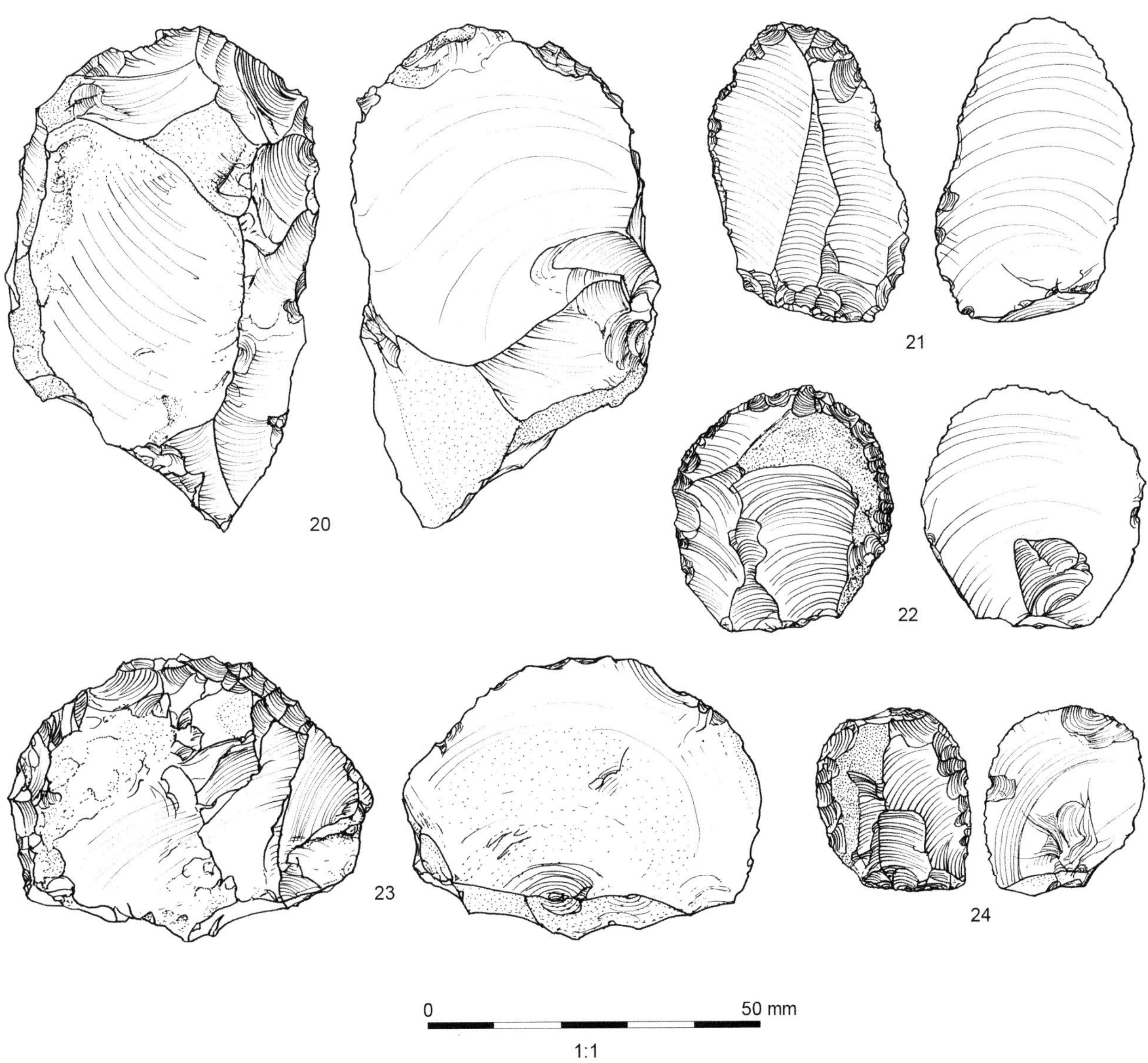

Figure 3.24. Flint scrapers (1) (drawn by S. Lambert-Gates).

Both of the two fabricators are rod shaped and have been reworked at one end. The example from Trench 28 is made from nodular flint and retains a small patch of coarse brown cortex.

There are two burins. One from Trench 25 resembles a microlith as it has a proximal and distal truncation with a removal from the side of the flake. The other, from Trench 38, has a single removal from a blade-like flake.

It is noteworthy that no arrowheads were recovered during the excavations, although a delicate barbed and tanged arrowhead was previously found in the southern field (Steve Walder pers. comm.).

Microliths

Eighty microliths are present in the lithic assemblage from Old Quay: seventy-one are classifiable forms, three fragments are tentatively classified and six small fragments are unclassifiable (Table 3.13; Figures 3.26–3.28). The classifiable microliths are not typical of the British Mesolithic and parallels have been sought in continental European assemblages (see also Anderson-Whymark et al. 2015). Given the similarities they share with the latter, for the sake of clarity we use continental European technological terminology in describing them. The 74 identifiable microliths can generically be termed *trapèze asymmétric* (asymmetric trapezoids or rhomboids in English terminology), but subtle variations in the angle of the small truncation (*petite troncature*) allow 67 artefacts to be classed as *trapèze à base décalée* (trapezoids with an offset base), and seven artefacts, which exhibit low angle truncations accounting for less than one-sixth of the artefact's length, are classed as *trapèze rectangle court*

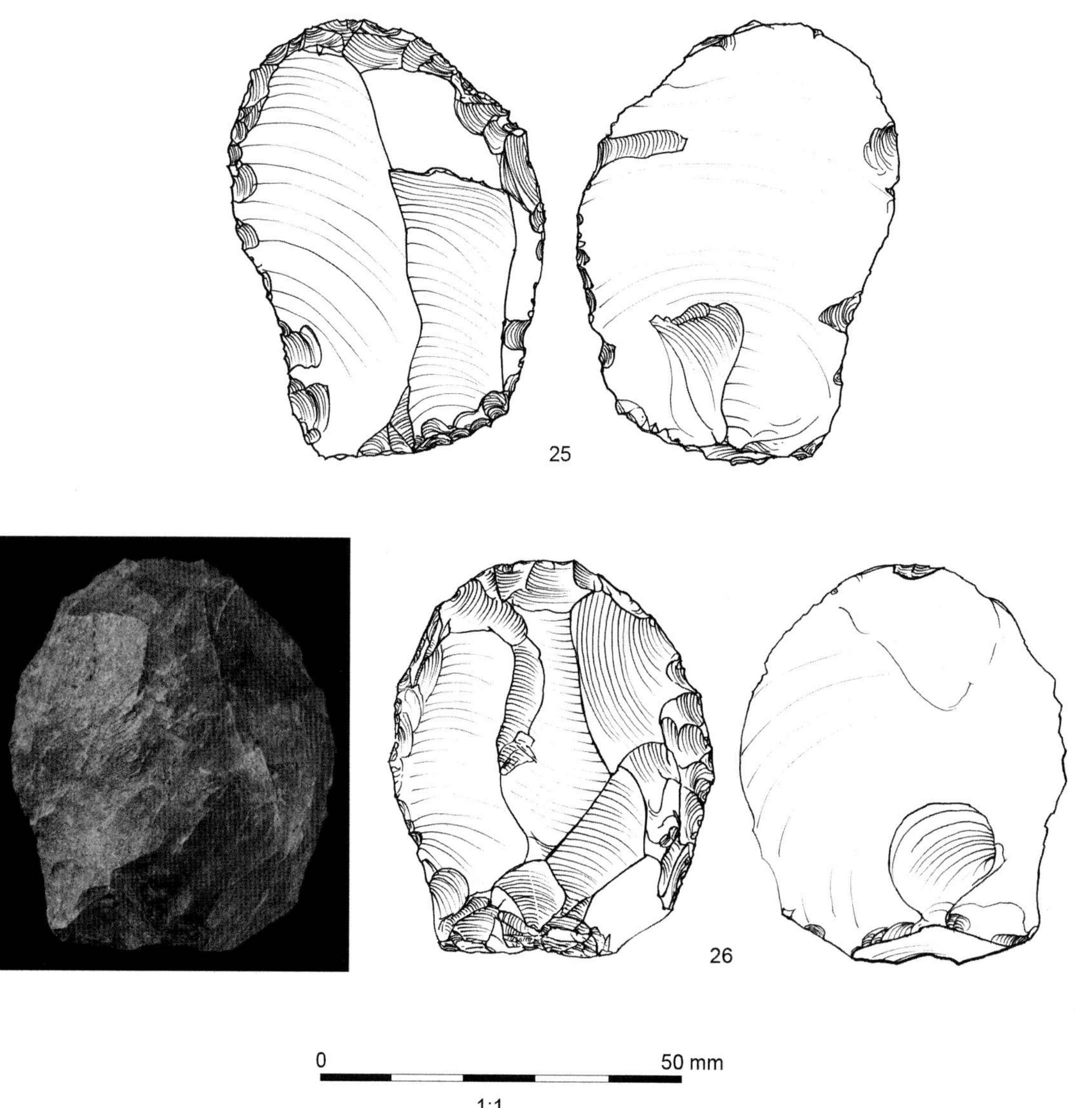

Figure 3.25. Flint scrapers (2) (drawn by S. Lambert-Gates).

(trapezoids with a 'short rectangle') (see Barrière et al. 1969 for definitions). These divisions are, however, rather arbitrary and it is preferable to consider all of the microliths from Old Quay as ultimately belonging to the same form. The four previously illustrated microliths from Old Quay (Ratcliffe & Thorpe 1991, 24; Dennis et al. 2013, 16) are all classifiable as *trapèze à base décalée*. In addition to the true microliths, four truncated flakes are of a comparable morphology although they lack retouch on their *petite troncature* and retain a proximal or distal end (SF 1, 29, 31 and 32).

Sixteen microliths were manufactured transversely (SF 13, 15, 21, 30, 34, 42, 45, 50, 52, 66, 71–3, 76 and 83–4) with a distal edge instead of a side forming the *grande base*. The overall form of the transverse microliths is, however, identical to those manufactured longitudinally and in this assemblage transverse production appears to be an idiosyncrasy resulting from microlith production on flake blanks rather than a distinct production strategy. As such transverse forms are considered within *trapèze à base décalée* and *trapèze rectangle court* classifications.

Table 3.13. The microliths – summary

Illus. no.	*Trench*	*Context*	*SF no.*
Trapèze à base décalée			
1	7	30	33
2	8	33	35
3	22	100	36
4	23	102	37
5	25	130	39
6	27	119	40
7	27	119	41
8	8	32	46
9	28	195	77
10	37	183	78
11	37	183	79
12	21	95	25
13	36	193	63
14	39	236	69
15	39	236	68
16	8	32	2
17	8	47	3
18	10	63	4
19	21	96	6
20	23	94	7
21	27	119	11
22	28	151	12
23	28	246	65
24	38	238	67
25	35	191	70
26	1	23	43
27	28	151	44
28	3	50	53
29	36	193	80
30	8	33	9
31	25	130	10
32	8	32	26
33	18	80	27
34	26	161	28
35	28	199	62
36	28	190	81
37	39	236	82
38	23	102	14
39	29	123	16
40	36	193	75
41	22	100	51
42	28	149	22
43	34	164	23
44	13	64	49
45	2	19	24
46	7	30	17
47	27	118	18
48	27	119	19
49	34	164	20
50	39	236	74
Trapèze à base décalée (transverse)			
51	8	33	34
52	29	123	42
53	34	165	45
54	37	183	66
55	39	236	76
56	35	189	71
57	1	28	13
58	28	150	15
59	28	190	83
60	28	190	84
61	27	119	52
62	18	80	21
63	26	162	50
64	39	236	72
Trapèze à base décalée?			
65	21	95	5
66	10	61	54
67	23	102	55
Trapèze rectangle court			
68	25	129	38
69	32	152	8
70	28	190	64
71	8	33	47
72	21	96	48
Trapèze rectangle court (transverse)			
73	21	95	30
74	36	193	73
Unclassified			
75	1	23	56
76	1	28	57
77	1	28	58
78	15	55	59
79	22	100	60
80	28	151	61

Figure 3.26. Flint microliths (1) (drawn by S. Lambert-Gates).

Figure 3.27. Flint microliths (2) (drawn by S. Lambert-Gates).

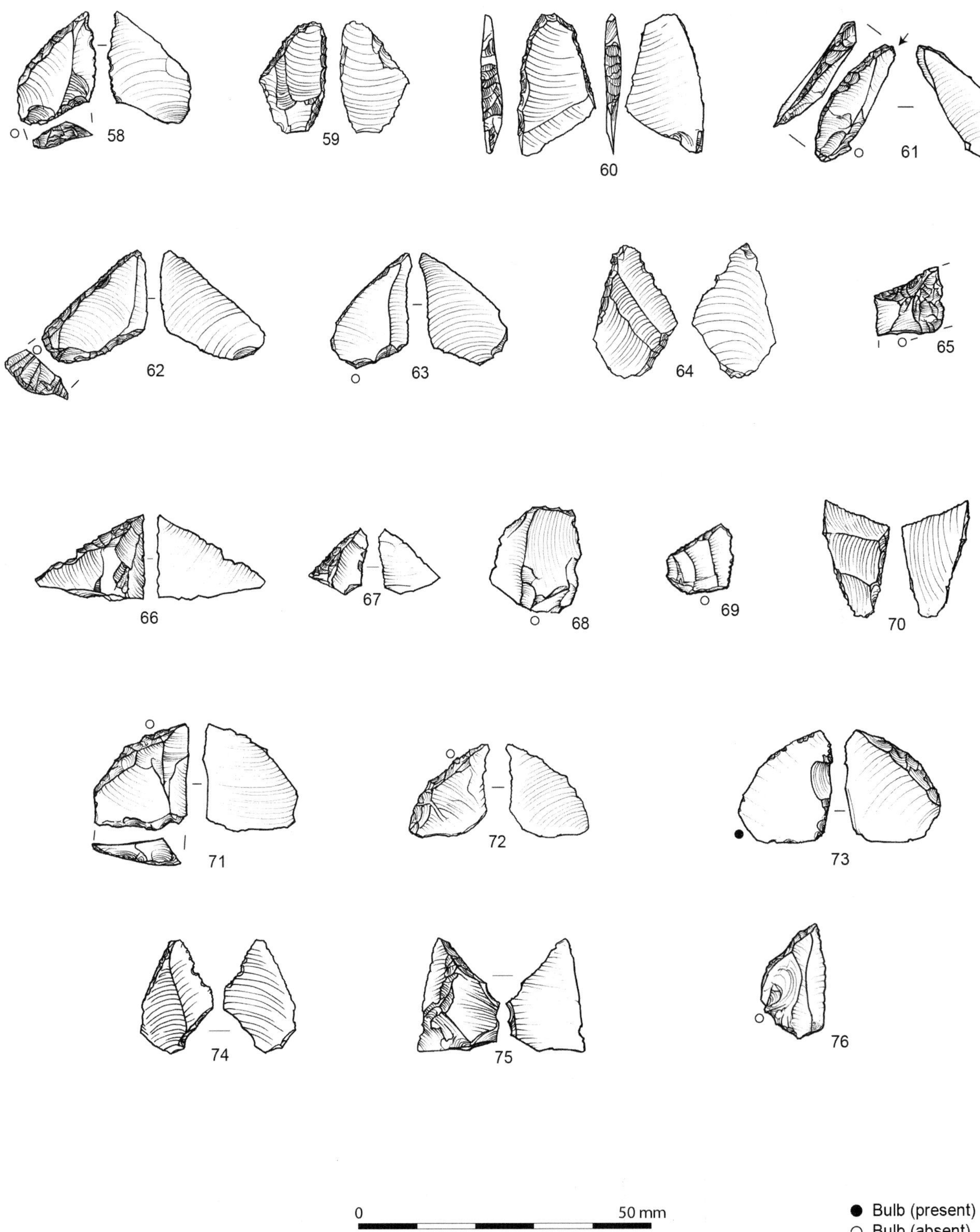

Figure 3.28. Flint microliths (3) (drawn by S. Lambert-Gates).

Twenty-eight microliths exhibit additional retouch on the shortest side (*petite base*) and these can be divided into three variations:

Variation 'A': *trapèze à base décalée* or *trapèze rectangle court* with straight retouch on the dorsal surface of the '*petite base*'. The angle at which the retouch on the *petite base* meets the retouch on the *petite troncature* is variable (SF 13–16, 30, 47–8, 71 and 81–2).
Variation 'B': As Variation 'A', but the retouch on the '*petite base*' is convex, forming a regular curve from the *grande* to *petite troncature* (SF 21–23, 51–2, 75 and 83–4).
Variation 'C': As Variation 'A', but the retouch on the '*petite base*' is on the ventral surface. In all cases this retouch is slight and cannot be classified as *retouch inverse plate* (SF 17–20, 24, 49, 50 and 72–4).

Variations in other characteristics may also be of typological significance; for example, the longest truncation (*grande troncature*) on 40 microliths is straight, while this retouch is convex on 31 examples. Similarly, the retouch on the small truncation (*petite troncature*) is straight on 66 microliths, but concave on five examples. The microliths at Old Quay are also predominately lateralized to the left (i.e. the *grand base* is on the right hand side when viewed from the ventral face with the *petite troncature* towards the bottom) (60 examples: 84.5%), rather than the right (11 examples: 15.5%).

The microliths provide some insight into the methods of their manufacture at Old Quay. One of the most striking idiosyncrasies of this assemblage is the use of flake blanks for the majority of the microliths. Only two microliths were definitively manufactured on blade blanks, although three further examples were probably manufactured from blades; the other 71 microliths were manufactured on small regular flakes. Notably, the Old Quay assemblage also provides very limited evidence for the use of the micro-burin technique for microlith production, with only seven artefacts exhibiting *piquant triédre* (the relic trace of a micro-burin notch). On the vast majority of microliths it was apparent that truncations were formed by simply retouching the flake edge, although in three cases retouch was applied to fragments of snapped or broken flakes. Again, this probably reflects the use of flake blanks that are not easily segmented using the micro-burin technique.

The dimensions of the 51 complete microliths can be summarised as:

Length: ranges between 10.9mm and 23.5mm; average 17.3mm (SD 2.3mm)
Breadth: ranges between 8.8mm and 21mm; average 15.1mm (SD 2.6mm)
Thickness: ranges between 1.6mm and 5.3mm; average 3.0mm (SD 0.8mm)

Overall, the microliths are typically slightly longer than they are broad, with length/breath indexes between 0.71 and 2.61, with and averages of 1.18 (SD 0.29). Notably only one microlith exceeded 2:1 length to breath ratio (No. 46) and only ten were below a 1:1 length to breath ratio (SF 2, 13, 18, 19, 24, 30, 33, 64, 66 and 84).

USE AND HAFTING DAMAGE

A high proportion of the microliths are broken (28: 35%), with damage concentrated on the leading tip and *petite base*. Eleven *trapèze à base décalée* (of 71 classifiable microliths: 15.5%) exhibit damage to the point formed between *grand troncature* and *grand base* (excluding breaks resulting from burning). In the majority of cases this point exhibits a flexion fracture, but in three cases the breaks are burin-type fractures initiated by impact to the tip: in two cases the spall has detached along the *grand troncature* (SF 2 and 84) while the other removed the *grand base* (No. 52). The pattern of damage to the tip supports suggestions that these microliths may have been mounted as armatures. The high incidence of breakage, including many snaps to the petite base, may result from hafting. It may also be of significance that a high proportion of microliths are burnt (10: 12.5%). This may relate to the loss of armatures within an animal's flesh that was subsequently cooked.

Distribution

In total 10,901 pieces of worked stone were recovered from the two seasons of excavations, 95% of which derived from topsoil or subsoil deposits. The overall density of finds by weight per metre square excavated shows two concentrations, one in the south of the investigated area adjacent to Old Quay itself and another in the north immediately south of Trench 28 (see also Section 3.3 and Figure 3.08). Broadly similar distributions appear when cores, microliths and truncated flakes are plotted while scrapers are more numerous within the northern concentration and burnt worked flint more common in the southernmost. The remaining stratified material was made up of 516 pieces (3858g) from 34 contexts within 25 features. One feature (F33), a large pit, produced 268 finds from four separate contexts, representing 52% of all stratified finds.

Large Pit F33

F33 is a large, somewhat irregular feature that fell only partially within Trench 28 (see Figures 3.10 and 3.11). It contained four fills [209, 210, 211 and 217]; the lower layers [211 and 217] seemed to be associated with burning. In contrast only five of the pieces of worked flint in F33 are burnt, four of which came from the upper fill [209]. Other notable finds from this feature are almost 600 sherds of Neolithic pottery and a pebble with an hourglass perforation in [210]. Since F33 produced the single largest stratified

Table 3.14. Lithics from large pit F33

	209		*210*		*211*		*217*		*232*	
	No.	*Weight (g)*	*No.*	*Weight (g)*	*No.*	*Weight (g)*	*No.*	*Weight (g)*	*No.*	*Weight (g)*
Primary Flake	3	17	3	4						
Secondary Flake			4	28	2	88	1	2		
Tertiary Flake	25	324	24	262	9	76	4	30	1	4
Non Cortex Flake	37	66	32	124	10	58	1	10		
Broken Flake	37	59	39	52	3	2				
Blade	2	5	1	1						
Burnt Flake	4	4							1	4
Single Plat Flake Core			4	133						
Core Fragment			1	12					1	15
End Scraper	4	76.5	4	145.5	4	110.5	2	47.5		
Serrated Flake					1	10				
Quartz			1	1						
Total	111	551.5	86	761.5	29	344.5	8	89.5	3	24

Following Andrefsky (1998, 104) dorsal cortex is divided into four categories: primary flake refers to those with cortex covering 100% of the dorsal face; secondary flakes have cortex on 50–99% of the dorsal face; tertiary flakes have cortex on 1–49% of the dorsal face; flakes with no dorsal cortex are referred to as non-cortical.

assemblage within a single feature, as well as material suitable for radiocarbon dating, finds from the four contexts were examined in extra detail.

Material from this feature reveals evidence for the reduction of several different stone types using a variety of techniques (Table 3.14). The tertiary flakes from [209] and [210] include two large pieces of flint conglomerate, the example from [209] weighing 117g (L = 94mm, W = 69mm) while that from [210] weighs 119g (L = 69mm W = 94mm). Clearly these derive from very large beach cobbles. In contrast there are two very small single-platform flake cores from [210] weighing 35g and 36g which exhibit simple but slightly different reduction strategies. One reveals basic flake removal without any form of core preparation. The second shows attempts to prepare a platform by detaching a large primary flake, after which smaller primary and secondary flakes are then struck at right angles to the initial removal. Thereafter flakes can be removed from the single platform but the original pebble is so small that it seems to be rapidly exhausted. A single much larger primary flake from [210] is evidence that the latter strategy may have been practiced on larger pebbles.

Two other single platform flake cores weighing 35g and 20g seem to be discarded remnants of worked out nodules but they retain sufficient of their original outer cortex, with its characteristic horn like projections, to identify them as originally chalk derived. There is also a single silcrete, non cortical flake in [210].

The tools from pit F33 are 11 complete scrapers, three broken scrapers and a serrated flake. Those from the upper fill [209] are three broken end scraper tips and a large scraper-like tool that is probably made on an unflaked piece of flint. The remaining scrapers are all intact but vary considerably in size and regularity of retouching. There are single examples of scrapers made from unflaked pebbles in both [210] and [211]. The finely made serrated flake is from [211].

Dating

The Old Quay assemblage is composed of 10,901 pieces of which 516 (4.7%) are from stratified contexts radiocarbon dated primarily to the Middle Neolithic. Two of these were from contexts [211] and [217], two of the four constituent contexts of pit F33. In addition there were a blade, a flake and a multi-platform flake core from pit F16, a bladelet and seven flakes from pit F23 and seven flakes, two single platform flake cores and a retouched flake from pit F56. The remaining dated assemblage was from post-hole F69, composed of seven chips, six flakes, an end scraper, a retouched flake, a fragmentary core and a split pebble. Two flakes were found in pit F22, which produced an EBA date associated with finds of EBA pottery.

The continental European-style microlith forms found at Old Quay can be paralleled with examples found in north-east France, Belgium and the Netherlands, during the Late and Final Mesolithic, c. 7th–5th millennia BC. Given that the Old Quay microliths have a length-breadth ratio of <1, are produced on flakes rather than blades and lack flat ventral retouch, it is perhaps most likely that they date to the 5th rather than the 7th or 6th millennium BC (Philippe Crombé pers. comm.), although it is impossible to say for sure. It is also important to point out that the continental comparators are not yet independently well-dated themselves (Crombé et al. 2009; Ducrocq 2009).

Many of the features excavated at Old Quay contained clearly Neolithic pottery (see Section 3.4) and thus it is reasonable to assume that the vast majority of features were of that date. However, dating the non-feature derived assemblage is problematic in that it probably represents at least three distinct phases of activity (Mesolithic, Middle Neolithic and EBA), the relative scales of which are unknown (see also Section 3.3).

Conventionally, in order to approach an understanding of chronology, the proportion of blades and/or narrow flakes within the overall flake assemblage could be considered together with the presence of certain chronologically significant artefacts, notably microliths and arrowheads. Mesolithic and Early/Middle Neolithic assemblages are often composed of a significant proportion of blades. However in the Old Quay assemblage, blades make up only 0.9% of the combined flake assemblage. Even if bladelets and blade-like flakes are included, the total rises only to 6%, although it is clear that the blade/bladelet-like component is greater in the 2013 assemblage (11%) compared to that of 2014 (1.7%). It would therefore seem that the 2014 excavations, centred in and around Trench 28, produced an assemblage with relatively few narrow flakes.

The dearth of blades in the assemblage results in part from the production of flake-based microliths, a reason why it is so difficult to determine the proportion of Mesolithic from later material. Another element could be the association of blades with mobility and the requirement to conserve raw materials (Bradley & Edmonds 1993, 185). Terrestrial mobility is obviously restricted on the Isles of Scilly while the abundant supplies of beach flint were always easily obtained.

The Mesolithic is most obviously represented by the 80 microliths and truncated flakes, but there are no clearly diagnostic Early/Middle Neolithic flint artefacts. No arrowheads were recovered and although serrated flakes are commonly associated with this period they do still occur in the later Neolithic, if relatively infrequently. There may also be an Early Bronze Age element within the assemblage to accompany the Trevisker style pottery, as evidenced by the thumbnail scrapers and the barbed and tanged arrowhead found previously (see above).

While it is impossible to determine how much of the unstratified material dates from the Mesolithic and how much from the Early/Middle Neolithic, it is possible to gauge the amount of residual Mesolithic material that occurs in Early Neolithic features. Of the 80 microliths only two are from within later stratified contexts. These are from F2, a possible Bronze Age ditch, and F45, a Neolithic post-hole.

A comparable site to Old Quay on the mainland is Poldowrian on the south coast of the Lizard peninsula, Cornwall, which had been first located by a combination of ad hoc and then gridded surface collection (Smith & Harris 1980). Subsequent excavation of the site produced an assemblage of 51,526 pieces of Mesolithic and Early Neolithic flint with a small element of Bronze Age pottery, most of which was unstratified although three small pits were revealed. Unlike Old Quay, of the 308 classifiable microliths recovered, 111 were lanceolate points, 104 convex backed points and 42 scalene triangles in addition to which there were 483 microlith fragments and 923 pieces of 'microlith by products'. Although the datable finds were overwhelmingly from the Mesolithic, the report could see no possibility of separating Mesolithic from Early Neolithic material.

Discussion

Previous Scillonian excavations have produced relatively small amounts of worked flint, chert and quartz. Fieldwork at Halangy Down between 1964 and 1977 produced an assemblage of 143 pieces and at Nournour, between 1969 and 1973, 275 pieces were found (Miles 1978). In addition, there have been other finds resulting from development led archaeology such as the Off-islands Electrification Project, the trenching for which produced over 2000 pieces of worked flint (Ratcliffe & Thorpe 1991). Thus the 10,901 pieces from the Old Quay site is by far the largest assemblage recovered to date on the Isles of Scilly.

Prior to these excavations the evidence for Mesolithic artefacts on the Isles of Scilly was restricted to a small number of individual and often unprovenanced finds (Section 1.6; Anderson-Whymark et al. 2015). Stray finds such as these indicated that the most promising of these various locations was the site at Old Quay; previous fieldwork had produced a number of microliths from the cliff area (Dennis et al. 2013; Anderson-Whymark et al. 2015).

Almost all of the worked stone from the current excavations was locally sourced, but that which appears to be imported from the mainland though small in number, remains significant. As has been observed in the context of maritime western Scotland, the occurrence of raw materials away from their source is the clearest indication of regular and extensive Mesolithic sea travel (Thomas 2013, 210). The link between the Isles of Scilly, the mainland and beyond is further attested by the assemblage of microliths (see also Section 3.10).

The specific rhombic/trapezoidal form of the microliths from Old Quay cannot be paralleled in any other Mesolithic assemblage from Britain or Ireland. While rhomboid/bi-truncated (as they would be termed in Britain) points are occasionally found in British assemblages, these bear very little resemblance to those found either at Old Quay or on the continent. Trapezoidal microliths of similar forms are, however, a common feature of Mesolithic assemblages across continental Europe, from the Black Sea to France and Belgium. As discussed in further detail below, the closest parallels for those from Old Quay come from north of the River Seine in France, Belgium, the Netherlands and Denmark.

In the Somme Basin, Belgium and the southern Netherlands, many sites have yielded microlith forms that can be paralleled at Old Quay (Ducrocq 2001, 46–51, 59–63, 88–94, 151–155; Robinson et al. 2011; 2013). Indeed, the additional retouch on the ventral surface of the *petite base* of the *trapèze à base décalée* and *trapèze rectangle court* at Old Quay (retouch variants A and B) make these forms comparable to *Flèche de Dreuil* (Ducrocq 1998). Morphological differences in the angle of the *petite base* and the presence of straight truncations on the *grande troncature* on the Old Quay microliths are, however, discernible.

Two other potentially significant differences between the Old Quay assemblage and those known from continental Europe should also be noted. First, the presence of flat invasive retouch on the ventral surface (*inverse retouch plate*) of trapezoidal microlith forms has recently been identified as a significant feature of Late–Final Mesolithic assemblages (Rozoy 1991; Robinson et al. 2011). The retouch on the ventral surface of seven *trapèze à base décalée* from Old Quay (retouch variation C) cannot be classed as *inverse retouch plate* as it is comparatively slight, rather than invasive, but the presence of this retouch may still be of chronological significance. It may also be of significance that the inverse retouch on the microliths at Old Quay is present on the *petite base* rather than the *petite troncature*, as is more common in the continental assemblages. The presence of additional dorsal retouch on the shortest side (*petite base*) is another difference: continental *Flèche de Dreuil* do not display a *petite base*, since it has been removed by retouching the *grande troncature* so that it intersects with the *petite troncature*. It could be argued that the examples from Old Quay should perhaps be seen as transverse arrowheads rather than real *trapèzes*, because the length–width ratio is <1.

The lateralisation of the microliths is also potentially of great significance when considering source areas. At Old Quay the microliths are predominantly (84.5%) lateralised to the left (i.e. the *grand base* is on the right hand side when viewed from the ventral face with the *petite troncature* towards the bottom), while the microliths from the Somme Valley are almost exclusively lateralized to the right. However, in the Rhine-Meuse-Scheldt region, a recent study revealed that a small but significant proportion (12%) of microlith *armatures* are lateralised to the left in the same fashion as those from Old Quay. The presence of left lateralisation in these assemblages may potentially indicate that the influence for the Old Quay microliths comes not from the Somme Basin, but the Rhine-Meuse-Scheldt region some 700km east of the Isles of Scilly (Robinson 2008; Robinson et al. 2013). This picture is, however, far from straightforward as other artefacts commonly associated with Late Mesolithic trapezes north of the Seine, such as Montbani blades or bladelets, are not present in the Old Quay assemblage.

The broader implications of this highly unusual Mesolithic assemblage are discussed in further detail within Section 3.10.

3.6. Worked stone

Henrietta Quinnell, with petrographic identification and comment by Roger Taylor

The worked stone from Old Quay can be divided into a number of artefact types, described in turn below (Figures 3.29–3.33).

Axes and artefacts with perforations

S1. Shafthole adze, [203] fill post-hole F29 Tr 28, 140 × 84 × 41mm, 760g (Figs 3.29 and 3.30). The shape, with one end narrower than the other, conforms to Roe's 'narrow butt' type (Roe 1979, 36). Surface apparently originally ground but now almost entirely eroded, hour glass perforation comparatively unweathered. Heavily weathered gabbroic greenstone with a coarse texture, amphibole elements up to 6mm. Not obviously from West Cornwall, possible sources further to the east in the south-west peninsula, or in Brittany. Absence of foliation also points to a source beyond west Cornwall. Dating for shafthole adzes is uncertain, given that their 'associations … are less than conclusive' (ibid.) and they could potentially be Neolithic or Early Bronze Age in date.

S2. Blade end of greenstone axe, good surface polish still surviving, [193], cleaning of [186] 'midden', Tr 36, 68+ × 75 × 36mm, 250g (Fig. 3.31). Weathered gabbroic greenstone, with amphibole clusters <3mm, within the Mount's Bay, Cornwall range of outcrops and Group 1 material: recent work on sourcing indicates that material

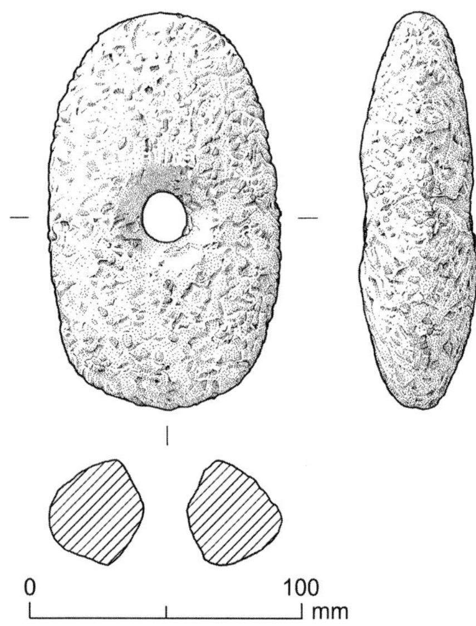

Figure 3.29. Stone adze (drawn by J. Read).

Figure 3.30. Worked and utilised stone (1) (photo: S. Lambert-Gates).

from a number of sources was used and that much of this may have been cobbles pecked into shape (Jones et al. 2013). Group 1 was used throughout the Neolithic (Davis et al. 1988, 16).

S3. Pebble with oblique hourglass perforation but no other modification, [210] fill F33, large pit, Tr 28, 66 × 38 × 17mm, 47g (Fig. 3.31). Some damage, caused during excavation (it was found during section cleaning with a spade). Hard siliceous siltstone, probably an erratic sourced from a local beach; varying iron content causes the banded appearance. It is unclear whether it should be described as a pebble hammer following Roe's 1979 definition, given its narrow and oblique perforation, its flat sub-rectangular shape and its size at the smallest end of the pebble hammer range. It could alternatively be regarded as a possible amulet. It was possibly chosen for its attractive banded colour (predominantly 5YR 4/4 reddish brown).

Comment

The records of and literature on finds of axes and related artefacts from Scilly are somewhat confused (see Hencken 1932, 8; Ashbee 1974, 236). Ransom (1993) provides illustrations of perforated items in an unpublished thesis. Two stone axes are included in the list published by Clough and Cummins (1988, 144–8), CO85 of greenstone from

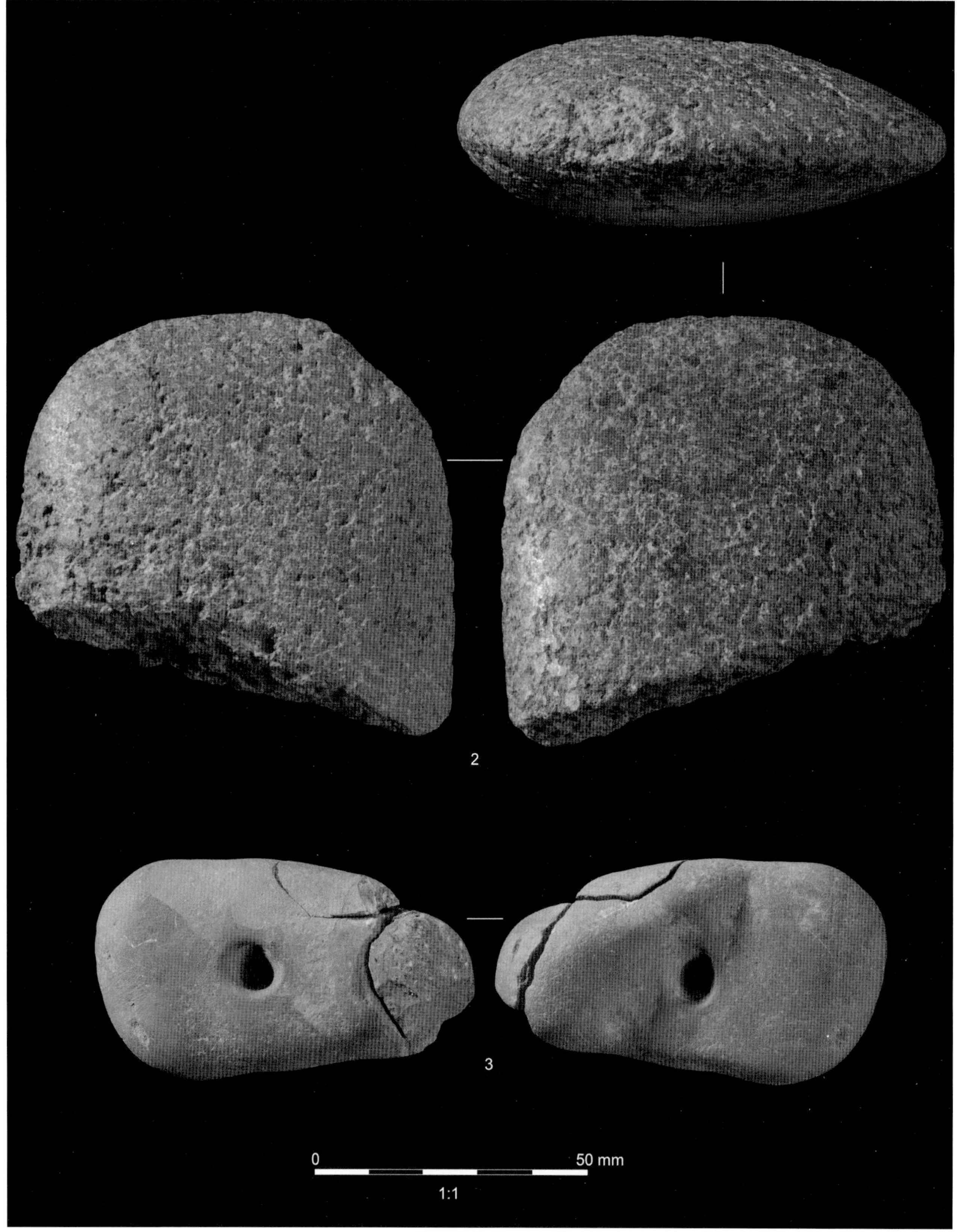

Figure 3.31. Worked and utilised stone (2) (photo: S. Lambert-Gates).

Gugh and CO 222 of altered slate from Peninnis Head, St Mary's, and are likely to be imports from the mainland. The axe fragment S2 is only the second artefact of Group 1 greenstone from Scilly, the other being a stone ball from the settlement at Nornour (Clough and Cummins 1988, 281): Nornour is only 2km east of Old Quay and would have been joined to St Martin's during the Neolithic. Two other greenstone axes in the Isles of Scilly Museum have been found by holiday makers and await petrological examination and publication: one is complete from Halangy Porth, St Mary's, found 1979 and one fragmentary from Pelistry Lane, St Mary's found 2014.

Part of an implement described as a shafthole adze, CO418 of decomposed dolerite (Clough & Cummins 1988, 148), was found in a fissure probably with a Bronze Age vessel at English Island Carn on St Martin's (Ransom 1993, no. 33; Robinson 2007, figure 5.7 no. 1, figure 8.1); however this had a cylindrical perforation and might be regarded as an axe hammer. The information on its context provided by Ransom and Robinson derives from notes in the Royal Cornwall Museum, Truro. It is likely to have come from the mainland. Part of a battle axe from Normandy Farm, St Mary's (Robinson 2007, figure 5.7 no. 4), CO261 is of tourmaline granite (Clough & Cummins 1988, 146) and could be island-made.

S3, if considered broadly as a pebble hammer, conforms with the majority of this group nationally as being made of quartzite. Four of these come from Normandy farm, with the granite battle axe referred to above (Robinson 2007, 66; Ashbee 1974, 237). CO257–9 are of impure (micaceous) sandstone imported to Scilly and CO262 of quartzite (Clough & Cummins 1988, 146). A broken quartzite pebble hammer was found effectively unstratified in the excavations at Halangy Down, St Mary's (Ashbee 1996, 100, figure 47) and another from Bryher is in the Isles of Scilly Museum (Hencken 1932, figure 18f; Robinson 2007, figure 5.7). As with S3, these quartzite objects may have been made from erratic material on Scillonian beaches. Pebble hammers appear to have been in use from the Mesolithic to the Early Bronze Age although firm associations appear to be nearly as rare today as when Roe (1979, 36) defined the type. There does not in fact appear to be secure evidence for perforated pebbles/cobbles in the 4th millennium BC. S3 can be regarded either as a component of the Middle Neolithic Old Quay assemblage, or to have derived from Mesolithic activities there. It is quite possible that there was one tradition of perforated tools relating to the Mesolithic, to which S3 may belong residually, and a second which developed with the groups of shafthole/macehead tools in the 3rd/2nd millennia BC.

Mullers and rubbing stones (Fig 3.32)

S4 [199] basal 'midden', Tr 28 Square E4. Roundish muller, convex working face moderately worn. 150 × 130 × 53mm, 3060 g. Coarse muscovite biotite granite beach cobble with small feldspar megacrysts showing some alignment up to 30mm.

S5 [242] fill pit/post-hole F43 Tr 28 (not illustrated). Half of roundish muller, 125mm across, 48mm thick, 766 g, worn convex working face, some damage possibly from hammerstone use around perimeter. Beach cobble, fine grained muscovite biotite granite with general grain size up to 2mm, rare feldspar megacrysts up to 15mm. Fracture probably deliberate with heavy impaction apparent.

S6 [190] A3 layer Tr 28. Cobble, worn flat from use as rubbing stone, end used for abrasion, some small diagonal grooves along one side, broken but possibly used after breakage. Top also has worn facet with pitted impact marks and oblique scratch marks apparent. 74+ × 57 × 27mm, 184g. Fine grained quartz rich sandstone with some mica, no evidence of foliation, perhaps erratic beach cobble.

Comment

S4 and S5 are good examples of the roundish mullers or rubbing stones appropriate for use with small saucer querns used during the Neolithic (see Smith 1965, 122–3, figure 52) and provided the earliest stratified items associated with grain processing on Scilly. Such items from south-west Britain have recently been discussed in detail by Watts (2014, chapter 6) and are infrequent even on sites such as the tor enclosures at Carn Brea and Helman Tor which retain large finds assemblages. Rubbing stone S6 is of a material and with a surface appropriate for working soft material such as leather: such items are found only occasionally in south-western Early Neolithic contexts, for example in a pit at Tregarrick Farm, Roche (Quinnell in Cole & Jones 2002/3, 122).

Tools used for abrasion and hammering

(Figs 3.32–3)

S7 [252] fill post-hole F47 Tr 28. Discoidal cobble, with one some surface used for abrasion and battering around periphery. 93 × 80 × 30mm, 353g. Fine grained muscovite biotite granite beach cobble, grain size up to 1.5mm.

S8 [306] fill post-hole F69 Tr 28 Irregular cobble with extensive areas of battering along two sides. 134 × 76 × 37mm, 354g. Fine quartzitic sandstone with some muscovite, probably erratic beach cobble similar to S6.

S9 [183] orange brown soil Tr 37 Small cobble, 75 × 58 × 40mm, 221g. Patch of fine battering on tip. Fine grained muscovite biotite granite beach cobble, unusual shape, possibly chosen for potential anthropomorphism.

S10 [183] orange brown soil Tr 37 (not illustrated). Small cobble 83 × 50 × 23mm, 180g. Patch of fine battering on tip and possible abrasion on opposite surface. Fine grained quartzitic erratic beach cobble.

Figure 3.32. Worked and utilised stone (3) (photo: S. Lambert-Gates).

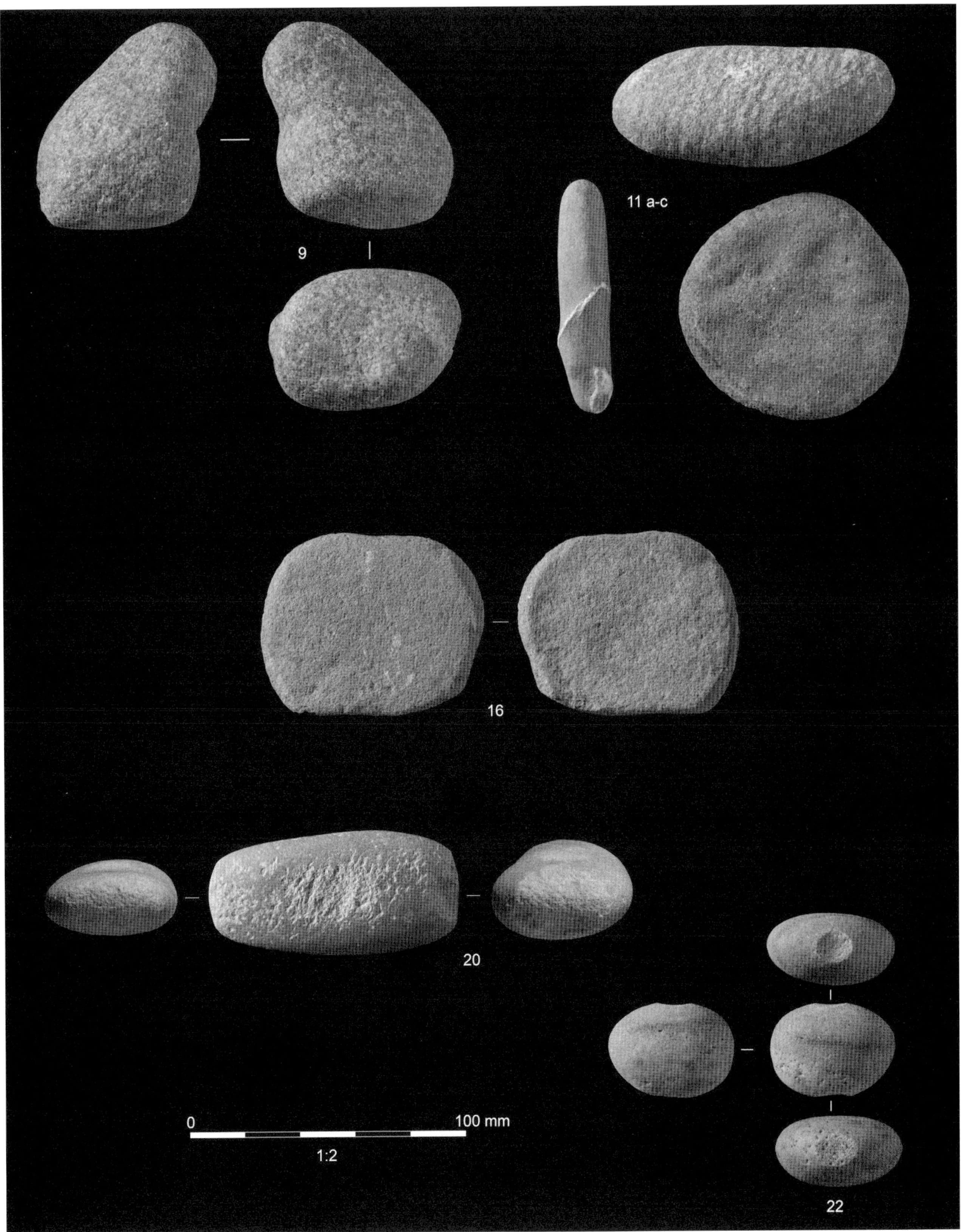

Figure 3.33. Worked and utilised stone (4) (photo: S. Lambert-Gates).

S11A–C [211] fill pit F33 Tr 28 Found together as Finds Group A. They appear to have been chosen for their unusual shape and lithology; S11A flat disc 80mm across 14mm thick, much periphery used for fine battering and abrasion, 140g, S11B narrow cobble, slight evidence of slight battering type usage on one end, 104 × 40 × 25mm 216g, S11C narrow cobble with two diagonal narrow quartz bands 80 × 16 × 14mm 37g. 11A very fine grained tabular beach cobble granite/aplite. 11B fine grained foliated greenstone elongated beach cobble, probably from the margin of Land's End granite. 11C elongated quartzose siltstone beach cobble penetrated by quartz veins, more likely to come from the Land's End area than to be an erratic.

S12 [151] pale yellow grey basal soil Tr 28 (not illustrated). Beach pebble 49 × 38 × 23mm, 66g. Abrasion/battering at both ends. Fine-grained granite with black tourmaline.

S13 [195] yellow basal layer Tr 28 D5 (not illustrated). Axe-shaped beach cobble, 72 × 46 × 19mm, 96g. Possible small area of grinding/abrasion on edge. Fine-grained muscovite granite.

S14 [22] layer beneath topsoil Tr 1 (not illustrated). Wedge shaped beach pebble 45 × 35 ×34mm, 440g. Two of the flatter surfaces abraded. Uniform muscovite granite with common black tourmaline.

S15 [19] yellow silt Tr 2 (not illustrated). Beach cobble, 84 × 59 × 30mm, 220g. Evidence of hammering at each end. Uniform fine-grained granite with muscovite and black tourmaline common,

S16 [18] gritty orange Tr 2 Tabular beach pebble, 52 × 37 × 16mm, 114g. Bevelled abrasion across one complete end, and partially across the other. Fine-grained aplitic granite with some muscovite.

S17 [33] yellow sandy layer Tr 8 (not illustrated). Triangular beach cobble, 81 × 65 × 37mm, 271g. Impact or abrasion facets on two corners and possibly slight wear on third corner. Fine-grained granite with sparse muscovite and tourmaline.

S18 [102] pale grey silty Tr 23 (not illustrated). Beach cobble, 84 × 57 × 48mm, 271 g. Patch of abrasion and some battering on one corner. Very fine-grained granite with scattered black tourmaline crystals.

S19 [102] pale grey silty Tr 23 (not illustrated). Beach cobble, 71+ × 1 × 33mm, 195g. Battering around most of edge indicates use as a hammer stone. Muscovite granite beach cobble.

S20 Recovered previously from cliff section after storm. Elongated beach cobble, 88 × 41 × 21mm, 125g. Evidence of hammering and abrasion at both ends, many indented hammering marks on both flat surfaces, the purposed of which is uncertain. Fine-grained silty sandstone, unlikely to be of Scillonian origin.

S21 (not illustrated). Beach pebble 56 × 45 × 14mm, 62g. Of similar material, apparently unused. Found with S20.

Comment

While most of the material used is local, the well stratified S11B (fine grained foliated greenstone elongated beach cobble) and S11C (quartzose siltstone beach cobble) are likely to come from the Land's End area. S20 and S21 of fine-grained silty sandstone, effectively not stratified, also probably come from Cornwall. There are also a few other pieces which have been 'imported'. There are two fragments from [32] Tr 8 62g of similar soft micaceous siltstone, probably from the same cobble, probably from Cornish mainland. From [130] Tr 35 is flat beach cobble fragment 72+ × 54+ × 17mm, 75g, fine-grained sandy siltstone, with narrow quartz veins, probably from the Cornish mainland. From [96] Tr 21 are a cobble 73 × 54 × 17mm, 99g, a with chip to the corner resulting from casual hammerstone use, and a flake, both of soft fine-grained sandstone fragment from Cornish mainland beach material, which is notably softer than the east Devon examples. These 'imported' items may link with the evidence for occasional distance sourcing for material in the lithic assemblage (see Section 3.5).

The fine battering on these pieces appears to come from some form of crushing on a harder rock, or processing some softer material on a hard surface. The wear is similar to that noticed on some cobbles from the Bronze Age settlement at Halangy Porth, St Mary's (Ashbee 1996, 98). It is not a feature of mainland prehistoric stonework assemblages and must reflect some aspect of island/coastal living. It is presumed that these pieces are Neolithic as S7 comes from F47, S8 from F69 and the group S11A–C from F33.

Pebble with pecked finger holds (Fig 3.33)

S22 [259] fill post-hole F.50 Trench 28 Banded quartz pebble with small oval areas pecked on opposing sides, probably forming finger holds. 44 × 31 × 23mm, 49g. Quarzitic sandstone beach pebble erratic, attractive banded colouring due to varying iron content. No evidence for use wear and no known parallels from prehistoric south-west Britain.

3.7. Pumice

Katharine Sawyer

A total of 23 pieces of pumice was found, five in 2013 and 18 in 2014 (Figures 3.34 and 3.35; Table 3.15). The finds cluster in two parts of the excavated area: trenches 7 and 8 in the southern part of the site and trenches 27, 28, 35, 37, 38 and 39 to the north. With the exception of a single unstratified piece, all the pumice is from contexts which yielded other finds, usually Middle Neolithic pottery and/or flints, but also quartz and worked stone.

All the pumice is of a grey-brown colour on the outer surface and, where cut or broken, a dark brown inside, suggesting that it has all come from a single source. Of the 23 pieces, seven appear to be unworked. There are nine

Table 3.15. Old Quay pumice

Trench	*Context*	*Sq.*	*Feature*	*No.*	*Weight (g)*	*Illus. no.*	*Details*
7	30	–	–	1	7	1	1 flat side – ?smoothed
7	72	–	–	1	2	8	Cut on one side
8	32	–	–	1	10	2	Unworked
8	Unstrat.	–	–	1	2	–	Cut or broken
27	119		–	1	10	3	Worked: groove 40mm long on 1 side. Cut.
28	195	A5	–	1	5.3	9	Cut
28	195	D5	–	1	10.1		Unworked
28	199	B3	–	1	5.5		Unworked
28	209	–	33	1	21.9	11	Cut
28	211	–	33	2	53	5, 6	Larger piece: 2 grooves at 1 end, longer 30mm; Smaller piece: 3 grooves in different directions, longest 45mm
35	191	–	–	4	23.4	10	3 pieces are cut, all join; 1 unworked
37	183	–	–	1	2.7	4	Small groove
38	238	–	–	1	2.8		Probably unworked
39	236	–	–	6	94.7	7	3 pieces have single grooves, 2 with cream-coloured residue on edges, 2 pieces probably join, 1 piece smoothed, 2 pieces probably unworked

pieces which show signs of having been cut or smoothed on one or more sides, three of these (from [191]) are from the same larger piece and join together.

The remaining seven have one or more grooves in them, with two pieces showing two grooves and one having three. The grooves are up to 45mm in length, between 4mm and 10mm wide and up to 4mm in depth. On two pieces (both from [236]) the edges of the grooves have a cream-coloured residue.

In Scilly, only five other pieces of pumice are known from prehistoric to Romano-British period sites: one from one of the Neolithic pits at East Porth, Samson (D. Neal pers. comm.), one from an entrance grave at Porth Hellick Down, St Mary's (Hencken 1932, 20), one from a Bronze Age settlement site at Little Bay, St Martin's (Neal 1983) and two from the multi-period site at Nornour (Dudley 1968, 18; D. Dudley site small finds notebook). A sixth piece was found by Alec Gray, probably in the 1920s or 1930s; this he described as a 'surface find, locality unknown, but not far from Bant's Carn, St Mary's' in the note which accompanies the object in the Royal Cornwall Museum, Truro (Sawyer 2015, 47). Three of these pieces have perforations through them but none is grooved.

3.8. Environmental analysis

Julie Jones, Ceren Kabukcu and Fraser Sturt

The sampling strategy and methods used at Old Quay followed those adopted at L'Eree (Chapter 2) and were in accordance with guidelines set out by English Heritage (Campbell et al. 2011). All excavated features were bulk sampled for floatation and wet sieving. For smaller discrete features 100% of the fill was retained, while for larger features (e.g. ditches, large pits) a minimum of 30 litres of dry deposit was recovered for analysis. During floatation sample sizes were updated, replacing the volume of dry sediment with a value gained from recording the amount of water displaced as the sample was added to the siraf floatation tank. In total 68 samples were taken, reflecting a volume of 808.5 litres.

The flot was collected on a sieve with a mesh size of 250μm, and residues on a mesh of 500μm. Both the flot and heavy residue were air dried and then hand sorted. Surviving organic remains were examined by Julie Jones with plant nomenclature following that given by Stace (2010). All recovered charcoal was analysed by Ceren Kabukcu at the University of Liverpool. Given the acidic, sandy soil conditions on site, it was unsurprising that only a small amount of material was recovered through this process.

Charcoal and charred plant remains

Julie Jones

In total 19 samples were examined under low powered magnification (×10) from OLQ13 and 49 from OLQ14. The sample floats varied from <1ml to 300ml in volume, with the bulk of most samples consisting of modern plant stem and root fragments, with the presence of bracken (*Pteridium aquilinum*) pinnules suggesting this formed the bulk of the modern plant debris. There was also a small, but consistent selection of modern seeds including red/oak-leaved goosefoot (*Chenopodium rubrum/glaucum*), fumitory (*Fumaria*), chickweed (*Stellaria media*), dock (*Rumex*), bramble (*Rubus*) and grasses (Poaceae).

Results

The results from each season are shown in Table 3.16. Details include the float volume and number of charcoal fragments extracted which may be suitable for dating purposes. Nomenclature and habitat information is based on Stace (1991).

Plant remains were sparse from OLQ 13 with a single hulled wheat (*Triticum* sp.) grain from a Neolithic pit (sample 15), with two accompanying charred weed seeds,

Figure 3.34. Pumice (1) (photo: S. Lambert-Gates).

Figure 3.35. Pumice (2) (photo: S. Lambert-Gates).

Table 3.16. Charred plant remains – summary

Sample	*Context*	*Trench/Feature*	*Flot (ml)*	*Charcoal fragments extracted*	*Plant macrofossils*	
1	47	Tr8/F2. ?BA ditch	80	0	no	
2	75	Tr 8. Scoop	20	0	no	
3	84	Tr19/F5. Neo. pit	300	0	no	
4	103	Tr19/F12. Neo. post-hole	20	0	no	
5	105	Tr19/F8. ?Neo. pit	300	0	no	
6	132	Tr25/F14. Prehistoric post-hole	<1	0	no	
7	144	Tr32/F13. ?natural	15	2	no	
8	120	Tr29. Layer.	10	5	no	
9	153	Tr 28/F17. Neo. post-hole	6	9	no	
10	115	Tr24/F18	8	9	no	
11	157	Tr28/F19. Neo. post-hole	12	5	no	
12	137	Tr19/F15. Neo. ?pit	80	0	no	
13	159	TR32/F20. Oval pit	1	4	no	
14	167	Tr32/F21. Trevisker pit	20	3	*Avena* (grain)	1
15	171	Tr28/F23. Neo. pit	20	21	*Triticum* (grain)	1
					Chrysanthemum segetum	2
					Plantago lanceolata	1
17	174	Tr28/F24. Neo. post-hole	8	0	no	
18	176	Tr28/F25. Neo. post-hole	13	8	no	
19	169	Tr32/F22. Trevisker pit	12	7	no	
20	179	Tr28/F26. Neo. post-hole	5	0	no	
21	196	Tr28/F27. Roman pit	40	0	*Triticum* sp. (grain)	239
					c.f. *Triticum* sp. (grain)	40
					Hordeum vulgare var. *nudum* (grain)	90
					Cereal indet (grain)	155
					Rumex sp.	1
22	203	Tr28/F29. Neo. post-hole	50	22	*Triticum* (grain)	1
					Avena/Poaceae	1
					Chrysanthemum segetum	1
23	201	Tr28/F28. Neo. post-hole	28	0	no	
24	207	Tr28/F30. Neo. post.hole	25	23	no	
25	171	TR 28/F23. Neo. pit	40	7	no	
26	207/8	Tr28/F30. Neo. pit	31	34	no	
27	201	Tr28/F28. Neo. pit	85	16	no	
28	153	Tr28/F17. Neo. post-hole	15	9	no	
29	179	Tr28/F26. Neo. post-hole	20	0	no	
30	176	Tr28/F25. Neo. post-hole	22	0	no	
31	212	Tr28/F31. Neo. post-hole	10	0	no	
32	211	Tr28/F33. Neo. pit	18	11	no	
33	214/5	Tr28/F32. Neo. pit	20	0	no	
34	221	Tr28/F36. Neo. post-hole	10	6	*Arrhenatherum elatius* (bulbil)	1
35	224	Tr28/F37. Neo. stake-hole	5	0	no	
36	219	Tr28/F34	0	0		
37	233	Tr28/F41. Neo. post-hole	8	0	no	
38	239	Tr28/F42. Neo. pit	30	0	no	
39	242	Tr28/F43. Neo. post-hole	20	22	no	
40	243	Tr28/F44. Neo. post-hole	10	0	no	
41	242	Tr28/F43. Neo. post-hole	15	9	no	
42	246	Tr28/F45. Neo. post-hole	50	39	no	
43	252	Tr28/F47. Neo. post-hole	50	35	no	
44	249	Tr28/F46. Neo. post-hole	26	13	no	
45	250	Tr28/F40. Neo. post-hole	60	74	no	
46	256/7	Tr28/F48. Neo. post-hole	40	55	no	
47	209	Tr28/F33. Neo. pit	20	13	no	
48	210	Tr28/F33. Neo. pit	30	25	no	
49	211	Tr28/F33. Neo. pit	60	9	no	
50	242	Tr28/F43. Neo. post-hole	10	9	no	

51	259	Tr28/F50. Neo. post-hole	3	0	no	
52	261/3	Tr28/F49. Neo. post-hole	160	40	no	
53	273	Tr39/F55. Neo. post-hole	19	0	no	
54	271	Tr39/F54. Neo. ?hearth	78	0	no	
55	217	Tr28/F33. Neo. pit	80	40	no	
56	275	TR38/F56. Neo. pit	50	19	no	
57	276	Tr38/F56. Neo. pit	22	0	no	
58	278	Tr38/F57. Neo. post-hole	80	49	no	
59	271	Tr39/F54. Neo. ?hearth	25	0	no	
60	291	Tr39/F63. Neo. feature	95	37	*Galium aparine*	1
61	232	Tr28/F33. Neo. pit	1	0	no	
62	288	Tr28/F61. Neo. stake-hole	2	0	no	
63	305	Tr39/F69. Neo. post-hole	75	21	*Arrhenatherum elatius* (bulbil)	1
64	306	Tr39/F69. Neo. post-hole	25	30	no	
65	297	Tr38/F66. Neo. post-hole	6	0	no	
66	299	Tr38/F67. Neo. post-hole	<1	0	no	
67	306	Tr39/F69. Neo. post-hole	10	0	no	
68	311	Tr28/F69. Neo. post-hole	<1	0	no	
70	227	Tr28/F39. Neo. post-hole	15	0	no	

corn marigold (*Chrysanthemum segetum*) and ribwort plantain (*Plantago lanceolata*). A single oat (*Avena* sp.) grain was also recovered from a further pit (sample 14), although this is likely to be from a wild rather than cultivated species.

Plant remains were similarly sparse in most samples from OLQ 14. The main exception was sample 21, context [196], recovered from a shallow pit fill. Around 90% of the 40ml float consisted of charred cereal grains, with many further fragments. Of the better preserved grains there were 239 hulled wheat with a further 40 poorly preserved grains (c.f. *Triticum*) and 90 naked barley (*Hordeum vulgare* var. *nudum*). A further 155 very poorly preserved cereal fragments were identified as Cereal indeterminate, but are thought likely to be wheat. The only charred seed was a dock (*Rumex* sp.). Interestingly a sample of what appears to be a cache of almost pure cleaned barley, with at least half identified as naked barley, was recovered from a cliff-face site at East Porth, Samson in 1990 (Ratcliffe and Straker 1996), which was dated to the EBA (2200–1770 cal BC). It was thus recommend that this seed assemblage from Old Quay be radiocarbon dated, the result of which returned a date from the 3rd/4th century AD (Section 3.9).

The only other cereal remains recovered were a single hulled wheat grain, an oat/grass (*Avena*/Poaceae) caryopsis and a corn marigold seed from the fill of a Neolithic post-hole (sample 22, with single onion couch (*Arrhenatherum elatius*) bulbils from further Neolithic post-holes (samples 34 and 63).

Anthracological analyses

Ceren Kabukcu

AIMS AND METHODS

The primary aim of this assessment was to provide suitable specimens for AMS dating from the Neolithic occupation at Old Quay. All submitted samples were examined for suitable specimens, and 5–10 fragments of wood charcoal greater than 2mm in size were picked out for further analysis. Following wood identification procedures listed in Schweingruber (1990) and Hather (2000), fragments were examined under a high power reflected light microscope (magnification range ×50–600) in order to observe the diagnostic wood anatomical features of the specimens. Individual fragments were sectioned using a single-edged razorblade and identifications were made following the wood anatomy keys in Schweingruber (1990) and Hather (2000) and also in consultation with the wood charcoal reference collection housed in the archaeobotany laboratory at the University of Liverpool. Since one of the aims of analysis was to provide specimens for AMS dating every precaution was taken to prevent cross-contamination between samples and therefore all fragments were handled while wearing latex-free gloves and petri-dishes were kept contaminant-free with regular cleaning. Specimens recommended for dating were weighed using a three decimal-point sensitive scale and were stored in contaminant-free PCR tubes.

Results

Twenty-one samples contained sufficiently well-preserved specimens to enable wood anatomical identification. The list of identifications is given in Table 3.17. Individual wood charcoal specimen weights are provided in milligrams.

Quercus (deciduous oak) was the most ubiquitous taxon, followed by Maloideae (apple/pear family), *Prunus* (wild plums/cherries) and Leguminosae (legume shrub, gorse). Specimens were relatively well-preserved, but were generally highly fragmented and encrusted with mineral inclusions. In some *Quercus* specimens fungal hyphae were noted. No twigs were present in the samples examined; however

Table 3.17. Charcoal: anatomical identifications

Sample no.	*Context*	*Feature*	*Trench*	*Specimen 1*	*Weight (mg)*	*Specimen 2*	*Weight (mg)*	*Specimen 3*	*Weight (mg)*	*Specimen 4*	*Weight (mg)*
7	144	13	32	Leguminosae	20						
19	169	22	32	Leguminosae	41						
15	171	23	28	Maloideae	64	Maloideae	18				
24	207	30	28	Leguminosae	20						
49	211	33	28	Leguminosae	20	Maloideae	93	Maloideae	62		
55	217	33	28	Leguminosae	41	Maloideae	98	Maloideae	79	Maloideae	77
50	242	43	28	Prunus	23	Prunus	18				
42	246	45	28	Leguminosae	42						
45	250	46	28	Leguminosae	18	Maloideae	51	Maloideae	38		
56	275	56	38	Prunus	19	Maloideae	24				
60	291	63	39	Maloideae	18						
63	305	69	39	Leguminosae	90	Leguminosae	60	Maloideae	240		
26	207, 208	30	28	Maloideae	49						
46	256, 257	48	28	Betula	71						
52	261, 263	49	28	Leguminosae	16	Prunus	32				

one sample contained a *Quercus* heartwood fragment with pith (sample 46, F48). More rarely fragments of *Juniperus* (juniper) and *Betula* (birch) were also recovered. A number of other fragments were recorded as indeterminate conifers as their wood anatomical features were not clearly visible due to preservation issues.

The preliminary analysis of the wood charcoal macro-remains indicate the presence of oak woodland on St Martin's, possibly close to the settlement. This evidence is in accordance with existing palynological spectra from the Isles of Scilly (see Wilkinson & Straker 2008; Ratcliffe & Straker 1996; Scaife 1984; Charman et al. 2016). Pollen spectra from St Mary's and St Martin's dating to the Early Neolithic suggest the presence of oak woodlands with an understorey of hazel. The absence of hazel (*Corylus*) wood charcoal at Old Quay is notable. Instead, the wood charcoal evidence suggests that oak woodlands used by the inhabitants of the Old Quay settlement possibly contained an understorey of various Rosaceae family trees and shrubs (e.g., Maloideae, *Prunus*) and gorse (Leguminosae, cf. *Ulex*). The Rosaceae family specimens identified in the charcoal assemblage are insect-pollinated, thus their absence in the pollen spectra is to be expected. The pollen evidence from St Martin's also suggests that by 3380–3010 cal BC (see references cited above), birch (*Betula*) had replaced the oak woodlands. *Betula* wood charcoal on the other hand, was very rare in the Old Quay assemblage.

3.9. Radiocarbon dating

Duncan Garrow & Seren Griffiths

Nine radiocarbon measurements in total were obtained from Neolithic, Early Bronze Age and Roman features at Old Quay (Table 3.18, Figures 3.36 and 3.37); three further samples were submitted for dating but failed due to low carbon yields. Since charred plant remains survived relatively well on site, it would have been possible to date more features; however these twelve were considered sufficient to establish a robust chronological sequence for the site. Unfortunately, since the microliths (and other potentially Mesolithic material) were recovered as a residual artefact scatter that was often mixed in with Neolithic material and/or in Neolithic (or later) features, it was not possible to obtain secure radiocarbon dates for them. The stratigraphic mixing of artefacts from different periods (see Section 3.4) would have rendered any dating samples obtained from the buried soils insecure in terms of their chronological relationship to the microliths.

The six Neolithic dates from features in Trenches 28, 38 and 39 suggest that the Neolithic phase of activity on site started *3460–3040 cal BC (95% probability; or 3340–3240 cal BC 28% probability* or *3210–3100 cal BC 40% probabaility; Start Old Quay, St Martins*) and ended *3110–2770 cal BC* (*88% probability; or 3270–3180 cal BC 8% probability* or *3110–2770 cal BC 88% probability; End Old Quay, St Martins).*

Table 3.18. Radiocarbon measurements and submitted samples from Old Quay

Lab No.	*Material*	*Species*	*Context*	*Radio-carbon age (BP)*	*δ¹³C*	*Calibrated date range (95% confidence)*
OxA-31872	Charcoal (wood)	*Prunus*; young roundwood	Pit F56, context [275], Tr 38	4511 ± 33	-24.0	3360–3100 BC
OxA-31868	Charcoal (seed)	*Triticum* (wheat)	Pit F23, context [171], Tr 28	4506 ± 31	-22.7	3350–3100 BC
OxA-31990	Charcoal (wood)	Leguminosae; young roundwood	Large pit F33, context [211], Tr 28	4451 ± 31	-25.6	3340–2950 BC
OxA-31871	Charcoal (wood)	Leguminosae; *ulex* (gorse); young roundwood	Large pit F33, context [217], Tr 28	4442 ± 35	-25.8	3330–2930 BC
OxA-29340	Charred ?food residue (external)	n/a	Post-hole F16, context [139], Tr. 28	4407 ± 30	-29.5	3270–2920 BC
OxA-31873	Charcoal (wood)	Leguminosae; young roundwood	Post-hole F69, context [305], Tr 39	4414 ± 30	-24.2	3310–2920 BC
OxA-32024	Charred ?food residue (external)	n/a	Oval pit F22, context [169], Tr 32	3413 ± 32	-27.6	1870–1630 BC
OxA-31870	Charcoal (seed)	*Triticum* (wheat)	Pit/Post-hole F29, context [203], Tr 28	1704 ± 27	-23.8	AD 250–400
OxA-31869	Charcoal (seed)	*Hordeum* (barley)	Post-hole F27, context [196], Tr 28	1724 ± 25	-23.3	AD 250–390
Failed – no carbon yield	Charred ?food residue (external)	n/a	Post-hole F23, context [172], Tr. 28	–	–	–
Failed – low carbon yield	Charred ?food residue (external)	n/a	Post-hole F26, context [179], Tr 28	–	–	–
Failed – no carbon yield	Charcoal (wood)	*Prunus*; young roundwood	Pit/Post-hole F43, context [242], Tr 28	–	–	–

Radiocarbon method: Brock et al. 2010.

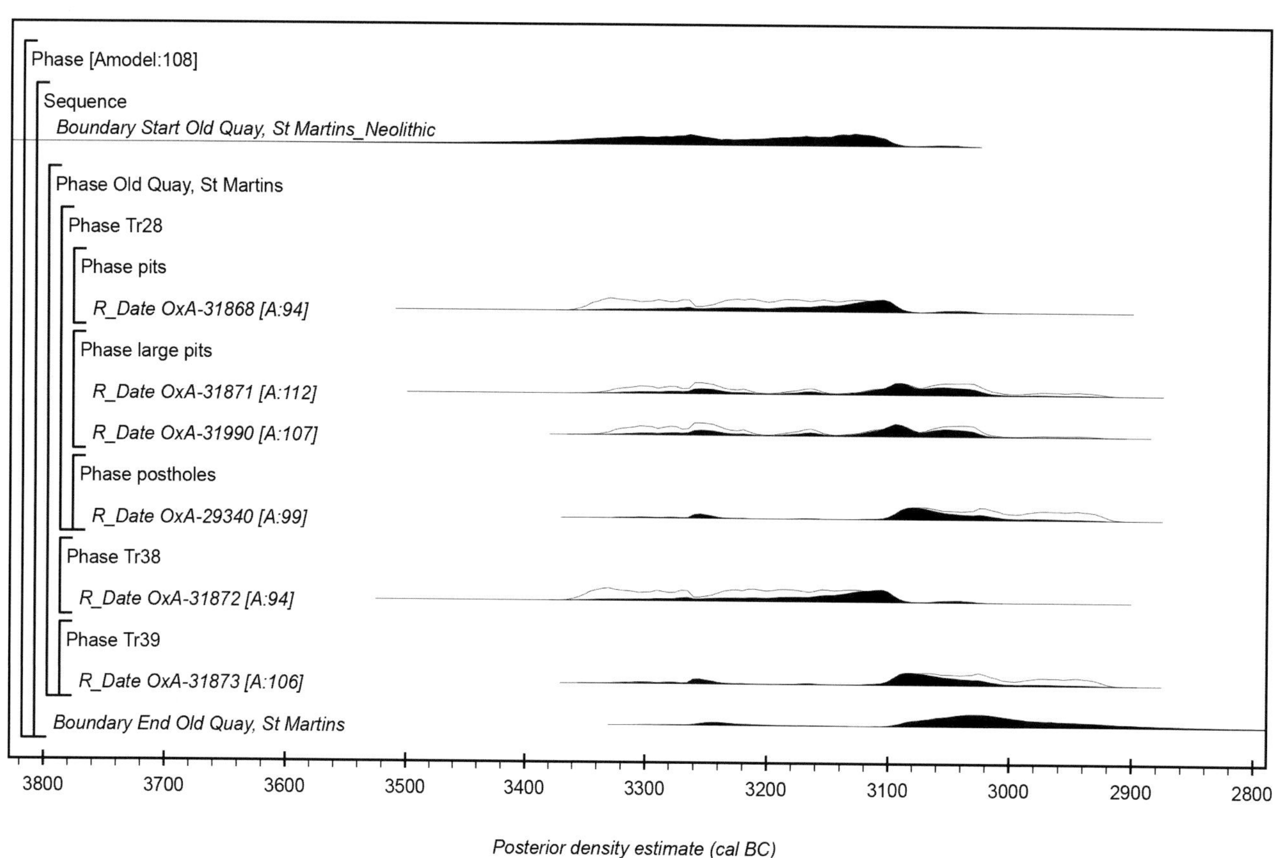

Figure 3.36. Model output for Neolithic radiocarbon dates obtained at Old Quay. These results have been presented within the model as a single bounded phase of activity at the site.

All six measurements, obtained either on young roundwood, cereal grains or from charred food residue on pottery, were statistically consistent and could therefore have been obtained from material of the same date (T' = 10.2; T'5% = 11.1; df = 5). Unfortunately, due to the nature of the calibration curve at this time, while it is possible that these measurements represent shortlived activity, an estimate for the duration of activity shown in Figure 3.36 means that this could have taken place between *1–330 years* (*95%* probability) or *180–220* years (*68% probability*). Neolithic occupation at Old Quay could potentially therefore have occurred within a decade or over the course of several centuries, it is impossible to say.

The single measurement from pit F22 in Trench 32 indicated that the Trevisker-associated EBA occupation recovered in that part of the site probably occurred c. 1870–1630 cal BC. This date range fits comfortably with dates associated with that pottery style elsewhere (Section 3.4). The final two measurements produced Late Roman period dates, somewhat to our surprise. As discussed in Section 3.3, post-hole F27 was known to be a late feature, having been cut from higher up stratigraphically than all other features in Trench 28. It was also unusual in that it contained hundreds of charred cereal grains (Section 3.8). By contrast, pit/post-hole F29 contained prehistoric material culture including, in its upper fills, the diagnostically Neolithic/BA shafthole adze. As things stand, the best explanation for the Roman radiocarbon date from this feature is that the seed was intrusive, perhaps having been deposited originally in F27 just a few metres away.

In summary, the radiocarbon dates from Old Quay suggest a phase of Neolithic activity during the latter centuries of the 4th millennium cal BC or early centuries of the 3rd millennium cal BC; a second phase of EBA activity early in the 2nd millennium; and a final, unexpected, phase of late Roman activity (not reflected by diagnostic material culture of that date) in the 3rd or 4th centuries AD. Unfortunately, due to its unsecure contextual location within the site, the significant Mesolithic lithic assemblage could not be radiocarbon dated.

3.10. Discussion: Mesolithic, Neolithic, Bronze Age and Romano-British occupation at Old Quay

The archaeology at Old Quay falls predominantly into two main phases: Late Mesolithic (c. 7000–4000 BC) and Middle Neolithic (c. 3350–2900 BC). The Bronze Age (c. 2000–1000 BC) and late Roman period (c. AD 250–400) were also represented.

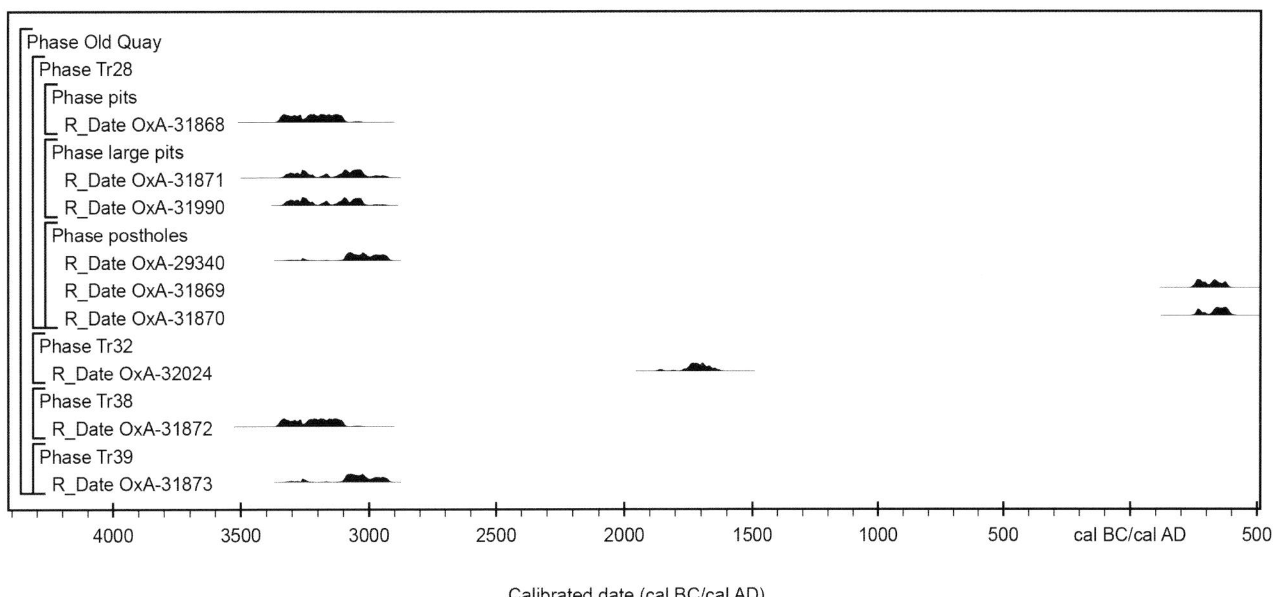

Figure 3.37. Model output for all radiocarbon dates obtained at Old Quay.

Mesolithic

The Mesolithic was represented entirely by an artefact scatter (contained within the ploughsoil and subsoils, and residually within later features). No features dating to this period were identified. As discussed above (Section 3.3), given that large quantities of Neolithic lithics (as well as pottery) and possibly also low levels of EBA material were found across the site, it is extremely difficult to establish what proportion of the overall flint assemblage was actually created as a result of Mesolithic occupation. The number of microliths recovered – 80 in total – is very substantial; given that only 11% of the area containing dense distributions of finds was excavated, we could in fact be talking about hundreds or possibly even thousands in total. On this basis, it can probably be assumed that a sizeable proportion of the nearly 11,000 flints recovered were Mesolithic.

These quantities imply persistent occupation probably over a lengthy period of time. As discussed in Section 3.5, the broken state of many of the armatures suggests that hunting took place on site; similarly, the fact that a high proportion of them was burnt implies that they may have been lodged in animal flesh which was subsequently cooked. This was a locale where a variety of tasks was carried out, which may well have been occupied many times. The analysis of charcoal from the excavation confirms the longer term perspective of landscape change presented by Charman et al. (2016). The Mesolithic occupation of the site is likely to have occurred within a well wooded landscape, in close proximity to the sea and within reach of an expanding inter-tidal and wetland area.

The microliths were in fact the only clearly chronologically diagnostic element of the scatter. Given that they were recovered within buried soils and features which also contained Neolithic and later material, no secure radiocarbon dates could be obtained for them. Precise typological dating, fairly difficult in itself in this case (see below), is rendered trickier by the fact that the microliths were very similar to, but not exactly the same as, those known in northern France and Belgium – even in those areas, microliths of this kind are not well dated independently (Crombé et al. 2009; Ducrocq 2009). Overall, however, they can be placed firmly within the Late/Final Mesolithic there, during the 7th–5th millennia BC. Given that the Old Quay microliths have a length–breadth ratio of <1, are produced on flakes rather than blades, and lack flat ventral retouch, it is most likely that they date to the latter part of this range (Philippe Crombé pers. comm.). In terms of the site's own internal sequence, it is interesting that the overall scatter appears to have two separate 'hotspots', which could conceivably relate to two separate phases of occupation.

Prior to the excavations at Old Quay described here, the otherwise very limited findspot evidence for the Mesolithic on the Isles of Scilly had been viewed as suggesting that the islands were only occasionally occupied by people visiting from the Cornish mainland (see Section 1.6). The evidence from Old Quay dramatically changes this picture in two key respects. Firstly, the site produced a totally different quantity of material, and thus arguably represents a totally different quality of site. Secondly, the character of the microliths suggests a completely different directionality of maritime travel – from continental Europe rather than south-west England. In order to understand the site fully, it is necessary to understand both of these elements in combination.

We have already discussed the broader implications of the continental European style microliths in a paper written after our first season of work at Old Quay (Anderson-Whymark et al. 2015). As highlighted there and in Section 3.5, the specific rhombic/trapezoidal form of the microliths from Old Quay cannot be paralleled in any other Mesolithic assemblage from Britain or Ireland; the closest parallels come from north of the River Seine in France, Belgium and the Netherlands (Thevenin 1995; Emmanuel Ghesquière and Erick Robinson pers. comm.), 550+km from Scilly. A more precise "origin" for the Old Quay assemblage is difficult to establish, as certain attributes (such as the use of flake blanks, the form of the *petite base*, and style of retouch on the ventral surface) are subtly different to continental European assemblages, which themselves show significant inter-regional variability at this time (Robinson et al. 2013). Interestingly, the trapezoidal forms known from Brittany and Normandy – the closest regions of France to the Isles of Scilly (c. 200km distant) – do not include *trapèze à base décalée* and *trapèze rectangle court* forms comparable to those at Old Quay (e.g. Cassen 1993; Marchand 2007).

The presence of a large assemblage of microliths on the Isles of Scilly, whose closest typological affinities lie not in southern England, or even in western France, but in northern France, Belgium and the Netherlands, is both puzzling and intriguing. It is, of course, theoretically possible that microliths typologically very similar to those produced on the near continent from the 7th to 5th millennia BC – and, importantly, very different to those made in south-west England during the Late Mesolithic – came to be manufactured on the Isles of Scilly independent of any social contact between the two regions. However, to us this seems a highly unlikely explanation. The fact that the potential region of origin and the location of their discovery are at extreme opposite ends of the Channel is a crucial aspect of the evidence to account for. Had the likely source region been Brittany, Normandy or the Channel Islands, their recovery on the Isles of Scilly would have been easier to interpret – the result of a much shorter north–south sea journey (or journeys). The evidence as it stands is most likely explained through one of three different scenarios: the first two view the material connections as essentially a consequence of a single, one-off journey, the third explores the possibility of more regularly maintained contact.

Scenario 1 suggests that a person or group of people living in Belgium or northern France travelled to the Isles of Scilly, establishing themselves there long enough to produce the potentially very large collection of microliths (and other Mesolithic flints) distributed across the site at Old Quay. If this period was fairly long, that duration could have resulted in 'drift' in the process of manufacture, leading to the few subtle differences observed between the assemblage found at Old Quay and those from the European mainland. It is also possible that this emigrating group chose to distinguish themselves intentionally from their founder community by making very similar-looking microliths in a subtly different way.

Scenario 2 places the dynamic of movement in the other direction. In this case, someone or a group living on the Isles of Scilly (or potentially even in south-west England or north-west France) could have travelled to Belgium or northern France, lived there for long enough to pick up the local manufacturing style and then returned (directly or indirectly) to Scilly. If this was the case, that person or group would have been very well travelled, but that is perfectly possible.

Scenario 3 suggests that people in (or visiting) Scilly and people in Belgium or northern France may have been in fairly regular contact in the medium to long term. As a result, the style of microlith manufacture in both regions stayed similar (if not exactly the same) over the duration of that period. The initial process(es) lying behind these long-term cross-Channel links may have been close to scenario 1 or 2.

Any journey between northern France or Belgium and Scilly certainly could have been undertaken in a single voyage; Callaghan and Scarre (2009), for example, have explored the possibilities of direct sea travel such as this in their models. It is also feasible that this single trip was never intended, with the weather and tides intervening to sweep a boat off course and the lucky mariners ending up on a small group of islands west of Cornwall, rather than meeting their collective end out in the Atlantic ocean. Equally, it is possible that the journey(s) was made in a series of shorter steps along the south coast of England, or even along the northern coast of France and then straight over from Brittany or Normandy.

Logically, it is not possible to distinguish between these three scenarios. Material connections can be identified, but who was responsible for them, how often they occurred or the exact route they took is essentially impossible to determine. Our feeling is that scenario 3 is perhaps the most likely, especially as it could potentially incorporate the possibility of scenarios 1 or 2 as well. Scenario 3 also arguably works best if a *social* interpretation is read directly from the similar-but-different *physical* evidence: the similar character of the microliths suggests an origin in northern France or Belgium and presumably also some level of maintained contact, while the differences imply a certain social distance, perhaps suggesting a community that did not return to the European mainland often, but which at the same time was keen to maintain a material identity separate from south-west England as well.

As Warren (2015) has argued in detail, in order for hunter-gatherers to maintain a viable population even on islands much larger than Scilly, a considerable degree of maritime interaction with those living elsewhere is necessary. The very low levels of Mesolithic activity so far identified elsewhere in Scilly make it hard to estimate the kind of occupation witnessed on the islands at this time: Old Quay represents a new scale of Mesolithic site. The material recovered there seems likely to have been created through multiple visits to the site over a long period of time. The persistent character of that material in the long term – clearly different both from its continental European 'origins' and from its British nearest neighbours – could potentially suggest a population focused, at least primarily, in the Isles of Scilly.

The evidence that the Old Quay microliths represent concerning maritime mobility is crucial in terms of our broader understanding of the Mesolithic–Neolithic transition in Britain and Ireland, especially so if they do indeed date to the 5th millennium BC. As discussed in Section 1.2, the 5th millennium was a crucial period of 'delay' during which Neolithic practices had arrived in north-west France but did not spread across the Channel. It has previously been suggested that this delay could have been due to a broad absence of maritime connectivity between Britain/Ireland and continental Europe at that time. The suggestion that at Old Quay we arguably have evidence for *persistent* contact between people living on (or regularly visiting) a group of islands 50km off the west coast of Cornwall, and northern France or Belgium 500km to the east, indicates substantial long-distance maritime connectivity at that time (even if perhaps only on a small social scale). The discovery of evidence for such connections implies that other comparable assemblages may well lie unexcavated (or unrecognised) elsewhere in southern England and beyond. The Mesolithic material uncovered at Old Quay was surprising, both in terms of its character and of what it implied. As we have discussed elsewhere (Anderson-Whymark et al. 2015), in order to move our understanding of the prehistoric past forwards, it is very important that we let the archaeological record surprise us sometimes, and incorporate the unexpected into our narratives.

Neolithic

The Neolithic at Old Quay is represented by numerous features – mostly within Trench 28 – as well as high densities of material culture contained within the buried soils – especially within Trenches 27 and 35–39. At a site specific level, even if the Mesolithic occupation at Old Quay was pushed as late as possible – to the end of the 5th millennium – there must still have been a hiatus in occupation there lasting several centuries; there is no question of any continuity between periods. The date span of Neolithic occupation at Old Quay during the latter part of the 4th millennium cal BC also ensures that, unfortunately, this phase of the site cannot contribute substantially to our understanding of the arrival of the Neolithic in the south-west more widely – it is simply too late. It nonetheless remains the earliest *radiocarbon dated* Neolithic site in the Isles of Scilly.

Altogether, the Neolithic archaeology at Old Quay is best interpreted as a site that witnessed significant levels of occupation, over the course of possibly several decades, or more. The absence of any clearly definable buildings, combined with the palimpsest of post-holes (interpreted as representing multiple phases of occupation-related structures), together appear to indicate repeated but probably not permanent settlement. The very different character (and contents) of the cluster of features uncovered in Trench 19, in comparison to those in Trench 28, seemingly also implies multiple phases of occupation. As with the Mesolithic phase(s) of the site, the large quantities of material recovered overall suggest that occupation at the site during the Neolithic was sustained and, cumulatively, fairly substantial. In this light, it is interesting to note that the strongest indication for land clearance for agricultural use identified in the pollen record from the islands occurs c. 3100–2900 cal BC in a core taken at Par Beach, just around the headland from Old Quay (Charman et al. 2016, 203), and also that charred wheat grains were recovered from a small (but, given the sandy soils, significant) number of excavated Neolithic features. It thus appears that the Neolithic inhabitants were making a significant impact on the ecology of the islands around this time. As the land area reduced as sea-levels rose so too did the complexion of the islands, with woodland making way for larger areas of open grasslands.

The Neolithic archaeology recovered at Old Quay would not look out of place on a site in south-west England (see for example Pollard & Healy 2007; Jones & Quinnell 2011) or indeed beyond. Similarly incoherent collections of post- and stake-holes, pits, evidence of burning, small midden-like deposits, etc. have been recovered at, for example, Carn Brea (Mercer 1981, e.g. figures 4 and 5), Helman Tor (Mercer 1997, e.g. figures 4 and 5) and Trenowah, St Austell (Johns 2011, 6–7). However, as discussed above, while Early Neolithic sites are relatively common in Devon and Cornwall, Middle Neolithic evidence is much rarer – Peterborough Ware has, for example, only been identified at all in the region in the last few years (see Section 3.4). The radiocarbon dated features at Old Quay all fall within a post-3400 cal BC, Middle Neolithic bracket (Section 3.9) – modelled to c. 3350–2900 cal BC – pushing the known date range for Hembury/South Western Bowl style pottery at least a little, and possibly a lot, later than that previously established (see Jones & Quinnell 2014, 128–129). As discussed in Section 3.4, this persistence of the pottery style into the late 4th millennium and possibly beyond could potentially be a trait unique to Scilly (if so, implying an established population on the islands that carried on doing things differently). However, given the very small number of sites involved, both there and on the mainland, meaning that the discovery and/or dating of a single new site could change this picture dramatically, it is at present necessary to be cautious in making any such assertions.

Material culture associated with the Neolithic phase of occupation at Old Quay indicates substantial movement of materials from – and thus presumably also regular maritime connections with – Cornwall and beyond. The site produced nodular flint, silcrete and gabbroic greenstone most likely to have come from Devon, along with Portland-type chert and greensand chert probably imported from Dorset and east Devon respectively (see Section 3.5). In addition, several of the worked stone tools must also have been imported from mainland south-west England (see Section 3.6). This kind of materially attested connectivity fits very well with the currently accepted model of impermanent occupation of the islands, from Cornwall, during this period; those that came would have brought some useful materials with them, but would also have made use of the plentiful supply of local beach flint at the northern end of St Martin's while they were there. It is important to stress that this evidence also does not contradict a model of permanent occupation on Scilly, as long as regular contact with the mainland is incorporated into that model as well. Ultimately, given the available evidence, it is possible that any such discussion of whether the islands were permanently occupied or not is largely missing the point. As in many other regions of Britain (see for example Whittle 1999; Garrow 2007), we may well be talking about a fluid settlement regime in which people settled down for varying amounts of time in various places. In this specific case, people may well have been moving between different sites in Scilly, and between Scilly and the mainland, at variable intervals – some staying on the islands for months or even years, others moving about much more.

Bronze Age

The Bronze Age was represented by three features recovered in Trench 32 (as well as pottery within the buried soils nearby) at the northern end of the investigated area, and by sherds in Fabric 2 recovered from the buried soils in several trenches within the southern part of the investigation area.

The two shallow, intercutting pits and somewhat amorphous gully-like feature in Trench 32 are hard to interpret. They may well represent part of a settlement, or some other form of occupation-related evidence, but it is difficult to say any more without further investigation. Internal residue on one sherd was dated to 1870–1630 cal BC, suggesting a firm EBA date for this feature. The fact that some of the sherds had strong Trevisker affinities (as opposed to the related 'Scillonian Bronze Age' style) makes the assemblage stand out as fairly unusual (if by no means unique) on the islands (see Section 3.4), perhaps suggesting closer links with the mainland than sometimes seen elsewhere. The fact that the date range of these features overlaps with the use of Knackyboy Cairn (see Sawyer 2015, table 8.1) which lies a few hundered metres to the north-west of Old Quay, is interesting. It is also possible that the four undated entrance graves or cairns immediately above the site on Cruther's Hill were also in use at that time.

Possibly prehistoric

A small collection of features in Trenches 8, 14 and 25 – a ditch (identified in two test pits and the beach section) and a post-hole – are also possibly prehistoric. The fact that one of the slots through the ditch produced two sherds in Bronze Age fabric 2 cannot be taken as conclusive evidence for its date, as similar sherds were found in buried soils across the vicinity. The post-hole contained a single flint flake (also found in large quantities nearby). Again, without substantial further investigation in the vicinity, it is impossible to say anything more.

Late Roman

The Late Roman period was represented by a single small pit that contained hundreds of charred wheat and barley seeds but no other finds. This feature (F27) was identified at a higher level in Trench 28 than any of the other features, and so stratigraphically it fits comfortably into the sequence. Given that it contained no artefacts, the fact that the single seed dated from it – along with another seed that must have got into an earlier feature nearby intrusively (presumably from F27) – produced a Late Roman date (cal AD 250–400) came as something of a surprise. No Roman period artefactual evidence was recovered from the site, either from features or from the buried soils. The fact that this feature therefore apparently exists in isolation from any other (surviving archaeological evidence for) contemporary activity nearby is difficult to explain. Given that Roman period evidence on Scilly is relatively slight overall (Johns 2012, 108–119), with very few substantial sites known, it is interesting to note that an unpublished hut circle site excavated at Par Beach just a few hundred metres to the east of Old Quay reportedly produced Roman period finds (ibid., 115).

Summary

The Mesolithic and Neolithic archaeology uncovered at Old Quay has transformed our understanding of the islands at this time. Previously, both periods were represented solely by occasional stray finds and small collections of artefacts. Consequently, it has broadly been assumed that the islands were occupied only occasionally, from mainland Cornwall (e.g. Robinson 2007; Johns 2012). As discussed above, the microliths and associated flint scatter present us with a completely different quality of Mesolithic site, appearing to suggest persistent occupation of the site over many years. The unique microlith forms recovered imply long-distance maritime connections not with Cornwall but with northern France or Belgium – a totally unexpected distance and direction of connectivity. Alongside the Ferriter's Cove cow bones in south-west Ireland (which were almost certainly imported from France – see Section 1.2), the material from Old Quay represents a crucial piece of evidence with which to try to understand the long-term processes of maritime conectivity and interaction that ultimately led to the arrival of Neolithic practices from the near continent. The substantial collection of Neolithic features at Old Quay also relates to persistent occupation at the site, perhaps over several decades towards the end of the 4th millennium cal BC. We have argued that, as in the Mesolithic, the site probably was not permanently occupied, but rather visited repeatedly at this time. Temporary structures were built and large amounts of debris accumulated in a substantial 'midden' nearby. During this phase, several different imported materials confirm (this time rather more expected) maritime connections with Cornwall, Devon and beyond. The Bronze Age archaeology at Old Quay adds new evidence to the established picture, with the radiocarbon date obtained suggesting that the site may have been occupied at the same time as the various EBA tombs nearby were in use. The small pit containing seeds dated to the Late Roman period adds to our knowledge of that period on the islands as well.

It would certainly be possible in future to carry out further profitable work at Old Quay. Ideally, one would be able to identify some Mesolithic features to accompany the wider artefact scatter (and with which to establish a firm date for that phase of occupation); whether or not any such features are actually there to be found is a good question. It would also undeniably be beneficial to excavate a second large open area in the vicinity of those Neolithic features identified in trenches 38 and 39; while this exercise may simply produce more incoherently organised post-holes and pits, and large amounts more material culture within the buried soils, surprises could also await. It would certainly be interesting to open up a large open area around the EBA features identified in Trench 32 in order to establish the context of that occupation, and it would also be nice to obtain some kind of contextual understanding of the pit containing Late Roman seeds. As with L'Erée, future work of this kind is not envisaged immediately, but would without doubt be immensely informative.

Chapter 4

An Doirlinn, South Uist, Outer Hebrides

Figure 4.01. An Doirlinn landfall view. This sketched image shows the 'landfall' view of the site at An Doirlinn as it would have looked from a boat approaching South Uist from the west c. 3500 BC. It is derived from 3D views of the palaeogeographic models (see Section 1.4) created in ArcScene and re-imagined by Rose Ferraby.

4.1. Introduction

This chapter outlines the results of excavation and survey work undertaken in June–July 2012 on the small tidal islet of An Doirlinn, off the west coast of South Uist in the Outer Hebrides. An Doirlinn is situated in between South Uist and the tidal island of Orosay which lies approximately 250m from the main high water shoreline (Figures 4.01–4.03). A 4-week excavation revealed a deeply stratified settlement site, dating to the Neolithic and Early Bronze Age; the settlement consisted of stone-built walls, hearths, post-holes, pits and midden-like occupation deposits. The earliest phases of the site produced substantial quantities of Earlier Neolithic Hebridean wares, the later phases Grooved Ware and Beaker pottery; a very large assemblage of flint and quartz was also recovered.

Geology, topography and environment

The Outer Hebrides lie between 40km and 90km off the mainland coast of north-west Scotland, and 24km off the Isle of Skye (Figure 4.02). Today, when considered together, the 119 named islands represent the third largest landmass in the British Isles, stretching 213km from the Butt of Lewis in the north to Barra Head in the south (Parker Pearson & Smith 2012, 1). To the west lies the vast expanse of the Atlantic Ocean, with the margin of the continental shelf marked by deep waters of the Rockall Trough, c. 160km west of Lewis. To the east, Lewis and Harris are separated from the mainland by The Minch, North Uist from the Isle of Skye by the Little Minch, and from Benbecula to the tip of Berneray by the Sea of the Hebrides (Figure 1.01).

These bodies of water are markedly different with regard to wave, tidal regime and exposure to storms. The next landfall to the west of the Outer Hebrides is Labrador, some 3000km away. This long fetch leaves the west coast exposed to increased significant wave heights (Wolf & Woolf 2006; Orme et al. 2016) and storm action. However, the relative proximity to the continental shelf and nutrient rich cold waters attract a host of marine life, making this an attractive maritime environment. The Minch, Little Minch and the Sea of the Hebrides are comparatively quieter waters with the islands acting as a barrier to westerly winds and waves. However, significant tidal races and confused sea-states are not uncommon, still posing a challenge to maritime transport today (Coll et al. 2013). As noted in Section 1.4, the palaeogeography of the islands and associated seaways has changed; however, the overarching contrast between a west coast exposed to high winds and storms and a more sheltered east coast remains valid (Orme et al. 2016) for the periods discussed in this chapter.

Just as the ocean and seas described above are discernibly different, so too are the islands that make up the Outer Hebrides – moving from the rounded glacial till landscapes of north Lewis, through more exposed mountainous terrain of Harris, to the generally low lying west coast of North Uist, Benbecula and South Uist, demarcated by a ridge of high ground and mountains on the east. Figure 4.04 presents the landscape characterisation of the islands as described by Richards (1998), illustrating the difference between the boggy moorland of the north and the extensive machair and peatlands of the south. In turn these differences offer an insight into the changes that have occurred across the islands, and the internationally significant environmental record it now preserves within both the machair and extensive 'blackland' peats (broadly shown as 'crofting' landscapes in Figure 4.04).

The machair is a low-lying coastal grassland that can be found across northern and western Scotland and Ireland (Young et al. 2015). It is composed of calcareous sand, with a calcium carbonate content of upto 80% (Dawson et al. 2004; Ritchie & Whittington 1994). This translates into low pH values (6.5–8) and thus low potential for recovery of bone within archaeological contexts (Parker Pearson & Smith 2012, 3). The formation of the machair is directly related to mid-to-late Holocene changes in sea-level. As Sharples notes (2015, 6) the machair has attracted detailed investigation since the 1960s due to the combination of archaeological sites located within it, and the compelling environmental history it physically represents. As Dawson et al. (2004, 284) describe, as the glaciers slowly began to melt c. 18,000 year ago they left behand a scoured landsurface whose depressions became filled with marshes and small lochs. As the glaciers melted, sea-levels rose and the land began to rebound recovering from the weight of ice that had been pressing it down (see Section 1.4). As this happened, glacially derived sands from offshore moved into circulation and became mixed with shell debris. These formed into ridge systems that migrated landwards, and when exposed were subject to Aeolian action, blowing them onshore. Here they could adhere to the scoured landsurface, providing a substrate on which a calcareous soil could form. Research by Ritchie and Whittington (1994) indicates that the exact timing and nature of this development can vary considerably up and down the coast, with stabilisation, erosion and redisposition events not being uncommon. Dating of offshore peats (Ritchie 1979) and the extent of previously exposed shallowly shelving coast illustrated in Section 1.4, indicate this process could have been occurring since the beginning of the Holocene, with a reduced rate as sea-level rise slowed post-4000 BC.

Interestingly, Edwards et al. (2005) have argued that the history of machair formation should not automatically be presumed to be entirely 'natural'. Instead, they argue that the presence of charcoal within machair deposits potentially indicates anthropogenic activity that may have shaped the distribution and stability of these deposits. As such, the history of machair may become more strongly related to histories of human activity. In particular Edwards et al. (2005, 446) argue that a Mesolithic presence on the islands could have been actively involved in destabilising soil surfaces through fires leading to remobilisation of fine sands. Similarly they document how grazing and removal of hazel scrub in the Neolithic may have further exacerbated this, leading to 'inundation of massive fane sand-size materials' at the site of Kallin on Grimsay (2005, 447).

Beyond the presence of machair and peat deposits, Brayshay and Edwards (1996, 16–23) lay out a broader environmental history through consideration of pollen and charcoal data. The picture they present is of a late glacial landscape dominated by open heath and grassland, slowly being replaced by a mosaic of blanket bogs, tall herbs and woodland (pine, birch and hazel) during the early–mid Holocene. Brayshay and Edwards (1996, 20) point to a slow decline in woodland species from c. 5470 cal BC, but this was regionally variable in nature. They also note that the replacement of woodland by herbaceous taxa could be for variable reasons from the extension of blanket bogs through climatic variation to anthropogenic activity. Far from being seen as bleak, Brayshay and Edwards (1996, 23) take time to point out that this was a productive landscape, well suited to supporting past populations: there was a range of edible plants (hazelnuts, wild strawberries, brambles, sorrel), heaths could be used to provide bedding material, marine resources drawn on.

The overall sense gained from the extensive previous research into the geology, palaeogeography and environmental history of the Outer Hebirdes is of a dynamic

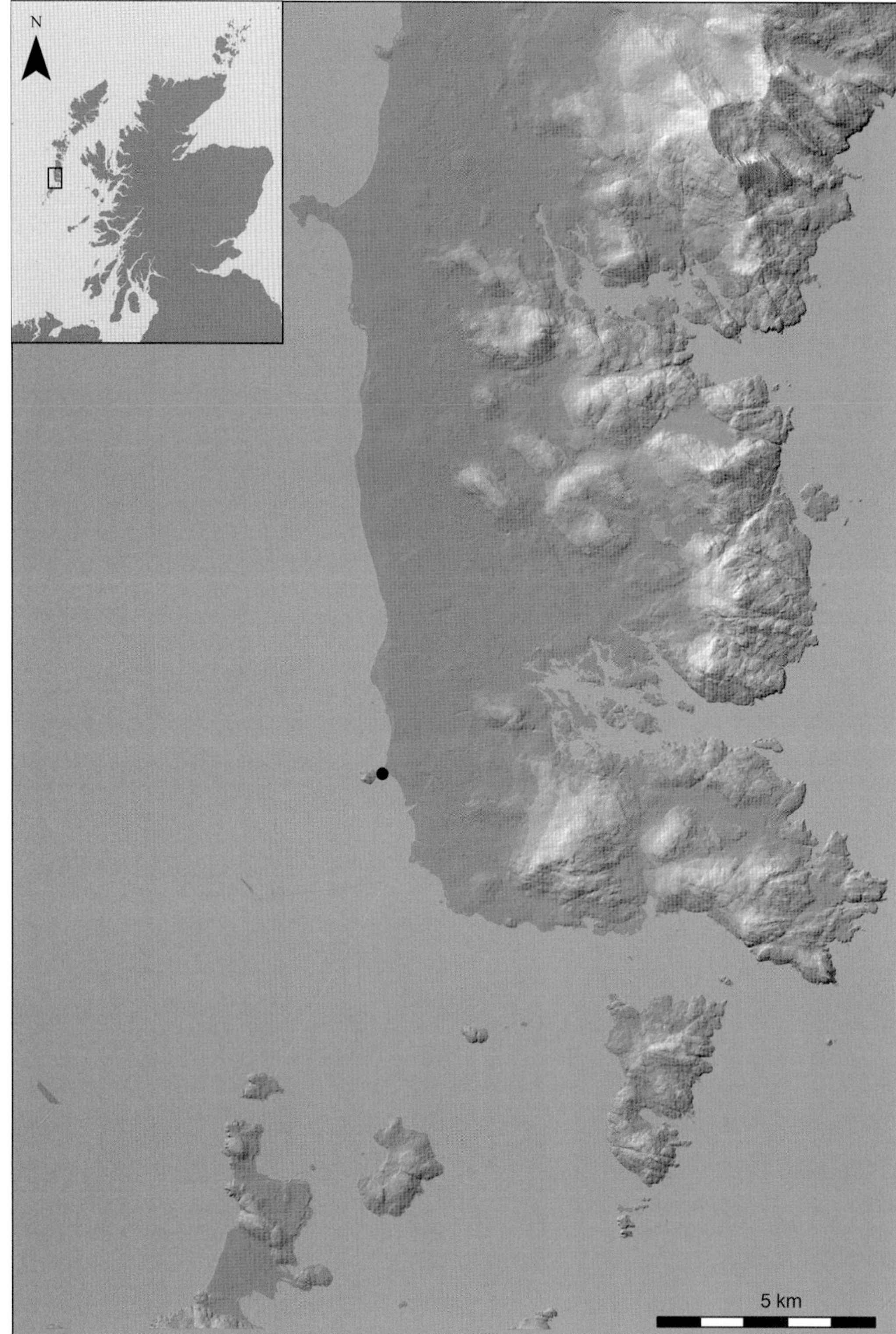

Figure 4.02. An Dorilinn site location. Topographic and bathymetric data from EMODnet (www.emodnet-bathymetry.eu) and the Ordnance Survey © Crown Copyright and Databse Right 2016.

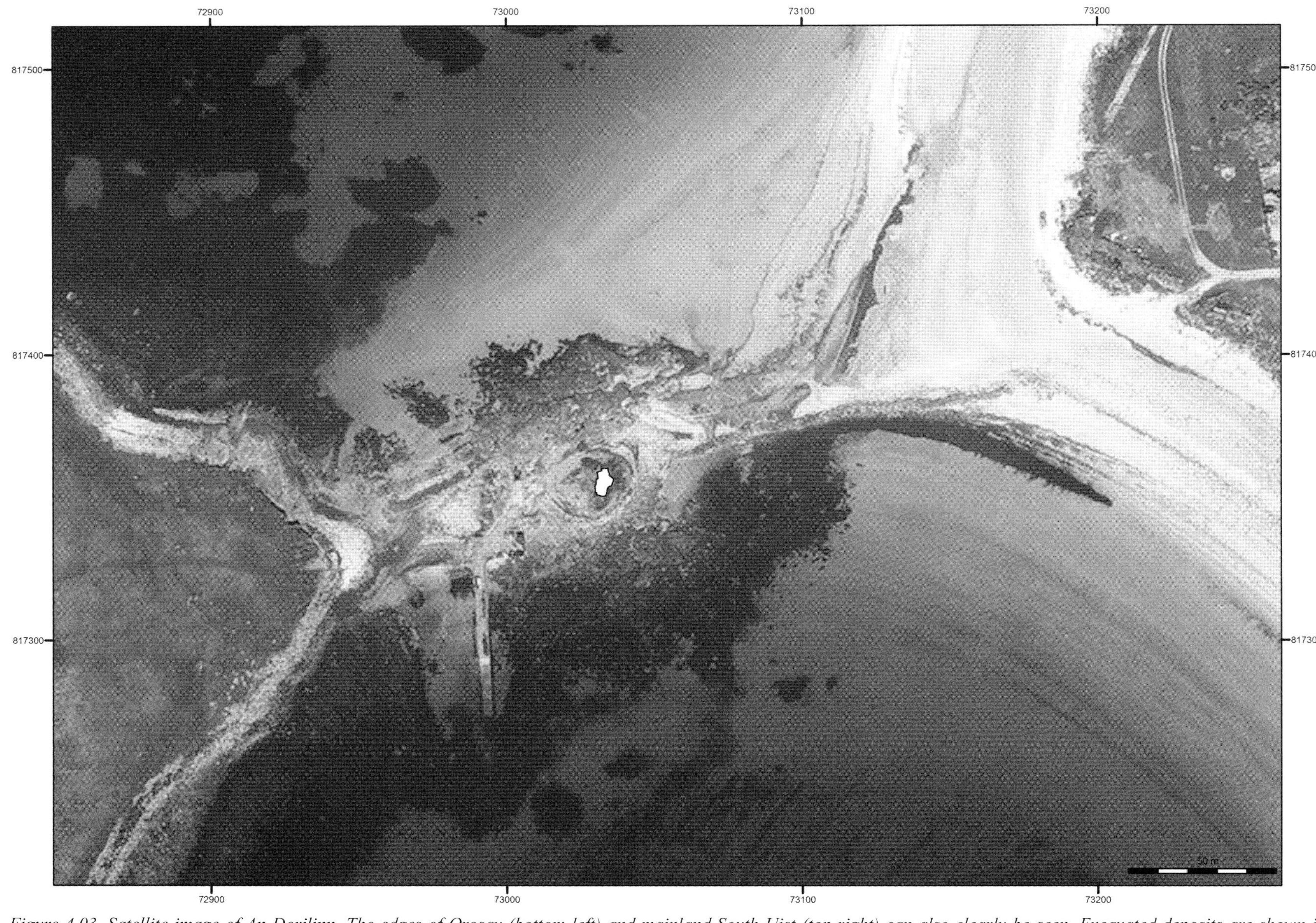

Figure 4.03. Satellite image of An Dorilinn. The edges of Orosay (bottom left) and mainland South Uist (top right) can also clearly be seen. Excavated deposits are shown in white with a black outline towards the centre of the image. Data from: Esri, DigitalGlobe, Earthstar Geographics, CNES/Airbus DS, GeoEye, USDA FSA, USGS, Getmapping, Aerogrid, IGN, IGP, and the GIS User Community.

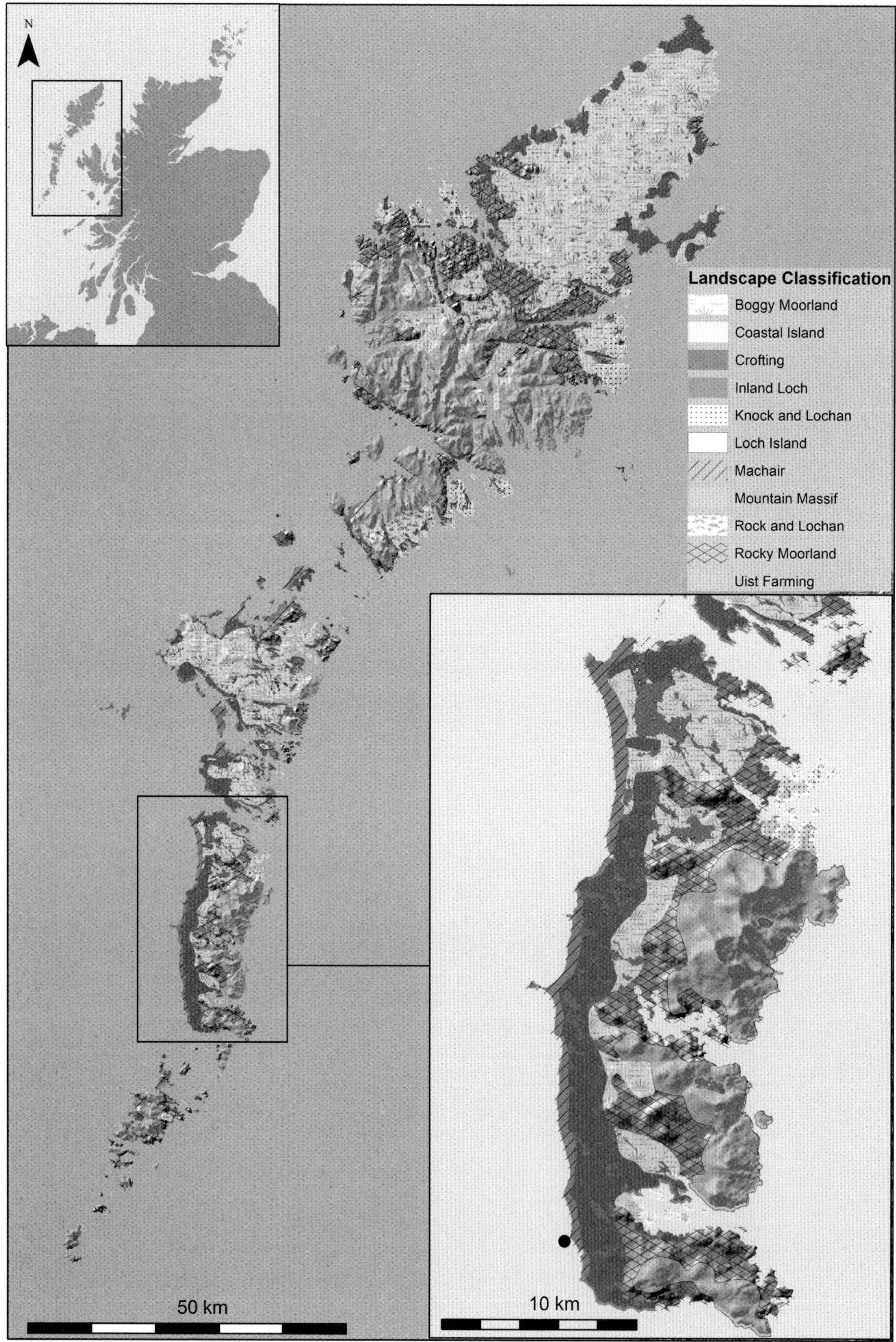

Figure 4.04. Landscape characterisation map of the Outer Hebrides (data from Richards 1998). Topographic data from the Ordnance Survey © Crown Copyright and Databse Right 2016. Ordnance Survey (Digimap Licence).

Figure 4.05. An Doirlinn: geographical location at the time of occupation. Topographic and bathymetric data from GEBCO14 (www.gebco.net), EMODnet (www.emodnet-bathymetry.eu) and the Ordnance Survey © Crown Copyright and Databse Right 2016. Ordnance Survey (Digimap Licence).

and changing landscape. However, as Sharples (2015, 10) notes, 'the 21st century will provide a whole new set of problems and opportunities, and the archaeology of the Western Isles should continue to provide an important resource for a range of interest groups'. These problems and opportunities relate to this complex and intertwined history of human and environmental change. The submerged peats, machair and blacklands represent an internationally significant resource that is capable of providing new insights into the nature and timing of environmental change, from longer term perspectives of landscape regeneration post-glaciation, through to an event based record of variability in storm frequency linked to climate and weather patterns (Orme et al. 2016). This same soil and sedimentary archive also contains more traditional archaeological data that offers the potential to transform our understanding of settlement, communication and the processes of social change. In the text below we have contributed to moving this discussion forward. However, as ever, the work we have carried out raises more and new questions, whilst also reinforcing the sense of value and potential discussed by Sharples (2015).

Figure 4.05 shows the coastline at the time of occupation for the site at An Doirlinn. The sea-level models described in Section 1.4 indicate a larger inter-tidal zone and more extensive coastal strip up the west coast of South Uist than at present. However, as we discuss in more detail below (Section 4.9), these renderings of the past coastline need to be treated with caution since the formation of machair and the rolling coastal dune system will have radically altered this coastline. As such, it is possible, indeed probable, that the more extensive coastal plain existed for a longer period of time. If so, the site at An Doirlinn would have been sheltered from the prevailing wind behind a pronounced headland (the modern island of Orosay), surrounded by a low lying plain, in close proximity to the sea.

Previous work at the site

An Doirlinn was identified as a site of potential archaeological interest as early as 1928, when the RCAHMS reported the presence of the small islet. They described it as being 'about 50 yards in length and 20 yards in breadth at its widest point … surrounded by a slight wall built round its margin', also noting the presence of 'a massive causeway … [that] connects it with the mainland' (RCAHMS 1928, 123). While it has since been suggested that the site was incorrectly identified as a dun in this publication (see below), it is worth noting that the original RCAHMS text does not in fact explicitly state this (although the site is included at the end of a list of other 'duns' of variable certainty). A few decades later, the Ordnance Survey reported that 'there is no trace of a dun on the islet. The causeway [noted in 1928] still exists but whether it is modern or formerly part of a dun, now destroyed, is impossible to say' (Ordnance Survey 1965). Thirty years later, Parker Pearson (1995) stated that the site had previously been misidentified as a dun/broch but, perhaps wisely, did not himself suggest a specific alternative identification.

Given the site's location, it is no surprise that it often bears the full force of severe storms. The damage caused by coastal erosion to the archaeology at An Doirlinn has long been recognised, but was made particularly clear in January 2005, when approximately two-thirds of the island was washed away following the worst storm seen in South Uist for many decades (Roddy Macleod pers. comm.; Woolf 2007). Unsurprisingly, in the Rapid Coastal Zone Assessment for the island which was carried out shortly afterwards, the site was mentioned specifically as being under threat (Moore & Wilson 2005, 17). The sections exposed by the sea were first examined formally at this time, with Moore and Wilson (2005, 17) noting 'a probable Iron Age settlement' (ibid., 22) with 'ample evidence of prehistoric activity … including anthropogenic surfaces containing flint-working scatters and others with decorated Iron Age [presumably, in fact, Neolithic] type pottery'. Later the same year, following identification of further flint eroding out of the site by Kate MacDonald, a team from Cardiff University led by Niall Sharples carried out a measured survey of the site and collected moderate amounts of material picked up during section-cleaning (Sharples 2005). It was as a result of this work that the site was first explicitly recognised as being of likely Neolithic date (ibid.). Their survey revealed possible Neolithic deposits across an area of approximately 20 × 8m; it is however impossible to compare these dimensions with those taken in 1928, as the earlier survey described the size of the islet itself rather than just the archaeological deposits. The site was subsequently monitored at regular intervals, with this work suggesting that erosion continued to be a problem. The most recent topographic survey carried out prior to the project described here was undertaken in 2011 (MacDonald & Rennell 2011).

Research objectives

Our work at An Doirlinn (Figure 4.06) was driven primarily by two main objectives. The first was to characterise and

Figure 4.06. Excavation in progress at An Doirlinn, looking E. The limited extent of surviving deposits on top of the islet can clearly be seen.

date more fully what was thought potentially to be amongst the earliest Neolithic settlements in the Outer Hebrides. The second was simply to record and recover material from the site before it was lost completely to the sea; as with L'Eree, this was in some senses a 'rescue' as well as a research excavation.

4.2. Excavation strategy and methodology

The first element of our 2012 work was to survey the site prior to excavation. Three types of site survey were undertaken at this point: GPS (Leica 1200 real time kinematic global positioning system connected to the Ordnance Survey Smartnet correction signal, transmitted via an internet server), measured hand-drawn plan and photogrammetry. In addition, the two main sections which had already been cut by the sea through archaeological deposits were drawn (Figures 4.07–4.09). This initial work revealed potential archaeology across an overall area measuring c. 12 × 11m with deposits possibly up to 1.5m deep.

As Sharples' 2005 survey noted, the site had been cut in two by a modern pipe trench, excavated by mini-digger a few years previously (Don MacPhee, pers. comm.). The main bulk (approximately 80%) of the surviving deposits lay to the south of this trench (best illustrated below in Figure 4.21); those to the north appeared less well preserved (in depth) overall, and were partly covered by a substantial layer of stones and boulders. Due to the relatively short, four-week time frame of the 2012 excavation, after initial removal of the uppermost layers, a decision was made to focus all of our efforts on the southern part of the site, as defined by the pipe trench, at least initially; in the end, there was no time to excavate the deposits to the north of the pipe trench, and they thus remain in situ.

All archaeological deposits were carefully hand-excavated and recorded using the single context system, occasionally combined with working sections. Separate feature numbers were used to group contexts by feature as well. Within this report, features are labelled with an 'F' (e.g. F10) and contexts are depicted in square brackets (e.g. [78]). Plans and sections were drawn at 1:10, 1:20 or 1:50 where appropriate. All contexts were also located digitally in three dimensions with GPS. Where extensive deposits were encountered, each stratigraphic context was divided further into smaller squares aligned on the site grid. The disturbed uppermost layers on the site were excavated in 2m squares, but once in situ occupation deposits were encountered, these were reduced to smaller 1m (and sometimes 0.5m) units. Deep, extensive deposits were excavated in 0.10m spits; in order to

Figure 4.07. Work underway and section being drawn (photo: C. Godwin).

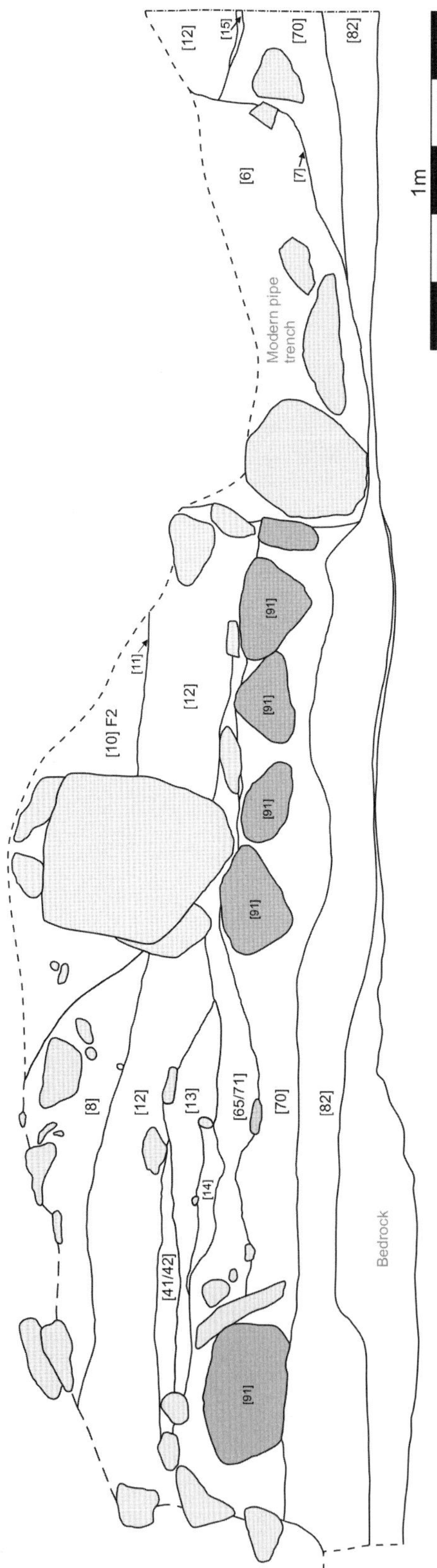

Figure 4.08. Drawing of south-east facing section prior to excavation.

Figure 4.09. Photo of cleaned south-east facing section prior to excavation (vertical scale: 1m).

avoid too many sub-divisions of the same numbered context, different spits of the same layer were usually attributed different context numbers. Each context was sampled for processing in a flotation tank. The quantity of deposit floated from each square varied depending on the volume of the deposit, varying between 5 litres and 15 litres. For features, 100% of the fills were retained for flotation. Of the remaining deposits, 50% of the excavated spoil from each square was passed through a 5mm mesh sieve; where notably high levels of flint/quartz were identified, the sample was increased to 100%. This strategy struck a balance between focused intensive sampling and careful assessment of the entire breadth of the site. It should be noted at the outset that the complex stratigraphy of the site (including features cut down into earlier layers, etc.), combined with erosion and disturbance of deposits caused by the sea at the edges of the site, may well have led to a limited amount of mixing of material between layers (see Section 4.3). The site archive has now been deposited with Museum nan Eilean, Stornoway (artefacts) and Historic Environment Scotland, Edinburgh (paper records) under the site code AND 12. Digital copies of the site records, finds tables and other data have also been deposited with the Archaeology Data Service (http://doi.org/10.5284/1016098).

4.3. Results

Three main phases of archaeology were identified during the excavation, relating respectively to Earlier Neolithic Hebridean (Phase 1), Grooved Ware (Phase 2) and Beaker (Phase 3) pottery; Phase 4 was modern disturbance. Each phase will be discussed in turn below, starting at the bottom of the sequence. Throughout the discussion, it is important to bear in mind that, due to erosion by the sea over many centuries, what remained to be excavated in 2012 was almost certainly a small portion of the original site which stood in the Neolithic.

Phase 1: Hebridean Neolithic

Phase 1a

The first features to be constructed on the site were four small post-holes (Fs 22–25), a small pit (F26) and a stone-built hearth (F15), all cut into or built directly on top of the eroded bedrock surface (Figure 4.10). None of these features produced material suitable for radiocarbon dating, but they probably date to a phase of occupation before (or possibly contemporary with) c. 3350–3030 cal BC, the dated span of the final Phase 1a deposit [82] (see below and Section 4.10 for details). The post-holes did not form a particularly coherent

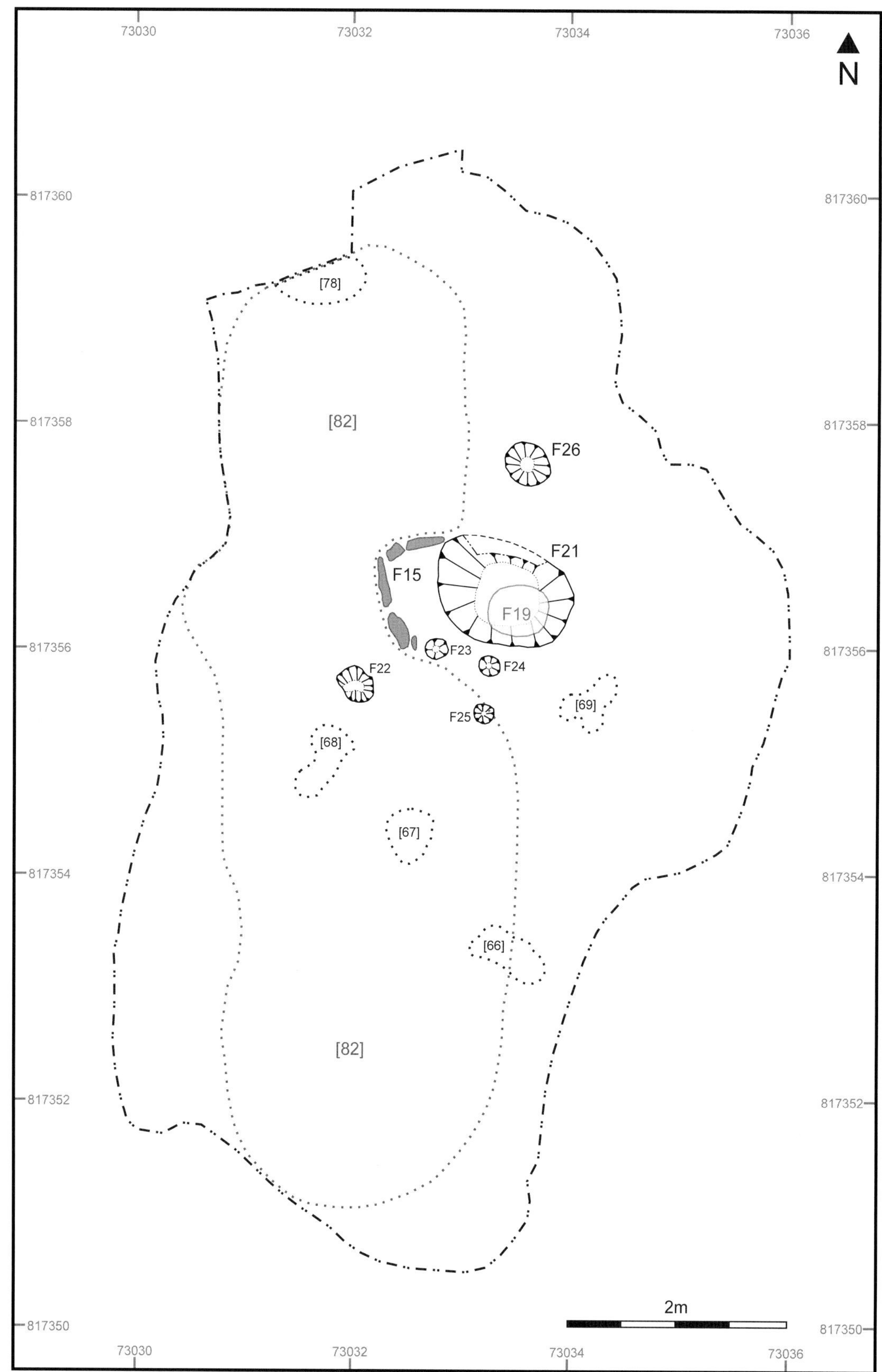

Figure 4.10. Phase 1a plan.

shape in plan; the largest measured 0.70m diameter × 0.18m deep, the others 0.20–0.30m diameter and 0.08–0.15m deep. Pit F26 was the most northerly feature of the group. It measured 0.40m in diameter and 0.15m deep, and was filled with a mid–dark grey silty sand. Intriguingly, it contained an almost complete, small pot (Pot H46) of unusual form (Figure 4.11) but no other finds; given that it was in the earliest group of features on the site, it is possible that it may have been a 'foundation deposit' of some sort. Other than this vessel, finds densities within all of the Phase 1a features were generally low.

The first phase of the hearth (F15) was constructed in stone (Figure 4.12). Two of its four original edges remained (following subsequent truncation), forming an L-shape 1.00 × 0.80m in size. The fill within the area of the stones was a bright orange-brown compact silt, the orange colour presumably a result of burning within the feature. At some point later in Phase 1a, the form of the hearth was altered. A large pit (F21 – 1.30 × 1.00 × 0.17m deep) was cut through its eastern side, presumably removing two of the four original stone edges in the process. The lower fill of this pit was a dark grey sandy silt, darkened by charcoal. Pit F21 was subsequently infilled, and a second 'hearth pit' (F19) placed in the top of it. This shallow feature (0.45 × 0.42 × 0.06m deep) contained a lower fill of compact orange-brown sand and an upper charcoal-rich fill, both the result of in situ burning. The two surviving stone edges of the first hearth were maintained throughout both subsequent remodelling episodes, presumably being kept to assist with the cooking process in some way.

This collection of features clearly relates to occupation of some kind, presumably relating to a building of some sort (Structure A). However, beyond that, they are slightly tricky to understand. The fact that they were constructed directly on top of exposed bedrock is difficult to comprehend (especially as a naturally-formed black, peaty deposit [92] also covered the rocky outcrop in places at this level, but no features had been cut into this). It was uncomfortable for us to excavate, and it must have been uncomfortable for the original occupants to have lived on top of a rock

Figure 4.11. Pit F26, containing the almost complete pot, under excavation.

Figure 4.12. Hearth F15 (scale: 0.5m).

(without any soil yet having formed on it) too. Nonetheless, the natural rise in the local landscape that An Doirlinn would have represented perhaps came to be a focal point for settlement, where cooking took place, and small structures were built. In this phase especially, the fact that we are dealing with a partial site, most of which has probably been lost to the sea, must be remembered – the site may well have been more comprehensible if we could see it all.

In contrast to the features just discussed, which produced just 17 sherds in total (plus the near-complete vessel in F26), the final layer attributed to Phase 1a [82] contained huge amounts of pottery (2090 sherds/39 kg). Context [82] was a black charcoal-rich sandy silt that extended across an area of 8 × 3m in the western part of the site (Figure 4.10). In amongst this material, five apparently substantially complete but highly fragmented vessels, which appeared to have been broken/smashed in situ, were recovered (Figure 4.13). These were assigned their own context numbers [66, 67, 68, 69 and 78]; four of these were found fairly close together towards the centre of the site [66–69], the fifth [78] was in the north-west corner. All five were substantial in size, and were either plain or minimally decorated. In addition to these, an estimated 25 other vessels were represented within the layer. In comparison to the pottery, there were only fairly small amounts of flint and quartz within the deposit (138 and 54 pieces respectively) – it is most likely, however, that this is a consequence of generally low usage of these materials during this phase (see below).

The manner in which layer [82] had accumulated is interesting to consider. The sheer amounts of material contained within it (53% by weight of the entire An Doirlinn pottery assemblage) and, perhaps even more importantly, the very fresh condition of the five broken vessels and large mean sherd weights within it overall (18.7g compared to an average of 9.4g for all other layers), suggests that it probably was not directly associated with the *occupation* of the Phase 1a site (at least the parts of it that survived) – any such activity would itself presumably have been hindered by the deposit, and would have led to the fragmentation of especially the substantially complete vessels much more than was the case. Rather, it seems more likely that the material was deposited (or redeposited) after occupation had ceased (temporarily) in that specific area of the overall site.

Overall, the distribution of pottery within deposit [82] was highly variable, with sherd numbers ranging from 4 to 189 per metre square. Equally, the proportion of burnt flint/quartz varied considerably across the deposit, with certain

Figure 4.13. Pot deposit [67] (scale: 0.1m).

squares producing high percentages of burnt material and others very low percentages. This variability, amongst all three materials, suggests that the deposit had perhaps been formed by multiple dumps of material of different character. Layer [82] is perhaps best seen as either (a) some kind of closing deposit, with material generated as a result of occupation associated with the Phase 1a (and perhaps other associated) features, but stored elsewhere, being dumped back into the area of settlement soon after abandonment; or (b) a midden, created once the focus of occupation had shifted elsewhere (to an area of the site that is now destroyed). The presence of five smashed pots perhaps fits best with the 'closing deposit' interpretation, but the location of the Phase 1b features (see below) supports the 'midden' interpretation fairly well too.

Phase 1b

The features assigned to Phase 1b were two substantial post-holes (F17 and F18) associated with the base of a stone wall (F20) and a stone-built hearth (F16) (Figure 4.14). This feature group was located right at the far north-eastern eroded edge of the site, and so no doubt other contemporary features had been lost to the sea. Radiocarbon dates suggest that these features were in use c. 2900–2800 cal BC.

Prior to the construction of this feature group, a layer of mid-grey sandy silt [70] was deposited across much of the site, covering most of layer [82] and the exposed bedrock elsewhere. Layer [70] was thickest towards the east, and thinned out towards the north and west, essentially counterbalancing the natural topography and previous archaeological layers to create a relatively level surface. It seems most likely that layer [70] represents an intentional levelling deposit, laid down to even out the site, and to cover over the midden-like layer [82], prior to the construction of the Phase 1b features. Layer [70] contained moderate amounts of material (324 sherds of pottery and 418 pieces of flint/quartz); it is possible that a portion of these could actually have been derived from the occupation-associated layers above and below it.

The two Phase 1b post-holes were very similar in size (F17 – 0.60 × 0.45 × 0.50m deep; F18 – 0.60 × 0.60 × 0.45m deep). Both were surrounded by stones that had been set around the edges of the cut, presumably used to support the posts. Both also contained interesting deposits – F17 a noticeably large amount of quartz, F18 a total of seventeen scrapers, interpreted as a cache or special deposit of some kind (Section 4.05). On the same NW–SE alignment as the two post-holes was a line of ten medium–large stones

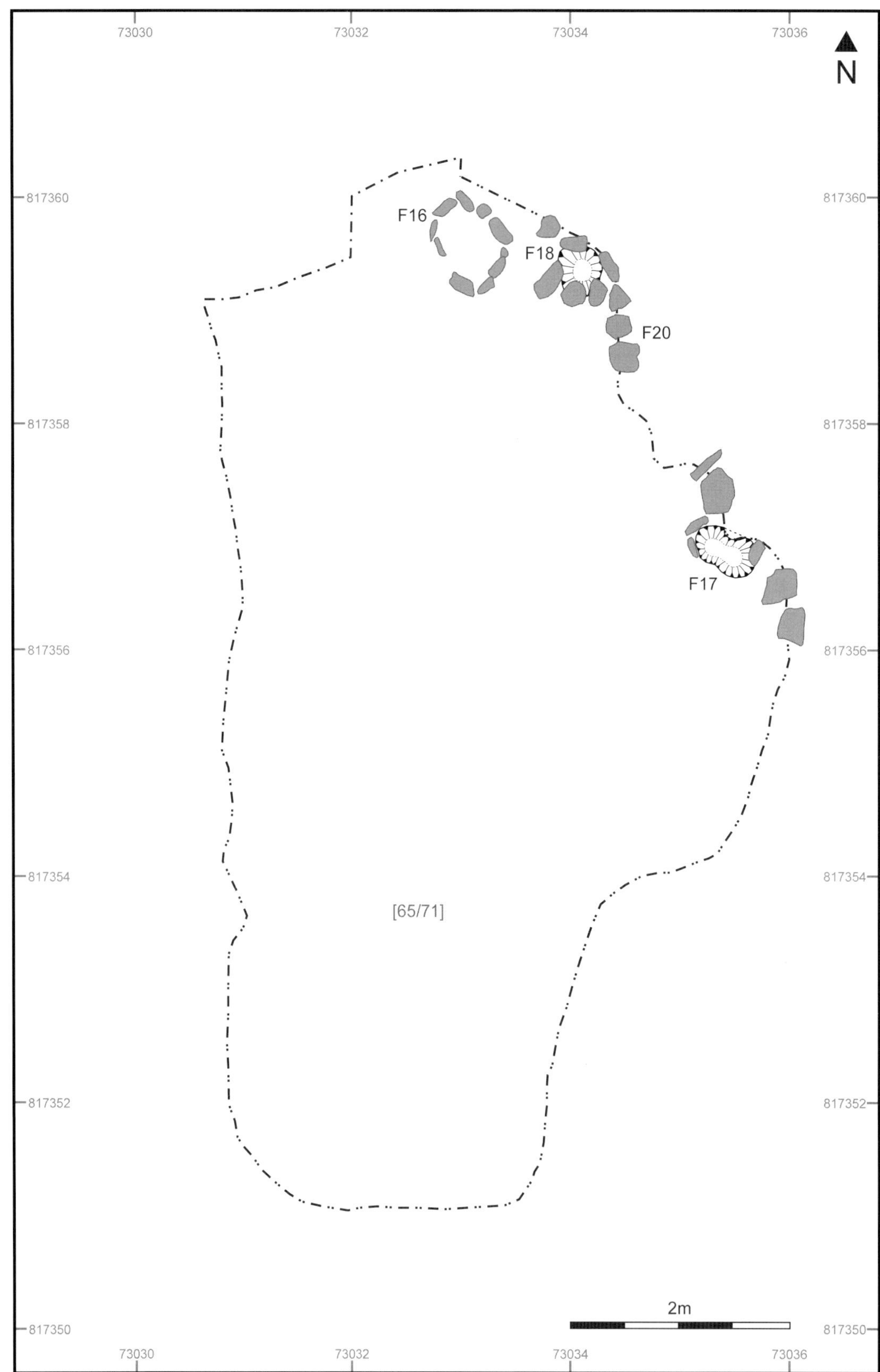

Figure 4.14. Phase 1b plan.

(F20) extending for 4.50m (see also Figure 4.08 where it is labelled as context [91]). This feature appears to be the remains of a wall, the upper parts of which may have been built in stone (now lost), or perhaps more likely out of turf. The wall was probably longer originally; some stones had certainly appeared to have been eroded from the middle section. Hearth F16 was located a small distance away from the north-western end of the wall, immediately adjacent to the northern edge of excavation. It was constructed from ten small-medium sized stones forming a rectangle 1.00 × 0.75m in size, set within a very shallow bowl-shaped cut (Figure 4.15).

It is likely that the wall created by Fs 17, 18 and 20 formed part of a structure (Structure B), perhaps a house of some kind. If it is assumed that hearth F16 would have been inside any such building, it is puzzling that no signs of the other three walls were detected within our excavation area. It is of course possible that the rest of the structure lay to the east (the area now lost to the sea). However, if so, hearth F16 would have to have been positioned *outside* the building, as an open air feature, or within a different building none of which survived.

The Phase 1b feature group was associated with a dark grey-black charcoal rich layer [65/71] which contained substantial amounts of material culture (559 sherds and 761 pieces of flint/quartz in total). Flint/quartz was much more prevalent than it had been in Phase 1a, and was found in higher densities towards the north and north-eastern edges of the site, adjacent to the hearth and next to/within the proposed structure. Given the character of this deposit and the distribution of material within it, it is likely that [65/71] was associated with the occupation of the Phase 1b building, wherever it was actually situated.

The final layer within Phase 1 (attributed to Phase 1c) was a brownish grey silty sand [53/54/59/62/63/64] that extended right across the site. Radiocarbon dates from this deposit suggest that it dates to c. 2840–2640 cal BC. Although this layer did not appear especially midden-like – it was not charcoal-rich at all – it contained very large amounts of material (595 sherds of pottery and 2601 pieces of flint/quartz). During excavation, given its relatively 'clean' sandy character, this was viewed as a possible storm deposit. However, the sheer quantities of material within it suggest that this could not have been the case. Interestingly, artefact distributions were highest towards the centre and south of the site, and so quite different to those in the occupation layer directly below it. It is hard to say whether it represents a second occupation deposit equivalent to [65/71] (with

Figure 4.15. Hearth F16 (scale: 0.5m).

the focus of activities/deposition having changed), or a deposit of waste material (notably *without* much charcoal) dumped into the area once it was abandoned. Notably, very small pieces of flint (<5mm) were broadly absent from this deposit, adding weight to the suggestion that the former was indeed redeposited material in a secondary context; almost all of the flint from this phase was burnt, potentially further supporting this suggestion.

Phase 2: Grooved Ware

Almost all of the Phase 2 features fell into two distinct groups (which appear to have related to two separate buildings), one in the south-west part of the site and one in the north-east (Figure 4.16). In between the two groups of features was a wall (F4). As a result of the presence of this wall, it was not possible to link up the two 'sides' of the site stratigraphically. During excavation, it was assumed that the two feature groups were probably from two contemporary buildings. However, subsequent radiocarbon dating of the associated deposits indicates that the south-western hearth (and its associated building) was earlier than, and probably succeeded by, the north-western hearth (and its associated building). The two buildings were thus probably in use successively rather than contemporaneously, probably from c. 2780–2480 cal BC (Structure C) and from c. 2480–2330 cal BC (Structure D) (see Section 4.10 for details).

Phase 2a (Structure C)

The earliest feature in the south-western cluster was a large pit (F14) cut into the final grey occupation deposit from Phase 1c. The pit appeared to relate directly to a stone hearth subsequently built on top of it (see below). Pit F14 was oval in plan (1.20 × 1.00 × 0.20m deep). It had two fills – the lower one [79] was a light orange-brown silty sand with frequent inclusions of burnt bone, the upper one [76] a dark grey-black silty sand containing further fragments of burnt bone and frequent small charcoal flecks. The two fills, whilst being quite different to each other, were both suggestive of burning. Unfortunately, the burnt bone contained within them – which, because it had been burnt, was virtually the only bone on the whole site to survive the acidic soils – was too fragmentary to be identified (see Section 4.8); we can perhaps presume that it was a by-product of whatever cooking process occurred within or around the pit. The pit's function is hard to ascertain.

Constructed immediately on top of the pit was a rectangular arrangement of stones, forming a two-part hearth (F8/9) (Figure 4.17). F9 was square, measuring 1.00 × 1.00m. Inside it, F8, a smaller, rectangular arrangement of stones (0.90 × 0.60m) had been created. The fills of both features were dark grey/black in colour and contained frequent charcoal. No layers had clearly accumulated in between the construction of F8 and F9, and it is possible that this was built as a two-part feature from the start. Hearth F8/9 was surrounded by a dark, charcoal-rich occupation layer [28] that extended across an area of approximately 3.50 × 3.00m. The distribution of artefacts within it was low (64 sherds and 136 pieces of flint/quartz) and showed no meaningful distribution.

Occupation layer [28] ended at a wall (F4), built using medium sized stones. It extended for 4.00m and was aligned NW–SE. As with Structure B (Phase 1b), it is probable that this wall represented the base of a building, whose superstructure may have been built in stone or turf. F4 was fairly well preserved in plan, perhaps because it was covered by large amounts of tumble towards the centre; it did not have any visible associated post-holes and had only a single course of stone. Presumably, other walls which would have gone with F4 to complete the building around hearth F8/9, had either been eroded by the sea or dismantled in prehistory.

Phase 2b (Structure D)

As with Structure C, the earliest feature in the Structure D sequence was a large pit, related to a hearth built on top of it. Pit F11 was a large, sub-rectangular cut (1.60 × 1.30 × 0.20m deep). Its main fill was a dark brown, compact silty sand. Integral to this deposit were a series of very clearly-defined, compact, brownish-yellow patches which are best interpreted as turves, and several large stones (Figure 4.18). In contrast to pit F14, the fill of F11 did not appear to have formed as a result of any 'use'. It was difficult to understand how and why turves had come to be deposited within the pit: they could perhaps have been part of some earlier, hearth-related feature (and its fuel?). The large stones, however – especially one particularly flat, slab-like rock close to the top of the pit – had potentially been placed in the pit as a kind of foundation layer for the hearth (F10) built on top; the stones were perhaps designed to reflect heat from underneath back into the fire.

The hearth constructed on top of the pit was similar in form to F8/9, but more substantial. In this case, F10 was the larger primary construction (1.40 × 1.00m) and F5 the smaller internal one (0.80 × 0.70m) (Figure 4.19). Although the internal fills of both features (F5 and F10) were not especially charcoal-rich, the occupation layers surrounding them [41/42/47] were. These extended across an area of approximately 4.00 × 3.50m. The lowest few centimetres of these occupation layers had built up around F10 prior to the construction of F5, indicating that some time had elapsed before the latter was added. Layer [41/42/47] contained moderate quantities of pottery (282 sherds) and very large amounts of flint/quartz (1798 pieces). Finds densities were at their lowest immediately around the hearth, and at their highest towards the eastern and western edges of the site (Figure 4.20), perhaps indicating that the interior of the building was regularly swept (a suggestion also made on the basis of the characteristics of the flint assemblage alone – see Section 4.5).

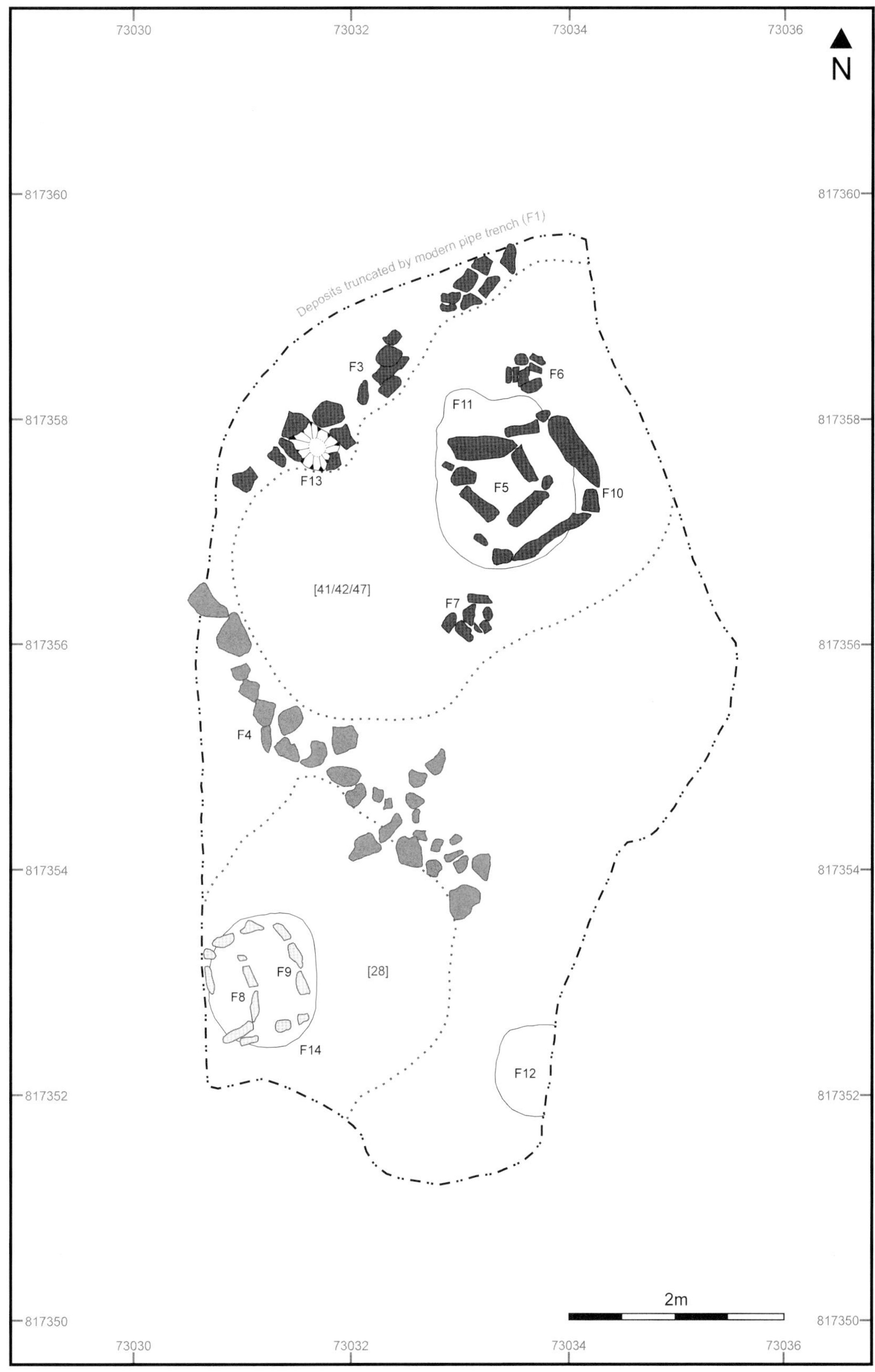

Figure 4.16. Phase 2 plan. The different sub-phases (identified by radiocarbon dating) are shown in different tones.

Figure 4.17. Hearths F8/9, looking N (horizontal scale: 0.5m).

Figure 4.18. Pit F11, half-sectioned. The turves can be seen as lighter patches especially towards the right-hand side of the remaining fill (scale: 1m).

Figure 4.19. Hearth F5/10, looking S (scale: 0.5m).

As in Structure C, these occupation deposits ended at a wall (F3) to the north. Wall F3 was built using medium sized stones, extended for 3.40m and was aligned NE–SW. This wall was somewhat fragmentary in plan, but had a large post-hole (F13) integral to it (0.70 × 0.40 × 0.40m deep) and was two courses high in some sections. F3 presumably formed one corner of a rectangular structure in combination with F4 (still used after Structure C went out of use).

It is worth noting that a third pit, F12, was identified in the south-eastern corner of the site, partly eroding out of the sea-cut section. Its surviving dimensions were 0.80 × 0.60 × 0.08m deep and it was filled with a very dark brown-black sandy silt. Its fill and likely original size were not dissimilar to the other two pits, and so it is conceivable that it too had been a hearth pit belonging to a third structure (or different phase) there; unfortunately, that part of the site's destruction by the sea makes it impossible to say any more about the pit with confidence.

Phase 2c

Two post-holes (F6 and F7) were added to the Structure D during its final phase (Phase 2c), when the Phase 2a/b walls must still have been in use; they were sited immediately to the north and south of hearth F5/10 (Figure 4.16). These post-holes comprised two neat clusters of stones (seven in each case) with a central void. No cut was visible for either feature and it is possible that they were simply rammed into the layer beneath. Their precise function is uncertain, but they may well have been added to support posts which themselves were used to support the structure's roof (which perhaps, in its final phase of use, was in need extra support). The post-holes were associated with the Phase 2c occupation layer [20] within the northern structure, as well as its equivalent to the east [27]. It is worth noting that Phase 2c produced no clearly Grooved Ware pottery (see Section 4.4).

Phase 3: Beaker

Four layers and a single pit (F2) were assigned to Phase 3 (Figure 4.21; Table 4.01). As a result of their physical position close to the upper surviving surface of the An Doirlinn islet, they had all been explosed to recent weathering, storms, etc. All four had the appearance of being naturally-formed deposits; they were all relatively 'clean' sandy or stone layers which, on excavation, seemed likely to have been created during storms or as a result of other natural processes. The currency of Beaker pottery in the Outer Hebrides is currently not well dated but is likely to be c. 2450 to 1750 BC (Alison Sheridan, pers. comm.).

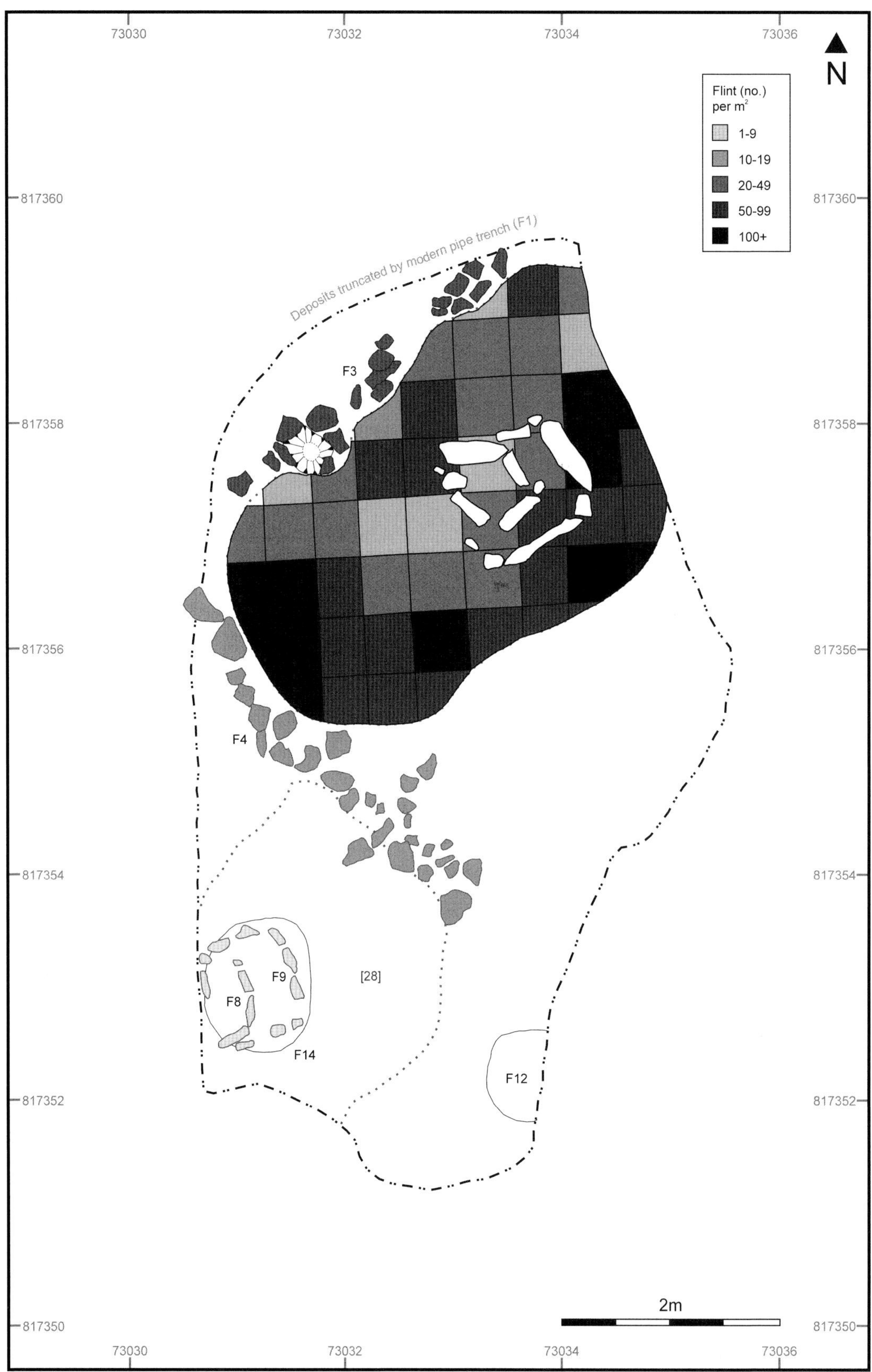

Figure 4.20. Finds densities plan for [41/42/47].

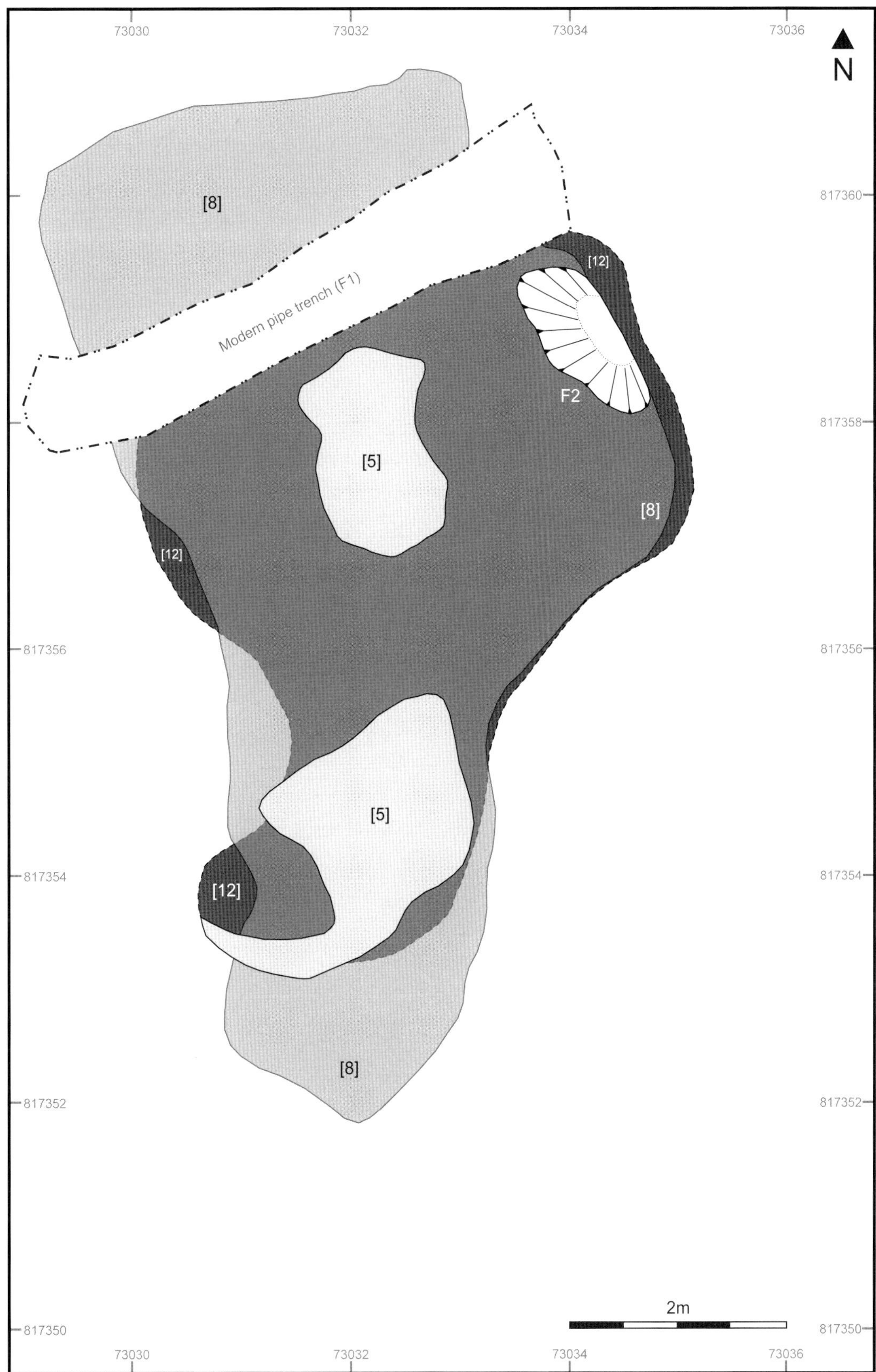

Figure 4.21. Phase 3 deposits.

Pit (F2) had been cut into layer [8] at the north-eastern edge of site (Figure 4.22; see also Figure 4.08). Its surviving dimensions were 1.30 × 0.40 × 0.70m deep, but it had been truncated to the east by the sea. It contained a single fill [10] of very dark brown silty sand. This contained several large rocks, some stood vertically on end, which appeared to have been intentionally dumped into the pit. Finds included a single undiagnostic sherd of pottery and 22 pieces of flint/quartz.

The Beaker phase of the site is difficult to interpret. Given their apparently naturally-formed character, it is not clear how or why the four main layers came to contain in some cases substantial quantities of flint and quartz, and a number of sometimes very large sherds of the site's only Beaker pottery. Equally, the function and broader context of the pit is also difficult to comprehend; its location close to the top of the site sequence, and the fact that it contained dumped stone which might originally have been structural, could suggest that it represents some kind of ritualised 'closing deposit' for the site (Niall Sharples, pers. comm.). It is quite possible that the Beaker phase of occupation on the site was, originally, substantial, and that other settlement-related features have subsequently been destroyed, with some of their contents ending up in the natural layers described above. However, if so, it is slightly unclear how the pottery within these came to be quite so well preserved. Unfortunately, the precise character of the Beaker occupation at An Doirlinn, ultimately, remains unknowable.

Table 4.01. Phase 3 layers – summary

Context	*Description*	*Pottery (no.)*	*Flint (no.)*	*Quartz (no.)*
5	Compact orange-brown sand	11	10	18
8	Clean golden sand	37	406	130
9	Irregular layer of large stones	–	–	–
12	Pale yellow shell sand	50	519	183
Total	–	*98*	*935*	*331*

Phase 4: Modern

Seven contexts, including the modern pipe-trench (which defined the northern limit of our excavations) were assigned to Phase 4. These were generally highly disturbed and contained mixed assemblages of redeposited material including Hebridean, Grooved Ware and Beaker sherds.

Figure 4.22. Pit F2, looking SW. The phase 1b wall (F20 = [91]) can be seen below the scale bar (scale: 0.5m).

4.4. Prehistoric pottery

Mike Copper

Introduction

The analysis of the pottery from An Doirlinn was undertaken at the University of Bradford between October 2012 and February 2013 and the digital catalogue filed with the main site archive. The ceramic assemblage comprises 4831 sherds together with 2465g of crumbs and small fragments, weighing just over 75kg in total. Three main styles of pottery were identified – Hebridean Neolithic (Figures 4.23 and 4.24; Table 4.02), Grooved Ware and Beaker (Figure 4.25; Table 4.02), corresponding with the three main phases of activity at the site. Most, if not all, vessels at An Doirlinn are of local manufacture and very well fired.

Aims

The assemblage from An Doirlinn is of considerable importance in furthering understanding of the nature and development of prehistoric pottery in the Western Isles: only one other Hebridean Neolithic site excavated in recent years (Eilean Dòmhnuill) has produced more pottery. With this in mind, the following report aims to characterise the assemblage and to highlight key aspects of the ceramic sequence at An Doirlinn in order to facilitate comparison with pottery from other Hebridean sites and contribute towards a better understanding of ceramic variation and sequence within the Western Isles.

Methodology

Analysis of the assemblage from An Doirlinn was undertaken with reference to the Prehistoric Ceramics Research Group's policies and guidelines (PCRG 2010). Four fabric types were identified and the number of sherds, vessel forms, attributes (particularly decoration) and rim and base diameters were recorded, together with any other significant diagnostic traits. It was not possible to reconstruct more than a few fragments of any of the vessels (despite a sustained attempt by Cardiff University's conservation department on two suspected near-complete but fragmented bowls – [66] and [69]); therefore overall vessel form was assessed largely of the basis of the presence or absence of formally diagnostic elements such as rim, carination/shoulder and neck sherds.

The size of the An Doirlinn assemblage, combined with the high degree of uniformity amongst fabrics, made estimation of vessel numbers very difficult and as such these must remain highly provisional. The estimate of a minimum of 135 vessels is made primarily on the basis of an examination of rim and body forms. It is important to note, however, that fragmentation and abrasion meant that it was difficult to assess the extent to which sherds from the same vessel were present within different contexts; therefore a working assumption was made that vessels would not be represented within different contexts unless there was clear evidence to the contrary such as the presence of cross-context joins. Nonetheless, it should be borne in mind that the presence of unidentified cross-context joins would reduce the actual vessel count while, conversely, the difficulty of separating vessels with very similar forms and fabrics may have led to an underestimation of vessel numbers. The extent to which one of these factors may cancel out the other is unknown.

Fabrics

Fabrics were assessed macroscopically and were initially divided into four groups. Within each group variations in sherd colour and the size of inclusions meant that fabric groups were further sub-divided during the analysis. However, as it is likely that taphonomic factors and the inherent heterogeneity resulting from open firing will be behind much of the variation in sherd colour, the original four categories are maintained in this report.

Fabric 1: Well-fired clay containing moderate to sparse, moderately well-sorted, sub-rounded, rounded and sub-angular grains of quartz and a dark, platy mineral – probably biotite. Sherds of this fabric, including the thickest sherds in the assemblage, were well oxidised and fully ceramic throughout. In the case of thinner sherds, inclusions may be rare rather than sparse. Colour varies from orange to pale yellow and creamy-white, although sooting means that a number of sherds are dark grey or black in colour.

Fabric 2: Fine, well-fired, dark grey clay with abundant, well-sorted, angular and sub-angular inclusions of quartz and mica. This fabric is primarily associated with finer, thinner sherds, although larger inclusions were associated with bigger vessels still considered to be of this fabric.

Fabric 3: Light grey clay with well-sorted, sub-angular grains of quartz and frequent mica and biotite particles. When held up to the light these inclusions can give this fabric a noticeable sparkle, probably due to the grains being brought to the surface by smoothing. This fabric is rare at An Doirlinn and is primarily associated with Grooved Ware sherds.

Fabric 4: In most respects this fabric closely resembles Fabric 1 but is distinguished by frequent voids giving it a distinctive 'corky' texture. This probably results from the former presence of organic inclusions and would not appear to be indicative of the leaching out of soluble minerals. Voids vary from around 1mm to over 10mm across and are of various shapes.

Taken as a percentage of the total sherd count, Fabric 1 is by far the most common fabric in all phases, accounting for 95% of the entire assemblage (Table 4.03). Large inclusions, some in excess of 5mm in diameter, were found within thicker sherds, but consist of the same minerals, in roughly

Table 4.02. Catalogue of illustrated pottery from An Doirlinn (Figs 4.23–4.25)

Illus. no.	*Description*
H1	Phase 1a, Context 82, Square C7. Decorated, everted rim with external incised lines and impressed decoration on internal bevel. Fabric 1.
H2	Phase 1a. Context 82, Square C7. Undecorated, rounded rim. Fabric 1.
H3	Phase 1a, Context 87, Square F5. Undecorated, rounded rim. Fabric 1.
H4	Phase 1a, Context 87, Square D5. Simple rim, undecorated. Fabric 1.
H5	Phase 1a, Context 87, Square C2. Undecorated, internally bevelled rim. Fabric 1.
H6	Phase 1a, Context 82, Square C2. Undecorated, everted rim with internal bevel. Fabric 1.
H7	Phase 1a, Context 67, Square C4. Simple rim, undecorated. Fabric 1. Probably part of the same vessel as H58.
H8	Phase 1a, Context 82, Square C4. Everted rim decorated with internal decoration of short, incised lines and external incised lines. Fabric 1.
H9	Phase 1a, Context 82, Square C4. Undecorated rim with slight rolled eversion. Fabric 1.
H10	Phase 1a, Context 82, Square B7. Everted rim with internal bevel. Bevel decorated with small impressions. Small slashes below rim externally. Fabric 1.
H11	Phase 1b, Context 65, Square C5. Everted rim with internal bevel decorated with horizontal incised lines. Fabric 1.
H12	Phase 1a. Context 82, Square C7. Undecorated everted rim with internal bevel. Fabric 1.
H13	Phase 1b, Context 65, Square C5. Undecorated everted rim of simple form. Fabric 1.
H14	Phase 1b, Context 70, Square B2. Everted rim with faint incised lines on internal bevel. Fabric 1.
H15	Phase 1b, Context 81, Feature 16. Undecorated rim of simple, everted form Fabric 1.
H16	Phase 1a, Context 78, Square unspecified. Undecorated, everted rim with flattened top. Fabric 1. Probably part of the same vessel as H47–52.
H17	Phase 1b, Context 70, Square B3. Undecorated, simple rim. Fabric 1.
H18	Phase 1a, Context 69, Squares D5 and E6. Undecorated simple rim. Fabric 1.
H19	Phase 1c, Context 63, Square C5. Undecorated, slightly expanded rim of inverted, flat topped form with possible carination. Fabric 1.
H20	Phase 1b, Context 70, Square C9. Undecorated, flat-topped rim with slight eversion. Fabric 1.
H21	Phase 1c, Context 63, Square C5. Undecorated, closed rim. Fabric 1.
H22	Phase 2a, Context 55, Feature 11. Everted rim with internal bevel decorated with lines of small stabs (possibly comb-decoration). Fabric 1.
H23	Phase 2a, Context 55, Square Unspecified. Everted rim with internal bevel decorated with short, incised lines. Fabric 1.
H24	Phase 1c, Context 59, Square E5. Slightly everted rim with internal bevel decorated with short, impressed lines. Fabric 1.
H25	Phase 1c, Context 54, Square D3. Slightly inverted, undecorated simple rim. Fabric 1.
H26	Phase 1c, Context 53, Square B5. Everted rim decorated with short, incised lines on probable internal bevel. Fabric 1.
H27	Phase 1c, Context 53, Square B5. Everted rim, probably with internal bevel, decorated with short, incised lines. Fabric 1.
H28	Phase 1c, Context 53, Square B5. Small rim fragment, probably everted with internal bevel, decorated with short, incised lines. Fabric 1.
H29	Phase 1c, Context 53, Square B5. Small fragment of everted rim with internal bevel decorated with short slashes. Fabric 1.
H30	Phase 1c, Context 52, Square D2. Undecorated, everted rim of simple form. Fabric 1.
H31	Phase 1a, Context 82, Square B8. Carinated bowl with slightly flattened simple rim decorated with two rows of short lines. Fabric 1.
H32	Phase 3, Context 12, Square H. Undecorated. Rolled rim Fabric 1.
H33	Phase 1a, Context 82, Square C7. Comb-decorated sherd. Fabric 1.
H34	Phase 1c, Context 64, Square B3. Sherd decorated with small stabs Fabric 2.
H35	Phase 1c, Context 64, Square B3. Sherd decorated with small stabs. Fabric 2.
H36	Phase 1c, Context 64, Square B3. Sherd decorated with small stabs. Fabric 2.
H37	Phase 1c, Context 64, Square B3. Sherd decorated with small stabs. Fabric 2.
H38	Phase 1c, Context 64, Square B3. Sherd decorated with small stabs. Fabric 2.
H39	Phase 1c, Context 64, Square B3. Sherd decorated with small stabs. Fabric 2.
H40	Phase 1c, Context 64, Square B3. Sherd decorated with small stabs. Fabric 2.
H41	Phase 1c, Context 64, Square B3. Sherd decorated with small stabs. Fabric 2.
H42	Phase 1c, Context 53, Square B4. Sherd decorated with incised, parallel lines. Fabric 1.
H43	Phase 1c, Context 53, Square B4. Sherd decorated with incised, parallel lines. Fabric 1.
H44	Phase 1c, Context 53, Square B4. Sherd decorated with incised lines Fabric 1.
H45	Phase 1c, Context 53, Square B5. Sherd decorated with incised/impressed lines. Fabric 1.
H46	Phase 1c, Context 53, Square B5. Sherd decorated with parallel lines of fingernail impressions. Fabric 1.
H47	Phase 1a, Context 78, Unspecified Square. Sherd decorated with shallow depressions. Fabric 1. Probably part of the same vessel as H16 and H48–52.
H48	Phase 1a, Context 78, Unspecified Square. Sherd decorated with shallow depressions. Fabric 1. Probably part of the same vessel as H16, H47 and H49–52.
H49	Phase 1a, Context 78, Unspecified Square. Sherd decorated with shallow depressions. Fabric 1. Probably part of the same vessel as H16, H48, H50, H51 and H52.

H50 Phase 1a, Context 78, Unspecified Square. Sherd decorated with shallow depressions. Fabric 1. Probably part of the same vessel as H16, H48, H 49, H51 and H52.

H51 Phase 1a, Context 78, Unspecified Square. Sherd with fingernail rustication. Fabric 1. Probably part of the same vessel as H16, H48–50 and H52.

H52 Phase 1a, Context 78, Unspecified Square. Sherd with fingernail rustication. Fabric 1. Probably part of the same vessel as H16 and H48–51.

H53 Phase 1a, Context 82, Square C7. Comb-decorated carination. Fabric 1.

H54 Phase 1a, Context 82, Square C9. Rim sherd with post-firing repair hole drilled from both sides. Fabric 1.

H55 Phase 1a, Context 82, Square C9. An unusual decorated, carinated bowl with everted rim decorated with impressed short lines on inner bevel and stabs along the flattened outer lip. A line of inverted 'Latin crosses' runs around the body of the pot above a line of fingernail impressions, itself just above the carination. Fabric 1.

H56 Phase 1a, Context 82, Square B8. Comb-decorated lug. Fabric 1.

H57 Phase 1a, Context 87, Square B2. Thin sherd with simple rim. Fabric 1.

H58 Phase 1a, Context 67, Square C4. Thick sherd with post-firing repair hole drilled from both sides. Fabric 1. Probably part of the same vessel as H7.

H59 Phase 1a, Context 66, Square D3. Large lug/knob. Fabric 1.

H60 Phase 1b, Context 65, Square E5. Lug decorated with a line of stabs. Fabric 1.

H61 Phase 1c, Context 64, Square B2. Sherd with pre-firing perforation. Fabric 1.

H62 Phase 1c, Context 64, Square B2. Sherd with impressed carination in distinctive 'corky' Fabric 4.

H63 Phase 1c, Context 64, Square B2. Undecorated rim or carination. Fabric 4.

H64 Phase 1c, Context 53, Square B5. Possible multiply-carinated sherd. Fabric 1.

H65 Phase 4, Context 2, Square N. Carinated sherd with incised parallel lines. Fabric 1.

H66 Phase 4, Context 2, Square N. Carinated sherd. Fabric 1.

H67 Phase 1a, Context 82, Square B7. Body sherd decorated with incised parallel lines. Fabric 1.

H68 Phase 1a, Context 105, Unspecified square. Small, undecorated, round-based pot with everted rim of simple form in a very sandy version of Fabric 1.

H69 Unstratified (material recovered 2005–2009). Undecorated everted rim. Fabric 1.

H70 Unstratified (material recovered 2005–2009). Undecorated rim sherd. Fabric 1.

H71 Unstratified (material recovered 2005–2009). Everted rim decorated with fingernail impressions on internal bevel. Fabric 1.

H72 Unstratified (material recovered 2005–2009). Everted rim with incised internal decoration. Fabric 1.

H73 Unstratified (material recovered 2005–2009). Flattened rim with row of stab marks along the top. Fabric 1.

H74 Unstratified (material recovered 2005–2009). Steeply everted rim with impressed herringbone motif on inner bevel, probably fingernail. Fabric 1.

H75 Unstratified (material recovered 2005–2009). Four sherds forming part of a carinated bowl with parallel, diagonal, incised lines between the carination and rim. The rim is everted with two concentric rows of fingernail impressions around the inner bevel. Fabric 1.

H76 Unstratified (material recovered 2005–2009). Undecorated everted rim with inner bevel. Fabric 1.

H77 Unstratified (material recovered 2005–2009). Body sherd with single impressed hollow. Fabric 1.

H78 Unstratified (material recovered 2005–2009). Body sherd with impressed hollow. Fabric 1.

H79 Unstratified (material recovered 2005–2009). Undecorated sherd with carination. Fabric 1.

H80 Unstratified (material recovered 2005–2009). Body sherd drilled from both sides after firing. Fabric 1.

GW1 Phase 1b, Context 74, Square B2. Rim with internal collar decorated with diagonal lines of shallow stabs. External decoration comprises incised, parallel diagonal lines alternating with lines of stab marks and blank zones. Fabric 3.

GW2 Phase 1c, Context 64, Square B2. Rim sherd of simple form decorated externally and internally with shallow stabs. Fabric 3.

GW3 Phase 4, Context 2, Square H. Simple rim with incised external horizontal grooves and a row of small stab marks along the top. Fabric 1.

GW4 Phase 1c, Context 59, Square D5. Rim sherd with internal decoration of horizontal lines and a single row of stab marks, and external decoration of horizontal lines immediately under the rim with diagonal lines below these. Fabric 3.

GW5 Phase 2b/c, Context 46, Square F6. Rim of unusual 'pinched' form with cordons below the rim both internally and externally. Fabric 1.

GW6 Phase 1c, Context 53, Square D6 and Phase 2a, Context 49, Square C4. Rim with internal collar decorated with two parallel, zigzag lines of shallow 'stabs'. External decoration consists of diagonal parallel lines and dots. Fabric 3.

GW7 Phase 1b, Context 65, Square B8. Flat-base sherd with smoothed outer surface. Fabric 1.

GW8 Phase 2c, Context 47, Square B5. Flat-base sherd. Fabric 1.

GW9 Phase 2c, Context 41, Square G4. Flat-base sherd. Fabric 1.

GW10 Phase 2c, Context 47, Square B5. Rim sherd of simple form, decorated internally with three horizontal lines. Fabric 3.

GW11 Phase 3, Context 12, Square J. Heavily abraded flat-base sherd. Fabric 1.

GW12 Unstratified sherd from cleaning of east section. Flat-base sherd. Fabric 1.

GW13 Phase 1a, Context 87, Square A7. Grooved Ware sherd incised with converging parallel lines (probably one corner of a lozenge or triangle) enclosing four impressed dots. Fabric 1.

GW14 Phase 2a, Context 76, Feature 14. Abraded sherd decorated with parallel lines. Fabric 1.

(*Continued on next page*)

Table 4.02. Catalogue of illustrated pottery from An Doirlinn (Figs 4.23–4.25) (Continued)

Illus. no.	*Description*
GW15	Phase 2a, Context 76, Feature 14. Abraded sherd decorated with parallel lines. Fabric 1.
GW16	Phase 2a, Context 76, Feature 14. Abraded sherd decorated with parallel lines. Fabric 1.
GW17	Phase 2a, Context 55, Unspecified Square. Sherd with converging incised lines. Fabric 1.
GW18	Phase 2c, Context 42, Square C2. Small sherd with cordon, incised line and row of stab marks. Fabric 2.
GW19	Phase 3, Context 12, Square J. Small sherd with incised line. Fabric 1.
GW20	Phase 3, Context 12, Square J. Small sherd with parallel, incised lines. Fabric 1.
GW21	Phase 3, Context 12, Square J. Small sherd with parallel, incised lines. Fabric 1.
GW22	Unstratified sherd from cleaning of south-east facing section. Sherd bears two low cordons or carinations, one decorated with a fingernail impression. Fabric 2.
GW23	Unstratified sherd from cleaning of Southeast facing section. Sherd bears two low cordons or carinations decorated with fingernail impressions. Fabric 3.
GW24	Unstratified (material recovered 2005–2009). Fine, undecorated body sherd of upright form with simple rim. Fabric 1.
GW25	Unstratified (material recovered 2005–2009). Decorated body sherd with applied cordons decorated with transverse fingernail impressions and infilling with random stab marks. Fabric 2.
GW26	Unstratified (material recovered 2005–2009). Body sherd with applied cordon. Fabric 2.
GW27	Unstratified (material recovered 2005–2009). Body sherd with infilling by random stab marks. Fabric 2.
GW28	Unstratified (material recovered 2005–2009). Flat–base sherd. Fabric 1.
GW29	Unstratified (material recovered 2005–2009). Flat-base sherd. Fabric 1.
GW30	Unstratified (material recovered 2005–2009). Flat-base sherd. Fabric 1.
GW31	Unstratified (material recovered 2005–2009). Flat-base sherd. Fabric 1.
B1	Phase 4, Context 2, Square J. Heavily abraded flat base sherd. Fabric 1.
B2	Phases 3 and 4, Contexts 5 and 3, Square G. Conjoining sherd from a large domestic Beaker with simple rim, external applied cordon below the rim and fingernail rustication. Fabric 1.
B3	Phase 2d, Context 28, Square L. Undecorated rim of simple form. Fabric 1.
B4	Phase 2d, Context 28, Square J. Undecorated rim of slightly pointed, upright form. Fabric 1.
B5	Phase 2d, Context 28, Square L. Abraded rim of simple form. Fabric 1.
B6	Phase 3, Context 8, Square G. Slightly everted rim with flattened top. Fabric 1.
B7	Phase 1a, Context 82, Square D3. Rim sherd with fine herringbone motif. Fabric 1.
B8	Phase 3, Context 5, Square H. Sherd with seashell impressions, probably limpet. Fabric 1.
B9	Phase 4, Context 8, Square I. Sherd with seashell impressions, probably limpet. Fabric 1.
B10	Phase 4, Context 8, Square G. Sherd with seashell impressions, probably limpet. Fabric 1.
B11	Phase 4, Context 8, Square G. Sherd with fingernail rustication. Fabric 1.
B12	Unstratified (material recovered 2005–2009). Body sherd with seashell.

Table 4.03. Pottery fabrics by phase (%)

	Phase 1a	*Phase 1b*	*Phase 1c*	*Phase 2a*	*Phase 2b*	*Phase 2c*	*Phase 3*	*Phase 4*	*Unstrat.*
Fabric 1	99	95	84	100	82	100	85	91	57
Fabric 2	1	5	12	N/A	4	N/A	15	9	43
Fabric 3	N/A	<1	<1	N/A	7	<1	<1	<1	<1
Fabric 4	<1	<1	4	N/A	7	N/A	N/A	N/A	N/A

the same proportions, as those found within finer sherds. Variety across the fabric types suggests that inclusions were being selected and added by the potters themselves, although some are likely to be naturally occurring within the clay itself. The nature of the inclusions within the clay employed for the manufacture of almost all of the pottery at An Doirlinn is consistent with derivation from a local source. A notable exception to the overall consistency in fabrics is Fabric 3, associated with a number of sherds identified as Grooved Ware, although there is no reason to believe that the clay for this fabric is not from a local source.

Fabric colour varies from pale yellow to black and, as noted above, includes various shades of orange, brown and grey. Fabric colour is a poor guide when assessing vessel numbers on account of the variation that can result from differences in firing conditions, even across a single vessel (Gibson 2002, 47; Gibson & Woods 1997, 52–53). Additionally, taphonomic factors can occasionally result in even conjoining sherds having totally different colours. It is of note, however, that grey cores, suggestive of low temperature firings or of short firing times, are conspicuous by their absence at An Doirlinn: pottery within the assemblage is almost invariably hard and well-fired. At Allt Chrisal and at Eilean an Tighe few waster sherds were identified (Gibson in Branigan & Foster 1995, 100), and a similar situation pertains at An Doirlinn, where no wasters were identified, suggesting that manufacture did not take place on the site itself, although this does not, of course, preclude it from having taken place close by.

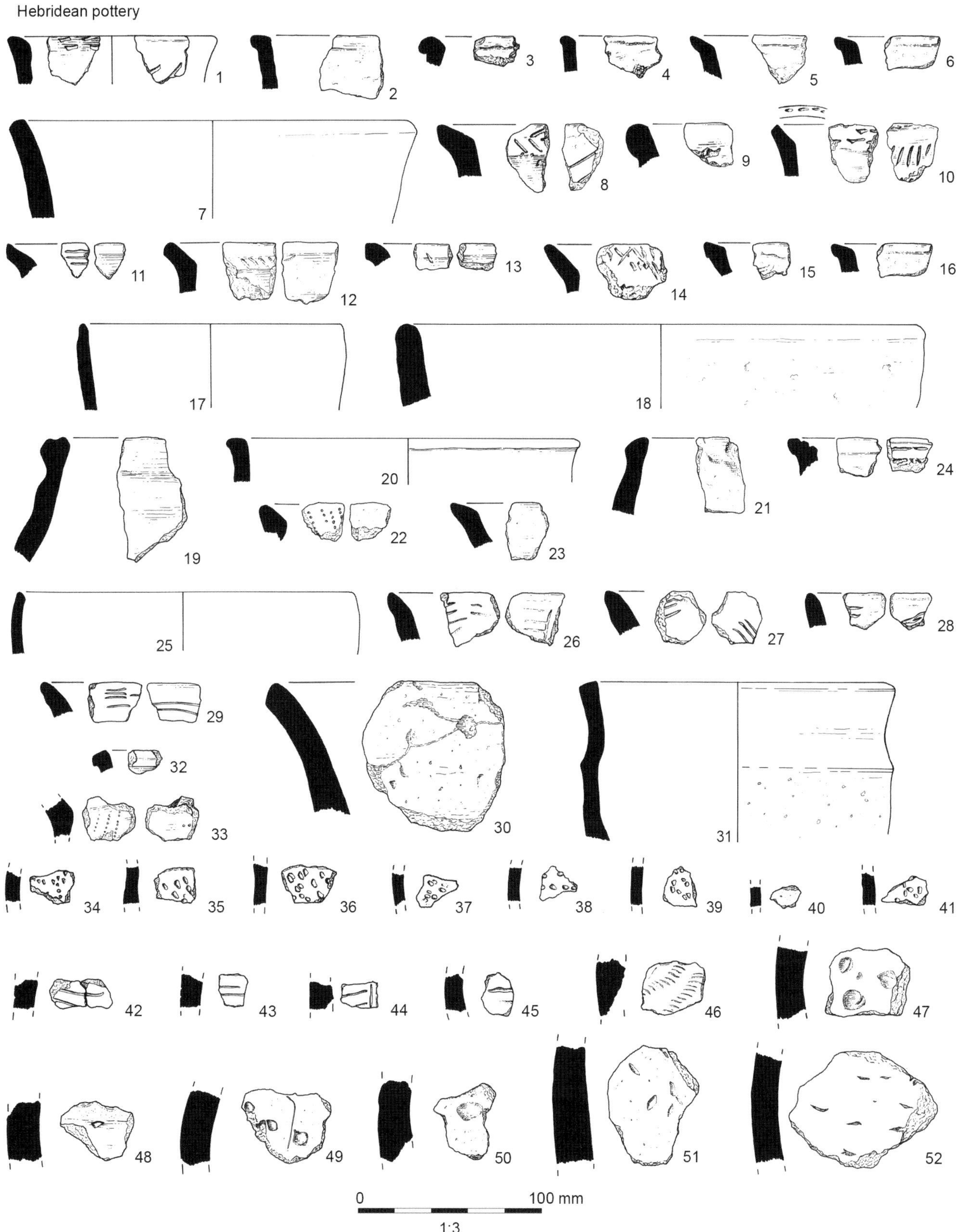

Figure 4.23. Hebridean pottery (1) (drawn by A. Wilkins).

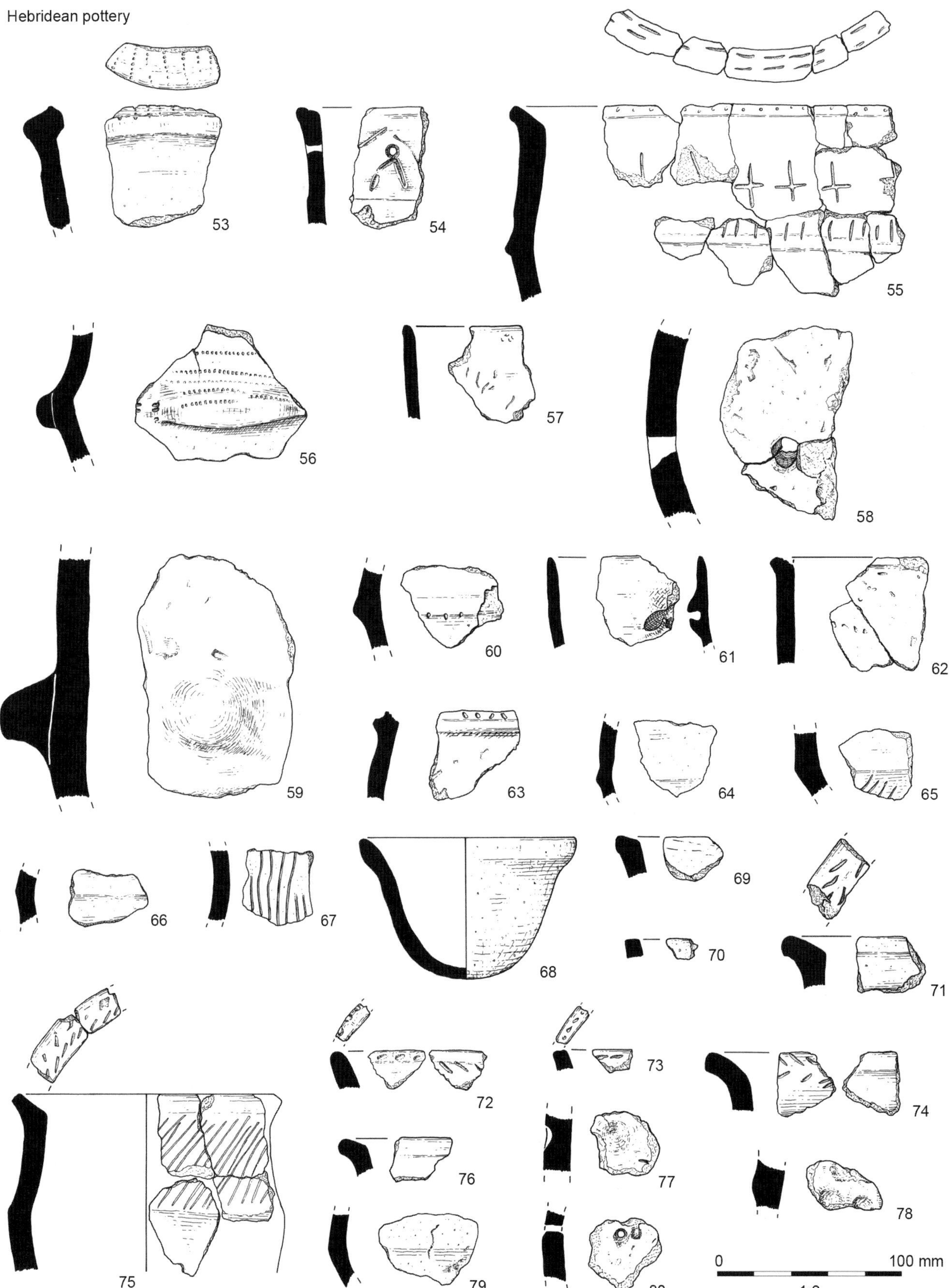

Figure 4.24. Hebridean pottery (2) (drawn by A. Wilkins).

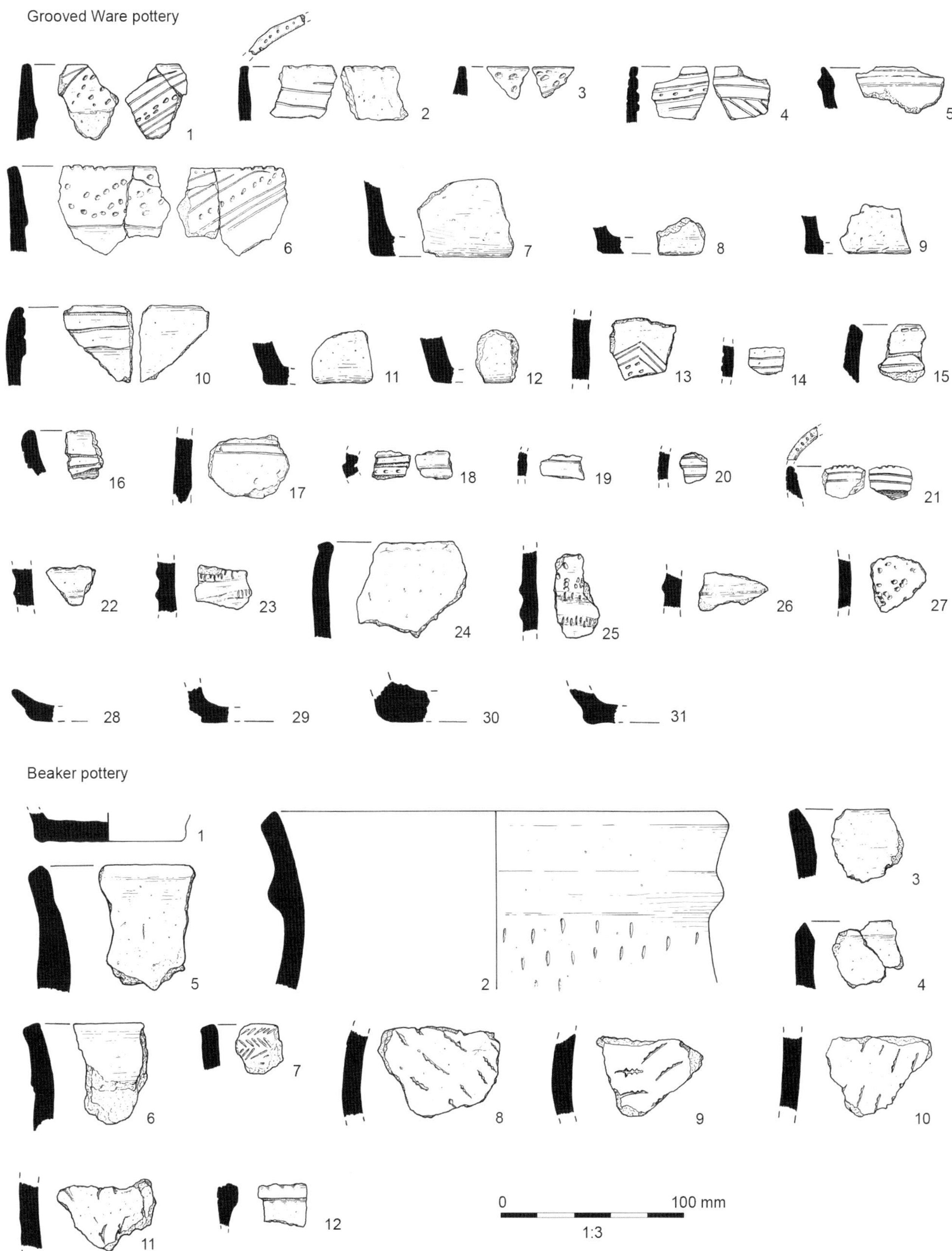

Figure 4.25. Grooved Ware and Beaker pottery (drawn by A. Wilkins).

Table 4.04. Rim forms by phase (decorated/undecorated)

Phase/form	*1a*	*1b*	*1c*	*2a*	*2b*	*2c*	*3*	*4*	*Unstrat.*
1a	1/18	1/4	4/5	1/0	1/5	0/0	0/0	1/2	0/0
1b	0/4	0/4	0/1	0/0	0/0	0/0	0/0	0/0	0/0
1c	1/34	4/1	2/2	0/0	0/0	0/0	0/0	0/0	0/0
1d	5/11	1/4	0/0	0/0	0/0	0/0	0/0	0/0	0/0
1e	0/0	0/0	0/0	0/0	0/1	0/2	0/0	0/0	0/0
1f	0/0	0/1	0/0	0/0	0/0	0/1	0/0	0/0	0/0
2a	0/10	0/3	0/4	0/0	0/0	0/4	0/1	0/0	0/0
2b	8/9	3/5	7/11	2/1	0/1	0/0	0/0	0/0	0/1
2c	2/4	0/2	0/1	0/0	0/1	0/0	0/0	0/0	0/0
2d	7/0	0/0	0/0	0/0	0/0	0/0	0/0	0/0	0/0
2e	0/0	0/0	1/2	0/0	0/0	0/0	0/0	0/0	0/0
3a	0/0	0/1	0/0	0/0	3/0	0/0	0/0	0/0	0/0
3b	0/0	0/0	0/1	0/0	0/0	0/0	0/0	0/0	0/0
3c	0/0	0/0	0/5	0/0	1/0	0/0	0/1	0/0	0/0
3d	0/0	0/0	0/0	0/0	1/0	0/0	0/0	0/0	0/0
Unclear	2/4	0/6	0/14	1	1	0/0	0/0	0/0	0/0

The condition of the sherds at An Doirlinn varies from very heavily abraded – particularly those from contexts likely to have been subjected to erosion and/or exposure – to smoothed and polished, although there is no evidence for burnishing, for example in the form of burnishing facets. Charred and sooty residues were identified on a number of sherds.

Six sherds, including two conjoining pieces, had been drilled after firing (e.g. H54 and H58). It is likely that this was for the purpose of repair as it is possible to close cracks within a pot wall by drilling holes either side of the crack and binding the two sides together. Locally, other examples of repair holes have been noted at Eilean an Tighe (Scott 1951, 19, figure 7:0.9), Eilean Dòmhnuill (Brown n.d.) and at Allt Chrisal (Gibson in Branigan & Foster 1995, 100 and figures 4.37.196 & 4.29.5).

The presence of coil breaks on a number of large and small sherds throughout all phases indicates that coil (or ring) building was at least one method of manufacture employed at An Doirlinn throughout the site's history. Coil building can, however, vary greatly in nature, and its presence does not rule out the use of other techniques such as beating or moulding (Gibson & Woods 1997, 37–44), although no unambiguous evidence was noted for these within the An Doirlinn assemblage.

Rims tend to be simple and either upright or everted in form, and the internal bevels associated with the Phase 1 pottery contrast with the externally bevelled collared rim mouldings found elsewhere in the Hebrides, which are not represented at An Doirlinn. Rims forms are summarised in Figure 4.26 and Table 4.04.

Pottery by phase

Phase 1 at An Doirlinn accounted for by far the greater proportion of the pottery assemblage, with 4326 sherds. Phase 2 produced a total of 473 sherds, with 163 and 108 sherds coming from Phases 3 and 4 respectively (Figure 4.27).

Phase 1

With a handful of exceptions – all apparently intrusive – all of the pottery from Phase 1 at An Doirlinn falls within the distinctly insular Hebridean Neolithic tradition and is dominated by simple, round-based vessels. A rough estimation of vessel numbers (taking into account the caveats set out above) would be 85, amongst which were a small number of sherds, including Beaker and Grooved Ware, whose presence almost certainly results from later disturbance.

As elsewhere on the site Fabric 1 is overwhelmingly the most common fabric, varying from 99% of sherds in Phase 1a to 84% in Phase 1c. The finer, darker Fabric 2 accounts for between 1% and 12% of the sherds (in Phases 1a and 1c respectively) and is associated with smaller, finer vessels. As with the Beaker and Grooved Ware sherds mentioned above, the handful of sherds of the distinctively 'corky' Fabric 4 is most likely intrusive, occurring within the possible occupation deposit or midden represented by Phase 1c.

Of the 3731 formally undiagnostic body/base sherds from Phase 1, over 97% exhibited no decoration whatsoever, while only 35 of the total of 4326 sherds from Phase 1 came from vessel shoulders or provided evidence for carination. Indeed, it is of note that the heavily incised, multiple-ridged vessels recognised elsewhere in the Western Isles are, with the possible exceptions of the H65, H67 and the unstratified H75 (probably a necked bowl or jar), conspicuous by their absence at An Doirlinn.

Rim forms also tend to be plain, and 77% of rim sherds were undecorated. Of these, 60% were of simple form and upright or slightly everted. The majority of the rims from the larger vessels represented within Phase 1 were of simple form. Everted rims of various forms accounted for 50% of all rim sherds in Phase 1. Of these, bevels – all internal – were a feature of 24% of the sherds. Flat tops were a feature of 14% of rim sherds, with 27% of these being decorated. There is no evidence from An Doirlinn for the 'flanged', T- and 7-sectioned rims known from other Hebridean assemblages (e.g. Allt Chrisal: Gibson 1995, 104 and figures 4.32.64 and 4.33.103; Eilean an Tighe: Scott 1951, 19, figure 7.O.1 and 17, figure 6 Y1 and Y3).

Rim diameters vary from 10cm to 28cm, and decoration occurs on rims of all sizes. Within Phase 1, 11 sherds had a rim diameter below 15cm, 29 between 16cm and 20cm, 27 between 21cm and 25cm, 22 over 26cm, while 120 were too small or fragmented/abraded to measure (Figure 4.28).

Thirty-nine of the 44 lug sherds from Phase 1 at An Doirlinn were undecorated. Where discernable, lugs – often elongated – tend to be located on carinations. Four lugs from Phase 1 display evidence of decoration, including comb-impression (on H53 and H56, and also recognised

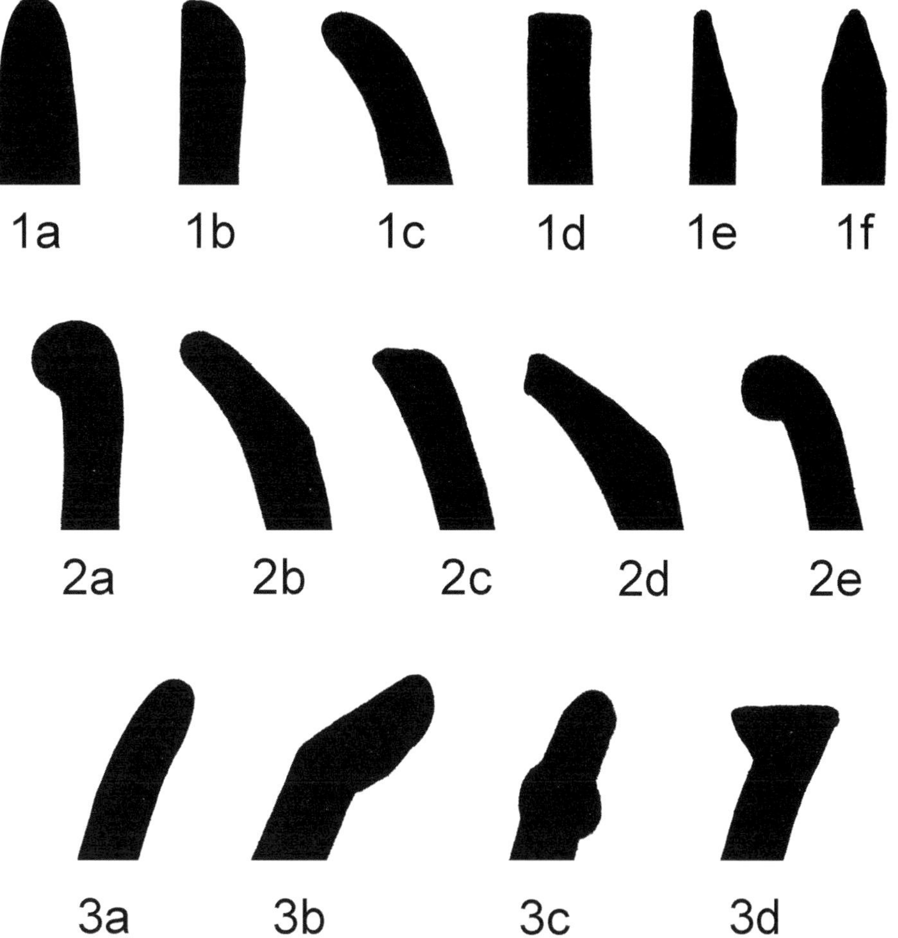

Figure 4.26. Rim types at An Doirlinn (Type 1: simple and/or upright; Type 2: everted; Type 3: inverted).

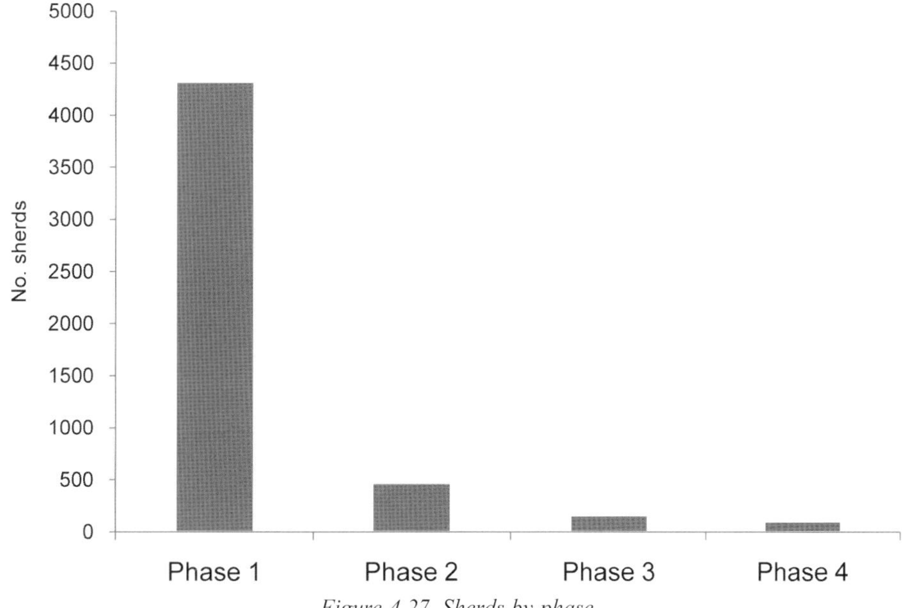

Figure 4.27. Sherds by phase.

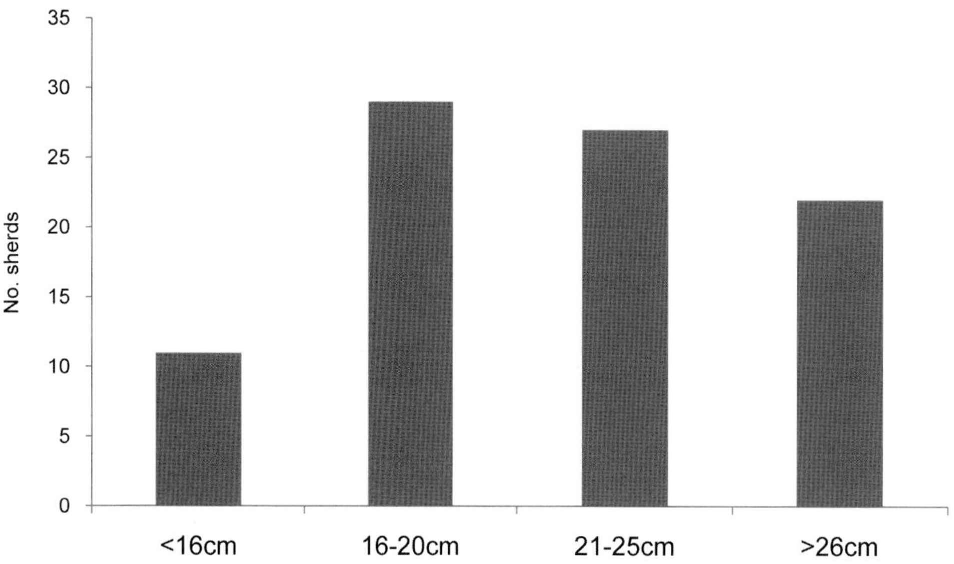

Figure 4.28. Phase 1 pottery: rim diameters.

on body sherd H33 and rim sherd H22). Comb impression is a very rare feature in pre-Beaker contexts but is possibly present elsewhere in Scotland at Eilean an Tighe on North Uist (Scott 1951, figure 7 no. Z7), Northton on Harris (Johnson 2006, 62–63) and at Luce Sands (McInnes 1963, 73, figure 8 no. 150) and, outside Scotland, on sherds of Mortlake-style Peterborough Ware at Ogmore, Glamorgan (Gibson 2001, 59 figure 3.5). Claims have also been made for comb impression on a lugged vessel from Beacharra in Argyll (Callander 1929, 53).

In addition to the four comb-impressed sherds, decoration is by both incision (present on 45% of decorated sherds) and impression (found on 38%). The most common motif, present on over 40% of all decorated sherds, is straight lines, including parallel lines. Other motifs include stabs (both random and in lines), shallow pits, fingernail impressions and, in one unusual case, a line of inverted 'Latin crosses' around the body of a carinated vessel just above the carination itself (H55, described below). A small number of sherds show evidence of applied cordons.

On rims and bevels decoration is mainly by incision, with impression (including one sherd (H46) decorated with fingernail impressions) accounting for the rest. Incised lines represent the most common motif, followed by stabs and lines of stabs. Herringbone patterns are also found, but are uncommon.

Three vessels stand out as noticeably different from the main assemblage in Phase 1. The first is the earliest vessel stratigraphically, a small, round-bottomed bowl of a sandy fabric with a slightly flaring rim (H68). The pot, with a rim diameter of 10cm, is undecorated. This is the only vessel whose complete form was discernible before reconstruction. It was deposited whole within a shallow pit (F46) in the bedrock.

The second vessel (H55) is notable on account of its unusual decoration, to the author's knowledge unparalleled elsewhere. The pot is a round-based, carinated bowl with an everted rim 24cm in diameter. The rim itself has an internal bevel decorated with two concentric, incised lines of short 'dashes'. The outer lip of the rim has been squared off and decorated with a line of stabs. The lower part of the neck of the vessel is encircled by a repeating pattern of inverted 'Latin crosses', below which, and immediately above the carination, is a line of vertically set fingernail impressions. This vessel was found within the occupation deposit or midden layer represented by context [82]. The third vessel is represented by a number of sherds (H34 to H41) of the unusual 'corky' Fabric 4. With the exception of this vessel, Fabric 4 is primarily associated with Phase 2. These sherds may therefore be intrusive from Phase 2a as they were also found within the sandy deposit that constitutes Phase 1c.

In addition to the three vessels noted above, five large pots seem to have been crushed *in situ* within the early occupation layer [82] and were assigned their own context numbers: [66] (H59), [67] (H7), [68] (not illustrated), [69] (H18), and [78] (H16). Vessel [66] (and possibly [78]) appears to be uncarinated, and no lug sherds were found with it. Lugs were also missing from vessel [78] but were present on the other pots. With the exception of vessel [69], which had an everted and internally bevelled rim, rim forms were all simple. Decoration was only present as simple incised lines on the rim of vessel [67] and as stabs, shallow pits and fingernail rustication on the body of vessel [78]. The weights of these potentially substantially complete pots are detailed in Table 4.05.

Overall, the pottery found within Phase 1 at An Doirlinn exhibits significant similarities with, but also differences to,

Table 4.05. Substantially complete vessel weights

Vessel	*Weight (kg)*
66	3.455
67	7.981
68	7.133
69	4.224
78	7.309

other Neolithic assemblages from the Western Isles, a point that will be discussed further below.

Phase 2

A significant proportion, if not all, of the pottery belonging to Phase 2 at An Doirlinn is Grooved Ware – an important discovery given the previous rarity of this style of pottery in the Western Isles.

As with Phase 1, it is hard to give a reliable figure for the number of vessels present, although examination of fabrics and rim forms would suggest a minimum of 26 pots in all. Most of the pottery from Phase 2 consists of small fragments, often heavily abraded, with plain body sherds and 'crumbs' constituting 92% of the sherds from this phase. Of the sherds from Phases 2a and 2b (from which the greater part of the pottery from Phase 2 as a whole derives), 82% are of Fabric 1, and it is significant that a quarter of these come from thinner sherds; while Fabric 2 constitutes 4%, and Fabric 3 and Fabric 4 (rare across the site as a whole) each constitute 7% of the sherds from these phases. Fragmented sherds of coarse fabric occur throughout Phase 2, although parts of a vessel – including heavy rim sherds of simple form – found within the Phase 2 occupation layers, and closely resembling vessels from Phase 1, are most likely redeposited. Sherds from Phase 2 are, on average, thinner than those from the preceding phase.

It was only possible to ascertain rim diameters for half of the vessels in Phase 2. These varied from 14cm to 28cm, but beyond this little can be added given the difficulty of discerning the number of vessels present. Quantifying percentages of pots with differing rim diameters was not possible, although both of the flat base sherds identified in Phase 2 had diameters of 12cm.

Decoration is almost exclusively by incision, with lines – often parallel – dominating the repertoire of motifs. Stab marks also occur, and one sherd has an applied cordon. Decoration on pottery from this phase will be considered more thoroughly in the discussion below.

Sixteen of the 26 rim sherds identified in Phase 2 were undecorated. Of these, simple rims were by far the most common. Of the decorated rims, two were of simple form, two had internal bevels and one appeared to come from a vessel with a closed mouth – a very rare feature at An Doirlinn.

Conspicuous by their rarity or absence in Phase 2 are neck sherds (4), shoulders/carinations (0) and lugs (1), and the contexts in which these were found suggest that these few examples were redeposited. This stands in contrast to Phase 1, where such features are rather more common.

The pottery from Phase 2 differs markedly from that of Phase 1, and the recognition of Grooved Ware in this phase is of great significance given the present rarity of this style elsewhere in the Western Isles. Indeed, Grooved Ware is the defining component of Phase 2 at An Doirlinn as no indigenous Hebridean-style pottery derives from a secure context within this phase.

Prior to the excavation at An Doirlinn only two Grooved Ware pots had been recorded from the Western Isles. One vessel is known from Calanais (Ashmore 2016) while a second was found in the Unival passage grave (Henshall 1972, 181–182 and 309; Scott 1948, 26–28 and plate vii). Recently, Grooved Ware has been recognised amongst the unpublished material from Iain Crawford's excavations at the Udal (Beverley Ballin-Smith, pers. comm.), meaning that the An Doirlinn Grooved Ware is now the second Hebridean Grooved Ware assemblage known from a domestic context. Like the Calanais and Unival vessels, diagnostic sherds from both An Doirlinn and the Udal would, in the past, have been considered to fall within the 'Clacton' style of Grooved Ware (Wainwright and Longworth 1971, 236–238) although it has been argued for some time that such styles are at best hard to apply in Scotland (Cowie and MacSween 1999, 53–54). The abraded or fragmentary condition of other likely Grooved Ware sherds would, in any event, preclude their attribution to any particular style.

Vessels GW1 and GW6 are of particular note. GW6 comprises sherds from context [53], a patchy (and possibly mixed) layer at the interface between Phases 1c and 2a, and context [49] in Phase 2b. The close similarity in decoration, combined with the fact that both GW1 and GW6 are of the same fabric (Fabric 3), strongly suggests that both may in fact belong to the same vessel. This vessel has a rim diameter of between 120mm and 160mm (probably 140mm) and a maximum wall thickness of 8mm. The rim is very distinctive, simple in some parts, but with a 'notched' form in others. A steep internal bevel runs to 3cm below the rim, and is decorated with two parallel zigzag lines of rounded stab marks. Externally, decoration comprises a pattern of incised diagonal lines (in threes) separated by lines of shallow stabs or blank spaces. This decoration may well be part of a pattern of triangles and/or lozenges similar to those on the Udal, Calanais and Unival pots. Sherds from contexts [64] and [87] (GW13), which are almost certainly intrusive into Phase 1 and probably come from the same vessel given the close similarity in both fabric and decoration, would seem to reinforce this conclusion.

Similarity in fabric and decoration also make it likely that sherds GW4 and GW18 come from a second vessel, once again resembling the Udal, Calanais and Unival pots, while a rim sherd of differing form (GW10, from occupation deposit

[47]) is also Grooved Ware. It is of note that one of the few flat-base sherds (GW8) also comes from the same context and grid square. A rim sherd from context [2] in Phase 4 (GW3) has probably been redeposited, but is of a different form from other Grooved Ware rims from An Doirlinn and may represent another vessel. Sherds of a distinctive, friable, mid-grey fabric (GW5 and GW9 – the former including a rim sherd of distinctive form and the latter a flat base) could well represent a fourth vessel.

Other possible Grooved Ware sherds include a smoothed, but otherwise undecorated, flat-base sherd (GW7) from context [65] Square B8, a possible cordon fragment from context [65] Square C5, and finely incised sherds from context [2] Square T, immediately beneath the modern turf line. Less certain are incised body sherds from context [76] (GW14 to GW16), [55] in F11 (GW17), [53] Squares B6 and D5. Given the presence of flat-base sherds (e.g. GW7) and probable straight-wall sherds (GW24) it may well be that many of the other undiagnostic sherds from Phases 2 are from Grooved Ware vessels, although fragmentation and abrasion make this hard to establish for certain.

The issues of redeposition and intrusion between layers (and, indeed, phases) discussed above, combined with the abraded nature of many of the sherds at An Doirlinn, makes it extremely difficult to quantify the number of Grooved Ware vessels present. A rough estimate, based on rim forms and decoration, gives a conservative figure of four to six vessels, but the total is likely to be be considerably higher. Although this is only around 25% of the total number of vessels suggested for Phase 2, fragmentation meant that most of the remaining sherds could not be attributed to any particular style and, as there is no clear evidence for the use of earlier Hebridean styles after Phase 1, these sherds may well also come from Grooved Ware pots. In the light of the dating of Phase 2a/b to 2780–2230 cal BC – with very little overlap with the dating of Phase 1, associated with Hebridean ceramic styles – it is suggested here that this is the most parsimonious explanation. The same redeposition issues and low numbers of vessels mean that it was not possible to identify any significant differences between the Grooved Ware from the various sub-phases within Phase 2, although the overall similarity of the Grooved Ware sherds at An Doirlinn suggests that there is likely to have been little variation in the character of the Grooved Ware throughout the phase. There is no good reason to believe that any of the An Doirlinn Grooved Ware originally belonged to anything other than Phase 2.

Phase 3

Diagnostic sherds from Phase 3 are indicative of 'domestic' Beaker, and include sherds from at least one large vessel. In all, around ten vessels are represented within this phase, mostly by small numbers of sherds. Fabric 1 and the finer Fabric 2 are represented in proportions of approximately 3:1. The domestic Beaker sherds discussed below are of a distinctively dark and sandy fabric high in quartz, although considered here to fall within the range of Fabric 1. Three rim forms are represented within the six rims from Phase 3, with most being of the everted and flat-topped form 2c, and with diameters of between 24cm and 30cm. Despite the varying rim diameters, it is probable that these all belong to a single pot: rim form can vary considerably in the case of hand built pots. No base sherds are known from this phase.

The large Beaker jar (B2) represented by sherds from contexts [3] and [5] (and possibly also from [8] in Phase 4) can be compared with others known from the Western Isles (e.g. Calanais, Ashmore 2016). It has a concave neck and upright or minimally flaring rim 24–26mm in diameter with a slightly flattened top. Four centimetres below the rim is an applied cordon, and below this at least one encircling line of fingernail impressions. Other sherds from the same context (e.g. B8) are decorated with seemingly randomly placed fingernail marks or seashell impressions and possibly come from the same vessel. It is most likely that the impressions were formed with a limpet shell (Simpson et al. 2006, 128–129). With the exception of a single intrusive sherd from a Phase 1 context (B7), no Beaker fine ware has been identified at An Doirlinn.

Phase 4

Seven vessels would appear to be represented within Phase 4. Unfortunately the nature of this phase, modern disturbance, means that probably all of the pottery is redeposited, accounting for the presence of at least one sherd of Grooved Ware (GW3: a thin rim sherd (max. 4mm) with incised lines on the body and a row of stab marks along the top of a simple rim) and another of Beaker, the latter – with fingernail impressions and an applied cordon – conjoining with sherds from Phase 3 (see Beaker B2). Additional 'domestic' Beaker sherds with fingernail and seashell (probably limpet) impressions also occur in Phase 4 contexts (B9, B10 and B11). As with previous phases Fabric 1 predominates, with Fabric 2 constituting 9% of the sherds. Also in keeping with Phase 3 no lugs are present in Phase 4. One heavily abraded flat-base sherd of 8cm diameter was found.

Unstratified material

Little can be said about the unstratified material found during the 2012 excavations at An Doirlinn beyond mentioning the presence of the same fabrics found in earlier phases, a single flat-base sherd of uncertain diameter, a single rim sherd with a plain internal bevel, a small number of decorated sherds (one incised with a single line, a second with fingernail marks) and two small sherds showing evidence of carination.

A number of sherds were collected during preliminary investigations at An Doirlinn between 2005 and 2009. These sherds, from surface collection and eroding sections, were examined alongside the pottery from the 2012 excavation and largely reflect the character of the main assemblage. Fabric 1 accounts for 95% of the sherds and Hebridean style pottery would appear to be the best represented at 85% of the sherds recovered before 2012, while Grooved Ware and Beaker sherds were also identified. One Hebridean-style sherd (H75) exhibits the closely spaced diagonal lines characteristic of vessels found at other Hebridean Neolithic settlement sites, although here the decoration does not appear to extend below the carination.

Contextualisation

Phase 1a

A minimum of 40 vessels is suggested for this phase, with 30 vessels of varying sizes coming from contexts [82] and [87] alone. Stratigraphically, the earliest pottery at An Doirlinn is represented by a single vessel (H68) found within a shallow pit that may well have been cut specifically for this simple, undecorated, round-based pot. The vessel was deposited whole and could conceivably have been intended (along with its contents?) as a foundation deposit.

The majority of the pottery from Phase 1a derives from [82] and [87], which may represent material deriving from a single phase of occupation. The rapid build up of [82] is evidenced by the presence of five large, undecorated pots within it (and, indeed, extending physically if not stratigraphically into the overlying layers [70] and [65]), and the nature of the deposition of these vessels may indicate that their significance extended beyond their potential as utilitarian domestic vessels. Although the character of the pottery from this phase has been discussed in more detail above, it is important to emphasise the relatively plain nature of the An Doirlinn pottery from Phase 1 in contrast to the much more extensively decorated pottery from other excavated settlement sites in the Western Isles, and the focussing of the limited decoration on rims (and particularly on internal rim bevels).

Phase 1b

There is little change in the character of the pottery between Phases 1a and 1b at An Doirlinn. A minimum of nine vessels, out of a total of nineteen for Phase 1b as a whole, was identified from context [70], which probably represents a levelling deposit. With one exception, very large vessels would appear to be absent, although rim forms and decoration are in keeping with the patterns established in Phase 1a. Larger vessels tend to be associated with simple rims, while decoration on other vessels is again found mainly on rims and bevels, the more elaborate forms of which tend to be associated with thinner and finer fabrics. A number of Grooved Ware sherds were identified within Phase 1b, although all are associated with contexts likely to have undergone later disturbance (e.g. at the sea-eroded edge of site) and should be considered as intrusive.

Phase 1c

The pottery from the various contexts that constitute Phase 1c can be regarded as belonging to a single layer [53/54/59/62/63/64]. This layer, excavated in spits, is likely to be occupation-related (possibly a redeposited midden). A minimum of twenty-six vessels was identified, although this figure should be regarded as highly provisional on account of the difficulty of identifying vessels across different spits/contexts. Three large, heavy pots are represented, and other vessels in a range of sizes continue the formal and decorative patterns found in earlier phases. Some of the material from Phase 1c is fairly heavily abraded and fragmented, supporting the suggestion that it could have been brought in from elsewhere.

Phase 2

A minimum of four vessels was identified from contexts associated with the earlier hearth pits in both Structure C and the later Structure D (F11 and F14). The sherds include examples of both Hebridean pottery of a similar character to that from Phase 1, and Grooved Ware. Although it could conceivably be argued that Hebridean vessels and Grooved Ware were in use contemporaneously during the use of these structures, the small number of sherds from F11 and F14 prevents firm conclusions from being drawn. It is argued here that the presence of the Hebridean-style vessels within these primary features is most parsimoniously regarded as resulting from the digging of hearth pits deep down into earlier material.

Pottery from Phase 2 is on the whole highly abraded and fragmentary although generally thinner than in preceding phases. A minimum of 26 vessels were identified, with all clearly diagnostic sherds being of Grooved Ware found in association with hearths or occupation deposits; a situation that will be discussed further below. Based on diagnostic sherds alone, there is a minimum of six Grooved Ware vessels, but it is likely that most, if not all, of the remaining vessels are also Grooved Ware.

Phases 3 and 4

Extensive modern disturbance means that the stratigraphic integrity of the later contexts at An Doirlinn is in doubt and, as such, they will be only briefly dealt with together here. One context, [28], proved hard to assign to a specific phase. Most of the pottery from [28] was highly abraded and fragmented, and many of the sherds would appear to come from at least one large 'domestic' Beaker pot, although variation in rim form may indicate that three vessels are actually represented. It is of note that although there is no clear stratigraphic break at this point there is no evidence of Grooved Ware in context [28].

Excluding context [28], a minimum of 11 vessels was identified from Phases 3 and 4, including a number of conjoining sherds forming part of a large 'domestic' Beaker. Seashell impressions and fingernail rustication occur on some sherds that probably come from this pot. Grooved Ware sherds also occur within Phase 3 contexts, but their association with Beaker pottery should be regarded as insecure given the degree of disturbance to this part of the site. Phase 4 comprises a number of highly disturbed contexts with a high degree of redeposited material that includes Hebridean, Grooved Ware and Beaker sherds, constituting a minimum of six vessels in total.

Discussion

Although a number of 20th century excavations in the Western Isles have produced considerable quantities of Neolithic pottery, poor stratification and a lack of precise dating means that the development of ceramic traditions in the region have remained relatively poorly understood. The largest assemblages have come from Northton (Johnson 2006), Allt Chrisal (Gibson in Branigan & Foster 1995), Eilean an Tighe (Scott 1951) and Eilean Dòmhnuill (Brown n.d.; Copper 2015). Additionally, a considerable quantity of pottery was excavated at the Udal on North Uist, but this complex and highly-fragmented assemblage awaits full publication (the most detailed discussion to date being Squair 1998, 435–469).

Unfortunately, the pottery from the Neolithic horizon at Northton lacks contextual information, meaning that the whole assemblage has had to be treated as if deriving from a single deposit. Johnson (2006, 63–64) suggested that the Northton pottery fell into four categories: uncarinated bowls, carinated bowls, multiple-ridged jars and Unstan-type bowls. Decorated and undecorated forms of the first two were found, with the great majority of the carinated bowls and all of the multiple-ridged jars and Unstan-type bowls being decorated. Unstan-type bowls would appear to form the majority of the vessels at Northton. However, as Johnson herself points out, it is possible that the relative ease of recognising this type of pottery may have led to an overestimation of its frequency at the site (Johnson 2006, 64). Johnson (2006, 67) went on to draw comparisons between the pottery from Northton and other Neolithic sites from the Western Isles, noting that at Eilean Dòmhnuill multiple-ridged jars and uncarinated bowls form the majority of the vessel types, followed by Unstan-type bowls. Analysis by the present author, however, suggests that Unstan-type bowls may account for over half of all identifiable vessels at the latter site.

On the basis of his interpretation of a number of features as kilns and of all of the potsherds as wasters, Scott argued that the small island site of Eilean an Tighe on North Uist was a pottery workshop (Scott 1951, 5–11 and 24). His proposed sequence for Hebridean pottery was reliant both upon his interpretation of the structures excavated at Eilean an Tighe as kilns and also upon his conclusion that the three postulated kilns succeeded each other and were in use for long enough to provide us with a developmental sequence for Hebridean Neolithic ceramics (Scott 1951, 13–29). Scott's interpretation of Eilean an Tighe has, however, been widely challenged (e.g. Gibson in Branigan & Foster 1995, 100; Simpson 1976, 222; Squair 1998, 314–321) and the published plans and sections are, from an interpretive point of view, ambiguous at best. In this respect it is unfortunate that the published report is the only extant record of Scott's excavation. It would now seem unwise to view this site as a workshop, although its exact nature remains contentious, and in consequence, the developmental sequence for Hebridean pottery proposed on the basis of the original interpretation of the site should be regarded as unreliable.

Brown (n.d.) noted the similarity between the assemblages from Eilean an Tighe and the small islet site of Eilean Dòmhnuill, also on North Uist, with necked bowls, decorated and undecorated open bowls and cups, ridged jars and bowls, and shouldered and Unstan-type bowls being key elements of both. The Eilean Dòmhnuill pottery also closely resembles that from Eilean an Tighe in being primarily coil-built, round-bottomed (with one exception) and profusely decorated using a variety of techniques (Armit 1987, 23). Although Brown was unable to propose any developmental sequence for the pottery from Eilean Dòmhnuill as no radiocarbon dates were available for the site at the time, work undertaken by the present author would suggest that the ceramic styles and decorative techniques in use at the at the site remained largely unchanged from before 3650 cal BC to after 2800 cal BC, with the exception of a general decline in the proportion of collared rims and a corresponding increase in everted rim forms (Copper 2015).

An estimation of just over 100 vessels was made for the pottery assemblage from Bharpa Carinish (Crone et al. 1993, 370–375), although this figure may well be too high given that the sherds were only grouped within contexts, meaning that vessels represented by sherds found in more than one context may have been counted more than once. Where it was possible to identify vessel shapes, only round-bottomed jars and bowls – mostly highly decorated – were present. Decoration was dominated by incised lines, with carinations, where present, forming divisions between decorated and undecorated zones. Plain, everted, and internally-bevelled rim forms are represented at Bharpa Carinish, but no clear chronological development could be discerned. Unlike at Eilean Dòmhnuill, no collared rims are known from Bharpa Carinish, a situation also reflected at An Doirlinn. Large standard deviations associated with the radiocarbon dates for Bharpa Carinish are problematical: an approximate date in the later 4th or earlier 3rd millennium cal BC is perhaps the best that can currently be proposed.

Gibson (in Branigan & Foster 1995) divided the Neolithic assemblage from Allt Chrisal into four groups: Undecorated bowls, Hebridean incised wares, Unstan ware and Impressed wares. All occur throughout the stratigraphic sequence, and Gibson suggested on the basis of the then available radiocarbon evidence, association of plain and decorated pottery at a number of Hebridean Neolithic sites, general uniformity in fabric types and the sharing of rim forms, that Hebridean Neolithic pottery had both a decorated and an undecorated component (Gibson in Branigan & Foster 1995, 104). Undecorated and incised vessels predominate at Allt Chrisal, and lugs and knobs also occur, as at An Doirlinn but in contrast to Northton and Eilean Dòmhnuill where they are very rare, while Unstan-type bowls form 'a small but distinctive element in the assemblage' (Gibson in Branigan & Foster 1995, 110). The impressed element of the Allt Chrisal assemblage includes examples of fingernail and fingertip decoration, twisted and whipped cord, seashell (cockle and limpet) and 'reed' marks and stabs. Internal rim bevels are often decorated, and carinations may be accentuated with lines of stab marks. In respect of our understanding of the nature and development of Hebridean Neolithic ceramics, however, it is unfortunate that the assemblage from Allt Chrisal is compromised by the presence of Beaker sherds throughout the stratigraphic sequence, suggestive of considerable mixing of material of different ages, and meaning that the Allt Chrisal pottery cannot be taken as unambiguous evidence for a heterogeneous Hebridean assemblage, as once appeared to be the case (Gibson in Branigan & Foster 1995, 115).

As well as at 'domestic' sites, Neolithic pottery has been found within megalithic tombs in the Outer Hebrides. The largest assemblages come from Clettraval (Scott 1935) and Unival (Scott 1948). The pottery from these sites comprises a mixture of shallow and deep bowls, including carinated and shouldered forms, while lugged pots are also known from Clettraval (Henshall 1972, 308–9). Rim types include simple and elaborated variants of upright and everted forms, and both plain and decorated internal bevels are present. Re-excavation of the chambered cairn at Geirisclett (Dunwell et al. 2003) has added more weight to the argument that pottery from mortuary contexts is distinctively different to that at some 'domestic' sites: although some features of the Geirisclett assemblage can be found at Eilean an Tighe, Allt Chrisal, Northton and Eilean Dòmhnuill, close parallels are harder to find. Interestingly, few unambiguous Unstan-type bowls and no multiple-ridged jars are currently known from megalithic tombs in the Outer Hebrides, although large examples of the former occur in tombs in Orkney (Davidson & Henshall 1989, 64–78). Unfortunately, the lack of dates from Unival and Clettraval mean that we cannot be certain if chronological factors may account for this difference.

Prior to the excavations at An Doirlinn only two fairly complete Grooved Ware vessels were recorded as coming from the Western Isles, one from the passage tomb of Unival (Henshall 1972, 309; Scott 1948, 26–7 and plate vii) and a second from Calanais (Ashmore 2016). Both are small, fine, thin-walled bowls with incised decoration of lozenges and triangles. Serpentine patterns are also employed on the Calanais vessel, and zones of dot-infilling on the Unival pot. The recognition of Grooved Ware amongst the unpublished assemblage from the Udal (Beverley Ballin-Smith, pers. comm.) has shown that this style of pottery is somewhat more widespread in the Western Isles than previously thought. Although mostly very small (<4cm), the fine and thin (<5mm thick) Udal sherds include examples with incised lozenges and with opposed triangles with dot and fingernail infill similar to that observed at An Doirlinn. They are smooth and well fired but, unlike the An Doirlinn Grooved Ware, are tempered with crushed shell, probably from a beach source. The significance of these vessels will be discussed further below.

The Neolithic pottery from An Doirlinn demonstrates significant similarities with, as well as important differences from, other assemblages in the Hebrides. Certain features are of particular note: the paucity of decorated sherds from An Doirlinn in comparison to sites such as Eilean Dòmhnuill, Northton, Allt Chrisal and Eilean an Tighe; the complete absence of Unstan-type bowls from the site; and, in Phase 2, the presence of a number of Grooved Ware pots within an apparently domestic context. In addition, the lack of the distinctive multiple-ridged jars and collared rim forms amongst the Hebridean vessels at An Doirlinn contrasts with their prevalence at other sites in the Western Isles.

Many attempts have been made over the years to place Hebridean Neolithic ceramic traditions within a broader context (important examples including Childe 1940; Henshall 1972; Piggott 1931; 1954; Scott J. G. 1964; 1969; Scott W. L. 1951). More recently, Sheridan has proposed that the indigenous pottery of the Hebrides developed from a fusion in western Scotland of two Early Neolithic traditions deriving ultimately from Brittany and Northern France (Sheridan 2000; 2003), and certainly some of the closest parallels for early Neolithic pottery from the Hebrides would appear to be with pottery from the tombs of Argyll, Arran and Bute (cf. Henshall 1972, 302–310) although the precise chronological relationship of Hebridean pottery to pottery from this part of Scotland remains uncertain. At Eilean Dòmhnuill the most distinctive Hebridean vessel forms – elaborately decorated ridged jars and Unstan-type bowls – were present from the earliest phases, dating to before 3650 cal BC (Armit in prep.). This would suggest that distinctively Hebridean ceramic styles developed fairly quickly after the first appearance of pottery in the Western Isles. However, the relatively plain decorative schemes and simple forms of the vessels from An Doirlinn contrast markedly with the considerably more elaborate ceramic assemblages from contemporary sites such as Eilean Dòmhnuill and Eilean an Tighe, suggesting that different elements drawn from a broader Hebridean repertoire were in use contemporaneously at different sites. An Doirlinn is not alone in this respect: pottery from Rubh' a'Charnain

Moir/Screvan Quarry (and possibly The Udal) also lacks the multiple-ridged jars and Unstan-type bowls, and presents a similar character in terms of form and decoration to the assemblage from An Doirlinn (Downes & Badcock 1998).

The deposition of substantially complete but fragmented vessels within an apparently 'domestic' context at An Doirlinn, and their rapid covering by the Phase 1 deposits, would seem to blur the division between the symbolic and the practical that is a feature of our own society. This in turn raises issues concerning the broader role of pottery within Hebridean Neolithic society, including why certain types of vessel – notably Unstan-type bowls and multiple-ridged jars – appear (on current evidence at least) to be very rare or absent from Hebridean Neolithic tombs. Overall, the evidence from An Doirlinn would seem to challenge the idea that Hebridean pottery comprised a single standard assemblage that persisted largely unchanged throughout the Neolithic, although all assemblages seem to draw on the same range of basic forms and decorative motifs. In this respect it is of interest that a number of sites producing formally and decoratively elaborate assemblages, including Eilean an Tighe and Eilean Dòmhnuill, or smaller numbers of elaborately decorated sherds, such as Pygmies Isle (MacKenzie 1904–5, 252–253), Dunasbroc (McHardy et al. 2009, 122–123) and even Saint Kilda (Fleming & Edmonds 1999), are located on islets, islands, or in other relatively inaccessible locations. Additionally, it is of note that Bharpa Carinish (Crone 1993) and Barpa Langais (which produced a single, round-bottomed decorated vessel: Sheridan 2008) are both located close to chambered tombs. In a discussion of Hebridean Neolithic pottery McSween notes that 'from the limited amount of stratified material available, it is perhaps more likely that there is a general ceramic sequence for the Hebridean Neolithic, and that within that general sequence, variations can be expected, depending on, for example, cultural preferences, or the activities being carried out on a site' (McSween in McHardy et al. 2009, 113). The evidence from An Doirlinn would certainly be consistent with such a view.

The recognition of Grooved Ware at An Doirlinn is of considerable significance given its previous rarity in the Western Isles. All identifiable pots from Phase 2 at An Doirlinn are thin-walled Grooved Ware vessels; many are made from a fine, occasionally almost sparkly, mica-rich clay that stands out against the background of the coarser, thicker-walled Hebridean vessels from Phase 1. It is likely that smoothing of the vessel surface has had the effect of bringing the grains of mica to the surface. Decoration on the An Doirlinn Grooved Ware pots closely resembles that on all of the other Grooved Ware vessels so far discovered in the Western Isles, at Calanais (Ashmore 2016), at the Unival passage grave (Scott 1948, plate vii), and at site RUX6 at the Udal (Beverley Ballin-Smith, pers. comm.). Grooved Ware at An Doirlinn was associated with hearths, hearth construction pits and occupation debris, and at the Udal with a likely Late Neolithic house (Squair 1998, 424–428), in contrast to the Calanais and Unival vessels, which come from a stone circle and a chambered cairn respectively. The presence of cross-context (indeed cross-phase) joins means that it is not possible to be absolutely certain that Grooved Ware was not in use at the same time as Hebridean vessels at An Doirlinn, although it is considered here that this is unlikely given that the Grooved Ware sherds from Phase 1 are all from disturbed contexts and that the small number of Hebridean sherds found in association with Grooved Ware in Phase 2 were found within hearth construction pits that had been cut into earlier material. Although new dates have since become available, the most recent Bayesian model for Hebridean pottery suggests that the Hebridean styles ceased to be produced after 2855–2460 cal BC (95% confidence) and probably after 2850–2690 cal BC (68% confidence) (Sheridan in Ashmore 2016).

As no radiocarbon dates are associated with the Unival, Calanais and Udal vessels, the dating of Phase 2 at An Doirlinn to 2780–2480 cal BC (Structure C) and 2480–2330 cal BC (Structure D) is significant in respect of the timing of the adoption of Grooved Ware along the Scottish Atlantic façade. The forms and incised decorative schemes of the Grooved Ware from An Doirlinn, as well as the Unival, Calanais and Udal vessels, are paralleled by vessels from other parts of Scotland, notably the Stones of Stenness (in particular SF 16: Ritchie 1978, 23), Balfarg (Henshall in Barclay & Russell-White 1993, 94–108) and Machrie Moor on Arran (Haggerty 1991, 65–66), and further afield (e.g. Knowth: Eogan 1984, 314–315). Dates from the Stones of Stenness suggest that this style of Grooved Ware was in use there by the second century of the 3rd millennium BC, and perhaps as early as c. 3000 cal BC, and incised Grooved Ware from Knowth is likely to be of a similar date, while dates for Barnhouse suggest that incised Grooved Ware was probably in use in Orkney before 3100 cal BC (Schulting et al. 2010a; Richards et al. 2016). Sheridan (2004) has linked the spread of Grooved Ware along the Scottish Atlantic façade and to Ireland with the spread of open-air ceremonial structures from Orkney at around 3000 BC. Although this scenario would make the An Doirlinn and Udal finds unusual in coming from seemingly 'domestic' contexts, it could also suggest that local communities could have been adapting new and exotic concepts and artefacts into established local practices, although precisely when this first began to occur in the Outer Hebrides remains to be ascertained. The presence of Grooved Ware at An Doirlinn and at the Udal has, however, confirmed that this style of pottery was more widely in use in the Western Isles during the Late Neolithic and that it was not confined to 'ceremonial' contexts.

The small quantity of Beaker pottery at An Doirlinn is associated with the final phases of occupation. Beaker pottery is known from many other sites in the Western

Isles (e.g. Northton, Simpson et al. 2006, 90–133) and the nature of the An Doirlinn Beaker pottery would suggest that, with the exception of sherd B7, it falls under the general heading of 'domestic' Beaker (Gibson 1982). Fabric and decoration, including fingernail rustication and seashell impression, recall the earlier pottery styles at the site and are indicative of local manufacture, and the large size of vessel B2, together with a number of thick-bodied sherds with seashell impressions and fingernail rustication, would suggest that the Beaker material from An Doirlinn represents at most a small number of fairly coarse pots.

Conclusions

The pottery from An Doirlinn adds considerably to our knowledge of ceramic traditions in the Outer Hebrides. The restricted range of forms and decoration associated with the earlier, Hebridean-style vessels on the site stands in sharp contrast to the assemblages from sites such as Eilean Dòmhnuill, Northton and Eilean an Tighe as well as the pottery from the few excavated Hebridean tombs, and suggests that differing elements drawn from a broader Hebridean repertoire were in use at different sites during the Earlier Neolithic. The presence of a number of Grooved Ware vessels at An Doirlinn has shown that this style of pottery was perhaps not as uncommon in the Outer Hebrides as previously believed, and demonstrates links with areas far beyond the Western Isles. The small quantity of 'domestic' Beaker sherds emphasises the continued significance of the site into the Early Bronze Age. The dating of the Grooved Ware phase at An Doirlinn to the period following 2780 cal BC, combined with the emergent stratigraphic and radiocarbon dating evidence (Section 4.10), strongly suggests that the Hebridean ceramic traditions are unlikely to have been a feature of the whole of the Neolithic in the Western Isles.

4.5. Chipped stone

Anne Pirie

Introduction

This report details the results of analysis of 10,613 chipped stone artefacts (flint and quartz) from An Doirlinn (Figures 4.29–4.31; Table 4.06). The vast majority of these were recovered during the 2012 excavations; 172 were collected from the site on a more ad hoc basis from 2005–2007.

Methodology

The entire assemblage was subject to initial visual inspection, with significant artefacts noted and recorded. On the basis of this preliminary scan, a sample of 5441 artefacts from key contexts throughout the sequence was selected for full cataloguing (51% of the total). This sample included all archaeological features, and then a representative selection of 1m grid squares from the larger occupation-related and 'levelling' layers. Exact details of the sampling strategy are set out in Appendix 1. The material within each grid square was bulk catalogued, with counts of artefact types, tool class/type, core type and material recorded. A small sample of blades and cores was measured, and tools and cores were studied/described in more depth. Identification of artefacts followed Inizan et al. (1999). All counts and comments below refer to the catalogued assemblage unless otherwise stated.

The assemblage

Overall, the assemblage is 85% flint, mainly greyish brown in colour and patinated, with quartz making up 15%. There are very few artefacts in other materials; these include quartzite and jasper from Phase 1; jasper, chalcedony and possible mudstone from Phase 2; and one pitchstone artefact from Phase 4 (Table 4.07). There were a few artefacts in dark grey/black flint, and one in pale grey flint. Cortex present suggests that raw materials were mainly derived from beach pebbles.

The entire assemblage is flake dominated, with smaller proportions of blades (Table 4.08). Most of the flakes and blades are irregular, and likely to have been largely the product of bipolar on anvil knapping. This is confirmed by the high proportions of bipolar cores (87% of all cores in the assemblage). These are often small pebbles that have been reduced down one striking face with cortex remaining on the opposite face, often flattish in form. Some have been reduced down three or four striking faces forming a thickish matchstick shape. The few platform cores present are often irregular with reduction from ad hoc platforms from previous removals. A few more prepared platforms exist, and some core tablets exist from more formal platform reduction. There is no sign of any change in core forms or use over the life of the site.

Most tools are on flint (96%) rather than quartz or other materials (Table 4.09). Tools are largely informal, with many defined only by macro-usewear rather than retouch. These include pièce esquillées which are usually irregular, with short esquillée removals down one or more faces. They sometimes have additional retouch or edge damage. Edge damaged pieces are also common, with some burins also probably formed through use damage.

Retouched tools are mainly scrapers and marginally retouched pieces. The scrapers are the most common formal tool in the assemblage, and are largely small thumbnail scrapers, with varying amounts of nicely made scraper retouch. All are quite small, but some are extremely small with diameters around 11mm. Many scrapers show signs of heavy use with esquillée type removals, burination and sometimes visible repairs/re-tooling.

Other tools include a number of nicely made knives usually on flakes (although note one knife on a blade in occupation deposit [65] (Phase 1b)), with low, sometimes

Table 4.06. Catalogue of illustrated chipped stone from An Doirlinn (Figs 4.29–4.31)

Illus. no.	*Context*	*Phase*	*Material*	*Description*
1	64	1	Flint	Single platform core (prepared)
2	28	2	Flint	Single platform core (prepared)
3	82	1	Flint	Bipolar core (elongated thick matchstick)
4	53	1	Flint	Bipolar core (flat, on pebble)
5	70	1	Quartz	Bipolar core
6	46	2	Flint	Bipolar core
7	20	2	Flint	Bipolar core (flat, cortical pebble)
8	46	2	Flint	Bipolar core (matchstick, bladelet removals)
9	31	2	Quartz	Bipolar core
10	42	2	Quartz	Bipolar core
11	8	3	Flint	Bipolar core
12	8	3	Flint	Bipolar core
13	12	3	Quartz	Bipolar core
14	65	1	Flint	Irregular platform core (learning?)
15	65	1	Flint	Core trimming element - cortical platform removal
16	65	1	Flint	Leaf shaped point
17	53	1	Flint	Plano-convex knife
18	65	1	Flint	Knife
19	67	1	Flint	Knife/pièce esquillée
20	12	3	Flint	Knife
21	71	1	Flint	Scraper
22	65	1	Flint	Scraper (small)
23	42	2	Flint	Scraper
24	42	2	Flint	Scraper (small)
25	46	2	Flint	Scraper/pièce esquillée
26	12	3	Flint	Scraper
27	12	3	Flint	Scraper
28	12	3	Flint	Scraper/Pièce esquillée
29	28	2	Quartz	Burin
30	12	3	Quartz	Notch
31	95	2	Flint	Marginally retouched piece (on spall)
32	41	2	Flint	Marginally retouched/pièce esquillée
33	8	3	Flint	Marginally retouched/pièce esquillée
34	65	1	Flint	Pièce esquillée
35	28	2	Flint	Pièce esquillée with tang
36	64	1	Flint	Used bladelet (regular)
37	47	2	Flint	Used bladelet (regular)
38	53	1	Flint	Flake (used)

Table 4.07. Locations of non-flint/-quartz lithic materials

Material	*Phase [context]*
Quartzite	Phase 1 [50], [70]
Jasper	Phase 1 [87], Phase 2 [64], [76]
Mudstone (?)	Phase 2 [29], [37]
Chalcedony	Phase 2 [41]
Pitchstone	Phase 4 [3]

inverse, retouch. These sometimes have a cortical edge opposite the retouched edge, possibly for hafting or holding. Knives often have signs of heavy use, with esquillée removals on their ventral faces. Other tools of note include one leaf point from the Phase 1b occupation deposit [65/71] and a plano convex knife from the Phase 1c equivalent [53].

Phase 1

In terms of raw material use, there are some striking differences within Phase 1 – the earliest levels show much greater use of quartz, with a ratio of one quartz artefact to every three flint ones (Table 4.10). Phases 1b and 1c, however, dip to a ratio of 1:18/17, and show variability between contexts in use of materials. Phases 1a and 1b have extremely variable levels of burnt artefacts, with occupation-related contexts sometimes more heavily burnt, sometimes not. Phase 1c is all quite heavily burnt.

While still dominated by irregular flakes, the assemblage from Phase 1 contains more blades overall (12%), and more of these are regular blades made using a dedicated blade technology (as high as 20% of all blades in Phase 1a). Blade proportions are higher in all context types and all sub-phases of Phase 1 with small, but consistent, proportions of most context type assemblages (>40 total artefacts) being regular blades. There are few regular blades that are sufficiently complete to allow measurement, but they are small, averaging 8.6mm in width (n = 10) and 28mm in length (n = 5). The blades present are of a size and material that suggest they

Table 4.08. Summary of the catalogued assemblage

Material	*Flint*		*Other*		*Quartz*		*Total*	
	No.	*%*	*No.*	*%*	*No.*	*%*	*No.*	*%*
Flakes	3071	66.6	16	88.9	555	68.4	3642	66.9
Blades	452	9.8	1	5.6	50	6.2	503	9.2
Spalls	199	4.3		0.0	7	0.9	206	3.8
Indeterminates	401	8.7	1	5.6	76	9.4	478	8.8
Core trimming elements	21	0.5		0.0		0.0	21	0.4
Cores	412	8.9		0.0	71	8.8	483	8.9
Small fraction	59	1.3		0.0	56	6.9	115	2.1
Total	4612	100.0	18	100.0	811	100.0	5441	100.0

Table 4.09. Summary of chipped stone tools

	Flint		*Other*		*Quartz*		*Total*	
	No.	*%*	*No.*	*%*	*No.*	*%*	*No.*	*%*
Marginally retouched	84	15.2			4	13.3	88	15.1
Notch	13	2.4			5	16.7	18	3.1
Denticulate	2	0.4				0.0	2	0.3
Scrapers	129	23.4	1	100.0	4	13.3	134	
Knife	8	1.5				0.0	8	1.4
Microlith	1	0.2				0.0	1	0.2
Truncation	2	0.4			3	10.0	5	0.9
Point	1	0.2				0.0	1	0.2
Awl	6	1.1				0.0	6	1.0
Other	11	2.0			2	6.7	13	2.2
Fragment	18	3.3			1	3.3	19	3.3
Total Retouched tools	275		1		19		295	
Pièces esquillée	146	26.5			6	20.0	152	26.1
Burin	41	7.4			3	10.0	44	7.6
Used piece	89	16.2			2	6.7	91	15.6
Total used tools	276		0		11		287	
Total tools	551		1		30		582	

were made on site rather than imported, although there are no signs of blade production in the cores, probably because of later use of bipolar working to extend the life of cores.

The only context type in Phase 1 to contain no regular blades was the levelling deposit in Phase 1b [70]. By contrast, the probable occupation deposit in Phase 1c [53/54/59/62/63/64] contained amongst the highest proportions of regular blades on the site (2.3% of the assemblage, or 15% of the blades).

In Phase 1, there are active signs that both flint and quarz were knapped on site, with cores and small numbers of core trimming elements present in flint in Phases 1a–c, and quartz cores present in Phases 1a–b. The small numbers of other materials present do not include cores or any other sign of knapping. While cores are ubiquitous in all types of Phase 1a contexts (14–15% of all contexts with assemblages >3 artefacts), in Phases 1b and 1c they are more heavily represented in the levelling deposit (10–11%), and more scarce in occupation levels (5–6%). This may reflect clearing of some lithic material from occupation areas at this time, or perhaps curation of cores which were subsequently disposed of elsewhere.

As throughout the entire site, Phase 1 cores are mainly bipolar on anvil. These are either abandoned at an early stage of exploitation or more thoroughly used with final removals bashed off leaving a small and irregular core. Many are flat with removals down one face and a cortical back. Only small numbers of cores show signs of non-anvil platform use, and these are mainly irregular and informal cores using cortical pebble faces as striking platforms. Scant signs of more formal platform technology include several core tablets. Another core trimming element removes a substantial part of a platform, but typically this platform, while showing controlled reduction, is simply the flat part of the external rind of a pebble. Some cores show awkward hinged removals, sometimes across a face that will have yielded hinged removals too small to be used; this could reflect either the process of learning to knap, or half-hearted 'doodling' in stone. Cores are mainly rather small, with an average length of 24mm (flint) and 37mm (quartz). Quartz cores are more variable in length, and if an outlier of 90mm in length is removed, the average length is 33mm. There is no significant difference in core dimensions across context types within Phase 1.

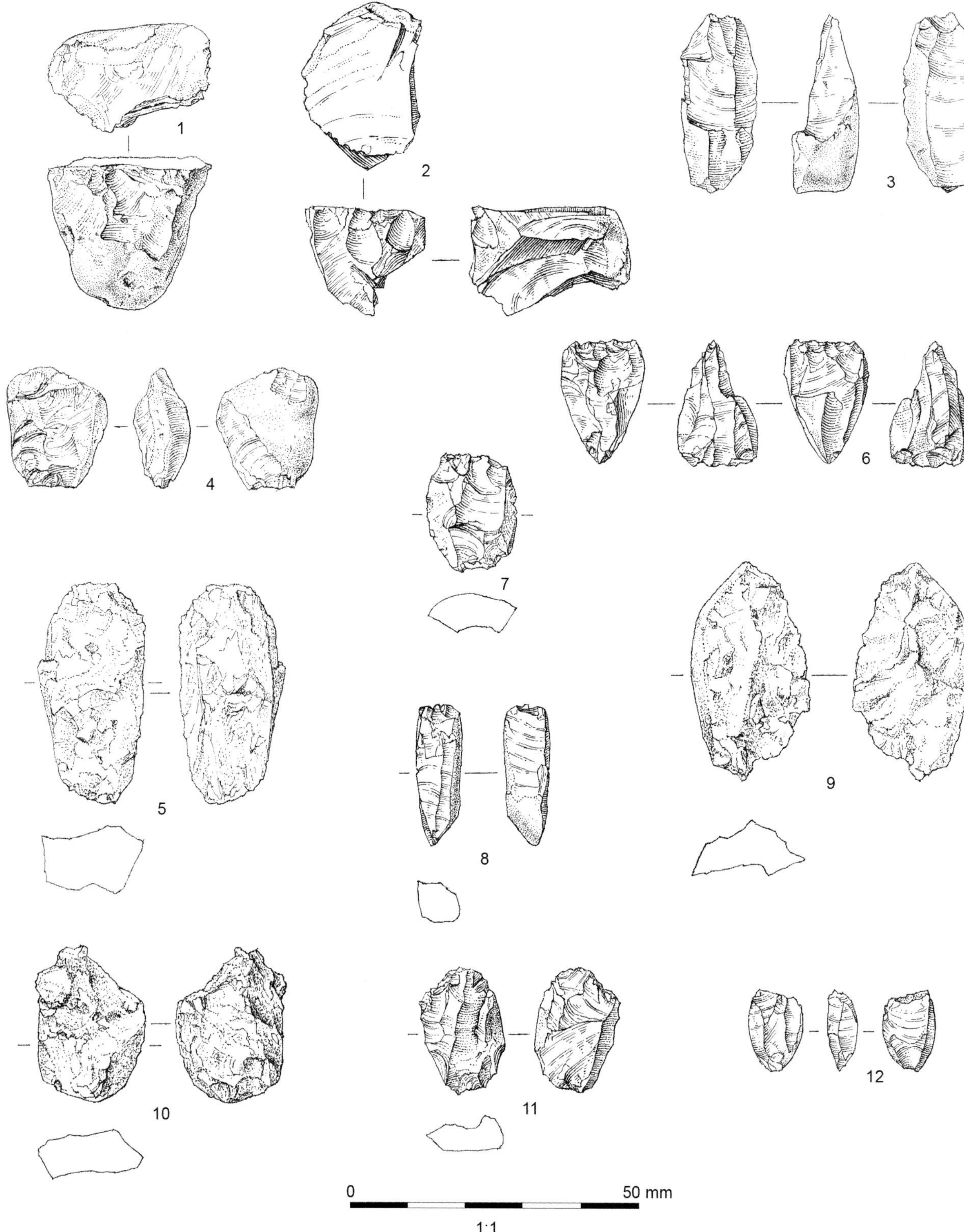

Figure 4.29. Flint (1) (drawn by J. Wallis).

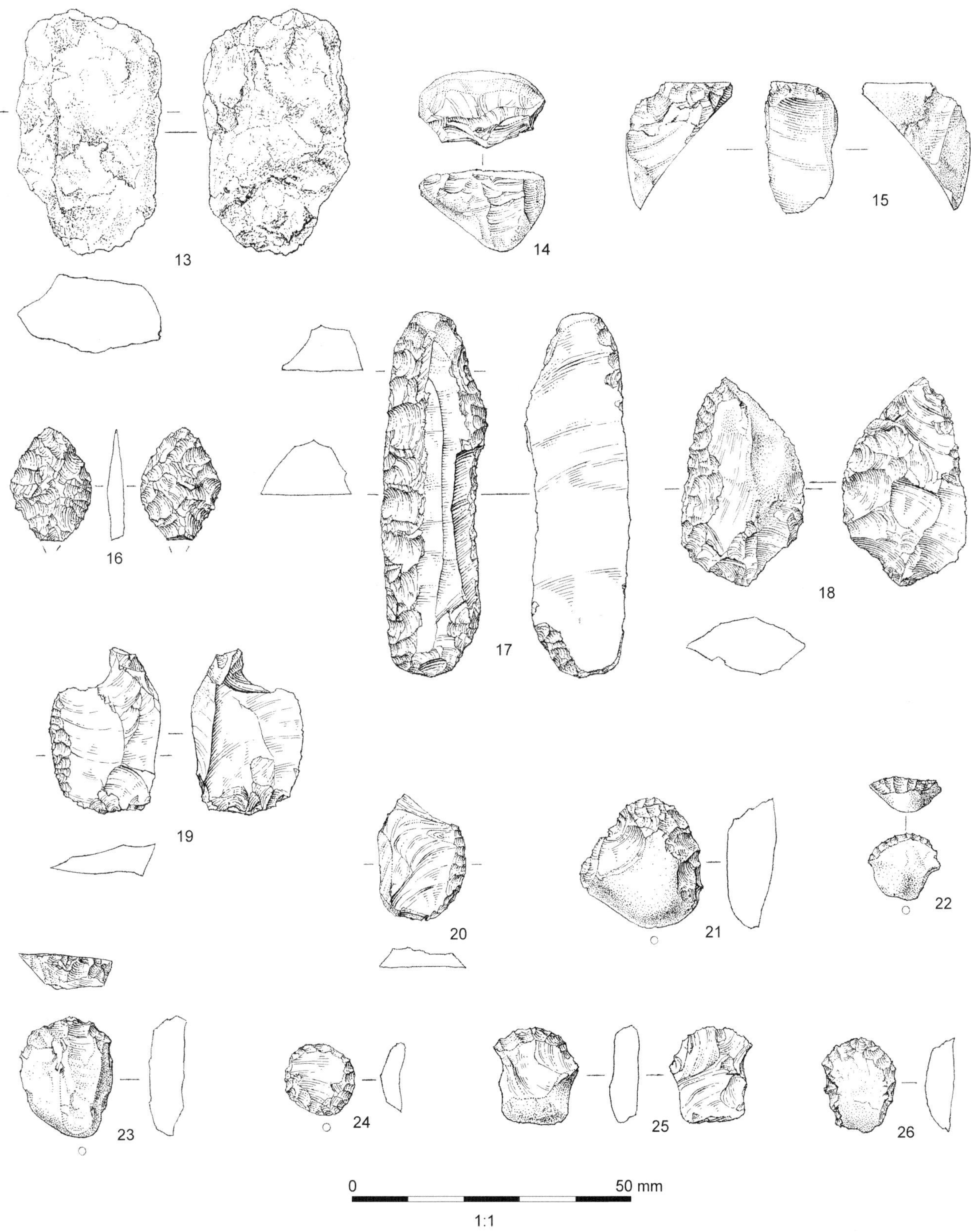

Figure 4.30. Flint (2) (drawn by J. Wallis).

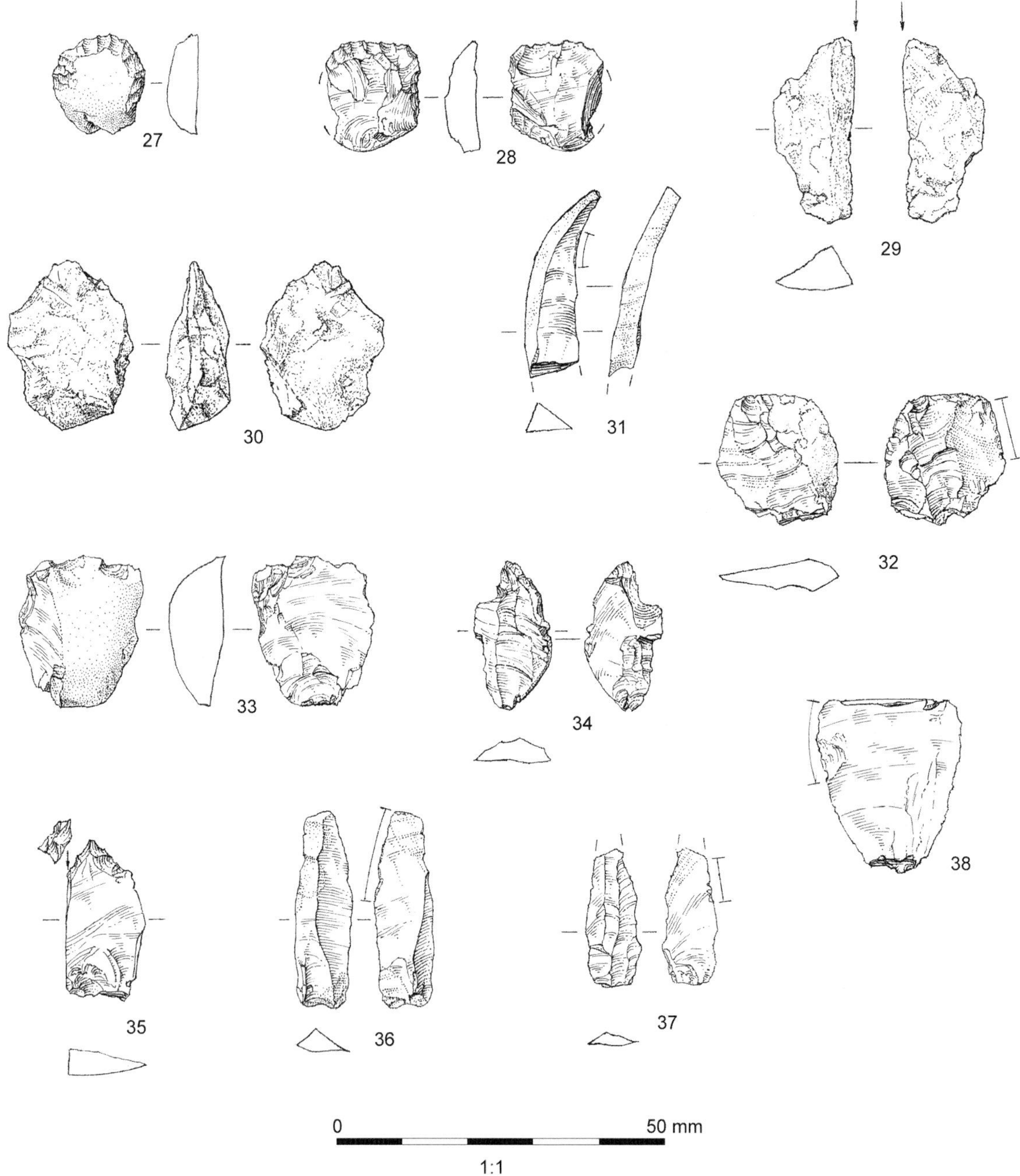

Figure 4.31. Flint (3) (drawn by J. Wallis).

Artefacts smaller than 5mm are differentially distributed across the context types in Phase 1, with higher levels in occupation layers, especially those in Phase 1a (3.7–4.8%). The small assemblages in features have little or no small fraction, while the larger levelling deposit of Phase 1b and the occupation-related deposit of Phase 1c have little or no small fraction either. This supports an interpretation of redeposition – possibly intentional deposition of certain artefacts in features, while the levelling/occupation deposits with low levels of small fraction may be comprised of redeposited material missing its small fraction through the redeposition process.

Tools

13% of the Phase 1 assemblage is either retouched or macro-used, but the various contexts show differences in proportions of tools, types of tool classes, and levels of tools modified by retouch (Table 4.11).

The Phase 1a assemblage was derived mainly from occupation deposits – these levels have lower proportions of tools (8%), with a mix of retouched and use-defined tools. Edge damaged pieces, marginally retouched pieces and pièces esquillées are common, as well as some irregular scrapers (but note that one regular thumbnail scraper was identified in [82]). The irregular scrapers found in Phase 1a are different from the more regular scrapers found in all other levels of the site. It was also interesting to note that the chipped stone found in amongst the deposits of substantially complete but fragmented pots [66, 67, 68, 69 and 78] included high numbers of often retouched tools (13%). These include an irregular scraper, and two knives which are the most formal/diagnostic part of the tool assemblage from these levels. In contrast, the two hearths contained chipped stone but no tools, and a pit and a post-hole contained small numbers of artefacts with no tools.

Phase 1b is comprised of a range of context types containing chipped stone. Most of the assemblage here came from occupation deposit [65/71], where again there are low proportions of tools (6.8%) including a mix of retouched and use-defined tools. A wide range of tool classes came from these levels, with used pieces and scrapers dominant.

Table 4.10. Summary of the Phase 1 catalogued assemblage

Phase 1	*Flint*		*Other*		*Quartz*	
	No.	*%*	*No.*	*%*	*No.*	*%*
Flakes	1296	61.7	8	88.9	125	63.1
Blades	272	12.9	0	0.0	23	11.6
Spalls	98	4.7	0	0.0	3	1.5
Core trimming elements	8	0.4	0	0.0	0	0.0
Indeterminates	208	9.9	1	11.1	19	9.6
Small fraction	28	1.3	0	0.0	12	6.1
Cores	191	9.1	0	0.0	16	8.1
Total	2101	100.0	9	100.0	198	100.0

These last included fine regular scrapers with varying amounts of retouch around often round tools; one scraper is nosed; some scrapers are tiny. The site's only leaf point came from these levels and is finely pressure-retouched on pale beige flint. Two knives are on larger than average flakes, and have widespread esquillée removals. There is a tanged truncation. As in Phase 1a, there appears to be patterning within the deposition of tools. Posthole F18 contained very high proportions of tools (31%; assemblage total 76); most of these were retouched, including a large number of well made scrapers (n = 17), some of which were very tiny (e.g. 11mm diameter in one case). A number of these tools have very heavy esquillée removals, including one which appears to be roughly tanged as well. The large number of scrapers in this post-hole form what is in effect a scraper cache/deposit. In contrast, the other post-hole (F17) contained mainly quartz and fewer tools, including a knife fragment. Hearth F16 produced a small number of artefacts but no tools. Levelling deposit [70] contained quite high tool proportions (13%) with a mix of retouched and use defined tools including especially non-formal tools such as marginally retouched pieces, and also high levels of scrapers.

The occupation-related deposit in Phase 1c [53/54/59/62/63/64] contained a fairly high proportion of tools (13%), with significant numbers of scrapers and a few marginally retouched pieces present. Several tools here are on regular bladelets, including a burin, a naturally backed bladelet, and an edge damaged bladelet. A plano convex knife was also retrieved, made on pale grey translucent flint. This large tool made on a chunky blade is likely to have been imported ready made, although possibly later repaired. A spall removal down one lateral side of one tool has been

Table 4.11. Summary of Phase 1 tools

Phase	*1a*					*1b*					*Phase 1*	
	hearth	*occu-pation*	*pit*	*post-hole*	*pot deposit*	*hearth*	*occu-pation*	*post-hole*	*levelling*	*Storm/ levelling*	*Total*	*%*
Marginally ret'd		8					8	1	10	7	34	15.7
Notch										3	3	1.4
Denticulate												0.0
Fabricator										1	1	0.5
Backed flake					1		1			2	4	1.8
Scrapers		11			1		25	17	13	13	80	36.9
Knives					2		2	1			5	2.3
Truncations												0.0
Points							1				1	0.5
Awls												0.0
Others							2			1	3	1.3
Fragments		3					3	1	1	1	9	3.7
Total ret'd		14			4		34	19	14	18	103	47.5
Pièce esquillée		2			1		6	3	5	17	34	15.7
Burins							5	1	1	12	19	8.8
Used		9			1		21	2	7	21	61	28.1
Total used		11			2		32	6	13	50	114	52.5
Total tools	0	25	0	0	6	0	66	25	27	68	217	

more roughly retouched, and at one end where the nose of the knife had been smoothed down (through usewear?), fresher inverse retouch has renewed the edge angle between ventral face and tool edge. A number of burins take the form of short spalls removed down one side, forming flat 'backed' edges, possibly for use in hafting (tangs?).

Discussion of phase 1

The first issue to discuss in Phase 1 is change over time. Use of raw materials certainly changes over this phase, with early levels having high proportions of quartz which drops off at the end of Phase 1a, to be replaced by more variable use of raw materials, with quartz overall lower, but higher in certain Phase 1b features. Scraper forms become more regular in Phase 1b, and remain so over the rest of the site's life. The dominance of non formal tools in general drops off somewhat by Phase 1b.

Deposition of cores also changes at the end of Phase 1a – cores are no longer ubiquitous in all deposit types and become rare in occupation levels, possibly reflecting a change in sweeping/clearing of occupation areas and/or of location of knapping areas. Cores are more common in levelling layers, which may have been derived from areas where cores were deposited (perhaps non-occupation areas?). Finally, blades, and especially regular blades, are more common in Phase 1a, dropping off to lower proportions in Phases 1b/c. This may reflect the subsequent focus on thumbnail scrapers as the main formal tool, but perhaps also the nature of activities carried out that resulted in damage even to these small, robust artefacts. Perhaps blades, especially of the size that could be manufactured on small beach pebbles, were just too fragile?

It is also worth considering the variable deposition of material across different contexts. In Phase 1a, the chipped stone assemblages associated with substantial pot deposits contain particularly high levels of retouched tools; likewise in Phase 1b, the two post-holes (F17/F18) have distinct characters, one containing high levels of quartz (unusual in this phase), the other dominated by flint retouched tools (including a possible scraper cache).

While the assemblage from occupation deposits contains small fraction and mainly debitage rather than tools (and seems most likely to form the detritus of knapping), assemblages from post-holes and hearths, and those associated with substantial pot deposits, contain far less knapping debris. This could suggest that this material may have been collected from elsewhere and deposited (minus the harder to collect small pieces) into these locations. The final occupation-related deposit [53/54] also has little debris, and higher tool levels (13% compared to 4% for underlying occupation levels), mainly scrapers and burins but also the plano convex knife. Redeposition of material by human action could result in the loss of small fraction debris from these levels, but the higher levels of tools suggests human action of some sort, either through distributing material that had more tools in it, or through adding tools as part of the process of deposition.

Table 4.12. Summary of Phase 2 catalogued assemblage

Phase 2	*Flint*		*Other*		*Quartz*	
	No.	*%*	*No.*	*%*	*No.*	*%*
Flakes	1029	66.9	8	100.0	129	62.3
Blades	97	6.3		0.0	8	3.9
Spalls	74	4.8		0.0	1	0.5
Core trimming elements	9	0.6		0.0	0	0.0
Indeterminates	177	11.5		0.0	25	12.1
Small fraction	31	2.0		0.0	19	9.2
Cores	121	7.9		0.0	25	12.1
Total	1538	100.0	8	100.0	207	100.0

Phase 2

Raw material use in Phase 2 is dominated by flint, but usually with sizeable amounts of quartz as well (Table 4.12). The ratio of quartz to flint usually ranges from 1:3 to 1:9 in each context. Phases 2a and 2b show high levels of burning in artefacts, while the Phase 2c assemblage had very low levels of burning.

The assemblage from Phase 2 is dominated by irregular flakes, with fewer blades (3–8% of each context >7 artefacts). Regular blades are particularly scarce, only appearing in the hearth and occupation layers, and even there in very small numbers (11% and 15% of the blade assemblages, respectively). There are few regular blades that are sufficiently complete to allow measurement, but they average 9.5mm in width (n = 8).

Cores are common in both flint and quartz in Phases 2a and 2b (especially in the hearth contexts at 12%) and in 2c's occupation layer (11%), even making up a significant proportion of the few quartz artefacts in Phase 2c (25%). Core trimming elements occur in Phases 2a/b in small numbers, but disappear in Phase 2c (but note this may be due to small assemblage size). Cores are usually bipolar on anvil, and include flat cores with removals down one face with a pebble back, and some with regular bipolar removals down two or three faces from regular ridge-like 'platforms', as well as more irregular and angular bipolar cores. Only very small numbers of cores show use of a platform technology, and these are usually irregular platform cores. One regular platform core has had several final removals taken off it. There are significant numbers of tested cores in Phase 2a pit F14 (17%), and in Phase 2a and 2b's hearth and occupation layers (7% and 4%); some of these have scant removals off very small pebbles, and may therefore be learning cores, or even 'doodles' (see above). Cores are rather small, averaging 28mm in length for flint cores, and 35mm in length for quartz ones. If one outlier of 255mm is removed from the flint figures, the average for flint cores becomes 23mm – very similar to those in Phase 1.

The small fraction is again differentially deposited across the context levels in Phase 2, with the 'hearth pit' (F11 and

F14) deposits containing high levels of small artefacts, and the hearths themselves variable small fraction, with F5 containing very high proportions (8.7%), and F8 and F10 somewhat less high (3% and 2.2%). The occupation levels in Phase 2 are rather low in small fraction (0–2.3%). This may suggest a different sweeping regime in comparison to Phase 1, or perhaps difference in knapping locations (but note the presence of cores in these deposits).

Tools

Phase 2 overall has similar tool proportions to Phase 1 (12.5%), but again there is considerable variation between sub-phases and contexts (Tables 4.13 and 4.14). Phases 2a and 2b show variability across context types. Hearth contexts have higher proportions of tools, especially [31] and [49] (17–18%), with more retouched tools amongst them. Tools include marginally retouched pieces and scrapers, with the latter being regular and thumbnail-like; one is on black flint and is larger than most others. There is also a range of other tool classes, including one marginally retouched bladelet.

Table 4.13. Summary of Phase 2 tools

Category	*No.*
Marginally retouched	34
Notch	6
Denticulate	2
Backed flake	2
Scrapers	37
Knife	2
Truncation	3
Point	0
Awl	1
Other	3
Fragment	8
Total retouched tools	98
Pièce esquillée	76
Burin	19
Used	26
Total used tools	121

Table 4.14. Summary of Phase 2 tools, by context type

Type	*Hearth*	*Pit*	*Occupation deposit*	*Post-hole*	*Wall*	*Total*
Marginally retouched	13	2	17	1	1	34
Notch	1	0	5	0	0	6
Denticulate	0	1	1	0	0	2
Backed flake	0	0	2	0	0	2
Scrapers	22	3	52	1	1	79
Knives	1	0	1	0	0	2
Truncations	1	0	2	0	0	3
Points	0	0	0	0	0	0
Awls	1	0	0	0	0	1
Others	2	0	1	0	0	3
Fragments	5	1	2	0	0	8
Total retouched	32	4	60	1	1	98
Pièces esquillée	22	12	41	1	0	76
Burins	6	1	12	0	0	19
Used	5	1	19	0	1	26
Total used	33	14	72	1	1	121
Total tools	65	18	132	2	2	219

Occupation layer [41/42/46/47] has somewhat lower levels of tools (11%), with equal proportions of use defined and retouched tools. A wide range of tools is presented, including pièces esquillées and high levels of scrapers, as well as marginally retouched pieces and small numbers of other classes. Several pièces esquillées and marginally retouched pieces are on core trimming elements. Scrapers are regular; some are small, many are heavily used; some have retouch limited to one end, and others are more heavily retouched round their circumference. It is interesting to note that two small assemblages (from post-hole F13 and wall context [29]) have very high proportions of tools.

The Phase 2c occupation layer [20/27/28] has very high levels of tools (25%), mainly made up of use-defined pieces including pièces esquillées and edge damaged pieces, as well as small numbers of scrapers and marginally retouched flakes. Two flakes have bipolar backing.

Discussion of Phase 2

The first element to note from Phase 2 is the redeposition of chipped stone. Assemblages in Phase 2 occupation levels have low proportions of small fraction, with higher numbers of cores and tools. This suggests that either knapping was not carried out in these locations, or that the knapping floors were swept out, with certain items like cores and tools curated, and debris swept into other areas. Pits in Phase 2 contain the small fraction of flint (with lower proportions of quartz than are found in other context types of this phase), with few cores or tools. This may also support the idea that these assemblages result from sweeping of flint knapping occurring elsewhere on the site. By Phase 2c, the lack of small fraction in any context may suggest that knapping was carried out elsewhere, with the small numbers of chipped stone present on site including especially high levels of tools in occupation levels brought in from elsewhere.

In terms of change over time, there are some differences from Phase 1 assemblages seen here. The use of quartz is more common than in Phase 1b/c, and fewer blades or regular blades are present. The organisation of technology changes over the phases as well. In Phase 1, there was widespread knapping residue, with deposition of certain items in deposits associated with substantial pot deposits and in pits. During Phase 2, debris may have been swept away with used tools into hearths and perhaps in some cases pits. By the end of this phase, knapping was carried out off site, with only curated items brought into the site's occupation levels. Otherwise, the assemblage remains very similar, with technology and tool types unchanging.

Phase 3

The Phase 3 assemblage was retrieved in large part from contexts [8] and [12], two sand horizons; and was most dense in [8] Square I and [12] Squares H and J – these three assemblages accounted for 47% of the entire Phase 3 total (Table 4.15).

Raw materials in Phase 3 continue to be dominated by flint (70%), but quartz is more important than in earlier phases, with the ratio of quartz to flint in this phase usually ranging from 1:2 or 1:3.

The assemblage from Phase 3 is dominated by irregular flakes to a greater degree than the earlier phases. There are fewer indeterminate pieces, possibly reflecting lower levels of burnt artefacts in Phase 3 than in previous levels, with the exception of Phase 1a. Blades levels are similar, as are the dimensions of blades and the scarcity of regular blades.

Cores are slightly more common overall, making up 10% of the flint assemblage. Cores are very similar to those in Phase 2, dominated by bipolar on anvil cores (87%), often worked down one face against a cortical back, or down both faces (45% of bipolar cores) or very irregular in form (23% of bipolar cores). Platform cores make up only 8% of the core assemblage, and are either single platform or more irregular multiple platform cores. Several cores are large flakes with multiple spall removals. Core form, technique and dimensions are very similar to those in Phase 2.

Small fraction is considerably less common than in previous levels – with none in any context in flint, and small amounts in quartz from contexts 8 and 12. While this might suggest that knapping was not carried out in these levels within the excavated area, the presence of cores and small numbers of core trimming elements would suggest otherwise. It is not clear if the lack of small fraction is due to post-depositional factors, or to differential deposition of different-sized artefacts.

Tools

Tools make up 13% of the Phase 3 assemblage (Table 4.16), a similar proportion to previous phases. But where previous phases showed variability between contexts, tool levels remain largely constant throughout Phase 3. The assemblage is dominated by thumbnail scrapers, with smaller numbers of pièces esquillées, and marginally retouched pieces. There are also small numbers of awls, notches, irregular scrapers, and edge-damaged pieces, with very small numbers of knives, truncations and burins. Most of the tools other than the scrapers are fairly ad hoc. The knives are small and show low retouch on irregular blanks, one of which is a core trimming element. A number of small cores were retouched into ad hoc tools such as a notch and a marginally retouched piece.

Table 4.15. Summary of Phase 3 catalogued assemblage

Material	*Flint*		*Other*		*Quartz*		*Total*	
	No.	*%*	*No.*	*%*	*No.*	*%*	*No.*	*%*
Flakes	742	76.7		0.0	301	73.4	1043	75.6
Blades	82	8.5	1	100.0	19	4.6	102	7.4
Spalls	27	2.8		0.0	3	0.7	30	2.2
Indeterminates	15	1.5		0.0	32	7.8	47	3.4
Core trimming elements	4	0.4		0.0		0.0	4	0.3
Cores	98	10.1		0.0	30	7.3	128	9.3
Small fraction		0.0		0.0	25	6.1	25	1.8
Total	968		1		410		1379	

Table 4.16. Summary of Phase 3 tools

	Flint		*Quartz*		*Total*	
	No.	*%*	*No.*	*%*	*No.*	*%*
Awl	5	3.1	0	0.0	5	2.8
Marginally retouched	18	11.3	2	10.0	20	11.1
Notch	5	3.1	4	20.0	9	5.0
Scrapers	79	49.4	9	45.0	88	48.9
Knife	2	1.3	0	0.0	2	1.1
Truncations	1	0.6	1	5.0	2	1.1
Fragments	2	1.3	0	0.0	2	1.1
Total retouched	112		16		128	
Pièce esquillée	39	24.4	3	15.0	42	23.3
Burin	5	3.1	1	5.0	6	3.3
Edge-damaged	4	2.5	0	0.0	4	2.2
Total used	48		4		52	
Total	160		20		180	

Overall, some 29% of the assemblage is made up of use-defined artefacts which are mainly pièces esquillées. There is little variability in tool class across contexts within Phase 3, although context [12] is more dominated by high numbers of pieces esquillees and scrapers, while context [8] has a slightly wider range of tool classes. F2 contained only two tools – one burin and one pièce esquillée.

This assemblage shows some significant differences from tools in Phase 2. There, higher proportions of the assemblage were use-defined, with both pieces esquillees and burins more common. In Phase 3, thumbnail scrapers become much more common, although they are similar in form – usually regular, and often heavily used (sometimes apparently made on pieces esquillees, and/or used as pièces esquillées after being retouched). They are often cortical, and have varying amounts of retouch around their circumference.

Discussion of Phase 3

The assemblage from Phase 3 overall was very similar to that from Phase 2, with some differences of degree in tool classes. Quartz is more heavily relied on than in the earlier phases, but overall assemblage composition is very similar. Use of bipolar on anvil technology continues, and irregular flakes and small numbers of largely irregular blades are present. There is little variability within Phase 3 between different contexts.

Phase 4

An assemblage of 150 artefacts was scanned from Phase 4 of the site (modern layers containing redeposited material). The condition of material was relatively fresh, with no sign of sand blown gloss. Artefacts are heavily patinated. Quartz and flint are similar in type and condition to that from previous phases. Other materials included several quartzite pieces and a pitchstone flake. The assemblage was dominated by irregular flakes that often formed large parts of small beach pebbles. Many artefacts have cortex from beach pebbles remaining. Two regular bladelets were found in [2], as well as a large, very regular blade fragment, and another blade fragment with retouch. Tools were rare, and included some pièces esquillées, several backed flakes and a quartz denticulate. Scrapers occurred throughout the assemblage. While most of the Phase 4 assemblage was bipolar on anvil in character, there were small numbers of flakes with very thick, regular platforms.

Discussion

Phases 1 and 2

This assemblage shows many characteristics of other Scottish Neolithic assemblages – the emphasis on use of bipolar on anvil technique seen in the west coast Neolithic, as at Allt Chrisal (Wickham-Jones 1995) on a mainly pebble sourced raw material, with a mix of flint and quartz, e.g. Dunnasbroc (McHardy et al. 2009), Eilean an Tighe (Scott 1951) and Auchategan (Marshall 1980).

There are very small numbers of blades present here, as at e.g. Geirisclett (Dunwell et al. 2003), but unlike e.g. Allt Chrisal (Wickham-Jones 1995), where no true blades were found. Despite the few blades, there is a lack of concern for blank form, and indeed tool form, as at Dunnasbroc (Barrowman 2009), with many tools utilised without retouch. The scraper is common as at many other sites (Eilean an Tighe, Scott 1951; Auchategan, Marshall 1980; Allt Chrisal, Wickham-Jones 1995) with very small numbers of other formal tools such as leaf shaped arrowheads and knives.

Arrowheads are often on special materials such as the orange flint leaf shaped arrowhead at Dunnasbroc (Barrowman 2009, illustration 68), but the one here is on a pale flint which could well have been pebble-sourced (as most of the rest of the assemblage was). However, the plano-convex knife found here was made on possibly imported pale grey flint and is on a chunky regular blade which is unlikely to derive from the usual pebble cores exploited. Plano-convex knives occur in some other assemblages in small numbers (e.g. Allt Chrisal, Wickham-Jones 1995). The one found here is elongated, as is the one from Achnacreebeag (Ritchie 1973, figure 4.13).

As has been pointed out by others (e.g. Warren 2006; Edmonds 1995), a common characteristic of Neolithic knapped stone assemblages is their purposeful deposition. This can be seen clearly in pits, caches, or, sometimes, funerary contexts as at Geirisclett (where small fraction was found, possibly suggesting knapping in the tomb, or very careful secondary deposition) (Dunwell et al. 2003), and many Neolithic assemblages, such as that from Allt Chrisal (Wickham-Jones 1995), are found without associated small fraction, suggesting secondary deposition. The An Doirlinn assemblage is very large and its distribution across the site and contexts is complex and varied, suggesting different deposition practices in different settings.

Organisation of technology

The place of knapping (literally) seems to shift over the life of the site. Phase 1 might be described as rather 'Mesolithic-like' with knapping debris widely distributed. However, the material associated with substantial pot deposits in Phase 1a and pits in Phase 1b contain artefact groupings with different characteristics from the rest of the assemblage, suggesting the possibility of intentional deposition. The possible larger-scale movement of deposits in the final levelling layer sees tool-rich assemblages possibly more similar to the substantial pot and pit deposits with less sign of knapping deposits seen across the site. By Phase 2, knapping debris is deposited in hearths, along with tools – possibly the swept by-products of activity areas near the hearths. Pits also contain some knapping debris, but no tools. By Phase 2c, the small assemblage, and lack of debris/debitage, suggests that knapping probably occurred off-site, with a few curated tools and cores brought into occupation areas on site. So knapping as an activity seems to move from ubiquity in the life of the site and its occupants, to a more structured use/manipulation of knapped products, clearing material from some areas and depositing certain items in others. Finally the activity of knapping is removed from the site altogether, with certain 'curated' objects reintroduced to it.

Unchanging character

Another feature of the An Doirlinn assemblage is the constancy of technology and most tool classes over time. This constancy is found in the knapping techniques that also characterise many Mesolithic assemblages (e.g. Mercer 1971; Wicks et al. 2014), and in the tool forms which persist over the life of the site. The only change in tool forms is seen in the slightly increasing formality of tools in Phase 1b – in the form of thumbnail scrapers and the rare diagnostic tools, which could be viewed as a 'Neolithic-ness' not seen in Phase 1a. It is interesting that these happen at the same time as an increase in the use of flint over Phases 1a/b that decreases in Phase 2. These raw material choices could relate to shifts in availability of beach pebbles in quartz or in flint, but seems more likely to relate to preferences, whether springing from functional needs or the cultural significance of different materials.

'Neolithic-ness'

Diagnostically 'Neolithic' items are noticeable for their very scarceness, here as at other west coast Neolithic sites. One leaf-shaped arrowhead, one plano-convex knife, and a scattering of other knives are their only presence here. They are the exception rather than the rule, and in some cases are likely to have been imported as tools or at least as blanks. They seem to be 'bolted on' to a much more long standing tradition of lithic use. Most are heavily used – like the plano-convex knife – and sometimes refurbished, although the arrowhead, while broken at the tip, does not show other signs of heavy use.

The only formal tool that seems completely embedded within the assemblage is the scraper. Probably made on small, round and often cortical blanks that are easily achieved from beach pebbles, these tools were, from phase 1b, very common, and used with some gusto judging by the obvious and destructive usewear on many pieces. But these are also the only common tools clearly made here that were carefully and beautifully retouched – and apparently at times collected and deposited in specific places.

Phase 3

The Phase 3 assemblage is, like many EBA assemblages, difficult to distinguish from the Late Neolithic. It has a typical dominance of thumbnail scrapers, often associated with Beaker deposits (Edmonds 1995). Knives are also present in small numbers which may sometimes be associated with Food Vessels and Collared Urns (e.g. Shepherd and Cowie 1977), but are also found in Later Neolithic assemblages. However, the assemblage lacks the classic EBA barbed and tanged arrowhead, present sometimes in significant proportions, as at Dalmore, Lewis, for example (Ballin 2009).

Quartz is present and significant within the assemblage, but plays a secondary role to flint, in contrast to some other nearby (but more northerly) assemblages which are dominated by quartz, at The Udal, North Uist, for example (Clarke 1997), and Rosinish, Benbecula where over 99% of the assemblage of over 3500 artefacts was in quartz (Ballin 2009). It is difficult to explain the higher levels of flint present here, but perhaps flint beach pebbles were particularly easily sourced at this coastal location in the southern part of the island chain (see Section 4.11).

The nature of the deposits in Phase 3 remains unclear. Having a naturally-formed appearance, the presence of large amounts of chipped stone concentrated in three grid squares is puzzling. The lack of small fraction in the chipped stone may support an interpretation of the deposits being formed through some sort of storm event. This might also explain the lack of differentiation in assemblage make up over the different contexts – although equally this could be the result of a different, more homogenous process of deposition from the patterning seen in the Neolithic levels.

Conclusion

The Neolithic/EBA chipped stone assemblage from An Doirlinn of 10,613 pieces represents by far the largest yet excavated in the Outer Hebrides. Allt Chrisal is the next largest, having produced 3621 pieces of flaked stone and just 138 pieces of worked quartz (Branigan & Foster 1995, 120). All of the other published sites have produced miniscule quantities of flint/quarz by comparison: 66 from Eilean an Tighe (Scott 1950, 35–37), 34 from Bharpa Carinish (Crone et al. 1993, 375) and 105 from the Neolithic and Beaker layers combined at Northton (Simpson et al. 2006, 70). Eilean Domhnuill also produced only very small quantities (Ian Armit, pers. comm.). It is difficult to ascertain why An Doirlinn should have produced so much flint in comparison to these other sites, and in some ways it is perhaps actually more pertinent to ask why they produced quite so little. Given the relatively large amounts of flint recovered from Allt Chrisal, it is possible perhaps that groups living in the south simply had better access to this raw material. Interestingly in this light, Wickham-Jones and Collins's survey of all geologically mapped Scottish flint sources places the only two locations identified in the whole of the Outer Hebrides on Vatersay, immediately south of Barra, and at Skiport in north-west South Uist (1978, 10–12); this suggests that flint could indeed have been more readily available in the southern part of the island chain than in the north.

The An Doirlinn chipped stone assemblage shares many similarities with other Neolithic and EBA assemblages on the west coast of Scotland – using local materials and long standing techniques, the assemblage is simple and seems more concerned with robustness than with investment in form. In Phases 1 and 2, it is however augmented by some elements that are of diagnostically Neolithic form and in a few cases imported. While the forms of tools and blanks do not change over time at An Doirlinn, the organisation of the technology of knapping changes substantially over the life of the site – not in materials or techniques used, but in how the activity of knapping and use of knapped products relates to the site. Despite its apparent simplicity of manufacture, chipped stone becomes something to be more consciously disposed of or collected, swept away or curated, chosen and moved across the site, or, possibly, the wider landscape. The role and significance of chipped stone becomes more spatially structured over the course of the site's occupation.

So, while tool forms at An Doirlinn may only occasionally reflect the 'new' world of the Neolithic, the role of chipped stone does shift (probably significantly in the lives of those who made and used this assemblage), continuing with age-old techniques and in many cases products, but seeing changes in organisation of technology and patterned distribution probably reflecting changes in when and where stone was knapped, perhaps in who knapped it, and why, and what this technology and its products meant to people.

4.6. Worked and utilised stone

Hugo Anderson-Whymark

Introduction

This report considers 16 worked or utilised stone artefacts recovered from the 2012 excavations and one stone tool exposed by coastal erosion in 2005 (Figures 4.32–4.34). These comprise three polished axe-heads, a fragmentary ovoid pebble-hammer or mace-head, seven facially pecked cobbles (anvils), a hammerstone, a facetted cobble (processor), two quernstones and four smoothers/rubbers. In addition to the worked stone, a large number of unworked igneous and metamorphic beach pebbles were identified during the excavation and a small sample (20 pebbles) were retained. Detailed examination revealed no traces of use on these pebbles, although it is possible that some or all of these pebbles functioned as ad hoc tools.

Methodology

The stone was macroscopically examined for evidence of shaping and use under bright lighting conditions. A ×10 hand lens was used where more detailed examination was required. The worked stone was catalogued using standard morphological descriptions (Clarke 2006). The catalogue was created in Microsoft Excel and has been deposited with the site archive.

Raw materials

The stone tools, with the notable exception of axe-heads, were manufactured from water-worn pebbles and cobbles of igneous and metamorphic rock. Detailed geological identification was not undertaken as these stones were probably obtained from local beach deposits. The stone used for the axe-heads was macroscopically identified by Rob Ixer (see below). The axe-heads were all manufactured from non-local stone imported to the Outer Hebrides.

Provenance

Stone artefacts were recovered from a variety of archaeological contexts, including occupation layers, levelling deposits, a shell sand horizon and a pit. The artefacts were widely distributed across the excavation area and there is no clear evidence for deliberate placement or special deposition practices. The range of artefacts is consistent throughout the stratigraphic sequence and no clear chronological variation was observed in the use of worked stone.

The assemblage

Axe-heads

Two polished stone axe-heads and a waisted axe-head-like implement were recovered from the excavations. These are described in detail below:

A once very fine stone axe-head with a long use-biography was recovered from surface cleaning of Phase 4 deposit [2] (Figure 4.32, No. 1). The raw material for this axe-head is a fine-grained acidic lava that is not local to the Outer Hebrides and must have been imported, but it does not belong to any known axe group and cannot be accurately located geologically (see Ixer, below). The original form of this axe-head cannot be determined due to extensive re-working, but it appears to have been a large finely manufactured implement with a lenticular cross-section, clear side facets (one partially survives) and a near perfect all over surface polish. At some point in its history the axe-head was broken in half, possibly in line with the haft; subsequently the sides and butt end of the artefact were crudely re-flaked to create a smaller implement measuring 97mm long by 70mm wide and 37mm thick. The blade-edge shows extensive use-damage including numerous small flake removals and one large scar 51mm in length. Many of these scars have been partially removed by polishing. The faces of the axe-head exhibit three small areas of fine pecking, measuring 11mm to 16mm in diameter; these indicate that this tool was used as an anvil in the same fashion as the facially pecked pebbles at the end of its use-life.

The second axe-head was recovered from Phase 1b occupation layer [65] Sq. B8 (Figure 4.32, No. 2). This implement was manufactured from Hornblende Lamprophyre, possible Group XXX, which probably originates from the west coast of Scotland (see Ixer, below). The artefact is roughly triangular in plan with a rounded butt, semi-circular convex sides and flat faces, and measures 107.5mm long by 70mm wide and 27mm thick. The sides and butt end were shaped by pecking and the blade edge has been finished by grinding and polishing. The blade edge is rounded and blunt, probably from use, but exhibits only a couple of minor flake scars. As with the axe-head described above, this implement was re-used as an anvil and each of the flat faces exhibit small sub-circular concave depressions 14–15mm in diameter.

The final axe-head-like implement was recovered from the Phase 3 Beaker associated shell sand layer [12] (Figure 4.32, No. 3). This implement was manufactured from a small weathered pebble of Hornblende Lamprophyre that also possibly belongs to Group XXX (see Ixer, below). The implement has been roughly flaked forming a semi-circular butt end and lateral notches. The blade edge was ground and polished to shape and prior to flaking damage

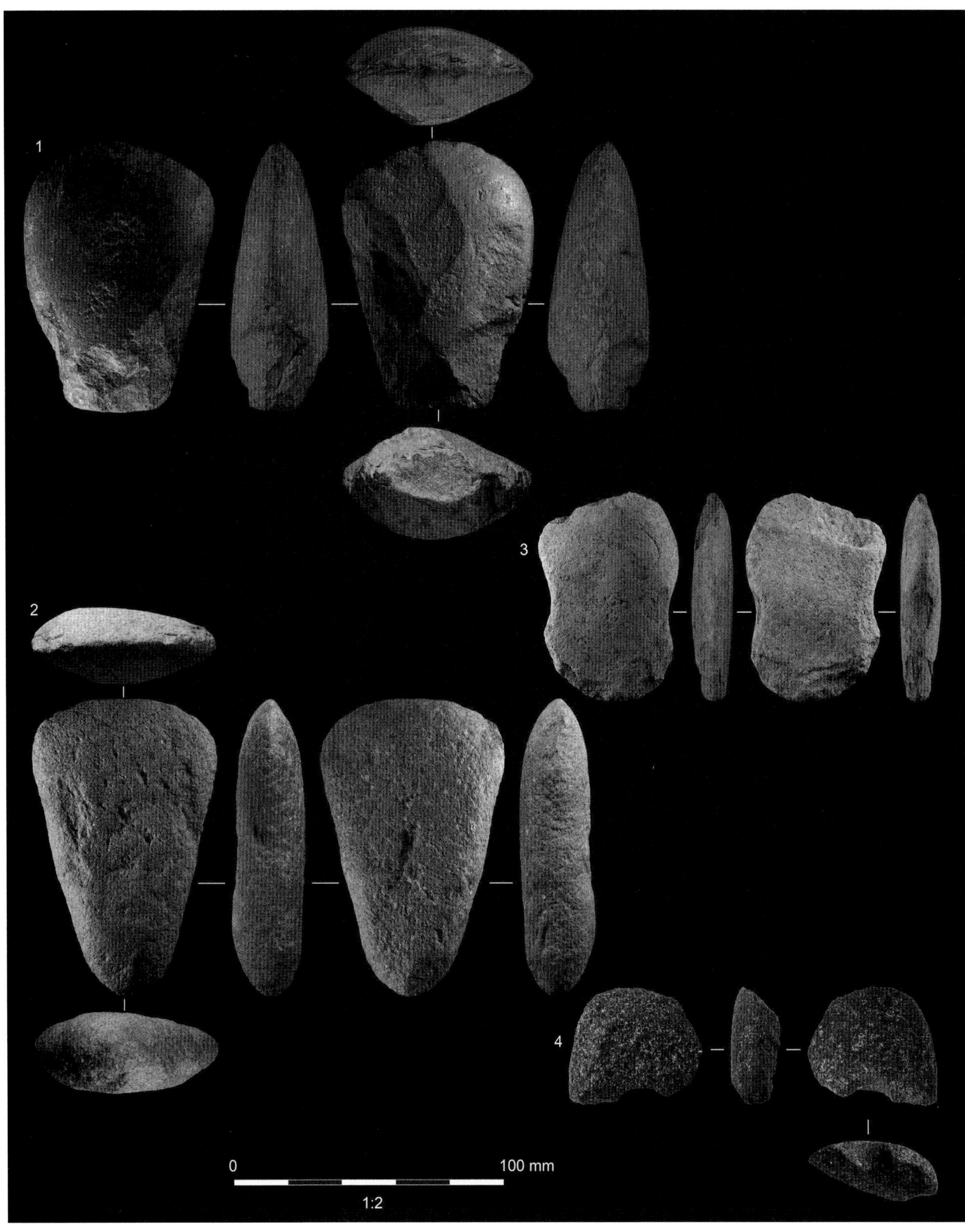

Figure 4.32. Worked stone (1) (photo: H. Anderson-Whymark).

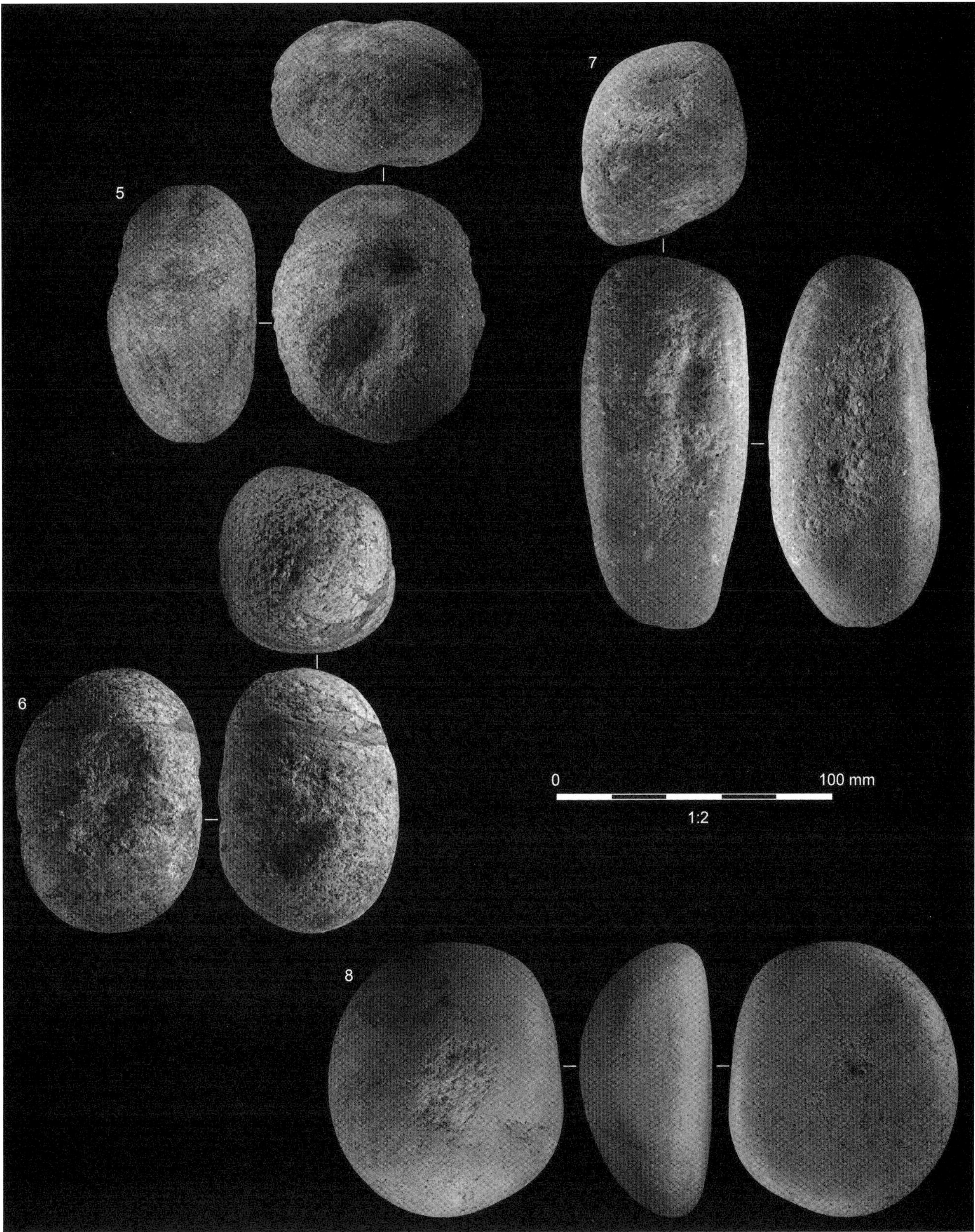

Figure 4.33. Worked stone (2) (photo: H. Anderson-Whymark).

Figure 4.34. Worked stone (3) (photos: H. Anderson-Whymark and S. Lambert-Gates).

from use it was probably semi-circular. The artefact measures 75mm long by 52.5mm wide and 15mm thick.

Ovoid pebble-hammer or mace-head

A small flake struck from an ovoid pebble-hammer or mace-head was recovered from Phase 1c occupation/ midden deposit [53] (Figure 4.32, No. 4). The artefact was manufactured from a distinctive highly metamorphosed black rock that is heavy flecked with fine (<0.4mm) white quartz. The artefact exhibits a smooth surface finish, but no definitive evidence for grinding or shaping, such as striations on the surface, was observed. A small area of the shaft-hole survives: this exhibits a rounded lip and tapers in the style of an hour-glass perforation for the surviving depth (12mm). Fine longitudinal striations are visible on the side of the shaft-hole; these probably result from production techniques. The absence of evidence for shaping or application of a surface finish, combined with the possibility of an hour-glass perforation point towards classification as a pebble-hammer, but as the artefact is fragmentary and the original form of the object and its shaft-hole cannot be determined with absolute confidence, a broad identification as a fragmentary ovoid pebble-hammer or mace-head is preferred.

Hammerstone

One sub-ovoid metamorphic pebble weighing 418g exhibited use-damage on one end, from shell sand layer [12]. Five of the six facially pecked cobbles, considered below, also bear evidence for use as hammerstones.

Facially pecked pebble/cobbles (anvils)

Seven pebble and cobbles exhibit discrete areas of facial pecking on their sides (Figure 4.33, Nos 5–8); five of these artefacts have also been used as hammerstones and two exhibit polished faces resulting from use as a grinding or burnishing tools (Nos 6 and 8). All of these tools utilised locally available rounded, ovoid, flattened ovoid or sub-rectangular, water worn pebbles of igneous and metamorphic rock, which weigh between 211g and 717g (average: 504g). The facially pecked cobbles exhibited 1–8 (average: 4) circular and sub-circular depressions on flat or convex sides. These depressions measure 10–35mm in diameter by 1–10mm deep and are either bowl-shaped or conical in form. These depressions all exhibit fine (<1mm) peck marks that probably result from use and imply contact with a hard sharp material. The coarse pecked damage resulting from the use of five of these pebbles as hammerstones was concentrated on the ends of the pebbles, with the exception of one example that exhibited more extensive damage around the lateral edge (No. 5).

Facetted cobble (processor)

One ovoid water worn pebble from Phase 3 shell sand layer [12] exhibits a distinct facet measuring 23mm long by 13.5mm wide on one end (Figure 4.34, No. 9). This facet results from grinding or abrasion against another stone during the processing of an unknown substance into a paste or powder.

Smoothers/rubbers

Two water worn pebbles, weighing 146g and 162g, and two cobbles, weighing 751g and 1260g, each possess one naturally flat face that exhibits a smooth to slightly polished surface resulting from use. The smaller pebbles may have been used as grinders or burnishing tools, while the larger artefacts may have been used as saddle quern rubbers, or in the case of the fragmentary stone from occupation/midden deposit [53] that is slightly concave along its long axis as a small saddle quern measuring 123+mm long by 80mm wide and 45mm thick (Figure 4.34, No. 10).

Quernstones

Two large stones, weighing 8.6kg and 13.3g. The first measures 295mm long by 263mm wide and 62mm thick. It has a very slightly dished (9mm deep) and clearly worn/polished surface resulting from use for grinding (Figure 4.34, No. 11). The second measures 358mm long by 248mm wide and 87mm thick. It has a concave surface (13mm deep) that is not obviously polished from use, but could nonetheless have been enhanced as a result of its use for grinding (Figure 4.34, No. 12).

Discussion

The range of tools from An Doirlinn is typical of Neolithic sites in the north of Scotland. Interim reports on excavations at Eilean Domhnuill indicate the recovery of comparable stone artefacts, but in the absence of comprehensive publication it is not possible to make detailed comparison with this important site. Stone assemblages from Orcadian Neolithic sites have been more comprehensively studied and parallels can be readily identified on many sites including Knap of Howar (Papa Westray), Barnhouse (West Mainland) and Pool (Sanday) (Clarke 2006). The assemblage from the late Neolithic settlement at Barnhouse is particularly comparable as all of the tool forms present at An Doirlinn are represented, while stone discs (pot-lids) and Skaill knives are absent from both sites. The absence of the two latter forms from Barnhouse is notable within the Orcadian Neolithic, but at An Doirlinn their absence may reflect the lack of suitable raw materials for these artefact types.

The stone tools reflect the performance of various activities, such as hammering, grinding and/or burnishing of various substances. The function of the small circular and sub-circular areas of pecking on the facially pecked cobbles and two of the axe-heads is, however, open to debate. One possible explanation is that these hollows represent areas of use-damage from the use of these stones as anvils for bi-polar flint knapping – the act of holding a flint against an anvil and striking to induce fracture from both ends. The flint industry at An Doirlinn was focussed on the working of small flint pebbles using bi-polar percussion (see Section 4.5). This technique is very effective for initiating fracture on rounded pebbles and controlling the reduction of small pieces of flint. As a hard material receiving a hefty blow, flint would have been more than capable of producing a peck mark as it was struck. Moreover, the development of a series of peck marks and eventually a hollow would provide 'grip' when the flint is struck. It is also possible to envisage a hollow becoming too deep to function effectively. This possible interpretation requires further experimental investigation, but represents a plausible explanation for the use of these tools.

Macroscopical geological description of the axe-heads

Rob A. Ixer

Three stone axe-heads were investigated macroscopically to determine their lithology. All three artefacts are exotic with regard to their find spot. Two are probably the same lithology and may belong to the very small, Scottish, Implement Petrology Group (IPG) axe Group XXX defined by Fenton (1988, 105) although one is very heavily altered. There are a number of geographical origins for this axe group lithology, which is rare and unusual; most are close to the west coast of Scotland (Fenton 1988, 106). The third implement is an acid-intermediate lava and belongs to no recognised axe group.

Waisted axe-head like implement from shell sand layer [12], Phase 3

Possibly a member of IPG axe Group XXX. Hornblende Lamprophyre. No specific geographical origin but probably from western mainland Scotland. The implement is very weathered/altered to a pale yellow brown (10YR 6/2 on the Geological Society of America rock-color chart). The fine-grained igneous lithology is uniform with randomly orientated, very small hornblende laths up to 1mm in length and small voids all within a fine-grained matrix. The lithology is very similar to the axe-head from occupation layer 65, but is heavily altered.

Axe-head from occupation layer [65], Sq. B8, Phase 1b

Possibly a member of IPG Axe group XXX. Hornblende Lamprophyre. No specific geographical origin but probably from western mainland Scotland. This axe fragment has weathered to a light olive grey (5Y 6/1 on the Geological Society of America rock-color chart). The fine-grained igneous lithology is uniform with randomly orientated, very small hornblende laths up to 1mm in length and rounded, 1–1.5mm diameter, pink-yellow feldspar in voids all within a fine-grained matrix. A thin section would be required to determine if this is a Group XXX axe head.

Axe-head from surface cleaning (2), Sq. G, Phase 4

A fine-grained acidic lava. No provenance suggested. No recognised axe group. The weathered surface of the axe fragment is a dark greenish grey (5GY 4/1 on the Geological Society of America rock-color chart). The fine-grained igneous lithology is uniform with pale-coloured feldspar microliths and microphenocrysts, 0.5–1.0mm in size; locally there is a feint planar fabric and the microliths lie within this suggesting the rock may be a lava. Small voids are present.

Catalogue (Figs 4.32–4.34)

ILLUSTRATED

1. Polished stone axe-head, heavily reworked and re-used as an anvil. Manufactured from a fine-grained acidic lava. Cleaning context [2], Sq. G. Phase 4. Weight: 291g. Dimensions: 97mm long by 70mm wide and 37mm thick.
2. Polished axe-head, re-used as an anvil. Manufactured from Hornblende Lamprophyre, possibly part of Group XXX. Occupation layer [65], Sq. B8. Phase 1b. Weight: 269g. Dimensions: 107.5mm long by 70mm wide and 27mm.
3. Waisted axe-head-like implement. Manufactured from Hornblende Lamprophyre, possibly part of Group XXX. Shell sand 'b' horizon [12], Sq. J. Phase 3. Weight: 76g. Dimensions: 75mm long by 52.5mm wide and 15mm thick.
4. Flake struck from an hour-glass perforated pebble-hammer or mace-head. Occupation deposit [53], Sq. B5. Phase 1c. Weight: 51g. Dimensions: 41.4+mm long by 47.6+mm wide and 17.9mm thick.
5. Facially pecked cobble (anvil)/hammerstone. Pit fill [76], F.14. Phase 2a. Weight: 493g. Dimensions: 90mm long by 73mm wide and 51mm thick.
6. Facially pecked cobble (anvil)/hammerstone with a slight use-polish on one side. Levelling deposit [70], Sq. C8. Phase1b. Weight: 559g. Dimensions: 91mm long by 69mm wide and 69mm thick.
7. Facially pecked cobble (anvil)/hammerstone. Shell sand 'b' horizon [12], Sq. H. Phase 3. Weight: 717g. Dimensions: 129mm long by 72mm wide and 55mm thick.
8. Facially pecked cobble (anvil) with burnishing on one face. Collected 8 Sep 2005 from erosion to N. side of the site. Weight: 536g. Dimensions: 94mm long by 82mm wide and 48mm thick.
9. Faceted cobble (processor). Shell sand 'b' horizon [12]. Sq. H. Phase 3. Weight: 315g. Dimensions: 97.5mm long by 59.5mm wide and 33.3mm.
10. Rubber/smoother. Occupation deposit [53]. Sq. F6. Phase 1c. Weight: 751g. Dimensions: 123mm long by 80mm wide and 45mm thick.
11. Quernstone. Occupation deposit [82], Sq. E8. Phase 1a. Dimensions: 295mm long by 263mm wide and 62mm thick.

12. Quernstone. Occupation deposit [82], Sq. B3. Phase 1a. Dimensions: 358mm long by 248mm wide and 87mm thick.

NOT ILLUSTRATED

13. Hammerstone. Shell sand 'b' horizon [12], Sq. K. Phase 3. Weight: 418g. Dimensions: 110mm long by 55mm wide and 46.5mm thick.
14. Facially pecked cobble (anvil)/hammerstone. Sub-spherical pebble with two small c. 15mm diameter areas of pecking on convex sides. Shell sand 'b' horizon [12], Sq. K. Phase 3. Weight: 404g. Dimensions: 71mm long by 70 mm wide and 58mm thick.
15. Facially pecked cobble (anvil)/hammerstone. Flattened ovoid pebble with two sub-circular areas of use-damage, 17mm in diameter and 1mm deep, present towards the middle of each of the flattened sides. A further sub-circular area of use damage, 20mm wide by 2mm deep is present on one of the narrow sides and slight damage from use as a hammerstone are present on both ends of the pebble. Occupation layer [20], Sq. S. Phase 2c. Weight: 637g. Dimensions: 110mm long by 78mm wide and 47mm thick.
16. Facially pecked cobble (anvil). Smooth sub-spherical water worn pebble that exhibits one area of very slight use-damage 18mm in diameter. Occupation layer [52], Sq. B4. Phase 1c. Weight: 211g. Dimensions: 60mm long by 52mm wide and 47mm thick.
17. Rubber/smoother. Sub-rectangular pebble with one face that is slightly smoother than others. Pipe trench F1, fill [6]. Phase 4. Weight: 1260g. Dimensions: 150mm long by 65mm wide and 70mm thick.
18. Rubber/smoother. Fragmentary pebble with one face smoother than the others. Layer [3]. Phase 4. Weight: 162g. Dimensions: 72+mm long by 51mm wide by 24mm thick.
19. Rubber/smoother. A sub-oval pebble with one flattened side that exhibits a slight polish compared to other surfaces. Pit F16, fill [76]. Phase 2a. Weight: 147g. Dimensions: 63mm long by 47mm wide and 33mm thick.

4.7. Pumice

Elise Fraser

The assemblage comprised of 165 fragments of pumice from 32 contexts, with a total weight of 2624g (Figures 4.35 and 4.36; Table 4.17). The average weight of each fragment was 15.9g. A small number of pieces show signs of modification and/or use; in total eleven fragments exhibit signs of working, approximately 7% of the total assemblage. This proportion of modified pumice is similar to those seen on sites in Shetland (Ballin-Smith 1999; Binns in Mercer 1974; Clarke & Dixon 1998; Newton 1999) where pumice is commonly found within archaeological excavations, and on other Neolithic sites in the Outer Hebrides (Gregory 2006, 69). The distribution of pumice along the northern and western fringes of Britain is most likely to be related to the dispersion and movement of erupted material from Iceland by marine currents along the Atlantic coast (Binns 1967).

Table 4.17. List of illustrated pumice from An Doirlinn (Figs 4.35–4.36)

Illus. no.	*Context*	*Square*	*Feature*	*Description of working*
1a	12	H	–	V-shaped groove
1b	12	H	–	V-shaped groove
1c	12	R	–	V-shaped groove
1d	82	B5	–	U-shaped groove
2a	8	K	–	Pierced hole
2b	46	E5	–	Pierced hole
3a	49	–	F10	Flat, abraded surface
3b	20	I	–	Carved

Of the modified pumice recovered from An Doirlinn, six fragments had deep grooves cut across the abrasive faces of the pebbles. These were 'V' shaped and most likely the result of use as sharpening stones for bone implements. Three of these examples were recovered from context [12] (Nos 1a–c). Another fragment from [82] (1d) showed evidence of a faint groove alongside a more deeply smoothed circular hole which stretched the length of the fragment. The shape and curved nature of this mark suggested extensive abrasive action upon the surface, possibly repeated smoothing of a shaft-like object rather than a sharpened edge.

Two fragments were pierced with a single hole. The first pebble had a pierced hole that appeared to have been drilled from both sides (2a). The second showed some evidence that the pebble had been split in half, with one surface being slightly rounded and the other flat and abraded (2b). It is possible that these objects may have been used as floats for fishing nets, being an ideal material and easy to manufacture (Batey & Newton in Brady & Batey 2008). The pierced holes do not appear to be centrally located on either fragment, which may also point to this function, allowing the pumice to float whilst the net was fully submerged beneath the water.

A single fragment from [49] showed evidence of being cut and polished, exhibiting a very flat and obviously abraded surface on one face (3a). One fragment also showed more extensive signs of working, having a central flat oval raised section carved in relief (3b). This fragment also had evidence of smoothing on the other external surfaces, which may suggest that this was being modified for a specific function.

4.8. Bone

Duncan Garrow with Jaco Weinstock

A total of 508 fragments of bone weighing 303g were recovered from 27 contexts across the site. Very small fragment sizes meant that these were recovered almost

Figure 4.35. Pumice (1) (photo: S. Lambert-Gates).

exclusively during wet sieving/flotation rather than during excavation. The only bone that had survived the acidic soil conditions on site was burnt; we can probably assume that quantities of unburnt bone were originally present but had not survived. The fact that the average fragment weight was <1g gives an indication of its condition; the single largest piece collected weighed 7g. As a result of the small fragment sizes involved, not a single piece was identifiable to species; however, many fragments appeared to be from long bones. The largest quantities were recovered from occupation deposits throughout the site's use, with highest overall amounts in Phase 1c [53/54/59/62/63/64]. Small amounts of burnt bone were also found in hearth fills (perhaps indicating meat cooking), and in the Phase 2 pits on top of which hearths had subsequently been constructed (F11 and F14).

Given the acidic soils prevalent across the islands (especially prior to widespread machair formation), it is not surprising that bone has not survived well, or indeed at all, on most other Neolithic sites in the region. None at all is recorded from Eilean an Tighe or Bharpa Carinish, while – as at An Doirlinn – a few tiny fragments of burnt bone were identified within hearths at Allt Chrisal (Branigan & Foster 1995, 85). Even at Northton, where preservation conditions were much better, fewer than 300 fragments (including sheep, cattle, pig, deer and seal) were recorded from the Neolithic layers (Simpson et al. 2006, 75). The presence of bone at An Doirlinn confirms that animals were kept and eaten by the occupants of the site, but frustratingly it is impossible to say any more than that.

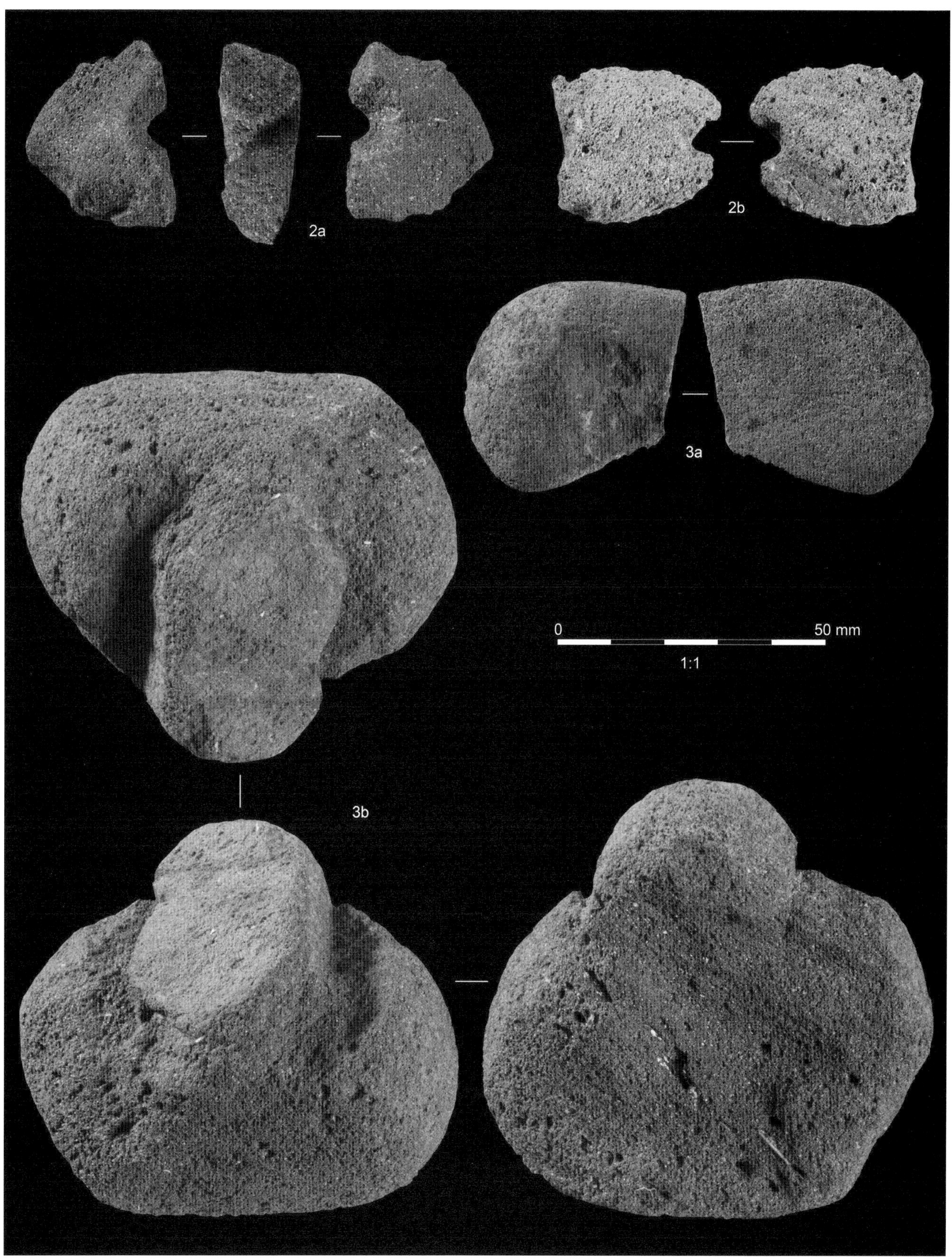

Figure 4.36. Pumice (2) (photo: S. Lambert-Gates).

4.9. Environmental evidence

Ceren Kabukcu, Julie Jones & Fraser Sturt

As noted in the introduction to this chapter, the environmental history of South Uist has received attention for a considerable period of time, with research intensifying over recent years. However, significant questions remain, particularly with regard to Mesolithic and Neolithic activity on the islands. As such, an intensive and extensive sampling strategy was adopted across the site. As in all our excavations this was undertaken with the understanding that the potential for recovery of floral and faunal remains was limited due to the acidic and abrasive sandy nature of the soils. The rationale was that any additional information that could be gained would make a significant difference to our understanding of occupation history and environmental change.

The sampling strategy and methods deployed at An Doirlinn followed guidelines set out by English Heritage (Campbell et al. 2011). One hundred percent of fills from features were collected for floatation analysis, and samples (varying in volume depending on the quantity of deposit) were taken from excavation squares for each context excavated. Monoliths and Kubiena tins were taken from key sections to provide archive samples in case questions emerged during post-excavation which required more detailed analysis.

Plant macrofossils

Julie Jones & Fraser Sturt

To retrieve plant macrofossils, charcoal and molluscs for identification, bulk samples were floated within a siraf system. The flot was collected on a sieve with a mesh size of 250μm, and residues on a mesh of 500μm. Both the flot and heavy residue were air dried and hand sorted in the field. Fifty-nine samples were identified as having possible organic or charred remains, and were subsequently examined by Julie Jones with plant nomenclature following that given by Stace (2010).

Results

The results are shown in Table 4.18, which details sample composition and charcoal fragments >2mm, a size suitable for species identification and therefore with potential for radiocarbon dating.

The samples are from occupation layers, hearths, pits, post-holes and some 'pot deposits' and are dominated by charcoal fragments. Many of the samples also have significant quantities of modern roots and occasional modern seeds. Charred plant remains only occured in six samples and are limited to individual occurrences of seeds from three taxa, sedge (*Carex*), spike-rush (*Eleocharis palustris/uniglumis*) and ribwort plantain (*Plantago lanceolata*). It is likely that these all occurred locally in grassland, with the spike-rush favouring wetter areas.

The only other remains were from snails which occurred in ten samples although with low numbers, (1–7 individuals), too small an assemblage for interpretation. Foraminifera also occurred in the 250μm mesh of seven samples, notably from occupation layers 65 and 41, with occasional ostracods also noted.

Charcoal

Ceren Kabukcu

Understanding the relationship between human societies and their environment is one of the oldest problems in archaeology. The way in which we aim to achieve a better understanding of the prehistoric environment is relatively straightforward: various methods of analyses are carried out by numerous specialists who examine unthinkable amounts and varieties of organic and inorganic residues left-over from past human activity. Even though results from different studies might not always agree unequivocally, a degree of confidence remains in the interpretation of data pertaining to reconstructions of prehistoric environmental and climatic conditions. A slightly more difficult and nuanced issue lies in the interpretation of how human societies might have used the environment, their perceptions of the flora, fauna and climatic conditions, and the way in which such external factors took meaning in their life-ways and world views. One of the aims of this study was to shed more light on the nature of vegetation around the site at An Doirlinn and in the greater landscape of South Uist using charred plant macrofossil evidence. A further aim was to address the question of how plant resources were used by the inhabitants of the site and in relation to this, to understand the nature of their relationship with their environment.

Study area

The present day vegetation of the island comprises grasslands, heath and wetland communities on the edges of lakes and bogs. With the exception of a few remnant woodlands, much of South Uist is treeless, a pattern reflected across the Outer Hebrides (Brashay & Edwards 1996; Edwards et al. 2005). Vegetation surveys on the island have identified remnant woodlands comprising of poplar, willow, birch, hazel and alder in a few localities such as Allt Volagir gorge and Meall Mor (Kenti et al. 1994, Brayshay et al. 2000; Pankhurst and Mullin 1991). The vegetation of the remainder of the Outer Hebrides is similar to the predominantly treeless grassland and heath found in South Uist. As discussed in the introduction, palynological evidence from various sites in South Uist, North Uist and elsewhere in the Outer Hebrides (Bennett et al. 1990; Edwards et al. 2005; Crone et al. 1993) and macroscopic identifications of fossil wood under blanket peat (Isle of Lewis, Wilkins 1984) suggests a more extensive woodland cover on the islands during the early–mid-Holocene including birch, alder, hazel, willow, poplar, heather, pine and possibly also oak, elm and ash. There are however some questions regarding long-distance

Table 4.18. Charred plant remains - summary

Context	*Sample*	*Feature*	*Vol (L)*	*Flot size (ml)*	*Sample composition*	*Charcoal >2mm*	*Macros*	*Foram/ ostracod/snails*
10	21	pit	9.5	4	predominant roots, rare charcoal			
20	23	occupation layer	5	<1	all roots			
37	24	hearth	8	28	100% charcoal, v freq roots	50+		1 s
37	25	hearth	1	8	100% charcoal, occ roots	30+		
31	26	hearth	12	5	pred roots, occ charcoal			
39	27	hearth	8	14	100% charcoal, freq roots	80+		
39	28	hearth	9	13	100% charcoal, freq roots	50+		
41	29	occupation layer	10	20	pred roots, freq. charcoal		*Carex* 1	freq f occ. o 1 s
46	30	occupation layer	8	50	100% charcoal, abund. roots	70+		
31	31	hearth	11	5	pred roots, occ charcoal	2		
42	32	occupation layer	10	8	pred roots, occ charcoal			
41	33	occupation layer	6.5	5	pred roots, occ charcoal			
42	34	occupation layer	9	8	pred roots, occ charcoal			
42	35	occupation layer	8	6	pred roots, occ charcoal			
42	36	occupation layer	12	23	pred roots, freq charcoal	15+		2 s
44	37	hearth	10.5	12	pred roots, v. freq charcoal	20+	*Eleocharis palustris/ uniglumis* 1	
49	39	hearth	14	5	pred roots, freq charcoal		*Plantago lanceolata* 1	
49	40	hearth	12.06	9	pred charcoal, bund roots	<10		
44	41	hearth	12	8	pred roots, freq charcoal	1		
52	42	occupation layer	11.5	8	pred roots, freq charcoal	20+		
52	43	occupation layer	8	28	100% charcoal, freq roots	80+		2 s
65	47	occupation layer	10	26	100% charcoal, freq roots	80+		
55	48	hearth	8	4	pred roots, occ charcoal		*Carex* 1	
60	49	post-hole	5	1	pred roots, rare charcoal			
65	50	occupation layer	8	10	100% charcoal, freq roots	10+		
74	51	hearth	9	110	100% charcoal, abund roots	400+		
76	52	pit	12	60	100% charcoal, freq roots	250+		
55	53	hearth	7	11	pred root/stem, occ charcoal			
65	54	occupation layer	9	10	freq roots, occ charcoal	20+		
60	55	post-hole	13	4	pred roots, occ charcoal			occ f occ o
54	56	storm/levelling deposit	11	37	100% charcoal, v freq roots	150+		occ f 2 s
47	57	occupation layer	6	14	100% charcoal, occ roots	50+		
71	58	occupation layer	8	31	100% charcoal, occ roots	160+		
65	59	occupation layer	6	11	pred roots, occ charcoal			freq f rare o 2 s
65	61	occupation layer	10	15	pred roots, occ charcoal			freq f 1 s
65	62	occupation layer	10	7	pred roots, v freq charcoal	15		freq f 2 s
76	63	pit	12	58	100% charcoal, freq roots	300+	*Carex* 1	2 s
92	64	natural	9	<1	all roots			
82	65	occupation layer	9	<1	occ roots	2		
85	66	post-hole	5	5	100% roots, rare charcoal flecks			
65	67	occupation layer	6	1	occ roots, occ charcoal	10		
88	68	hearth	2.5	15	pred roots, freq charcoal	<10		
65	69	occupation layer	6	9	100% charcoal, abund roots	40+		
96	70	post-hole	5	6	pred roots, occ charcoal	6		
82	71	occupation layer	7	38	100% charcoal, v freq roots	200+	*Carex* 1	

(*Continued on next page*)

Table 4.18. Charred plant remains - summary (Continued)

Context	*Sample*	*Feature*	*Vol (L)*	*Flot size (ml)*	*Sample composition*	*Charcoal >2mm*	*Macros*	*Foram/ ostracod/snails*
70	72	storm/levelling deposit	8	8	pred roots, occ charcoal	4		
93	73	pit	4	<1	pred roots, occ charcoal	2		
83	74	post-hole	6	2	pred roots, occ charcoal			
94	75	pit	6	<1	all roots			
76	76	pit	11	150	100% charcoal, occ roots	500+		
60	76	post-hole	?	15	100% charcoal, freq roots	75+		
82	77	occupation layer	5	1	pred roots, occ charcoal	15+		
76	78	pit	9	4	pred charcoal, occ roots	30+		
67	79	pot deposit	0.5	7	pred charcoal, freq roots	10+		v.freq f 7 s
82	80	occupation layer	10	4	occ charcoal	15+		
76	81	pit	5.5	65	100% charcoal, occ roots	200+		
	82	Feature 16	?	55	100% charcoal, freq roots	200+		
69	83	pot deposit	0.5	1	pred roots, occ small charcoal			
105	84	pit	6.5	<1	pred roots, rare small charcoal			

pollen deposition, especially with regard to the presence of oak, elm and ash, since these taxa appear in generally low abundance and are completely absent from the island flora today. Therefore, examinations of macro-remains from archaeological sites provide invaluable insights into the possible presence of these trees in the South Uist landscape during the early–mid Holocene. Furthermore, the use of specific woodland resources and any shifts over time evidenced through the analysis of wood charcoal macro-remains gives us the opportunity to assess environmental and woodland change on the island.

The prehistoric occupation at An Doirlinn spans the Neolithic and EBA. Ten radiocarbon dates have provided a well stratified chronology spanning over a millennia, occupied c. 3590–3100 to 2480–2050 cal BC (see Section 4.10). Evidence from pollen analysis on the island suggests that there was a period of later woodland decline, starting in the 3rd millennium cal BC (Bennett et al. 1990; Fossitt 1996), with most woody taxa being replaced by heath shrubs (i.e. *Calluna vulgaris*) and extensive wet and dry grasslands forming throughout much of the Outer Hebrides (Edwards et al. 2005; Fossitt 1996; Bennett et al. 1990).

Methods of analysis

Following the sorting and identification of seed macro-remains by Julie Jones, sorting and identification of wood charcoal remains were carried out in the Archaeobotany laboratory at the University of Liverpool. Scanning and sorting was carried out using a stereo-zoom microscope (magnification range ×7–80). From the contexts submitted for wood charcoal analysis all fragments greater than 2mm in size were picked out for further analysis.

Following wood identification procedures listed in Schweingruber (1990) and Hather (2000), fragments were examined under a high power reflected light microscope (magnification range ×50–600) in order to observe the diagnostic wood anatomical features of the specimens in all three planes. Clean sections from the wood charcoal fragments were obtained using a single-edged razorblade and identifications were made following the wood anatomy keys in Schweingruber (1990) and Hather (2000) and also in consultation with the modern wood and charcoal reference collection housed in the Archaeobotany laboratory at the University of Liverpool. Due to the poor state of preservation and the small size of the wood charcoal assemblage, sub-sampling was not applied and all fragments >4mm were examined for species identification and dendro-ecological qualities.

Results

A range of context types including occupation layers, hearths, pits and post-holes were examined. Charred plant remains of seeds were found only in six samples and are limited to individual occurrences of seeds from three taxa, sedge (*Carex*), spike-rush (*Eleocharis palustris/ uniglumis*) and ribwort plantain (*Plantago lanceolata*) (see above). No cereals at all were recovered from the site. Fragments of wood charcoal were more ubiquitous and abundant, occurring in 40 out of 63 samples examined. Ten charcoal rich contexts were analysed in full, covering all stratigraphically secure phases of occupation (1a–c, 2a–c). 171 fragments of charcoal were identified to species, genus or family level representing 12 different woody taxa (Table 4.19). Sixteen fragments were not preserved well enough to permit any identification and were classified as indeterminate. A great majority of the remains exhibited signs of fungal decay, evidenced by the presence of the imprints of fungal mycelia on cell walls and collapsed

Table 4.19. Wood charcoal – summary

Context	*82*	*74*	*71*	*65*	*54*	*76*	*37*	*39*	*44*	*60*			
Sample	*71*	*51*	*58*	*47 & 50*	*56*	*76*	*24 & 25*	*28*	*37 & 41*	*76*			
Context type	*Occ. layer*	*Hearth fill*	*Occ. layer*	*Occ. layer*	*Levelling deposit*	*Pit fill*	*Hearth fill*	*Hearth fill*	*Hearth fill*	*Post-hole fill*	*Total*	*Ubiquity*	*% abundance*
Phase	*1a*	*1b*	*1b*	*1b*	*1c*	*2a*	*2b*	*2b*	*2c*	*2c*			
Taxon													
Pinus cf. *sylvestris*		7	6	3	1	2	3	4	1	1	28	90	16.4
Larix/Piceae		1	2	1	3	6	3			1	17	70	9.9
Taxus				1							1	10	0.6
Quercus		8		1	1	1	1	5	1	3	21	80	12.3
Betula	3					2					5	20	2.9
Alnus	3		1		3		1	1		1	10	60	5.8
Corylus avellena	4	3				1				2	10	40	5.8
Maloideae				1							1	10	0.6
Fraxinus		2	1	5		2				1	11	50	6.4
Salicaceae	3	1		1	1					1	7	50	4.1
Calluna vulgaris	21			1					1		23	30	13.5
Indeterminate conifer		1	9	5	4	4	7	1		5	36	80	21.1
Indeterminate rootwood						1					1	10	0.6
Indeterminate	4		2	2	3			1	1	3	16		
Total identified	34	23	19	19	13	19	15	11	3	15	171		100.0

vessels/tracheids as a result of degradation (cf. Moskal-del Hoyo et al. 2010 for identification criteria).

The wood charcoal assemblage consists of 48% conifer remains based on fragment counts, pine (*Pinus sylvestris/mugo*) being the most commonly found and abundant taxon, present in nine out of ten of the contexts studied (Table 4.19). In addition, spruce/larch (*Picea/Larix*) was present in seven contexts. These specimens also contained insect boreholes. Similar remains from other archaeological sites in the western coastal regions of Scotland have been interpreted as representing driftwood since neither species is native to the British Isles (Church 2002; Dickson 1992). A majority of the pine charcoal fragments exhibited traces of fungal mycelia and collapsed tracheids suggesting that this taxa might have been collected as deadwood. A number of other fragments were recorded as indeterminate conifers as their wood anatomical features were not clearly visible on the radial section due to their poor preservation condition and heavy mineral deposits throughout.

In terms of abundance, oak (*Quercus*) and ling (*Calluna vulgaris*) remains are also an important component of the assemblage. However, a majority of the ling fragments come from one context [82] (see Table 4.19), an occupation-related layer, which might therefore contain elements of construction debris, roofing or bedding. Remains of deciduous oak on the other hand are more ubiquitous (found in eight contexts) and appear to have been used as part of the fuel economy as well since they are found in hearth deposits along with conifers.

Alder (*Alnus*), ash (*Fraxinus*) and willow/poplar (Salicaceae) are also moderately ubiquitous occurring in about half of the contexts examined, but are found in lower abundance. Occupation layers, pit and post-hole fills are the most taxonomically diverse deposits, which usually reflect the long-term accumulation of a mix of fuel waste, various structural wood elements and in some cases, remains of wooden artefacts. The rare occurrence of yew (*Taxus*) and apple-family wood (Maloideae, including crab apple, hawthorn, rowan etc.) in occupation deposit [65] could point out to the use of these taxa for a non-fuel purpose.

While a majority of the wood charcoal fragments examined displayed indications of fungal decay or post-depositional degradation as a result of soil conditions leading to heavy mineral deposits, a number of fragments were preserved in a much better condition. For example, twigs with pith and bark preserved were observed in pine, willow/poplar, alder and heather, while twigs without bark were observed in hazel and apple-family wood. Based on growth ring morphology, the remains of conifers (including pine, spruce/larch and yew) came from mostly trunk wood or large branches. Compression wood, possibly resulting from bending of the trunk due to strong winds was also observed in pine. A number of fragments of pine and spruce/larch also displayed wood anatomical properties (sudden reduction in growth lasting several years, cf. Schweingruber 2007, 64) suggesting that these fragments might have come from trunks in the dying phase. One fragment of spruce/larch root wood was also identified.

Fragments of hazel wood in the assemblage come mostly from branch wood and twigs and also show signs of heavy mineral deposits. It was not possible to assess the growth ring curvature of most fragments of alder, birch and willow/poplar due to the fact that these remains generally had a limited amount of the transverse section preserved. Some fragments of ash showed signs of unfavourable growth conditions as they contained traumatic cell growth and narrow, discontinuous growth rings. Ash wood fragments came from both branch wood and trunk wood. Remains of oak were also heavily degraded and came from both branch wood and trunk wood of a larger size.

Discussion

While there have been previous palynological investigations on the island, there are no previous studies on wood charcoal macro-remains from a Neolithic site in South Uist. Therefore, the evidence from An Doirlinn provides instrumental insights into the use of woodland resources while also validating the presence on the island of taxa identified through pollen analysis. There are, however, a number of studies on wood charcoal macroremains and on subfossil wood from elsewhere in the Outer Hebrides including North Uist, Barra and Lewis dating to the Neolithic period.

Neolithic woodland use in the Outer Hebrides, evidence from wood charcoal macroremains

At Bharpa Carinish on North Uist, the mid-5th to late 4th millennium occupation provided evidence for the use of various woodland and scrub resources including crab apple pips and hazel nutshell present in the macroremain assemblage, in addition to wood charcoal from hazel, birch, apple-family and willow found in the Neolithic hearth complexes (Crone et al. 1993). Pollen analysis conducted at the same site identified a sequence with a late Bronze Age base, indicating the presence of dry heath vegetation in the vicinity of the site with possible minor presence of alder, birch, hazel, pine, sloe, oak, willow and elm. At the Neolithic chambered cairn of Geirisclett, North Uist, wood charcoal remains of birch, pine, hazel and heather were identified (Dunwell et al. 2003). At Eilean Domhnuill, North Uist, wood charcoal macroremains of birch, hazel, and willow, and waterlogged larch, are reported (Mills et al. 2004; Armit 1996). Similarly, at Allt Chrisal, Barra, occupation dating to c. mid-4th millennium cal BC provided evidence for alder, birch, hazel, pine, sloe and apple-family wood charcoal (Boardman 1995). Similarly, the site of Aird Calanais, Lewis (mid-4th millennium cal BC) provided evidence for the use of birch, hazel and willow/poplar wood (O'Brien et al. 2009).

Holocene vegetation dynamics in the Outer Hebrides, palynological evidence

Pollen evidence from Loch Lang in eastern South Uist indicates an early phase of woodland development at around 9600 cal BC with birch, juniper and a component of heather in the landscape (Bennett et al. 1990). When hazel begins to colonize the island c. 8600 cal BC an open birch-hazel woodland forms with a minor component of oak and elm. After about 6000 cal BC, alder and pine also become more important components of woodlands on South Uist. After the mid-3rd millennium cal BC, a decline in tree cover is observed with lower arboreal pollen values and increasing heather pollen in the sequence, matched with an increase in herbaceous cover, suggesting the development of heath and grassland ecosystems (Bennett et al. 1990).

Another pollen core in eastern South Uist, at Loch a'Phuinnd, provided evidence similar to Loch Lang, with an early phase of birch and juniper pioneer vegetation at the beginning of the Holocene, followed by hazel (Fossitt 1996). The evidence at Loch a'Phuinnd suggests that between c. 8200–6000 cal BC, woodlands diversified with pine, oak and elm. In the latter part of this woodland diversification, alder (between c. 6800–5700 cal BC) also became a component of woodlands, followed by ash shortly after 6000 cal BC. Fossitt (1996) also dates the woodland decline in South Uist to around 2600 cal BC. Similarly, at Loch an T-sil (South Uist), the pollen spectra begins earlier and shows a similar development of hazel-birch open woodlands, later diversified with the addition of alder, ash and oak (Edwards & Whittington 1994). Blanket peat formation on the island began around the same time when woodland spread was at its maximum (between 8200–6000 cal BC) and seems to be driven as part of a natural process as a result of cool and wet climatic conditions and the acidic bedrock and soils of the island. This pattern is repeated in the rest of the Outer Hebrides and blanket peat vegetation likely co-existed with woodlands for several millennia (Fossitt 1996).

Palynological evidence from elsewhere in the Outer Hebrides places the initiation of woodland decline at an earlier date. Evidence from western Lewis, Loch Buailaval Beag, suggests two phases of woodland decline, the earlier beginning around 6600 cal BC, with a possible second decline beginning c. 4000 cal BC and lasting until around 2600 cal BC (Fossitt 1996). Evidence from this core suggests that hazel, willow, poplar, pine and apple-family trees were present in the early–mid-Holocene landscape of Lewis, with the possible presence of oak, elm, alder and ash. Complementing this evidence, subfossil remains of pine, birch, heather and willow were identified on Lewis (Wilkins 1984) under blanket peat, dating broadly to the early and mid-Holocene. At Benbecula and Grimsay, Edwards et al. (2005) report the presence of willow, heather and grasses prior to machair development (c. mid-5th millennium cal BC) in the low coastal areas of these islands. Changes in arboreal pollen concentrations from a pollen core at Loch Olabhat in North Uist suggest the beginning of woodland decline between 4000–3300 cal BC (Mulder 1999).

Vegetation dynamics in the Outer Hebrides, a combined perspective

The timing of woodland development and decline during the Holocene on the Scottish mainland is slightly different, however the species involved and woodland types are somewhat similar. The main difference between the Outer Hebrides and the mainland is in the establishment of oak and elm woodlands (Tipping 1994). A number of factors could have contributed to this, including the limited range of dispersal of oak acorns and ash seeds and unfavourable soil types (Lowe et al. 2005). However, hazel, which has a similar dispersal mechanism, does not seem to be affected by this and is one of the earlier colonisers of the islands. Therefore, it is possible that one of the most important limiting factors in woodland development on the islands would have been climate and soil conditions.

According to Gilbertson et al. (1999) aeolian deposition and sand drift in the Outer Hebrides was continuous throughout the Holocene with notable periods of heavier deposition or sand drift. However, by the early Holocene a variety of soil types including podzolic brown earths and peat soils were established on the islands. As indicated by OSL dating of the sediments, carbonate sands (associated with machair vegetation) had started developing by the mid-8th millennia cal BC in North Uist and slightly later in South Uist (Gilbertson et al. 1999). These carbonate sand formations would have limited the spread and growth of woodlands, especially in the coastal regions which are exposed to wind and sand drift. It seems however that these areas of early machair formation were used by early communities since midden-like soil deposits rich in organic materials were found within the carbonate sands. The authors argue that these soils are anthropogenic in origin suggested with the results of micromorphological analyses (Gilbertson et al. 1999). It is likely therefore that human settlement on the island did not necessitate woodland clearance, but rather utilized a range of habitat types including the coastal machair/sand dunes, a situation which has been supported by the locations of archaeological sites. In such locations, small patches of woodlands would have been accessible such as wet woodlands around lake and marsh margins including alder, willow/poplar or open pine-birch-hazel woodlands on drier ground with better soils.

As discussed above, a number of Neolithic settlements on North Uist, spanning a time frame between the 5th and mid-3rd millennium, provided evidence for the use of hazel, birch, willow, apple-family, pine and larch wood. Palynological evidence from this time period confirms the presence of these taxa on the island, with the exception of larch, which is likely to represent driftwood, similar to those found at An Doirlinn. If the dates for the beginning of woodland decline on North Uist are accurate, then the span of Neolithic habitation on the island largely coincides with this period. The situation is slightly different at An Doirlinn, as the earlier phases (1a, 1b, 1c) of the site occupation pre-date the woodland decline (c. 2600 cal BC) and the later phases (2a, 2b, 2c) would have been more or less contemporary. Therefore, the woodland vegetation around An Doirlinn would be expected to be more diverse when compared to many other Neolithic occupation sites in the Outer Hebrides.

Conceivably, the woodland decline phase detected in pollen spectra reflects the beginning of woodland degradation, with increasing environmental stress on woody taxa, more intensive use by humans and perhaps increasing grazing pressure, along with the spread of blanket peat. Potential evidence of grazing pressure and grassland fires is inferred from the Benbecula and Grimsay cores during the machair development phase (Edwards et al. 2005). Stunted and shrubby growth in woody taxa, which could stem from environmental stress and/or animal browsing, could result in markedly lower pollen production. The presence of *Plantago lanceolata* in the macro-remain assemblage at An Doirlinn could also be indicative of such grazing pressure on the surrounding grassland vegetation, however the remains are too few to make a stronger case for this.

Through evidence provided from pollen, sub-fossil wood and charcoal it is evident that pine, hazel, birch and heather were present in the woodland vegetation of the Outer Hebrides. The presence of certain taxa however, such as oak and ash, has been called into question due to their low arboreal pollen sums in the sequence, and it has been suggested that a certain amount of pollen rain could be coming in from the Scottish mainland. The work of Brayshay et al. (2000) on modern pollen rain concluded that a great majority of pollen deposition on South Uist comes from on-island sources, while only a small fraction (~1.3%) comes from off-island sources. In the light of this, the evidence from An Doirlinn confirms the presence of more diverse woodlands including pine, hazel, birch, alder, willow, poplar, oak, and ash on South Uist during the mid-Holocene when compared to the other islands. In fact, the oak and ash charcoal remains are the earliest finds of these taxa from the Outer Hebrides. Furthermore, the dendro-ecological qualities of a majority of the examined specimens signal environmental conditions marginal for tree-growth and it is highly likely that a majority of the specimens came from scrub-like stunted individuals.

Conclusions

The site assemblage from An Doirlinn contains several remains of coniferous wood used as fuel, including pine which was collected as deadwood and spruce/larch driftwood. Other elements of the fuel wood selection reflect the diversity of trees and scrubs surrounding the site including birch, hazel, alder, willow/poplar, oak and ash wood charcoal remains. Pine was probably one of the most common woody taxa in the vicinity of the settlement, with perhaps a number of these taxa growing close to the wind-exposed coastal areas as suggested by their wood anatomy. The earlier phases of the site occupation pre-date the phase of woodland decline detected in palynological spectra from South Uist lakes, while the later phase of occupation is contemporaneous with the initial woodland decline period. However, the wood charcoal assemblage does not reflect any significant changes in composition or species diversity. Therefore, it is likely that the use of woodland and woody resources by the inhabitants of An Doirlinn did not have any significant effects on the surrounding landscape. The macroremains analysis did not provide any indication of agricultural activity. However, on this sandy, heavily-eroded site, it is impossible to know whether this is a consequence of taphonomic processes (whereby cereals or other crops simply have not been preserved) or of past cultural choice.

4.10. Radiocarbon dating

Duncan Garrow & Seren Griffiths

Twelve radiocarbon measurements in total were obtained from Neolithic and Early Bronze Age layers and features at An Doirlinn (Table 4.20). All contexts on site with appropriate material were dated; two layers were dated twice using separate samples (charred plant remains and residue on pottery in both cases).

The samples submitted were from deposits which could be clearly stratigraphically related during excavation. Modelling the radiocarbon results to reflect all of the stratigraphic relationships between sampled deposits produces a model with a poor agreement index (model not shown). Given the complexity of site formation processes at An Doirlinn (see Section 4.3) – whereby many features were cut into earlier occupation deposits, some deposits were redeposited in a secondary or tertiary location, and the sea had eroded layers at the edge of site potentially mixing them stratigraphically – it is very likely that at least some of the dated charred plant remains were themselves either redeposited in later contexts or reworked in other ways.

Consequently, for the model presented here, we have treated results on samples from unsecure contexts (i.e. they were either from pits/post-holes cut down into earlier deposits or in layers that had clearly been redeposited) that seem to be too old for their position in the stratigraphic sequence as *termini post quos*.

Table 4.20. Radiocarbon measurements from An Doirlinn

Lab No.	*Material*	*Species*	*Context*	*Site phase*	*Radio-carbon age (BP)*	*$\delta^{13}C$*	*Calibrated date range (cal BC) (95% confidence)*
OxA-29156	Wood charcoal	*Calluna* sp. (heather); twig	Occupation layer [82]	1a	4501 ± 31	-27.7	3350–3100
OxA-28950	Charred residue	n/a	Occupation layer [82]	1a	4505 ± 29	-26.6	3350–3100
OxA-29161	Wood charcoal	*Alnus* (alder); twig, 2 years old	Post-hole F13, context [60]	2b*	4334 ± 31	-26.1	3020–2890
OxA-29159	Wood charcoal	*Pinus sylvestris/mugo*; twig	Hearth F14, context [76]	2a*	4290 ± 31	-26.2	3010–2880
OxA-28907	Wood charcoal	*Alnus* (alder); age uncertain	Levelling layer [54]	1c	4269 ± 27	-26.6	2920–2880
OxA-28906	Wood charcoal	*Corylus* (hazel); young roundwood	Hearth F16, context [74]	1b*	4185 ± 28	-28.4	2890–2670
OxA-28910	Wood charcoal	*Alnus* (alder); young roundwood	Hearth F8, context [37]	2a	4141 ± 27	-26.0	2870–2630
OxA-29158	Charred residue	n/a	Levelling layer [55/64]	1c	4126 ± 32	-27.0	2870–2580
OxA-28909	Wood charcoal	*Alnus* (alder); young roundwood	Hearth F8, context [37]	2a	4110 ± 27	-25.9	2860–2580
OxA-29160	Wood charcoal	*Alnus* (alder); age uncertain	Hearth F9, context [39]	2a	4063 ± 30	-25.2	2850–2490
OxA-29157	Wood charcoal	Malvidae (apple/pear); twig	Occupation layer [65]	1b	4056 ± 30	-26.0	2840–2480
OxA-28908	Wood charcoal	*Calluna* (heather); twig	Hearth F10, context [44]	2b	3908 ± 26	-27.6	2470–2300

Instances where radiocarbon dates may relate to redeposited material (and could thus be out of sequence stratigraphically) are indicated with a * in the 'Site phase' column. Radiocarbon method = Brock et al. 2010.

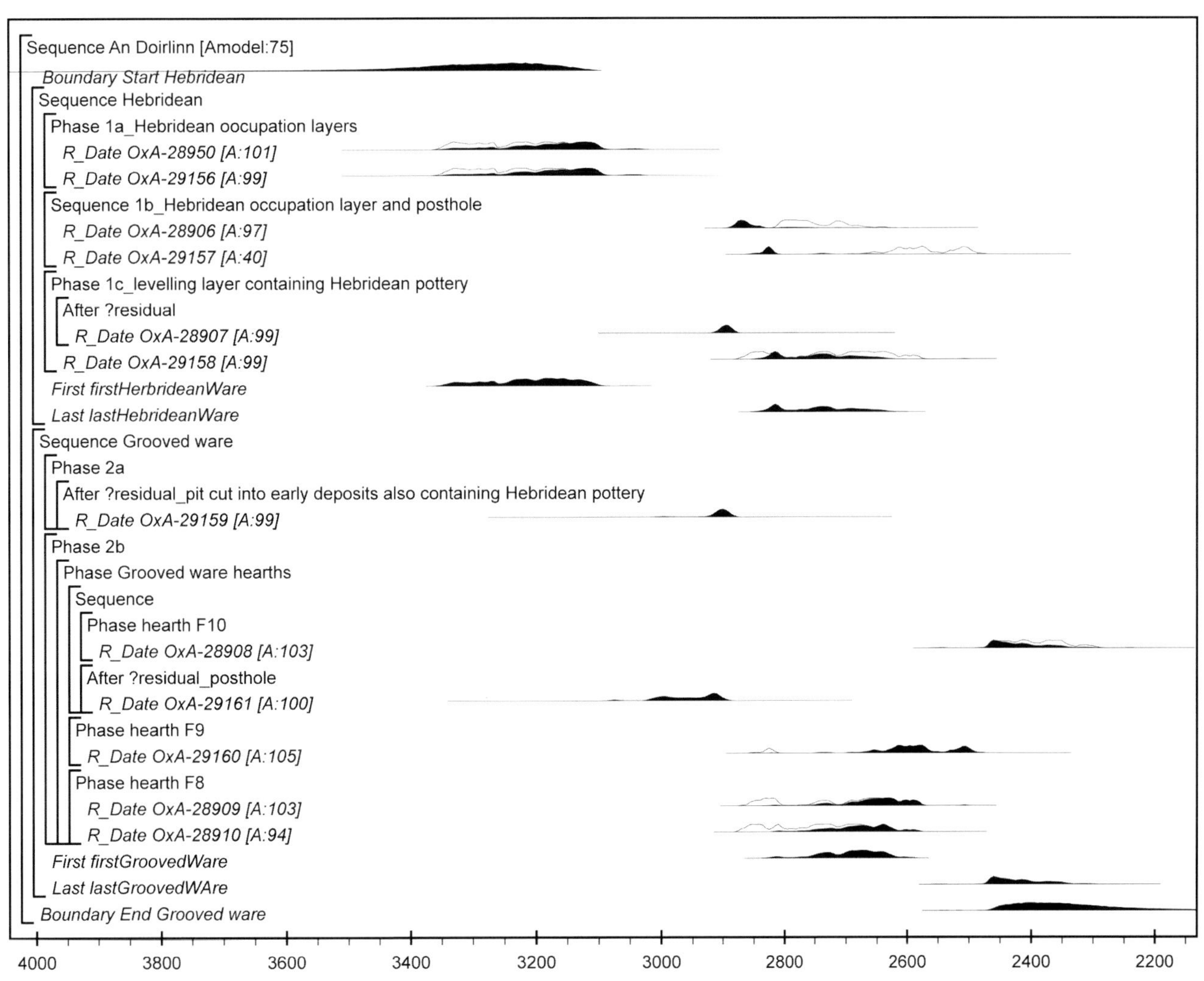

Figure 4.37. Model output for radiocarbon dated phases at An Doirlinn. Note that in the model presented here we have presented samples which derived from stratigraphically unsecure contexts (i.e. they were either from pits/post-holes cut down into earlier deposits or in layers that had clearly been redeposited) as termini post quos.

Within this model, the first dated evidence for activity at the site occurs in *3530–3100 cal BC* (*95% probability; 3340–3140 cal BC 68% probability; Start Hebridean*; Figure 4.37), and is associated with the use of Hebridean pottery. The end of use of Hebridean pottery is estimated to have occurred in *2840–2640 cal BC* (*95% probability; 2830–2800 cal BC 21% probability,* or *2780–2660 cal BC 48% probability; lastHebridean*; Figure 4.37). It is worth noting that the earliest elements of phase 1a produced no dateable material (see Section 4.3), so it is likely that the estimate for the start of Neolithic activity on site represents a *terminus ante quem* for the earliest elements of phase 1a.

The first dated event for Phase 2, associated with Grooved Ware pottery, is estimated to have occurred in *2830–2600 cal BC* (95% probability*; 2750–2630 cal BC 68% probability; firstGrooved*; Figure 4.37). The last use of the site for which we have scientific dating evidence is associated with the end of use of Grooved Ware, estimated to have occurred in *2480–2330 cal BC* (*95% probability; 2470–2400 cal BC 68% probability; End Grooved ware*; Figure 4.37). Unfortunately, no suitable samples for dating were available from the Phase 3 Beaker-associated deposits.

In summary, the total span of *dated* occupation at An Doirlinn is estimated to have occurred over *680–1410 years* (*95% probability;* or *770–1080 years*; *DurationAnDoirlinn*). As discussed above (see also Section 4.11), it is likely that the actual span of occupation extended both earlier and later than that, since the earliest and latest stratigraphic phases on site could not be dated as they did not produce datable material.

4.11. Discussion: Early Neolithic to Early Bronze Age occupation at An Doirlinn

At the start of this final discussion, it is important to remind ourselves of the fact that, even more obviously than usual, we are dealing with a *partially surviving* site, now located on a small islet which has seen considerable erosion by the sea over the years, and is known for certain to have been reduced considerably in size within living memory. Given these issues, and its relatively small overall size, it is even more impressive that, on excavation, the site produced quite so much evidence – a deeply stratified sequence of deposits accumulated over perhaps 1000 years and architectural remains to rival most other Neolithic settlement sites in the region, as well as the largest assemblage of chipped stone, and the third largest assemblage of pottery, yet excavated in the Outer Hebrides. It may be a small, partial site, but there is still a great deal to discuss.

As a result of the deep stratification of deposits, and good preservation of wood charcoal remains, it proved possible to obtain a sequence of radiocarbon dates for the majority of the site's phases, and to model these in order to refine the sequence. The *dated* elements suggest a sequence of c. 680–1420 years from the final deposit of material in Phase 1a to the penultimate hearth in Phase 2b. Deposits that were stratigraphically both earlier and later but could not be radiocarbon dated indicate that this sequence should be extended further in either direction, especially at the end into the Beaker phase: the site's overall occupation probably dates from the second half of the 4th millennium cal BC to perhaps the early centuries of the 2nd millennium cal BC. As we discuss below, the evidence recovered from An Doirlinn was a lot like other sites in the region architecturally, but not so similar in terms of material culture; this discrepancy is a key contradiction to resolve in terms of the site's overall interpretation.

The earliest phase of occupation (1a) is difficult to comprehend – a collection of post-holes and short sequence of three hearths (perhaps a little generously termed 'Structure A') built directly onto bedrock. Contemporary with these features was a small pit containing an unusual, almost complete pottery vessel, interpreted as a possible foundation deposit for the site as a whole. On top of this group of ephemeral features, the most substantial layer (materially) on the site [82] had been deposited across the entire western side of the excavation area. It contained 62% (by weight) of the total pottery assemblage, and included a number of substantially complete pots that appeared to have been smashed in situ. It was radiocarbon dated to c. 3350–3030 cal BC. The ceramic assemblage was notable for its plain forms and general lack of decoration – in stark contrast to most other Hebridean Neolithic sites. The discrepancy between this massive deposit and the much more minimal group of features it overlay suggests that further substantial buildings may originally have been situated nearby but had not survived.

This sense of 'missing' structures at An Doirlinn is made particularly acute in the next two sub-phases (1b and 1c). In Phase 1b, the single wall line and hearth that survived of Structure B were located at the extreme north-eastern limit of the surviving deposits (the wall identified by Sharples eroding out of the sea-cut section in 2005). In this case, the rest of at least one and possibly two buildings had very clearly been lost to erosion. Radiocarbon dates suggest that these features were in use c. 2900–2800 cal BC. Phase 1c consisted only of a (possibly redeposited) occupation layer, overlying Structure B and its associated deposits. This was presumably associated with buildings that simply had not survived at all. Phase 1c was dated to c. 2840–2640 cal BC.

Phase 2 consisted of more substantial architectural remains, in the form of two adjacent, but successively constructed and used, structures (Structures C and D). Radiocarbon dates from the hearths within these buildings suggest that they were in use perhaps for one or two centuries each, over the period c. 2780–2330 cal BC. Each structure was defined primarily by a substantial double hearth feature, and accompanying low-level stone wall(s) within which occupation deposits were identified. Both structures were associated with Grooved Ware pottery, importantly representing the first published settlement, and only the fourth excavated site, in the Outer Hebrides to be associated with that ceramic type (see Section 4.4).

The Phase 3 archaeology from An Doirlinn was difficult to interpret: a series of what appeared on excavation to be naturally-formed, 'clean' sandy layers containing quantities of domestic Beaker pottery. It is conceivable that this material originally related to a structure of some sort or to a midden deposit, but ultimately it is impossible to know. These layers could not be radiocarbon dated, but probably date to within the c. 2450–1750 BC bracket (the currency of Beaker pottery in the Outer Hebrides is currently not well dated (Alison Sheridan, pers. comm.)).

The radiocarbon dates secured from the site sequence at An Doirlinn do not themselves indicate any clear hiatus in occupation from c. 3350 to 2330 cal BC. However, in saying this, it is of course important to note that the calibrated date ranges involved could easily mask any such absence to a considerable degree. In addition, the fact that the site was substantially altered/remodelled several times, and that various 'levelling' layers (and other comparable deposits) were laid down at various intervals, perhaps in themselves suggest that shorter hiatuses in occupation did occur.

Especially on this very clearly partial site, it is difficult to estimate the precise character and 'texture' of that occupation. Domestic dwellings of some sort probably were in evidence throughout the life of the site. Whether or not, and when, these were permanently or seasonally occupied it is impossible to say. The coastal location of the site may have made it a more attractive (or viable) place to inhabit at certain times of the year. It is a shame that no substantial animal bones or charred seeds were recovered through which to gain a richer understanding of what happened at the site. The extensive range of species represented in the wood charcoal assemblage suggests that it may have been situated in a key location with access to several different ecozones. The absence of animal bone is undoubtedly a consequence of the acidic soils. The absence of charred cereals is more difficult to understand given the presence of small charcoal fragments, but again could be the result of poor preservational conditions.

It is possible, albeit to a limited extent, to gain some insight into the 'amounts' of occupation that the site witnessed through the quantities of material recovered there. However, the clearly highly differential character of depositional practice within different phases and across space make this an uncertain game to play. Figures 4.38 and 4.39 show the changing amount of pottery and flint/quartz deposited throughout the site's life. Notable discrepancies between the two main categories of material remind us that here we are not dealing simply with overall 'amounts' of occupation, but with the more subtle nuances of living, of practice and of resource availability in the prehistoric past as well. The fact that changes between different phases in relation to the presence/absence and location of flint debitage may suggest subtle changes of 'normal' practice on site was discussed in Section 4.5. Similarly, isolated 'odd' deposits (the near-complete 'foundation deposit' pot at the start of Phase 1a, the possibly complete but smashed vessels at the end of Phase 1a, the cache of scrapers in a post-hole in Phase 1b) hint at other practices that alter the 'average' deposition of material culture through time as well. Nonetheless, the fact that we are dealing here with the largest chipped stone assemblage and third largest pottery assemblage from a site of this date in the Outer Hebrides – despite its generally ephemeral architectural remains – suggests that we must be dealing with a settlement that saw significant occupation, whatever that occupation was like.

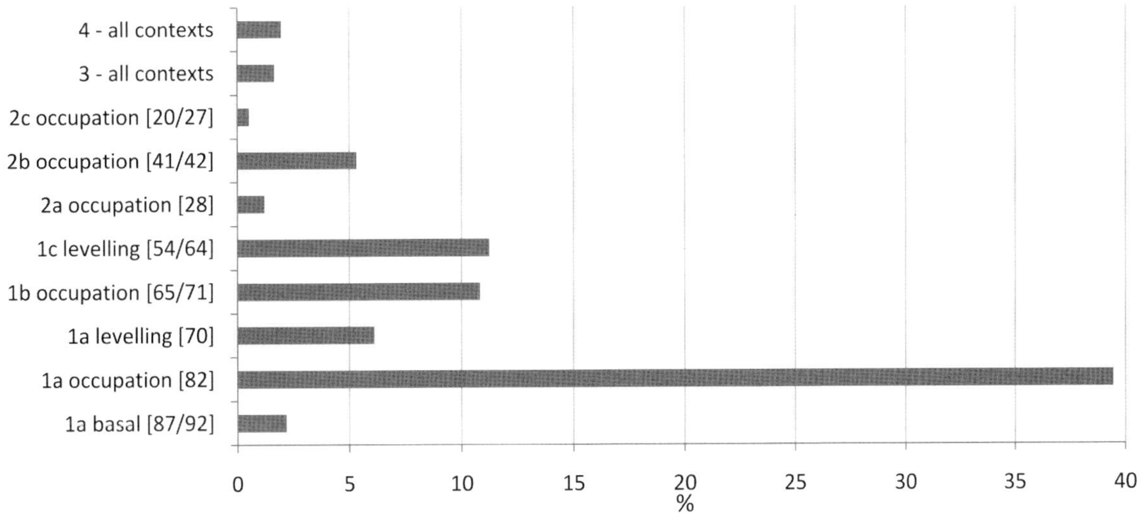

Figure 4.38. Pottery: percentage of total site assemblage (by number) in each main layer group.

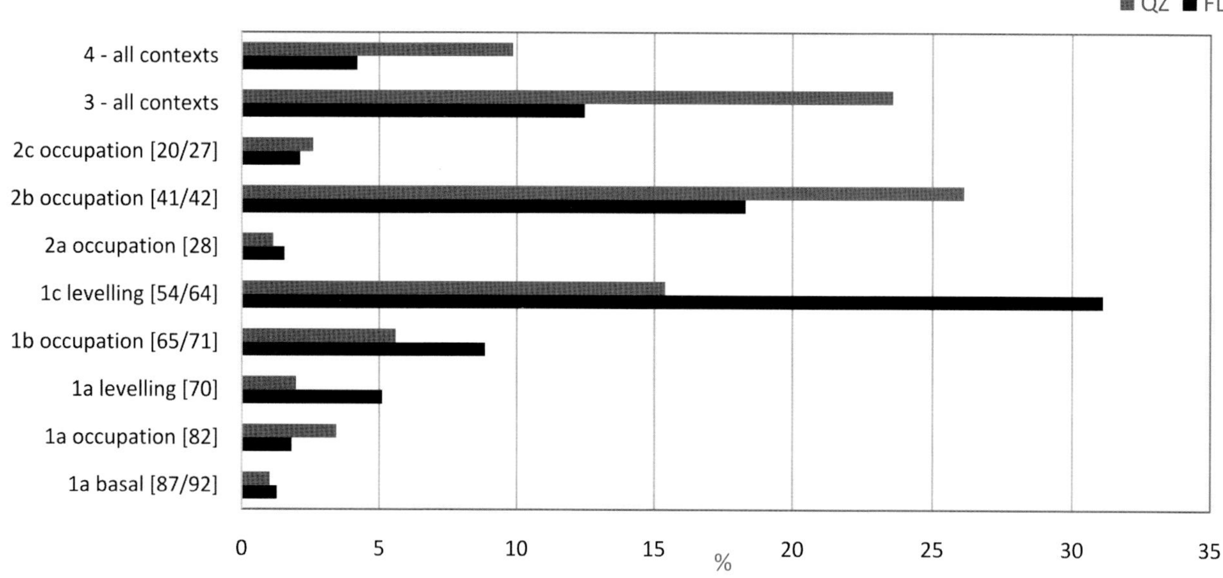

Figure 4.39. Flint/quartz: percentage of total site assembage in each main layer group.

An Doirlinn in its regional context

The site excavated at An Doirlinn adds significantly to our knowledge of Neolithic/EBA settlement in the Outer Hebrides. The archaeology uncovered there was similar in many ways to other known sites in the region. Its very long lifespan is comparable to several other Neolithic settlements (Figure 4.40; see Garrow et al. 2017 for details): Eilean Domhnuill was in use for approximately 1000 years; at Allt Chrisal the Neolithic radiocarbon dates span 800 years, with the Beaker phase extending the site's overall life for perhaps up to another millennium; at Northton, the dated range of Neolithic occupation is 500 years, again with the Beaker phase possibly extending it for up to a millennium; the three dates from Eilean an Tighe do not date the settlement there very accurately, but it seems likely that, there too, the three successive buildings would have been in use for several centuries. As at An Doirlinn, it is uncertain whether these sites were occupied permanently over these very extensive durations, at both macro- (centuries/decades) and micro- (years/months) temporal scales – the general consensus has been that they probably were not (see Section 1.6).

The architecture uncovered at An Doirlinn shared many distinct characteristics with other extensively excavated sites in the region. Its low, partially surviving stone walls with occasional integral post-holes were directly comparable to those seen at Eilean an Tighe, Eilean Domhnuill and Allt Chrisal. The fact that much of each structure appeared to have been dismantled or destroyed in the past, leading to somewhat incoherent building forms in the present, was also a common trait on all of these other sites. The presence of very obvious – and, seemingly therefore, very important – stone-built hearths was also key at all of these other sites;

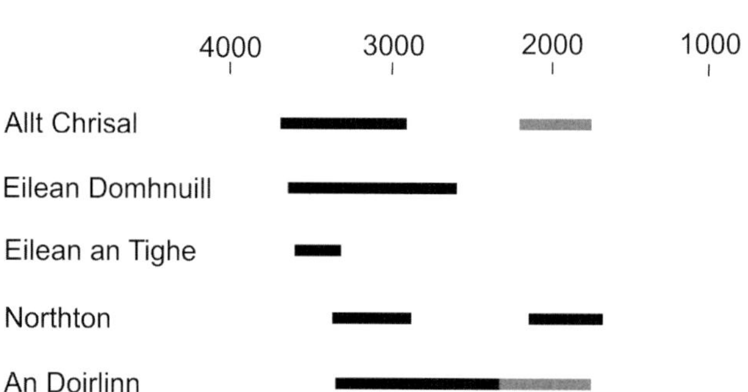

Figure 4.40. Timespans of extensively excavated Neolithic/EBA settlement sites in the Outer Hebrides (black = radiocarbon dated phases; grey = estimated Beaker phase dates).

elsewhere, however, they had often been constructed successively on top of each other in stacks (something not seen at An Doirlinn after Phase 1a). The presence of very rich occupation deposits producing large assemblages of material culture was also a feature at all other sites. Overall, the most similar site to An Doirlinn is probably Allt Chrisal, which is also the closest extensively excavated site geographically. There, in various different ways and at various different scales – the fine details of hearth construction technique, the presence of burnt bone flecks in those hearths, the relatively low proportion of decorated pottery, the large amounts of flint – many elements were closely reminiscent of the archaeology uncovered at An Doirlinn.

As well as these abundant similarities with contemporary sites elsewhere in the Outer Hebrides, key differences were noted as well. Other sites have differed significantly in their landscape locations, with Eilean an Tighe and Eilean Domhnuill being islet/loch sites and Allt Chrisal being in the uplands. An Doirlinn can certainly be described as coastal (in the Neolithic as well as the present day), a location shared by Northton (apparently a quite different kind of site) and the Udal.

A second key difference is the composition of the pottery assemblage at An Doirlinn. As discussed at length in Section 4.4, the pottery was very plain, with no Unstan whatsoever and minimal quantities of decorated Hebridean Neolithic pottery identified from an assemblage of 4831 sherds. This plainness contrasts radically with Eilean an Tighe, Eilean Domhnuill and Northton, and to a lesser extent with Allt Chrisal (which had a smaller but still significant highly-decorated element) as well (see also Copper 2015, 458–468). While An Doirlinn may have been established a little later than most of these sites, their datespans of use nonetheless overlap for several centuries at the end of the fourth millennium (see Figure 4.40). Interestingly, the unchangingly *highly-decorated* character of the pottery from Eilean Domhnuill (the largest and best-dated assemblage elsewhere) was noted as a characteristic feature of that assemblage (see Section 4.4). It is very difficult to explain this very clear difference between An Doirlinn and all of these other contemporary sites. It is possible that it came about for functional reasons – as discussed, the site is in a different landscape location to these other sites, and could conceivably therefore have been used differently as a result. Perhaps the activities that involved decorated pots in Hebridean Neolithic life simply did not take place there. Copper has suggested elsewhere that, in contrast to Eilean Domhnuill and possibly also other islet sites – which he argues may have been central gathering places for large numbers of people – An Doirlinn may only ever have been used by a small family group, and thus the need to signal social messages through highly-decorated pottery was not as great (Copper 2015, 459). A second possibility is that some other kind of social meaning lay behind the material differences. It is possible that the occupants of An Doirlinn chose to distinguish themselves materially, asserting their identity and difference through use of non-decorated ceramics. Equally, it is possible that they may not have had access to the exchange networks through which such pots were secured. Given the relative dominance of undecorated pottery at Allt Chrisal as well, it is conceivable that these social elements could have had a geographical aspect to them as well – the highly decorated assemblages all come from sites a considerable distance to the north.

A third significant difference between An Doirlinn and most other substantially excavated sites is the quantity of flint and quartz recovered there. Interestingly, again Allt Chrisal is the only comparable site, having produced several thousand pieces in contrast to the handful of pieces from all other sites (see Section 4.5). It was suggested in Section 4.5 that this discrepancy may have come about through differential access to the raw materials, which may have been much more readily available in the southern part of the island chain. As with the pottery, however, there could of course have been a social aspect to this difference as well.

The absence of cereals from An Doirlinn is also intriguing, given their relative abundance on most comparable sites. This may simply be a taphonomic pattern, created through different soil conditions on site. However, the possibility that it too may have come about through different practices and different social preferences at An Doirlinn is also worth considering.

A final, very notable difference between An Doirlinn and other contemporary settlement sites is the presence of a clear Grooved Ware phase, and indeed the presence of Grooved Ware on site at all. As discussed in Section 4.4, this pottery has only been found previously in the Outer Hebrides at Calanais stone circle, Unival chambered cairn and the Udal. Its absence from all of the other comparitor sites for An Doirlinn is notable. It is certainly possible that this discrepancy is meaningful, representing a continuation of the material distinctions drawn in the Hebridean pottery phase. However, given the chronological information we currently have for Neolithic settlement sites, it is important to be cautious in making too much of the distinction in the Grooved Ware phase. At An Doirlinn, this pottery was in use c. 2780–2570 to 2480–2330 cal BC. Not one of the other sites has radiocarbon dated (or ceramic) evidence of occupation between the late Hebridean phase (at Eilean Domhnuill c. 2600 cal BC at the latest) and their mostly undated Beaker phases (where they occur) which are likely to date to c. 2450–1750 BC (see Figure 4.40). Consequently, it seems that An Doirlinn is the only settlement occupied from c. 2600 cal BC to the Beaker-using phase c. 2450–1750 BC, during which Grooved Ware may have been in use. Sharples (2009) has suggested that the Beaker period in the Outer Hebrides saw a significant shift in settlement practice, with most sites moving into the Machair shell sand zone; the reasons for this move are at present unclear. It is possible that, prior to this shift, significant changes had already occurred on most sites – other than An Doirlinn – leading to a general invisibility of settlement sites during the middle and later centuries of the 3rd millenium BC.

Turning to the main themes of this volume, as at Old Quay (Section 3.10), the site at An Doirlinn is established too late in the Early Neolithic to help with our understanding of the Mesolithic–Neolithic transition on the islands. Equally, the Late Mesolithic in the region in itself is not as yet well understood (see Section 1.6). An Doirlinn does, however, provide us with considerable insight in relation to the other main themes we have chosen to explore – the variable nature of settlement across the western seaways and the conectedness/isolation of island communities.

As discussed in Section 1.6, the Early Neolithic settlement record – and, perhaps even more, the Beaker evidence – in the Outer Hebrides rivals anything known in Britain as a whole in terms of surviving architecture. Differences between

Neolithic sites have been much discussed (see Section 1.6) – while some writers have emphasised the differences between settlements in different parts of the landscape, especially between islet sites and those elsewhere (e.g. Armit 1996; Henley 2003; Sharples 2009), others have suggested that those differences could at least partly have arisen as a result of the differential levels of preservation on different sites (Simpson et al. 2006). The latter issue in particular is made very apparent by the significant erosion and clearly 'missing' buildings at An Doirlinn. It is our feeling that, given the glimpses of directly comparable features on many sites, differential preservation has certainly exaccerbated apparent differences between sites. Nonetheless, key material differences between them are also apparent, and these are certainly meaningful as we have discussed.

The presence of 'foreign' materials at An Doirlinn – quartzite, jasper, mudstone, chalcedony and pitchstone – all of which were certainly or probably imported across the sea from the Inner Hebrides and beyond, demonstrate that at one level, the occupants of An Doirlinn were clearly tied into very long distance networks of exchange or maritime mobility. Yet at the same time, at a more local level, comparable exchanges do not appear to have taken place. The occupants of An Doirlinn do not appear to have exchanged their seemingly abundant flint resources with their contemporaries living in North Uist and beyond. Conversely, the latter perhaps did not exchange their highly decorated pots with the former. No doubt a complex set of social relations lies behind these material differences. Yet the potentially high levels of independence and/or isolation (depending on how you choose to look at it) between sites do seem significant – an independence mirrored perhaps in the construction of isolated islet settlements, distanced even from near neighbours by a stretch of loch water and a narrow, defensible causeway.

Summary

In summary, the site at An Doirlinn has provided a wealth of new, well-dated evidence with which to continue piecing together the material and social dynamics of Neolithic and EBA life in the Outer Hebrides. Importantly, in many respects it provides a *different* perspective on the period in the region to other sites. It is located in a different kind of place and produced a very different material repertoire. Yet at the same time, key similarities between these sites enable us to envisage shared practices and social connections. As discussed at the beginning of this section, it is in attempting to understand the interplay between these similarities and differences that the key to fuller social interpretations of the great wealth of evidence from the region lies.

In contrast to both of the other sites described in this volume, the surviving site at An Doirlinn was almost completely excavated. It would have been nice to have more time to excavate the remaining 20% (left in situ north of the pipe trench), and it would, of course, have been good to explore the full extent of the original settlement (since destroyed by the sea). In this case, however, future work possibilities lie mostly elsewhere in the South Uist landscape and beyond.

Chapter 5

Discussion: 'insular connectivity' across the western seaways

5.1. Introduction: 'islandness' – a context-specific concept

> '"Islandness" is a relative, contingent, situtational matter' (Fleming 2008, 19).

At the end of this book investigating three newly-excavated island sites across the western seaways, along with the wider archaeological and landscape contexts into which they fit, it is important to take a step back to reflect on our findings. The 'Stepping Stones' project was always conceived as a geographically disparate endeavour, indeed that was in many ways its very essence – the distance from Orkney to the Channel Islands is 2400km and would have taken two to three weeks of paddling in a Neolithic boat to achieve (Callaghan & Scarre 2009, 364). Nonetheless, despite this distributed spatiality, the fact that our focus has been almost exclusively on islands and that all of our excavations took place in very clear island/seaside contexts have somehow served to connect those sites together in many and various ways. Even in the present, despite their being hundreds of kilometres apart, their status as islands ensured that, ironically, they felt somehow linked – by the western seaways.

Over the course of the project, we have been very privileged to work in a series of fantastic places, meeting a very wide range of generous and helpful people along the way, most of whom did us the huge favour of being interested in what we were doing. Our focus was on settlements, which are often overlooked in Neolithic archaeology at the expense of easier to find and more glamorous (if that is the right word) monuments. On all three sites, our methodology was broadly the same. We always started where we knew that Early Neolithic (and sometimes also Mesolithic) material had been found, building directly on the work of others before us. However, in every case, no-one had any real sense of what kind of sites they might be – an assemblage of pottery and lithics eroding out of a cliff may signify a Neolithic presence, but it provides very few further clues as to what else might be there. At L'Erée and Old Quay, we then went on to dig multiple test pits in order to establish the presence (or not) of related features and to acquire further material; An Doirlinn was so small that this phase was not necessary. In all three cases, the site turned out to be a clear settlement of Neolithic (and, interestingly, also EBA) date. Evidence of other periods, previously undetected, was found as well. The amounts of archaeology recovered – particularly in terms of the quantities of finds – were significant, producing, in some cases, assemblages multiple times bigger than we had expected. This fairly simple method of approaching unknown sites could *not* have worked – there could well have been very little there on all three sites – but thankfully, luckily, it did. Neolithic settlements can be hard to find, but if you look, there are certainly sites out there to be explored.

In order to reflect on the broader success of the excavation elements of the Stepping Stones project, we will first revisit our original motivations for investigating those three sites in the first place, and then move on to re-visit this book's central themes as set out in Chapter 1.

Essentially, our main stated aim was to excavate three key sites (in Guernsey, the Isles of Scilly and South Uist) in order to enhance the existing archaeological record of the Early Neolithic in those island groups. Our secondary aim was to recover associated material (a) in order to enhance our wider radiocarbon dating programme of key sites across the western seaways zone (Garrow et al. 2017) and (b) through which to assess material connections and culture-historical links with other regions. All of these aims were achieved. It is also important to stress that, while the project was driven primarily by these academic goals, the fact that all three sites had been discovered as a result of coastal erosion and were thus, to varying degrees, in danger of being lost altogether to the sea was also clear in our minds from the outset.

The four themes we set out to explore in Chapter 1 were: 'island-ness' and the sea, material signatures of connectivity, settlement variability across the western seaways and differential traditions of research in different regions. In order to link up the next section and this, we will begin with the latter, investigating the ways in which different traditions of research on our island groups – in comparison both to each other and to the mainland – have led to particular understandings of their respective archaeological records.

5.2. Differential traditions of research

In Guernsey and across the Channel Islands more broadly, the long-term focus of Neolithic excavation has been predominantly on tombs rather than settlements, as in many other parts of Britain. This situation is entirely understandable – tombs are much more visible than settlements – but in the Channel Islands particularly it has led to a somewhat incomplete understanding of the Early Neolithic. The reason for this is that, both in north-west France and the Channel Islands, tombs do not feature until the mid-5th millennium BC at the very earliest, firmly within the French Middle Neolithic. In the east, the earliest Neolithic is associated with a remnant post/final-Linearbandkeramik (LBK) (Villeneuve Saint Germain) longhouse tradition. Further west, however, across most of Brittany and into the Channel Islands, the Neolithic arrives slightly later, in association with somewhat less visible occupation-related archaeology (Marcigny et al. 2010; Garrow & Sturt 2017; Garrow et al. 2017). Glimpses of Early Neolithic settlements have occasionally been caught in the Channel Islands (see Section 1.6), but without exception these have been through small and often somewhat opaque windows. At L'Erée, our glimpse was especially narrow, comprised only of artefacts with no contemporary features detected. If we are to understand the Early Neolithic of the Channel Islands better, it seems we will need to maintain the recent focus on settlements (and other related sites) in future.

The Isles of Scilly have seen very little sustained research into, and excavation of, the islands' Mesolithic and Neolithic archaeology. This certainly has not been for lack of interest, but more as a consequence of there being very few glimpses to follow up – a situation which led to a broad consensus that the islands were occupied only intermittently until the Bronze Age (see Section 1.6). This in turn led to a position whereby the Neolithic archaeology of Scilly could not easily be compared to that of the mainland, which was far better known and explored (Pollard & Healy 2007). It is true to say, without exaggeration, that our work at Old Quay has completely transformed our knowledge of both the Mesolithic and the Neolithic in Scilly, producing a site of an entirely different magnitude (in terms of both features and artefacts) to any known before. This has had the knock-on effect of making the evidence for both periods on the islands seem more substantial, raising new questions about the character of occupation seen there at that time (Section 3.10). The large assemblage of microliths, in particular, forced us to ask new questions – questions that we had certainly never expected to ask before encountering those artefacts in the field. As the closest parallels for them were to be found not in south-west England, and not even in Brittany and Normandy, but in northern France (north of the Seine) and Belgium, our preconceptions as to the likely geographical route(s) of connectivity between the Isles of Scilly and elsewhere were completely shattered. Questions remain about the origins and long-term maintenance of the proposed relationship between the two regions, and indeed its very validity (depending as it does entirely on typological comparisons). Nonetheless, if we *are* talking about a social relationship between people in Belgium and people in Scilly, then it can perhaps be argued that our understanding of seafaring and sociality during the Mesolithic as a whole, not just of the islands, has also been transformed.

The Outer Hebrides, in comparison to most other regions of Britain, have a Neolithic settlement record that survives fairly well and is thus relatively well known. That is not to say that it is necessarily well understood – the archaeology that is preserved is often difficult to comprehend, mixed stratigraphy making many sites difficult to radiocarbon date accurately (Garrow et al. 2017). By contrast, the impressive burial monuments of the Outer Hebrides, whilst certainly visible and well-recorded (at least in some cases), have seen very little recent work. Not a single tomb on the islands has been well-dated (Garrow et al. 2017) and consequently it must be said that our knowledge of the timing of the Early Neolithic in particular is far from fully understood.

5.3. Settlement variability

In any consideration of settlement variability across and between our island groups, it is important to take into account two parallel variables – differences and similarities between the different island groups, and between those same islands and the mainland regions closest to them.

The Channel Islands settlement record during the Neolithic is interesting. As we and others have discussed elsewhere (Marcigny et al. 2010; Scarre 2011; Garrow & Sturt 2017), while the Early Neolithic across much of northern France is associated with the highly visible, final LBK (or Villeneuve Saint Germain) longhouse-associated Neolithic, as you move (in space) west into Brittany and the Channel Islands, and (in time) forwards towards the end of the 5th millennium BC, this clarity of architecture largely disappears. Across the Channel Islands, the earliest Neolithic does appear to have been related to occupation sites rather than monuments, but these have generally been tricky to define architecturally – those sites we do see consist of disparate post-holes, hearths, pits and midden deposits. At L'Erée, our glimpse of the site was small (and heavily truncated by the sea), yet we were able to be fairly confident that we had indeed characterised the archaeology there well, due to its similarity to many other sites across the wider region at that time (see Section 2.10). This style of domestic architecture (or rather broad absence thereof) in the Channel Islands continues through the Late Neolithic and into the EBA, again echoing patterns across much of northern France (Hénaff 2002; Scarre 2011) and Britain (Whittle 1999; Brück 1999), where clear house structures are, for most areas, difficult to find. The question as to whether this post-LBK transformation of Neolithic settlement practices in France was in some way a necessary prerequisite to the British Mesolithic–Neolithic transition remains a very interesting issue that would certainly benefit from further sustained investigation in future.

For the Isles of Scilly, it would be mistaken to attempt to discuss the settlement record of the islands as a whole on the basis of our findings at Old Quay. Nonetheless, the archaeology recovered there, in combination with the two pits found at East Porth, Samson (Johns 2012, 59–60) and *relatively* low level of Neolithic material culture found across the archipelago in general, does perhaps suggest a fairly mobile settlement regime, as argued by many others previously (see Section 1.6). As the numerous stone walls seen across the islands today testify, stone was accessible to people in the Neolithic with which they could have constructed more permanent settlement architecture; yet apparently they chose not to do so. Nonetheless, at the same time, the scale of Neolithic archaeology and material culture deposition at Old Quay is also sufficient to raise questions about those previous narratives – as work progresses in future, it is possible that we may need to revisit our assumptions about the longevity of sites and about what exactly we mean by impermanent occupation of the islands as a whole. As discussed in Section 5.2, very clear differences in the scale of archaeological work undertaken in Cornwall and on Scilly make it difficult to compare the two regions meaningfully. While the islands, perhaps unsurprisingly, appear to lack the large ceremonial enclosure sites of the south-west peninsula, in many other respects the pits and post-holes found at Old Quay and East Porth are comparable to many other sites of a similar nature on the mainland (Jones & Quinnell 2011). As the Old Quay microliths and, to a lesser but still significant extent, the imported Neolithic stone tools from the site make very clear, it is also extremely important that we do not focus too closely only on neighbouring Cornwall when investigating maritime connections with the mainland.

The architecture of Neolithic and EBA settlements in the Outer Hebrides is very clearly different to both the Channel Islands and Scilly – and, it must be said, to most other regions of Britain. Stone domestic buildings were a prominent feature of the settlement record of the region, and while house walls do not seem to have been built very high in stone (most of the height may have been achieved with turf), substantial stone hearths were a significant feature of most buildings. While these structures echo, to some extent, those of Orkney just around the coast to the north, the similarities between the two regions are not necessarily that striking. Hearths do feature prominently in both, but the scale of Late Neolithic settlements in Orkney and the character of the architecture itself, cannot really be seen as directly comparable; on present evidence, this does not seem to be only an accident of preservation and/or recovery. Even within the Outer Hebrides, as discussed in Section 4.11, variability between settlements is significant – in terms of landscape locations and material culture as well as architecture. The recent identification of potentially widespread Neolithic islet settlements or 'crannogs' on the Isle of Lewis (Garrow, Sturt & Copper 2017), added to the well-known islet site at Eilean Domhnuill and possible island site at Eilean an Tighe (Armit 2003; Scott 1951), suggests that certain groups or families may have chosen to separate themselves off physically and socially from the wider community almost from the start of the Neolithic. Equally, distinct material culture differences between our site at An Doirlinn and most others – in terms of the complete absence of heavily decorated, multiple-ridged vessels and Unstan pottery, and presence of large quantities of flint (largely absent from most other sites) – suggests a breakdown or disjuncture in material (and social?) relations in other respects as well. Potentially, some people living in the Outer Hebrides were communicating more regularly with people in Orkney (leading to the co-presence of Unstan pottery, etc.) and other Scottish mainland regions nearby (leading to shared tomb architectures) than they were with those living a lot closer by.

5.4. Material signatures of connectivity and 'islandness'

Our two final themes – 'islandness' and 'the material signatures of connectivity' – can arguably be seen as representing two different sides of the same coin. The process of studying them together often results in the emergence of contradictory messages about islands, which somehow captures the essence of these places – apart from, yet connected to, the mainland (and often also each other) – very well. As a result, we will discuss both sets of material messages – of connection and of separation – together in this section. Archaeological signatures of connectivity can be divided into *actual* (i.e. materials, usually stone, which have demonstrably been moved physically from elsewhere) and *inferred* (i.e. artefacts that share similar stylistic traits and thus can be seen as suggesting social connections between the two areas) types. On every island group, the degree of connectedness with other regions ebbs and flows through time, yet, at any one time, those very same connections can occur simultaneously with other patterns that suggest the opposite. Exactly what we mean by this rather complex statement will, we hope, become clearer as we flesh out some concrete examples below.

On the Channel Islands, the insularity of the island landscape setting is in evidence from the Mesolithic onwards. After what appears to have been a well-populated period of occupation during the Middle Mesolithic, almost all signs of human activity on the islands disappear during the Late Mesolithic (Conneller et al. 2016), a pattern that is not clearly seen in the mainland regions nearby or in fact on other French islands to the south (ibid.). The reasons for this change are currently difficult to ascertain (ibid.), but could be viewed as reflective of the islands' status as insular, separated pieces of land becoming much more pronounced during the Late Mesolithic, resulting in a dramatic drop in connectivity with the mainland and thus a related drop in population. The Early Neolithic, however, sees a renewal both of population on the Channel Islands and of connections with the mainland (the two processes are, of course, related). In terms of the kinds of connection seen at this time, it is possible to discern *inferred* relationships (in the form of 'VSG cordons' style pottery and similar settlement forms to those found on the mainland) as well as *actual* ones (in the form of 'Cinglais' flint and polished stone rings that must have been imported from France). Moving into the Middle Neolithic, the picture is complicated again. Settlement practices continue to be similar to those in France, but the styles of material culture in evidence in the two regions diverge. This trend is most notably seen in the development of 'Pinacle-Fouaillages' pottery, a Channel Islands-specific sub-style that, at some level, must have symbolised a developing islands-wide identity in opposition to neighbouring mainland regions. Ironically, however, as Marcigny et al. (2010) have argued very effectively, that very transformation in fact represents a local instantiation of what is actually a widespread trend across north-west France towards regionally specific sub-styles of pottery during the Middle Neolithic. Immediately following these developments, however, we see the widespread adoption of directly comparable passage graves across the entire region. Moving forwards into the Late Neolithic and Early Bronze Age, the picture of comparable occupation practices continues, with such sites becoming increasingly difficult to define everywhere. The importation of flint from the mines at Grand Pressigny onto sites like L'Erée represents a clear *actual* connection with the mainland. Similarly, the use of Beaker pottery occurs across France and the Channel Islands at approximately the same time. Typically, however, on the islands, a related but very distinctly insular style of pottery – Jersey Bowl – also emerges at that point.

On the Isles of Scilly, such ebbs and flows through time, and apparently contradictory mixed messages of simultaneous similarity and difference, can certainly be seen as well. Again, from the Mesolithic onwards, connections across the sea can be identified in the archaeological record. As we have dicussed at length elsewhere (Anderson-Whymark et al. 2015; see also Section 3.10), the microliths found at Old Quay suggest *inferred* connections with northern France and Belgium. If the clear material similarities between the microliths found in that region and at Old Quay do indeed relate to a connection (or series of connections) in terms of people moving from one to the other, this particular flow of maritime contact certainly represents the most surprising of any we encountered. Nonetheless, true to their island location form, subtle differences between the microliths from Scilly and those from the continent (see Section 3.5) suggest a degree of insularity as well. These differences may have come about through unintentional drift, or as a result of an explicit intention on the part of those making these objects in Scilly to distinguish themselves from their 'founder' population, it is impossible to say which. Moving forwards into the Early Neolithic, the material from Old Quay clearly demonstrates *actual* connections with south-west England – stone had been brought in from Cornwall, Devon and beyond. In this instance, it is very important to recognise the fact that, even in Cornwall, the flint sources on St Martin's are likely to have been the best available for many kilometres. Flint is therefore very likely to have travelled back across the sea in the other direction – islands are not, and must not be seen as, merely constant *recipients* of materials and/or change. The South-Western Bowl pottery found at Old Quay fits comfortably within the wider south-west England style, but at the same time is arguably notable – distinctive even – for its plainness (Section 3.4). Given the lateness of the radiocarbon dates with which some of the pottery at Old Quay was associated, it is possible that the style continued in use for longer on the islands than on the mainland (ibid.); on present evidence, however, this intriguing suggestion must remain a possibility only. The picture for the Bronze Age is similar – vessels with clear mainland-derived, Trevisker traits have been identified, whilst at the same time the strongly regional 'Scillonian Bronze Age' style comes into use.

Across the Outer Hebrides, as in both the Channel Islands and the Isles of Scilly, the presence of 'exotic' materials on various Neolithic sites (including An Doirlinn) which can only have been sourced from the Inner Hebrides and beyond provides us with clear *actual* evidence of the maritime networks within which those islands were caught up. We can infer regular sea travel around the northern part of the western seaways as a result. As discussed above, it may have been the case that certain communities on the islands had much stronger connections with people far away across the sea than they did with those living close by. While it is important not to speculate too much on the basis of equivocal evidence, if this was indeed the case, it could potentially tell us something significant about the manner in which the islands were settled during the Early Neolithic, with old contacts in distant places perhaps being maintained for many years. As already discussed, further *inferred* connections (such as the co-presence of Unstan and Grooved Ware pottery in the Outer Hebrides and Orkney) invite us to discuss other such relationships across the sea. Yet, at the same time, the subtly different uses to which both Unstan and Grooved Ware were put in the two regions, and the development of a distinctive 'Hebridean Neolithic' pottery style, completes the standard, contradictory picture on islands that we have come to expect. Similar patterns are maintained into the EBA. Whilst, as in other regions, the use of Beaker pottery demonstrates *inferred* connections with mainland Britain and far beyond, again the uses to which these vessels were put, and contexts within which they were used, are very different – the settlements associated with Beaker pottery in the Outer Hebrides are perhaps the most visible in Europe (Hamilton & Sharples 2012), while, in direct contrast to mainland Britain, Beakers are only very rarely used in funerary contexts on the islands. Ebbs and flows, contrast and contradictions again.

5.5. Summary: ebbs and flows, contrasts and contradictions, connections and separations

The preceding sections have made the complexity of our task in trying to decipher what was going on, both on our three main island groups and across the western seaways more generally, very clear. It has often been suggested that islands can be seen as microcosms of the wider world; while they may be 'good to think' (Fleming 2008, 20), it must be said that, as this chapter has very clearly demonstrated, they can also be 'complicated to think' as well. Following on from Fleming's point, it must be said that, in addition to the concrete, material results described above, over the course of the project we were also lucky enough to be made to *think* differently as well. The process of working on an island – and especially on multiple, very different islands – places you in a new position, geographically (of course) but also conceptually. As Fleming (2008, 11) noted, islands are different spaces, and they should not be treated simply as extensions of the mainland no matter how closely networked with it they were. Archaeologically, we found ourselves thinking about material connections with other places much more than we would have done in excavating a land-locked location, even though – as we have argued more than many – the presence of the sea may in fact have represented a connecting routeway rather than a separating barrier during prehistory. This was a positive thing, especially within a project designed to investigated cultural connections and long-distance change. Equally, we also found ourselves thinking harder about change and the 'origins' of new technologies: the 'arrival' of farming practices or pottery technologies on an island seems somehow more worthy of consideration, again even despite the caveats just outlined. As we stated in Chapter 1, steps across water to the stepping stones can appear more significant than those taken on land up to the bank of the river. Finally, as discussed at the start of this chapter, despite the fact that we were working on (admittedly at times strikingly similar) sites hundereds of kilometres apart, their locations on islands and comparable date-ranges leant them a familiarity and comparability that we had not really expected, facilitating broad-scale comparison at a macro geographical level. While all of these thoughts may have been evoked as a result of our modern conceptualisation of islands, the sea, the mainland and more, nonetheless they did have a positive effect in terms of making us think differently, and about different things.

The aim of the Neolithic Stepping Stones project was to focus attention onto the western seaways zone which, whilst being viewed by many as a crucial corridor of interaction over the course of the Mesolithic–Neolithic transition, had been investigated less, and consequently was much less well understood than the mainland islands (Britain and Ireland) on either side. We achieved this goal, with our work on all three island groups certainly enhancing the archaeological records, and in turn our wider interpretations, of their Mesolithic, Neolithic and Bronze Age archaeology.

Since the start of the project, we sought to address the question of whether those island groups acted as 'stepping stones to the Neolithic' – island stopping points that somehow facilitated the much broader process of change early on – given that Neolithic things and practices *must* have come across the sea to Britain and Ireland in various forms. While the project's radiocarbon dating programme (Garrow et al. 2017) was able to shed considerable light on this issue – broadly confirming the model of Whittle et al. (2011) in *Gathering Time* – none of our three sites, as it turned out, fell within the earliest Neolithic phase of their island group or the wider region. With hindsight, it was perhaps overly hopeful to expect to identify strategically, to excavate successfully and then to date accurately three earliest Neolithic sites – especially given that so little was known about each one prior to our work. Nonetheless, the archaeology uncovered on all three sites was substantial, materially rich, informative and interesting, sometimes producing transformative results.

As we have said at various points elsewhere in this book, in order to understand maritime connectivity across the Mesolithic–Neolithic transition period better, it is important that we make the most of the glimpses of contact (both actual and inferred) that can be seen; and in order to understand Neolithic settlement better (in comparison to the better known, if not always better understood, monumental record), you have to take a risk and look at potentially unrewarding sites. It is also vital that we let the archaeological record surprise us (as the Old Quay microliths in particular did), challenging our preconceptions and hinting at a past that is not as we might expect. Finally, it is important that we embrace the ebbs and flows, contrasts and contradictions, connections and separations summarised in this chapter – that is, after all, what the past within the western seaways and beyond was like.

Appendix 1

Chipped stone post-excavation analysis sampling strategies

L'Erée

Catalogued (highlighted in grey) and scanned artefacts were as follows:

Trench	*Grid*	*Med.*	*EBA*	*Marbled*	*Basal*	*Basal up*	*Basal low*	*Features*	*Ditch*	*Natural*	*??*	*Scanned*	*Catalogued*
3			4									4	
4		24	37	49	195							24	281
5		4	37	65		394						500	
6		21	145	202		117	313	8				21	785
7		28	37	50		75	330		45			235	330
8		13	48	52		156	58					327	
9		12	7	94				37				113	37
10		21		5								26	
11	a		583	61								644	
11	B		375	126				11				501	11
11	C		183	48				31					262
11	D	80	254	64				8				398	8
11	E		299	437								736	
11	F		278	251				1				529	1
11	G		39	123				9				162	9
11	H		47	70								117	
11	I		178					29			4	211	29
11	J		184			237							421
11	K		275	577		8						860	
11	L		54	406		52						512	
11	M		52	259		16						327	
11	N		31	168		66							265
11	o		13	88		1						102	
11	p		41	154		38		8				233	8
11	q		20	347		267		78					712
11	R		15	129		65						209	
11	s		22	176		34		12				232	12
11	T		17	103		24		9				144	9
11	u		93	128		55						276	
12		9	27			303						339	
13		4		62	53							119	
15			4	295								299	
16		20	187	479				154				686	154
17	?			22								22	
17	a			614								614	
17	b			720								720	
18			54	247						8		309	
Total		236	3640	6671	248	1908	701	395	45	8	4	10551	3334

An Doirlinn

The focus of this study was the Phase 1, Phase 2 and Phase 3 lithics, with the later Phase 4 lithics subject to scanning only. Sampling strategy for the Phases 1–3 lithics was to catalogue:

- All material from the earliest Phase 1a occupation levels and features including hearths, pits, post-holes and pot deposits
- The assemblages from a sample of grid squares across the site from the Phase 1b occupation levels including hearths and post-holes, and from levelling/storm deposits
- A 50% sample of the assemblages from a sample of the grid squares from the very dense Phase 1c levelling/storm deposits
- All material from Phase 2a (all contained in features including hearths and pits)
- The assemblages from a sample of grid squares across the site from the Phase 2b occupation levels, a sample of the assemblage from one of the occupation contexts, and all material from features including hearths, post-holes and a wall
- The assemblages from a sample of grid squares across the site from the Phase 1c occupation levels and a post-hole.
- All of the Phase 3 material

Phase	*Context*	*Feature*	*Total*	*Sample*
1a	66		31	Entire assemblage
	67		12	Entire assemblage
	68		1	Entire assemblage
	78		2	Entire assemblage
	82		162	Entire assemblage
	87		125	Entire assemblage
	72	15	36	Entire assemblage
	89	19	7	Entire assemblage
	94	21	3	Entire assemblage
	96	22	3	Entire assemblage
1b	65		881	Sample of grid squares (B3, B8, C5, D8, E5, E7)
	71		94	Sample of grid squares (C9)
	70		198	Sample of grid squareas (A2, C9, E7)
	74	16	15	Entire assemblage
	83	17	42	Entire assemblage
	85	18	76	Entire assemblage
1c	52		140	50% sampled from certain grid squares (B3, B4)
	53		185	50% sampled from certain grid squares (B4, C5, C6)
	54		147	50% sampled from certain grid squares (B3)
	63		17	50% sampled from certain grid squares (C5)
	64		129	50% sampled from certain grid squares (B3, B4)
2a	55	11	190	Entire assemblage
	57	12	5	Entire assemblage
	76	14	372	Entire assemblage
	79	14	21	Entire assemblage
2b	41		39	Sample of grid squares (C2, C5, G2)
	42		129	Sample of grid squares (C2, C5, G2)
	46		185	50% sample from entire context
	47		395	Sample of grid squares (B6, C5)
	29	3	5	Entire assemblage
	31	5	46	Entire assemblage
	37	8	66	Entire assemblage
	44	10	2	Entire assemblage
	49	10	93	Entire assemblage
	95	13	9	Entire assemblage
2c	20		55	Sample of grid squares (H)
	27		26	Sample of grid squares (T)
	28		113	Sample of grid squares (K, L)
	35	7	1	Entire assemblage
3	5		29	Entire assemblage
	8		548	Entire assemblage
	10	2	19	Entire assemblage
	12		773	Entire assemblage
	19	2	10	Entire assemblage

Bibliography

Anderson-Whymark, H. & D. Garrow 2015. Seaways and shared ways: imaging and imagining the movement of people, objects and ideas over the course of the Mesolithic–Neolithic transition c. 5000–3500 BC. In H. Anderson-Whymark, D. Garrow & F. Sturt (ed.) *Continental Connections: exploring cross-channel relationships from the Mesolithic to the Iron Age*: 59–77. Oxford: Oxbow Books.

Anderson-Whymark, H., D. Garrow & F. Sturt 2015. Microliths and maritime mobility: a continental European-style Late Mesolithic flint assemblage from the Isles of Scilly. *Antiquity* 89: 954–971.

Andrefsky, W. 1998. *Lithics: Macroscopic Approaches to Analysis*. Cambridge: Cambridge University Press.

Antoine, P., J. Catt, J.-P. Lautridou & J. Somme 2003. The loess and coversands of northern France and southern England. *Journal of Quaternary Science* 18: 309–318.

Armit, I. 1986. *Excavation at Loch Olabhat, North Uist, 1986: 1st Interim Report*. Edinburgh: Department of Archaeology, University of Edinburgh.

Armit, I. 1987. *Excavation of a Neolithic Island Settlement in Loch Olabhat, North Uist, 1987: 2nd Interim Report*. Edinburgh: Department of Archaeology, University of Edinburgh.

Armit, I. 1988. *Excavations at Loch Olabhat, North Uist, 1988: 3rd Interim Report*. Edinburgh: Department of Archaeology, University of Edinburgh.

Armit, I. 1990. *The Loch Olabhat project, North Uist, 1989: 4th Interim Report*. Edinburgh: Department of Archaeology, University of Edinburgh.

Armit, I. 1992. *The Later Prehistory of the Western Isles of Scotland*. British Archaeological Report 221. Oxford: Tempus Reparatum.

Armit, I. 1996. *The Archaeology of Skye and the Western Isles*. Edinburgh: Edinburgh University Press.

Armit, I. 2003. The drowners: permanence and transience in the Hebridean Neolithic. In I. Armit, E. Murphy, E. Nelis & D. Simpson (ed.) *Neolithic Settlement in Ireland and Western Britain*: 93–100. Oxford: Oxbow Books.

Armit, I. 2006. *Anatomy of an Iron Age Roundhouse: the Cnip Wheelhouse Excavations, Lewis*. Edinburgh: Society of Antiquaries of Scotland.

Armit, I. in prep. *First farmers in the west: excavations at Eilean Dòmhnuill, Loch Olabhat, North Uist*. Edinburgh: Society of Antiquaries of Scotland/National Museums Scotland.

Ashbee, P. 1974. *Ancient Scilly*. Newton Abbot: David & Charles.

Ashbee, P. 1983. Halangy Porth, St Mary's, Isles of Scilly, Excavations 1975–6. *Cornish Archaeology* 22, 3–46.

Ashbee, P. 1996. Halangy Down, St Mary's, Isles of Scilly, Excavations 1964–1977. *Cornish Archaeology* 35: 9–201.

Ashmore, P. 2016. *Calanais Survey and Excavation, 1979–88*. Edinburgh: Historic Environment Scotland.

Ashmore, P. 2016. *Calanais: excavation and survey 1979–88*. Edinburgh: Historic Environment Scotland. Available online at https://www.historicenvironment.scot/archives-and-research/publications/publication/?publicationId=b6aee5fd-5980-4872-a2e0-a63c00cc7b68. Accessed 21.11.16.

Bailiff, I., C. French & C. Scarre 2014. Application of luminescence dating and geomorphological analysis to the study of landscape evolution, settlement and climate change on the Channel Island of Herm. *Journal of Archaeological Science* 41, 890–903.

Ballin, T. 2009. Quartz in Scottish Prehistory. *Scottish Archaeological Internet Reports* 26.

Ballin, T. & J. Faithfull 2014. Stotfield 'cherty rock'/silcrete. A 'new' lithic raw material from Scotland. *Chartered Insititute of Archaeologists Finds Group Newsletter*, 3–8.

Ballin-Smith, B. 1999. Pumice. In B. Crawford & B. Ballin-Smith (ed.) *The Biggings, Papa Stour, Shetland: the History and Archaeology of a Royal Norwegian Farm*: 177–178. Edinburgh: Society of Antiquaries of Scotland.

Barclay, G. & C. Russell-White 1993. Excavations in the ceremonial complex of the fourth to second millennium at Balfarg/Balbirnie, Glenrothes, Fife. *Proceedings of the Society of Antiquaries of Scotland* 123: 43–210.

Barrière, C., R. Daniel, H. Delporte, M. Escalon de Fonton, R. Parent, J. Roche, J. Rozoy, J. Tixier & E. Vignard 1969. Epipaléolithique-Mésolithique. Les microlithes géométriques. *Bulletin de la Société Préhistorique Française* 66: 355–366.

Barton, K. 1984. Excavations in the middle ward, Mont Orgeuil, Jersey. *Archaeological Journal* 141, 216–42.

Bennett, K., J. Fossitt, M. Sharp & V. Switsur 1990. Holocene vegetational and environmental history at Loch Lang, South Uist, Western Isles, Scotland. *New Phytologist* 114: 198–281.

Berridge, P. & A. Roberts 1986. The Mesolithic period in Cornwall. *Cornish Archaeology*: 7–34.

Besse, A.-M. 1996. *Le Campaniforme en France: analyse de la céramique d'accompagnement*. British Archaeological Report S635. Oxford: Tempus Reparatum.

Binns, R. 1967. Drift pumice in Northern Europe. *Antiquity* 41: 311–312.

Bishop, R., M. Church & P. Rowley-Conwy 2014. Seeds, fruits and nuts in the Scottish Mesolithic. *Proceedings of the Society of Antiquaries of Scotland* 143: 9–72.

Blott, S. & K. Pye 2001. GRADISTAT: a grain size distribution and statistics package for the analysis of unconsolidated sediments. *Earth Surface Processes and Land Forms* 26: 1237–1248.

Boardman, S. 1995. Charcoal and charred plant macrofossils. In K. Branigan & P. Foster (ed.) *Barra: Archaeological Research on Ben Tangaval*: 149–57. Sheffield: Sheffield Academic Press.

Booth, P., T. Champion, S. Foreman, P. Garwood, H. Glass, J. Munby & A. Reynolds 2011. *On Track: The Archaeology of High Speed 1 Section 1 in Kent*. Oxford: Oxford Wessex Archaeology.

Bradley, R. 1984. *The Social Foundations of Prehistoric Britain*. London: Longman.

Bradley, R. 2013. Houses of commons, houses of lords: domestic dwellings and monumental architecture in prehistoric Europe. *Proceedings of the Prehistoric Society* 79, 1–18.

Bradley, R. & M. Edmonds 1993. *Interpreting the Axe Trade: Production and Trade in Neolithic Europe*. Cambridge: Cambridge University Press.

Bradley, S., G. Milne, I. Shennan & R. Edwards 2011. An improved glacial isostatic adjustment model for the British Isles. *Journal of Quaternary Science* 26: 541–552.

Brady, K. & C. Batey 2008. Excavations and survey on Brei Holm and Maiden Stack, Papa Stour, Shetland. *Scottish Archaeological Journal* 30: 1–64.

Branigan, K. & P. Foster 1995. *Barra: Archaeological Research on Ben Tangaval*. Sheffield: Sheffield Academic Press.

Branigan, K. & P. Foster 2002. *Barra and the Bishop's Isles: Living on the Margin*. Stroud: Tempus.

Brayshay, B., D. Gilbertson, K. Edwards, P. Wathern & R. Weaver 2000. Surface pollen-vegetation relationships on the Atlantic seaboard: South Uist, Scotland. *Journal of Biogeography* 27, 359–378.

Brayshay, B. & K. Edwards 1996. Late-glacial and Holocene vegetational history of South Uist and Barra. In D. Gilbertson, M. Kent & J. Grattan (ed.) *The Outer Hebrides: the last 14,000 years*: 13–26. Sheffield: Sheffield Academic Press.

Brock, F., T. Higham, P. Ditchfield and C. Bronk Ramsey 2010. Current pretreatment methods for AMS radiocarbon dating at the Oxford Radiocarbon Accelerator Unit (ORAU). *Radiocarbon* 52, 103–112.

Brooks, A., S. Bradley, R. Edwards & N. Goodwyn 2011. The palaeogeography of Northwest Europe during the last 20,000 years. *Journal of Maps* 7: 573–587.

Brophy, K. 2007. From big houses to cult houses: early Neolithic timber halls in Scotland. *Proceedings of the Prehistoric Society* 73: 75–96.

Brown, N. no date. Eilean Dòmhnuill, Loch Olabhat pottery. Unpublished specialist report.

Brück, J. 1999. What's in a settlement? Domestic practice and residential mobility in Early Bronze Age southern England. In J. Brück & M. Goodman (ed.) *Making Places in the Prehistoric World: Themes in Settlement Archaeology*: 53–75. London: UCL Press.

Bukach, D. 2004. The Mesolithic–Neolithic transition on the Channel Islands: adopting agriculture in an emerging island landscape. *Environmental Archaeology* 9: 155–162.

Bullock, P. and Murphy, C. 1979. Evolution of a paleo-argillic brown earth (Paleudalf) from Oxfordshire, England. *Geoderma* 22, 225–252.

Bullock, P., N. Fedoroff, A. Jongerius, G. Stoops & T. Tursina 1985. *Handbook for Soil Thin Section Description*. Wolverhampton: Waine Research.

Burns, R. 1988. *Excavations at Jerbourg, Guernsey*. St Peter Port: Guernsey Museum.

Burrow, S. 1997. *The Neolithic Culture of the Isle of Man*. British Archaeological Report 263. Oxford: Archaeopress.

Butcher, S. 1978. Excavations at Nornour, Isles of Scilly, 1969–73: the pre-Roman settlement. *Cornish Archaeology* 17: 29–112.

Butler, C. 2005. *Prehistoric Flintwork*. Stroud: Tempus.

Callaghan, R. & C. Scarre 2009. Simulating the western seaways. *Oxford Journal of Archaeology* 28: 357–372.

Callander, J. G. 1929. Scottish neolithic pottery. *Proceedings of the Society of Antiquaries of Scotland* 63: 29–98.

Campbell, G., L. Moffett & V. Straker 2011. *Environmental Archaeology: A Guide to the Theory and Practice of Methods, from Sampling and Recovery to Post-excavation*. London: English Heritage.

Campbell, J. 2000. Holocene Palaeoenvironments of Guernsey and Alderney, Channel Islands. Unpublished PhD thesis, Coventry University.

Case, H. 1969. Neolithic explanations. *Antiquity* 43: 176–186.

Cassen, S. 1993. Le Néolithique récent sur la façade atlantique de la France. La différenciation stylistique des groupes céramiques. *Zephyrus* 44–45: 167–182.

Cazenave, P. 2012. Sediment Transport of the North-west European Continental Shelf. Unpublished PhD thesis, University of Southampton.

Chancerel, A. & B. Masson 1991. Nouveaux sites campaniformes de la basse vallée de la Seine: présentation et localisation des sites. *Gallia Préhistoire* 33, 172–184.

Chancerel A., C. Marcigny & E. Ghesquière E. 2006. *Le plateau de Mondeville (Calvados): du Néolithique à l'Âge du Bronze*. Paris: DAF.

Charman, D., C. Johns, K. Camidge, P. Marshall, S. Mills, J. Mulville & H. Roberts 2016. *The Lyonesse Project. A Study of the Historic Coastal and Marine Environment of the Isles of Scilly*. Truro: Cornwall Council.

Cherry, J. 1981. Pattern and process in the earliest colonization of the Mediterranean islands. *Proceedings of the Prehistoric Society* 47: 41–68.

Childe, V. G. 1940. *Prehistoric Communities of the British Isles*. London: W. R. Chambers.

Childe, V. G. 1946. *Scotland before the Scots*. London: Methuen.

Church, M. 2002. The archaeological and archaeobotanical implications of a destruction layer in Dun Bharabhat, Lewis. In B. Ballin-Smith & I. Banks (ed.) *In the Shadow of the Brochs: the Iron Age in Scotland*: 67–75. Stroud: Tempus.

Church, M, R. Bishop, E. Blake, C. Nesbitt, A. Perri, S. Piper, P. Rowley-Conwy & L. Snape-Kennedy 2012. Temple Bay. *Discovery and Excavation in Scotland* 13, 186

Church, M. & P. Rowley-Conwy 2013. Pabaigh Mòr. *Discovery and Excavation in Scotland* 14, 198.

Clarke, A. 1997. *A report on the quartz and stone assemblages from the Udal, RUX6, North Uist*. Unpublished Historic Scotland report.

Clarke, A. 2006. *Stone Tools and the Prehistory of the Northern Isles*. British Archaeological Report 406. Oxford: Archaeopress.

Clarke, A. & D. Dixon 1998. The coarse stone. In N. Sharples (ed.) *Scalloway: a Broch, Late Iron Age Settlement and Medieval Cemetery in Shetland*: 93–95. Oxford: Oxbow Books.

Cleal, R. 2004. The dating and diversity of the earliest ceramics of Wessex and South-West England. In R. Cleal & J. Pollard (ed.) *Monuments and Material Culture: Papers in Honour of an Avebury Archaeologist Isobel Smith*: 164–192. Salisbury: Hobnob Press.

Clifton Antiquarian Club 2015. *Rousse Tower (RH93): draft interim report*. Unpublished Clifton Antiquarian Club report.

Clough, T. & W. Cummins 1988. *Stone Axe Studies (Volume 2): The Petrology of Prehistoric Stone Implements from the British Isles*. London: Council for British Archaeology.

Cohen, K., P. Gibbard & H. Weerts 2014. North Sea palaeogeographical reconstructions for the last 1 Ma. *Netherlands Journal of Geosciences* 93: 7–29.

Cole, D. & A. Jones 2002–3. Journeys to the Rock: archaeological investigations at Tregarrick Farm, Roche. *Cornish Archaeology* 41–42: 121–122.

Coles, B. 1998. Doggerland: a speculative survey. *Proceedings of the Prehistoric Society* 64: 45–81.

Coles, B. 1999. Doggerland's loss and the Neolithic. In B. Coles, J. Coles, & M. Schon Jorgensen (ed.) *Bog Bodies, Sacred Sites and Wetland Archaeology*: 51–67. Exeter: Wetlands Archaeological Research Project.

Coll, J., D. Woolf, S. Gibb & P. Challenor 2013. Sensitivity of ferry services to the Western Isles of Scotland to changes in wave and wind climate. *Journal of Applied Meteorology and Climatology* 52: 1069–1084.

Conneller, C., M. Bates, R. Bates, T. Schadla-Hall, E. Blinkhorn, J. Cole, M. Pope, B. Scott, A. Shaw & D. Underhill 2016. Rethinking human responses to sea-level rise: the Mesolithic occupation of the Channel Islands. *Proceedings of the Prehistoric Society*, 1–45.

Constantin, C. 1985. *Fin du Rubané, céramique du Limbourg et post-Rubané, le Néolithique le plus ancien en Bassin parisien et en Hainaut*. Oxford: British Archaeological Reports International Series 273.

Copat, V., M. Danesi & G. Recchia 2010. Isolation and interaction cycles: small central Mediterranean islands from the Neolithic to the Bronze Age. *Shima: The International Journal of Research into Island Cultures* 4: 41–64.

Copper, M. 2015. *The same but better: understanding ceramic variation in the Hebridean Neolithic*. Unpublished PhD thesis, University of Bradford.

Cowie, T. & A. MacSween 1999. Grooved Ware from Scotland: a review. In R. Cleal & A. MacSween (ed.) *Grooved Ware in Britain and Ireland*, 48–56. Oxford: Oxbow Books.

Crawford, O. G. S. 1927. Lyonesse. *Antiquity* 1, 5–14.

Crawford, O. G. S. 1936. Western seaways. In L. Buxton (ed.) *Custom is King. Essays presented to R. R. Marett on his Seventieth Birthday*: 181–200. London: Hutchinson's Scientific and Technical Publications.

Crombé, P., M. Van Strydonck & M. Boudin 2009. Towards a refinement of the absolute (typo) chronology for the Early Mesolithic in the coversand area of Northern Belgium and the Southern Netherlands. In P. Crombe, M. Van Strydonck, J. Sergant, M. Boudin, & M. Bats (ed.) *Chronology and Evolution within the Mesolithic of North-West Europe: Proceedings of an International Meeting*: 95–112. Newcastle: Cambridge Scholars.

Crone, A., I. Armit, S. Boardman, B. Finlayson, A. MacSween & C. Mills 1993. Excavation and survey of sub-peat features of Neolithic, Bronze and Iron Age date at Bharpa Carinish, North Uist, Scotland. *Proceedings of the Prehistoric Society* 59: 361–382.

Cummings, V. & C. Richards 2013. The peristalith and the context of Calanais: transformational architecture in the Hebridean early Neolithic. In C. Richards (ed.) *Building the Great Stone Circles of the North*: 186–200. Oxford: Windgather Press.

Cunliffe, B. & P. de Jersey 2000. Rescue excavations on coastal sites on Guernsey and Herm, 1998 and 1999. *Report and Transactions of La Société Guernesiaise* 24: 867–944.

Davidson, J. & A. Henshall 1989. *The Chambered Cairns of Orkney*. Edinburgh: Edinburgh University Press.

Davis, V., H. Howard & I. Smith 1988. The petrological identification of stone implements from south-west England. In T. Clough & W. Cummins (ed.) *Stone Axe Studies (Volume 2)*: 14–20. London: Council for British Archaeology.

Dawson, S., D. Smith, J. Jordan & A. Dawson 2004. Late Holocene coastal sand movements in the Outer Hebrides, N.W. Scotland. *Marine Geology* 210: 281–306.

Dennis, I., J. Mulville & C. Johns 2013. New evidence for Mesolithic occupation and environments in the Isles of Scilly *PAST: The Newsletter of the Prehistoric Society* 73: 14–16.

Dickson, J. 1992. North American driftwood, especially *Picea* (spruce), from archaeological sites in the Hebrides and Northern Isles of Scotland. *Review of Palaeobotany and Palynology* 73: 49–56.

Downes, J. & A. Badcock 1998. *Berneray Causeway: Archaeological Watching Brief and Excavations at the Screvan Quarry Site and Otternish, North Uist*. Sheffield: Archaeological Research and Consultancy at the University of Sheffield (ARCUS Report 231c).

Ducrocq, T. 1998. Le *Mésolithique du bassin de la Somme*. Unpublished PhD thesis, Université des Sciences et Technologies de Lille.

Ducrocq, T. 2001. *Le Mésolithique du bassin de la Somme*. CREP Number 7. Lille: Centre d'Etudes et de Recherches Prehistoriques, Université des Sciences et Technologies de Lille.

Ducrocq, T. 2009. Eléments de chronologie absolue du Mésolithique dans le Nord de la France. In P. Crombé, M. Van Strydonck, J. Sergant, M. Boudin, & M. Bats (ed.) *Chronology and Evolution within the Mesolithic of North-west Europe*: 245–362. Newcastle: Cambridge Scholars.

Dudley, D. 1968. Excavations on Nor'Nour in the Isles of Scilly, 1962–6. *Archaeological Journal* 124: 1–64.

Dunwell, A., M. Johnson & I. Armit 2003. Excavations at Geirisclett chambered cairn, North Uist, Western Isles. *Proceedings of the Society of Antiquaries of Scotland* 133: 1–33.

Edmonds, M. 1995. *Stone Tools and Society*. London: Batsford.

Edwards, K. 1996. A Mesolithic of the Western and Northern Isles of Scotland? Evidence from pollen and charcoal. In T. Pollard & A. Morrison (ed.) *The Early Prehistory of Scotland*: 23–38. Edinburgh: Edinburgh University Press.

Edwards, K. & G. Whittington 1994. Lateglacial pollen sites in the Western Isles of Scotland. *Scottish Geographical Magazine* 110, 33–39.

Edwards, K. & G. Whittington 2000. Multiple charcoal profiles in a Scottish lake: taphonomy, fire ecology, human impact and inference. *Palaeogeography, Palaeoclimatology, Palaeoecology* 164, 67–86.

Edwards, K., G. Whittington & W. Ritchie 2005. The possible role of humans in the early stages of machair evolution: palaeoenvironmental investigations in the Outer Hebrides, Scotland. *Journal of Archaeological Science* 32: 435–449.

English Heritage 2004. *Geoarchaeology: using earth sciences to understand the archaeological record*. London: English Heritage.

English Heritage 2011. *Geoarchaeology: Using Earth Sciences to Understand the Archaeological Record*. London: English Heritage.

Eogan, G. 1984. *Excavations at Knowth 1: Smaller Passage Tombs, Neolithic Occupation and Beaker Activity*. Dublin: Royal Irish Academy.

Evans, J. 1973. Islands as laboratories for the study of culture process. In C. Renfrew (ed.) *The Explanation of Culture Change*: 517–20. Pittsburgh: University of Pittsburgh Press.

Evans, J. 1977. Island archaeology in the Mediterranean: problems and opportunities. *World Archaeology* 9: 12–26.

Evans, J. 2003. *Environmental archaeology and the social order*. London: Routledge.

Fedoroff, N. 1968. Génèse et morphologie des sols a horizon B textural en France atlantique. *Science du Sols* 1, 29–65.

Fenton, M. 1988. The petrological identification of stone battle axes and axe-hammers from Scotland. In T. Clough & W. Cummins (ed.) *Stone Axe Studies (Volume 2)*: 92–132. London: Council for British Archaeology.

Fergusson, J. 1872. *Rude Stone Monuments*. London: John Murray.

Fieldhouse, J. 1984. Final Remarks. In G. Till (ed.) *The future of British sea power*, 255–259. London: Springer.

Fleming, A. 2008. Island stories. In G. Noble, T. Poller, J. Raven & L. Verrill (ed.) *Scottish Odysseys: the Archaeology of Islands*: 11–22. Stroud: History Press.

Fleming, A. & M. Edmonds 1999. St Kilda: quarries, fields and prehistoric agriculture. *Proceedings of the Society of Antiquaries of Scotland* 129: 119–159.

Flitcroft, C. & A. Heald 1997. Aird Callanish, Lewis. *Discovery and Excavation in Scotland*: 85.

Fossitt, J. 1996. Late Quaternary vegetation history of the Western Isles of Scotland. *New Phytologist* 132: 171–196.

Fox, C. 1932. *The Personality of Britain: its Influence on Inhabitant and Invader in Prehistoric and Early Historic Times*. Cardiff: National Museum of Wales.

French, C. 2011. *The Holocene soil and landscape development of northern part of the island of Herm*. Unpublished report submitted to Prof C Scarre, Durham University.

Fromont, N. 2008. Les anneaux du Néolithique bas-normand et du nord-Sarthe: production, circulation et territoires. *Bulletin de la Société Préhistorique Française* 105: 55–86.

Fromont, N. 2013. *Anneaux et cultures du Néolithique ancien: production, circulation et utilisation entre massifs ardennais et armoricain.* British Archaeological Report S2499. Oxford: Archaeopress.

Frouin, M., D. Sebag, A. Durand, B. Laignel, J. Saliege, B. Mahler & C. Fauchard 2007. Influence of paleotopography, based level and sedimentation rate on estuarine system response to the Holocene sea-level rise: the example of the Marais Vernier, Seine estuary, France. *Sedimentary Geology* 200, 15–29.

Gaffney, V., S. Fitch & D. Smith 2009. *Europe's Lost World, the Rediscovery of Doggerland*. York: Council for British Archaeology.

Gaffney, V., K. Thomson, S. Fitch & S. Finch 2007. *Mapping Doggerland: The Mesolithic Landscapes of the Southern North Sea*. Oxford: Archaeopress.

Gale S. & P. Hoare 1991. *Quaternary sediments: petrographic methods for the study of unlithified rocks*. New York: Wiley.

Garrow, D. 2006. *Pits, Settlement and Deposition during the Neolithic and Early Bronze Age in East Anglia*. British Archaeological Report 414. Oxford: John and Erica Hedges.

Garrow, D. 2007. Placing pits: landscape occupation and depositional practice during the Neolithic in East Anglia. *Proceedings of the Prehistoric Society* 73: 1–24.

Garrow, D. & F. Sturt 2011. Grey waters bright with Neolithic argonauts? Maritime connections and the Mesolithic–Neolithic transition within the 'western seaways' of Britain, c. 5000–3500 BC. *Antiquity* 85: 59–72.

Garrow, D. & F. Sturt 2015. Introduction. In H. Anderson-Whymark, D. Garrow, & F. Sturt (ed.) *Continental Connections: Exploring Cross-Channel Relationships from the Mesolithic to the Iron Age*: 1–6. Oxford: Oxbow Books.

Garrow, D. & F. Sturt 2017. The Mesolithic–Neolithic transition in the Channel Islands: maritime and terrestrial perspectives. *Oxford Journal of Archaeology* 36, 3–23.

Garrow, D., F. Sturt & M. Copper 2017. *Submerged Neolithic of the Western Isles Interim Report (March 2017)*. Unpublished report. Available online at: http://cma.soton.ac.uk/submerged-neolithic-western-isles/.

Garrow, D., S. Griffiths, H. Anderson-Whymark & F. Sturt 2017. Stepping stones to the Neolithic? Radiocarbon dating the Early Neolithic on islands within the 'western seaways' of Britain. *Proceedings of the Prehistoric Society* 83.

Ghesquière, E. & J.-N. Guyodo 2008. Les industries lithiques taillées des IVe et IIIe millénaires avant J.C. dans le quart nord-ouest de la France. In M.-H. Dias-Meirinho, V. Léa, K. Gernigon, P. Fouéré, F. Briois & M. Bailly (ed.) *Les industries lithiques taillées des IVe et IIIe millénaires en Europe occidentale*: 113–33. British Archaeological Report S1884. Oxford: Archaeopress.

Ghesquière, E. & C. Marcigny 1998. Le débitage lithique au Cerny en Basse-Normandie. *Internéo* 2: 57–68.

Ghesquière, E. & C. Marcigny 2011. *Cairon. Vivre et mourir au Neolithique. La Pierre Tourneresse en Calvados*. Rennes: Universitaires de Rennes.

Gibson, A. 1982. *Beaker Domestic Sites: a Study of the Domestic Pottery of the Late Third and Early Second Millennia BC in the British Isles*. British Archaeological Report 107. Oxford: British Archaeological Reports.

Gibson, A. 2001. Neolithic pottery from Ogmore, Glamorgan. *Archaeologia Cambrensis* 147: 56–69.

Gibson, A. 2002. *Prehistoric Pottery in Britain & Ireland*. Stroud: Tempus.

Gibson, A. & A. Woods 1997. *Prehistoric Pottery for the Archaeologist*. Leicester: Leicester University Press.

Gilbertson, D., J. Schwenninger, R. Kemp & E. Rhodes 1999. Sand-drift and soil formation along an exposed North Atlantic coastline: 14,000 years of diverse geomorphological, climatic and human impacts. *Journal of Archaeological Science* 26: 439–469.

Giot, P.-R. 1960. Une station du néolithique primaire Armoricain: Le Curnic en Guissény (Finistère). *Bulletin de la Société préhistorique de France* 57, 38–50.

Godfray, A. & F. Burdo 1949. Excavations at the Pinnacle, Parish of St Ouen, Jersey (1930–1936). *Société Jersiaise Bulletin* 15, 21–100.

Godfray, A. & F. Burdo 1950. Excavations at the Pinnacle, Parish of St. Ouen, Jersey, 1930–1936. *Société Jersiaise Bulletin* 15: 165–238.

Goslin, J., B. Van Vliet Lanoë, G. Spada, S. Bradley, L. Tarasov, S. Neill & S. Suanez 2015. A new Holocene relative sea-level curve for western Brittany (France): Insights on isostatic dynamics along the Atlantic coasts of north-western Europe. *Quaternary Science Reviews* 129: 341–365.

Gregory, R. 2006. Drift pumice. In D. Simpson, E. Murphy, & R. Gregory (ed.) *Excavations at Northton, Isle of Harris*: 69 and 133. British Archaeological Report 406. Oxford: Archaeopress.

Gregory, R., E. Murphy, M. Church, K. Edwards, E. Guttmann & D. Simpson 2005. Archaeological evidence for the first Mesolithic occupation of the Western Isles of Scotland. *The Holocene* 15: 944–950.

Griffith, F. & H. Quinnell 1999. Neolithic settlement, land use and resources. In R. Kain & W. Ravenhill (ed.) *Historical Atlas of South-West England*: 51–54. Exeter: University of Exeter Press.

Griffiths, S. & C. Richards 2013. A time for stone circles, a time for people. In C. Richards (ed.) *Building the Great Stone Circles of the North*: 281–91. Oxford: Windgather Press.

Guyodo, J.-N., A. Noslier, P. Madioux & C. Bizien-Jaglin 2001. L'assemblage lithique du site Néolithique Moyen II de Lillemer (Ille-et-Vilaine). *Bulletin de la Société Préhistorique Française* 98: 647–662.

Haggerty, A. 1991. Machrie Moor, Arran: recent excavations at two stone circles. *Proceedings of the Society of Antiquaries of Scotland* 121: 51–94.

Hamilton, M. & N. Sharples 2012. Early Bronze Age settlements at Machair Mheadhanach and Cill Donnain. In M. Parker Pearson (ed.) *From Machair to Mountains: Archaeological Survey and Excavation in South Uist*: 199–214. Oxford: Oxbow Books.

Hardy, K. & C. Wickham-Jones 2009. Mesolithic and later sites around the Inner Sound, Scotland: the work of the Scotland's First Settlers project 1998–2004. *Scottish Archaeological Internet Reports* 31.

Hather, J. 2000. *The Identification of Northern European Woods: a Guide for Archaeologists and Conservators*. London: Archetype.

Hawkes, J. 1937. *The Archaeology of the Channel Islands II: The Bailiwick of Jersey*. London: Methuen.

Hawley, D. 2017. *Lithics, landscape and people: life beyond the monuments in prehistoric Guernsey*. Unpublished PhD thesis, University of Southampton.

Hénaff, X. 2002. *Les habitats au Néolithique en Bretagne*. Rennes: Institut Culturel de Bretagne.

Hencken, H. 1932. *The Archaeology of Cornwall and Scilly*. London: Methuen.

Henley, C. 2003. *The Outer Hebrides and the Hebridean World during the Neolithic: an Island History*. Unpublished PhD dissertation, Cardiff University.

Henley, C. 2012. Loch a'Choire Neolithic settlement. In M. Parker Pearson (ed.) *From machair to mountains: archaeological survey and excavation in South Uist*, 189–98. Oxford: Oxbow.

Henshall, A. 1972. *The Chambered Tombs of Scotland*. Edinburgh: Edinburgh University Press.

Hijma, M. & K. Cohen 2010. Timing and magnitude of the sea-level jump preluding the 8200 yr event. *Geology* 38: 275–78.

Hodgson, J. 1997. *Soil Survey Field Handbook*. Harpenden: Soil Survey of England and Wales.

Holderness, H. 2007. A865/A867 road improvement scheme, North Uist. *Discovery and Excavation in Scotland* 8, 202.

Hood, A. 2009. *Land adjacent to Tresprison, Helston, Cornwall: archaeological strip, map and sample post-excavation assessment*. Unpublished report. Swindon: Foundations Archaeology.

Inizan, M.-L., M. Reduron-Ballinger, H. Roche & J. Tixier 1999. *Technology and terminology of knapped stone*. Naterre: Cercle de Recherches et d'Etudes Préhistoriques Maison de l'Archéologie et de l'Ethnologie.

Innes, J., J. Blackford & P. Davey 2003. Dating the introduction of cereal cultivation to the British Isles: early palaeoecological evidence from the Isle of Man. *Journal of Quaternary Science* 18: 603–13.

Johns, C. 2011. The excavation of a multi-period archaeological landscape at Trenowah, St Austell, Cornwall, 1997. *Cornish Archaeology* 47: 1–48.

Johns, C. 2012 (ed.). *Isles of Scilly Historic Environment Research Framework. Resource Assessment and Research Agenda*. Truro: Cornwall Council.

Johns, C., J. Ratcliffe & A. Young forthcoming. Results of archaeological recording during the 1996 Coast Protection Scheme at Porth Killier and Porth Coose, St Agnes, Isles of Scilly. *Cornish Archaeology*.

Johnson, M. 2006. Pottery. In D. Simpson, E. Murphy, & R. Gregory (ed.) *Excavations at Northton, Isle of Harris*: 44–69. BAR British Series 406. Oxford: Archaeopress.

Jones, A. & H. Quinnell 2011. The Neolithic and Bronze Age in Cornwall, c. 4000 cal BC to c. 1000 cal BC: an overview of recent developments. *Cornish Archaeology* 50: 197–229.

Jones, A. & H. Quinnell 2014. *Lines of Archaeological Investigation along the North Cornish Coast*. BAR British Series 594. Oxford: Archaeopress.

Jones, A., S. Taylor & T. Sturgess 2012. A Beaker structure and other discoveries along the Sennan to Porthcurno Southwest Water Pipeline. *Cornish Archaeology* 51: 1–69.

Jones, A. & C. Thomas 2010. Bosiliack and a Reconsideration of Entrance Graves. *Proceedings of the Prehistoric Society* 76: 271–96.

Jones, A., A. Tyacke, A. Lawson-Jones, H. Quinnell, G. Hill, R. Taylor & B. Tapper 2013. Landscapes of stone: contextualising greenstone working and lithics from Clodgy Moor, West Penwith, Cornwall. *Archaeological Journal* 170: 2–29.

Jones, R., D. Keen, J. Birnie & P. Waton 1990. *Past Landscapes of Jersey: Environmental Changes During the last Ten Thousand Years*. Saint Helier: Société Jersiaise.

Jones, R., C. O'Brien & G. Coope 2004. Palaeoenvironmental reconstruction of the Younger Dryas in Jersey, UK Channel

Islands, based on plant and insect fossils. *Proceedings of the Geologists' Association* 115: 43–53.

Keen, D. 1978. *The Pleistocene deposits of the Channel Islands*. London: HMSO.

Keen, D. 1981. *The Holocene deposits of the Channel Islands*. London: HMSO.

Kendrick, T. 1928. *The archaeology of the Channel Islands: Volume 1 - The Bailiwick of Guernsey*. London: Methuen.

Kenney, J. 2008. Recent excavation at Parc Bryn Cegin, Llandygai, near Bangor, North Wales. *Archaeologia Cambrensis* 157: 9–142.

Kenti, M., B. Brayshay, D. Gilbertson, P. Wathern & R. Weaver 1994. A biogeographical study of plant communities and environmental gradients on South Uist, Outer Hebrides, Scotland. *Scottish Geographical Magazine* 110: 85–99.

Kinnes, I. 1982. Les Fouaillages and Megalithic Origins. *Antiquity* 57: 24–30.

Leary, J. 2015. *The remembered land*. London: Bloomsbury.

Lee, D. & N. Woodward 2009. Links House, Stronsay: excavation. *Discovery and Excavation in Scotland* 10: 141.

Lowe, A., C. Unsworth, S. Gerber, S. Davies, R. Munro, C. Kelleher, A. King, S. Brewer, A. White & J. Cottrell 2005. Route, speed and mode of oak postglacial colonisation across the British Isles: Integrating molecular ecology, palaeoecology and modelling approaches. *Botanical Journal of Scotland* 57: 59–81.

Lucas, G. 2012. *Understanding the Archaeological Record*. Cambridge: Cambridge University Press.

MacArthur, R. & E.O. Wilson 1967. *The theory of island biogeography*. Princeton: Princeton University Press.

MacDonald, K. & R. Rennell 2011. *An Doirlinn*. Unpublished Report. Lochboisdale: Uist Archaeology.

Mackenzie, W. 1905. Notes on the Pigmies Isle, at the Butt of Lewis, with results of the recent exploration of the "Pigmies' Chapel" there. *Proceedings of the Society of Antiquaries of Scotland* 39, 248–58.

Mackinder, H. 1902. *Britain and British seas*. New York: D. Appleton.

Macphail, R., M.-A. Courty & A. Gebhardt 1990. Soil micromorphological evidence of early agriculture in north-west Europe. *World Archaeology* 22, 53–69.

Malinowski, B. 1922. *Argonauts of the Western Pacific: an account of native enterprise and adventure in the archipelagoes of Melanesian New Guinea*. London: Routledge.

Marchand, G. 2007. Neolithic fragrances: Mesolithic–Neolithic interactions in western France. In A. Whittle & V. Cummings (ed.) *Going over: the Mesolithic–Neolithic transition in north-west Europe*: 225–42. London: British Academy.

Marchand, G. 2013. Le Mésolithique insulaire atlantique: systèmes techniques et mobilité humaine à l'épreuve des bras de mer. In M.-Y. Daire, C. Dupont, A. Baudry, C. Billard, J. Large, L. Lespez, E. Normand & C. Scarre (ed.) *Ancient Maritime Communities and the Relationship between People and Environment along the European Atlantic Coasts*: 359–69. BAR International Series 2570. Oxford: Archaeopress.

Marcigny, C., E. Ghesquière, L. Juhel & F. Charraud 2010. Entre Néolithique ancien et Néolithique moyen en Normandie et dans les Iles anglo-normandes: parcours chronologique. In C. Billard & M. Legris (ed.) *Premiers néolithiques de l'Ouest, 28e Colloque interrégional sur le Néolithique, Archéologie et culture*: 117–62. Rennes: Presses Universitaires de Rennes.

Marcigny C., X. Savary, A. Verney, G. Verron 2010. L'âge du Bronze en Basse-Normandie (-2300/-2000 à -800 av J.C.). In Anon. *Bilan de la recherche archéologique Basse-Normandie (1984–2010), du Paléolithique à la fin de l'âge du fer*, 93–142. Caen: Direction régionale des affaires culturelles.

Marshall, D. 1980. Excavations at Auchategan, Glendaruel, Argyll. *Proceedings of the Society of Antiquaries of Scotland* 109: 36–79.

Marshall, P., C. Bronk Ramsey, G. Cook, A. Bayliss, J. Meadows, D. Hamilton & M. Perez 2016. Scientific dating. In D. Charman, C. Johns, K. Camidge, P. Marshall, S. Mills, J. Mulville, H. Roberts, & T. Stevens (ed.) *The Lyonesse Project: A study of the historic coastal and marine environment of the Ilses of Scilly*: 89–150. Truro: Cornwall Council.

McHardy, I., C. Barrowman & M. Macleod 2009. STAC: The Severe Terrain Archaeological Campaign - investigation of stack sites of the Isle of Lewis 2003–2005. *Scottish Archaeological Internet Reports 36*.

McInnes, I. 1963. The Neolithic and Early Bronze Age pottery from Luce Sands, Wigtownshire. *Proceedings of the Society of Antiquaries of Scotland* 97: 40–81.

Mercer, J. 1971. A regression-time stone-workers' camp, 33ft OD, Lussa River, Isle of Jura. *Proceedings of the Society of Antiquaries of Scotland* 103: 1–32.

Mercer, R. 1974. A regression-time stone-workers' camp, 33ft OD, Lussa River, Isle of Jura. *Proceedings of the Society of Antiquaries of Scotland* 103, 30–31.

Mercer, R. 1981. Excavations at Carn Brea, Illogan, Cornwall: a Neolithic fortified complex of the third millennium bc. *Cornish Archaeology* 20: 161–85.

Mercer, R. 1997. The excavation of a Neolithic enclosure complex at Helman Tor, Lostwithiel, Cornwall. *Cornish Archaeology* 36: 29–37.

Mills, C., I. Armit, K. Edwards & P. Grinter 2004. Neolithic land-use and environmental degradation: a study from the Western Isles of Scotland. *Antiquity* 78: 886–895.

Mithen, S. 2000. *Hunter-Gatherer Landscape Archaeology: The Southern Hebrides Mesolithic Project 1988–1998. Volume 1*. Cambridge: McDonald Institute.

Moore, H. & G. Wilson 2005. *Western Isles (South). Coastal zone assessment survey: Grimsay, Benbecula and South Uist*. Edinburgh: EASE Archaeology.

Moore, P., J. Webb & M. Collinson 1991. *Pollen Analysis*. 2nd edition. London: Blackwell.

Moskal-del Hoyo, M., M. Wachowiak & R. Blanchette 2010. Preservation of fungi in archaeological charcoal. *Journal of Archaeological Science* 37: 2106–16.

Mulder, Y. 1999. *Aspects of vegetation and settlement history in the Outer Hebrides, Scotland*. Unpublished PhD thesis, University of Sheffield.

Murphy, C. 1986. *Thin section preparation of soils and sediments*. Berkhamstead: A.B. Academic.

Neal, D. 1983. Excavations on a settlement at Little Bay, St Martin's, Isles of Scilly. *Cornish Archaeology* 22: 47–80.

Needham, S. 2009. Encompassing the sea: 'maritories' and Bronze Age maritime interactions. In P. Clarke (ed.) *Bronze Age Connections: Cultural Contact in Prehistoric Europe*: 12–37. Oxford: Oxbow.

Neighbour, T. 2005. Excavation of a Bronze Age kerbed cairn at Olcote, Breasclete, near Calanais, Isle of Lewis. *Scottish*

Archaeological Internet Report 13.

Newberry, J. 2002. Inland flint in prehistoric Devon: sources, tool-making, quality and use. *Devon Archaeological Society Proceedings* 60: 1–32.

Newton, A. 1999. Report on the pumice. In B. Crawford & B. Ballin-Smith (ed.) *The Biggings, Papa Stour, Shetland: the history and archaeology of a royal Norwegian farm*: 178. Edinburgh: Society of Antiquaries of Scotland.

Nicolas, C. 2011. Artisanats spécialisés et inégalités sociales à l'aube de la métallurgie: les pointes de flèches de type armoricain dans le nord du Finistère. *Bulletin de la Société Préhistorique Française* 108: 93–125.

Nowakowski, J. 1991. Trethellan Farm, Newquay: the excavation of a lowland Bronze Age settlement and Iron Age cemetery. *Cornish Archaeology* 30, 103–131.

Nowakowski, J. and H. Quinnell 2011. *Trevelgue Head, Cornwall: the importance of C.K. Croft Andrew's 1939 excavations for prehistoric and Roman Cornwall*. Truro: Cornwall Council.

O'Brien, C., M. Church & H. Ranner 2009. Aird Calanais, Lewis, Scotland. Unpublished report, Archaeological Services Durham University No. 2170.

Ordnance Survey 1965. Canmore entry, 16 May 1965. Available online at: https://canmore.org.uk/site/9797/south-uist-an-doirlinn.

Orme, L., L. Reinhardt, R. Jones, D. Charman, A. Barkwith & M. Ellis 2016. Aeolian sediment reconstructions from the Scottish Outer Hebrides: Late Holocene storminess and the role of the North Atlantic Oscillation. *Quaternary Science Reviews* 132: 15–25.

Pailler, Y., G. Marchand, S. Blanchet, J.-N. Guyodo & G. Hamon 2008. Le Villeneuve-Saint-Germain dans la péninsule Armoricaine: les débuts d'une enquête. In L. Burnez-Lanotte, M. Ilett & P. Allard (eds.) *Fin des traditions Danubiennes dans le Néolithique du bassin Parisien et de la Belgique (5100–4700 av. J.-C.)*, 91–111. Paris: Société Préhistorique Française.

Pankhurst, R. & J. Mullin 1991. *Flora of the Outer Hebrides*. London: Natural History Museum.

Parker Pearson, M. 1990. The production and distribution of Bronze Age pottery in south-west Britain. *Cornish Archaeology* 29, 5–32.

Parker Pearson, M. 1995. Canmore entry, 1995. Available online at: https://canmore.org.uk/site/9797/south-uist-an-doirlinn.

Parker Pearson, M. & H. Smith 2012. Introduction. In M. Parker Pearson (ed.) *From Machair to Mountains: Archaeological Survey and Excavation in South Uist*: 1–11. Oxford: Oxbow.

Patton, M. 1984. Excavation of a Bronze Age enclosure system at La Moye. *Société Jersiaise Bulletin* 23, 532–538.

Patton, M. 1990. Neolithic stone rings from the Channel Islands. *Société Jersiaise Bulletin* 25, 347–352.

Patton, M. 1991. An early Neolithic axe factory at Le Pinacle, Jersey, Channel Islands. *Proceedings of the Prehistoric Society* 57: 51–60.

Patton, M. 1992. Entre Cerny et Castellic: le Groupe Pinacle/Fouaillages. *Revue Archéologique de l'Ouest* Suppl. No. 5, 147–151.

Patton, M. 1993. The Mesolithic of the Channel Islands: Economy and settlement in a changing landscape. *Oxford Journal of Archaeology* 12: 9–17.

Patton, M. 1995. *Neolithic communities of the Channel Islands*. BAR British Series 240. Oxford: British Archaeological Reports.

Patton, M. & M. Finlaison 2001. *Patterns in a prehistoric landscape: the archaeology of St Ouen's Bay, Jersey*. St Helier: Société Jersiaise.

PCRG 2010. *The study of prehistoric pottery: general policies and guidelines for analysis and publication*. 3rd edition (revised). Available online at http://www.pcrg.org.uk/Publications1-2.htm. Accessed 21.11.16.

Perez, M. 2013. *A Palaeoecological approach to understanding the impact of coastal changes in Late Holocene societies using the Isles of Scilly as a case study*. Unpublished PhD thesis, University of Plymouth.

Perez, M., R. Fyfe, D. Charman & W. Gehrels 2015. Later Holocene vegetation history of the Isles of Scilly, UK: coastal influence and human land use in a small island context. *Journal of Quaternary Science* 30: 764–78.

Piggott, S. 1931. The Neolithic pottery of the British Isles. *Archaeological Journal* 88: 67–158.

Piggott, S. 1954. *The Neolithic cultures of the British Isles*. Cambridge: Cambridge University Press.

Pioffet, H. 2013. Des vases et des îles: étude de la céramique des Fouaillages à Guernesey dans son contexte (Néolithique ancien et début du Néolithique moyen). In M.-Y. Daire, C. Dupont, A. Baudry, C. Billard, J.-M. Large, L. Lespez, E. Normand, & C. Scarre (ed.) *Ancient maritime communities and the relationship between people and environment along the European Atlantic coasts*: 391–400. BAR International Series 2570. Oxford: Archaeopress.

Pollard, J. 1999. 'These places have their moments': thoughts on settlement practices in the British Neolithic. In J. Bruck & M. Goodman (ed.) *Making Places in the Prehistoric World: Themes in Settlement Archaeology*: 76–93. London: UCL Press.

Pollard, J. & F. Healy 2007. Neolithic and Early Bronze Age. In C. Webster (ed.) *The Archaeology of South West England. South West Archaeological Research Framework: Resource Assessment and Research Agenda*: 75–102. Taunton: Somerset County Council.

Quinnell, H. 1994. *Isles of Scilly Coastal Erosion Project 1989–93: The Pottery and Other Significant Artefacts from Sites with Recorded Stratigraphy*. Unpublished Archive Report. Truro: Cornwall and Scilly HER, ER 557.

Quinnell, H. 2012. Trevisker pottery: some recent studies. In W. Britnell and R. Silvester (eds). *Reflections on the past: essays in honour of Frances Lynch*. Welshpool: Cambrian Archaeological Association.

Quinnell, H. 2014. Neolithic and Bronze Age Pottery. In A. Mudd & S. Joyce (ed.) *The Archaeology of the South-West Reinforcement Gas Pipeline, Devon*, 48–55. Cirencester: Cotswold Archaeology.

Quinnell, H. 2016. Appendix 3: Pottery. In Anon. *Land at Tregunnel Hill, Newquay, Cornwall: post-excavation assessment and updated project design*. Cotswold Archaeology Report 14315.

Rainbird, P. 2007. *The Archaeology of Islands*. Cambridge: Cambridge University Press.

Ransom, R. 1993. *A Catalogue and Analysis of Perforated Implements from Cornwall and the Isles of Scilly*. Unpublished MPhil thesis, University of Exeter.

Ratcliffe, J. 1989. *The Archaeology of Scilly: An assessment of the resource and recommendations for its future*. Truro: Cornwall Archaeological Unit.

Ratcliffe, J. 1994. *Fieldwork in Scilly: July 1993*. Unpublished report. Truro: Cornwall Archaeological Unit.

Ratcliffe, J. & V. Straker 1996. *The Early Environment of Scilly*. Truro: Cornwall Archaeological Unit.

Ratcliffe, J. & C. Thorpe 1991. *Lighting Up the Past in Scilly: Archaeological Results from the 1985 Electrification Project*. Truro: Cornwall Archaeological Unit.

RCHAMS 1928. *Royal Commission on the Ancient and Historical Monuments of Scotland: ninth report with inventory of monuments and constructions in the Outer Hebrides, Skye and the Small Isles*. Edinburgh: HMSO.

Reid, C. 1913. *Submerged Forests*. Cambridge: Cambridge University Press.

Reimer, P., E. Bard, A. Bayliss, J. Beck, P. Blackwell, C. Bronk Ramsey, C. Buck, H. Cheng, R. Edwards, M. Friedrich, P. Grootes, T. Guilderson, H. Haflidason, I. Hajdas, C. Hatté, T. Heaton, D. Hoffmann, A. Hogg, K. Hughen, K. Kaiser, B. Kromer, S. Manning, M. Niu, R. Reimer, D. Richards, E. Scott, J. Southon, R. Staff, C. Turney. & J. van der Plicht 2013. IntCal13 and Marine13 Radiocarbon Age Calibration Curves 0–50,000 Years cal BP. *Radiocarbon* 55: 1869–87.

Renouf, J. 1985. Geological excursion guide 1: Jersey and Guernsey, Channel Islands. *Geology Today* 1: 90–93.

Richards, J. 1998. Western Isles landscape character assessment. *Scottish Natural Heritage Review* 92.

Richards, C., A. Challands & K. Welham. 2013 Erecting stone circles in a Hebridean landscape. In C. Richards (ed.) *Building the Great Stone Circles of the North*: 201–23. Oxford: Oxbow.

Richards, C., Jones, A., MacSween, A., Sheridan, A., Dunbar, E., Reimer, P., ... Whittle, A. 2016. Settlement Duration and Materiality: Formal Chronological Models for the Development of Barnhouse, a Grooved Ware Settlement in Orkney. *Proceedings of the Prehistoric Society* 82, 193–225.

Richards, C. & R. Jones (eds) 2016. *The development of Neolithic house societies in Orkney*. Oxford: Windgather.

Ritchie, J.N.G. 1978. The Stones of Stenness, Orkney. *Proceedings of the Society of Antiquaries of Scotland* 107: 1–60.

Ritchie, J.N.G. 1973. Excavation of the chambered cairn at Achnacreebeag. *Proceedings of the Society of Antiquaries of Scotland* 102: 31–50.

Ritchie, W. 1979. Machair development and chronology in the Uists and adjacent islands. *Proceedings of the Royal Society of Edinburgh. Section B. Biological Sciences* 77: 107–22.

Ritchie, W. & G. Whittington 1994. Non-synchronous aeolian sand movements in the Uists: The evidence of the intertidal organic and sand deposits at Cladach Mor, North Uist. *Scottish Geographical Magazine* 110: 40–46.

Roach, R. 1991. *Outline and guide to the geology of Guernsey.* St Peter Port: Guernsey Museums & Galleries.

Robinson, E. 2008. Scratching the surface: surface scatters, armatures and forager-farmer contact in a 'frontier zone'. *Notae Praehistoricae* 28: 55–62.

Robinson, E., L. Lombaert, J. Sergant & P. Crombé 2011. Armatures and the question of forager-farmer contact along the North-Western fringe of the LBK. *Archaologisches Korrespondenzblatt* 41: 473–90.

Robinson, E., J. Sergant & P. Crombé 2013. Late Mesolithic armature variability in the southern North Sea basin: implications for forager-Linearbandkeramik contact models of the transition to agriculture in Belgium and the southern Netherlands. *European Journal of Archaeology* 16: 3–20.

Robinson, G. 2007. *The Prehistoric Island Landscape of Scilly.* BAR British Series 447. Oxford: Archaeopress.

Roe, F. 1979. Typology of stone implements with shaftholes. In T. Clough & W. Cummins (ed.) *Stone Axe Studies*: 23–48. York: Council for British Archaeology.

Rozoy, J.-G. 1991. Nature et conditions de la néolithisation au nord de la Loire: la fin de l'Epipaléolithique ("Mésolithique") au Nord de la Loire. *Actes des congrès nationaux des sociétés savantes* 113: 403–23.

Salanova, L. 2000. *La question du Campaniform en France et dans les îles anglo-normandes: productions, chronologie et roles d'un standard ceramique*. Paris: Mémoire de la Société Préhistorique Française.

Sawyer, K. 2015. *Isles of the Dead? The Setting and Function of the Bronze Age Chambered Cairns and Cists of the Isles of Scilly.* Oxford: Archaeopress.

Scaife, R. 1980. *The vegetational history of the Isles of Scilly I: pollen analysis of Higher Moors, St Mary's, Isles of Scilly.* AML Report 3047. London: English Heritage.

Scaife, R. 1984. A history of Flandrian vegetation in the Isles of Scilly: palynological investigation of Higher Moors and Lower Moors peat mires, St Mary's. *Cornish Studies* 11: 33–47.

Scarre, C. 2011. *Landscapes of Neolithic Brittany*. Oxford: Oxford University Press.

Schulting, R., A. Sheridan, R. Crozier & E. Murphy. 2010. Revisiting Quanterness: new AMS dates and stable isotope data from an Orcadian tomb. *Proceedings of the Society of Antiquaries of Scotland* 140: 1–50.

Schulting, R., H. Sebire & J. Robb 2010. On the road to Paradis: new insights from AMS dates and stable isotopes at Le Déhus, Guernsey, and the Channel Islands Middle Neolithic. *Oxford Journal of Archaeology* 29: 149–73.

Schweingruber, F. 1990. *Anatomy of European Woods: An atlas for the identification of European trees, shrubs and dwarf shrubs*. Stuttgart: Haupt.

Schweingruber, F. 2007. *Wood structure and environment*. Berlin: Springer.

Scott, J.G. 1964. The chambered cairn at Beacharra, Kintyre, Argyll, Scotland. *Proceedings of the Prehistoric Society* 30: 134–58.

Scott, J.G. 1969. The Clyde cairns of Scotland. In T. Powell (ed.) *Megalithic Enquiries in the West of Britain: a Liverpool symposium*: 175–222. Liverpool: Liverpool University Press.

Scott, W.L. 1935. The chamber tomb of Clettraval, North Uist. *Proceedings of the Society of Antiquaries of Scotland* 69: 480–536.

Scott, W.L. 1948. The chamber tomb of Unival, North Uist. *Proceedings of the Society of Antiquaries of Scotland* 82: 1–49.

Scott, W.L. 1951. Eilean an Tighe: a pottery workshop of the second millennium BC. *Proceedings of the Society of Antiquaries of Scotland* 85: 1–37.

Scourse, J. 1986. *The Isles of Scilly: field guide*. Coventry: Quaternary Research Association.

Sebire, H. 2005. *The Archaeology and Early History of the Channel Islands*. Oxford: Tempus.

Sebire, H. 2012. Excavations at the Royal Hotel Site, St Peter Port,

Guernsey. *La Société Guernesiaise Report and Transactions* 27, 190–257.

Sebire, H. & J. Renouf 2010. Sea change: new evidence for Mesolithic and Early Neolithic presence in the Channel Islands with particular reference to Guernsey and the rising Holocene sea. *Oxford Journal of Archaeology* 29: 361–86.

Selkirk, A. 1996. The Udal. *Current Archaeology* 147, 84–94.

Sharples, N. 1992. Aspects of regionalisation in the Scottish Neolithic. In N. Sharples & A. Sheridan (ed.) *Vessels for the Ancestors: Essays on the Neolithic of Britain and Ireland in Honour of Audrey Henshall*: 322–27. Edinburgh: Edinburgh University Press.

Sharples, N. 2005. *A Late Neolithic settlement at An Doirlinn, Orosay, South Uist - and some other erosion problems*. Unpublished report. Cardiff: Cardiff University.

Sharples, N. 2009. Beaker settlement in the Western Isles. In M. Allen, N. Sharples, & T. O'Connor (ed.) *Land and People: Papers in Memory of John Evans*: 147–58. Oxford: Oxbow.

Sharples, N. 2015. A Short History of Archaeology in the Uists, Outer Hebrides. *Journal of the North Atlantic* 9: 1–15.

Shennan, I. & B. Horton 2002. Holocene land- and sea-level change in Great Britain. *Journal of Quaternary Science* 17: 511–526.

Shennan, I., S. Bradley, G. Milne, A. Brooks, S. Basset & S. Hamilton 2006. Relative sea-level changes, glacial isostatic modelling and ice-sheet reconstruction from British Isles since the Last Glacial Maximum. *Journal of Quaternary Science* 21: 585–99.

Shephard, I. & T. Cowie 1977. An enlarged food vessel urn burial and associated artefacts from Kiltry Knock, Alvah, Banff and Buchan. *Proceedings of the Society of Antiquaries of Scotland* 108: 114–23.

Sheridan, A. 2000. Achnacreebeag and its French connections: vive the 'auld alliance'. In J.C. Henderson (ed.) *The prehistory and early history of Atlantic Europe: papers from a session held at the European Association of Archaeologists fourth annual meeting in Göteborg 1998*: 1–15. BAR International Series 861. Oxford: British Archaeological Reports.

Sheridan, A. 2003. French connections I: spreading the marmites thinly. In I. Armit, E. Murphy, E. Nelis & D. Simpson (ed.) *Neolithic settlement in Ireland and western Britain*: 3–17. Oxford: Oxbow.

Sheridan, A. 2004. Going round in circles? Understanding the Irish Grooved Ware 'complex' in its wider context. In J. Bradley, J. Coles, E. Grogan & B. Raftery (ed.) *From megaliths to metals: essays in honour of George Eogan*: 26–37. Oxford: Oxbow.

Sheridan, A. 2008. *Pottery from Barpa Langais*. Unpublished specialist report prepared for ARCUS, University of Sheffield.

Sheridan, A. 2010. The Neolithisation of Britain and Ireland: the big picture. In B. Finlayson & G. Warren (ed.) *Landscapes in transition: understanding hunter-gatherer and farming landscapes in the early Holocene of Europe and the Levant*: 89–105. Oxford: Oxbow.

Sheridan, A. 2011. The Early Neolithic of south-west England: new insights and new questions. In S. Pearce (ed.) *Recent archaeological work in south western Britain. Papers in honour of Henrietta Quinnell*: 21–39. BAR British Series 548. Oxford: British Archaeological Reports.

Sheridan, A., C. Murray, D. Garrow & H. Anderson-Whymark 2014. Spectacular Neolithic finds emerge from the lochs of Lewis. *PAST: The newsletter of the prehistoric society* 76: 1.

Sibesson, E. 2009. *The petrology of a Neolithic assemblage from L'Eree, Guernsey*. Unpublished MSc dissertation, University of Southampton.

Simpson, D. 1976. The later Neolithic and Beaker settlement at Northton, Isle of Harris. In C. Burgess & R. Miket (ed.) *Settlement and economy in the 3rd and 2nd millennia BC*: 221–31. BAR British Series 33. Oxford: British Archaeological Reports.

Simpson, D., E. Murphy & R. Gregory 2006. *Excavations at Northton, Isle of Harris*. BAR British Series 408. Oxford: Archaeopress.

Smith, G. & D. Harris 1982. The Excavation of Mesolithic, Neolithic and Bronze Age settlements at Poldowrian, St Keverne, 1980. *Cornish Archaeology* 21: 23–62.

Smith, I. 1965. *Windmill Hill and Avebury. Excavations by Alexander Keiller 1925–1939*. Oxford: Clarendon.

Smith, O., G. Momber, R. Bates, P. Garwood, S. Fitch, M. Pallen, V. Gaffney & R. Allaby. 2015. Sedimentary DNA from a submerged site reveals wheat in the British Isles 8000 years ago. *Science* 347: 998–1001.

Smyth, J. 2014. *Settlement in the Irish Neolithic: New discoveries at the edge of Europe*. Oxford: Oxbow.

Snape-Kennedy, L., M. Church, R. Bishop, C. Clegg, L. Johnson, S. Piper & P. Rowley-Conwy 2013. Tràigh na Beirigh 9. *Discovery and Excavation in Scotland* 14, 199.

Squair, R. 1998. *The Neolithic of the Western Isles*. Unpublished PhD thesis, Glasgow University.

Stace, C. 1991. *New Flora of the British Isles*. 1st edition. Cambridge: Cambridge University Press.

Stace, C. 2010. *New Flora of the British Isles*. 3rd edition. Cambridge: Cambridge University Press.

Stewart, R. 2012. The role of chert in later lithic industries with specific reference to south-west England. *Geoscience in South West England* 13: 123–30.

Stoops, G. 2003. *Guidelines for analysis and description of soil and regolith thin sections*. Madison, Wisconsin: Soil Science Society of America.

Sturt, F. 2006. Local knowledge is required: a rhythmanalytical approach to the late Mesolithic and early Neolithic of the East Anglia Fenland, UK. *Journal of Maritime Archaeology* 1: 119–39.

Sturt, F. 2015. From sea to land and back again: understanding the shifting character of Europe's landscapes and seascapes over the last million years. In H. Anderson-Whymark, D. Garrow, & F. Sturt (ed.) *Continental connections: exploring cross-channel relationships from the Mesolithic to the Iron Age*: 7–27. Oxford: Oxbow.

Sturt, F. & D. Garrow 2015. Continental Connections: concluding discussion. In H. Anderson-Whymark, D. Garrow & F. Sturt (ed.) *Continental connections: exploring cross-channel relationships from the Mesolithic to the Iron Age*: 166–72. Oxford: Oxbow.

Sturt, F., D. Garrow & S. Bradley. 2013. New models of North West European Holocene palaeogeography and inundation. *Journal of Archaeological Science* 40: 3963–76.

Taylor, R. & C. Johns 2009–10. Archaeological recording of a multi-period site at Dolphin Town, Tresco, Isles of Scilly, 1999–2003. *Cornish Archaeology* 48–49: 109–16.

Taylor, S. in prep. *Down the bright stream: the prehistory of*

Woodcock Corner and the Tregurra Valley. Leiden: Sidestone Press.

Thevenin, T. 1995. Mésolithique récent, Mésolithique final, Néolithique ancien dans le quart nord-est de la France: pour une réinterprétation des données. *Revue Archéologique de Picardie* 9: 3–15.

Thomas, C. 1985. *Exploration of a drowned landscape: archaeology and history of the Isles of Scilly*. London: Batsford.

Thomas, J. 2013. *The Birth of Neolithic Britain: An Interpretive Account*. Oxford: Oxford Univeristy Press.

Tingle, M. 1998. *The Prehistory of Beer Head. Field survey and excavations at an isolated flint source on the South Devon coast*. BAR British Series 270. Oxford: Archaeopress.

Tipping, R. 1994. The form and fate of Scotland's woodlands. *Proceedings of the Society of Antiquaries of Scotland* 124: 1–54.

Uehara, K. & J. Scourse 2006. Tidal evolution of the northwest European shelf seas from the Last Glacial Maximum to the present. *Journal of Geophysical Research: Oceans* 111: 1–15.

Wainwright, G. & I. Longworth 1971. *Durrington Walls: excavations 1966–1968*. London: Society of Antiquaries.

Waller, M. & J. Kirby 2002. Late Pleistocene/early Holocene environmental change in the Romney Marsh region: new evidence from Tilling Green, Rye. In A. Long, S. Hipkin & H. Clarke (ed.) *Romney Marsh: Coastal and Landscape Change through the Ages*: 22–39. Oxford: Oxbow.

Warren, G. 2006. Chipped stone tool industries of the Earlier Neolithic in Eastern Scotland. *Scottish Archaeological Journal* 28: 27–47.

Warren, G. 2007. Mesolithic myths. In A. Whittle & V. Cummings (eds). *Going Over: The Mesolithic-Neolithic transition in north-west Europe*, 311–28. Oxford: Oxford University Press.

Warren, G. 2015. Britain and Ireland inside Mesolithic Europe. In H. Anderson-Whymark, D. Garrow, & F. Sturt (ed.) *Continental connections: exploring cross-Channel relationships from the Mesolithic to the Iron Age*: 43–58. Oxford: Oxbow.

Warton, R. 1913. Report on exploration work carried on at 'La Motte' (Green Island) in the month of April 1912. *Société Jersiaise Bulletin* 38, 289–94.

Watts, S. 2013. *The life and death of querns*. Southampton: Highfield Press.

Westerdahl, C. 1992. The maritime cultural landscape. *The International Journal of Nautical Archaeology* 21: 5–14.

Whittle, A. 1999. Moving on and moving around: Neolithic settlement mobility. In P. Topping (ed.) *Neolithic Landscapes*: 15–22. Oxford: Oxbow.

Whittle, A., F. Healy & A. Bayliss 2011. *Gathering Time: Dating the Early Neolithic Enclosures of Southern Britain and Ireland*. Oxford: Oxbow.

Wickham-Jones, C. 1995. The flaked stone tools. In K. Brannigan & P. Foster (ed.) *Barra: Archaeological Research on Ben Tangaval*: 120–39. Sheffield: Sheffield Academic Press.

Wickham-Jones, C. & G. Collins 1978. The sources of flint and chert in northern Britain *Proceedings of the Society of Antiquaries of Scotland* 109: 7–21.

Wicks, K., A. Pirie & S. Mithen 2014. Settlement patterns in the late Mesolithic of western Scotland: The implications of Bayesian analysis of radiocarbon dates and inter-site technological comparisons. *Journal of Archaeological Science* 41: 406–22.

Wilkins, D. 1984. The Flandrian woods of Lewis (Scotland). *Journal of Ecology* 72: 251–58.

Wilkinson, K. & V. Straker 2008. Neolithic and Early Bronze Age Environmental Background. In C. Webster (ed.) *The Archaeology of South West England. South West Archaeological Research Framework: Resource Assessment and Research Agenda*: 63–74. Taunton: Somerset County Council.

Wolf, J. & D. Woolf 2006. Waves and climate change in the north-east Atlantic. *Geophysical Research Letters* 33: 1–4.

Woodman, P. & M. McCarthy 2003. Contemplating some awful (ly interesting) vistas: importing cattle and red deer into prehistoric Ireland. In I. Armit, E. Murphy, E. Nelis & D. Simpson (ed.) *Neolithic settlement in Ireland and western Britain*: 31–39. Oxford: Oxbow.

Woolf, J. 2007. *Modelling of waves and set-up for the storm of January 2005*. Liverpool: Proudman Oceanographic Laboratory. Available online at http://nora.nerc.ac.uk/2672/. Accessed 21.11.16.

Young, E., B. McKenzie, J. McNicol, A. Robertson, R. Wendler & S. Dawson 2015. Spatial trends in the wind abrasion resistance of cultivated machair soil, South Uist, Scottish Outer Hebrides. *Catena* 135: 1–10.